Historiography in the Middle Ages

Historiography in the Middle Ages

Edited by

Deborah Mauskopf Deliyannis

BRILL

LEIDEN • BOSTON
2012

Library of Congress Cataloging-in-Publication Data

Historiography in the Middle Ages / edited by Deborah Mauskopf Deliyannis.
    p. cm.
    Includes bibliographical references and index.
    ISBN 9004118810
    1. Middle Ages—Historiography. 2. Civilization, Medieval—Research. 3. Medievalism—
History. 4. Biography—Middle Ages, 500-1500. 5. Europe—History—476-1492—
Historiography. I. Deliyannis, Deborah Mauskopf, 1966-

    D116 .H575 2002
    909.07'07'2—dc21

                                                                          2002028389

This paperback was originally published in hardback under ISBN 978 90 04 11881 2.

ISBN 978 90 04 22677 7

CONTENTS

ACKNOWLEDGMENTS

I am extremely grateful to all the authors for their enthusiasm and patience. I would particularly like to thank Leah Shopkow, who has generously provided advice on almost every aspect of this book. I am also very grateful to Kristin E. Thomas and Daria Michelle Roche for translating three of the articles, and to Susan Steuer for assisting me with the index. Finally, I am indebted to Julian Deahl and Irene van Rossum of Brill for commissioning this book and then bearing with me through the publication process.

INTRODUCTION

Deborah Mauskopf Deliyannis

> *... medieval historiography, by all critical odds, is inauthentic, unscientific, unreliable, ahistorical, irrational, borderline illiterate, and, worse yet, unprofessional.*[1]

In recent years, much has been written about the 'memory' of the past in the Middle Ages.[2] Taken broadly, this includes a consideration of any sort of memorialization of events or persons of the past, from the recitation of the names of the dead at funerary masses, to the production of images and monuments, to the creation of public ceremonies and rituals, to the recitation of narratives, to the writing of texts. All of these represent strategies by which people, sometimes publicly, sometimes more privately, appropriate the past for their own purposes.

Of these strategies, the one that most explicitly claims to be performing this function is the writing of historical texts. *Historia* was a type of writing that had a long tradition in classical antiquity. Moreover, the Jewish and Christian religions were both by definition historical, in that they were based, at least in part, on historical and biographical texts. Medieval authors inherited both these traditions. There was thus no question, in the Middle Ages, that history should be written, as one suitable strategy for remembering a particular set of events or people. However, history was not recognized as an independent branch of study; it was usually classified as a branch of grammar or rhetoric. Historians came from many different backgrounds and wrote for many different purposes. New forms, and new ideas of what the content should be, were introduced at various points. Sometimes medieval authors consciously imitated classical or biblical models, but most authors were more interested in imitating each other.

---

[1] Spiegel (1983), 43–44.
[2] See Geary (1994); Coleman (1992); Wickham and Fentress (1992); Clanchy (1993).

Much of our knowledge of 'what happened' in the Middle Ages is based on these historical texts. Whether or not we admit it, the way a society is presented by a historian or historians often colors our interpretation of that society: sixth-century Francia from Gregory of Tours, for example, or fourteenth-century France and England from Froissart. Scholars have long realized that all such texts are constructed, even (especially) if they seem to be transparent narrations of events, and that it is important to understand the author's sources and literary models, the contexts in which he wrote, his purposes for writing and his presumed audience, before evaluating the information contained in the text. Historical texts can thus be approached as objects created by the efforts of individuals, and/or as products of collective memory, reflections of contemporary *mentalités*.

Naturally, each historical text has its own history, sometimes a very complex one. In this volume, we ask whether it is possible to generalize about the way history was written, given a very disparate body of historical texts from the Middle Ages. In order to provide a summary and synthesis of medieval historiography, we must consider the ways in which historical texts can or should be meaningfully categorized, subdivided, and discussed. There are two ways to pose this question: how do *we* categorize these texts, and how were they categorized when they were written? Both ways of looking at the material are useful. By looking at the entire body of medieval historiography, we are able to see patterns, paths of influence and similarities that allow us to draw conclusions about the function and meaning of the texts. The question is, did medieval authors themselves notice such similarities; did they categorize the products of their scholarship in the same ways?

Medieval Understanding of Historiography

In the Middle Ages, the use of the word 'historia' was not restricted to historiography.[3] *Historia* literally means 'story'. In the Middle Ages it could refer to narrative works of art, saints' lives, parts of the Bible, the literal sense of scriptural texts, liturgical offices, epic poems,

---

[3] See especially Knape (1984).

and other texts and objects.[4] The common thread is 'narrative', which is perhaps useful to remember, but without any specific connotation of the form or factuality of the given story.

Nevertheless, many medieval authors who wrote works that we consider historiographical did have some idea that *historia* was a particular type of narrative. It is difficult to assess precisely what all medieval historians thought they were doing, because there are very few theoretical treatises devoted to the writing of history. Isidore of Seville's discussion of the place of *historia* is probably the most frequently quoted, partly because Isidore's exposition was so clear, and partly because his work was so widely consulted in the Middle Ages. Isidore discusses history in book I of the *Etymologiae*, which is devoted to grammar.[5] After explaining parts of speech and rules of syntax and poetic meter, Isidore comes to *fabula* and *historia* as the two basic types of writing. *Fabulae* are fables, fictional accounts (such as those about speaking animals) intended to prove a point. History, as the parallel to *fabula*, likewise is intended to prove points. "*Historiae* are things which really have been done; *argumenta* are those thing which in fact have not been done, but could be done; *fabulae* are things which neither have been nor could be done, since they are contrary to nature".[6] Isidore notes that the etymological root of the word in Greek means 'to see or to know':[7]

> Among the ancients, no-one wrote history unless he was present and had seen what he was writing about. For we discover what happened

---

[4] Cf. Ray (1974), 36.

[5] The place of *historia* in the *trivium* was not clear; Alcuin, like Isidore, assigned it to grammar, but Honorius Augustodunensis, in *De Animae exsilio et patria*, and others after the twelfth century assigned it to rhetoric. See Boehm (1957); Goetz (1985).

[6] Isidore of Seville, *Etymologiae* I.44.5, ed. W. M. Lindsay (Oxford, 1911): "Nam historiae sunt res verae quae factae sunt; argumenta sunt quae etsi facta non sunt, fieri tamen possunt; fabulae vero sunt quae nec factae sunt nec fieri possunt, quia contra naturam sunt". This is based on the classical tradition, inherited from (pseudo) Cicero, in the *Ad Herennium* and *De inventione*: history was a genre of prose writing, one of the three main parts of *narratio*, alongside *fabula* and *argumentum*. "Fabula est, quae neque veras neque veri similes continet res, ut eae sunt, quae tragoedis traditae sunt. Historia est gesta res, sed ab aetatis nostrae memoria remota. Argumentum est ficta res, quae tamen fieri potuit, velut argumenta comoediarum" (*Ad herennium* 13); see Roest (1999), 51.

[7] Isidore, *Etymologiae* I.41.1–2: "Apud veteres enim nemo conscribebat historiam, nisi is qui interfuisset, et ea quae conscribenda essent vidisset. Melius enim oculis quae fiunt deprehendimus, quam quae auditione colligimus. Quae enim videntur, sine mendacio proferuntur. Haec disciplina ad Grammaticam pertinet, quia quidquid dignum memoria est litteris mandatur".

better with our eyes, than we learn from hearing others. For what is seen can be reported without lying. This discipline pertains to grammar, since whatever is worthy of being remembered is committed to writing.

Isidore then divides *historia* into three genres: diaries or ephemerida, which recount actions day by day; calendars, which tell things month by month; and annals, which record events year by year. *Historia* deals with events from many years or periods of time, and differs from annals in that "history is about those times which we have seen, but annals are about those years which our age does not know".[8] Interestingly, the primary distinction for Isidore seems not to be *historia* vs. *annales*, but the unit of time that is the base of the narrative.

After Isidore, theoretical writing about history ceases. We are therefore dependent upon the statements, usually quite brief, found within historical texts, in which the authors explain what they are doing. Bede, in the preface to his *Historia ecclesiastica*, notes that "as is a true law of history, I have endeavored to commit to writing those things which I have gathered from common report for the instruction of posterity".[9] Some modern scholars have taken the *vera lex historiae* to mean that Bede thought there were rules for writing history, which involved checking sources and reporting facts accurately (all things that Bede is known to have done). However, Roger Ray has argued that Bede meant not that there was one true law for writing history but that one of the laws used in writing history allowed for the use of evidence from hearsay if it is thought to be true.[10] The focus on 'truth' as a characteristic of history-writing, based on the definitions of Cicero, Isidore, Bede, and other authorities, did form part of the definition understood by most historians throughout the Middle Ages. For example, Hugh of St. Victor noted that "historia est rerum gestarum narratio quae in prima significatione litterae continentur".[11]

---

[8] Isidore, *Etymologiae* I.44.4: "historia est eorum temporum quae vidimus, annales vero sunt eorum annorum uos aetas nostra non novit".

[9] Bede, *Historia ecclesiastica gentis Anglorum*, preface, my translation: "ui, quod vera lex historiae est, simpliciter ea quae fama vulgante collegimus ad instructionem posteritatis litteris mandare studuimus".

[10] Ray (1980).

[11] Hugh of St. Victor, *De sacramentis*, prologue, *PL* 176, col. 185A.

But historical truth itself was not necessarily understood in the same way by every author, as many scholars have pointed out.[12]

Scholars have attempted to look at the nominal terms used by and about medieval historians, such as 'historia', 'chronica', 'annales', 'gestae', to see whether they had particular meanings that were commonly understood over time.[13] The conclusions seem to be negative. Bert Roest notes that:[14]

> It can be proposed that throughout the middle ages *historia* in the broad sense of the word was seen (1) as a way of knowing (either depicted as an activity: *historia est videre vel cognoscere*; or as the medium by which is known: *narratio per quam ea, quae in praeterito facta sunt, dignoscuntur*); (2) as something like a literary genre (a *narratio rerum gestarum*); or (3) as the object of cognition itself (*res verae quae factae sunt*).

The only sort of distinction that sometimes appears is between *historia* and *chronicon*, with the former meaning a continuous narrative, and the latter a type of writing organized by years.[15] This goes back to Eusebius, who wrote both types of text; and the tradition was continued by Isidore, Bede, and others who wrote both narrative histories and chronicles or annals. Guenée used this distinction, derived from statements in various texts from the twelfth to the fourteenth centuries, to distinguish these as two main types of historical writing, and moreover as a conceptual tool which enabled historians to make choices about forms of presentation and format.[16] The distinction was between chronicle's *brevitas* and history's *prolixitas*, as stated by, for example, Gervase of Canterbury:[17]

---

[12] See, among others, Beer (1981); Morse (1991); Otter (1996); and Ainsworth's article on "Legendary history" in this volume.

[13] See Roest (1999); Knape (1984); Guenée (1973).

[14] Roest (1999), 51.

[15] Guenée (1973); Roest (1999), 53.

[16] Guenée (1973).

[17] Gervase of Canterbury, *Chronicle*, Prologue, ed. W. Stubbs (London, 1879–80), 1:87–88; cited by Roest (1999), 54: "Cronicus autem annos incarnationis Domini annorumque menses computat et Kalendas, actus etiam regum et principum qui in ipsis eveniunt breviter edocet, eventus etiam, portenta vel miracula commemorat. Sunt autem plurimi qui cronicas vel annales scribentes, limites suos excedunt, nam philacteria sua dilatare et fimbrias magnificare delectant. Dum enim cronicam compilare cupiunt, historici more incediunt, et quod breviter sermoneque humili de modo scribendi dicere debuerant, verbis ampullosis aggravare conantur.

> The chronicler counts years of the incarnation of the Lord and months and days within years, and briefly recounts the deeds of kings or princes which took place in them, and also records events, portents, or miracles. There are, however, many authors writing chronicles or annals who exceed those limits . . . for while they want to compile a chronicle, they proceed in the manner of historians, and what they should say briefly, with a simple manner of writing, they try to swell with elaborate words.

Note that this was *not* the same as the distinction between *historia* and *annales* given by Isidore, which had to do with subject matter, not format.

However, only some medieval historians announced that they were observing this distinction, and for many, these rules were not followed. Moreover, this distinction omits other forms of writing about the past, such as biography (including saints' lives).[18] Many historians mixed format or subject matter or both in one text—a little hagiography, a little annal, a little universal history, a little eyewitness account, a little brevity, a little prolixity. No one seems to have played by any "rules" for writing history. This is perhaps fundamentally because there was no such thing as a professional historian at any time during the Middle Ages. In the earlier Middle Ages, people who wrote historical texts were scholars, monks, bishops, clerks, and government officials, and they wrote exegesis, poems, panegyrics, scientific or computational texts, and legal documents in addition to works that memorialized the past. Even in the later Middle Ages, when scholarly professionalization began, there was no place for the historian as such, although certainly historical texts were welcomed, and even frequently commissioned for particular purposes.[19]

There is considerable criticism of 'positivist' ideas about genre, and modern scholars tend to reject the idea that there were such things as historiographical genres in the Middle Ages.[20] But in fact, what constitutes a genre? Can a historian write in a genre if he doesn't know he is doing so? Can a historian think he is writing in a genre but actually be missing most of its constituent elements? In other words, to what extent does the existence of a genre presup-

---

[18] See Lifshitz (1994).
[19] Cf. Guenée (1980), 44–76.
[20] See, for example, Lifshitz (1994); Roest (1999); etc.

pose active participation by the author, and to what extent is it a category in which an author passively participates? Is it "a system of rules for writing as well as for the evaluation of what is written"?[21] Is it a literary format or style? Is it dependent upon subject matter? Is it dependent on the function of the text, or the author's purposes for writing it, or the way it was to be presented to its audience?

Most historians, when they sat down to write, were doing so in response to another text or texts. In some cases these models are acknowledged, in some cases they are not, although we can often recognize them, and we assume that contemporary readers would also have caught the allusions. Whether they thought beyond that to larger questions of genre may not be the point for their writing, but it is the point for our analysis of groups of similar texts. When a certain number of texts are all based on one model, then modern scholars usually group them together as a genre. Certainly it is significant that many authors wrote the same sort of text, whatever they may have thought of the 'rules' of writing such a text. If authors *did* think that they were writing in a genre, the stylistic or methodological assumptions they used might have shaped their narratives. And, if we can make statements about certain features common to members of a genre, we can then use these assumptions to tell us what the history-writers meant.

Modern Analysis of Medieval Historiography

Until the 1940s, relatively few scholars had seriously considered general aspects of history-writing in the Middle Ages.[22] Those who had were usually concerned with one genre of historical writing,[23] one text,[24] one period,[25] or one geographical area.[26] Many of the known historical texts were published in series such as the *Monumenta Germaniae Historica* or the *Rerum Italicarum Scriptores*, with a certain amount of

---

[21] Roest (1999), 48.
[22] See Ray (1974) for a summary of research through 1974.
[23] For example, Büdinger (1900), on universal history; Poole (1926), on chronicles and annals; von Rad (1930), on chronicles.
[24] Beumann (1950), on Widukind of Corvey.
[25] Hoffmann (1958), on the Carolingians.
[26] Balzani (1883–84), on Italy; Dübler (1943), on Spain; Jones (1947), on England.

critical study devoted to them individually.[27] Synthetic works were few.[28]

The study of medieval historical texts began to intensify after the 1957 publication of Herbert Grundmann's *Geschichtsschreibung im Mittelalter: Gattungen, Epochen, Eigenart.* Surveying medieval historiographical texts relatively briefly, Grundmann divided his study into two sections, one based on genre (he included oral poetry, ethnic history, world chronicle, annal, *vita, gesta,* national and urban chronicle, and Latin poetry), and one on chronology (Germanic, Carolingian, Ottonian/Salian, Investiture, Barbarossa, and late Middle Ages). This format allowed him first to examine texts of the same basic type from different periods, and then to explain which genres were more popular in the different periods. Focused mainly on Germany, Grundmann nevertheless attempted to draw generalizations and formulate categories for the whole of medieval historiography.

Since 1957, the study of medieval historiography has snowballed. Articles, dissertations, conference proceedings, and monographs on individual texts, groups of texts, and/or theoretical aspects of medieval historiography have appeared at an accelerating rate, as a glance at the bibliography of the present volume makes clear. In 1974, Roger Ray published a survey of research on medieval historiography, in which he noted that scholars writing about medieval historiography had three main concerns: "genre, the impact of the Bible, and the influence of classical literature".[29] Since Ray wrote, each of these approaches has been continued by large numbers of scholars, and broadened and expanded. Today, one might add to Ray's list topics such as audience reception, concepts of historical consciousness, notions of truth, narrative structures, literary and fictional aspects of history-writing, and the role of gender.[30]

---

[27] See Vasina (in this volume).

[28] An exception is Marie Schulz's *Die Lehre von der historischen Methode bei den Geschichtschreibern des Mittelalters (VI–XIII Jahrhundert),* published in 1909.

[29] Ray (1974), 35. Genre, for Ray, included studies in which scholars attempted to decide into what genres medieval historiography should be divided, and also studies of a particular genre as a whole. For the former, projects such as that of van Caenegem and Ganshof (1978), as well as the survey by Grundmann (1957); for the latter, for example, Anna Dorothea von den Brincken's study of universal history (1957).

[30] See, for example, Beer (1981); Pizarro (1989); Morse (1991); Goetz (1999); van Houts (1999).

In 1980, Bernard Guenée published *Histoire et culture historique dans l'Occident médiévale*. In 1985, Franz Josef Schmale published *Funktion und Formen mittelalterlicher Geschichtsschreibung: eine Einfuhrung*. The two books are quite similar in many ways. In each book, the author considers the whole range of medieval historiography in chapters on the place of history in medieval knowledge, the way the author learned about the past, the ways time was marked, the relationship to religious writing, and the nature of historical truth, function, and audience. By taking a topical approach to the historical texts, rather than one based on genre or chronology, Guenée and Schmale are able to examine much more clearly the place of history-writing in medieval intellectual life, and ways that medieval historians thought about their subject matter.

Other than these comprehensive works, there have been numerous studies on more focused groups of historical texts. Generally these studies center on a particular geographic area in one particular period, or even on one text, and to look at the factors (political, personal, institutional, etc.) that went into the texts' construction. National surveys have appeared for England, Italy, and Spain.[31] Five volumes devoted to individual genres of texts have appeared in the series *Typologie des Sources du Moyen Age occidental*, on early medieval annals, universal chronicles, hagiographical manuscripts, *gesta episcoporum et abbatum*, and local and regional chronicles.[32] As noted above, all of these different types of categories are modern conceptions created for the purpose of studying a group of texts, rather than necessarily corresponding to what medieval historians were doing.[33]

Conclusions

It is much easier to write an analysis of an individual text than to attempt to survey medieval history-writing as a whole. As the idea that medieval historians did not think in terms of genre has taken

---

[31] England: Gransden (1974); Spain: Dübler (1943) and Linehan (1993); Italy: Zanella (1984).
[32] McCormick (1975); Krueger (1976); Philippart (1977); Sot (1981); van Houts (1995).
[33] Cf. Roest (1999), 48–49.

hold, scholars have shied away from writing surveys of medieval historiography, instead focusing on more theoretical aspects of history writing. The purpose of the present volume is to attempt to fill that void, by introducing the whole variety of medieval historical texts, as well as the ways that modern scholars have approached them.

Since genres, either medieval or modern, are now held in such disrepute, this book takes as an organizational framework the subject matter of the texts: whose pasts were being written down in the Middle Ages. In some cases, the texts discussed in a chapter will represent only one or two of the traditional historiographical genres, but in other cases many different sorts of texts might be considered, for example in the chapter by Joaquin Pizarro. By considering the texts in this way, we can do two things at once. First, we can see which entities were considered worthy of having their history written down (and, by extension, which were not) at various periods. Second, we can examine how the histories of these entities were written, which conventions and genres were considered suitable for them, and thus ultimately understand something about historical genres as well. At certain points we can see that a genre *has* developed, with assumptions and rules, and based on a recognized model.[34]

Rather than simply understanding the place of history in medieval intellectual culture, by looking at the different types of subject matter memorialized in these texts, we reach a broader understanding of what mattered at different times and in different contexts, of what sorts of individuals, groups, and sets of events were considered worthy of having their history recorded. The book is divided into two parts, early and later Middle Ages. For the early period, there are four chapters, whereas for the later period there are seven. This is partly because many more texts survive from the later period, and in order to give greater coverage to them, more chapters were deemed necessary. But a look at the chapter titles also indicates the wider array of subject matter that was covered by history in the later period.

For the early Middle Ages, historiographical texts can be divided into four main subject areas. Universal history was very popular since

---

[34] Allen (in this volume) notes this for universal history; Pizarro (in this volume) for the *origo gentis*, which, however, only exists as a conscious genre after the tenth century.

Eusebius of Caesarea invented the genre; as also in the later Middle Ages, universal histories usually start with creation, and then become more local as they approach the time of their composition. In a sense, they thus function as both universal and local histories, in this case with 'local' being the bishopric or the kingdom or the territorial unit.[35] The early Middle Ages was a period that saw many new political entities come into being; of these, it seems to have been particularly 'peoples' who had their histories written, which was sometimes, but not always, analogous with kingdoms. This ambiguity of subject matter reflects the ambiguity of the identities of the 'peoples' and kingdoms themselves. Curiously, the Carolingian empire, which saw a large amount of historiography and the development of some new forms (notably the annal), was not the subject of major narrative histories.[36] Institutions in the early Middle Ages whose histories were written down were almost exclusively bishoprics and individual monasteries, whose pasts were universalized by demonstrating their divine origins.[37] And of the biographical writing produced, there were only a very few Lives of exceptional rulers (Charlemagne, Alfred); otherwise it was all hagiography.[38]

As institutions, governments, cities, and families developed, arose, became more complex and perhaps more politically or socially important, they too began to become the subject of historical writing. The genres used for the new subjects were often the same as in the early Middle Ages, but they were adapted to highlight the new subject matter. What is interesting about the "new" subject matter in the later Middle Ages is that the area which saw the greatest expansion in terms of subject matter was local and institutional history. For the early Middle Ages, this was one category, and it almost always covered the history of a bishopric or monastery. In the later Middle Ages, in contrast, various different subjects on the local level were deemed worthy of having their own histories, such as ruling families, cities, and religious institutions. An interesting development is that in the later Middle Ages, some religious institutions have become transnational; thus histories of mendicant orders, for example, are

---

[35] See Sot and Allen, in this volume.
[36] See Pizarro, in this volume.
[37] See Sot, in this volume.
[38] See Heffernan, in this volume.

now institutional but no longer local.[39] Another type of history that was not new, but was rediscovered, was the writing about recent events such as a military campaign, a crusade, or a war, written by a participant or someone who interviewed eyewitnesses. This was the classical subject for history, but had been neglected in the early Middle Ages, at least in the Latin West. There was also the development of texts which present material in a historical manner, although the subject matter is considered fictional by us (and was by people in the Middle Ages also). It is important to consider those epic and legendary texts alongside more "factual" historiographical ones, to remind us how interrelated were the literary forms.[40] Nonetheless, some categories—like universal history, biography and hagiography, and national history—continued as subjects for historians, although of course with changes in focus and purpose.[41]

The writing of history required someone to say that the history of something needed to be written down, and then someone had to research and write the text. The choice of subject matter thus informs us of the self-awareness of entities, and of the general cultural values that made the idea of writing such a history possible. For example, Augusto Vasina defines urban historiography as not just histories which focus on cities, but histories that actually recognize or deal with the consciousness that they are writing about cities; in other words, not just people writing about their own localities, but people writing in a way that shows that they are aware that the important subject of their histories is the urban collective. What we see throughout this volume is that history was written when its subject mattered to someone. Sometimes history was just written as an exercise in scholarly curiosity, and certainly it was often considered entertainment;[42] it also usually had a purpose in the larger world of ideas, to create, establish, or justify an institution, a lineage, a kingdom, a saint. By studying the types of history that were written, we can learn what mattered to whom, and when.

When does medieval historiography end? Forms and types of subject matter developed by medieval historians continued to be written

---

[39] Cf. van Houts (1995). See Shopkow, Roest, and Vasina, in this volume.
[40] See the two chapters by Ainsworth, in this volume.
[41] See Sprandel, Kersken, and Goodich, in this volume.
[42] Cf. Partner (1977).

for centuries after the end of the Middle Ages (whenever that is to be defined). Certainly new ways of writing history began to be added in the fifteenth and sixteenth centuries: the humanistic focus on classical antiquity led to a new phase of writing history following classical models; the Protestant challenge to the universality of the Church led to histories written for specifically polemical religious purposes; a new interest in applying scientific principles to historical learning led to the development of text criticism (including criticism of historical source texts), and auxiliary studies such as numismatics.[43] None of these marks a clear break with the medieval tradition; after all, new historiographical forms and classical revivals had appeared during the Middle Ages also. Perhaps the most significant break is pointed out by Norbert Kersken for national histories, but is also valid for other types: until the sixteenth century, historical texts were produced in the territory which was their subject, and were written for, and usually by, its own inhabitants. It is thus the humanist interest in other peoples' histories, and especially the writing of histories by foreigners, which marks the end of the medieval historiographical tradition.[44]

---

[43] See Breisach (1994), 153–70.
[44] In this volume.

PART ONE

EARLY MEDIEVAL HISTORIOGRAPHY

CHAPTER ONE

UNIVERSAL HISTORY 300–1000: ORIGINS AND WESTERN DEVELOPMENTS

Michael I. Allen

For Peter White

Beginnings

The practice of universal history from A.D. 300 to 1000 reflects basic
tenets and wider concerns of Christian belief. Adherents to the faith
received in baptism a sacramental cleansing from Original Sin, inherited by all humanity from Adam and Eve. The baptized, whatever
their personal stories, gained forgiveness and kept, for that, a nature
shared with the first parents in their fallen state. Ambrose of Milan
evoked the common origin of all in his sermons on the *Hexaemeron*,
or "Six Days of Creation", which he delivered in A.D. 386 during
the paschal week that culminated in the new and annually reaffirmed
christenings of the Easter Vigil. To aspirants who had applied for
baptism, the bishop preached other sermons on Abraham and the
patriarchs.[1] For new and established believers, there lay—beyond
kith, kin, locality, and perceived time—an inherited community and
history rooted in the Bible: to believe was to assent to a divine plan
whose origins Moses had written and whose end the prophets and
the resurrected Christ had foretold. Yet, if Christian leaders like
Ambrose harked back to a common beginning, or "principle" (*prin-
cipium*), promptly allegorized into Christ himself,[2] the task of elabo-
rating what was simple and all-embracing was often complex and
time-bound. Genesis set the beginning of history, and St. Paul, for

---

[1] Cf. Introduction to *Sancti Ambrosii Opera*, ed. C. Schenkl, *CSEL* 32/1 (1897),
2:vi–viii.
[2] Ambrose, *Hexaemeron* I.4.15, ed. C. Schenkl, *CSEL* 32/1 (1897), 2:13.

one, emphasized the goal and the quality of its trajectory when he
wrote to the Philippians (3:20): "Yet our citizenship[3] is in heaven,
whence also we look for the Saviour, the Lord Jesus Christ". The
universal history of the Christian dispensation was a matter of common origin and desired end, of self-definition, and also of intuited
and perscribed strategies for the present.

Classical Antiquity had known its own universal histories, cut to
the contours and needs of its leading cultures.[4] Christians did not
ignore these writings and their facts, but focused of necessity on the
dynamic of their own community, the paradox of its continued existence in the absence of Jesus's return, and the mystery of its increase,
even in the teeth of persecution. From very early, there was need
to address the spectre of the messianic promise and, also, to shape
and root a viable communal identity within a sometimes hostile social
context. The body of scripture inherited from the Jews and the emergent canon of holy texts connected with Jesus provided the basis for
understanding and attempted explanation. Believers, confirmed by
Jesus's own use of allegory and typology, took for granted the unity
and coherence of Scripture, subject to the use of the right exegetical methods. Biblical utterance in its diverse aggregate and presumed
unity of intent amounted to a single universal history and also invited
various acts of interpretive reconciliation.

Jesus's promise to return and the goad of alternate, competing
wisdoms set the actual backdrop for the first Christian translations
of biblical historical data into the lineaments of a distinct universal
history. St. John's *Apocalypse* (ca. A.D. 95) had first raised against
Rome the force of biblical allegory (Rome as the harlot Babylon)
and pointed to the persecutor Nero under the figure "six hundred
threescore and six".[5] Attention to analogous historical data, suggested
in the Old Testament and its Christian supplements, gave believers
tools to stir or still eschatological fears. As vigorous churches emerged
in cultivated urban centres, Christian apologists used biblical chronology

---

[3] Or "way of life" for the Latin *conversatio*, as found before and in Jerome's Latin
Vulgate (ca. A.D. 400); from St. Paul's Greek, πολίτευμα, '(practice of) citizenship'.
All biblical references follow the Vulgate and its numbering.

[4] E.g., Diodorus Siculus, *Bibliothêke* (ca. 50 B.C.), and Justin's *Epitome* (3rd cent. A.D.)
of the *Philippic Histories* of Pompeius Trogus (1st cent. B.C.).

[5] Cf. Rev. 17–18; Rev. 13:18, the key example of Hellenistic *gematria*, or mystical
number science, in Christian scripture.

positively to advance claims to authority and antiquity. By the end of the second century A.D., Clement of Alexandria could build on the efforts of numerous predecessors, including co-opted Jewish learning, to assert the temporal and logical priority of Christian revelation. He compared biblical time-spans with parallel evidence for Assyrian, Egyptian, and Greek history and showed that God's revealed truth predated and nourished Greek philosophy. Outward-looking argument claimed title by precedence and suggested the practical reach of sacred chronology and the common human roots traced in Bible. Both the origin and end of time figured in the *Chronography* of Julius Africanus, who, after schooling in Alexandria, elaborated the first, broadly framed Christian treatement of world-historical data (ca. A.D. 217). In addition to showing Old Testament priority by means of its synchronies with other world history, Africanus explicitly fixed Christ's birth in the year 5,500 from Creation, based on biblical sums that he confirmed—as Nero's identity is revealed in the *Apocalypse*—by symbolical substitution. The coherence of biblical history invited typological proofs, whose hallmark was to bridge the divide of the Incarnation, where ancient foreshadowings resolve in the Christian "fullness of time".[6] To start, Africanus presupposed a lifespan for the world of 7,000 years, and followed in that an established cosmic remapping of the Six Days of Creation, plus a Sabbath of Rest, which literally accounted "a day in God's sight as a thousand years" (cf. Ps. 89:4; 2 Pet. 3:8). Christ, the Beginning and End of Creation (cf. Rev. 21:6), thus died in his Passion at the half point of the sixth day of the week (John 19:14), and so the Incarnation of the 5,500th year coincided with its own sacramental fulfillment in the final week and day of the Saviour's earthly work. Africanus, a layman in imperial service, cribbed this ambitious typological key from the *Commentary on Daniel* (ca. A.D. 204) of Hippolytus, a rigorist presbyter and later schismatic bishop of Rome, who himself issued a tightly focused *Chronicle* in A.D. 234, near the end of a life marked by confessional strife, secular persecution, and his own major summation of church liturgy and discipline, the *Apostolic Tradition* (A.D. 215). Hippolytus and Africanus together bear witness to an intense preoccupation with the details of history, as number and symbolical confirmation, deployed to address the situation of believers in time.

---

[6] Gal. 4:4. On the Bible and its interpretation, see de Lubac (1959–64).

From the flux of the agreed sixth millennium, Hippolytus fixed his
followers, and a wider readership, in the 5,738th year of the world
and, thereby, removed to an emphatically unnamed (and perhaps
unknowable) distance the spectre of the cosmic end (cf. Acts 1:7).
The bishop's pronouncement on time bent attention back to the
imperatives of continued communal existence.[7] Where Hippolytus
acted with pastoral specificity, Africanus integrated broader historical detail, the rhetoric of precedence, the logic of typology, and even
fresh, if sketchy, speculation on a safely distant seventh millennium.
Africanus wrought the first comprehensive, if now fragmentary, vision
of world time, and meant therein to push its end from proximity.
In doing both, he drew together the possibilities suggested by the
fundamental biblical narrative and also the time-bound concerns and
exegetical methods of his contemporaries. These, in rapid sketch,
were the terms and beginnings of a new historical idiom.

Eusebius

This Christian universal history embraced the inhabited world (the
Hellenistic *oikoumênê*) and counted time from Creation, based on the
Bible and parallel secular evidence. It showed a pragmatic engagement with this same world, both as a place of learning and as the
vessel of salvation. One century later, Eusebius of Caesarea still
praised Africanus's monumental exactitude,[8] but, more important, he
followed and greatly expanded his exemplar. The translations and
re-applications of Eusebius's results and ideas, especially by St. Jerome
(†ca. 419), would determine the content and shape of most strands
of universal historical writing in the Latin West.

   Eusebius (ca. 260–339) first approached history from the standpoint of a biblical exegete and only afterwards as a leading ecclesiastic in a new, assertively Christian imperial dispensation. During
the scholar's long tenure as bishop (from ca. 312), Constantine the
Great (306–337) successively snuffed out competing co-rulers and
definitively ended the recurrent and recently disastrous state-spon-
sored persecutions that had always complicated Christian-Roman

---

[7] Haeusler (1980), 7–11; Altaner and Stuiber (1966), 166–67, 209–10.
[8] *Historia ecclesiastica* VI.31.2.

relations. Constantine attributed his decisive victory at the Milvian Bridge in 312 to a battle standard revealed to him by the Christian God, and he richly acknowledged that divine favour, and others, for the rest of his life. This sea-change in Christian fortunes did not seem arbitrary to its beneficiaries, and Eusebius's formulation of Christian universal history helped to conceptualize the meaning of events.[9]

After excellent scholarly training at Caesarea, Eusebius first composed his *Chronological Canons*, or *Chronicle*, in the shadow of the Great Persecution initiated by Diocletian in the early 300s. He had assembled an extensive dossier, or *Chronography*, of regnal lists and historical extracts, and this he reshaped into a companion volume of parallel chronologies and world history from the year of Abraham's birth. It sufficed merely to sum up earlier biblical times, since a tandem Greek or barbarian record, that is "Gentile history", was lacking.[10] Eusebius thus asserted sacred precedence, lifted from Creation the liability of anchoring a cosmic chronology, and laid out a novel synchronic table that reconciled biblical time with other major systems. He shared the outward-looking concerns of earlier Christian apologists, and plausibly intended to address eschatological fears stirred by persecution. His revised account of biblical chronology moved the Incarnation to the year 5,199 from Creation, and silently broke with the earlier millennial typologies and their eschatological baggage.[11] The *Chronicle* set the decades from Abraham's birth in its leftmost margin and, under those auspices, laid out known history as synchronous vertical columns of regnal dates and coordinated statements or judgments of fact. For nineteen major peoples, the columns appear, continue, or disappear in step with their associated regnal tallies, from four vertical rows initially, to a maximum of nine, and finally to the lone column of the Romans. The rows nestle around interior spaces reserved for concise historical notes, first on two-page openings, with sacred matters to the left and secular ones to the right, until the flow of significant data reduces to one field in a progression of single pages.[12] There, sacred and secular data commingle

---

[9] Cf. Momigliano (1963); Barnes (1981).

[10] Eusebius, Prologue to Eusebius-Jerome, *Die Chronik des Hieronymus (Hieronymi Chronicon)*, 2nd rev. ed., ed. R. Helm, Griechische Christliche Schriftsteller 47 [= Eusebius Werke 7] (Berlin, 1956), 15: "in quibus [temporibus] nulla . . . gentilis inuenitur historia". [3rd ed. repr. with Preface by U. Treu (Berlin, 1984).]

[11] Cf. Landes (1992), 359–60.

[12] For the layout, see Helm's edition: over two pages, four columns, p. 20, and

until and beyond "the peace granted to Christians by Constantine",
at least in Eusebius's final version of the work down to what we
would call A.D. 325.[13] In its completion, this "epitome of universal
history"[14] elaborates myriad particular facts and sets them in the
context of a new whole. The Christian scholar might learn from it
to order major dates and events, and found pagan holy lore reduced
to an innocuously uncelestial retelling.[15] More important, no reader
could avoid the implications of the overall articulation, which was
unprecedented.[16] If Eusebius could lump barbarians and Greeks into
a proto-historical Gentile commonality, the graphical movement of
history itself later resolved all peoples and temporal conventions into
Rome and the presiding count from Abraham. Eusebius knew the
practical advantages of the Saviour's birth under the newly wrought
monarchy and stability of Caesar Augustus. But he chiefly emphasized the dawn of Jesus's public life and his call to all peoples as
the fulfilment and enlargement to the Gentile world of the ancient
biblical promises first made to the Hebrews.[17] Eusebius's ecumenical
digest of time charted the course and integration of many histories
as the unfolding of God's single providential plan for all mankind.

Constantine's new Christian allegiance expressed this divine providence as a symptom reveals its cause, yet in the *Chronicle*, Eusebius
preferred to exploit arrangement and matter-of-factness, to illustrate
a historical dynamic rather than to commentate its latest effect. The
legacy to future writers included, of course, the effect, whose story
Eusebius told in his *Church History* along with earlier Christian travails and triumphs. That amply documented narrative gave his "most
full account", but only of the end-game of a vastly longer unfolding of God's intentions.[18] For the future, the *Chronicle* itself provided
a cosmic dynamic and framework, a store of ancient fact and lore,

---

later nine, p. 83; with a single-page format from p. 106, narrowed to the single
Roman regnal column on p. 187.
    [13] Eusebius-Jerome, *Chronicon* 2330, 2342, pp. 230, 231.
    [14] So Eusebius in his *Eclogae propheticae* I, *PG* 22, col. 1024A.
    [15] Analogous chronological guides are still published, e.g., Finegan (1998). Eusebius,
for instance, reduces the origins of Trojan War to the squabble of three women,
one of whom promises Helen to the shepherd asked to rate their beauty: Eusebius-
Jerome, *Chronicon* 826, p. 60b.
    [16] Burgess (1999), 80–82; Croke (1983); Mosshammer (1979), 29–37.
    [17] Cf. Eusebius-Jerome, *Chronicon* 2015, 2044, pp. 169, 173.
    [18] *Historia ecclesiastica* I.1.6. Cf. Momigliano (1963); Barnes (1981), 126–47.

and a model of rhetorical discretion. All these St. Jerome conveyed in his Latin translation and extension of the work to A.D. 378.

Jerome and His Continuators

The Latin *Chronicle* of Eusebius-Jerome widely disseminated the messages of its now-lost Greek original. Jerome carefully preserved Eusebius's exacting layout and historical breadth, which he supplemented with added Western details for the specific needs of a contemporary Latin readership.[19] He engaged his translator's task as a biblical specialist and ended his forward temporal projection with the still-lingering upset brought upon the Roman world through the defeat and murder of the Arian emperor Valens by Gothic forces at Adrianople in A.D. 378. In his final summation of chronology, Jerome clearly followed Eusebius in accenting Christ's preaching to the world, yet he spoke differently when he then continued to mark time back to Creation itself from the world's troubled 5,579th year.[20] Whether or not the Gothic turmoil loosed new communal fears, the end of the millennial week was plainly nowhere to hand. More important, Jerome set the alpha of time squarely into view, paced off his place from it, and emphatically broadened the province of all-embracing history to its biblical start. He also set, as translator and continuator, the example of reflecting on the flux and continuities of time, or providence, down to the present.

Actual manuscripts of the *Chronicle* of Eusebius-Jerome tended likewise to extend the work in one direction or more. Accounts of pre-Abrahamic biblical history often fill out the preliminary void left by Eusebius and merely bridged by Jerome, and one, the prefixed exordium of a *de luxe* edition used in early sixth-century Italy, shows the adaptive reach of the Christian universal idiom in new circumstances. While it had suited Eusebius to fuse Greeks and barbarians into an amorphous protohistory, Genesis itself also traces, along with the cardinal line of sacred genealogy, Gentile origins in the offspring of Noah. A tabular translation of that history places the Gentiles, too, in their biblical origins, and neatly anticipates, as though in

---

[19] Cf. Burgess (1999), 90–98.
[20] Cf. Eusebius-Jerome, *Chronicon*, Prologue and 2394, pp. 1–7 and 249.

reverse, their later re-integration into sacred history, which was the actual or inherited experience of most Christian readers.[21] At the near end of the *Chronicle*, Jerome himself pointed the way for future continuators, whose additions now often chiefly rate as independent historical documents. The *Chronicle of 452*, in its earliest and best copy, from the early tenth century, continues an adapted Jerome to the eponymous date, where the manuscript then briefly shifts to an alternate continuation by Prosper of Aquitaine to A.D. 455, and thereafter finishes with the *Chronicle* to A.D. 581 of Marius of Avenches (†A.D. 594). Each of these linked additions, like Eusebius-Jerome itself, preserves unique factual information and has attracted focused attention.[22] The problem of the whole, however, remains, since a major ninth-century use of the implicated variant of Jerome and its otherwise unknown appendix by Marius simply ignores the intervening *Chronicle of 452*. Without prejudice to their factual substance, the still-murky history of the medieval Eusebius-Jerome allows little certainly as to when and how some continuations were added, spliced, or replaced, and the date of the present assemblage may be closer to the tenth century than one expects.[23] Like the grafts, the stalk too could vary. The altered Eusebius-Jerome, among other adjustments, elevates Rome, from her first strength, into a proleptic and privileged opposition vis-à-vis the diverse nations (*diuersae gentes*) that she eventually subsumes.[24] The change complicates the sober division of sacred and secular in the original epitome of world history but accurately reflects St. Jerome's own mature and influential understanding of the mechanisms of providence.

Christian universal history was, for Jerome and his Latin successors, both a matter of schematic, epitomized content and also of purposive theological reflection. The expression of universal historical

---

[21] Cf. Schöne (1900), 25, 276. The exordium is published in Schöne (1875), 43–49.

[22] Cf. Muhlberger (1990); Favrod (1993); Burgess (2001).

[23] The ninth-century complication arises from the *Histories* (A.D. 830) of Frechulf of Lisieux, on which more below. On the still unwritten history of Eusebius-Jerome in the early Middle Ages, cf. Schöne (1900), 39–41, 135–37.

[24] Consider, for instance, the new arrangement and rubrication of Eusebius-Jerome at *Chronicon* 1504 (p. 106), where the adapted text joins, to the left, prospective Roman with actual Persian leadership ("Reges Persarum et Romanorum") opposite, to the right, the "other peoples" ("Reges gentium diuersarum"); see also MS London, British Library, Add. 16974, fol. 87ᵛ.

thought varied from the skeletal but meaningful arrangement of historical data, to the focused treatment of the logic and particular
expressions of divine providence, often in the context of biblical exegesis. Jerome's engagement with Eusebius reflected his preoccupation to explain and translate the Bible, as well as the need to interpret
the roots and terms of the history that Christians had acquired and
made. His contemporary Sulpicius Severus also traced a seamless yet
relentlessly sacred *Chronicle* (A.D. 400) from Creation to the present,
and especially emphasized the continuum of recent holy experience
by joining the travails of the prophets to those of the church in a
single narrative.[25] Sulpicius worked out the prophetic vision of Daniel
2 for the first time in a historiographical context: he parsed the metal
colossus of Nebuchadnezzar's dream into the four great historical
monarchies, from the golden head of Chaldea, via the silver and
bronze of Persia and Macedonia, to Rome's feet of clay and iron,
all of which Christ, as the smiting stone, brings to nothing. Sulpicius's
sectarian focus and even prudery toward alien, secular forces—be
they heretics, Jews, or the Roman state—almost never widen beyond
the narrow path to salvation, and left his eloquent but promptly forgotten narrative unsuited for more broadly engaging what God and
men had wrought.[26]

   Jerome's efforts had the reach to deal positively with both, and
triggered interpretive echoes. His own concise exegesis of Daniel (A.D.
407) reconfigured the basic identifications followed by Sulpicius in
light of the real progress, as it seemed to many, that the Roman
world had witnessed in and since Constantine's conversion. Jerome
explicitly accented God's hand as the force behind the sweep of
world empires, and emphasized the confluence of the prior ones in
the final monarchy of Rome, under which Christ himself had established worship of the true God for many and Jewish cult had expired.[27]
Without illusions as to setbacks, Jerome could see, with Eusebius,
the progress of God's purposes under the aegis of imperial Rome.[28]
For the future, his exegesis vested the continuance of the empire

---

[25] Sulpicius arranged his work as two parts separated at the end of Old Testament
histories, 2 Kings and 2 Chronicles.
[26] Cf. von den Brincken (1957), 71–76.
[27] Cf. Jerome, *In Danielem* 2, 21a; 2, 31/35; 7, 7b; 11, 24; ed. F. Glorie, *CCSL*
75A (Turnhout, 1958), 787, 794, 843, 875.
[28] Kelly (1975), 72–75, 175–77.

with a new cosmic significance: Rome's feet of iron and clay stood, with unknown tenure, at the doorstep of Antichrist and the world's end.[29] In the near term, Jerome decisively influenced the tone and articulation of Orosius's major account of world history from a Christian perspective.

Augustine and Orosius

In place of an epitome or mnemonic chart, Orosius (†ca. 419) proposed a narrative reckoning with the content and meaning of time. His *Histories against the Pagans* (ca. 417) traces human experience from its beginning in Adam's Fall to the present, and proclaims the watershed marked by the Saviour's advent and effect in privileged Roman times. Orosius had arrived in North Africa from Spain, as a refugee, in the mid-410s, and Augustine of Hippo (†430) promptly enlisted his help, among other roles, in compiling a dossier meant to illustrate, not relativize, recurrent human catastrophes: these had often equalled the trauma of recent barbarian incursions, and even the specific anguish of Rome's sack by the Goths in A.D. 410. Augustine himself, in the on-going composition of his *City of God* (412–426), reacted to pagan recriminations that Rome fell because the abandoned gods had deserted her. The catalogue of disasters, which the bishop had neither the taste nor perhaps the sources to pursue, became Orosius's project.[30] Theological business led to a mission by the Spaniard to Jerome in Bethlehem, and that encounter proved fateful. Orosius would follow Augustine's lead in fixing sin as the source and motor of human misery, but in other key regards he followed Jerome and ignored his sponsor's mistrust of equating God's hidden purposes with external circumstance. Augustine's episcopal office included battling schismatics raised by former persecutions, and he spent Mondays judging cases sequestered from the venality of civil courts. For him, the practical consequences of sin showed the

---

[29] Jerome, *In Danielem* 7, 7c–8; ed. Glorie, 843–44.

[30] Cf. Augustine, *De ciuitate Dei* IV.2, ed. B. Dombart and A. Kalb, *CCSL* 47–48 (Turnhout, 1955), 47:99–100; Orosius, *Historiae aduersus paganos* I Prol., 10, ed. and trans. M.-P. Arnaud-Lindet, 3 vols. (Paris, 1990–91), 1:8. On the sources of the two works, cf. Angus (1906); Lacroix (1965), 59–62. On the early literary impact of Rome's fall, see Feichtinger (1998).

instability and basic indifference of any links between secular power and the purely spiritual promise of redemption in Christian times. The bishop dismissed the facile triumphalism and convenient presumptions of some fellow believers, and Orosius joined Jerome as one of them.[31]

Nonetheless, Orosius salvaged from his tale of calamities a creative statement of Christian Roman confidence, expressed as a masterly reconfiguration of universal history. He exploits the possibilities of narrative not only to trace the misfortunes of the world from their start but also to shape the telling through argument and allegory into a new historical vision. Orosius follows Jerome's framework and provides a place for all peoples in the pre-Abrahamic landscape by means of a comprehensive survey of geography.[32] He moves from sin as common root, to the world as common theatre, for the economy of calamity, chastisement, reward, and salvation that he means to trace. Orosius addresses Augustine's original brief by recounting the recurrent slaughters and natural disasters of ancient history. His seven books unfold both the depths and breadth of human miscreance and God's unfailing punishments: misery as its own reward and as the consequence of divine justice. That would have sufficed for the assigned task, but Jerome's *Chronicle*, among other prods, invited more than a mere expansion of its most sombre cues. A fundamental insight was to seize upon and virtually sacralize the concurrence of Christ's transformative entry into history and the rise of the Roman imperial dispensation under Augustus. Orosius configured Jesus's public advent and call to all peoples in terms of the monarchy that ruled them, and that monarchy itself, whatever the failings of its leaders, assumed from its distant origins the aura of a pre-ordained benefaction and historical culmination. The years from Rome's founding pace the subsequent chronology of the world.[33] The arrival of Christ under Augustus begins Orosius's final book and a new dispensation of favour in which even secular disasters weigh lighter for the coming of the Redeemer.

This rosy conceptualization emphasized the progress of Christian times over the past, and reflected both a wide optimism and particular effort by Orosius. Hippolytus of Rome also had noticed the

---

[31] Cf. Mommsen (1959a); Markus (1988), 1–71; Mommsen (1959b), 287, 297.
[32] Orosius, *Historiae* I.2, ed. Arnaud-Lindet, 1:13–42. Cf. Janvier (1982).
[33] Orosius, *Historiae* II.3.5–10, ed. Arnaud-Lindet, 1:89–90.

coincidence of Augustus's empire and Christ's birth, and had seen
in the former an earthly, Satanic foil to the Saviour's heavenly kingdom.[34] Jerome's rereading of Daniel updated the gloomy, third-cen-
tury judgment, and Orosius built on his findings. Jerome had mapped
the four empires of Daniel 7 onto the successive kingdoms of Babylon,
the Medes and the Persians, Macedonia, and, finally, imperial Rome.
Orosius's revision configured the series in light of his Iberian homeland and its past experience of Carthaginian sway, and it adapted
the temporal paradigm to embrace earthly and human geography.
He replotted the succession with a directional focus: first, the realm
of the Assyrians, Medes, and Persians to the east; succeeded by that
of Carthage to the south, and then of Macedonia to the north; all
finally subsumed from the west by the world monarchy of Rome.
For the Middle Ages, Orosius thus framed the best-known expression of the cosmic paradigm of the "Four Kingdoms", which led to
Rome and presupposed the continuance of her rule lest the world
itself come to an end.[35] For mankind, he posited the single present
empire under whose aegis God had set all nations in order to call
them to salvation. Not least for himself, Orosius bound up his spiritual faith with the worldly dominion where he, a refugee, was everywhere a citizen and where all might be as much by virtue of creed.[36]
Therein lay solace, faith in assimilation, and seeming paradox.

Apart from the questionable blessing of barbarian upheaval, it
required creativity to argue away the shadows of persecution. If
Orosius privileged the Roman Empire through biblical allegory and
compliant mystical numbers, he also meant to prove the final alliance
of spiritual faith and secular state that his Christian Roman citizenship presupposed. To this end, he resorted to an ambitious typological reading of the Bible to reckon with the pagan persecutions
and to spotlight spiritual progress even *within* Christian times. He
expounded the ten plagues inflicted on Egypt in the Exodus (cf.
Exod. 7–11) as foreshadowings of God's punishments against the ten
pagan imperial persecutors. Constantine's conversion had changed
all that: leading temples became churches, and "thereafter God's

---

[34] Markus (1963), 342.
[35] Orosius, *Historiae* II.1.5–6, ed. Arnaud-Lindet, 1:84–85. Cf. Krüger (1976),
24–25 and notes.
[36] Cf. Orosius, *Historiae* V.2 and VII.32.12–13, ed. Arnaud-Lindet, 2:86–87 and
3:87.

people was nevermore forced to idolatry".[37] The Empire, too, reaped divine rewards for the emperor's piety. Yet, without prejudice to facts, the argument presumed against the narrative closure of scriptural prophecy, which Christ himself had fulfilled. Moreover, such progress seemed to qualify the original fullness of the work of salvation. For Augustine, Orosius's historical effort amounted to bad theology, and the bishop disavowed his poignantly unnamed disciple: the thesis and method showed "not the spirit of prophecy, but rather the conjecture of a human mind, which sometimes arrives at the truth and sometimes errs".[38]

Unlike Orosius, Augustine mistrusted the world, its ways, and its citizenship. A key effort of his *City of God*, which Orosius purported to complement, was to argue for Christian detachment from the world, not least from the state. Orosius salvaged and spoke to the political order by emphasizing the dynamic of God's retributions and rewards; he worked out a christianized *do ut des* religious economy for a Roman Empire proved destined to survive.[39] Augustine focused on the independent completeness of Christ's salvation, which left no place and no need for spinning biblical typologies into the secular present or for pretending to fathom God's mysterious purposes. In books 14–18 of the *City of God*, he unfolded the origin and course of human history as the segmented story of the heavenly city and its earthly counterpart. His vision embraces all mankind in its shared original sin, its dissemination over the earth, and, above all, in the originary, overriding spiritual and social fracture that defines two distinct communities—the *civitas Dei* and the *civitas terrena*—by virtue of their love of God or the world.[40] Although neither city ever lacked, the Bible itself is unclear as to the shape of those who worshiped the true God before Abraham.[41] Because God's Covenant thereafter creates an interim historical identity for his city, Augustine proceeds by unfolding a nearly exclusive account of Hebrew history from

---

[37] Orosius, *Historiae* VII.27.4–16, ed. Arnaud-Lindet, 3:70–74.

[38] Augustine, *De ciuitate Dei* XVIII.52, ed. Dombart and Kalb, 48:650–52. Orosius is explicitly identified as the target by Augustine's friend, Quodvultdeus, *Liber promissionum et praedicationum Dei* III.36, ed. R. Braun, *CCSL* 60 (1994).

[39] Cf. Tanz (1983), 344–46; Hillgarth (1992), 158–59.

[40] Cf. Augustine, *De ciuitate Dei* XIV.28, and XV.1, ed. Dombart and Kalb, 48:451–54.

[41] Cf. Ibid. XVI.1 and 10, ed. Dombart and Kalb, 48:498, 512–13.

Abraham and God's promises up to the Incarnation.[42] As if to melt that history and its Christian fulfillment into the meaning he intends, Augustine only then traces, as a single book, the surrounding and contrasting story of the earthly city from Abraham up to his own day.[43] The Saviour's work extended God's promises to all humanity in Christian times, and changed their quality and expectation. However, for that, the broadened sociology of heavenly longing no longer reduced straightforwardly to any earthly assembly.[44] The enemies of God's city included some of her yet unknown future citizens, whereas some companions of her earthly pilgrimage, even joined in her sacraments, would prove alien to the eternal reward of the saints.[45] Augustine warily understood his fellow Romans and Christians, and set his stock by the heavenly citizenship of the angels and their right love and worship of the true God.[46]

Two very different understandings of human circumstances thus emerged with the help of universal historical narrative. Augustine's metahistorical categories, if clearly understood, made familiar earthly constructs unreliable for the needs of God's city. Orosius, who claimed Augustine's sponsorship, powerfully asserted the providential construct of Rome's empire and made all history, pagan or sacred, into a means of instruction, subject to the historian's power of exegetical prophecy. Orosius met and vastly exceeded the apologetic goal of cataloguing ancient disasters. For subsequent historical expression, his work brilliantly commended the narrative form of books and chapters, and its trove of data became an omnipresent authoritative reference.[47] Readers prized its analysis of unfailing divine punishment and reward, which invited the extension of Christian ethics into the political sphere through the use and new creation of historical writing.[48] The practical clarity and force of Orosius's engagement mostly overrode Augustine's subtle theological vision. The claim

---

[42] Cf. Ibid. XVIII.1, ed. Dombart and Kalb, 48:592–93.

[43] Ibid. XVIII, ed. Dombart and Kalb, 48:592–656.

[44] For an analysis of Augustine's understanding, with a survey of important literature, see Staubach (2002), 345–58.

[45] Cf. Augustine, *De ciuitate Dei*, I.35, ed. Dombart and Kalb, 47:33.

[46] Cf. Ibid. X.7, ed. Dombart and Kalb, 47:279–80; XVIII.54, ed. Dombart and Kalb, 48:656.

[47] Hillgarth (1992).

[48] Cf. Werner (1987), 7–16.

of sponsorship drew the master's authority to his student and commended the mistake of reading the *City of God* through Orosius's lens and seeing the heavenly city in the Christianized empire.[49]

Augustine influenced the idiom of universal history less ambiguously through his cosmic periodization according to the "Six Ages". The *City of God* presupposed rather than repeated the chronology of Eusebius-Jerome.[50] Its theological purposes required a temporal framework that reflected the milestones of sacred history, and the bishop possessed such a scheme. The Six Ages recur in many works by Augustine, and they show plainly how an historical tool could develop and migrate across generic divides. Augustine's most detailed statement of the Ages occurs in his early *Commentary on Genesis against the Manichees* (ca. A.D. 388), a polemic directed at one group with resonance for others. Since the second century, Christians had understood the Six Days of Creation, with the appended Sabbath of Rest, as typological shorthand for the world's duration of six, or seven, thousand years. On the latter assumption, as we saw, Julius Africanus had mapped universal time partly to set the troubling prospect of the year 6,000 and the ensuing millennium beyond the horizon. Augustine disarmed the typology by means of biblical history and adapted classical understandings of the phases of human life. Analogous temporal cadences existed, but Augustine minted something essentially new. He matched the successive days of Creation to periods of sacred history, as defined by persons or events, and added comparisons between those historical phases and the stations of an individual life. Thus, the first Age, from Adam, was infancy (*infantia*); the second, from Noah, childhood (*pueritia*); the third, from Abraham, adolescence (*adolescentia*); the fourth, from David, youth (*iuventus*); the fifth, from Captivity in Babylon, maturity (*gravitas*); the sixth, from Christ's preaching, old age (*senectus*); and last, the seventh, the final rest to come. World time as lifetime-writ-large immediately opened the gates to socially useful moral allegory based on sacred history. Equally important, the facts of biblical chronology eroded the disruptive potential of the original millennial week, since each Age, as

---

[49] Cf. Marrou (1970), 85–87.
[50] So the source notes to *De ciuitate Dei* XVIII, ed. Dombart and Kalb, 48:592 ff. Augustine took care, however, to state correct regnal chronology where Orosius grossly stretched it: Marrou (1970), 75 and n. 38.

Augustine underscored, embraced a different span of time.[51] Augustine redeployed this scheme in the later, historically minded books of his *City of God*, and there, as elsewhere, he emphasized the vanity of striving in the Sixth Age "to know the times which the Father has set" for the Seventh (cf. Acts 1:7).[52] Believers, he argued, lived already in the symbolical "millennium" of God's earthly kingdom by virtue of their spiritual resurrection from sin and acknowledgement of the Saviour.[53] Their need, or at least one need, was to apply themselves to the promise of heavenly fulfillment, undistracted by times known only to God. Augustine thus worked to channel eschatological aspiration into a patient yet demanding present. The scheme of the Ages helped to disarm reductive chronology and kept the ultimate goal of time plainly in view. Augustine concluded his *City of God* with a capsule account of the Six Ages of the world and the subsequent unfolding of Man's Sabbath of Rest into the Lord's Day, the unending Eighth Age of the corporeal resurrection.[54] That concise statement, if not Augustine's richest exposition, showed the practical background and reach of what became a key instrument of universal historical organization.

Isidore and Bede

Unlike Eusebius-Jerome or Orosius, Augustine's historically minded reflections offered no real purchase for continuation as such. The conceptualizations of the Two Cities and the Six Ages each presented their respective visionary completeness, which could be more

---

[51] Augustine, *De Genesi contra Manichaeos* I.33–43, *PL* 34, cols. 34, cols. 190–94. Cf. Schmidt (1956), 292–97.

[52] Cf. Augustine, *De ciuitate Dei* XVI.43, and XVIII.53, ed. Dombart and Kalb, 48:550, 652–53.

[53] Ibid. XX.7–9, ed. Dombart and Kalb, 48:708–19.

[54] Ibid. XXII.30, ed. Dombart and Kalb, 48:862–66, esp. 865–66. Augustine here changes one important point vis-à-vis the earlier treatment of the Ages sketched above. The *Commentary on Genesis against the Manichees* I.40 emphasizes, with Eusebius-Jerome, Christ's preaching as the dawn of the Sixth Age: "Mane autem fit ex praedicatione euangelii per Dominum", *PL* 34, col. 192. The conclusion of the *City of God* shifts the pivot to the Nativity ("ad Christi carnalem natiuitatem"), in a way reminiscent of Orosius. There were, however, other currents of theological discussion on the Incarnation that may have influenced the shift, on which see Barnes (1982).

readily adapted than developed. The scheme of the Ages spoke in particular to concerns rooted in exegesis and chronology, and where these persisted, they invited the re-application of Augustine's solution in conjunction with other arguments or chronological evidence. Churchmen in positions of leadership adapted, condensed, and continued Eusebius-Jerome to frame their own situation in time, and from the early seventh century, the scheme of the Ages regularly appears as an organizing superstructure in updated compendia of universal history. As he did with so much else, Isidore of Seville (†A.D. 636) takes credit for amalgamating and popularizing Augustine's temporal conceit. Isidore analyzed and applied it in the discussion and *Lesser Chronicle* (A.D. 627) given in his *Etymologies*, and there built on the use found in his *Greater Chronicle*, whose re-editions (from A.D. 615) meld several sources, including the *City of God*.[55] In both settings, Isidore filled out Eusebius-Jerome for the two pre-Abrahamic ages and extended the underlying chronology in a single-column distillate of universal history, now matched with running dates configured to the Creation. Augustine's stature may have recommended the Ages even where polemical needs were not acute, but the *Greater Chronicle* did underscore his warning about the uncertain remainder of earthly time, with concluding advice that "each should look to his own passing", since "that is for him the end of the world".[56] Isidore's cosmic numerical datings showed as well that the world's ages varied considerably in extent. Nevertheless, reliance on the Greek Septuagint's chronology, followed since Eusebius-Jerome, still placed the start of the Sixth Age in the year 5,196, a figure easily rounded into a troublesome spectre.

In reaction, Bede the Venerable (†A.D. 735) seized on the counting of the "Hebrew Truth" of Scripture to place Christ's birth in the year 3,952 from Creation. He significantly developed the allegory of the Ages to introduce and articulate his own renumbered summary of universal history. He built on the temporal scheme's original function, and also played out a palpable desire to overlay Isidore's encyclopedic and partly uncritical treatment of "times". In a multiple

---

[55] Isidore of Seville, *Etymologiae*, ed. W. M. Lindsay, Oxford Classical Texts (Oxford, 1911), V.38.5; V.39 (= *Lesser Chronicle*). The latter is edited with the *Greater Chronicle* by T. Mommsen, in *Chronica minora*, vol. 2, MGH AA 11 (1894; repr. Munich, 1981), 424–81.

[56] Isidore, *Chronica*, § 418, p. 481.

effort, Bede meant to end lingering uncertainty about the *computus*,
or rules for Easter-reckoning, needed to translate the high feast's
lunar dating, from the Hebrew calendar, into its complex yet predictable annual shifts in the solar calendarical system inherited by
Christians from Rome. Isidore's *Etymologies* passed along confused
information on the relevant lunar and solar cycles and helped to
protract upset about a key matter of Christian time-keeping. Bede
reworked the entire field in two discussions, his *On Times* of A.D. 703
and his *Reckoning of Time* of A.D. 725, which respectively conclude
with his *Lesser* and *Greater Chronicle*.[57] The redating of the Incarnation,
based on Jerome's Vulgate Latin translation of Scripture, occurred
first in the earlier work and merited Bede an ill-considered charge
of heresy. This prompted a pointed reply that showed the teacher's
indignant irritation at millennial questioning and spurred studies
that culminated in the highly sophisticated later monograph.[58] Bede
there set the standards for medieval Easter-reckoning, and the associated *Greater Chronicle*, with its revised dates, became a norm in its
own right.

Bede's mature discussion bound universal history into a whole that
reflected the unity of the physical, spiritual, and moral worlds. His
use of the Ages articulated history so as to seal the preceding theoretical discussions of times and their markers with positive particular information: the *Greater Chronicle* thus affirmed, for instance, the
practitioners of correct Easter-reckoning, just as it recounted the triumphs of the saints in times of persecution; its revised datings and
applications of the Ages ploughed away the potential for millennial
unclarity left by Isidore; and Bede's own discussion of continuing
earthly time emphatically asserted its unknown and unknowable duration. Once again, Bede reconfigured and extended the basic data of
Eusebius-Jerome and kept universal history, for the changes of context and content, keenly relevant to contemporary theological reflection
and practical questions. The success of his computistical solutions

---

[57] The complete texts with the included chronicles (as edited by T. Mommsen)
have been published by C. W. Jones, in *CCSL* 123B (1977), pp. 263–544 (= *De
temporum ratione*, with the *Chronica maiora* in chapters 66–67, pp. 463–537), and *CCSL*
123C, pp. 585–611 (= *De temporibus*, with the *Chronica minora* in chapters 17–22, pp.
601–11). For Bede's deployment of the Ages, see especially *De temporum ratione* 10
(*De hebdomada aetatum saeculi*); 66.1–9, 20, 38, 81, 143, 268 (the earthly Ages in the
Chronicle); 67 (*De reliquis sextae aetatis*); 68–71 (on the final Ages).
[58] Jones (1943), 120–21, 131–35.

favoured his tandem but separable universal framework, which folded together cosmic time based on Hebrew Truth, the paradigm of the Ages, and wide-ranging yet concise historical annotations.[59] Bede bulks large today for his pioneering but spare use of A.D. and B.C. dating in his *Church History of the English People*.[60] His importance for universal historical idiom was different. Along with Isidore, Bede preached the cadence of the world's ages according to Augustine's model and concerns, and Bede's adjusted chronology helped to set those concerns at least partly to rest.[61]

Models for Subsequent Historiographers

Since Clement of Alexandria, the idiom of universal history had provided Christian thinkers with a highly adaptable means for knowing and stabilizing their place and even their moral duties in the continuum of time. Jerome's *Chronicle* set the background and the terms for virtually all subsequent Latin engagements with historical peoples and events from Abraham and, by implicit embrace, from Creation. Even where Bede revised datings according to "Hebrew Truth" (itself known from Jerome's Vulgate), the sweep of his early historical notices followed the contours and cues of Jerome's chronistic model. In the interval between Jerome and Bede we see, in effect, the emergence of a grammar of universal historical expression rooted in early needs, learned achievement, and innovation. Other authors promptly built on the primary foundation of sacred and secular fact laid by Eusebius-Jerome, Orosius, Isidore, and Bede, in order to situate new elaborations of regional or communal history in their wider Christian and cosmic perspective. In addition to content, these continuators and creators of history emulated the rhetorical examples and devices of their predecessors. These ranged from the succinctly commentated, columnar chronistic form, with or without multiple threads to begin, to the narrative mode of Augustine or Orosius, or even the Latin versions of Greek church histories devoted to Christian times. Structure,

---

[59] Cf. Borst (1998), 511, 754.
[60] Bede, *Historia ecclesiastica gentis Anglorum* I.2, and V.24. Cf. Jones (1943), 120–22.
[61] Cf. Haeusler (1980), 24–32; Schmidt (1956), 293–94.

chronology, and periodization themselves claimed or implied meanings that attested or disproved specific eschatological, providential,
or other postulates. For Orosius, his work marked an advance also
because he superseded pagan historical discourse by starting world
history from Original Sin. Following Augustine and the Bible, Bede
began still earlier, in the week of the Creation, which he dated less
remotely and deployed in its allegorical translation to silence millen-
nialist questioning, as well as to set his nuts-and-bolts *Reckoning of Time*
into its ultimate spiritual and moral perspective. Altogether, we can
discern in these early efforts the normal and mostly normative patterns
that universal historiographical efforts followed when medieval Christian
authors tried to set their time and place into cosmic perspective.

In practical terms, Latin universal history embraced time from the
beginning and embraced the multitude of the world's peoples. Christ's
preaching, or even his birth, heralded the extension of Abraham's
promises to all humanity. Individual historical expression might thereafter narrow its focus, even to local events, but Christian circumstances presupposed, no less than Creation, the transformative spiritual
enlargement that Rome's empire had accompanied, and fostered, by
uniting humanity and geography.

The origins of universal historical idiom consecrated the habit of
lapidary concision. The most obvious major divide among the sources
in question emerges from the occasional choice to expand the meanings of contour and fact by the use of narrative exposition. Universal
history usually takes the form of *epitomized* universal history: the larger
story reduced to essential data, shaped and presented as a universal
chronicle. Augustine presented the larger story in theological terms
for part of his *City of God*, while his follower Orosius worked out a
different account tailored to reinforce and project accumulated
Christian confidence, in a forced alliance with Roman patriotic hope.
The narrative of both writers amounted to a commentary on human
experience and included the usual Christian hermeneutical tools of
allegory and typology. These, when applied to the Bible, had produced defining terms of reference for the earliest engagement with
time and history, as a means not just to show precedence but also
to teach communal patience and individual ethical focus before the
prospect of the world's end. Augustine and Bede continued in the same
educative effort, and Bede's discursive generosity about the Ages, in
the midst of chronistic spareness, emphasizes their message and the
value of narrative style. Augustine was a model of such commentary,

but he disavowed its terms and results when Orosius manipulated biblical typology as if earthly politics, not Christ himself, had been the object and fulfillment of Old Testament prophecy. Nevertheless, Orosius's scheme of reward and punishment and his identification of earthly rulership with God's design ensured his brand of admonitory narrative an important medieval future, not least as the type of historical writing offered to princes and configured for their instruction.[62] Lapidary concision sufficed for the study hall. Charlemagne, Einhard tells us, preferred Augustine's *City of God* for meal-time listening.[63] Narrative extended the applications of universal history without displacing the appeal of more concise rhetoric.

The models for the future themselves reflect an accretion of outlooks and possibilities, and later choices illustrate both lines of dependence and new aspiration. The multiple threads of Eusebius-Jerome, whether recopied to start over two pages or compressed onto one, remained ever-present. The work provided tell-tale facts. Its terse notice that "Pericles died" defined, for instance, the sum total of medieval knowledge of the great Athenian statesman and shows, where it recurs, a direct or indirect act of faith about a matter that no medieval copyist or writer could have fully understood.[64] The tapering contour was itself a message, which could be retained or collapsed into a single column of historical notices, with immediate effect for the interplay between sacred and profane history and, not least, for the implicit dynamic of imperial Rome at the Incarnation. Such alterations meant choices, and not merely simplification,[65] since the sheer complexity of Jerome's layout could actually favour its intact survival.[66] In his single-column epitome and extension of Eusebius-Jerome and Orosius, Prosper of Aquitaine deployed, in fact, a structure that helped to reassert his Augustinian "sense of history as the theatre of God's hidden purposes".[67] Conversely, in the absence of the visual armature of a multi-threaded chronicle, Orosius's narrative required an exegetical paradigm like the "Four Kingdoms" to

---

[62] For a good discussion of this strand of universal history as the genre *historia*, as distinct from universal chronicles, see Werner (1987) and Werner (1990).

[63] Einhard, *Vita Karoli Magni*, ch. 24.

[64] Eusebius-Jerome, *Chronicon* 1588, p. 115. The reuse of this entry is a *leitmotif* in von den Brincken (1957).

[65] *Pace* von den Brincken (1957), 67.

[66] Cf. Introduction to Eusebius-Jerome, *Chronicon*, xxi–xxv.

[67] Cf. Markus (1986), 40–41.

articulate his particular vision of historical progress. Jordanes's restate-
ment of imperial optimism for the mid-sixth century, in his *Roman
and Gothic Histories*, likewise began as a single-column condensate of
Jerome's *Chronicle*, here now pointedly cast in terms of the Four
Kingdoms.[68] The paradigm, where used, offered a statement in place
of a graphic configuration, and prepared the way for later medieval
preoccupation with the continued transfer of Rome's empire (*translatio imperii*) as the stabilizer of earthly existence.[69] The Four Kingdoms
and the corollary of triumphal continuance built on inherent tendencies in Jerome, yet Prosper of Aquitaine had managed to filter
these from other content to create a quite different solution. Isidore
and Bede knew and cumulatively reworked his single-column form
under the new superstructure of the Six Ages, and they achieved
both ethically relevant and compact formulations in their separate
universal chronicles. Whatever their differences, their widely received
works made the Six Ages virtually an obligatory feature in subsequent
medieval efforts to chart human history.[70] As it happened, Bede's
revision of Jerome's chronology proved correct to the extent that the
world, in what we call A.D. 800, continued to exist beyond its 6,000th
year as reckoned from the Septuagint. But perhaps more important,
contemporary scholars, who still sometimes followed Jerome's numbers, faced the approaching juncture tautly mindful of the essence
of Bede's message: that every dawning day decided the fate of the
world and of man. If the years numbered nearly 6,000, or even far
less, the duties of Christian life remained the same.[71]

In their discrete variety, the early elements of universal historical
grammar defined the options for the near medieval future. There
were gradients between narration and configuration, degrees of worldly
versus heaven-centered emphasis, varied dispositions for relating sacred
and secular experience, the schemes of the Kingdoms and the Ages,
and the alternatives of Greek versus Hebrew biblical chronology. For
recognizing these, modern scholarship has served us well in summary
handbooks, generic typologies, and even accounts of particular gram-

---

[68] Jordanes, *Romana* ¶ 11, ed. T. Mommsen, *MGH AA* V.1 (1882), p. 4.
[69] Goez (1958).
[70] For a useful conspectus of formal filiation and source dependency, see the
tables published in von den Brincken (1957), 249 ff.; repr. in Krüger (1976), 37–42.
[71] Borst (1998), 460–61.

matical elements.[72] Most subsequent universal history builds very directly on the past. Yet the merging of old history into new, as background to present, still requires us to look beyond what seems familiar, and one particular example combines so much that is strictly old that scholarship has yet to appreciate fully what is new.

New Interpretations: Frechulf

Frechulf of Lisieux addressed his *Histories* (ca. 830) to the Carolingian court. He combined all the writers we have mentioned, and ended his summary of time since the Fall more than two hundred years before his own day. His work shows the quiet force of a mind at pains to mark a fresh trail without rejecting any useful source. Some careful readers have praised him as a prodigious compiler devoid of guiding historical ideas, but have done so too hastily.[73]

Frechulf traced the first two Ages of the World as a prelude to a vast narrative enlargement on the factual cues of Jerome's *Chronicle*. He worked out the origins of history as the establishment of Augustine's Two Cities, and these he presents as the segmented but intersecting circles of a single humanity.[74] At the outset, he emphasizes a sociology of intention, an aspiration to angelic citizenship, centered in the cult of the true God. The dynamic is neither closed nor clearly delimited to the external eye, and it is authentically Augustinian.[75] Not insignificantly, Frechulf absorbed as much of it straight from Augustine as indirectly via the writings of his own suspect contemporary, the

---

[72] In general, e.g., von den Brincken (1957), Krüger (1976); on the narrative subtype (*historia*), Werner (1987), Werner (1990); on the motifs of Kingdoms and Ages, respectively, Goez (1958), Schmidt (1956).

[73] Notably, Schelle (1952), 139–44, who looked for usual ideas; more temperately, Brunhölzl (1991), 151–52. Other optimists perplexingly misconstrue the evidence, e.g., McKitterick and Innis (1994), 212–13. Staubach (1995) positively transformed the landscape. For Frechulf's sources, see my edition (Frechulf of Lisieux, *Historiarum libri XII*, in *Opera omnia*, ed. M. I. Allen, CCCM 169 [Turnhout, 2002], 17–724), which I cite according to chapter and line number. I expand on points made herebelow in the volume of studies that will complement the edition.

[74] See the middle and concluding chapters of Frechulf, *Historiae* I.1, which variously parse and distinguish humanity based on lineage, language, and affection.

[75] Frechulf, *Historiae* I.1.3 [11/15] (angelic aspiration); I.1.7–9 (origins of the Cities and their different worship); I.1.33 (their sociological presence and partial indistinction). Cf. Staubach (1995), 183–88, 190–93.

iconoclast Claudius of Turin (†ca. 827).[76] Among the outer segments of humanity, there were both future citizens of God's City and writings useful for an historian.

Frechulf's cultic focus makes temple-based worship, both Hebrew and pagan, the key *leitmotif* of his work. In the first installment of seven books, he paces history, where possible, by the pivotal moments in the call to worship fixed in God's people. In the five books of the second part that begins from the Incarnation, he calibrates the extension of salvation in Christian times by the successive demise of superseded temples, in Jerusalem and elsewhere. The topos of the Temples punctuates his books.[77] The final conversion of the Pantheon at Rome into the Church of St. Mary and All the Martyrs caps the consecutive narrative at the moment when "the Franks and the Lombards have succeeded Roman officials and Goths" as the rulers of Gaul and Italy.[78] Frechulf thus sealed his story of religious transformation and affirmed Carolingian readers by halting his *Histories* when the spatial foundations of their world were laid.[79] Not least, his account of "imperial deeds, saintly triumphs and teachings" aimed at challenging his readers, since he cast the work explicitly as a "mirror" in which "all should know to find themselves" and there "discover how to act and what to avoid".[80] As a Carolingian writing about the past, Frechulf traced a history of anecdotes, facts, and exempla whose actors and readers shared a common possibility, if not an equal grace, to discern and help make their own place in God's City. It was a rich, if understated, call to learn and measure up.

Far from confusing the Ages or omitting the Kingdoms, Frechulf set them aside to chart a new course. Beyond Abraham, he adhered to a division of Hebrew history that had been recommended but not followed by Eusebius, with divides at the Exodus, Solomon's

---

[76] Namely, his *Commentary on Genesis*. Cf. Allen (1998), 288–89, 305.

[77] Allen (1994), 69–73.

[78] Frechulf, *Historiae* II.5.26 [4/8] (conversion of the Pantheon); II.5.27 [22/24] (closure of the work).

[79] The phrase "kingdoms of the Franks and Lombards" echoes Charlemagne's titulature after his conquest of the Lombard Kingdom of Italy in A.D. 774. Cf. Wolfram (1967), 217–24.

[80] Frechulf, *Historiae* I.7.19 [63]: "Vt omnes sciant: in me sunt" (the explicit of Part I); II Prol. [28/32]: "His [scil. *libris*] enim uelut in speculo . . ."; II Prol. [43/46]: imperatorum gestis sanctorumque triumphis atque doctorum magnificentium doctrinis inlustratus, cautius quid agendum sit siue subtilius inueniet quid sit uitandum".

Temple, and then from the Second Temple to Christ.[81] This division better highlighted the functional pivots of sacred history, and Frechulf effaces the normal alternatives where necessary but admits them beforehand and later. He uses mentions of the Ages to emphasize the Flood, Abraham, and Christ's coming into the world, yet skirts the incongruity of his result in order to quote Bede on the advent of the "Sixth Age" at what stands, in effect, as the seventh.[82] Although kingdoms and rulers inexorably succeed one another, and Orosius appears in massive quotation, Frechulf eliminates all traces of the allegory of the Four Kingdoms.[83] His purpose seems clear when we observe how he knows to quote from and report about Jerome's *Daniel Commentary* but takes no account of the particular exegesis that lay behind Orosius's historical vision.[84] Frechulf did not presume against God's good order but, rather, found new means to express it, which refined or effaced the systems we might expect.

In the early medieval afterlife of Latin universal history, Frechulf stands apart by the massiveness of his narrative result and the careful effort he set to cutting old cloth to new meaning. Within the constraints of a retrospective compilation built of books and chapters, he traced a vision that marked for his readership their historical place and inheritance, which he offered as a treasure house and a prod. Good came even from examples to avoid, and chronological disagreement, which he left unresolved and perhaps cultivated, served to highlight the inner moment of the religious milestones he emphasized.[85] Within Christian times, it was the milestones themselves, not counted years, that paced his books and marked temporal advance, and the interstices of good teaching and saintly virtue that filled them.

It was possible to build on the prior tradition of Christian universal history by extending a branch, reframing and updating a current, or, as in the exception of Frechulf, by reweaving accumulated expressions into something wholly derived yet new. Most subsequent engagements depended easily on recognized forms, and these, to the

---

[81] Cf. Eusebius, Prologus to Eusebius-Jerome, *Chronicon*, pp. 16–17; Schmidt (1956), 304–05, without notice of Frechulf.

[82] Frechulf, *Historiae* I.1.25 [4]; I.1.35 [19/21]; II.1.2 [41].

[83] He also purges the typological deployment of the ten plagues of Egypt, which Augustine had sharply dismissed.

[84] Frechulf, *Historiae* I.7.13 [32/46] (quotation); II.5.3 [68/70] (with the addition, as a recensional variant, of the *Daniel Commentary* to the listing of Jerome's works).

[85] See my complementary annotations on chronology in the *CCCM* edition.

extent that they merely repeated schemes and content, often easily pale for us in comparison to what was added new and not derived. Yet as they emerged, the early forms and habits show a reach for social and ethical self-definition often as broad as the chronological stretch to Creation. Universal history provided facts and times and, by content or form, helped to intimate the terms for Christian citizenship.

CHAPTER TWO

ETHNIC AND NATIONAL HISTORY CA. 500–1000

Joaquín Martínez Pizarro

Introduction

The works usually studied under the heading of ethnic histories, some of which are among the most widely read productions of the early Middle Ages, do not belong to one genre or share a common approach to their subject. They continue to be treated as a group only because scholars have done so for a long time, describing what they call *origines gentium* as a distinct genre of historiography, with antecedents in classical ethnography, that was taken up across Europe in the early medieval period by writers moved by ethnic self-awareness.[1] No matter that the texts show none of the common formal characteristics that distinguish a literary genre, or that among the most famous works of the group, one, the *History* of Gregory of Tours, is clearly a universal history in the tradition of Orosius, while another, Bede's *Ecclesiastical History*, follows faithfully the generic model for church history set by Eusebius of Caesarea: somehow, these texts were thought to be bound by ideological and emotional factors that went much deeper than any literary considerations. Since all of them were concerned, to some extent, with the early history of Germanic tribes, the national passions of nineteenth- and twentieth-century Europe became implicated in their study from very early. The question to which the ethnic histories were believed to hold the answer was that of the role of Germanic culture in the formation of medieval Europe, vis-à-vis the Roman Empire and its overwhelming legacy.

However, nationalism alone will not explain the misunderstandings and distortions to which these works have been exposed. Scholarship has been haunted by other agendas, among them a yearning for cultural otherness that is as old and as powerful as the need for national

---

[1] Grundmann (1965), 12–17.

self-affirmation. When a scholar as critical and as alien to all cultural nationalism as Arnaldo Momigliano can write, after having discussed Cassiodorus's lost *History of the Goths*, "Not long afterwards the
Barbarians of the West began to speak for themselves. There are
less than forty years in the chronology I have adopted between
Cassiodorus's *Gothic History* and the *History of the Franks* by Gregory
of Tours"[2] we are not only surprised—how can a Gallo-Roman
bishop of senatorial ancestry represent the barbarians of the West
speaking for themselves?—but genuinely at a loss. Gregory of Tours'
background is perfectly well known: what could have led Momigliano
to characterize him, if only in passing, as a barbarian? Would
Gregory's notorious grammatical deficiencies have seemed sufficient
ground to make him a spokesman for the new protagonists of European
history in the sixth century? What is evident here and in many similar formulations is the need for an alternative to Roman sources,
the longing to hear the genuine voice of the barbarians, the desire
for a narrative that might rightly be called *The History of the Franks*,
as Gregory's cannot.

New developments in historical ethnography should allow us to
approach these early medieval texts with a greater measure of critical detachment, and may do so by emphasizing the limitations of
the available data. The very definition of what is Germanic is found
to be highly unstable, determined by linguistic and archaeological
criteria that are neither univocal nor always coherent with each
other.[3] The influential concept of ethnogenesis makes it possible to
look at such ethnic markers as language, weapons, and national cos-
tume, but also at the discourse of the ethnic histories as strategies
by which a new nationality is created and affirmed, rather than as
traces of a pre-existent and established tribal identity.[4] Ethnicity in
this new light turns out to be not a single monolithic factor but a
complex option that must be constructed, negotiated, and performed.

Valuable as these theoretical revisions appear, they may not be by
themselves powerful enough to liberate the study of the early medieval
origines gentium from the ideological imperatives that have plagued it
for so long, in particular, the tendency to subordinate the analysis

---

[2] Momigliano (1955), 198.
[3] Wenskus (1986).
[4] Pohl (1998) and (1998b).

of these narratives to the search for kernels of ancient Germanic tradition that may be connected to pagan cults and ancestral pieties. The quest for what is referred to as "Germanic continuity" can easily be made compatible with ethnogenesis: it is enough to argue that the presence, deliberate or accidental, of these archaic elements in the late antique or early medieval *origines* triggered an irrational identification with a myth of origins, thereby serving to shape and buttress an emergent group identity.[5]

The pursuit of Germanic continuity, a subterranean survival of vernacular myths and loyalties under what is usually represented as a thin veneer of Latin culture, runs through the record of twentieth-century scholarship on this subject. Its logic has derived interdisciplinary credibility from Germanic philology and the comparative study of religions.[6] The philology, however, is often highly speculative and involves questionable procedures such as projecting the information in Tacitus's *Germania* into the early Middle Ages, on the assumption of an undisturbed constancy of Germanic tradition. Even more frequent has been the retrojection of data taken from Nordic literature of the thirteenth century and later, on the unlikely premise that Scandinavian, especially Icelandic, literature constitutes one great quarry of cultural fossils. The theories of myth and religion used in this enterprise are at least equally problematic: the most frequently invoked authority is that of Georges Dumèzil, who finds numerous exact correspondences between Indo-European mythologems and theologems on one side and the legendary sagas and stories preserved by Saxo Grammaticus and Snorri Sturluson, both writing in the first half of the thirteenth century, on the other.[7] A startling picture of early medieval history arises from these reconstructions. The Holy Spear of the Ottonians, described by Liutprand of Cremona and Widukind of Corvey in the tenth century, goes back not only to the True Cross, nails from which were embedded in its blade, and thus to Constantine and Helena, but also, more deeply, to the spear of Wodan, god of kingship, and ultimately to the rock carvings of Bronze-Age Sweden, where spears are represented serving obviously

---

[5] Cf. Pohl (1994).
[6] Cf. Hauck (1955); Wolfram (1994). *Contra* von See (1972); Goffart (1995); Amory (1997), 326–31.
[7] Dumèzil (1959). *Contra* Page (1978–79); von See (1988), 63–68.

ritual functions.[8] Royal charisma, the *fortuna* or *felicitas* ordinarily
attributed to divine grace in medieval sources, is in fact always the
manifestation of a sacral Germanic *Königsheil* traceable to the presence of a pagan divinity in the ruler's genealogy.[9] Demonstrations
of such archaic survivals are impossible to disprove precisely because
the evidence offered, often with much philological and antiquarian
erudition, is uncommonly flimsy. An analogy of form is sufficient for
a well-attested Christian and Latin source to be set aside in favor
of a pagan Germanic one, which is automatically assumed to be the
one that really counts.[10]

The ancient Germans retrieved from the *origines* in the name of
continuity are a peculiar lot, occupied exclusively with cultic activities and the preservation of sacred lineages (*Geblütsheiligkeit*). It is not
possible, of course, to isolate historical scholarship from the illusions
of its own epoch, but the barbarian ancestors thus exhumed are
more reminiscent of early twentieth-century creations, of the irra-
tionalist heroes of Ernst Jünger and Gottfried Benn, caught in the
Spenglerian dialectic of culture and civilization, than of the shrewd
politicians and able careerists documented by Ammianus, Procopius,
and the ethnic histories themselves.[11]

The chief objection to *Kontinuitätstheorie* as an approach to the ethnic histories is that, because of its exclusive interest in a few passages that can be used to establish the persistence of a native culture
under the forms of Latin Christianity, it dismisses any study of these
works as wholes and as products of late antiquity and the early
Middle Ages, periods in which the writing of history was always also
a literary undertaking, and when literature was never "mere literature" but could be expected to serve political, social, or religious
purposes. This rejection of literature reaches back at least as far as
the denunciation of Eduard Norden's 1920 study of the *topoi* in the
Germania.[12] Literature, like Latinity and Christianity, is held to be

---

[8] Höfler (1938).
[9] E.g., Beumann (1950), 236–42; Bosl (1962), esp. 92. *Contra* Picard (1991).
[10] Beumann (1950), 253–54, provides an excellent illustration of this kind of
reasoning.
[11] Cf. for instance Stroheker (1955) and (1961), 9–53.
[12] Cf. von See (1981), 31–37. The pedigree of this prejudice is remarkable and
awakens echoes remote from—but not unconnected with—the realm of academic

only a husk, a thin formal cover in itself unworthy of investigation, and recent attempts to go back to the texts are still waved aside as the reduction of history to pure literature, to fiction, to "the prejudices of a few literate churchmen".[13] Such charges involve a misrepresentation of the aims of scholars such as Walter Goffart,[14] whose identification of plots and genres in the ethnic histories concerns only the formal organizing principles of each narrative and in no way implies a blanket denial of the historical truth of the information framed by means of these genres and plots.

One purpose of the outline that follows is to bring out the heterogeneity of these texts, not an unexpected feature if we keep in mind that the authors of some of them did not belong to the *gentes* they wrote about (Gregory of Tours, Isidore of Seville), that some wrote about peoples who had ceased to be sovereign—and without necessarily taking their side (Jordanes, Paul the Deacon), while others focused on particular groups or tribes within the larger nation (Fredegar, the *Liber historiae Francorum*), and the last author in the series used the history of his people only as a brief introduction to an account of the larger territorial confederacy by which they had been absorbed (Widukind).

Jordanes and the Goths

The author of *On the Origin and Deeds of the Goths*[15] introduces himself (*Getica* 266) as a Moesian Goth, the grandson of a Goth who had been secretary (*notarius*) to a king of the Alans established in Moesia, and himself a *notarius*, even though *agrammatus*, i.e., lacking the conventional school training in grammar and rhetoric. Jordanes often refers to Constantinople as "the city" (*urbs*) and adopts Justinian's

---

scholarship: cf. Thomas Mann, *Reflections of a Nonpolitical Man* (1918), trans. W. D. Morris (New York, 1983), 32:

> The Roman West is literary: this separates it from the Germanic—or more exactly—from the German world, which, whatever else it is, is definitely not literary.

[13] Pohl (1994), 9; cf. also Wolfram (1994).
[14] Goffart (1988).
[15] Jordanes, *Romana et Getica*, ed. T. Mommsen, *MGH, AA* V.1 (Berlin, 1882).

official grounds for the campaigns against the Vandals and the Goths (170–71, 305–07); he states that he once borrowed Cassiodorus's *History of the Goths*, his main source, for three days from Cassiodorus's steward, a loan that could hardly have taken place outside of Constantinople (preface). It is certain, therefore, that he wrote in the capital of the Eastern Empire, and from a strong Constantinopolitan perspective. The preface, in the form of a letter to Castalius, a friend who lives "close to the Goths", i.e., in Italy, informs Castalius that his request for a short version of Cassiodorus's *History* has caused Jordanes to interrupt his work on "a summary of the chronicles", that he does not have the *History* at hand, but can remember it well from the three-day loan, and that he has added a considerable amount of material that is either his own or taken from various Greek and Latin authors. The *Getica* is not a wholly independent work but part of a diptych. It shares a preface addressed to Vigilius, another friend, with the *Romana*, a two-part text consisting of a chronicle of world history from the Creation to the age of Augustus, plus a Roman history that reaches from the legendary founding of Rome to the Gothic wars of Jordanes's own day. The *Romana* is that "summary of the chronicles" that Jordanes had had to interrupt in order to compose the *Getica* and to which he clearly returned.

Jordanes wrote early in 551, after the patricius Germanus had died as he was preparing to leave for Italy at the head of the Imperial armies. A posthumous son, named after his father, had just been born to Germanus's wife Matasuntha, granddaughter of Theoderic and former wife of Vitiges. Jordanes mentions only the defeat of Vitiges, not the subsequent victories of Totila or the appointment of Narses to replace Germanus and lead the army sent against the Goths. It is difficult to draw any conclusions as to the reasons for his silence about Totila, since he does mention him briefly in the *Romana* (383–85). The absence of Narses from both works and the author's constant praise of Belisarius suggest that in one respect Jordanes did not agree with Justinian's strategy and may have belonged to a faction that wished to keep Belisarius in command of the Gothic war.[16] This point excepted, Jordanes appears to be strongly in favor of government policies at this moment of increased imperial intransigence and explicitly subordinates the greatness of the Goths to that

---

[16] Croke (1987), 128–29.

of the Romans, making it only a further claim to glory on the part of Justinian and Belisarius that they were able to conquer such a warlike nation (315–16).[17]

Jordanes quotes from many Greek and Latin sources: Pompeius Trogus, Dio Chrysostom, Ptolemy, Josephus, Dexippus, an unidentified Fabius, Rufinus of Aquileia, Prosperus, Priscus, the *Roman History* of Symmachus, and the Gothic histories of Ablabius and Cassiodorus, although it is likely that some of these authorities are not used first-hand.[18] His Latinity and literary skills in general have been judged adversely by many scholars, from his editor Theodor Mommsen who wrote that if Cassiodorus had taken the origin of the Goths and made it Roman history, then Jordanes had rendered it Moesian[19] to a recent scholar who describes the *Getica* as "the illiterate epitome made and supplemented by Jordanes".[20] These harsh evaluations, which overlook the varieties and possibilities of sixth-century Latin, have made it easier to dismiss Jordanes himself, his political views, and his conception of the *Getica* as crucial factors in the interpretation of the work.

The design of the *Getica* is simple: it is divided into three sections of comparable length. The first of these (4–130) consists largely of legends of origin combined with geographic-ethnographic descriptions of the various lands inhabited by the Goths on their way to the Mediterranean. The narrative reaches from the tribe's first mythic migration from the island of Scanzia (Scandinavia) to the Hunnish conquest of the Gothic kingdom north of the Black Sea circa A.D. 370. The second section (131–245) follows the fortunes of the Visigoths to Jordanes's own time, which finds them rulers of southern Gaul and Spain. The third section (246–316) goes back to A.D. 370 and relates the history of the Ostrogoths, first under Hunnish overlordship and then as a free people settled in Pannonia and later in Italy.[21]

The *Getica* has always been read in terms of its relation to Cassiodorus's lost *History of the Goths*. One school has searched in it for

---

[17] Jordanes also shows intense awareness of the danger to Constantinople from various barbarian nations (*Romana* 388) and is clearly in favor of harsh military measures to keep them in line.

[18] Mommsen, Preface to *Romana et Getica*, xxx–xliv.

[19] Mommsen, Preface to *Romana et Getica*, xliv.

[20] Barnish (1984), 336.

[21] An outline is provided in Appendix 1.

long-lost vernacular traditions of the Goths, which it would interpret as a dynastic oral tradition (*Hausüberlieferung*) of the Amals, learned by Cassiodorus at the court of Ravenna and incompetently summarized by Jordanes.[22] This approach, which in its speculative handling of legendary materials and its reconstruction of missing oral traditions often comes close to the literary ethnography of antiquity, favors linguistic evidence, chiefly onomastics and etymology. Thus, for instance, the story of the origin of the Huns from banished Gothic witches who mated with evil spirits of the desert (121–22) is interpreted as a misunderstood account of a religious/ideological change undergone by the early Goths as they settled in Scythia, whereby those conservative elements who held to the old tribal *religio* were cast out from the community and eventually perceived and remembered as demonic. Although the story has well-known scriptural sources,[23] it is read as somehow reflecting authentic Gothic traditions on the strength of the Gothic word *haliurunnae*, 'witches', used by Jordanes. But *haliurunnae* proves nothing other than that Jordanes, or perhaps Cassiodorus, knew some Gothic vocabulary. In the *Getica* the word clearly serves as an authenticating device and also to provide a plausible explanation for the name of the Huns.[24]

A second school has read the *Getica* primarily in terms of Cassiodorus's own views and the political sentiments of the court of Ravenna in the early sixth century.[25] The chief argument for this insistence on the standpoint of Cassiodorus is the fact that the last event mentioned in the text is the birth of Germanus, son of the patricius Germanus and Matasuntha. Instead of emphasizing the father's kinship with Justinian, whose nephew he was, the *Getica* stresses his family connection to the powerful Roman *gens* of the Anicii, to which Cassiodorus may have belonged, and the significance of an alliance, at this critical moment in Roman-Gothic affairs, between the Anicii and the Amals. It has been argued that this slant could come only from Cassiodorus himself. It also has been suggested by Momigliano that this reference to a late event (the child was born in 551) implies that, while in exile in Constantinople, Cassiodorus revised his his-

[22] Wolfram (1980), 454–55, and (1990), 58.
[23] Maenchen-Helfen (1945).
[24] Wolfram (1994), 30–31; Goffart (1995), 27–28.
[25] Momigliano (1955); Barnish (1984); Heather (1991).

tory, usually dated early in the second quarter of the century, in the light of recent developments and brought it up to date. This revision would account for those sentiments in the *Getica* that appear incompatible with the politics of the Gothic court in the 520s: its violent anti-Arianism for instance. A recent reading has brought back Gothic oral tradition, though from a new angle.[26] It is known that a function of oral tradition in illiterate societies is to align the past with the present by projecting present circumstances into remote antiquity. The argument is that this is exactly what the *Getica* does in dating the division of the Goths into Visigoths and Ostrogoths back to their early settlement north of the Black Sea, which contradicts all earlier evidence on the subject, and in placing the Amals at the head of the Goths from very early and making Ermanaric an Amal, which is equally unsupported.[27] These beliefs may not be archaic, but they are what we might expect from Theoderic's courtiers in Ravenna and, hence, from Cassiodorus at second hand.

The textual basis for Momigliano's argument is weak: the *Getica* mentions the child Germanus and his ancestry three times (81, 251, 314) and the *Romana* once (383), at considerable length given the dimensions of the work, and two of these references are made far in advance of the child's birth. The Anicii are mentioned only once (314), Germanus's status as nephew of the emperor twice (81, 251). Clearly, these allusions do not come from an earlier text that Jordanes summarizes but are a conspicuous element of his own design and his political agenda. The third and most recent tendency in scholarship about the *Getica*, accordingly, is to read it as the considered work of Jordanes and not the incoherent abbreviation of another work.[28] Its account of Roman-Gothic relations can be understood as reflecting the values of a strongly assimilated Goth of Constantinople, Catholic and anti-Arian, writing in 551 in full support of Justinian's Italian policy (though wishing the emperor were sending Belisarius and not Narses), proud of the historical achievements and the antiquity of his people, but even more certain of the need for them to yield to the authority of the empire.

---

[26] Heather (1991).

[27] On the antiquity of Visigoths and Ostrogoths, see *Getica*, 19. Jordanes repeats the information, attributing it to Ablabius, in 82, but contradicts it to some degree in 98; cf. Heather (1991), 12–18.

[28] Goffart (1988), 20–111; Croke (1987).

Gregory of Tours and Merovingian Gaul

Although Jordanes did not place the Goths first in the scheme of things, he did make them and their doings the subject of the *Getica*. This is by no means the case with Gregory of Tours and the Franks. Gregory, a Gallo-Roman bishop of senatorial ancestry, writes for a public that lived mainly south of the Loire. He shows no interest in ethnicities, not even his own, let alone that of the Franks. Aside from a few casual remarks about Frankish customs and language,[29] he has nothing to say about them and their culture in particular. If he focuses on the Merovingian rulers of Gaul, it is because they are in power and not because they happen to be Franks. Today there is a measure of agreement that Gregory is not a national or ethnic historian.[30] The misleading title *Historia Francorum* is found only in late Carolingian manuscripts; Gregory's own title for his work was *Historiae* or *Ten Books of History*.[31]

Gregory probably was born in 538, the son of an Auvergnat father and a Burgundian mother, and retained all his life a deep attachment to the city of Clermont and its vicinity. There had been numerous bishops in his family, at Lyons, Langres, and Tours. From his parents Gregory inherited a passionate devotion to the cult of certain saints, most importantly St. Julian of Brioude. When in 573 he was appointed—uncanonically—bishop of Tours, he transferred his devotion to Martin of Tours, of whose sanctuary and reputation he had become the custodian. As one of the leading bishops in Merovingian Gaul, Gregory found himself involved in the religious and secular affairs of Austrasia, Neustria, Burgundy, and their dependent territories. He died most probably in 594.[32]

Gregory's literary work, most of which has come down to us, is entirely in prose. It comprises, in addition to the *Historiae*, seven books of *miracula*, one of biographies or *vitae* of holy men, a version

---

[29] Goffart (1983).
[30] Vollmann (1983), col. 903; Heinzelmann (1994b); cf. also Rouche (1977). James (1998) argues, largely *e silentio*, that Gregory thought of himself as a Frank, i.e., an inhabitant of Gaul who was a subject of the Frankish kings.
[31] Gregory of Tours, *Libri historiarum X*, ed. B. Krusch and W. Levison, *MGH*, *SSRM* I.1 (Hanover, 1951). On the original title see Goffart (1987) and (1988), 119–27.
[32] Verdon (1986); Wood (1994).

of the legend of the Seven Sleepers of Ephesus, a short treatise on chronology and the stars, and another (now lost) on the interpretation of the psalms. These other works are of considerable relevance to the understanding of the *Historiae*, which combine the narrative of secular affairs with innumerable miracles and hagiographic sketches and with descriptions of omens and natural "signs".

In both his historical and hagiographic writings, Gregory deplores his shortcomings as a stylist and even lists the grammatical mistakes of which he is guilty; he then counters that his simple language reaches a wider public because it is easily understood (cf. general preface to the *Historiae*, preface to *Glory of the Confessors*, preface to *Miracles of St. Martin*). In a much-cited afterword to the *Historiae*, he exhorts future bishops of Tours to keep the text of his works unchanged, whatever may be wrong with its Latinity. These passages have often been read as conventional modesty topoi and as the expression of a realistic self-appraisal on Gregory's part, since scholars tended to agree that his Latin represented a dramatic drop in standards compared to that of other authors of his age (Caesarius of Arles and Venantius Fortunatus, for instance). Recent students of his work have found these issues less straightforward and raised the question whether modern editors, by preferring the more "Merovingian" manuscripts of the *Historiae*, have not distorted our sense of the Latin Gregory actually wrote.[33] An equally important question is whether Gregory's endorsement of a simpler language is not part of a Christian polemic against standards of Latinity associated with pagan and secular literature.[34]

The *Historiae* opens with a general prologue followed by ten books of historical narrative of which I, II, III, and V also have individual prefaces. Between the end of Book X and his invocation to his successors to respect the integrity of the text, Gregory has inserted an account of the bishops of Tours in the form of a series of very brief biographies. This may well be the earliest instance of what was to become the genre of *gesta episcoporum*.[35] The ten books with their prefaces are clearly conceived as a single work, but Heinzelmann has argued persuasively that the first four, which cover an enormous

---

[33] Vollmann (1983), cols. 124–28; See also Auerbach (1946); du Plessis (1968).
[34] The best discussion remains Beumann (1964).
[35] Sot (1981), 16 and 33.

range of time from Creation to 575, show signs of having been composed separately, as a self-contained narrative intended for publication.[36] Among other traces of earlier composition, the computation
of the age of the world at the end of Book IV, which matches the
one at the end of X, and Gregory's frequent addresses to the public in I–IV seem to indicate that his initial project did not include
the events of his own time. Books V–X, which cover a mere fifteen
to sixteen years of Merovingian history, with Gregory himself in a
leading role, involve a sharp narrowing of the geographic and chronological scope of the *Historiae* and possibly a decision on Gregory's
part not to make the longer work public in his lifetime. The ten
books have been carefully edited to form a new continuous unit in
spite of the transition from history of the past to history of the present at the beginning of Book V.[37]

   Among the chief sources of the *Historiae* are Jerome's translation
and continuation of Eusebius's chronicle, the chronicle and Martinian
writings of Sulpicius Severus, the historians of the late empire Renatus
Profuturus Frigiredus and Sulpicius Alexander, from whose otherwise
lost histories Gregory quotes at length in Book II, and, most importantly, Orosius's *History Against the Pagans*. Gregory also makes use of
a broad range of Merovingian hagiography and, for the contemporary books, especially IX and X, of various charters and documents,
some of which he incorporates into his text (e.g., the text of the
Treaty of Andelot [IX,20], Saint Radegund's letter of foundation for
her Convent of the Holy Cross at Poitiers [IX,41]). Occasional quotations from Vergil (e.g., VIII,22; IX,6) and from Sallust's frequently
cited opinions on the writing of history (e.g., IV,13; VII,2) are thought
not to imply familiar knowledge of these pagan authors but to be
taken from *florilegia* to raise the tone of the narrative.

   Gregory's credibility as a historian has generally been judged high,[38]
but recent scholars have made sharp attacks on his coverage of the
Arian kingdoms, distorted by Catholic zeal,[39] his portrayal of Clovis
and particularly of the Frankish king's conversion,[40] his account of
the invasion of Gaul by the Huns in 451, which assigns to the Franks

---

[36] Heinzelmann (1994), 96–102.
[37] An outline is provided in Appendix 2.
[38] Vollmann (1983), cols. 915–16.
[39] Moorhead (1995).
[40] Wood (1985).

an important role in the defense of Gaul that they could not have played,[41] and his biased characterization of Chilperic I, which ignores the king's remarkable cultural dynamism and originality.[42]

Contemporary interpretations of the *Historiae* have tended to center on two problems generated by Gregory's narrative practice. The first is a matter of technique, namely the extreme discontinuity of the text, which shifts constantly from political episodes to reports of miracles to stories of violent crimes and descriptions of portents. It has been suggested that the apparent chaos of his narratives reflects the moral and political disorder of his age and the inability of writers at that time to provide a coherent and organized account.[43] A new reading, however, places Gregory's narrative style in line with the Christian critique of the rhetorical organization of late-antique historiography and the advocacy of a simple language that would give access to the events themselves. In juxtaposing dramatic incidents of very different sorts, Gregory is reaching for a rhetoric of events as opposed to words.[44] The setting side by side, *mixte confusaeque*, of miracles and slaughter by a narrator who does not editorialize but maintains an honest, detached, and possibly ironic tone proves Gregory's chosen genre to be prescriptive satire.[45] In identifying the genre of the *Historiae*, this argument addresses the second major interpretive issue, namely Gregory's ideological aim and its translation into a narrative scheme. The deliberate alternation of crimes and miracles creates a picture of life in the world, morally uncertain and incoherent and the proper subject of satire. A weakness of this solution is that evidence for the cultivation of satire in sixth-century Gaul is scanty. In addition, satire in the form of a prose history in ten books would have been so unprecedented in Gregory's time (as in any other) that it would have obscured and blunted the moral message associated with the genre.

The literary form of Gregory's narrative has been identified more convincingly by K. F. Werner, who characterizes *historia* as a late antique/early medieval kind of Christian historiography that takes its inspiration from Orosius and the historical books of the Old

---

[41] Banniard (1978).
[42] James (1988), 165–68.
[43] Auerbach (1946).
[44] Goffart (1988), 162–83.
[45] Goffart (1988), 197–203.

Testament, especially the Books of Kings. *Historia* is not national or ethnic in subject, but centers instead on the functioning of a Christian society and very particularly on the duties of its rulers, who—in association with the priests of God—lead the people towards salvation.[46] Drawing on Werner's definition of *historia*, a recent study of Gregory solves the problem of narrative discontinuity by tracing throughout the *Historiae* a non-chronological pattern of antitheses combined with a typological interpretation of history.[47] The work as a whole, but also each individual book, must be read with these paradigmatic symmetries in mind and particular attention must be paid to the first and last chapters of each book, which represent the terms of the antithesis, and to the thematic middle chapters, which often involve a mediation between those terms. This complex structure would explain Gregory's passionate opposition to any abbreviation or "improvement" of his text. The elaborate pattern would convey a definition of *ecclesia* as Christian society in its entirety and a plea for full collaboration in its government between rulers and bishops, a collaboration that Chilperic I rejected and that his antithesis, the *bonus rex* Guntram, apparently was willing to practice.[48]

Of the historians of the early Middle Ages, Gregory always has been considered the only one to give his readers a sense of the actual life of the period, its daily realities and its emotional climate. This ability of Gregory often has been presented as a function of his literary naivety: the realism of his narrative was wholly unstudied, an effect of his chaotic and spontaneous reproduction of what he witnessed. With the rise in appreciation of Gregory's literary originality and artfulness, pioneered by Auerbach in 1946,[49] it also has become apparent that Gregory's fascinating 'reality', his world of dramatic contrasts of sanctity and violence, is largely a product of his art and not to be taken at face value by critical historians.

---

[46] Werner (1987).

[47] Heinzelmann (1994), esp. 84–135.

[48] Heinzelmann (1994), 158–67. Ian Wood has proposed external (i.e., nonliterary) reasons for some of the discontinuities in the *Historiae* and particularly in the moral characterization of the leading figures (Wood [1994] and, more generally, [1994b]). He identifies numerous erasures, delays, and diplomatic suppressions (e.g., in the portrayal of Chilperic before and after his murder) dictated by the course of events and political expediency.

[49] Pp. 81–97, English edition 77–95. See also Auerbach (1958), 78–83 [English edition (1965), 103–12]; Thürlemann (1974); and Pizarro (1989).

Isidore of Seville and the Visigoths, Vandals, and Sueves

The encyclopaedic bishop of Seville (570–636) left behind two versions of the *Historia Gothorum* (*HG*),[50] a shorter one, finished during the reign of Sisebut (612–21), probably in 621; and a longer one, dated 624, extending into the reign of Suinthila (621–31), with jubilant praise of this king's re-conquest of Cartagena, occupied by imperial troops since 552.[51] The history of the Goths proper opens with the "Praise of Spain", in which these former Roman provinces are described as an exceptionally rich and temperate territory and then personified as a beautiful woman, once desired and married by imperial Rome but now seized and enjoyed by the rising power of the Goths. The "Praise" is followed by sixty-five short chapters focusing exclusively on the history of the Visigoths, from their first encounters with Rome to the foundation of the kingdom of Toulouse in the early fifth century and then to the conquest, settlement, and unification of Spain. After this narrative comes a "Recapitulation" in five chapters (66–70) praising the achievements of the Goths and attributing their success—presented as a triumph over Rome—to their valor in combat and their love of freedom. The *History of the Vandals* and *History of the Sueves* (chapters 71–84 and 85–92 respectively) are brief appendices attached to the *HG* as concerning other *gentes* who once inhabited Spain. They provide brief summaries of their history from their arrival in the peninsula to the imperial re-conquest of the Vandal kingdom in North Africa in 533 and the incorporation of the Sueves into the Visigothic realm under Leovigild in the 570s.

The *HG* is a tissue of borrowings from previous histories and presents itself as such ("de historiis libata retexere" [2]). It draws many of its materials and some ideological inspiration from Orosius, but otherwise its chief sources are universal chronicles: Jerome's continuation of Eusebius, Hydatius, Prosper of Aquitaine, Victor of Tunnuna (for the Vandals), John of Biclar. There is no evidence that the author knew Jordanes's *Getica*. These sources have been subjected to considerable generalization for the sake of elegant *brevitas*, losing in

---

[50] Rodriguez Alonso (1975), 26–49.
[51] Isidore of Seville, *Historia Gothorum Wandalorum Sveborum ad DCXXIV*, ed. T. Mommsen, *MGH, AA* XI (Berlin, 1894).

the process much significant information, so that as a historical source
the *HG* tells us much less than the works from which it is derived.
Ideologically, however, and as a work of literature, it is of considerable originality and deserves more attention than it has received.

Its chief claim to distinction is its extreme Gothic patriotism, manifest in a systematic revision of the historical record. The Goths
fought on Pompey's side at Pharsalia and came close to defeating
Caesar (3). The victories of Claudius and Constantine over the Goths
are counted primarily as shining additions to the fame of these emperors, now illustrious for having defeated "such a powerful people"
("tam fortissimam gentem", 4–5). Following Orosius, the *HG* presents Alaric's sack of Rome in 410 as remarkably merciful and
restrained, particularly in the treatment of churches and their property (15–17). Most remarkably, perhaps, the Goths are said to have
taken the lead against the Huns in the battle of the Catalaunian
Fields in 451, with Aetius and his Roman forces participating as
mere supporters ("auxiliante Aetio duce Romano", 23). As might be
expected, the Arianism of the Goths is the one serious mark against
them ("superstitio idolatriae" . . . "malum blasphemiae", 8; "inoliti
erroris labes", 52). The *HG*, once again echoing Orosius, blames this
on the emperor Valens, who had sent them Arian missionaries (7)
and elsewhere bypasses this difficult subject with moderate blame or
with indications that the Goths, though heretical, had shown much
piety. Throughout, the author presents his protagonists as victorious
over Rome, which he portrays as a declining power, closely associated with paganism and heresy. One immediate occasion for the
HG, Suinthila's recovery of the last imperial holdouts in Cartagena,
is of special significance for Isidore, whose family came from that
region, as it marks the beginning of undivided Visigothic rule over
a Catholic kingdom.

The brief chapters of the *HG* are dated according to the Spanish
era and the year of an imperial reign.[52] In most of them, a stage in
the political destiny of the Gothic nation is embodied in the biography
of a king.[53] It is striking, given the minimal scope of these chapters,
that Isidore always describes the exact circumstances of the king's
end, whether assassinated ("His throat was cut in the middle of a

---

[52] The sections on the Vandals and Sueves are dated by the Spanish era only.
[53] Reydellet (1981), 523–54.

feast", 44) or, far less often, from natural death ("morte propria", 59).

The genre of the work has never been satisfactorily defined. It makes no use of vernacular legends, as would be expected in an *origo gentis*. On the other hand, despite its title and the dominant influence of Orosius, its exclusive concentration on the Visigoths makes it impossible to classify the *HG* as a *historia* in the late antique/ early medieval sense proposed by Werner.

It has been argued that the *HG* marks the literary and ideological birth of the Spanish nation, created and led by the Goths and unified under their rule and in this sense the earliest of the European nations of today.[54] This reading of the text is contradicted by the total absence from its pages of the Hispano-Roman majority, an absence so pronounced that the *Spania* of the famous "Praise of Spain" with which the work begins has to be presented in purely geographical terms, almost as if it were uninhabited.

The originality of the *HG*, surprising in an encyclopaedist such as Isidore, lends credibility to the argument made of late that the short version of the *HG* is in fact either identical with or else very close to a *historiola* of the Goths ascribed to Maximus of Zaragoza and long believed lost.[55] In this case, the long version would be Isidore's revision of Maximus in light of the events of the early 620s and, in particular, of the achievements of Suinthila.

Two Historians of the Franks A. Fredegar

The author known as Fredegar[56] composed his chronicle circa 658–60, some seventy years after Gregory completed the *Historiae*. The present form of the text, four books divided into chapters, does not originate with the author but was introduced later. The author had arranged it as a series of chronicles, five of them abbreviated from earlier historians, the sixth his own; the present fourth book, identical with this last chronicle, still bears the heading "In nomine domini nostri Iesu Christi incipit chronica sexta".[57]

---

[54] Teillet (1984), esp. 463–501.
[55] Collins (1994), 345–58.
[56] Evidence for this name goes back to the sixteenth century only.
[57] *Chronicarum qui dicuntur Fredegarii scholastici libri iv*, ed. B. Krusch, *MGH, SSRM* II (Hanover, 1888; repr. 1956).

Scholarship on Fredegar long was dominated by two questions: whether the chronicle as a whole was the work of one or several authors, and when it was composed. Authorship was made particularly difficult to establish by the fact that two thirds of the text consist of extracts and summaries from other works, all systematically interpolated by the author. Recent studies of Fredegar have returned to the hypothesis of a single author, in part because the case for multiple authors has not been proved, but mainly because the evidence from stylistic analysis points strongly in this direction.[58] The date of composition helps determine the authority of Fredegar's own chronicle (i.e., Book IV), the greater part of which centers on the 620s and 630s. A dating circa 658–60, supported by references to events after 657 and 658 (IV,76; IV,81; IV,84), agrees with the sense of several scholars that the chronicle contains an unusually high proportion of legendary and fictional materials.[59]

A general prologue, which has survived as prologue to Book IV, describes Fredegar's original project: a world history compiled from five other authors and followed by a chronicle of his own. The sources listed are Jerome, Hydatius, "a certain wise man" who turns out to be Hyppolitus of Porto, Isidore, and Gregory of Tours. The distribution of these materials in the present four-book format is as follows: Book I is taken largely from Hyppolitus of Porto's *Liber generationis*, to which are added lists of Roman emperors and kings of the Jews as well as a computation of the age of the world. A few of the materials at the end of I are derived from Isidore; others are very similar to the lists and computations in Isidore's universal chronicle, and Fredegar may have believed them to be Isidore's work. Book II consists of extracts from the chronicles of Jerome and Hydatius, with important interpolations. Book III is based on Gregory's *Historiae*, Books II–VI (to the death of Chilperic I in 584). Book IV begins with a characterization of King Guntram in the twenty-fourth year of his rule over Burgundy (584) and continues with information about the Frankish kingdoms and a number of foreign countries until about 658.

---

[58] Hellmann (1935), esp. 40–59; Goffart (1963), 339–45; Erikson (1965). For important arguments in favor of two authors, see Gerberding (1987), 13–17.
[59] Wallace-Hadrill (1958), 84–88; Goffart (1963), 345–54; Wood (1994b).

Unlike Gregory, Fredegar is a historian of the Franks: he brings them on stage as early as II,4–8 (and again in III,2), providing them with the first Trojan *origo gentis* in medieval historiography,[60] and Frankish history is dominant from Book III on. But the design of the work as a whole indicates that Fredegar understood the history of the Franks as a part of world history, and this is confirmed by Book IV, his original contribution, which sets the events of Burgundy, Austrasia, and Neustria in a richly developed frame of international information, not only from Spain, Italy, and Byzantium, but also from Slavic eastern Europe and the territories north of the Rhine (see esp. his account of the Wends and their Frankish leader Samo, IV,48 and 68). A second reason why Fredegar can be considered an ethnic historian is the decidedly secular cast of his chronicle. Church history, with its imperial and international frame of reference, gets a very modest share of attention; hagiographic elements are also few, though omens and portents are frequently described.

Beginning in the days of Guntram and Childebert II, Book IV centers primarily on the reigns of Chlothar II (584–629), the son of Chilperic I, and of his son Dagobert I (623–39), though it extends into the early years of Dagobert's sons Clovis II and Sigibert III. To refer to the inhabitants of Merovingian Gaul, Fredegar uses territorial or political categories: "Auster", "Austrasia", "regnum Austrasiorum", "Neuster", "consilium Neustrasiorum", "regnum Burgundiae", etc. He makes use of ethnic terms when introducing characters in positions of power, for instance the commanders (*duces*) of an expedition against the Basques in 637/638: "Arinbertus, Amalgarius, Leudebertus, Wandalmarus, Waldericus, Ermeno, Barontus, Chairaardus ex genere Francorum, Chramalenus ex genere Romano, Willibaldus patricius genere Burgundionum, Aigyna genere Saxsonum" (IV,78). Most significantly, he often introduces the mayors of the palace on their rise to power by specifying their ethnicity: Bertoald "genere Francos" (IV,24), Claudius "genere Romanus" (IV,28), Flaochad "genere Franco" (IV,89).

Fredegar's collage of extracts and interpolations is so heterogeneous that it has been described as "not historiography in the strict

---

[60] It is not his own creation, as it occurs also in the *Liber historiae Francorum* (see below), whose author was unacquainted with Fredegar. On the myth of Trojan descent in medieval histories, cf. Reynolds (1983), 376–78.

sense of the word, but a juxtaposition of literary forms".[61] From a great variety of genres and rhetorical configurations, two are of particular historical and literary interest. Books II and III contain novelistic biographies of Theoderic the Goth (II,57–59), Justinian (II,62), and Clovis I (III,11–27). The selection in itself throws light on Fredegar's understanding of world history and its protagonists. The narratives, filled with prophetic dreams, loyal friends, military and political stratagems, bridal quests and marriages, constitute an important link between the Hellenistic romances of late antiquity and the medieval *roman*. Ian Wood has pointed out that they are all in some sense "buddy" stories, tales about rulers and loyal counselors.[62] It is likely that much in these tales goes back to Fredegar himself, as their novelistic themes are also present in Book IV.[63] There, in addition, Fredegar's concern with the dynamics between kings and their advisors is expressed by another literary device, a series of *notationes* or brief sketches of the various mayors of the palace: Warnachar (IV,18); Genialis (IV,21); Protadius (IV,27); Claudius (IV,28); Aega (IV,80); Erchinoald (IV,84); Flaochad (IV,89). Traced by means of these short and formulaic notes, the increasing power of their office is singled out as one of the essential transformations from the late Merovingian period to the Carolingian.

B. *The* Liber historiae Francorum

This short work, also known as *Gesta Francorum*, covers the entire history of the Franks from legendary Trojan origins to the sixth year of Theuderic IV (727) in fifty-three chapters. Extremely popular in its time, it survives in numerous manuscripts and in two redactions: A, dated 727; and B, a longer version based on A and composed no later than 737.[64] The anonymous author was a Neustrian with little interest in the doings of Austrasians and Burgundians and practically none for whatever happened outside the Frankish kingdoms.

---

[61] Scheibelreiter (1984), 269.

[62] Wood (1994b), 362–63.

[63] An especially striking similarity is the use of animal fables by royal advisors to convey political messages; cf. Theoderic and Ptolomaeus II,57; King Theuderic and Bishop Leudegasius of Mainz IV,38.

[64] *Liber historiae Francorum*, ed. B. Krusch, *MGH, SSRM* II (Hanover, 1888; repr. 1956).

The sources of the *LHF* have not all been identified; they appear to include many oral traditions of the Neustrians.[65] The Trojan *origo* in chapters 1–4, however, is a learned invention. It traces the Franks back to those Trojans led by Priam and Antenor who, after the fall of the city, made a fresh start in Pannonia. Characteristic of the narrow ethnic range of the author's interests is the fact that neither the Roman Empire nor any of the leading nations of antiquity plays much of a part in the early history of the Franks. A few clashes with Rome serve the purpose of driving them to the furthest reaches of the Rhine, where they choose Faramund to be their first long-haired king (4).

The sixth century (8–34) is covered by a summary of Gregory of Tours's *Historiae* I–VI. The seventh century (35–47) is rich in dramatic legendary episodes but uses no identifiable sources and appears to be based largely on oral lore. The author was unacquainted with Fredegar's chronicle. For events of the turn of the seventh to the eighth century and to 727, he is a contemporary. This gives particular value to the final chapters, which are our chief source for Merovingian obsolescence[66] and the rise of the Carolingians.[67]

The *LHF* has nothing to say on ecclesiastical and hagiographic matters and limits itself throughout to military and dynastic history presented in an epicizing manner, with abundant use of direct speech and anecdotal form. Unlike the novelistic compositions in Fredegar, which integrate such incidents into complex plots and heroic biographies, the *fabulae* in the *LHF* stand by themselves, brought in at different points of the narrative without further coordination with each other. This suggests that they were taken directly from oral tradition, or in any case had not undergone much literary elaboration.

The term *Franci*, as in Fredegar, is largely reserved for the nobility but, in this case, restricted further to the Neustrian nobility. There are, however, occasional reminders that Austrasians and Burgundians are also Franks: after the death of Theuderic II in 613, "Burgundians and Austrasians made peace with the other Franks" ("cum reliquis Francis", 40). The Austrasian nobility is referred to as "Austrasii Franci superiores" (41).

---

[65] Gerberding (1987), 155, 163.
[66] Geary (1988), 179–220.
[67] Gerberding (1987), 92–145.

The author of the *LHF* has been described as a Merovingian legit-
imist,[68] but he presents a remarkably balanced account of the rise
of the Pippinids. Clearly, the king is a necessary presence and also
must be a genuine descendant of Merovech, but perhaps no more
than that is required. The author's sympathy with the nobility and
his constant invocation of the *consilium Francorum* would appear to
indicate that strict limitations on royal power met with his approval.
Aside from the coup of Grimoald in 656, which he condemns as
treason and usurpation (42), he describes the rise of the palace mayors with respect. Towards the end of the *Liber*, he begins to refer to
the office as a *principatus*; of Ebroin: "ipse principatum sagaciter
recepit" (45); of Pippin: "erat Pippino principe uxor nobilissima" (48),
"Pippinus . . . obtenitque principatum sub suprascriptos reges annis
27 et dimidio" (51). Pippin II's son Carolus (Charles Martel) is characterized as a "virum elegantem, egregium atque utilem" (49).

Coming after Gregory of Tours and Fredegar, with their vast
postimperial scope and their sense of the Franks as players among
other nations in a complex international scene, the *LHF* with its
total concentration on one Frankish kingdom and its exclusive interest in politics and war marks an evolution towards a more narrowly
focused historiography. Its success in its own time and later among
the Carolingians confirms that the author was attuned to the contemporary audience of history and had produced what the times
were calling for.

Bede and the Anglo-Saxons

Bede (673–735), a monk at Benedict Biscop's great Northumbrian
foundation of Wearmouth-Jarrow, was a learned and prolific scriptural exegete. His commentaries on numerous books of the Old and
New Testaments contributed decisively to the study of the Bible in
the early Middle Ages. His historical works—a world chronicle, *vitae*
of St. Cuthbert in verse and prose, a history of the abbots of
Wearmouth-Jarrow, and his five-book *Ecclesiastical History of the English
Nation* (*HE*)[69]—were written relatively late, most of them in the last

---

[68] Gerberding (1987), 162.
[69] Bede, *Historia ecclesiastica gentis Anglorum*, ed. C. Plummer (Oxford, 1896; repr.
1969).

two decades of his life. The *HE* generally is believed to have been completed by 731.[70] It covers the history of Britain and the English from Julius Caesar's first attempt to conquer the island in 60 B.C. to the death of Archbishop Bertwald in A.D. 731. It is remarkable that Bede pays little attention to the first three decades of the eighth century, i.e., to his own times, about which he could have written with the authority of a witness; these years are treated summarily in a few final chapters of Book V. Bede's interest centers primarily on the conversion of the English and their unification—with the other inhabitants of Britain: Scots, Picts, and Britons—under the Roman model of Christianity.

The epistle dedicating the *HE* to King Ceolwulf of Northumbria enumerates at length Bede's informants for the various regions of Britain as well as the sources of their knowledge: Roman and local archives, oral tradition, personal experience. Throughout the *HE*, Bede specifies the sources of many segments of his narrative, introducing the famous story of Pope Gregory and the English slaves (II,1), for instance, as a "traditio maiorum", and his account of the sinful goings-on in the monastery at Coldingham as having been told him by the priest Edgils, a resident of Coldingham at the time (IV,25). This measure of methodological caution has earned Bede the applause of twentieth-century historians, who find him to be aware of the requirements of historical evidence to a degree otherwise unexampled in the historiography of the period.

The *HE* begins from the territory, with a description of Britain and Ireland and their native inhabitants before the coming of the Anglo-Saxons. Book I is by far the most important from the standpoint of secular history, unfolding as it does the centuries of Roman rule, the eventual withdrawal of the Romans, with the construction of the Hadrianic and Antonine walls, the coming of the Angles, Saxons, and Jutes and their eventual takeover of the island, as well as Gregory the Great's organization of a first mission to the English, the arrival of Augustine and his fellows in Kent in 597, and the beginnings of English Christianity. Bede's is the fundamental early medieval account of these events and has provided the accepted representation of the coming of the English until very recently. His portrayal of the Britons is essentially negative, while the Anglo-Saxons

---

[70] Though a reference in V.23 to a Saracen defeat in Gaul may concern the battle of Poitiers (732).

are introduced as a providential nation sent by God to take Britain away from an unworthy and sinful people. This is a point Bede makes even when the Britons are known to be Christians of long standing and the English have not yet converted: the raids of the pagan king Ethelfrid of Northumbria on the Britons are described approvingly, with typological parallels from the Old Testament to make sense of the apparent paradox (I,34). What modern historical scholarship has had to correct in Bede's account of the Anglo-Saxon *Landnahme* is precisely this sense of alienation and lack of contact and mutual assimilation between Britons and English, together with the idea that the spread of the latter pushed the former into Wales and areas of the North.[71]

With Christianity in place, the *HE* becomes more exclusively ecclesiastical in focus, covering political developments and secular affairs thinly and unsystematically, only as they impinge on the life of the church. Book II is largely dedicated to the conversion of Northumbria under King Edwin, Book III to the clash of Roman and Irish missions over the Easter controversy and the eventual victory of the Romans at the synod of Whitby in 664 (III,25). Book IV describes the institutional birth of an English church under Archbishop Theodore, who arrived in England in the year of Whitby and brought the branches of the new church together at the synods of Hertford (673) and Hatfield (680). Book V covers more recent matters, such as Willibrord's mission on the Continent, the tempestuous career of Bishop Wilfrid of York, and, somewhat triumphalistically, the final acceptance of the Roman Easter by the Irish and the Picts (the Britons remained unpersuaded at the time of writing). The work closes with a diffident appraisal of the situation of Britain in 731, a chronological summary, and a famous personal statement by the author: an account of his career followed by a list of his works.

Bede writes Christian history, molding his narrative on typological schemes borrowed from exegesis—redemption history (*Heilsgeschichte*) and the theory of the six ages of the world—and on contemplative ideals characteristic of his own monastic background.[72] A feature of the *HE* that often has disturbed modern historians is the frequency of hagiographic episodes, more numerous and important in Bede's

---

[71] Cf. Collins (1991), 162–82.
[72] Hanning (1966), 63–90; Davidse (1982).

masterpiece than in any other historical narrative of the period. Alongside the chapters on ecclesiastical and political history, Bede has set up a parallel series of saints' lives, miracles, and visionary episodes that trace the spiritual transformation of Britain as opposed to its institutional incorporation into the Roman church: the martyrdom of St. Alban and the miracles of Germanus of Auxerre in Book I, the posthumous miracles of King Oswald, the life and miracles of Aidan, the Irishman Fursey's vision of the hereafter in Book III, the life of St. Chad, the miracles of the nuns of Barking, the life of St. Hilda of Whitby, the story of Caedmon and his miraculous gift of poetry, the life and miracles of St. Cuthbert in Book IV, the life and miracles of John of Beverley, and three successive visions of heaven and hell (by Drycthelm and two anonymous visionaries) in Book V. While the many miracles create a sense of the gradual sanctification of Britain, the visions add an apocalyptic perspective confirmed later on by dire omens in Bede's appraisal of the state of the country (V,23).

In historiography, Bede's chief model was Eusebius of Caesarea, whose *Ecclesiastical History* he knew in the Latin translation of Rufinus.[73] The most distinctive structural trait of the genre created by Eusebius was the incorporation of many documents, whole or in part, into the text. Bede follows him in this practice, reproducing the entire *libellus responsionum* sent by Pope Gregory to Augustine of Canterbury to answer questions of pastoral policy that had come up in the early days of his mission[74] in Book I, and many letters from the *registrum* of Gregory's correspondence and from the correspondence of later popes in Books I, II, and III. In Book IV he incorporates the acts of the synods of Hertford and Hatfield (the latter only in part), and Book V contains the lengthy and erudite letter of Abbot Ceolfrid of Wearmouth-Jarrow to Nechtan, king of the Picts, explaining the superiority of the Roman Easter and tonsure over the Irish. Among Bede's other literary sources we may count Orosius, Gildas's *De excidio Brittaniae*, and several hagiographic works of Northumbrian origin: the anonymous Lindisfarne life of Cuthbert, the Whitby life of Gregory the Great, and the *vita* of Wilfrid of York attributed to Eddius Stephanus. His celebrated narrative style owes much to the example

---

[73] Barnard (1976).
[74] Cf. Meyvaert (1986).

of the Latin Bible and to the "stylisation biblique" of late antique and early medieval saints' lives,[75] but also to his familiarity with ancient rhetoric, especially in its postclassical Christian incarnation.[76]

Bede has been praised so highly for his superior Latin, English common sense, and quasi-modern standards of scholarship that it has taken modern historians a very long time to express dissatisfaction with certain aspects of the *HE*. Dissatisfaction is now the dominant note in studies of Bede as a historian,[77] and not only because of his relative lack of interest in secular matters or his attention to miracles. It is difficult to say, when reading the *HE*, whether the author is painting an idealized, unproblematic picture of Christian origins among the English or whether, in ascribing particular holiness to the customs of an earlier time (e.g., IV,27: "Erat quippe moris eo tempore populis Anglorum ut . . .") and occasionally voicing disappointment with the Christianity of his own day (e.g., III,5: "In tantum autem vita illius [Aidan] a nostri temporis segnitia distabat, ut . . ."), he is proposing his vision of the early church as a measure of the height from which the English have fallen. Such uncertainties are laid to the account of Bede's discretion, i.e., the uncompromising way in which he eliminates overt criticism and every negative note from his historical canvas. As a quality, Bede's discretion is the more questionable because of the sharp contrast between the *HE* and the letter he addressed to Bishop Egbert of York in November 734, only months before his death. In it, Bede reviews a series of church abuses—primarily the neglect of episcopal visitations and the proliferation of pseudo-monasteries ruled by private owners—of which there is hardly a trace in his ecclesiastical history.

The *HE* has often been read as a national history *malgré soi*, and scrutinized for intimations of national consciousness or a less definable "Englishness".[78] Bede, however, writes from within a wholly imperial institution and, unlike Isidore, projects no sense of alienation or secession from the Roman world. In fact, his constant argument against the Irish Easter is that it constitutes the religious tradition of a single, remote nation. In a passage that long has been taken as evidence for the early existence of an English state, Bede lists seven

---

[75] Van Uytfanghe (1987), 17–60; Kendall (1979).
[76] Kendall (1978); Ray (1986).
[77] Cf. especially Wormald (1978).
[78] Cowdrey (1980–81).

"overkings" who have had power over many nations of the English south of the Humber (II,5). Taken over from Bede by MS. A (Parker) of the Anglo-Saxon Chronicle, this office is attributed there to a "Bretwalda" or "brytenwalda" ('ruler of the British,' or 'wide ruler'). Recent studies, however, show convincingly that Bede's list of rulers includes widely different sorts of overlordship and that his use of the word *imperium* for power over various English groups indicates that he did not see the English as forming one nation or *gens*.[79] The ideology of national unity found in this passage and elsewhere in the *HE* can be traced more plausibly to Canterbury and the ecclesiastical authorities, given that the English church had been one from the time of Archbishop Theodore.[80]

Of late, more attention has been paid to Bede's Northumbrian bias. A good half of the *HE* is exclusively dedicated to the affairs of the historian's native kingdom, and it has been pointed out that he often identifies the Northumbrians with the English.[81] This privileging of the country he knew best may be explained by the unavailability of sources and information for the other Anglo-Saxon realms.[82] Bede's sustained effort to tell the history not only of East Saxons, East Angles, West Saxons, Mercians, and men of Kent but also of such elusive groups as the Middle Angles, Hwiccas, Gyrwas, and Gewissae becomes even more significant and deserving of study in light of his struggle to obtain reliable information on the kingdoms to the south.

A recent and much debated study has added to the new picture of Bede as rooted Northumbrian historian, aloof neither from his own narrower ethnicity nor from the church politics of his time, by providing considerable evidence that the *HE* follows a precise agenda: it is intended to contradict on every point of substance the account of Northumbrian church history in the *vita* of Wilfrid of York attributed to Eddius Stephanus.[83] Even Bede's unwavering Romanism can be read as a response to the Wilfridians: since they claimed the triumph of Roman ways in Northumbria as an achievement of their leader, Bede had to argue from the same premises, but only in order

---

[79] Fanning (1991).
[80] Wormald (1983).
[81] Fanning (1991), 21.
[82] Kirby (1965–66).
[83] Goffart (1988), 235–328.

to attribute the final victory of the Roman cause to every ecclesiastic of note except for Wilfrid and his disciples.[84]

Paul the Deacon and the Lombards

The author of the *Historia Langobardorum* (*HL*)[85] was a noted and many-sided literary figure before he—late in life—came to write his most famous book. A poet, grammarian, and lexicographer, Paul had already published a *Historia Romana* based on the *Breviarium* of Eutropius and dedicated to Adalperga, duchess of Benevento, a brief *History of the Bishops of Metz* written at the request of Bishop Angilram of Metz, and a *vita* of Gregory the Great. Of these earlier historiographic works, the *Historia Romana* is of particular importance for the study of the *HL*, as Paul's own continuation of Eutropius (Books XI–XVI) brings Roman history to the reign of Justinian, which is precisely where the *HL* takes up the history of Italy. Although more than two decades separate the composition of the *Romana* from that of the *HL*, there is every appearance that the latter was conceived as a continuation of the former.

The circumstances of Paul's life have played a significant role in the interpretation of *HL*. Born at some time between 720 and 730, Paul belonged to a noble Lombard family of Friuli and had spent his youth at the court of Pavia. After the suppression of the Lombard kingdom by Charlemagne in 774, a brother of his, involved in a rebellion against the Franks, was arrested and sent captive into the Frankish kingdom. In 782 Paul visited the Frankish court to move its ruler to clemency. He stayed until 787 as a member of Charlemagne's court circle, and the commission to him of the short Metz history suggests that he was highly regarded, as this text touches on dynastic issues of importance to the Carolingians.[86] Paul had been a monk at Monte Cassino before his stay in Aachen, and on his return to Italy he went back to the great monastery in the still-Lombard duchy of Benevento. It is there that he wrote Books I–VI

---

[84] See Mayr-Harting (1994) for a rejoinder in favor of the aloof Bede.
[85] Paul the Deacon, *Historia Langobardorum*, ed. L. Bethmann and G. Waitz. *MGH Ss. Rer. Lang. et Ital.* (Hanover, 1878; repr. 1966), 265–391.
[86] Goffart (1986).

of the *HL*, and it is likely that he was interrupted by death and that the *HL* was left unfinished.[87]

To the development of national or ethnic historiography the *HL* brings a new generic self-consciousness and deliberation. In addition to his specifically Lombard sources—the seventh-century *Origo gentis Langobardorum* and the equally seventh-century *Historiola de gestis Langobardorum* of Secundus of Trent, now lost, as well as (it is thought) a rich supply of oral tradition—Paul uses all the works and authors discussed so far, with the single exception of the *Liber historiae Francorum*, to provide a panoramic view of Italy and the Lombards, but also of the Franks, the Byzantines, the Anglo-Saxons, Visigoths, and Avars. He is far removed from the ethnocentricity of an Isidore.[88]

Paul's orientation and point of view are anything but transparent, and recent interpretations of the *HL* show few areas of agreement.[89] Certain large questions come up regularly: writing when the Lombard kingdom no longer exists, does Paul design the *HL* as a memorial to a vanished culture? If we keep in mind his years among the Franks and his careful record of Frankish history in the *HL*, should we expect to find an anticipation of the Lombard downfall in his narrative, perhaps even a justification of Frankish triumph? What makes it particularly difficult to answer such questions is that Paul moralizes only about events and actions, rarely or never about characters or national communities in general. His Lombard kings may be great leaders of their people, brave in battle and politically astute, but they nonetheless are guilty of usurpation, treachery, perjury (the best example is Grimoald I in IV.51 and V.1–4), and Paul neither apologizes for their crimes, of which he gives highly dramatic accounts, nor tries to draw coherent moral portraits. The same is true of nationalities. Though he obviously dislikes the Greeks, he praises Justinian lavishly. He does not characterize the Franks negatively, though he acknowledges that they often were at odds with the Lombards, and he presents King Guntram, Queen Brunhild, Arnulf of Metz, and Charles Martel in a favorable light.[90] Less often noticed

---

[87] *HL*, VI.58, the final chapter, contains a reference to an episode to be narrated later, a miracle performed by Peter, bishop of Pavia.

[88] An outline is provided in Appendix 3.

[89] Vinay (1978), 25–49; Bullough (1986); Goffart (1988), 328–431.

[90] *Contra* Bullough (1986), 97: "The Franks figure in his narrative almost entirely as enemies".

is the fact that, on the rare occasions when Paul refers to the non-Lombard inhabitants of Italy, he makes it very plain that for them the coming of his people has been an unqualified disaster. In the kingless years after Alboin's death, under the power of the Lombard dukes "many of the noble Romans were killed for love of gain" and "the churches were sacked, the priests killed, the cities ruined, the people who had grown up like crops annihilated" (II.32). He comments later on a letter of Gregory the Great concerning the Lombards that they "indeed were unbelievers and were stealing everything" (IV.29). Writing in a Monte Cassino that he knew had been pillaged and left vacant by the Lombards (IV.17), Paul hardly will have had an unqualified sense of his people's achievement in Italy or an unwavering dislike of a foreign invader who had come to defend the interests of the church.

There is a strong possibility that Paul, after the fall of the Lombard kingdom (cf. V.6: "Ante Langobardorum perditionem"), may have placed his hopes for the persistence and national survival of the Lombards on Benevento, where he wrote the *HL*. Friuli and Benevento receive a disproportionate amount of attention in comparison to other regions of Lombard Italy. Paul's portrait of Grimoald I, the Friulan prince who became duke of Benevento and then ruler of the Lombards, stands at the center of his narrative, and this king was the ancestor of Grimoald III, duke of Benevento while Paul wrote the *HL* and son of the same Duchess Adalperga for whom he had composed his *Historia Romana* many years before.[91] It can be argued that in tracing the history of his people Paul had in mind Grimoald III and his court as a possible audience. References to Liutprand's collaboration with Charles Martel (VI.54) and to his great care to keep peace with the Franks (VI.58; final words of the *HL*) can be read as suggesting a conciliatory policy to be followed with the new masters of Italy.

Of great importance in the study of the *HL* is its enduring reputation as a storehouse of Lombard oral traditions. Many famous stories, among others those of how the Lombards acquired their name, of how Alboin received his arms from the Gepid king Turisind, whose son he recently had slain in battle, and of how Alboin as king of the Lombards came to be murdered at the instigation of his wife,

---

[91] Krüger (1981).

long have been regarded as authentic survivals of various early Germanic genres, notably the heroic lay, purportedly preserved in Paul's Latin prose.[92] This view would lend considerable support to the reading of the *HL* as a monument to a vanished culture, the product of feelings of loss and ethnic nostalgia. The chief difficulty is that the early Germanic narrative genres are so poorly documented that they cannot be identified with certainty by either thematic or formal criteria.[93] In addition, Paul's legends show so many signs of novelistic treatment, with loosely attached subplots and narrative motifs and with supporting characters who end up rivaling the ostensible protagonists in importance, that it is hard to see them as pristine survivals of a single ethnic tradition. They have much in common with the historical romances of Fredegar's chronicle, which have never been suspected of authenticity. Goffart's recent reading of the *HL* has established that the individual books of Paul's narrative follow patterns of elaborate symmetry that convey the author's interpretation of Lombard history by means of prolepsis and typology. These patterns are obviously Paul the Deacon's creations, and the allegedly traditional legends fit into them too neatly to avoid the suspicion that they too are devised, or in any case reformulated, so as to confirm the design presented by the work as a whole, the outline of a national destiny as projected by an artful alignment of episodes and narrative sequences.[94]

Franks and Anglo-Saxons in Other Genres

Several works written before A.D. 1000 are rich sources of information on ethnic groups, and notably on the Franks and the Anglo-Saxons, but have not been studied together with the national histories because they belong to different genres. Chief among these are annals, which in the early Middle Ages derive from an Anglo-Saxon tradition of marginal notations on Easter tables.[95] Ideally, such annals

---

[92] Gschwantler (1976) and (1979).
[93] Cf. Haug (1975); Schröder (1991). Comparisons with the lays of the *Poetic Edda* composed in Iceland and Norway between the tenth and the thirteenth century are anachronistic, though frequently proposed.
[94] Goffart (1988), 425–28.
[95] McCormick (1975).

were compiled year by year and entries made immediately after the events, or in the same year. In reality, however, whole sequences were often reconstructed many years later, and archetypes created in one region, within a specific community, were incorporated into other annals or used to start a record of the same type somewhere else. Texts of this nature, whose original function was to support a chronological scheme by labeling the different years with memorable happenings, have been said to lack the defining characteristics of narrative: unity of design, closure, and the totalizing force that comes with an individual author and his conception of history.[96] These reservations apply better to ideal annals, put together diachronically in a strict year-by-year sequence, than to the early medieval texts that have come down to us, which frequently owe large blocks of entries to a single annalist and are even more often revised and supplemented to reflect an institutional or personal point of view.

Noteworthy and a case in point are the *Royal Frankish Annals (RFA)*,[97] which cover Frankish history from 741 (the death of Charles Martel) to 829 and are a source of fundamental importance for the reigns of Charlemagne and Louis the Pious and for imperial expansion under the Carolingians. Language and style show them to be the work of three authors: one who was active between 787 and 793 and who was also responsible for the retrospective entries from 741, which he drew from earlier annals and the continuators of Fredegar's chronicle, a second one who wrote the entries from 794 or 795 to 807, and a third one who composed the sequence 808–29. Their approach to Frankish history, however, is remarkably uniform: the events related are almost exclusively matters of policy, especially military and diplomatic, and the annalists systematically ignore or attenuate the errors and defeats of the Frankish rulers and their armies. This optic, which strongly suggests an official point of view, would appear to place the authors in the Carolingian royal chapel rather than in a monastic community, which would have projected its own more local interests and predilections.[98] What separates the *RFA* most

---

[96] White (1980), esp. 6–14.

[97] *Annales regni Francorum inde ab a. 741 usque as a. 829, qui dicuntur Annales Laurissenses maiores et Einhardi*, ed. G. H. Pertz, revised by F. Kurze, *MGH, SRG* (Hanover, 1895).

[98] Wattenbach-Levison (1953), 245–53. More recently Collins (1998) has argued for a less linear and uniform tradition behind the *RFA*: the 741–87 section, for

evidently from the ethnic histories is their thoroughly imperial out-look: rather than focus on the Franks and their traditions, the authors center their attention on the accomplishments of Charlemagne and his heir in turning Saxons, Slavs, Danes, and Lombards into subjects.

The *RFA* are *annales maiores*, a highly developed offshoot of their genre,[99] and show a marked formal consistency that sets them apart from the basic format of Easter annals. Although, as in most texts of this kind, the earliest entries, composed synchronically, are much shorter than the later diachronic ones, they are from the beginning summaries of the year's events rather than single sentences register-ing one or two remarkable happenings chosen to identify a year.

Far more difficult to classify generically is the four-book *Historia* of Nithard,[100] written between 841 and 843 with the explicit aim of supplying posterity with an accurate record of the wars between the sons of Louis the Pious—Lothair, Louis the German, and Charles the Bald—and the division of the empire. The author is hardly impartial: a grandson of Charlemagne himself through his mother Bertha, he took up this assignment in contemporary history at the request of Charles the Bald, Louis the Pious's youngest son, whose supporter he declares himself to be and whom he addresses directly in the brief prologues to the first three books.

Nithard is very much a part of the story he tells, going on impor-tant military and diplomatic missions for Charles. Although Sallust's historical monographs have been mentioned as a possible model, the action of Nithard's narrative is too episodic and drawn-out to make the parallel persuasive. One important formal feature it shares with the *RFA* is the function of Book I, a competent outline of the reign of Louis the Pious (814–40), clearly intended as a backdrop or pref-ace to the dynastic conflicts that follow. Nithard's perspective, how-ever, is the very opposite of that of the Frankish annals, as he advocates a division of the Frankish territories and clearly regards the empire as a thing of the past. Yet ethnic factors have no part in his conception of a fair division, which is exclusively territorial and concerns borders and not national traditions.

---

instance, would have been grafted to the text and not composed originally to serve as its prologue.

[99] McCormick (1975), 16–18.

[100] Nithard, *Histoire des fils de Louis le Pieux*, ed. and trans. P. Lauer (Paris, 1964).

Recently the case has been made that Book IV, the prologue of which is not addressed to Charles, moves away from the focus on public history that distinguishes the previous books to dwell on Nithard's own predicament and especially on his loss of the benefice lands that Lothair had taken away from him in July 840 when he refused to betray Charles. When Charles and Louis the German later returned those lands to Lothair in the course of peace negotiations, Nithard would have reacted with bitterness and composed this last book in the genre of a political complaint or polemic, possibly for his intimates at St. Riquier, where he had retired as lay abbot.[101] This reading credits Nithard's work with an unusual degree of generic diversity—from history proper (Book I) to contemporary history (II and III) to political polemic (IV)—which one is tempted to connect with the author's exceptional standing in his age as a lay historiographer.

The chief source of information on the Anglo-Saxons from the eighth to the eleventh century (i.e., after Bede) is the group of Old English annals known collectively as the *Anglo-Saxon Chronicle* (*ASC*).[102] They are bound together by a common archetype or core, an annalistic work composed in the late ninth century, during the reign of Alfred. The choice of the Old English language points in the direction of this king's renewal of learning, with its stress on vernacular literacy and on translation from Latin into English. However, there are indications that the author(s) of the archetype should be placed in the southwest (Dorset, Somerset), about which this earliest core of the *ASC* supplies very specific data.[103] Beginning sixty years before the Incarnation with Julius Caesar's first expedition to Britain, the archetype runs to the ninth century, possibly to 855. Copies were distributed throughout England in the wake of the Alfredian revival, and are found—with various additions and alterations—as the basis of chronicles associated with Winchester, Abingdon, Worcester, and Peterborough. The Winchester (or Parker) chronicle was continued to 1070; the Abingdon chronicle to 1066; the Worcester chronicle

---

[101] Nelson (1985).
[102] *The Anglo-Saxon Chronicle. A Collaborative Edition*, ed. D. Dumville and S. Keynes (Cambridge, 1983–).
[103] Stenton (1925). This local focus is particularly clear in the *Chronicle of Aethelweard*, which has been shown to derive from a fuller version of the prototype than any of the extant versions of the *ASC*.

to 1079; the Peterborough chronicle to 1154. The narrative style of these texts is anything but uniform, nor do they simply evolve, as might be expected, from initial annalistic brevity to greater copiousness and particularity. Over the centuries, the entries shift back and forth between laconic objectivity, usually paired with extreme syntactic simplicity, and an interpretive, moralizing attitude coupled with rhetorical elaboration and a more ambitious vocabulary.[104] More importantly, the focus of the narrative keeps changing, as does the generic profile of the text. If the protagonists of history are at first the early Christians, the Romans, and the Britons, in an outline that owes much to universal chronicles, these are soon replaced by a great number of royal and ecclesiastical lineages whose rise to power and eventual decline become the annalists' almost exclusive concern. Once the Scandinavian raids begin, strategy emerges as the dominant subject and the comings and goings of the invading army are covered in considerable detail. Occasionally, the concerns of the religious houses and communities where the various chronicles were compiled take center stage and receive as much attention as matters of national importance.[105] This constant diversity of approach is probably the main reason why the *ASC*, despite its use of the national language and its sustained interest in the Anglo-Saxon *gentes*, rarely is discussed as a national history. It is a cumulative, heterogeneous text with more seams than continuities and is therefore difficult to place in a specific generic tradition.

Widukind and the Saxons

Widukind, a monk at the Carolingian-founded monastery of Corvey on the Weser since 941/42, almost certainly was a member of the Saxon nobility and a descendant of the famous chieftain of the same name who in the late eighth century had led the Saxon resistance against enforced conversion and incorporation into the Frankish empire. His death must be dated after 973. After composing a few saints' lives that have not survived, Widukind took up a major work

[104] Clark (1971).
[105] Cf. Stenton (1971), 692–93: "... when compared with the great Frankish annals of the ninth century, which seem to descend from an official record, the *Chronicle* has definitely the character of private work".

of secular history, the *Rerum gestarum Saxonicarum libri tres* (*RGS*) or
"Three Books of the Deeds of the Saxons".[106] Scholars agree that
Widukind produced three versions of this work. A first one, completed by 967/8, is sometimes referred to as the monastery version.
A second one, adapted from the first version almost immediately and
dedicated to Mathilda, a daughter of Otto I who at the age of eleven
had just become abbess of Quedlinburg, adds pompous prefaces to
each book, rephrases some of the earlier chapters, and provides
justifications for sections that have little to say about the glory of
the dedicatee's Liudolfing ancestors. A third version, finished in 973
or shortly thereafter, brings the narrative to the death of Otto I on
that same year.[107]

As a whole, the *RGS* cannot be described as an ethnic history.
Only the first fourteen chapters of Book I focus on the Saxons and
sketch out a brief legendary *origo*. The remainder of Book I covers
the passing of the kingdom of the East Franks from the Frankish
Conradines to the Saxon Liudolfings and the rule of the first Saxon
king, Henry I (Henry the Fowler). Books II and III give a very full
account of the reign of Henry's son Otto I, with particular attention to the civil wars he was forced to fight with his nobility and
most often against his own near relatives, his military successes on
the eastern borders against Magyars and Slavs and, towards the end,
his achievements in Italy and increasingly confident dealings with
the court of Constantinople. The optic of the narrative after I,14 is
thoroughly imperial: Widukind never loses sight of the fact that Henry
and Otto are ruling a Frankish realm and can, in the best of cases,
only claim to have been elected to their position by "the peoples of
the Franks and the Saxons".[108]

Widukind's Saxon *origo* is largely made up of legendary materials,
some of it reflecting the author's considerable learning, as when he
speculates that the first Saxons may have been relicts from the
Macedonian armies of Alexander the Great (I,2), or when he has
recourse to etymology and onomastics to account for the name of
the Saxons (I,7) or that of their war-god (I,12). Two legends (I,2–7)

---

[106] *Die Sachsengeschichte des Widukind von Korvei*, ed. P. Hirsch and H. E. Lohmann,
5th ed., *MGH, Scriptores rerum Germanicarum in usum scholarum* (Hanover, 1935; repr.
1977).
[107] Beumann (1970), 857–62.
[108] Cf. Eggert (1994).

serve to explain the Saxon *Landnahme* or conquest of their territory from the Thuringians, who held it before them. This is accomplished by means of a legal stratagem, but the acquisition is secured later when the Saxons invite the Thuringian leaders to a banquet that turns into a deadly ambush. At this point (I,8), Widukind inserts a brief narrative of the Saxon conquest of Britain, derived entirely from Bede, as if to establish that his people had an imperial vocation even before they became part of a Frankish empire. The remainder of this ethnic sequence is taken up by an account of the wars between the Frankish king Thiadric and Irminfrid, ruler of the Thuringians. Thiadric asks the Saxons to fight on his side, promising them the lands now owned by the Thuringians. When he is later persuaded by an adroit Thuringian envoy to make peace with Irminfrid and turn on his new allies, the Saxons discover that they are about to be betrayed and move on by themselves, led by a heroic and eloquent old warrior, to exterminate the Thuringians. This complex episode appears to combine what must have been independent legends to begin with: that of the Saxon leader Hathagat and his saving initiative and that of the later betrayal of Irminfrid by Iring, his envoy to the Franks, an interesting tale with little or no relevance to Saxon history.[109]

These early chapters of the *RGS* suggest that by the mid-tenth century *origo gentis* had taken on, if not the status of a genre (here it would be an embedded genre), at least a distinctive profile as an identifiable complex of legendary subject matter. Following in the steps of Paul the Deacon, Widukind is fully aware of his predecessors and refers to them pointedly: Bede (I,8), Paul himself (I,14), and Jordanes (I,18). It generally is believed that he drew on vernacular oral tradition throughout the work, which would explain the dramatic form of much of his narrative.[110] But Widukind also wrote under the influence of the Latin classics, especially Sallust's works, and this source of inspiration helps to account for at least two important characteristics of the *RGS*: the tendency of the characters to express themselves in lengthy, fully expository speeches; and Widukind's own strongly developed sense of *Realpolitik*, or "neutrality", as Beumann calls it, which makes him singularly understanding of the ambitions

---

[109] Uecker (1972), 131–34.
[110] Beumann (1950), 66–93.

of high-born pretenders and conspirators.[111] Recent scholars tend to see the deliberative assemblies of the *RGS*, with their many eloquent speakers, as more classicizing than tribal or 'Germanic'. However, Widukind's uncommon attention to ritual and ceremony has been associated with a post-Carolingian breakdown of literate culture and a return to the expressive forms of a primarily oral civilization.[112]

An important question about the ethnic portico to the *RGS* concerns the measure in which it is organic to the work as a whole. In his preface to Book I, addressing Mathilde, Widukind justifies this section as an entertainment on an edifying and noble subject, however unconnected to the greatness of her lineage. But there are at least two fundamental ways in which this section sets the stage for the dynastic and imperial history that is to follow. The early collaboration of Franks and Saxons against Thuringians, though enforced at the last moment by a Saxon initiative, serves as heroic-legendary precedent for their later partnership as *Reichsvölker* in East Francia: as soon as the destruction of the Thuringians is an accomplished fact, the Saxons are called "partners and friends of the Franks" (I,13, repeated in I,14). This myth of an ancient *amicitia* allows Widukind to gloss over the extreme violence of Charlemagne's Saxon wars— as he puts it, the wise Frankish ruler converted the Saxons to Christianity "in part by wise persuasion, in part by force of arms", making them brothers of his own people in faith (I,15).

In addition, Hathagat, the venerable warrior who renders this first alliance possible by forcing the hand of the Franks, is referred to as "pater patrum" by his fellow Saxons in honor of earlier deeds of prowess (I,11) and serves as a clear forerunner of Henry I, who after his victory over the Magyars at Riade in 933 is honored as "pater patriae, rerum dominus imperatorque" (I,39), and of Otto I who, after his decisive triumph over the Magyars at the Lechfeld (955), is acclaimed as "pater patriae imperatorque" by his troops on the battlefield (III,49). It is from this point on that Widukind refers to Otto as "the emperor", ignoring entirely his imperial coronation by the pope, which he passes over in silence and which had taken place in Rome seven years after the Lechfeld, on February 2, 1962.

---

[111] Beumann (1950), 94–100.
[112] Leyser (1993).

By Way of Conclusion

The development of *origo gentis* does not run its course within the early Middle Ages; it reaches if not its high point at least its fullest definition in Saxo Grammaticus's massive *Gesta Danorum* ("Deeds of the Danes"), composed between 1200 and 1220. Though he relies primarily on Nordic sources, Saxo, with a keen sense of the unfolding of ethnic themes in European historiography, cites the chief texts of the tradition: Jordanes, Bede, Paul the Deacon, as well as the eleventh- and twelfth-century historians of the Normans. His grasp of what is called for in the way of subject matter is no less assured: of the sixteen books of the *Gesta*, he dedicates the first nine to heroic-legendary prehistory.

Saxo's predecessor in these respects is Paul the Deacon, whose knowledge of the tradition of ethnic history was even more comprehensive and who, for the first time since Jordanes, chose to open his narrative with a tissue of vernacular legends, stories that he derides as silly popular creations but nevertheless tells in full. Between Paul and Saxo stands Widukind, whose ability to produce a miniature *origo* along the same lines and use it as a prelude to what is no longer a national but a dynastic history indicates that in these representatives the historiography of *gentes* may have begun to move, albeit slowly, towards generic form.

Appendix 1: Outline of Jordanes's Getica

The first section is punctuated by set descriptions of remote northern localities: the limit of the world-ocean, Britannia, the Gothic homeland of Scanzia, the Goths' first settlement on the European mainland, known later as Gothiscanzia, Scythia, Dacia, eventually Moesia and Thrace. There are constant references to oral traditions preserved in the *carmina* and *fabulae* of the Goths (28, 43, 72, 79), but in fact most of the legendary history narrated here has a bookish and fanciful appearance, much like that of the classical and late-antique literature on *origines gentium* (Bickerman [1952]; the notion that the earliest sources of history are songs is a well-documented cliché of classical historiography, cf. Momigliano [1957]). There is a clear intention to attribute to the Goths a considerable antiquity by involving them in wars with the Egyptians (47), the Trojan war (60), wars against the Persians or Parthians led by Cyrus, Darius, and Xerxes (61–64), and in wars against the Macedonian empire (65–66). At the same time, and often by means of the speculative etymology of his age, Jordanes manages to turn the Parthians (48), the Amazons (49), the Gepids (94–95), and the Huns themselves (121–22) into descendants of the Goths. This move is made easier by Jordanes's assumption that the Goths were identical with the Getae or Thracians, an opinion common in late antiquity (Jordache [1983]). If the Goths do not struggle against the rising Roman Empire, it is because they are at the time being educated by their philosopher-king Diceneus (69–72). The first clash with Rome comes under Domitian, and not long after that the empire is paying the Goths a regular subsidy. Whenever this is withheld, the Goths devastate Eastern provinces. They are adopted into the Roman army under Constantine and make it possible for the emperor to dedicate himself to the raising of his new capital. Under the Amal Ermanaric, the Huns conquer the Gothic territories north of the Black Sea; while the Visigoths move into imperial lands, the Ostrogoths are forced to become satellites of the Huns.

The second section, on the Visigoths, presents what is on the whole a favorable view of this tribe, starting from their settlement in Moesia and conversion to Arian Christianity (for which Jordanes, following Orosius VII, 33, 19, blames the emperor Valens; 131–33). Alaric's sack of Rome in 410 is explained by a treacherous attack against him led by Stilicho at Pollentia (154–55). The narrative center of this section and of the book as a whole is a very full account of the battle of the Catalaunian Fields in 452, with Aetius and the Visigoths together on one side and the Huns, led by Attila and supported by his Ostrogothic subjects, on the other (184–218). Various episodes are narrated dramatically, which contrasts with Jordanes's usual style: Athanaric's visit to Constantinople and his extravagant praise of the city and the empire (143–44) and Attila's speech to his troops at the Catalaunian Fields (202–06) are especially notable. The *Getica* has been regarded as a relic of Ostrogothic traditions (presumably going back to Cassiodorus and the court of Ravenna), but this section on the Visigoths is in fact longer and more favorable to its subjects than the chapters on the Ostrogoths that follow. It has been suggested recently (Heather [1991], 63–66) that Jordanes may have used here a separate Visigothic source that has not survived.

The third and final section takes us back to the collapse of the Ostrogothic kingdom at the death of Ermanaric and traces the further history of his tribe and his lineage, the Amals, under Hunnish power. The death of Attila (254–58) allows them to settle in the imperial province of Pannonia as a free people. There are recurrent episodes of Gothic rampaging, especially in Illyricum, when imperial subsidies are not paid (271, 285–86), but from the introduction of Theoderic and his childhood as a hostage in Constantinople (271), Jordanes emphasizes the closeness and harmony of the Ostrogoths and the Eastern Empire. The one significant episode that is dramatized is a conversation between Theoderic and Emperor Zeno in which the Goth asks the emperor's permission to take over Italy from Odoacer in his name (290–92). After summarizing the events that led to Justinian's war against the Goths, Jordanes closes the *Getica* stating that he has written it not so much in praise of the Goths as of the ruler who conquered them (316).

Appendix 2: Outline of Gregory's Historiae

Book I, which reaches from the Creation to the death of Martin of Tours in 397, serves as a world-historical backdrop to the other books, which are concerned primarily with the Merovingian kingdoms. Gregory emphasizes the role of Christ in the Creation, in harmony with the recurring anti-Arian polemic of the *Historiae*. His account of ancient history concentrates almost exclusively on the Jews and on biblical narrative, except for I,17, where he enumerates the world-empires of antiquity. With the Christian missions to the gentiles and the first persecutions and martyrdoms he blends some information on the Roman Empire and its rulers. Book II extends to the death of Clovis in 511 and of all the books of the *Historiae* pays the most attention to the Franks as a people, as it must describe their first appearance in Gaul and their rise to power. Especially important is II,9; in it Gregory analyzes all the information available to him from historical sources on the question of whether the early Franks had been ruled by kings: it is a *tour de force* of sustained historical criticism. His biography of Clovis outlines his gradual conquest of Gaul, culminating in his victory over the Arian Visigoths in 507 and the Frankish takeover of what had been the Visigothic kingdom of Toulouse. Gregory sets side-by-side Clovis's profile as God-appointed king (probably derived in part from early propaganda on his behalf, cf. Wood [1985] and Hen [1993]) with his systematic elimination of his own relatives and other potential rivals. Book III covers the disastrous reigns of the sons of Clovis; his grandson Theudebert emerges as a model king, courageous, effective, and deferential to the church. His death in 548 marks the end of the book. Book IV describes the later reigns of the sons of Clovis and the coming to power of the children of Chlothar: Charibert, Guntram, Sigibert, and Chilperic, the fateful Visigothic marriages of the latter two, and the murder of Sigibert in 575, allegedly engineered by Chilperic's wife Fredegund.

Books V to X relate events from 575 to 591, with a strong concentration on the affairs of Central and Southern Gaul. Gregory's interest rarely extends to the northern Franks or to the lands north and east of the Rhine. On the other hand, there is occasional coverage of Spanish developments (e.g., V,38 and VIII,28: the conversion and rebellion of Hermengild), Byzantine politics (V,30; VI,30: reign of Tiberius), and news from Rome (X,1: plague; Gregory the Great becomes pope). Books V and VI revolve around the figures of Chilperic I and Fredegund, portrayed very negatively by Gregory, who refers to the king as "the Nero and Herod of our times" (VI,46). VII to X follow the reigns of Sigibert's son Childebert II (with the Visigothic Brunhild as queen mother) and of his uncle Guntram and their various alliances, betrayals, and reconciliations with each other, culminating in the Treaty of Andelot (November 587). Among the important events in these books of contemporary history is the campaign of Gundovald, an alleged son of King Chlothar who had been living in Constantinople and was summoned back by a group of nobles (VI,24). Gregory gives a nuanced and even equivocal account of this pretender's claims, which he appears to have considered legitimate, and his dramatic narrative of the betrayal of Gundovald by the very men who had brought him to Gaul and of his wretched death at Comminges shows genuine compassion (VII,34–38). Gregory himself appears as a protagonist in several major episodes, notably his own trial at Berny-Riviere for treason and slander against Chilperic and Fredegund (V,47–49) and his appearance before King Guntram on behalf of Childebert II, to reassure Guntram that his nephew was not breaking the clauses of the Treaty of Andelot (IX,20).

Alongside of these political episodes, the *Historiae* include abundant information about ecclesiastical matters, for instance the Vandal persecution of Catholics in North Africa, of which Gregory gives a partisan account (II,2), or the trial of Bishop Praetextatus of Rouen for conspiring against King Chilperic (V,18). In particular, Gregory keeps track of everything concerning the churches of Tours, Clermont, and Poitiers. There is a steady stream of hagiographic episodes, miracles, and portents, as well as coverage of the more notorious crimes, scandals, and episodes of violence in the Frankish realms (e.g., VII,47; IX,19, 27, 35).

Appendix 3: Outline of Paul the Deacon's Historia Langobardorum

Though Paul foregrounds the Italian territory as focus of his narrative, the *HL* begins outside Italy, with the largely legendary history of the Lombards in Northern and Eastern Europe before their crossing of the Alps. Book I, which has been characterized as an "ethnic prologue" to the *HL* (Goffart 1988, 379) describes the exodus of one third of the Winnili from the overpopulated northern island of Scandinavia, their adoption of the name Langobards, or Lombards, in the course of their early migrations on the continent of Europe on the occasion of a battle with the Vandals, their victorious war with the Heruli, settlement in Pannonia, and equally victorious war with the neighboring Gepids. The book ends with the youthful *gesta* of Alboin, destined to lead his people into Italy, and with accounts of St. Benedict's foundation of Monte Cassino and of the military, cultural, and juridical achievements of Justinian.

Book II brings the Lombards into the larger world of imperial politics: Narses, humiliated by Justin II and his empress after winning Italy back from the Goths, takes revenge by inviting these newcomers, former allies of his in the Gothic war, into the reconquered land. Alboin, now their king, surveys the new country Moses-like from the top of a mountain and on the spot creates the Lombard duchy of Friuli to protect the northeastern marches of his realm. There is, even at this early point, some account of the affairs of the Franks, whose vicinity, Paul knew, would prove fateful to his people. But Book II is primarily taken up by a survey of the Italian territory, presented as a list of seventeen provinces and their cities, a symbolic inventory of the country with all its regions and landscapes. The book ends with a highly novelistic narrative of the murder of Alboin, instigated by his wife the Gepid princess Rosimund. The

Lombards were so daunted by the loss of this great leader that—
after the brief reign of Cleph—they remained kingless for ten years,
during which they were ruled by dukes.

Book III surveys the hostilities between Lombards and Franks in
the period between Cleph and Authari (574–83): the Lombard dukes
invaded Gaul and were driven out; then the Franks led raids into
Italy. Authari, chosen king in 584, won great victories over the Franks
and married the Bavarian princess Theodelinda; his bridal quest and
other prowess are narrated in anecdotal and romantic form. On his
death Theodelinda, beloved of the people, was allowed to select the
new king of the Lombards to be her husband, and her choice fell
upon Agilulf, duke of Turin. Book III also traces the origins of the
duchy of Benevento (III,33) and gives considerable attention to extra-
Italian matters, covering the succession of emperors at Constantinople
from Justin II to Maurice, who moves the Frankish Childebert to
attack the Lombards, as well as the dawn of Christianity among the
English with the mission of Augustine (III,25).

Book IV handles the longest period of time, from Agilulf (590–616)
to Grimoald's taking of power in 662. Agilulf has a tumultuous reign,
fighting against rebellious Lombard dukes and against the Roman
(i.e., Byzantine) armies of the patricius of Ravenna. Occasionally, he
must also make war against the Avars, former neighbors of the
Lombards in Pannonia, though more often the two are allies. About
some of the kings of this period, Paul confesses that he has found
no information at all (e.g., Arioald, 626–36; *HL* IV,41). Aside from
the Lombard sack of Monte Cassino, which remains uninhabited for
years, and the affairs of Benevento, the most notable incident of this
book is the Avar invasion of Friuli, told dramatically and seasoned
with Paul's favorite themes of feminine treachery and youthful heroism on the battlefield. After the invasion, the duchy falls to the
brother of Duke Gisulf, who had been killed by the Avars, and
Gisulf's sons move to Benevento. Grimoald, the youngest, will become
duke of Benevento before taking the Lombard crown by force at
the end of the book. On the international front, the narrative covers
the reigns of Phocas and Heraclius in Constantinople.

Book V is primarily concerned with Grimoald I's battles against
the Franks, the Avars, but chiefly against Constans II, who leaving
the imperial capital sets up his court in Sicily and lays siege to
Benevento, then ruled by Grimoald's son Romoald. This book is of
decisive importance in Paul's argument against the Byzantines, whom

he calls "Greeks" throughout and shows to be wholly indifferent to the welfare of Italy, even in the territories of Roman/Byzantine obedience. The symbolic nub is a scene in which one of Romoald's Lombards puts an entire Byzantine army to flight by brandishing a *graeculus* impaled at the end of his spear. Grimoald's prosperous reign is followed by the return to the throne of the dynasty he had ousted, with Perctarit and his son Cunincpert, and by the conflict of Cunincpert with Alahis, duke of Trent and Brescia, who wrests the throne from him for a while only to lose it again, defeated by a coalition of alienated former allies and resentful clergy.

Book VI makes a scattered impression: it follows the reign of Cunincpert to its end and then the intrusion of a Torinese dynasty, eventually succeeded by Ansprand, the former tutor of Cunincpert's heir, and by Ansprand's son Liutprand (712–44). Much attention is given to Friuli and Benevento, the former as before threatened by incursions of Avars and Slavs. There is also much foreign information, from the rise of the mayors of the palace among the Franks, for which Paul furnishes a classic Carolingian justification (VI.16), to the evils of monotheletism and iconoclasm in Byzantium, which, already blamed for the Schism of the Three Chapters, is made to look like the birthplace of all heresies. Book VI also describes the Arab invasion of Spain and the great victory of Charles Martel at Poitiers, achieved with the collaboration of Liutprand. The book ends with the death of the latter in 744 and does not cover the last thirty years of the Lombard kingdom or the first decade of Frankish rule.

CHAPTER THREE

LOCAL AND INSTITUTIONAL HISTORY (300–1000)

Michel Sot

When investigating local history, the twentieth-century researcher thinks of a particular place: a town, a city, even a region. Historians from French universities speak somewhat condescendingly about 'erudite locals', those who are very knowledgeable about certain details but who often lack an understanding of the big picture. In this perspective, 'local history' is opposed to 'general history'.

When investigating institutional history, today's scholar thinks of the different structures that allow society to function: political institutions first, such as representative assemblies; judicial institutions with the various courts; religious institutions, with churches preeminent; and, finally, institutions for education and research. It is in reference to the latter that the word *institute* has been preserved in the French and the English languages.

In the period with which we are concerned (300–1000), what might local and institutional history mean? The most important place, that which appears in history and which is the object of historiography, is the city (*civitas*). The city is considered based on its various aspects: the topographic dimension of the land itself, organized between inhabitants and buildings; the Roman administrative dimension of territorial subdivision; and, finally, its religious dimension as the seat of a bishop at the head of a diocese. The most elementary form of local history is the list of bishops of a city. Over the centuries, this list has been enriched with various types of information to become, in the ninth and tenth centuries and beyond, the *Gesta episcoporum*.[1] In this genesis of local history, one place in particular has played an important role: the city of Rome, where the *Liber pontificalis* was created and put into place for the first time in the sixth century.[2]

---

[1] Sot (1981); Kaiser (1999).
[2] *Liber pontificalis*, 3 vols., ed. L. Duchesne and C. Vogel (Paris, 1955–57).

As for institutional history, for this period of study it can only be the history of ecclesiastical institutions, at the head of which, again, stands the episcopal institution in the city. And yet the bishop is at the head of a church that is local but belongs to the universal Church. The bishop of Cologne, of Reims or of Canterbury is at the head of the 'one Catholic and apostolic' Church, 'which is in Cologne, in Reims or in Canterbury'. Local history being a history of the Church, it has necessarily a universal dimension. Due to the type of institution with which it deals, local history pertains to universal history. What has been said here concerning an episcopal city is equally valid concerning the history of a monastery. One is less surprised to note that the models of local history and those of universal history are the same. In the middle of the tenth century, Flodoard borrowed from Eusebius of Caesarea the general schema for his *History of the church of Reims*.[3]

The elementary form of universal history, from Eusebius in the fourth century and for the entire period of this study, is the *chronicle*, a simple chronological table, not to be confused with a *history*, which introduces elements of analysis and explanation in order to draw out the sense of the events. Eusebius's *Chronicle* was translated into Latin and continued up to 378 by Jerome, and his ecclesiastical *History* was translated by Rufinus.[4] These two works are the basis of every library of the High Middle Ages, and all historical work, even 'local and institutional', draws its inspiration from them. In the *Chronicle* Eusebius conserves the sharp sense of chronology, the concise style (*brevitas*), and the concern with establishing lists or catalogues. In the *History*, he maintains the desire to demonstrate the development of the Church in the general context, to establish its origins during the time of Christ and the Apostles, and to show how the apostolic tradition was transmitted without rupture all the way up to the time when the work of history was written: this is the case particularly in regard to the exemplary churches which are the four great sees of Jerusalem, Antioch, Alexandria, and Rome.[5]

---

[3] Flodoard, *Historia Remensis ecclesiae*, ed. M. Strattmann, *MGH SS* 36 (Munich, 1998); Sot (1993), 92.

[4] *Eusebius Werke, Die Chronik des Hieronymus*, ed. R. Helm, Die griechischen christlichen Schriftsteller der ersten drei Jahrhunderte (Leipzig, 1913–26); *Eusebius, Kirchengeschichte. Die lateinische Übersetzung des Rufinus*, 3 vols., ed. E. Schwartz and T. Mommsen (Leipzig, 1903–09).

[5] Guenée (1980), 203; Kaiser (1999), 463–64; Zimmermann (1960), 11–24.

The elementary form of local and institutional history is the list: martyrology, episcopal diptych, chronological catalogue of bishops, and, later, the catalogue of abbots. The primary historical concern lay in establishing the chronological catalogue of the holders of the episcopal or abbatial authority: one can write local and institutional histories only after these catalogues have been established. This includes the special place of Rome. We shall see first how the catalogues were established, how they were developed progressively into a history, the *Liber pontificalis* being the first history of a local church. But this church is also the head of the universal Church, and its history illustrates well the paradox of local and institutional history between 300 and 1000, local, without doubt, because it was rooted in a precise area, but universal due to the institution with which it dealt.

We will first examine what appears to be the most ancient and the most elementary form of local and institutional history, that is, the list or the catalogue. Next we will see how the *Liber pontificalis* of Rome developed, for this seems to be the prototype of local and institutional histories. Finally, we will treat the diffusion and the characters of local and institutional history such as it was written in particular after the eighth century, in the form of *gesta episcoporum* and *gesta abbatum*.

The List, Elementary Form of Local History: Martyrologies, Diptychs, and Catalogues

Definitions

In principle, martyrologies[6] are narratives or praises of martyrs. But in a stricter sense, this word stands for catalogues, organized in chronological order, with directions to the locations of the martyrs. It is in this form that local martyrologies developed in the first Christian communities, demonstrating the heroes who were remembered and, in particular, celebrating the anniversaries of their deaths. In Africa, Tertullian mentions such martyrology annals as early as

---

[6] Leclercq (DACL); Dubois (1978).

the second century, and one century later, Saint Cyprian of Carthage recommends that they be brought up to date.[7]

Diptychs are lists of the bishops of a church. But a high number of the first bishops were also martyrs, and their names can be found on both lists: *depositio martyrum* and *depositio episcoporum* tend to merge together to make up the local martyrologies. A very ancient calendar of Carthage is introduced in the following manner: "Hic continetur dies nataliciorum martyrum et depositiones episcoporum quas Ecclesia Cartagenis anniversaria celebrant".[8]

From this point exchanges of martyrs develop gradually between churches, and the glory of the local martyr is passed on to the universal Church, while the local martyrology grows with the saints of other churches and also has a tendency to become universal. Various elements are added to this: anniversaries of monument dedications, those of the transfers of relics, of the names of founders of basilicas where martyr relics are kept, and all of the important people of the local church: abbots of monasteries, ascetics or penitents, and confessors in general. In the fifth and sixth centuries the martyrology would become the register of illustrations of the local church with this tendency toward the universal that characterizes all Church phenomena.

This traditional presentation, while satisfying for the mind, contains however a serious flaw: we have not conserved this type of local martyrologies. The great martyrology that we know well is the martyrology called 'hieronymian', attributed to Saint Jerome (347–420), translator of the Bible and of Eusebius's *Chronicle* into Latin, the Father of the Western Church who always will be considered the historian *par excellence*.

Martyrologies

The hieronymian martyrology is a general, not a local, martyrology. It appears slightly before Saint Jerome because it was first written in Greek, in Nicomedia in the middle of the fourth century, with the help of Eusebius's writings, of local martyrologies, and probably

---

[7] *S. Thasci Caecili Cypriani Opera omnia*, *Epist.* XII.2, ed. W. Hartel, 3 vols. *CSEL* 3 (Vienna, 1868–71), 503.
[8] Leclercq (*DACL*), col. 2523.

also with the help of oral traditions. In the first half of the fifth century it was translated into Latin by a cleric from northern Italy, and it was enriched with analogous Western documents from Rome and Africa. At that point it was attributed to Jerome, which granted it great authority. At the end of the sixth century this text came to Auxerre, where it was recopied and probably embellished under Bishop Aunarius (561–604). All known copies of this martyrology derive from the inventory of Auxerre.

This martyrology is probably no longer local history, but it seems likely to be a synthesis of local histories. For its editors, the hieronymian martyrology is a general collection of primitive calendars of the Eastern and Western Churches, classified according to the divisions of the Empire in the fourth century.[9] The inventory of Auxerre added names of the most illustrious bishops of Gaul up to the end of the sixth century, and a certain number of historical memories from Auxerre, in particular the dedication of monuments. Historical notes and summaries of the acts of the martyrs were added to the laconic text of local martyrologies, then necrological notes were again inscribed in the margin of the manuscripts. The hieronymian martyrology is the necessary starting point of all of the hagiographic tradition that followed it.

But the great era of martyrologies is the ninth century, the century of the 'historical martyrologies', new compositions that contain biographical notes of fewer saints but more details on each of them. Bede had written the first composition of this type in the eighth century. It was followed in the ninth century by Florus, Ado, Hrabanus Maurus, Usuard, Notker, and a certain number of anonymous authors, without counting the different copies more or less revised. It is no longer a piece of local history but from then on it is of general, even universal, history: it was on the basis of the martyrology of Usuard that the official martyrology of the Roman Catholic Church would be established in the sixteenth century.

From this examination of the history of martyrologies let us first retain the concern of commemoration and of the celebration of martyrs and saints that illustrated the Church (both local and universal). It is fundamental to the historical *démarche*. Let us also retain the procedure by which it progressively evolved from a simple list with

---

[9] De Rossi and Duchesne (*AS*).

dates to a group of entries including information on the sacred places and various general information.

We must add some observations on the chronology of the composition of martyrologies and on the places where they were copied and preserved. The hieronymian martyrology was recopied in Auxerre at the end of the century during which the first version of the *Liber pontificalis* of Rome was completed, at the precise time when Gregory of Tours received a copy of it and added to Book X of his *Histories* a short *Liber pontificalis* of Tours.[10] In Auxerre in the ninth century, the canons of the cathedral composed particularly elaborate *Gesta pontificum*.[11] The ninth century is the great period of historical martyrologies: it is also the period when, as we shall see, the genre of the *gesta episcoporum* is definitively established.

And if one is interested in manuscripts, it is notable that the hieronymian martyrology was recopied in Metz at the end of the eighth century (*Bernensis* 289), at the time when Paul the Deacon was composing a *Libellus de episcopis mettensibus* (789–91)[12] and when another copy originates in the abbey of Fontenelle (*Wissemburg*, 23), where the first *Gesta abbatum* are completed (834–45).[13] It is hardly possible, in the current state of our knowledge, to establish here anything more than coincidences, but they call for complementary research.

It remains to note that the martyrologies are organized *per circulum anni* and not according to chronological order strictly speaking. This leads us to consider the second great type of list that we wish to study: diptychs.

Diptychs and Episcopal Catalogues

Diptychs may be defined as 'the list of the living and the dead for whom we pray during the canon of mass'. The idea became accepted

---

[10] Gregory of Tours, *Libri historiarum X*, ed. B. Krusch and W. Levison, *MGH SSRM* 1.1 (Hanover, 1951).

[11] *Gesta pontificum autissiodorensium*, ed. L. Duru, in *Bibliothèque Historique de l'Yonne*, vol. 1 (Auxerre, 1850), 309–509; *Les Gestes des évêques d'Auxerre*, ed. and trans. M. Sot (Paris, 2002).

[12] *Liber de episcopis mettensibus*, ed. G. H. Pertz, *MGH SS* 2 (Hanover, 1829).

[13] *Chronique des abbés de Fontenelle (Saint-Wandrille)*, ed. and trans. P. Pradié (Paris, 1999).

that those people inscribed in the diptychs were saints, hence the use of the words *to canonize* to designate the process through which they are recognized as saints. These diptychs would have been kept in most cathedrals, but, as is the case with the local martyrologies called 'primitive', none remain today.[14]

It appears to have been a longstanding practice in Gaul to recite during the offertory of solemn masses the names of bishops, the faithful, and the saints: this practice was forbidden by Pope Innocent I (d. 417), but Venantius Fortunatus and Saint Germanus of Paris witnessed it in the fifth century. In 789, in order to conform to Roman practice, Charlemagne ordered "that the names not be recited publicly before the canon" (*ordinatio imperii*, ca. 54), and in the *Gesta of the abbots of Lobbes* around 980, Folcuin indicated that, during mass, Archbishop Adalbero of Reims had the under-deacon read the names of his predecessors, the archbishops, in "a commemoration of the dead named on the diptychs".[15]

Léopold Delisle developed the hypothesis that the diptychs at first consisted of simple nomenclatures, meant to be read quickly during the canon of the mass, and that in these lists of names were included the durations of pontificate, then the date of the death of the prelate, his place of burial, and other historical details. In that way the practices allegedly moved from the catalogue to the *Gesta episcoporum*, as, we shall see, they moved from the Roman catalogues to the *Liber pontificalis*. Dom Jacques Dubois established the fragility of this hypothesis by showing that Folcuin's mention of a recitation 'on the diptychs' was unique.

Nevertheless, it is certain that, very early on, local churches established catalogues of city bishops, perhaps in order to read them during the liturgy of the mass, or in order to remember them silently, or simply in order to place them on the altar. They were sometimes written in verse, and metric catalogues existed in Metz in the ninth century and Strasbourg in the tenth century, for example. Many of these lists can be found in various types of manuscripts, not only in liturgical manuscripts. As early as the middle of the ninth century, we have even found collections like the one from Angers (*Vat. Lat.*

---

[14] Delisle (1885); Duchesne (1907–15); Dubois (1967) and (1976).
[15] Folcuin, *Gesta abbatum Lobiensium*, ed. G. H. Pertz, *MGH SS* 4 (Hanover, 1841), 58–59.

465), which gathers together the lists of bishops of Angers, Nantes, Sens, Orleans, and Mans, with a group of saints' lives.

During the intense literary activity of the Carolingian era, just as the ordinary martyrologies developed into historical martyrologies, so were the diptychs and the simple catalogues of bishops developed into *Gesta episcoporum*. But the process had been established much earlier in the city of Rome, where we can observe it thanks to Louis Duchesne's work on the *Liber pontificalis*.

The Prototype of Local and Institutional History: The Roman Liber pontificalis[16]

In Rome, at the beginning of the sixth century, an anonymous cleric began to establish catalogues of bishops again, in a series of biographical entries on Roman pontiffs since Saint Peter. In order to lend authority to his work, this cleric attributed it to Pope Damasus (378–84), allegedly upon the request of Saint Jerome. After the sixth century, the work was continued regularly, most often by contemporaries of the popes, up to Martin V (d. 1431).

This work plays a crucial role in medieval historical literature, and it can be considered the prototype of local and institutional history for two reasons: first, because it was developed, as would be the *gesta episcoporum* and the *gesta abbatum*, from a catalogue that was progressively enriched and continued; and second, because it served as a formal model for the development of those texts. Before we look at the form and contents of the *Liber pontificalis*, let us first look at its evolution.

Evolution of the Liber pontificalis

As early as the second and third centuries, lists were drawn up of the bishops of Rome, just as, traditionally, lists of the consuls had been drawn up. But in establishing these lists, there appeared the apologetic concern to establish the continuation of ecclesiastical teaching from the apostles up to the contemporary bishop. It is in this

---

[16] *Liber pontificalis*, ed. Duchesne and Vogel; Noble (1985).

spirit that the lists of Hegesippus or Irénaeus were composed in the second century.[17] In the third century, the chronicle of Hippolytus (*Liber generationis*) was continued until 235 and then from 235 to 254. It probably contained a list and presents entries that prefigure those in the *Liber pontificalis*, but these entries were to be discontinued. Earlier in this paper we noted the importance of the episcopal lists for the *Chronicle* and the *Ecclesiastical History* of Eusebius of Cesaraea and their Latin translations. It is from Eusebius that we know the lists of Hegesippus, Irenaeus, and Hippolytus.

The catalogue of Pope Liberius (352–66) establishes the first veritable work on the chronology of the popes. It takes up Hippolytus's catalogue and improves upon it but does not include biographies. This catalogue is placed in a chronological collection with lists of consuls and of emperors.[18] It was taken up again by Optatus of Milevis and Augustine, who used it against the Donatists. It is continued by Jerome in his *Chronicle* up to Pope Damasus (378–84), and then by Jerome's followers.[19]

In the sixth century, a series of isolated catalogues appear in the manuscripts—often at the head of canonical collections written or copied in the two centuries that followed—these catalogues play the role of the helpful document to the user, with lists of provinces and cities that allow us to date and locate the councils and ordainments. Louis Duchesne established a list of canonical manuscripts, at the head of which is found the catalogue of the popes from the seventh to the ninth centuries (Arras, Corbie, Chieti, Reims, Lyon, Cologne, Albi). Duchesne showed that, with only a few exceptions, the *Libri canoni* are always preceded by catalogues of the popes.

Two additional phenomena in the sixth century reveal the growing interest placed on the pontifical succession: first, at the basilica of Saint Paul-outside-the-walls, a series of images of bishops of Rome were painted, with inscriptions that identify them; second, the antipope Laurence (514–18) had a catalogue created that is considered schismatic because it leads to his pontificate.

These elements attest to the interest in the pontifical succession in the sixth century. The list is considered a guarantor of the legitimacy of orthodoxy; it can be magnified on the walls of a basilica,

---

[17] *Liber pontificalis*, ed. Duchesne and Vogel, Intro., ch. I, I.
[18] In *Chronica minora*, ed. T. Mommsen, *MGH AA* 9 (Hanover, 1892); Stern (1953).
[19] *Liber pontificalis*, ed. Duchesne and Vogel, Intro., ch. I, II.

and it has been listed in catalogues. All of these concerns are taken
up again, amplified, and rendered more explicit in the *Liber pontificalis*.
Louis Duchesne showed that its primitive version, which is known
only through cross-checking between its second edition and the abbreviated segments from this first version, must be attributed to the time
of Pope Hormisdas (514–23) and of his two successors, John I and
Felix IV (d. 530).

Form and Content

This first version of the *Liber pontificalis* is introduced by two apocryphal letters, one from Saint Jerome to Pope Damasus (†384) and
the other from Damasus to Jerome, according to a rhetorical formula that is not without examples. Jerome wrote to Damasus that
he wanted to know the names of the martyred popes and the popes
who transgressed the canons. Damasus replied that he was sending
to Jerome what he was able to find, that is, the series of documentation on his predecessors from former times and the collected accounts
on the more recent predecessors.[20]

The entries concerning each pope are organized according to a
outline format[21] that reflects the concerns of all former local history.
First, the name of the pope and his number are given in chronological order, beginning with the catalogue of Liberius (up to 354)
and other catalogues whose common sections appear to have ceased
in the fifth century. It was crucial for the author to be able to spec-
ify which figures could be included in the rank of pope and to establish the order in which they followed one another. Next comes the
origin and family of the pope: his nation and the name of his father,
according to an arrangement taken from Jerome's *de Viris illustribus*.
Then the duration of the pontificate in years, months, and days borrowed from the previous catalogues.

The popes' status as martyrs is explained next, in order to answer
the first question asked in the letter of Pseudo-Jerome: the author
places here the passions and the oral traditions that are linked, instead

---

[20] *Liber pontificalis*, ed. Duchesne and Vogel, Intro., ch. II.
[21] *Liber pontificalis*, ed. Duchesne and Vogel, Intro., ch. IV.

of the martyrs. He does not use the *Gesta martyrum* but points out the institution of ecclesiastical notaries who were given the duty of collecting depositions from the persecutor tribunals. He gives details on the reconstitution of the Church after the two great persecutions of Decius and Valerian (250–59) under Pope Dionysius, and of Diocletian (303–11) under Pope Marcellus I. To this he adds other historical elements: narratives of the transfer of relics from Peter to Paul, discovery of the True Cross, or more political information on the role of the emperor Constantine in relation to Pope Sylvester, for example.

Many entries add disciplinary or liturgical decrees known from the decretals that the popes sent to the other bishops, often in response to consultations, of which a first collection had been established in the fifth century; or from conciliary documents that had been grouped together and translated into Latin by Dionysius the Short around 500, beginning with the fifty canons called 'apostolic'. Canons and decretals constituted the *Liber canonum* of the Church of Rome, with which the author of the *Liber pontificalis* was surely familiar because, in his preface, he has the Pseudo-Jerome ask Pope Damasus for the names of the pontiffs who had transgressed the canons.

Next the foundations and the endowments of the churches are included, probably in part following collective memory but also by reading the inscriptions and, in regard to the possessions and the treasures, by using the documents (foundation charters) preserved in the *vestiarium* of the Church of Rome. Finally, the place of burial and the anniversary of the pope's death are always mentioned, as well as the number of ordinations officiated by the pope and the duration of the vacancy of the papal seat after his death.

The information included is very important for many areas, on the discipline and the liturgy in force in Rome in particular, on Christian topography, too, but one must not trust the dates or the numerical figures, of ordinations, for example. However, the author appears to be more trustworthy than the author of the *Gesta martyrum* compiled after the end of the fourth century. His language is natural and evokes that of the contemporary inscriptions. This character of the author of the *Liber pontificalis*, honest and modest, a bit hardworking and not always skillful, can also be found with the authors of local histories. Louis Duchesne thought he was a subordinate cleric of the *vestiarium*, utilizing the language of the archives

rather than the refined style of the *scrinium* (chancery). Today we
believe instead that he was a cleric of the *scrinium*,[22] but the question is secondary: the author of the first *Liber pontificalis* remains modestly anonymous.

The rigorous arrangement in entries, without using a refined style,
is common to a certain number of works that were circulating at
that time, like Jerome's *de Viris* or a *Small Chronicle of the Roman Kings
and Emperors*, which was associated with the catalogue of Liberius in
the chronographical collection of 354.[23] This form of notice and the
questions that it raises would become exemplary for local and institutional history. The very fact of continuing the work after a first
edition of the series and upon the death of each pontiff is also exemplary. We know that in Rome, as early as the middle of the seventh
century, in regard to Martin I, the entry on the pope was begun
while he was still living, and we observe that in some of these entries
there are several periods of writing.[24]

Let us add that the title that is habitually attributed to the *Liber
pontificalis* is attested only in the twelfth century and does not become
widely accepted until the fifteenth century. The best manuscripts
refer to this work as the *Episcopale* or the *Liber episcopalis*, then the
Gesta pontificum or the *Chronica pontificum*:[25] these are the titles of works
of local history that will be taken up again.

Gesta Episcoporum *and* Gesta Abbatum[26]

We have arrived at the study of works of local and institutional history called by scholars the *gesta episcoporume* and *gesta abbatum*, whose
genre flourished in the Carolingian period. We would like to show
first how, after the Roman model, this historiographical literary genre
spread in the West up to the twelfth century, in close relation, it
seems, with the affirmation of the imperial power, first Carolingian,
then Ottonian and Salian. Next we will describe the characteristics
of these works, where we are going to find not only a fundamental

---

[22] Noble (1985).
[23] *Chronica minora*, ed. Mommsen; Stern (1953).
[24] *Liber pontificalis*, ed. Duchesne and Vogel, Intro., ch. VI.
[25] Monfrin (1994).
[26] Sot (1981); Kaiser (1999).

preoccupation with the list of bishops or of abbots but also a tension between the history of the city and of its pontiffs on the one hand and the universal history of the Church on the other.

Spread of the gesta Genre

From Gregory of Tours to Paul the Deacon

At the beginning of the decade in 590, Gregory of Tours added to the tenth of his *Ten Books of History* a *libellus episcopalis* of the city of Tours.[27] Although it was much more brief, it was organized in entries like the *Liber pontificalis*, from which it seems to have borrowed a certain number of expressions and, especially, the typology of information to be given about each bishop: his homeland, his family, his character, the churches he had built, the disciplinary and liturgical regulations that he provided, the duration of his episcopate, the location of his burial, and the duration of the vacancy of his seat after his death. Louis Duchesne has showed that Gregory of Tours possessed one of the summaries of the first version of the *Liber pontificalis* called the "Felician summary".

The most convincing hypothesis is that this text was given to him by his deacon Agiulfus, who had been on a pilgrimage to Rome in 589. While there he was witness to the plague epidemic that was to kill Pope Pelagius, who was succeeded by Gregory the Great in 590. He stayed for a long time, and we know from Gregory of Tours that he brought back information on the monuments of Rome and on some of the saints, in particular those whose relics he had been given by the pope. We can imagine the deacon Agiulfus given a mission by his historian-bishop to bring him back relics, of course, but also documents and, among the latter, the Felician summary of the *Liber pontificalis*.

However, it has not been dismissed that this text may have been known in Gaul earlier, since it is featured at the head of a canonical collection whose first edition would have been in 549, or even in 530, and on which a Frankish continuation of the *Chronicle of*

---

[27] Gregory of Tours, *Libri historiarum X*, ed. Krusch and Levison.

Marcellinus Comes, going up to 558, appears to depend.[28] Nevertheless, the Roman *Liber pontificalis* was imitated for the first time in Gaul by Gregory of Tours in 590–91.

We do not find any more local history of this type before the end of the eighth century. In the seventh century, the Roman book does not appear to have given rise to emulators. At the beginning of the eighth century, we know that Bede, in his monastery in Jarrow between 717 and 724, had a manuscript. He had written a *History of the Abbots of Wearmouth and Jarrow*, notably of the latter, and in this domain, as in many others, he is the precursor. But it is not until 784 and the *Libellus* of the bishops of Metz, composed by Paul the Deacon,[29] that we find a local and institutional history inspired by the Roman *Liber pontificalis*.

Paul the Deacon's work is part of the great movement of the Carolingian renaissance, at the heart of the region of origin of the Carolingian family, of its possessions and its history. Commissioned by the bishop Angilram, the *Libellus* traces in part the history of the church of Metz, from its first bishop Saint Clement, sent from Rome by Saint Peter. It even begins with the story of the Ascension of Christ and that of Pentecost, events that were considered to have marked the beginning of the story of the universal Church. Next comes the catalogue of bishops, which stops with Saint Arnoul, the bishop at the beginning of the seventh century, who is the ancestor of the Carolingians. Paul the Deacon then establishes a genealogy of Charlemagne and of his children since Arnoul, before returning to the succession of bishops. He develops the notice on the last one, Chrodegang, following exactly the model of the *Liber pontificalis* of Rome. Chrodegang was the reformer, the one who re-established a close link between Rome and the Frankish church, especially on the liturgical level. This link is so well established that this local history, whose origins are with Christ himself, leads both to the glorification of the bishops of the time, who were chaplains for Charlemagne and promoted the Roman liturgy, and to the glorification of the Carolingian family, whose usurpation in 751 thus is justified. His vocation in the Empire is perhaps even suggested.[30]

[28] Duchesne (1882).
[29] *Liber de episcopis mettensibus*, ed. Gh. H. Pertz, *MGH SS* 2 (Hanover, 1829).
[30] Sot (1978); Goffart (1986).

Texts of the Ninth Century

In the decade of 830, Bishop Aldric of le Mans, who was educated in the cathedral school of Metz and who fulfilled important duties in the emperor's court, had the *Actus pontificum* of le Mans written,[31] the second of our local histories. The founder of the Church of le Mans was Saint Julian, one of the '72 disciples' of Jesus, and again the origin of the local church and the origin of the universal Church become confused. The successive entries allow for the cathedral church of le Mans to establish and affirm its rights against usurpers, in particular against the abbey of Saint-Calais.[32] The *Liber pontificalis* was known in le Mans in the period of the 830s.

At the same time and in the same strictly Carolingian context was undertaken the *Gesta sanctorum patrum Fontanellensis coenobii*, recently re-edited and translated into French under the title *Chronicle of the Abbots of Fontenelle (Saint-Wandrille)*.[33] The sponsor was Ansegisus, abbot from 823 to 833, after having fulfilled important duties at the palace of Aachen. His predecessor at the abbey was none other than Einhard, Charlemagne's biographer. These *Gesta abbatum* of Fontenelle show that the founder, Saint Wandrille, was related to the first Ansegisus, the son of Saint Arnoul of Metz in the seventh century, and he is therefore related to the imperial family.

The monk Ratpert of Saint-Gall composed in the 880s a *De origine et diversis casibus monasterii Sancti Galli*[34] in order to show the links between the abbey and the imperial family and to affirm the rights of the monastery against the bishops of Constance. It is a piece of local history that brings us somewhat away from the Roman model but which was composed in the same spirit of justification by proximity to the Carolingian family as the preceding works.

We must consider separately two texts of the ninth century that were both produced in Italy: the episcopal histories of Naples and of Ravenna. The first,[35] composed around 800 or 850 according to

---

[31] *Actus pontificum Cenomannis in urbe degentium*, ed. L. Busson and A. Ledru (LeMans, 1902).

[32] Goffart (1966); Van der Straeten (1967); Le Maître (1980).

[33] Laporte (1971); *Chronique des abbés de Fontenelle (Saint-Wandrille)*, ed. and trans. P. Pradié (Paris, 1999).

[34] *De origine et diversis casibus monasterii Sancti Galli*, ed. I. von Arx, *MGH SS* 2 (Hanover, 1829) 61–74.

[35] *Gesta episcoporum Neapolitanorum*, ed. G. Waitz, *MGH SS rer. Lang. et. Ital* (Hanover, 1878); Granier (1998).

the authors, is only in part a local history: it takes up a universal chronicle that it divides up according to the catalogue of bishops of Naples, adding only some Neapolitan elements, of religious topography in particular. The *Liber pontificalis* dictated by Agnellus of Ravenna[36] in the 830s was greatly influenced by the Roman *Liber pontificalis*. In the prologue, Agnellus indicates that he composed a book "on the order of succession of the bishops who have occupied the see of Saint Apollinaris". The desire to establish the catalogue from the origins is set up immediately. For each bishop, the author states what he was able to find out, either having heard it from his elders; after having seen it in observing the monuments of the city and, in particular, the images and inscriptions; or, finally (but this is less important to him), after having read about it in the 'authorities' or the archives. We have here a local history, loaded with the pretensions of the local church, which demands a dignity equal to that of the churches of Rome and of Constantinople.

After 870: Auxerre, Reims and the Others

Another collection of local and institutional histories may be distinguished, written after 870 and up to the eleventh century in the radius of the cities of Auxerre and Reims. The Carolingian school of Auxerre in the second half of the ninth century was illustrated by the monks of the abbey of Saint-Germain, Haymon, Heiric and Remi.[37] But it is at the cathedral that the two canons Alagus and Rainogala, no doubt in connection with the monk Heiric, as the most recent edition of the text suggests, composed the *Gesta pontificum autissiodorensium* between 873 and 876.[38] The canons are a part of the scholarly culture of the school of Auxerre, even if their work does not have the qualities of those of the masters of the abbey of Saint-Germain. They possessed a copy of the *Liber pontificalis*, from which they borrowed chronological information, especially for their entries. The work does not claim to trace the origins of the church of Auxerre back to Christ or his apostles, only to the persecutions.

---

[36] Agnellus, *Liber pontificalis ecclesiae Ravennatis*, ed. O. Holder-Egger, *MGH SS rer. Lang. et. Ital* (1878), 265–391; Fasoli (1970); Pizarro (1995).
[37] Iogna-Prat, Jeudy, Lobrichon (1987).
[38] *Gesta pontificum autissiodorensium*, ed. Duru; *Les Gestes des évêques d'Auxerre*, ed. Sot.

The entries were written carefully, with a great concern for the chronology. In the eyes of the reader the church of Auxerre grows little by little just as it did in the ninth century, illuminated by the prestige and the sanctity of its successive bishops, enriched with their talents that constitute its heritage, organized by the liturgical regulations that they set into place and used to decorate the monuments that they had built.

At the end of the century, around 893, Bishop Foulques of Reims, in order to restore the schools of his city, makes an appeal to the scholar Remi of Auxerre and to the monk Hucbald of Saint-Amand, who had been a student of Heiric in the Auxerre school. The Auxerrois culture gives a new start to the school of Reims, whose beginning had been launched by the great Hincmar (845–82). Furthermore, the canon Flodoard was educated in this school in the years around 810. In the middle of the century, between 848 and 852, he wrote his *History of the church of Reims*,[39] which is the most complete realization of local and institutional history in the West.[40]

Previously, Hucbald had participated in the reform of the monastery of Saint-Bertin at the time of Abbot Raoul. This monastery, in the province of Reims, received an oblate by name of Folcuin, who composed the *Gesta abbatum sancti Bertini Sithiensium* in 961.[41] Four years later, in 965, the same Folcuin, having become abbot of the monastery of Lobbes in the diocese of Cambrai, composed the *Gesta abbatum* for this abbey.[42]

Among the monks of Lobbes, disciples of Folcuin, we find Heriger, who succeeded the former as abbot. It is Heriger who was commissioned to write the *gesta episcoporum* for the city of Liège by the bishop Notger of Liège (972–1008). His work was taken up again later, at the time of Bishop Wazo (1042–48), by another monk of Lobbes, Anselm, who dedicated his work to Archbishop Anno of Cologne, of which Liège is a suffragan.[43]

The bishopric of Cambrai was in East Francia since the division of Verdun and thus in the empire restored by the Ottonians in 962.

---

[39] Flodoard, *Historia Remensis ecclesiae*, ed. Strattmann.

[40] Sot (1993).

[41] Folcuin, *Gesta abbatum sancti Bertini Sithiensium*, ed. O. Holder-Egger, *MGH SS* 13 (Hanover, 1881).

[42] Folcuin, *Gesta abbatum Lobiensium*, ed. Pertz.

[43] *Gesta episcoporum Leodiensium*, ed. R. Koepke, *MGH SS* 4 (Hanover, 1841).

But it still belonged to the ecclesiastical province of Reims, and
Lobbes Abbey was in its jurisdiction. Bishop Gérard I had his *Gesta
episcoporum* written there around 1024–25.[44] This Gérard came from
the region of Liège. He was the nephew of the archbishop Adalbero
of Reims, and he was educated in the cathedral school of Reims,
where he became canon. We remain, therefore, in the same cultural
and political circle.

Coming back to the Auxerre school, it maintained close relations
with the monastery of Fleury-sur-Loire. In the last quarter of the
tenth century, we find in this monastery an abrupt flourishing of historiography[45] under the impetus of Abbo (989–1004), who gave a
summary of the Roman *Liber pontificalis*, and especially due to his
disciple Aimoin, who wrote, after 1007, the *Gesta of the abbots of Fleury*.
Aimoin's work is not extant today, but we believe that it was inspired,
at least in composition, by the *Liber pontificalis* summarized by Abbo
and the *Gesta of the bishops of Auxerre*.

In Eleventh-Century Saxony

A third group of local histories in the form of *gesta episcoporum* appeared
in Saxony, at the very end of the tenth century, which we can put
in relation to the Ottonian restoration. The first known editions of
the *Gesta episcoporum* of Halberstadt[46] and of Magdeburg[47] are from
the period around 1020, but it has been established that some elements existed as early as the end of the tenth century.[48] Around
1080 the texts of Hildesheim and Hamburg[49] appear. These Saxon
bishoprics are of Carolingian imperial foundation, and their history
highlights this imperial origin. The prologue of the *Gesta* of Magdeburg
states that the city owes its enormous prosperity to three emperors:
Julius Caesar who founded it, Charlemagne who brought faith to it,
and Otto the Great who established it as an archbishopric. The *Gesta*

---

[44] *Gesta pontificum cameracensium*, ed. G. Bethmann, *MGH SS* 7 (Hanover, 1846);
Van Mingroot (1975).
[45] Bautier (1975).
[46] *Gesta episcoporum Halberstadtensium*, ed. L. Wieland, *MGH SS* 23 (Hanover, 1874).
[47] *Gesta archiepiscoporum Magdeburgensium*, ed. G. Schum, *MGH SS* 14 (Hanover,
1883).
[48] Jäschke (1970); Schlochtermeyer (1998).
[49] *Chronicon Hildesheimense*, ed. G. H. Pertz, *MGH SS* 7 (Hanover, 1846); *Gesta
Hammaburgensis ecclesiae pontificum*, ed. G. Waitz, *MGH SS* 7 (Hanover, 1846).

of the bishops of Hildesheim include, in parallel to the list of bishops, those of the Carolingian and then the Ottonian emperors. In this Saxon development of local history, the role of Halberstadt appears to have been crucial: we can see in fact that Archbishop Adalbert I of Hamburg (1043–72), the one who had the *gesta* of his predecessors written, was educated in Halberstadt. He came to Hamburg following Herimann, dean of Halberstadt who became archbishop of Hamburg in 1032. These Saxon texts were to be rewritten and expanded in the twelfth century, after the period that we are treating here.

We can conclude that local history flourished in relation to the model given by the *Liber pontificalis* of Rome, but especially from the moment when Rome became of importance in the West, first due to the Carolingians, then due to the Roman-Germanic emperors. This is confirmed by the fact that scarcely any local history exists south of the Loire in France, very little in Italy and in England, and even less in the Iberian peninsula.

Characteristics of Local History in the Ninth, Tenth and Eleventh Centuries

Still and Forever the Catalogue[50]

The authors of local histories create their work around the list of bishops or abbots who provide the chronological axis. The list remains the elementary form of local history up to the end of our period of study. We can cite as an example the *Catalogus abbatum de Fulda* (tenth century)[51] and the *Series episcoporum* of Bremen and Hamburg (eleventh century),[52] which must not be confused with the *Gesta pontificum Hammaburgensium*. Older lists can exist independently of the *gesta*, then. The author of the *gesta episcoporum* of Verdun at the beginning of the tenth century points back to a catalogue completed before it.[53] Elsewhere the lists were established using the same historiographical

---

[50] Duchesne (1907–1915); Dubois (1976).
[51] *Catalogus abbatum Fuldensium*, ed. G. Waitz, *MGH SS* 13 (Hanover, 1881).
[52] *Series Bremensium et Hammaburgensium episcoporum*, ed. J. M. Lappenberg, *MGH SS* 7 (Hanover, 1846).
[53] *Gesta episcoporum Virdunensium*, ed. G. Waitz, *MGH SS* 4 (Hanover, 1841), 40.

108 MICHEL SOT

method. The bishop Angilram of Metz had requested the composition of a metric catalogue of his predecessors several years before he commissioned Paul the Deacon to write the *gesta*, and at le Mans the catalogue and *Actus pontificum* appear to have been composed simultaneously. In order to offer details on the local lists, it was necessary to establish dating, generally with respect to other lists of prelates and in particular with respect to those of Rome. We find at Auxerre, as at le Mans, a *Liber pontificalis* that gives not only the dates of the popes but also those of the consuls and emperors for the beginnings of the churches—and, in addition, dates of the kings. In the *Gesta abbatum* of Saint-Bertin, Folcuin relies on three lists at once: that of the abbots, of course, but also that of the kings, which confirms the donations made to the abbey, and that of the bishops of Thérouanne, upon whom the abbey depended.[54] In Fontenelle's *Gesta abbatum*, datings are written with particular care: the beginning of each abbacy is dated from the year of the Incarnation and of the year of indiction, followed by the correspondence between the reign of the Frankish king and that of the pope. For each donation to the abbey, the same careful attention to chronology can be observed.[55]

The proof that this concern with the catalogue and with chronology is fundamental to local history is contained in the titles that the authors give to their works. Paul the Deacon wrote for Metz a *Libellus de numero sive ordine episcoporum* and Agnellus for Ravenna an *Ordinatum libellum de ordine pontificalis successionis*.[56] This concern with chronology was the same for Gregory of Tours when he added a *Libellus* of the bishops of Tours to his *Ten Books of History*: "I considered it fitting", he writes, "to go back and note their succession and to calculate their years; and I have done this beginning with the first time that an evangelist came to the city of Tours".[57] It is indeed a matter of establishing the chronological continuity of the institution from its establishment.

The *gesta* have the advantage over the simple list in being able to show how the succession took place, how it was a normal succes-

[54] Folcuin, *Gesta abbatum sancti Bertini Sithiensium*, ed. Holder-Egger, 619.
[55] *Chronique des abbés de Fontenelle*, ed. Pradié, ex. Benignus, 39–57.
[56] Paul the Deacon, *Liber de episcopis mettensibus*, ed. Pertz, 261; Agnellus, *Liber pontificalis ecclesiae Ravennatis*, ed. Holder-Egger, 278.
[57] Gregory of Tours, *Libri historiarum X*, ed. Krusch and Levison.

sion. From that point, they can organize all of the information that the author has been able to find and that he believes is useful for the church. Two moments of local history are emphasized, in the two chronological extremities: the origins and the contemporary period. The period of the origins is treated with particular care to show that the local church is rooted in the origins of Christianity; the development of local history between the eighth and the ninth century was contemporary with the invention of the apostolic origins of a good number of churches.[58] In a general manner, there must be at least one saint at the origin of the list of the prelates: in the case of the abbots, it is the founder who became the patron saint of the abbey—Wandrille or Bertin for example. The saintly origins impart to the whole episcopal or abbatial lineage a particular strength that is transmitted and enriched up to the period during which the history was written.

Hence the importance granted to the contemporary prelate. His entry is developed a great deal and often forms a large portion of the work. Most likely, the information on him was easier for the author to gather. But we also must attribute to the author the desire to create a work that was useful to the church of his time. All of the history of the local church converges around its latest prelate. We might evoke here the *History of the church of Reims* by Flodoard, which goes back to the founding of Rome but is, for more than half of its volume, devoted to the last one hundred years, in particular to the prestigious Hincmar.[59] In the *Gesta episcoporum* of Cambrai, the first book is devoted to the successive bishops, the second book is devoted to the monasteries which depended on the cathedral in the eleventh century, and the entire third book is devoted to the bishop Gérard (1012–51).[60] In Hamburg, the fourth book of the *Gesta* is entirely devoted to Adalbert (1043–72), the bishop who commissioned the work.[61] The local history ends with the last prelate.

Let us note that, for the author, the history only stops there momentarily. He knows that his work is going to be continued.

---

[58] Duchesne (1907–15); Sot (2001).
[59] Sot (1993) 626 ff.; 721 ff.
[60] *Gesta pontificum cameracensium*, ed. Bethmann, 465–88.
[61] *Gesta Hammaburgensis ecclesiae pontificum*, ed. Lappenberg, 335–67.

Local Information

The sources of local history are of three types: archeological sources, oral traditions or direct observations, and archival documents. The sources that we call 'archeological' are the tombs of prelates, or the monuments those prelates built, or the treasures they collected. Knowledge of the locations of the prelates' burials and, eventually, of the inscriptions upon their tombs is very important in affirming the truth of the prelate's existence and of his deeds. The author of the *Gesta* of the bishops of Verdun is very upset not to have located the tomb of the founder Sanctinus, all the more so since the city of Meaux claims him, too, and has been able to present a tomb for Sanctinus.[62] Similarly, at Ravenna, Agnellus is quite embarrassed not to have found out the location of the tomb of Bishop Peter I: a miracle occurs just in time, which reveals its location to him.[63] In Naples, le Mans, and Auxerre the excavations and transfers of saintly bishops' bodies took place shortly before or after the *gesta* were composed. It was due to an archaeological dig around the tomb of Saint Julian, reputed to be the first bishop of le Mans, that other sarcophagi were discovered, on which could be read in the ninth century the names of those who were considered his first successors.[64] The authors of the *gesta* describe also the monuments and the treasures such as they might have seen them and such as their contemporaries might have observed them. They are always integrated into the entry of the bishop whose memory they observe.

Our authors belong most often to the college of the cathedral's canons or come from an area near that of the bishop, where memories have been maintained by the elders, the old men, those who have seen many things. The questioning of witnesses is justified by Agnellus of Ravenna in his prologue in which he points to the Bible's example: it is upon questioning his fathers that Moses was able to put into writing the story of the Creation; it is upon questioning the apostles that Mark and Luke were able to write their Gospels of Jesus, whom they had never seen.[65] Adam of Bremen collected a large portion of the fourth book of his *Gesta* on the bishops of

---

[62] *Gesta episcoporum Virdunensium*, ed. Waitz, 40.
[63] Agnellus, *Liber pontificalis ecclesiae Ravennatis*, ed. Holder-Egger, 290–91.
[64] *Actus pontificum Cenomannis in urbe degentium*, ed. Busson and Ledru, 328.
[65] Agnellus, *Liber pontificalis ecclesiae Ravennatis*, ed. Holder-Egger, 278.

Hamburg from the very mouth of the king of Denmark, Svend Estriden, around 1067–70. As for Berthaire of Verdun, he insists that he was the direct witness of the last three episcopates about which he writes.[66]

The authors of the *gesta* also had recourse to the archives of their churches, which allowed them to establish in detail the evolution of the heritage and to date the acquisitions and the dismembering of various bishops. The *gesta* are able to play a role close to that of the church's collection of charters and property deeds. Those of Verdun were written because the archives had just been lost in a fire,[67] and the *Actus* of le Mans publish the complete donations and royal confirmations "so that, if by chance or negligence the original were to become lost, one might look at this copy and know from it what occurred and, if necessary, through this document one might recover the property".[68]

In comparison to the archaeological or archival sources, the portion of literary sources in the *gesta* is modest. Probably, if a *vita* of a certain holy prelate existed, it was exploited by the author, but only the authors of more important texts of local history, such as the *History of the church of Reims* or the *Gesta of the bishops of Hamburg*, had recourse to Roman historians or to the Fathers of the Church. And with that their history loses, in part, its local dimension and becomes more a part of general history. Flodoard of Reims cites Livy, Caesar, or Sallust, then Jerome, Augustine, and Isidore of Seville, but he does so in order to situate his *History of the church of Reims* in a history of the Roman world which had become Christianized.[69] In the same manner Adam of Bremen cites Sallust, the Fathers, and the Venerable Bede.[70] Because of their ambitious nature, these two works go beyond the concerns of local history.

The authors of works of local history organize, around the strictly chronological axis of the catalogue of bishops or abbots, the material that they collect through the archaeological, oral, and archival sources, principally. This material is organized into a narration that

---

[66] *Gesta episcoporum Virdunensium*, ed. Waitz, 44.
[67] *Gesta episcoporum Virdunensium*, ed. Waitz, 40.
[68] *Actus pontificum Cenomannis in urbe degentium*, ed. Busson and Ledru, 162.
[69] Sot (1993), 634 ff.
[70] *Gesta Hammaburgensis ecclesiae pontificum*, ed. Lappenberg, 267 ff.

is oriented based on a certain number of the authors' concerns and objectives, a point at which we must now stop.

The Goals of Local History: The Effectiveness of Memory

The primary goal of a local history is to show the saintliness of a church and thus the sacred character of all that it encompasses. We have shown that a local history seeks its origin in the time of Christ, or the apostles for a diocese, or in the time of a great founding saint for a monastery. Over the course of history other great saints live, who reactivate the original claims to saintliness. On the other hand, some of them are bad bishops or bad abbots, and the entries written about them demonstrate what must be avoided: such is the case with the entry-foil of Archbishop Theodore in the *Liber pontificalis* of Ravenna.[71] But globally the history of the Church is a saintly history, despite the absence of saintliness of certain individuals.

We may add that this history is full of the cult of the dead whose memory is maintained. The entries devoted to the bishops of le Mans in the *Actus* are called *commemorations*, and each one ends with an invocation.[72] The bishop Dado of Verdun undertook the composition of *gesta* "so that the memory of the orthodox pontiffs would be eternally with us, those whose names we believe are eternally written in heaven".[73] *Commemoratio* and *memoria* point to liturgical practices and to constructions in relation to relics, tombs, and the cult of the dead in general.

The tombs of the bishops are their locations of memory, but so, too, are the monuments of the city or of the monastery that they had built or frequented. By extension, each possession that belonged to him, that he received or gave to his church, becomes a place of memory. We noted earlier the authors' concern to include archival documents in order to justify the possessions of the local church: these documents are integrated into the chronological framework of sacred history, which reinforces their purely juridical effectiveness through its memorial and sacred dimension.

---

[71] Agnellus, *Liber pontificalis ecclesiae Ravennatis*, ed. Holder-Egger, 335–60.
[72] *Actus pontificum Cenomannis in urbe degentium*, ed. Busson and Ledru, 39, 46.
[73] *Gesta episcoporum Virdunensium*, ed. Waitz, 37.

We find everywhere the desire to found the possession of the church's wealth on the prestige of the saints inscribed in local history. Thus, in the *Gesta pontificum* of Auxerre, Bishop Amator, the predecessor of Saint Germanus in the fifth century, obtained from a rich Christian a house from which he made the cathedral of Saint Stephen, but it was Germanus who established the patrimony of the church by leaving it the collection of his possessions, the inventory of which is listed by the authors. Similar inventories are made regarding Bishop Aunarius's (572–603) legacy and that of Bishop Deusdedit (603–21), who also gave a valuable treasure of goldwork carefully described in the *Gesta*.[74] These domains and these precious objects belong to the church of Auxerre "up to today", state the authors around 875. The usurpation of these possessions, in particular those performed by great laymen, is thus sacrilegious.

Local history also serves to defend its rights. The *Actus pontificum* of le Mans attributes to the founder Saint Julian the division of the diocese into thirty-three parishes and the dedication of the main churches such as they are presented in the ninth century, when it was written. From the origins the annual diocesan council was also established.[75] As for the monasteries, they were all said to have been established by bishops, based on the possessions that they owned. Thus, history 'proves' that all of these parishes and all of these monasteries are under the jurisdiction of the bishop. This is what the monks of the abbey of Saint-Calais objected to in the ninth century, in violent conflict with the bishops of le Mans.[76]

As for the *Liber pontificalis* of Ravenna, it intends to justify, among other things, the right of this great metropolitan church to autocephaly, that is, juridical autonomy from the church of Rome. In order to show this, Agnellus demonstrates that it is the emperor and not the pope who granted the archiepiscopal dignity to the seat of Ravenna and established its jurisdiction over the fourteen dependent cities, dignity and jurisdiction that were maintained, during the history of the different pontiffs, "up to our time".[77] He adds that, if Rome is the city of Peter whose body it possesses, Ravenna also has

[74] *Gesta pontificum autissiodorensium*, ed. Duru, 317, 332, 334–40.
[75] *Actus pontificum Cenomannis in urbe degentium*, ed. Busson and Ledru, 37–38.
[76] Le Maître (1980).
[77] Agnellus, *Liber pontificalis ecclesiae Ravennatis*, ed. Holder-Egger, 304–05.

numerous relics of apostles and martyrs, whom he lists, and he shows that Ravenna nearly obtained the body of the apostle Andrew, which was finally brought to Constantinople.[78] Ravenna, through its history, has a dignity nearly equal to that of Rome and Constantinople.

Local history is oriented toward an affirmation of the authority of the local church. Local memory written in a book of history allows for a justification of the possessions and the rights of the local church in relation to the competing powers, secular or ecclesiastical.

But, we note again, even in these particular claims, local history is never purely local. The history of a local church always has a universal dimension, given the institution that it covers. Let us remark also, in conclusion, that within the context of universality the notion of empire also is included. Indeed, we have seen that local historiography developed in imperial contexts. It is in Rome that the first *Liber pontificalis* was composed; the Carolingian renaissance spreads the model to the west, particularly in the regions of strong imperial establishment; it is in Saxony, original haunt of the 'Roman-Germanic' emperors, that the genre spreads next. In the case of Ravenna, we have just seen how its *Liber pontificalis* had played its relationship to Rome and Constantinople, the two imperial and ecclesiastical cities par excellence. The paradox of this study is arriving at the conclusion that, from the third to the tenth centuries at least, local and institutional history always possesses a universal dimension.

---

[78] Agnellus, *Liber pontificalis ecclesiae Ravennatis*, ed. Holder-Egger, 327–29.

CHAPTER FOUR

CHRISTIAN BIOGRAPHY: FOUNDATION TO MATURITY

Thomas J. Heffernan

For those who wish to enter upon the narratives of history . . . we have aimed . . . to profit all readers. (2 Macc. 25)

Prologue

Christian history begins with the biographies of Christ in the gospels. These theological proclamations of the messianic kingship were modeled on earlier Semitic and classical biographies.[1] The genre of biography was a deliberate choice for the proclamation of this message, since contemporary audiences—Jewish, Christian, and pagan alike—were accustomed to such presentations of idealized characters. Early Christians especially believed it best represented their cult, since their oral *kerygma* was particularly biographical, focused on an incarnate god who lived among men as a man.[2] Biography's popularity with audiences also provided Christians with a vehicle to celebrate and proselytize the virtue of new converts.[3] The early church's effort to evangelize through the lives of the martyrs and saints was in part motivated by the precedent of the gospels and the emerging theology of a hellenized church.[4]

Biographical narrative in the Hebrew Bible contends that the highest moral good is that which promotes an intimacy between human act and divine will. This synchrony of resolution is the foundation of a theology that causally links righteousness and lawful rewards. Behavior that exemplifies such an ideal is praised.[5] Classical biography,

---

[1] Talbert (1977).
[2] Kermode (1987), 378.
[3] Kennedy (1984), 101.
[4] Brown (1993), 5–47.
[5] Gunn (1993), 4.

in contrast, constructs a narrative that celebrates a subject (often in panegyric) capable of independent agency, who may act outside the story of god and tribe. The good life is one spent in service to the family and state.[6] Christian sacred biography is an uneasy syncretism of these two traditions. Neither tradition represents a life with the understanding of the self and its attendant scrutiny of motive that we find in modern biography.

While the Hebrew Bible privileges certain individuals, e.g., Joseph, or Moses, the narrative subordinates intention and action to divine will, employs disruptive and a-synchronous chronologies, uses parataxis, elevates tribal interests at the expense of the individual, and views human virtue as contingent on God's mercy.[7] Memorable biographical anecdotes, e.g., Abraham's willingness to sacrifice Isaac (Gen. 22: 1–19), are signs of the covenantal relationship of the subject with God. There is no interest in exploring the relationship of father and son after the abortive execution. There is but a single line of dialogue between Abraham and Isaac concerning the location of the ram and none from that point until the tale is told. Religious teleology governs the narrative. Abraham's faith has been tested and verified; the absolute gratuity of divine judgment and man's need to accept that judgment has been confirmed. The representation of a 'life' in biblical narrative serves to illustrate one's dynamic relationship with God or its lack. The narrative axis is vertical, not horizontal, and rarely uses description to create verisimilitude. The message is clear: if you follow God's will, you will become powerful and have dominion over the world; if not, you will suffer and die in poverty.[8]

If we compare a Greek story that also presents a parent's sacrifice of a child, for example, Euripides' *Iphigenia at Aulis*, the differences are stark. Agamemnon is overwhelmed with guilt about his decision to kill his daughter, he deceives Klytemnestra, fights with Menelaus, jeopardizes the reputation of the spotless Achilles, plots to deceive the army, knows that Calchus's oracle is prompted by revenge, and even questions the existence of the gods. Yet he kills his child because he is afraid of confronting the army. The narrative is dense with description, motives, action, and fateful decisions. The comparison

---

[6] Momigliano (1987), 159–77.
[7] Brown (1968), 608.
[8] Gunn (1993), 97–100; Westermann (1985), 356.

between the Hebrew and Greek texts, both of which have a father's sacrifice of his child as the crux of the story, notwithstanding their different genre, speaks to the differences of the nation's relationship to the deity. The gods are a remote presence for Euripides: the narrative axis is entirely horizontal, and volition and fate are the chief players. In contrast the author of Genesis is unable to imagine life lived in harmony outside of God's will. The moral choices depicted in Greek representations of biography emerge from the individual's struggle to balance competing claims on the good, while in the Bible such claims issue from the apodictic (often oracular) commands of God.

Virtue in the Hebrew Bible requires the subordination of human volition to God's plan. Events in the life of Abraham and Isaac—or in those of Joseph, Moses, Samuel, Ruth, or Jesus, for that matter—are important only as they illustrate that the proper role for humans is as faithful servant to God. Lives only have meaning in the frame of the larger story of God's covenant with his chosen people. Notable biographical studies by Jews—for example, Philo's *Life of Moses* and Josephus's epitomes of Jewish lives in *Jewish Antiquities*—are hardly Semitic in character but, rather, a complex joining of Platonist and Stoic sensibilities with a learned Jewish tradition. Jewish biography's legacy to later Christian biography was its devotion to an exploration of the intersection of the human and divine, its interest in transcendence, and its promotion of the ideal of a theocratic eschatological state led by God-anointed leaders, i.e., saints.[9]

Greco-Roman biography gave to Christian sacred biography a model of the virtuous life endowed with agency and not one simply subordinated to the will of God.[10] Human freedom, freed from sanction by the gods as a self-sustaining good, was the goal of the citizen. Where the pious Jew believed that the measure of moral conscience was doing God's will as evident in Torah, Greeks and Romans viewed civic responsibility as the ground of virtue. Classical biography was believed to be a hybrid genre. Although designed to focus on the deeds done by an individual in a social setting, it was not history, since it celebrated these acts as indicators of moral good in panegyric. Nepos, among others, expressly argued that panegyric was

---

[9] Colson (1935), 1:27–29.
[10] Cox (1983).

largely absent from historical writing but was obligatory in biography. Nor could biography be covered by the epic genre, since it was written chiefly in prose and promoted the volitional act over that of providence or fate. Biography inhabited a rhetorically ambiguous place. Such liminal status allowed the form a freedom it would not have otherwise enjoyed. Historical writing recorded what an individual did; biography celebrated what he was. Biography emphasized virtue inherent in action outside the act's meaning as a socio-political event. Therefore, the rules governing evidence in biography were different, although not necessarily less rigorous, than those governing historical writing. The focus of biography was on epideisis rather than authentication, on mimesis rather than reporting.[11]

In his *Life of Pericles*, Plutarch makes this distinction clear when he says his purpose is to present virtuous deeds for contemplation so that the reader will be filled with an eager desire to imitate them Καὶ προθυμίαν ἀγωγὸν εἰς μίμησιν ἐμποιεῖ τοῖς ἱστορήσασιν.[12] Classical biography recorded the exemplary deeds of virtuous men as models for conduct. Men could aspire to imitate Pericles; God called Moses. Christian sacred biography fuses these two traditions, and the product is the righteous servant who by God's grace chooses to imitate Christ. This twining of grace and will is fundamental to the construction of agency in Christian sacred biography.

Biography could serve as a forum of public moral suasion. Its encomiastic tenor was a constant of the tradition from the earliest times. The Athenian orator Isocrates claimed his *Evagoras* (ca. 365 B.C.) was the first to use this panegyric form in depicting a *bios*. Xenophon borrowed from *Evagoras* in his encomium of the Spartan king Agesilaus. Both authors depicted the life of their subject in two distinctive ways: (1) with a chronological summary of the deeds, the *praxeis*; and (2) with an interpretative scrutiny of the subject's character, the *ethos*.[13] With the emergence of the Peripatetic School, and leading practitioners such as Aristoxenus, the emphasis shifted to the illustration of the ethical nature of heroic behavior, one's *ethos*. In *Bioi Andron*, Aristoxenus's lives of Socrates, Plato, and others, the

---

[11] Stancliffe (1983), 88; Heffernan (1988), 145–50.
[12] Plutarch, *Lives* III.2–3, ed. and trans. B. Perrin, vol. 3, Loeb Classical Library (Cambridge, 1916).
[13] Leo (1901), 91–92.

author proposes that the scrutiny of actions reveals true character.[14] All acts are not equal in their ability to reveal character, however. Actions believed especially redolent with character are those of the subject when faced with suffering and death. Thus there grew up a literary form—a form crucial to the evolution of Christian biography—the so-called *exitus illustrium virorum*, designed to explore these epiphanic moments.[15]

Sacred biography from late antiquity to year 1000 depicts individuals from every walk of life—martyrs and apostates, kings and commoners, children and elderly, warriors and clerics, bishops and bureaucrats, ascetics, abbots, prostitutes, pilgrims, miracle workers, virgins, demons, devils and fictional personages of every ilk and species. Every segment of the populace (though female lives are a distinct minority), real or fanciful, is represented. Aside from the thousands of anonymous texts, authors as varied as Luke, Tertullian, Eusebius, Athanasius, Jerome, Baudonivia, Gregory the Great, Adomnán, Bede, Alcuin, and Ælfric wrote sacred biographies. A few memorable autobiographies survive, most notably those of Perpetua and Saturus of Carthage, Patrick of Ireland, Augustine of Hippo and that of Boethius.[16] My review must be highly selective and will consider only those few texts that have played a role in shaping the evolving tradition of saints' lives. The *Bibliotheca Hagiographica Latina*, which alone lists 8,989 saints' lives, and the sixty-nine volumes of the *Acta Sanctorum* attest that saints' lives were the most favored of narratives. Many thousands more were written in Greek, Syriac, Coptic, and in all the western vernacular languages; there are innumerable texts no longer extant. Although the differences amongst these compositions are considerable and appear resistant to a synoptic presentation, the traditional religious character of their enterprise—one continually subject to the church's *magisterium*—provided a frame that became canonical for these biographies and allows for such diachronic study.

---

[14] Stuart (1967), 131–54.
[15] Ronconi (1966), 1258–60.
[16] Misch (1949–69).

The Beginning of the Tradition

Therefore be imitators of God. (Eph. 5.1)

My survey begins with the earliest Christian sacred biography, the depiction of Christ in the gospels. The Incarnation proposed that God took human form and lived on earth. If one wished to be a follower of Christ, one had to follow the example of Jesus in the gospels. The imitation of Christ's behavior is a structural principle that underlies all Christian sacred biography. The paradox of the Incarnation, the human in the divine, made human transcendence possible. Since Christ could not be wholly bound by his humanity, the saint who imitated Christ and thus participated in the *vita Christi* was, likewise, less subject to the laws of nature. The miracles of the *vita sanctorum* recall the challenge of the Incarnation and legitimate belief in these supernatural events through an appeal to God's all-powerful presence. The miracle is a multivalent sign: it becomes the marker of sanctity, a tool to promote a particular cult, create support for a political initiative, legitimate the claims of a monastery against a predatory or competing authority, or praise a particular ruling dynasty.

Although the *vita Christi* was the rule for Christian life, how Christians were to live that life was hotly debated. Did Jesus really intend his followers to live lives of voluntary poverty or to practice celibacy? This and other questions vexed the faithful. The teachings of the gospels were mysterious. Augustine, among others, commented on the difficulty of apprehending the truth of Scripture despite its rhetorical simplicity.[17] Despite often-contentious disputes, ideologies of the sacred emerged in late antiquity and informed the tradition of sacred biography. These teachings are extensions of three positions: a positive view of self-sacrifice, including martyrdom and radical asceticism; an avoidance of civic life; and an eschatological view of human history. If you would be Christ's disciple, you must 'put on' his life, since he is the paradigm for correct living. The saint is the embodiment of these teachings. But questions of legitimacy invariably arose: how were the faithful to know that this specific saint did

---

[17] Augustine, *Confessions* III.5 (90) and VI.4 (6), trans. H. Chadwick (New York, 1991).

indeed 'put on' the Christ? The Church provided the answer through its promotion of hagiography. The narrative of the holy life provided the documentary evidence of sanctity.

The gospel narratives present a soteriology of the holy that is indebted to this imitation of the incarnate divine. Christians redefined the holy and virtuous life as someone in whom the teachings of Christ were manifest. Athanasius of Alexandria attributes this comment to Anthony of Egypt: "The Kingdom of Heaven is within you. Virtue, therefore, has need only of our will, since it is within us and springs from us".[18] The individual who sought virtue through a responsible civic life in the late Roman Empire, who revered the ancestral gods and the genius of the emperor, was now outside the pale. Men and women who would be saints had to represent the *imitatio Christi*, even if it cost them their lives. There are no saints' lives or Christian biographies that do not make mimesis central to the narrative. It was the constitutive rhetorical principle of the genre.

Mimesis functions in the saints' lives through recursive structures intended to excite memory. Recursive structures, or tropes, might appear as anecdotes, metaphors, events, or even exact language from Scripture or new canonical Christian biographies. These structures were built into the narrative to remind the listener that this biography was part of the idealizing tradition of Christian biography and drew its legitimacy from the gospels. Recursive structures facilitate patterns of correspondence as multiple layers of recognition (*anagnorisis*) emerge from the shuttling back and forth between the old and the new biographies.[19] Such rhetorical tropes fuse mimesis and ideology and move us from ignorance to knowledge, "Ἀναγώρισις δέ, ὥσπερ καὶ τοὔνομα σημαίνει, ἐξ ἀγνοίας εἰς γνῶσιν μεταβολή".[20]

The biographer—whether he is extolling the prophetic wisdom of St. Polycarp, the heroism of Perpetua of Carthage, or Adomnán's celebration of Columba—employs such recursive tropes to remind his audience of the presence of the divine in his subject. This recursive principle of Christian sacred biography is crucial and has its *locus classicus* in Christ's dying lament.

---

[18] *St. Athanasius: The Life of St. Anthony*, trans. R. T. Meyer, Ancient Christian Writers 10 (New York, 1978), 37.
[19] Dörrie (1938), 274.
[20] Freese (1975), 1452a, 36.

The Gospels

> While all can read it [scripture] with ease it also has a deeper mean-
> ing in which its great secrets are locked away. (Augustine, *Confessions*
> VI, 5)

Jesus's haunting cry on the cross "Eloi, Eloi, lama sabachthani" is
the most shocking and dramatic moment in the gospels (Mk. 15:34;
Mt. 27:46). Jesus utters a final cry and dies. The paradox of the
Incarnation has come full circle. The hideous death on the cross is
accomplished. The man is dead. Such torment prepares one to expect
a cry from the heart but not this agonized cry of abandonment. Has
the Messiah been deceived; does he believe himself abandoned by
his God? His cry, while filled with apparent despair, is actually a
quotation of Psalm 22:1, a psalm that combines two literary types,
viz., lament and thanksgiving. Scriptural commentators argue that
this cry is not one of heart-felt despair. Rather, they argue that Jesus
identifies himself with the iconic biblical figure of the innocent vic-
tim who, despite following the Lord's proscriptions, is made to suffer,
e.g., Job. Psalm 22 traditionally was understood to represent exemplary suffering and deliverance. Rabbinical exegesis during the time
of Christ expected the listener to grasp the entire psalm; their teaching on the use of scriptural quotation emphasized a gestalt understanding.[21] Thus Jesus turns at the last minute to God not with a
despairing lament but as the source of his consolation after a period
of trial.

   While many scholars have labored over the human and theological intent of Jesus's cry, few have considered its narrative and historiographic implications. His quotation of Psalm 22:1 proved to be
crucial for the development of Christian sacred biography. Mark and
Matthew—the only two to record the cry—knew that their audience
would recognize the citation from Psalms and would derive the appropriate meaning from the psalm. If they did not act on such an understanding, their decision to feature Jesus's cry would lead one to
conclude that they believed he despaired, that in his last hour he
felt abandoned. Such an idea would not only have been theologi-
cally unsupportable but also would have been intolerable for the
early Jewish-Christians who required a triumphant messianic Jesus.

---

[21] Marcus (1992), 177–82; but see Brown (1994), 2:1044 ff.

Biblical exegesis notwithstanding, the fact that in his most ago-nized moment Jesus quotes a passage from Scripture does violate verisimilitude. The drama of his death is diminished, even if but for a moment. The recognition of the verse from the psalm moves atten-tion away from the particular, the death of the Galilean Jesus, to the general, a theology that promotes the saving mercy of God. The humanity of Christ's death is compromised by his quotation. The psalm proclaims that God looks after those who are faithful to him and will vindicate the suffering of his servant. The actual biograph-ical detail has been subordinated to a theological or, perhaps more accurately, moral historiography. If the quotation is recognized, as the synoptic authors intended, the cerebration it insists on puts at risk the personal historic drama of the crucifixion. This anguished moment is swallowed in a larger cosmic struggle. Personal history is consumed by the structure of sacred history. This is effected through the theology of the Incarnation that insists the exemplary life is an invitation to the indwelling of the divine. Philo suggests as much in his *Life of Moses*.[22]

The saint—following the model of the cross—embodies a para-doxically dualist nature, simultaneously human and divine. Christian sacred biography and history will ever after seek to root the partic-ular in the general. Even when constructing the most apparently unique moments—moments as unique as Jesus's cry—the gospel authors and later hagiographers shared an understanding of human psychology, biography, and history that is trans-personal. From this understanding they promoted a genre that sought to privilege the universal ethical lesson inherent in the individual behavior. Jesus's quotation from Psalm 22:1 is the foundation on which the entire edifice of the rhetoric of recursivity is built.

At the moment of his death, Jesus's cry to his father is a procla-mation of his faith despite the horror of the cross; his crucifixion emphasizes the salvific power consequent on the imitation of God's will. Jesus was the faithful servant and led his exemplary life fol-lowing the prophecies of Scripture. His fearsome cry is the first appli-cation of recursivity in Christian biography. For most Jews of the first century, the psalms were King David's personal reflections and were, therefore, his biography. Jesus's quotation of Psalm 22:1 is his

---

[22] Colson (1935), 1:27–29.

identification with his ancestor David. Why would Matthew and
Mark highlight such a correspondence? The question is not easily
answered, since Jesus and David, although they share the roles of
kingship and are types of deliverers, make very different claims on
their audiences. Certainly both synoptic authors wish to illustrate the
continuity of Judaism to their audiences. The answer may lie in the
gospel authors' intent that David and Jesus's shared responsibility to
do God's will, to imitate his commands for the redemption of his
people, is a responsibility inseparable from pain and suffering. Jesus's
quotation of Psalm 22:1 unites Christ with his heroic but tragic ancestor David. His utterance signifies the presence of a larger reality,
one that bridges chasms of time and culture. The employment of
recursive linguistic signs and the multivalent levels of recognition it
stimulates, beginning in the gospels but employed throughout Christian
sacred biography, is an authenticating principle that testifies to the
presence of God's favor in an individual. It is used frequently in the
lives of the martyrs, the earliest of Christian sacred biographies and
the first series of lives we shall consider.

Religio Illicita: The Church of the Martyrs

> . . . to feed on human blood while the people cheer. (Petronius, *Satyricon*
> 119.18.)

The account of Stephen's death is the first Christian biography after
that of Christ and, although brief and lacking narrative complexity,
it is the first Christian saint's life. (Acts 6:8–8:1a). The book of Acts
depicts Stephen as the first martyr, a thaumaturge, one "full of grace
and power, [who] did great wonders and signs among the people"
(Στέφανος δὲ πλήρης χάριτος καὶ δυνάμεως ἐποίει τέρατα καὶ σημεῖα
μεγάλα ἐν τῷ λαῷ; 6:8). His power comes from the abundance of
the spirit in him. Stephen was very likely the leader of the hell-
enizers in the Jerusalem Christian community. He opposed the
Sanhedrin, which was prepared to tolerate the church led by James.
Stephen's life follows, although epitomized, Christ's: he preaches
against the rigidity of the law; he is believed to be a blasphemer;
he is forcibly brought before the judicial tribunal and questioned by
the high priest; he preaches about the prophets and patriarchs; he
condemns the council; and he has a vision of Christ as the "Τὸν

υἱὸν τοῦ ἀνθρώπου" in heavenly glory. He is dragged to the place of execution, where he receives the prescribed Jewish punishment for blasphemy, viz., stoning. During his execution, Stephen paraphrases the words Luke attributed to Jesus on the cross: "Κύριε Ἰησοῦ, δέξαι τὸ πνεῦμά μου". Luke constructs these final moments of Stephen's life as an *imitatio Christi*, and he makes the connection explicit: the particularity of Stephen's final moments is subsumed into the larger paradigm of Christ's life. The imitation of Christ through a sacrificial death in which the very language returns us to the *vita Christi* is the guarantee of Stephen's sanctity and the legitimacy for his cult.

The early church revered those who, following the examples of Jesus and Stephen, died as witnesses for their faith. The word *martyr* used denotatively as a blood witness has a complicated history. For centuries, μάρτυς referred to the act of witness in a judicial setting (see Plato's *Phaedrus* 244d).[23] By the period of the New Testament, its meaning broadened to include witness as a sign of religious faith. However, save for the instance of Stephen in Acts (Acts 7:56–58), it was not unambiguously coupled with the idea of blood witness in the Christian scriptures. Some locate the antecedent of Christian sacrifice in the Semitic tradition, particularly in the depiction of Eleazar, the pious Jew who is killed for refusing to eat pork, and in the figure of the Maccabean mother and her seven sons, all of whom died under the rule of the Seleucid Antiochus Epiphanes (4 Macc. 5:1–6:3 and 8:3–18:24).[24] Others, like Bowersock, suggest that the depiction of Christian martyrdom that exists in the *Acta Martyrum* is a new phenomenon cobbled from a syncretism of hellenized Judaism and played out in an empire whose tradition sanctioned principled suicide, e.g., Seneca's despair at being unable to remedy Nero's excesses.[25] By the mid-second century, in the Christian community the word μάρτυς had ceased to have a legal meaning and referred exclusively to blood sacrifice.

Minorities suffer abuse in most societies. The Christian community, like other minorities, also suffered, even though Christians were indistinguishable from the rest of the citizenry. The anonymous

[23] Liddell and Scott (1968), 1082.
[24] Grabar (1946), 2:20–21; Downing (1963), 279–93.
[25] Bowersock (1995), 1–39.

Christian *Epistle to Diognetus* (ca. 150) makes this very point: "Christians are not distinguished from the rest of humanity by country, language or custom".[26] They differed from other citizens, however, by their refusal to participate in many public rituals that required sacrifice to the gods and to the genius of the emperor. As the Roman State grew in complexity and became ever more ethnically and linguistically diverse, the figure of the emperor functioned as a totem to promote political and social stability. Rome's insistence that Christians sacrifice to the emperor was an effort to legislate Roman customs in an ever-burgeoning and diverse empire. Christians, however, saw resistance to such legislation as a measure of fidelity to their religion and an opportunity to repudiate the values of the state. As long as Romans viewed Christians as apostate Jews, they were well within the law regarding the legitimacy of established religions. However, this all changed by the middle of the second century, when sporadic persecution of Christians became intense.[27]

In the *Laws* Cicero remarked: "Let no one have separate gods, either new or foreign, unless they are officially allowed" (II, 19). Such sentiment underscored a traditional hostility for any religion that would deter individuals from revering their ancestors. Prominent Romans believed that the success of Rome was indebted in part to the 'custom of these ancestors', the *mos maiorum*. New cults would jeopardize not only these revered traditions but also the very state itself. Tacitus believed that Christians were another eastern cult that would undermine the purity of Roman tradition and argued that fear was the only remedy to hold them in check (*Annals*, xiv, 445). Juvenal's comment that "the Syrian Orontes has been pouring into the Tiber for a good while now" identifies the east as the birthplace of these superstitions that pollute the quality of life in Rome with their unspeakable oriental vices (*Satires*, iii, 62). In the *Martyrdom of Fructuosus* (ca. 259), Aemilianus, the Roman governor, makes the connection among the gods, the state, and the emperor crystal clear: "If the gods are not worshipped, then the images of the emperors are not adored".[28] These sentiments were to harden as the empire expanded and the eternal city became a world that incorporated

---

[26] *The Epistle to Diognetus* V.1–4, ed. J. J. Thierry (Leiden, 1964).
[27] Barnes (1981), 136–39.
[28] Musurillo (1972).

devotees of Tanit, Isis, the cult of Mithras, Dea Syria, and the Christ. It was inevitable that Christianity would become an outlawed sect. Beginning with Trajan's famous receipt to Pliny (*Epis.* 10, 96, 97), the official status of Christianity was to seesaw for two centuries from outright persecution to that of benign neglect. The most severe of these persecutions took place in the urban areas of the eastern provinces and North Africa. The repression of Christianity, however, appears to have been a local event dependent upon the will of the local community and the provincial leaders, until the time of the Decian persecutions 250–51.[29]

The *Acts of the Martyrs* are the first Christian biographies written after the scriptures that record these persecutions. Under the general rubric of *Acta* we also can place the *Passiones*, records that emphasize the actual persecutions of the martyrs. For simplicity's sake, I will use *Acta* here to designate both types of work, whether they were genuine historical records, *Acta sincera*, or apocryphal fictions.[30] The *Acta* served the beleaguered communities in many ways. They showed that Christians were powerful and could resist the barbarisms of the state that they stigmatize; they were consolations, promising immortality to the condemned; and they were used liturgically in memorial services on a martyr's anniversary. Of the many texts that survive this early period—including those historic and those fiction—all use the central strategy of mimesis to legitimate their authenticity and accomplish this through narrative recursive structures that stimulate memory.

The Trial and Structure of Debate

> We shall narrate a selection from the life and actions of each and display through the selection the character of the whole life. (Theodoret of Cyrrhus, *Historia religiosa* Prol. 8)

Aside from the early depiction in Acts of Stephen—who is called the most perfect of martyrs in the *Letter of the Churches of Lyons and Vienne* (Στέφανος ὁ τέλειος μάρτυς)—the great majority of the *Acta Martyrum* narrate events of the second and third centuries. Although

---

[29] Frend (1965), 406–07.
[30] Delehaye (1962), 86–98.

the narratives of the martyrs are written over a period of two centuries in different languages and from regions as different as Thessalonica in Greece and Cirta in Africa they share similar narrative structures, rhetoric, and theology.

Central to all the martyr stories is the use of the trial transcript (*commentarius*) of the actual trial (*cognitio extra ordinem*). The transcript provided—whether a fabrication of the actual trial or an eyewitness account—the text with three essential elements: a display of the heroism of the martyr; the cruelty of the inquisitor; and the bankruptcy of the Roman system. The *cognitio* was an expedient way to handle malefactors and was used only during the empire. Under the provisos of the *cognitio*, the local official who presided could initiate legal action by summoning the litigants and appointing himself as judge. Ironically, this piece of purely expedient legislation was to provide the *Acta* a unifying and dramatic focus. Aside from the obvious use of the *commentarius* to provide historical legitimacy, the *cognitio*—since it allowed the prosecutor to serve as summoner, judge, and jury—provided authors of the *Acta* with a vehicle to display the martyr in intellectual debate with the single representative of the state. After the age of historical persecution had passed, the inquisitional, testing aspect of the *cognitio* and *commentarius* was retained in hagiographic narratives. Moreover, the figure of the corrupt and cruel Roman jurist in dialogue with the saint was to evolve into a demon-like persecutor.

The *commentarius* is prominent even in the earliest *Acta*. In the *Martyrdom of Polycarp* (ca. 156–59) the governor himself is the judge:

> Governor: "Swear by the emperor's genius"!
> Polycarp: "If you delude yourself into thinking that I will swear by the emperor's genius, as you say, and if you pretend not to know who I am, listen and I will tell you plainly: I am a Christian/Χριστιανός εἰμι".[31]

This interchange shows the pattern that was to become a formula in the *Acta*. The judge asks the accused to swear by the emperor's genius, the Christian refuses, often with a stinging rebuke, and then pronounces what became a ritual part of the *commentarius*, the declaration of the name "I am a Christian/Χριστιανός εἰμι". The dia-

---

[31] *Acts of the Christian Martyrs*, 10–11.

logue between single judge and single accused afforded the author great latitude to present the drama of opposing points of view and to supply biographical information. *Acta*, like the *Martyrdom of Carpus, Papylus, and Agathonicê* (ca. 170?), actually begin with the *commentarius*. Here the dialogue between the anonymous proconsul of Pergamum and Carpus illustrates vividly the degree to which the author used the legal transcript to polarize sentiments:

> Proconsul: [He] became angry and said: "Sacrifice to the gods and do not play the fool".
> Carpus: with a gentle smile, said: "May the gods be destroyed who have not made heaven and earth".
> Proconsul: "You must offer sacrifice," said the proconsul. "These are the emperor's orders".
> Carpus: [He] said: "The living do not offer sacrifice to the dead".[32]

The use of *commentarius* and *cognitio* occur throughout the *Acta*. The *Martyrdom of Pionus and Companions* (ca. 300?) has a very effective interchange between Pionus and Quintillian, the proconsul for Africa. The *commentarius* was used in the latest of the historical martyrdoms as in the *Passio Sanctae Crispinae*. Crispina was found guilty of violating Diocletian's fourth edict of January/February 304 that compelled sacrifice to the gods under pain of death. The *commentarius* presents what by now has become a predictable and polarizing *mise en scène:*

> Proconsul Anullinus: "I will put before you the sacred edict. You must obey it."
> Crispina: "I will obey the edict," replied Crispina, "but the one given by my Lord Jesus Christ."[33]

In some martyrdoms, especially those in which the martyr is a woman, the threats also involve sexual violence. For example, Crispina is threatened with disfigurement:

> Anullinus then turned to the court notary and added: "Let her be completely disfigured by having her hair cut and her head shaved with a razor till she is bald, that her beauty might first be shamed/*ad ignominiam deueniat*".[34]

---

[32] *Acts of the Christian Martyrs*, 24–25.
[33] *Acts of the Christian Martyrs*, 304–05.
[34] *Acts of the Christian Martyrs*, 306–07.

In Eusebius's account of the *Martyrdom of Potamiaena and Basilides*, the Alexandrian virgin Potamiaena is threatened with sexual assault by her judge, Aquila: ". . . [he] subjected her entire body to cruel torments, and then threatened to hand her over to his gladiators to assault her physically".[35] Later fictive hagiographies, showing the influence of Greek romance, highlight the sexual threats. In the apocryphal *Life of St. Eustace*, set in the time of Trajan, the saint's wife is kidnapped by pirates and threatened with violence and rape, anecdotes that I have shown elsewhere were borrowed from Achilles Tatius's *The Love of Leucippe and Clitophon* and Helidorus of Emesa's *Aethiopica*.[36] There, the role of the judge is often a pastiche of the Roman jurist and a Satan-like figure. In Athanasius's biography of Anthony, the figure of the judge has been transformed into a demon who resorts to physical abuse: "So he [Satan] came one night with a great number of demons and lashed him so unmercifully that he lay on the ground speechless from the pain".[37]

Authorship in the *Acta* often is difficult to determine and frequently is of interest from a narrative point of view. The text can be anonymous, as in the *Martyrdom of Bishop Fructuosus, and his Deacons, Augurius and Eulogius*; the narrator may claim eyewitness status as an actual participant in the story, as in *Passio Sanctorum Mariani et Iacobi*; the text may be an autobiography imbedded in a larger anonymous narrative, as in the *Passio Sanctarum Perpetuae et Felicitatis*; and, lastly, it may take the form of an epistle written by one church to another, as in the *Letter of the Churches of Lyons and Vienne*. In the Donatist account of the *Acts of the Abitinian Martyrs*, the narrator reports that he has had access to the actual court transcript from which he has fashioned his account.[38] Although the issue of authorship varies considerably and plays a part in the unique history of each text, the *Acta* do share a singular point of view, which is the construction of a literature able to show to the Greco-Roman and Jewish cultures that the Christians have men and women equal to, if not more powerful than, any of their heroes and heroines because they worship a more powerful God whom they are endeavoring to imitate. The mil-

---

[35] *Acts of the Christian Martyrs*, 132–33.
[36] Heffernan (1988), 142.
[37] *St. Athanasius: The Life of St. Anthony*, 26.
[38] Tilley (1996), 28.

itantly propagandistic tone of many of the *Acta* appears to have been designed as a consolation to give heart to the Christians who continued to suffer persecution. The documents illustrated the worst that could happen and showed how faith could turn tragedy into triumph. The *Acta* create a Christian ethos that shows the only true salvation is opposition to the existing order, even if that requires suffering and death. In the *Martyrdom of the Saintly and Blessed Apostle Apollonius*—a martyrdom of the Christian equivalent of a Stoic philosopher—the text ends with a moving doxology: "So then because of his [Apollonius] heroic deeds (*tois ekeinou kalois andragathemasin*), brothers, strengthening our own souls in faith, let us show ourselves lovers of the same grace".[39]

The martyrdom of Polycarp (69–155) is vividly described in the anonymous *Letter of the Church of Smyrna to the Church of Philomelium*. The old Polycarp has a vision of his death by fire. He decides that flight is futile and gives himself up to his pursuers. At the outset in the letter we read the following: "Just as the Lord did, he [Polycarp] waited that he might be delivered up, "that we might become his imitators/ἵνα μιμεταὶ καὶ ἡμεῖς αὐτοῦ γενώμεθα".[40] Notice that the emphasis on Polycarp's imitation of Christ is made at the very beginning of the letter, before the narrative of his persecution. Although we are at the very dawning of the tradition of sacred biography, the idea of imitation has become a precondition for Christian sacred biography.

Religio Licta

> We give to Christians and all the freedom to follow the religion they desire. (Lactantius, *De Mortibus Persecutorum* 48)

Not only did Constantine's recognition of Christianity legitimate the church, but also his policies, especially those implemented in the East after 324, changed the ideology of the sacred and the representation of the self in Christian biography. It was now no longer necessary, as St. Anthony's life makes clear—indeed no longer possible—to seek martyrdom as a way of imitating Christ. This emancipation

---

[39] Tilley (1996), 103.
[40] Tilley (1996), 2.

brought new problems and solutions. A singular question the Christians now faced was what new structures could substitute as an appropriate model for those pious Christians who saw suffering and martyrdom as the greatest test of faith. Eusebius suggests in his *Oration on the Tricennalia of Constantine* that the change from martyrdom to a new form of witness was inevitable and providential, a position Constantine himself avowed.[41] Eusebius argued that the dictates of God's plan were evident in Constantine's life. He proposed that God ordained the demise of the martyrs coincident with the emergence of a new and triumphant Christian State. Constantine was his means of effecting this change.[42] Living the Christian life was to substitute for dying the Christian death. As Wilson aptly put it, "Ideal lives rather than ideal deaths were called for".[43] The change had far reaching implications for the construction of a new ethos governing sanctity and its literary representation. Where most of the *Acta Martyrum* had been focused on the testimony, passion, and death of the subject, the new freedom afforded the Church radically widened the possible focus of Christian biography. If the martyr followed the hallowed archetype of Christ's death, the saints of the fourth century had the entire fabric of Christ's life as their model. Suddenly the opportunity presented itself for priests, monks, bishops, lay men and women, virgins, and soldiers to seek sanctity through their living and not through their death. For example, notable female figures—such as Macrina, *ancillae Domini* like Paula the Elder and her daughter Eustochium, and Melania the Elder and Younger—began to take their place in sacred history.[44]

Emergence of the Charismatic Ascetic

> The desert was made a city by monks, whose citizenship was that of heaven. (Athanasius, *Life of St. Anthony*)

Christian biographies from the second half of the fourth century were no longer limited to a narrative summary of a martyr's suffering

---

[41] Lieu (1998), 142.
[42] Binns (1994), 39.
[43] Lieu (1998), 108.
[44] Petersen (1996), 89–279.

and death but, instead, celebrated individuals who best embodied the presence of God in their daily lives. Although the emphasis on living for Christ rather than dying ideally enfranchised all walks of life, the emerging popularity of the radical renunciate—who lived a type of living death—was the first to dominate the new paradigm. The new players in the pages of Christian biography are ascetic monks and monastic women. The origin of asceticism as a wholly Christian idea has been exaggerated. Abstinence was widely practiced in the Greco-Roman world. Sexual activity was believed by some to be a disease, an internal burning of the vital spirit. Stoics, like Zeno or Seneca, went one step further and extended the metaphor of disease to the sexual desire itself. Self-control and well-being, *eudaimonia*, meant a rejection of desire, *epithymia*. While Christians such as Tatian, Marcion, and Irenaeus supported a severe encraticism, many non-Christian contemporaries also approved of their efforts. However, there was a profound philosophic difference between their ideologies of abstinence. The Christian ideal of abstinence is best exemplified in Paul's understanding that Christians cannot achieve a stoic-like self-sufficiency (*hikanoi*) since they are in all things dependent on God; our truest self is realized not in the achievement of self-control over body and mind but in a union with God made possible by grace (2 Cor. 3:5–6).

Men like Anthony of Egypt, who lived lives of exoticized renunciation—practicing morbid fasting, not bathing, and going about half-naked—were seeking not simply self-sufficiency and *eudaimonia* but, further, a greater intimacy with God on whom their every action depended. They became powerful intermediaries of the sacred, in Peter Brown's phrase "arbiter[s] of the holy".[45] The lives of the women, in contrast, like Macrina—known to us only through male authorship—depict women as domesticators of asceticism. Although dwelling in a social community, they nonetheless transformed conventional mores. Gregory of Nyssa says that his sister Macrina "put herself on the level with the many by entering into a common life with her maids, making them her sisters and equals rather than her slaves and underlings".[46] Despite the differing social contexts of their renunciation, these men and women were equally charismatic leaders. Like the martyrs, they rejected the world and all it represents.

---

[45] Brown (1995), 60.
[46] Petroff (1986), 79.

Although Christians had earlier fled to the desert to escape persecution, the movement to the wilderness was greater after Constantine
than before. The rise of monasticism is a complex phenomenon that
appears to have benefited from a number of factors—contemporary
disenchantment with the very success of the Church, earlier influential
biblical models that promoted communal life, and possibly the prestige of groups such as the Pythagoreans. For some, monasticism represented an alternative to the union of Church and State, a union
that did not provide an apt model of the Christian life. For these
individuals, the new Christian Empire lacked rigor; it turned its back
on those who proclaimed the 'name' and died for the faith. They
were ever mindful of Tertullian's ringing comment "Quid Athenae
Hierosolymis?". In his prologue to the *Life of St. Malchus* St. Jerome
remarks ". . . [how the church] was crowned with martyrdoms, and,
after it came into the hands of Christian emperors, how it became
greater in power and riches indeed, but meaner in virtue".[47] The
emergence and triumph of the ideology of these ascetic monastics
was an acknowledgement that suffering still held a central place in
the Christian imagination.

The spirit of martyrdom was reborn in Athanasius's *Life of St.
Anthony*.[48] While Anthony's life depicts the life of the ideal Christian
monk, the ancient ideal of suffering remains vigorous, as Anthony is
repeatedly referred to as a martyr. The figure of Anthony is indebted
to both Old and New Testaments, to depictions of Moses and Christ,
and to images of the philosophical sage, e.g., Philostratus's biography of Apollonius of Tyana, Iamblichus's study of Pythagoras, and
Porphyry's life of Plotinus. Unlike the earlier narratives of the martyrs, this new direction in a saint's biography chronicles, albeit selec-
tively, the deeds of Anthony's life from birth to death. The entire
fabric of his life—and by extension that of all Christians—bears testimony to his witness. The life opens with a prologue urging the
reader to admire Anthony and emulate his resolve. His conversion
is presented as a literal imitation of Christ's injunction to leave material things and follow him. Anthony's asceticism is the new heroism.
The monk is not a miracle worker but a "daily martyr to his con-

---

[47] Jerome, "Life of Malchus", in *Early Christian Biographies*, trans. M. L. Ewald, ed.
R. J. Deferrari, in The Fathers of the Church (Washington, 1964), 283–97, at 287.
[48] Barnes (1993), 240 n. 64; but see Anatolios (1998), 166.

science".[49] Athanasius couples Anthony's asceticism with wisdom. His authority and power are manifested in his control over his body and his extended Socratic-like discourses on the perfect life. The life of extreme asceticism (*askesis*) is celebrated as an achievement of the very highest athleticism (*athlesis*). The athletic metaphor, although used in earlier Christian biography, was amplified by Athanasius and used to dramatize the severity of Anthony's struggle with temptation, frequently personified as Satan. Athletic striving, that is asceticism, was required if the struggle was to be successful. (Heb. 10:32; 1 Cor. 9:24–27) Anthony is depicted battling demons in his cell. For Anthony, the model of Christ's renunciation was central. Pilgrims, skeptics, and even pagan philosophers flocked to his hermitage, and his fame spread throughout the East. Athanasius was able to build onto this reputation and shrewdly constructed a composite character of Anthony as a Christian type of the pagan sage who skillfully mediated between the sacred and the profane.[50] The persona of the classical sage is just a scratch beneath the patina of Athanasius's Anthony. For example, Anthony's refusal to bathe is a deliberate borrowing of an anecdote in Porphyry's remarks about Plotinus (*Vita Plotini*, 2).

The model of the philosopher hermit was to prove a seminal figure for Christian biography. Augustine's conversion owes much to his learning of Anthony from his friend Ponticianus (*Confessions* 8.6–7). Jerome's biographical compositions are also deeply indebted to the depiction of Anthony.[51] Jerome's biographies of Saints Paul, Hilarion, and Malchus, written over a period of twenty years while he himself was living as a hermit, are an important step in the evolution of Christian biography. Jerome acknowledges his debt to Athanasius and to Evagrius's translation of the *Life of Anthony* (ca. 360) in his *Life of St. Paul the Hermit* (ca. 376). Although it appears that Jerome likely prompted Evagrius to translate Athanasius, his *Life of Paul* is a work different both in spirit and in execution. Where Athanasius wrote of Anthony as a philosopher dispensing wisdom in long discourses while choosing to live the exacting life of a Christian ascetic, Jerome rejects the model of the learned pedagogue as a character

[49] *St. Athanasius: The Life of St. Anthony*, 60.
[50] Binns (1994), 60.
[51] Cameron (1993), 23.

type in his narratives. Paul, Hilarion, and Malchus fail to appropriate the figure of the classical teacher to the extent that Anthony does. Although Jerome's saints' lives are rich in citations from his favorite authors (Cicero, Sallust, Vergil, and Florus), by the time he composes the *Life of Malchus* his allusions are chiefly scriptural. Jerome moves away from the model of the rational sage to distance himself from the classics and to dramatize the power of God's grace and its ability to reshape the natural world. The world of wonder and miracle is the arena where Jerome finds grace and faith cooperating.

Although Athanasius does underscore the devil's place in Anthony's struggle, he rarely dramatizes the attributes of Satan. Jerome, however, to an unprecedented degree depicts fantastic visions, speaking beasts, the ravages of asceticism, fantastic depictions of Satan, and fearful exorcisms. The immediacy with which we grasp the horrible rigors of Hilarion's diet may reflect Jerome's own struggles with his self-debasement. In Jerome's three saint's lives, for the first time in Christian biography, a deliberate effort is made to bridge the epistemological barrier separating the historical and the fictive, the fantastic and the factual. Jerome absorbed the opposing forces of these two experiential planes of the real and the meta-real, yet struggled to maintain the "historical sequence of my narrative", as he says in the *Life of Hilarion*.[52] For example, in his *Life of St. Paul* Jerome depicts St. Anthony's journey to find the hermit Paul, during which he meets a fantastic horned Manikin. The saint asks him to identify himself. The beast replies that he worships Christ. This provokes in Anthony a prayer in celebration of Christ and a curse on Alexandria where they worship beasts as gods. Here in the purity of the desert the uncontaminated beasts worship Christ: "Woe to you, Alexandria, because you worship monsters for God! [Here] Beasts speak the name of Christ".[53] Jerome, aware of the possible ridicule such anecdotes might cause, offers a two-fold defense: first, he appeals to history and notes that a fantastic beast was recently brought and displayed in Constantinople; second, he paraphrases Scripture that ". . . all things are possible for God and those who have faith".[54] The new

---

[52] Jerome, "Life of St. Hilarion", in *Early Christian Biographies*, 241–80, at 251.
[53] Jerome, "Life of St. Paul, the First Hermit", in *Early Christian Biographies*, 225–38, at 231.
[54] Jerome, "Life of St. Paul", 231.

emphasis on living a life of daily martyrdom through ascesis and the variety of experiences Jerome saw in the depictions of Christ's life in the gospels provided the basis for his interest in portraying the temptations, healings, visions, and interaction with disciples of Paul, Hilarion, and Malchus.

Miles Christi

Imperauit potius quam rogauit/He commanded rather than requested
Sulpicius Severus, *Life of Saint Martin.*

Sulpicius Severus (ca. 363–420?) wrote his influential *Life of St. Martin* (ca. 396) little more than four years after Jerome completed his *Life of St. Hilarion.*[55] Sulpicius, an educated Gallo-Roman from a good family, was trained in the traditions of Latin rhetoric, perhaps in Bordeaux, and displayed his considerable skill in his *Life of St. Martin.* Ambitious, Sulpicius used his study of law combined with his obvious gifts in rhetoric to gain employment in the imperial administration. He married into a senatorial family. On the unexpected early death of his wife, he retired from public life. Listening to his friend Paulinus of Nola describe Martin likely prompted his first trip to visit the saint in 393–94. Sulpicius may have become a monk before 395, possibly following the example of Paulinus. He was working on his biography of the saint shortly after that date, and it was clearly finished before Martin died in November 397.

Called the "Christian Sallust", Sulpicius was indebted to the Roman historian, likely sympathized with his repugnance with and withdrawal from public life, and, following Martin's example, became a monk. Suetonius's influence is also apparent, especially the latter's use of the narrative technique of *divisio,* used most notably in his *Life of Caesar.* Sulpicius took from Suetonius the practice of briefly representing the salient moments in a subject's life, chronologically until maturity. After that was accomplished, the biographer was free to select at random the anecdotes that best reflect the argument being made. Sulpicius's *Life of Martin* follows this pattern, beginning with Martin's birth in Pannonia, his time in the army and subsequent

---

[55] Sulpicius Severus, *Vie de saint Martin,* ed. and trans. J. Fontaine, *Sources Chrétiennes,* 3 vols. (Paris, 1967–69).

resignation, his choice of monasticism, his election as bishop, the founding of Marmoutier (chapters 2–10), the fourteen chapters on his miracles (11–24), and the last three chapters that report his inability to portray accurately the majesty of the man and his inner spirituality. In his *Dialogues*, Sulpicius reports how inspiring he found the tales of the great Christian ascetics depicted in Jerome's *Life of St. Hilarion*, Evagrius's translation of Athanasius's *Life of St. Anthony*, and Pontius's *Life of St. Cyprian*. All influenced his *Life of St. Martin*. Yet for all the literary influences on his *Life of St. Martin*, Sulpicius's Martin remains a very personal document written while the saint was alive, and during the time that their friendship was formed "I burned with the fire to write his life/*iam ardebat animus uitam illius scribere*".[56]

Sulpicius's Martin is crucial in the history of Christian biography because it does something not done before this time; namely, it presents three disjunctive and competing ideologies in the Church in the figure of one man, thereby legitimating models of alternate routes for later biographers to exploit. Sulpicius's first ten chapters depict the chronology of Martin's life, recounting in turn each of its three vocational stages, as a soldier, ascetic/thaumaturge, and bishop. While Sulpicius's Martin is among the earliest of the *vitae episcoporum*, Sulpicius, unlike his near contemporary, Possidius, author of the earliest *Life of St. Augustine of Hippo* (ca. 430), or Paulinus of Milan's *Life of St. Ambrose* (ca. 417?), does not concentrate on Martin's episcopal career. The latter two Christian biographies present their subjects principally as defenders of the Church against schismatics and the corruption of the state. Indeed in Possidius's *Life of St. Augustine* the saint—true to his intellectual leaning—is depicted as being ambivalent about miracles, telling the sick man who sought a cure "He [Augustine] replied that if he had any powers of that kind he would surely have used them on himself first".[57]

Although the charismatic ascetic, whether eremitic or coenobitic, was the dominant icon of sanctity at the end of the fourth century and dear to Sulpicius's heart, Martin's life legitimated other vocations as routes to sanctity: bishop, warrior, abbot, ascetic, thau-

---

[56] Sulpicius Severus, *Vie de saint Martin*, 1:310.

[57] Possidius, *Life of Augustine*, in *Soldiers of Christ: Saints and Saints' Lives from Late Antiquity and the Early Middle Ages*, ed. and trans. T. F. X. Noble and T. Head (University Park, Penn., 1995), 63.

maturge, and a combination of these vocations. Sulpicius's *Life of Martin* fits into none of the univocal category of lives, whether of bishops, monks, or ascetics. Such classificatory systems, while helpful, often require emendation, since *vitae* rarely belong to a single category. For example, Paulinus's *Life of St. Ambrose*, while focusing on his role as bishop, is filled with anecdotes of Ambrose's supernatural powers, while there are no such anecdotes in Possidius's *Life of Augustine*.

Martin—as the ex-military, uneducated holy man from Pannonia who settled in Tours, was consecrated bishop, founded a monastery at Marmoutier, was an enemy of paganism, and a maker of miracles—was a thorn in the flesh of the Gallic episcopacy. Their obvious disapproval of Martin provided Sulpicius a model with which to promote a more inclusive view of sanctity while serving as a sharp reminder to the bishops of Gaul that asceticism and service were an integral part of their ministry. For example, Sulpicius's depiction of Martin's nine years in the army show him reversing the role separating superior from subordinate: "it was the master who performed the services/*dominus seruiebat*".[58] And despite his real difficulties with his fellow bishops, Sulpicius's *Life of St. Martin* did underscore the potential for sanctity present in that of the clerical hierarchy, provided they followed this model of humility and service.

Martin's military career, conversion while a soldier, and resignation from the service—despite Sulpicius's efforts to minimize it—is nonetheless present in his metaphors and highlighted in his depiction of Martin's refusal to remain a soldier. Martin's decision to resign his commission and refuse the bonus for re-enlistment has antecedents in the *Acta martyrum*, especially in such military lives as the *Martyrdom of St. Marinus*, the *Acts of Maximillian*, the *Acts of Marcellus*, and the *Martyrdom of Julius the Veteran*. Martin makes his resignation to the Caesar Julian with a thundering affirmation that he is a soldier of Christ: "I have been your soldier up to now. Let me now be God's. Let someone who is going to fight have your bonus. I am Christ's soldier/*Christi ego miles sum*; I am not allowed to fight".[59] In the anonymous *Acts of Marcellus* (ca. 298?), the Christian centurion Marcellus, questioned about his reason for refusing his commission by

---

[58] Sulpicius Severus, *Vie de saint Martin*, 1:254.
[59] Sulpicius Severus, *Vie de saint Martin*, 1:260.

the praetorian prefect Aurelius Agricolanus, responded: "I answered . . .
that I was a Christian, and that I could not fight by any other
oath, but solely for the Lord Christ Jesus, Son of God almighty"[60]—
Such debates became standard topoi in saints' lives, and Sulpicius
knew them.

Sulpicius uses military metaphors and settings to characterize many
of Martin's miracles. Martin is depicted as a scourge of pagan custom, destroying the centers of pagan cults and ending the rituals
practiced by the rustics. Sulpicius reports that after his first miracle
he was "looked upon as a man of power/*potius etiam et uere apostoli-
cus haberetur*".[61] Even when angels are sent to help him destroy a successful pagan temple, they come as fellow soldiers "looking like
heavenly warriors, with spears and shields".[62] On those occasions
when Martin was forced to petition the emperor on behalf of someone, Sulpicius says that "he commanded rather than requested".[63]
Sulpicius's language underscores Martin as the premier *miles Christi*
who sought to honor his Lord as soldier, monk/thaumaturge and
bishop.[64]

His life was enormously influential and was instrumental in com-
bating heresy and extending the opportunity of sanctity to include
different vocations. Eustochius, the second after Martin to lead the
community at Marmoutier, used Martin's reputation to champion
Catholic Christianity over Visigothic Arianism.[65] Martin became the
patron saint of the Merovingians. In his *Life of Charles the Great*, Nokter
the Stammerer reports that the Merovingians always went into battle bearing the cope of St. Martin. Sulpicius's depiction of Martin
as a thaumaturge and ascetic, combined with his use of military
metaphors and anecdotes depicting Martin as a powerful combatant
against paganism and heresy, provided Christian biography with a
newly invigorated model of the Christian warrior. Constantius of
Lyon's *Life of Saint Germanus of Auxerre* (ca. 475–80) nicely illustrates
this influence from Sulpicius. Military metaphors and epithets are
common in this work. Germanus, formerly a married military com-

[60] *Acts of the Christian Martyrs*, 255.
[61] Sulpicius Severus, *Vie de saint Martin*, 1:268.
[62] Sulpicius Severus, *Vie de saint Martin*, 1:284.
[63] Sulpicius Severus, *Vie de saint Martin*, 1:296.
[64] Rousseau (1978), 404–19.
[65] Van Dam (1993), 17.

mander who becomes a monk, bishop, ascetic, and thaumaturge (thus closely following the model of Martin), is called after his conversion a "leader of the soldiers of God". Constantius depicts Germanus leading a battle ("leader of the battle"/*dux proelii*) against the combined forces of Saxons and Picts while chanting *alleluia*.[66] For Constantius there was no contradiction in Germanus's episcopal ministry incorporating the role of warrior and miracle worker. He was both a "protector in the court of heaven and in the tempest of this world".[67] And, like Martin, he was an exorcist casting out demons and raising the dead to life.

Although the example of the warrior saint is as old as the *Acta martyrum*, the ideal that military personnel, even former soldiers, could achieve sanctity had languished until Sulpicius's biography of Martin. Beginning with Sulpicius's creation of Martin, however, an idea took root and grew slowly at first—to wit, that it was now possible to live fully in the 'world' and yet achieve sanctity. This shift in the paradigmatic model of sanctity, from self-sacrificing ascetics and clergy to include the laity, is, however, not fully realized until the tenth century. By the tenth century laymen are the subjects of hagiography—even those busily engaged with their fellow citizens as military and secular rulers—and could aspire to sanctity, provided that their primary concern was to live as a model of Christ and to imitate him in all things. This new dimension is present in Odo of Cluny's *Life of St. Gerald of Aurillac* (ca. 930?). Odo opens his narrative skeptically, voicing his concern about the historicity of the deeds attributed to Gerald—a rhetorical pose that is partly a literary device to gain credulity for his narrative and partly a result of his awareness of the problem that writing a saint's life of a warrior layman might cause. Odo justifies Gerald's vocation by appeals to the patriarchs: "Let no one be worried because a just man sometimes made use of fighting, which seems incompatible with fighting . . . [since] King David . . . sent his forces even against his own son".[68] After an accounting of Gerald's portentous *in utero* miracles (a traditional topos), Odo depicts Gerald's pious youth and moves quickly to present him as a just ruler, going so far to refer to him as a "blessed prince".

---

[66] Constantius of Lyon, *Life of Saint Germanus of Auxerre*, in *Soldiers of Christ*, 90.
[67] Constantius of Lyon, *Life of Saint Germanus of Auxerre*, 91.
[68] Odo of Cluny's *Life of St. Gerald of Aurillac*, in *Soldiers of Christ*, 302–03.

Although Odo extends the idea of confessor and martyr to encompass not only Gerald's lay status but also "all those who carry the cross by resisting vice, or who glorify God by doing well", he does not portray Gerald as responsible for a single miracle until Book two, after the count has left his lay status and joined the clergy. As a member of the clergy Gerald now is able, through grace, to constrain natural law, heal the sick, exorcise demons, and, notably, to accomplish these tasks even posthumously. He was capable of performing none of these deeds as a layman. Despite Odo's insistence that the bounds of sanctity be extended, he was reluctant to extend to the lay individual the status of thaumaturge.

Gregory of Tours: Posthumous Miracles and Cult Centers

Two centuries after Sulpicius finished his *Life of Saint Martin*, the custodian of his cultic center, Gregory of Tours, completed his *Life of the Fathers*. Gregory is indebted to Sulpicius's depiction of sanctity, yet his view of the sacred reflects the momentous changes that Gallic society had undergone in the two centuries since Sulpicius's death. In his *Liber vitae patrum* Gregory recounts the lives of twenty saints: six bishops, nine abbots, one nun, and four recluses.[69] The figure of Martin in Sulpicius's life is that of an unlettered, brilliant, and charismatic healer who moves among the world of the hermitage, the episcopal palace, and the imperial court with ease. Martin is a public miracle worker whose acts proclaim his sanctity. Sulpicius does not record a single posthumous miracle. While Gregory does not argue that doctrinally the life of the recluse, monk, or bishop has a greater claim to sanctity, he shows a greater interest in the lives of the bishops, at least three of whom were his relatives. He devotes approximately twice as much of his narrative to their lives than to the lives of abbots or recluses, and he seems principally interested in the miracles that they do posthumously.

Gregory's lives of the bishops are saints' lives about men drawn from the best families, frequently aristocrats, who enjoyed the arena of power, were well educated, politically well connected, and sometimes members of his family. His bishops were public servants, like,

---

[69] Gregory of Tours, *Life of the Fathers*, trans. E. James (Liverpool, 1985).

for example Nicetius, bishop of Lyons, who was frequently involved in disputes with his lay overlord. Such men often had to walk a fine line between principle and politics. Discretion in everyday affairs was undoubtedly a watchword for the successful prelate, and prudent compromise often proved a necessary evil. Power, politics, ego, and compromise are not the typical ingredients of sanctity, but these elements were inseparable from a maturing Gallic church. Accordingly, Gregory has a jaundiced view of the power to perform miracles and their quality while the saint was alive, since the political arena frequently compromised principle. In his *About Saint Illidius* Gregory makes this perfectly clear:

> the virtue that comes from the tomb is much more worthy of praise than those things which a living person has worked in this world, because the latter could be blemished by the continual difficulties of worldly occupations, while the former were certainly free from all blemish.[70]

Accordingly, all twenty of his lives in the *Life of the Fathers* avoid public display of supernatural powers, or of behaviors that might draw undue attention to one's piety while the saint is alive.

Although the narrative of the posthumous miracle has a pedigree as old as the gospels, the important early hagiographers like Athanasius, Jerome, and Possidius do not use them. Such miracles appear in the West in the fifth century, are used sparingly at first, and are associated thematically with the saint's reputation in life. For example, in Paulinus's *Life of St. Ambrose* the single posthumous healing, that of the blind man, underscores Ambrose's connection with miraculous sight restorations and the metaphor of illumination associated with Ambrose's interpretation of Scripture. Gregory promotes a different model, however, contending that such supernatural actions in life, although they should not be avoided, are subject to egoism, politics, or even the deeds of the devil. This shift privileged the numinal power of the tomb over the miracles of the charismatic holy man. Gregory promotes the idea of humility and hidden virtue. For example, in his *About Saint Gregory, bishop of Langres*, Gregory records the following incident:

---

[70] Gregory of Tours, *Life of the Fathers*, 37.

so that the people would not think that he took pride in it [his asceti-
cism], he used to hide his meager loaves of barley under the wheaten
loaves, and when he broke wheaten loaves and offered them to people
he was able to take a barley loaf for himself without anyone knowing.[71]

Gregory's championing of posthumous miracles promoted the growth
of cultic centers and patronage to an unprecedented degree. Favors
were now bestowed on the living from the dead mediated by divine
grace. The petition was more efficacious the more the penitent showed
faith in the saint. Such faith was measured through the hardships
suffered for the saint, the degree of difficulty a pilgrim suffered to
reach the cult center, and the gifts offered to the saint. The burial
site became the most hallowed place of association, since the closer
the contact one had with the saint, the more likely the petition would
be granted. These sacred precincts grew in power and prestige. They
were lavishly decorated with multi-colored murals, wall hangings,
and flickering candles by the hundreds, with clouds of incense bil-
lowing in the cramped space. Throngs of pilgrims would surge forward, jostling one another, trying to get as close as possible to the
relics as they sought favors from the saint. In his *About Saint Illidius*
and *About St. Gregory, bishop of Langres*, Gregory reports that cults grew
so rapidly that the old crypts that previously had held their relics
provided insufficient ease of access and had to be expanded. St.
Avitus, bishop of Clermont, enlarged the old structure, building "an
apse of circular shape and admirable workmanship" to display the
saint's bones.[72] Gregory's lives promoted the value of visiting the cultic sites. Being custodian of the shrine of St. Martin was profitable
for Gregory, and the ecclesiastical and lay power that the dead saint
conferred on his see was palpable. In his *About St. Nicetius* he describes
the epileptic servant of Bishop Phronimius of Agde who sought cures
unsuccessfully for years. On the bishop's order, the servant visited
the tomb of St. Nicetius, threw himself in front of the tomb, and
was permanently cured. Such powerful commendations increased the
popularity of these centers, as well as the revenues they provided
the local administrator and his authority. Gregory's support for the
posthumous miracle promoted an important change and facilitated
the growth of cult centers administered by a powerful clerical hierarchy. The cult of St. Martin became so powerful that the Frankish

---

[71] Gregory of Tours, *Life of the Fathers*, 60–61.
[72] Gregory of Tours, *Life of the Fathers*, 39, 63.

kings avoided visiting the city lest they give the impression that they were subservient to the cult and its episcopal administrators.

Benedict of Nursia

Knowingly ignorant and wisely unlearned. (Gregory the Great, *Dialogues*)

It would be difficult to imagine Gregory the Great (ca. 540–604) composing his life of Saint Benedict in Book II of his *Dialogues* without the earlier models of Sulpicius's Martin and Gregory of Tour's *Life of the Fathers*.[73] Yet, although Pope Gregory and Gregory of Tours are near contemporaries and the influence of Sulpicius's Martin is apparent in Gregory's hagiographies—even borrowing miracles from Gregory of Tours for his life of Saint Benedict—Gregory's life of Saint Benedict, marks another shift in the representation of the sacred. Gregory's incorporation of dialogue is a narrative innovation in Christian biography. His use of the dialogue is indebted to two traditions: the first is the polarized court room inquisitions of the *Acts of the Martyrs* presented in the *commentarius*; the second is the classical model, best exemplified by Plato. The personae of Gregory as the benevolent teacher and Peter as the zealous, inquisitive student create a dramatic setting that provides an audience with multiple frames of reference: Benedict and all the individuals he interacts with, as well as Gregory and Peter. The audience receives the story of Benedict through the conversation of Gregory and Peter. Their commentary on the nature of Benedict's miracles, the presence of grace, the saint's concern for his monastery, and his asceticism, makes Gregory and Peter central in the construction of this sacred biography. Peter's questions and Gregory's answers, while pedagogic devices, also serve through synecdoche as the questions and answers of the audience. Miraculous anecdotes are reviewed, questions proposed and interpretations given. The audience, drawn into the narrative, sits, along with Peter, at the feet of Gregory the teacher, becoming participants in constructing the representation of the holy man.[74]

---

[73] Gregory the Great, *Dialogues*, trans. O. J. Zimmerman, ed. R. J. Deferrari, in *The Fathers of the Church* (New York, 1959).

[74] O'Donnell (1995), 70.

What were Gregory's new emphases? For Gregory of Tours, the figure of saint as thaumaturge, as a reservoir of almost magical power, as a posthumous miracle maker who intercedes for his devotees, was central. In Gregory's *Life of Saint Benedict*, however, the emphasis is on the saint as a pastoral mediator of God's grace, whose power is always subordinated to God's and whose deeds focus almost exclusively on the betterment of his new foundation. Of the thirty-six miracles that Gregory attributes to Benedict, only one is posthumous, and even that miracle is accomplished without the woman's knowledge that it was the saint who cured her (II.38). Gregory the Great underscores that Benedict's miracles are *res gestae* done while he lived, sometimes mediated by other worthy individuals, but utterly dependent on God's grace.[75] Most of Benedict's miracles are not dramatic healings or exorcisms but have a pragmatic bent. These miracles typically illustrate his concern that his monastery prosper: the restoration of a lost scythe iron, the removal of a devil who sat atop a large rock and thus impeded the building project, the private healing of the monk hurt while building a wall, or the creation of a well for the use of a monastery. Such utilitarian depictions undoubtedly appealed to a pope beset with a thousand different worldly cares, who likely saw Benedict as an alter ego and longed himself for an opportunity to live the contemplative life. When Gregory does illustrate Benedict's healing power, he does it by shrouding the incident with God's mysterious power. He clarifies the opacity of these anecdotes of the conjunction of the divine in the world through dialog, interrupting the narrative for a colloquy between the fictive figures of Gregory and Peter. For example, in the single resurrection miracle Gregory records, that of Benedict raising the dead peasant child, Benedict, when asked to help, first acknowledges his limitations, claiming that he is unable to work such miracles: "Such miracles are not for us, but for the holy apostles". Benedict prays over the child's body; he does not touch the body, but appeals to God to overlook his sinfulness and acknowledge the faith of the father who asks for the favor: "O Lord, do not look at my sins, but consider the faith of the man who asks that his son be revived". The boy is restored to life. At this point Gregory breaks into the narrative, addresses Peter and comments: "Obviously, Peter, this miracle was not in his

---

[75] Ward (1981), 2.

power. He [Benedict] knelt in prayer and asked that he might per-form it".[76] This comment and Peter's ensuing agreement underline that the power of healing is shared between the holy man and the faithful father, who both receive the gift by God's grace.

Gregory shifts the emphasis from an ideology of the sacred—which depicted the holy man as a powerful, charismatic, spirit filled, mir-acle-worker whose mighty spirit performs miracles—to one that places saintly power within the grasp of the peasant father, the elderly nun, or perhaps even an elderly pope working to maintain his piety beneath an avalanche of secular concerns. Furthermore, Gregory extends this location of God's salvific power even beyond the personal. For exam-ple, Gregory's interest in representing Benedict's primary interest as caregiver for the monastery broadens the emphasis in the life from the figure of Benedict as saint and miracle worker to include the monastery as a center for God's grace. The worshiping community, the ecclesiastical structure, and the Church Triumphant all become the locus of God's mercy and power. Gregory's intent to feature the Church as a principle locus of the divine is indicative of the Church's maturity and his own heart-felt need to illustrate the possibility of realizing the divine in the profane. His life of Benedict is not, how-ever, a repudiation of the saint as charismatic holy man (in figures like that of Anthony, Martin, or in some of Gregory of Tour's bish-ops) but a domestication of the model. Gregory intended his depic-tion of Benedict—and by analogy his own life—to serve as a rebuttal to the traditions of an increasingly bureaucratic papacy that grace and the miraculous can thrive in the tumult of a worldly life.[77]

Far Away Across the Sea

> His face showed a holy gladness because his heart was full of the joy of the Holy Spirit. (Adomnán, *Life of St. Columba*)

The Island of Iona in the late sixth century was the edge of the known world. Europeans who knew of it believed it to be the end of the earth, perched on the edge of the primeval abyss of Genesis (Gen. 1.9), surrounded by a hostile sea inhabited by monsters and

---

[76] Gregory the Great, *Dialogues*, 101.
[77] O'Loughlin (1997), 13.

perils of an unspeakable sort. Orosius in his *Historia Adversus Paganos* considered even the large islands of Ireland and Britain of little importance. St. Patrick, writing in his autobiography, believed Ireland to be in the western sea, the sea of the setting sun at the end of the earth (*Confessio* 23, 34). Bede, writing from the comparative wilderness of Northumbria, noted that the island monastery of Iona was ". . . situated in a remote corner of the world".[78] Although impossibly remote for non-Irish contemporaries, the monastery founded by Columba (ca. 521–97) became a renowned center of spirituality and learning. Columba, according to his biographer Adomnán, was copying a manuscript of the psalms hours before his death.

Little is known of St. Columba, and what we do know is chiefly from Adomnán's (ca. 628–704) life of the saint, written a century after Columba's death (hereafter VC, ca. 688–97), the most nuanced saint's life written in the enormously rich Celtic hagiographic tradition.[79] Columba was a high-born member of the Cenél Conaill family, which ruled much of County Donegal. The first forty years of Columba's life are a mystery, save that a priest/foster father named Cruithnechán raised him. His religious studies would have begun as an adolescent. He subsequently studied theology with a teacher in the prominent school in Leinster and, after being ordained a deacon, studied with a Bishop Uinniau (Findbarr?). Adomnán writes that Columba left Ireland with twelve disciples in 563 for Scotland, wishing to be a pilgrim for Christ/"pro Christo perigrinari uolens enauigauit".[80] Columba's reasons for leaving Ireland for Scotland are unclear and unimportant for our discussion, except Adomnán's insistence that Columba was a pilgrim. The idea of penitential pilgrimage is an early and important part of Irish spirituality and frequently depicted in Irish saints' lives, e.g., St. Brendan the Navigator. Columba's reputation as a prominent, well-connected individual preceded him. Shortly after his arrival in Scotland, he was given the island of Iona (ca. 563–65) by Conall mac Comgaill, king of the Dál Riata (Annals

---

[78] Bede, *A History of the English Church and People*, trans. L. Sherley-Price, rev. R. E. Latham (Harmondsworth, 1986), 147.
[79] Bieler (1962), 248. See also Adomnán of Iona, *Life of St. Columba*, trans. R. Sharp (London, 1991).
[80] Adomnán, *Life of Columba*, ed. and trans. A. O. Anderson and M. Ogilvie (Oxford, 1991), 6.

of Ulster ca. 561; see also the Annals of the Four Masters ca. 555).[81]
He became a force in western Scotland, possibly converting Bridei,
the king of the Picts. He performed the first Christian consecration
of a Celtic king, that of Aedán mac Gabráin of the Dál Riata.[82] He
founded monastic dependencies in the Hebrides, in Scotland and
Ireland, and created from a windswept island on the edge of the
world a center with an international reputation whose brethren, like
Colman, became Abbot of Lindisfarne.[83] His foundations left such
masterpieces as the Book of Kells, the Book of Durrow and his own
Catach.[84]

Adomnán's depiction of Columba borrows liberally from the lives
of Anthony, Martin, Benedict, Germanus, Sylvester and Hilarion, to
name the most important, and was massively influential in later
hagiographies. While the VC illustrates his asceticism, charisma, and
healing gifts—gifts he shared with these worthy predecessors—Adomnán stresses his role as a founder, very possibly reflecting Gregory's
depiction of Benedict. Columba began the monastic settlement on
Iona and was responsible for the spread of its dependent houses and
its international reputation. The VC reads like a literary palimpsest
of these saintly predecessors. Like Athanasius's Anthony, Columba
embodied an ascetic ideal, leaving his native land for a 'desert' island;
like Jerome's Hilarion, his ministry required frequent and arduous
travel; like Sulpicius's Martin he was a miracle worker who evan-
gelized non-Christians, and, like Gregory's Benedict, he founded a
great monastic tradition and nurtured his brethren as their first abbot
to ensure the success of his dependencies throughout the British Isles.
Lastly, like four of these saintly predecessors, Columba's undertaking was most original, according to Adomnán.

It is unclear if copies of these lives were available on Iona in the
late sixth century. Certainly Gregory's *Dialogues* reached Iona by the
early seventh century. Adomnán knew them and used them in constructing the life of his founder and spiritual father. The VC specifically
shows the influence from these lives, from the Gospels and from
Virgil and Juvencus.[85] Since Adomnán believed that Columba shared

---

[81] Bieler (1963), 65; O'Neill (1997), 96.
[82] Macquarrie (1997), 76.
[83] Macdonald (1984), 272.
[84] O'Neill (1997), 96.
[85] Brüning (1917), 241.

in the same grace given to his saintly predecessors, he used encomium, recursivity, *anagnorisis*, and mimesis throughout to make important connections between Columba and these earlier heroes of the Church and, thus, to solidify the reputation of his monastery and founder.

The VC has at least three specific goals: to present Columba as a great saint, equal to any of his predecessors; to deflect criticism of Columba by the Northumbrians and others, concerning the Irish date for the celebration of Easter; and, lastly, to refute the idea, gaining ground at the time, that Iona was a backward center, "barbarous and rustic" according to Bede.[86] Moreover, Adomnán, as the ninth Abbot of Iona (ca. 679–704) and a member of the same family as Columba, was obliged to protect the reputation of the monastery and maintain the dignity of the family name, an important issue since the practice in Irish monasteries was to appoint the abbot from the founding family. A monastery's poor reputation would reflect badly on the family and could damage the family's political standing. Adomnán used the continental tradition of hagiography to illustrate to the civilized world that Iona was a community of great learning, second to none and blessed by God.

Adomnán intended that those who read the VC recognize his scholarship and Columba's rightful connection to the existing tradition of Christian biography.[87] He makes these associations obvious from the outset. For example, the VC's three books deliberately follow the three-fold structure of Gregory's *Dialogues*. There are fourteen clear allusions to the *Dialogues* in the VC. Adomnán opens his life with two prefaces, a calculated borrowing from Sulpicius *Life of Martin* who, in turn, borrowed it from Evagrius's translation of Athanasius's *Life of Anthony*. There are ten references in the VC to Sulpicius's *Life of St. Martin*, his *Dialogues* and *Epistles*.[88] The VC, again like Sulpicius's *Life of St. Martin*, exhibits the influence of hellenistic biography. Columba's life is presented in a three-fold manner, examining deeds (*praxeis*), virtues (*aretai*), and relationships with others (*politeia*). Adomnán begins with a nod to Sulpicius in his adoption of the classical *captatio benevolentiae* trope, taking ideas and sentences, sometimes verbatim, from Sulpicius. For example, Adomnán's second

---

[86] Picard (1984), 60.
[87] Picard (1982), 170. See also Picard (1985), 69.
[88] Brüning (1917), 244.

sentence—"They should be mindful that the kingdom of God comes not from the exuberance of rhetoric but from the flowering of faith"— is from the ninth line of Sulpicius's prefatory remarks to his friend Desiderius in the *Life of St. Martin*. The appropriation is clear as these two selections illustrate:

> VSM: ... qui regnum Dei non in eloquentia, sed in fide constat.
> VC: ... que regnum dei non in eloquentiae exuberantia sed in fide florulentia constare.[89]

If Adomnán was to rehabilitate the reputation of Columba's monastery, he had to associate his predecessor with the most unimpeachable saints.

There are a few instances when Adomnán's narrative raises interesting epistemological issues. For example, in the Second Preface he makes the traditional claim that he will write only the truth and report nothing "doubtful or uncertain"/*quaedam dubia uel incerta scripturum*.[90] Most of the miracles in the VC are drawn from oral testimony. Adomnán rarely claims to have been an eyewitness to Columba's miracles. Yet in his retelling of one of the more important posthumous miracles he claims to have witnessed, he has made significant use of a similar miracle from Book III of Gregory's *Dialogues*. The incident is worth amplifying. Adomnán reports the existence of a severe drought and its miraculous end in God-sent rain. (II.44) After acknowledging that he had been an eyewitness to this miracle (*nostris temporibus factum propriis inspeximus oculis*), he fixes the approximate time of its happening, seventeen years before his writing about it, or approximately 575–80 (*Ante annos namque ferme xuii*).[91] He carefully places these specific historical markers before the anecdote is told. He then tells the story: the monks, suffering from a severe drought, fearing that there would be no harvest, took Columba's white tunic, the tunic he died in, and those books he had personally written, and, after choosing some from among the elders, they caused them to walk around the ploughed land raising the tunic in the air and shaking it three times. They then took his books and read from them atop the hill of the angels where Columba was seen conferring with

---

[89] Adomnán, *Life of Columba*, 2,1a; Sulpicius Severus, *Vie de Saint Martin*, 248.
[90] Adomnán, *Life of Columba*, 6; Sulpicius Severus, *Vie de Saint Martin*, 253–54.
[91] Adomnán, *Life of Columba*, 172.

these divine beings. That very day the sky clouded over and the rain fell. Adomnán underlines the veracity of these events in the next chapter (II.45) by repeating that he witnessed it (*quae ipsi perspeximus fidem indubitanter confirmant*).[92] The actual event he described is, however, closely related to, and was likely borrowed from, an incident reported by Gregory the Great in the *Dialogues* (III.15). Gregory tells his disciple Peter of a posthumous miracle performed with the tunic of the monk St. Eutychius of Noricia. There are a number of interesting parallels between Eutychius and Columba: both were monks, both became abbots, and both nurtured their respective monasteries for many years before their deaths. Gregory reports that there was a serious drought in the area. Eutychius's cloak was brought out by the citizens of the region and held aloft, and prayers were offered while citizens processed through the fields. Invariably the rains would fall shortly after the ceremony concluded.

The miracles are virtually identical. Why would Adomnán insist on being an eyewitness to an account that bore so close a correspondence to Gregory's account of Eutychius and not acknowledge the correspondence? If we accept Adomnán as a reliable narrator, then we must conclude that both events could have taken place. However, that does not adequately explain the similarity of language in the two accounts (*eius tunicam levare Dial.* III.15; *circumirent tunica . . . leuarentque* VC II.44) and the order of events in the two different narratives. It is plausible that the miracle in the *Dialogues* was used by the community of Iona, possibly prompted by Adomnán himself, and ritually performed in order to end their drought. Adomnán then would have reported this event to which he was indeed an eyewitness in the VC. Since the earlier miracle served as the prompt for this event at Iona, Adomnán wished his readers to know—and hence the obvious use of the familiar borrowed language and order—not only that the founder of the Iona community was capable of ending the drought but also that Columba—this representative of a community that some would think rustic and barbarous—possessed the same power as the great leaders of Benedictine monasticism. Adomnán is making use of the rhetorical principle of recursive structures discussed above. The recognition facilitated by the recursive structure subordinates the importance of the actual event on Iona to Columba's

---

[92] Adomnán, *Life of Columba*, 174.

participation in the same grace that Benedict was heir. In this manner it is typologically similar to the attribution to Jesus of the verse from Psalm 21. The historiography is a thoroughly religious one.[93]

The longest episode in the three books of the VC is Adomnán's presentation of Columba's death. The passage is indebted to the Johannine depiction of Christ's death. Columba has just returned to his lodging after vespers. He turned to his companion of many years, Diarmait, and said "I commend to you, my little children, these, my last words: Love one another unfeignedly. Peace. . . ."[94] His last words are a direct quotation of Jesus's farewell remarks to his disciples after the celebration of Passover (John 13:33). Like the miracle of the tunic shared between Columba and Eutychius/Benedict, the repetition of Christ's remarks confers authority on the moment and likewise places the abbot in an unimpeachable place, the bosom of his Lord. Such deathbed farewells follow the Antonian model. Imbedded allusions to the gospels and other saints are common and designed to shroud the penitent in the grace and power of Christ and his saints. For example, in his *Life of St. Cuthbert* Bede appears to have modeled Cuthbert's last moments on that of Columba and places Columba's final words concerning mutual fellowship in the mouth of Cuthbert.[95] Such deliberate rhetorical association is rich with theological and political purpose, as I have been arguing throughout. Adomnán required that Columba's sanctity have an unimpeachable pedigree. The community of Iona had suffered a loss of prestige ever since the Roman position on the dating of Easter and the appropriate tonsure had been decided at Whitby (664) a generation earlier. This quotation from John serves a number of purposes: it shows the intimacy of Christ and Columba; it underlines Adomnán's efforts at illustrating the orthodoxy of Columba and Iona; and, lastly, it provides a basis for reconciling those at Iona and their dependencies, who still did not adopt the Roman position, with Rome, while reminding the world of the importance of Iona.

The tradition of Christian sacred biography would continue to delight and educate medieval audiences. The depiction of Christ in the gospels continued to provide the model (mediated, of course,

---

[93] O'Reilly (1997), 90–94.
[94] Adomnán, *Life of Columba*, 224.
[95] *Two Lives of Cuthbert*, trans. B. Colgrave (Cambridge, 1940), 282–83.

through other saints' lives) for new saints, and, hence, the taxonomy of Christian sanctity was to change only incrementally after the millennium. The saint still had to manifest holiness through a well-established pattern of recognizable topoi: asceticism, miracles, great humility, and/or pastoral ministry. One notable change in the hagiographies of the high Middle Ages, however, is the increased presence of lay people and women as the subjects of Christian sacred biography. For example, while the early Middle Ages did have a number of notable female saints (e.g., Perpetua, Agatha, Macrina, Brigit, and Radegunda), their numbers are comparatively few when compared with their male counterparts. By the early thirteenth century, however, there appears a considerable increase in the composition of lives of lay (aristocratic as well as non-aristocratic) and female saints, possibly under the impetus of the mendicant orders and their zeal to create Third Orders. It is difficult to consider the life of St. Francis without that of Clare, or the importance to Sweden of Bridget (†1373), the mother of St. Catherine (†1381), and the importance to Scotland of Margaret (†1093). Indeed even local cultic heroes who were not members of the clergy and lived according to their own rule—individuals like Richard Rolle of Hampole (†1349), Simon de Montfort (†1265), or Juliana of Norwich (†1416), to take three examples from England—were celebrated as saints and liturgies were sometimes written for them, despite the fact that they never received official canonization from Rome. The narrative tradition of Christian sacred biography continued to make use of the principle of *imitatio* and the use of recursive tropes to bring about *anagnorisis* in the audience. Christian sacred biography remained strong throughout the Middle Ages and was even used to good effect by the sixteenth-century reformers in celebrating their own holy men and women.

PART TWO

LATER MEDIEVAL HISTORIOGRAPHY

.

CHAPTER FIVE

WORLD HISTORIOGRAPHY IN THE LATE MIDDLE AGES

Rolf Sprandel
(Translated by Kristin E. Thomas)

Introduction and Delineation

This article concentrates on world history writing in late medieval Germany, the particular field of research of the author. Mentions are also made of neighboring lands and periods. Using Martin of Troppau and his influence as a point of departure, fundamental questions are addressed which are also valid for other countries.

Martin of Troppau's Pope-Emperor-Chronicle, which extends into the middle of the thirteenth century, marks the end of the historiography of the High Middle Ages.[1] Its object is the world and the crowning figures of that world: pope and emperor. Martin of Troppau relies mainly on sources from Italy and France. Noteworthy is the alignment of the German king and emperor as one of the two poles of world history. (In what follows 'emperor' should be understood as including both king and emperor.)

Additionally, there is a Latin-language world history in Germany, in which a two-pole portrayal is not attested. In this Latin world history, the history of the world extends from Creation to the German empire of the High Middle Ages. This world historiography is written by a series of authors, ranging from Frutolf of Michelsberg to Ekkehard of Aura and Otto of Freising to Burchard of Ursperg. While Martin of Troppau delivers only a short survey of Roman history and otherwise limits himself to Christian times, the afore-mentioned authors reach further back. Since traditionally two world history models competed with one another, namely that of the six

---

[1] Martin von Troppau, *Chronicon pontificum et imperatorum*, ed. L. Weiland, *MGH SS* 22 (1872), 377–475.

epochs of the world and that of the four empires of the world, there are also variations in this respect amongst the authors named above. The world-epochs model is more prevalent. However, Burchard of Ursperg prefers the world-empires model and begins first with the Assyrians. Manuscript C of Frutolf and Ekkehard takes a third route and begins with Charlemagne. This version has been characterized as a Frankish-German folk and imperial history.[2]

In addition to the Latin world historiography, a vernacular world historiography in prose and verse is also attested in the German High Middle Ages. This vernacular historiography, similar to the Latin one, reaches back to pre-Christian times and extends to the German empire.

All three types of world history—Martin of Troppau's and the Latin as well as the vernacular in Germany—are continued in the late Middle Ages, whether written anonymously as in the Codices, or written by attested authors with their own individual conceptions. This is not self-explanatory. The European world suffered a blow as a result of the collapse of the Staufer Empire and the fate of the papacy after 1303. The attempts by German emperors to re-associate themselves with the history of the high medieval empire do not carry much persuasive power. The council movement of the fifteenth century is also too short to provide a new basis for world history.

If one is to examine the motives for the continuation of world history, one must differentiate several layers. In a foundational layer there is, to a certain extent, the autonomous task of continuation, which is addressed, called-upon, and awakened time and again by the chroniclers. The author of the *Saxon World Chronicle* calls for the continuation of his work.[3] Johan Spies of Rattenberg collects, as he states, notes for those who wish to continue the *Flores Temporum*.[4] In the codex of the world chronicle of Johannes of Utino there are blank pages intended expressly for later additions.[5] Conversely, Johannes of Viktring wishes to name his work a *subplementum* [*sic*], because it is intended to expand upon *alia chronicalia*,[6] and the Italian

---

[2] Wattenbach/Holtzmann (1948).
[3] *Sächsische Weltchronik*, verses 77–87, ed. L. Weiland, *MGH Dt. Chron.* 2 (1877).
[4] Riedmann (1970).
[5] Ott (1980/1981); Melville (1980).
[6] Johannes von Viktring, *Liber certarum historiarum*, II.242, ed. F. Schneider, *MGH SS rer. Germ.* 36 (1909).

chronicler Jacobus of Bergamo, influential for Germany, gives his entire work the name *Supplementa Chronicarum*.[7] Heinrich Taube begins his continuation of the *Flores Temporum* with the words: "cupiens . . . gesta supra scripte materie continuanda".[8] Mathias of Neuenburg links his chronicle to the chronicle of Martin of Troppau with the words: "Item incipit cronica . . . a tempore Friderici imperatoris, quo precedens cronica et alie cronice dimittunt".[9]

This task of continuation is not as clearly formulated in the High Middle Ages as it is in the late Middle Ages. It developed to a certain extent out of three other topoi, which appear in the forewords of the high medieval chroniclers: "[the task is] to offer raw material for a later writer to complete, in order that mistakes may be corrected and missing material added".[10] At the same time there is the task of preserving the *res memorabiliores*, whatever these are. Linked to this is the belief in chronology. Only that which can be chronologically ordered and thus inserted remains permanently in the *memoria*.[11] Twinger of Königshofen writes, following Hugo of Fleury: "That which is not fixed remains fable".[12] The reigns of popes and emperors traditionally offer a framework for the chronological ordering.

Part of the foundation of any medieval chronicle, on which world chronicles also rest, is moral doctrine. Indeed, this pedagogic purpose exists with the same fortitude as formulated by Johannes Rothe in the rhymed foreword of his world chronicle: "Present and future are deceitful, elusive, illusory, only the past bears true witness".[13] According to Andreas of Regensburg, as he writes in the foreword of the world chronicle, comprehensive chronicles, among which world chronicles may be counted, are better suited than others for the

---

[7] Jacobus Philippus Foresti von Bergamo, *Supplementum chronicarum orbis* (Venice, 1483).

[8] Heinrich Taube von Selbach, *Chronik, 1294–1362*, ed. H. Breslau, *MGH SS rer. Germ.*, N.S. 1 (1922), 1–132.

[9] Mathias von Neuenburg, *Cronica, 1241/1273–1350 and continuation to 1378*, ed. A. Hofmeister, *MGH SS rer. Germ.*, N.S. 4,1 and 4,2 (1924/1940), 1–500.

[10] Simon (1958–60).

[11] Von den Brincken (1978); Lemke (1953).

[12] Jacob Twinger von Königshofen, *Chronik, bis 1400/1415*, ed. K. Hegel, *Die Chroniken der oberrheinischen Städte, Straßburg* 1 and 2; *Die Chroniken der deutschen Städte* 8 and 9 (Leipzig, 1870/1871), 230–498; 499–910, at 231.

[13] Johannes Rothe, *Thüringische Weltchronik, bis 1440 (= Düringische Chronik)*, ed. R. von Liliencron, *Thüringische Geschichtsquellen* 3 (Jewa, 1859), 1–686, at 4; trans. in part by E. Fritsche, *Chronik von Thüringen* (Eisenach, 1888), 11–254.

aforementioned purpose.[14] The Good, when it is confirmed through many testimonies, *plurimorum noticia*, appears *quanto communius, tanto divinius*.

One layer beyond these motives one finds the ubiquitous *ressentiments* and biases, which may be explained on the basis of the author's experiences and political affinities. These will be elaborated in what follows. Another theme of the following pages is the motivations of an even higher layer, which we will characterize as conceptions. Which ideas could carry such conceptions? The oldest concern of medieval world chronicles is the expectation of the end of the world. A conception that developed from that perspective could be said to have validity independent of the views of the popes and emperors. In contrast, a conception indebted to *Heilsgeschichte* can lend a function to pope and emperor, regardless of the positions of power, which the tradition continues.

Martin of Troppau is more pragmatically, less eschatologically oriented than other world chroniclers of the High Middle Ages. The latter begin with the creation of the world or with the first world empire. One must be cognizant of which of the late medieval writers reach further back than Martin of Troppau in their continuations and thus represent Old Testament and Greek world history.

Whether with weak pope and strong council and in spite of any intervening schism and also despite the more or less recognized splitting-off of the Greeks, the Church remains institutionally Catholic and ecumenical. Among and alongside the authors who continue the work of Martin of Troppau there are pope chronicles that have a world-historical horizon of events, which in turn however relate that horizon exclusively to the papacy. They latch onto either the papal section of the Martin of Troppau chronicle or they continue the older type of church historiography that goes back to Eusebius and with which the *Liber pontificalis* is connected as well, even if the latter belongs simultaneously to the *Gesta* of public officials. In addition to the papal historiography of Avignon, one should mention the Italian Tholomeus of Lucca, whose work is continued in Germany especially by Heinrich of Diessenhofen and Martin of Fulda.[15]

---

[14] Andreas von Regensburg, *Chronica pontificum et imperatorum Romanorum, bis 1438*, ed. G. Leidinger, in *Andreas von Regensburg, sämtliche Werke*, Quellen und Erörterungen zur bayerischen und deutschen Geschichte, N.F. 1 (München, 1903), 1–158; 461–501.
[15] Tholomeus of Lucca, *Historia ecclesiastica nova*, ed. L. A. Muratori, *Rerum Italicarum*

This papal and church historiography does not belong to the world history examined here. In our opinion, it stands in a historiographic tradition that claims not the status of world history but, rather, that of a history of the Church in and against the world. The course is set early for this differentiation. One need only recall that Eusebius published a church history separate from a world history and thereby founded a tradition.[16]

Then one recalls the imperial idealism of Henry VII and Ludwig of Bavaria and the imperial reform plans of Charles IV through Frederick III and Maximilian.[17] To what extent do these provide impetus and foundation for conceiving post-Staufer history as a world empire history? On the other hand, one must consider the rise of regional institutions and authorities. Can one not continue the traditional world history by giving special consideration to the local dynasty, the diocese or cloister, and the city, thereby enhancing their status in relation to others?

The French continuation of Martin of Troppau's history reduces world history first of all to a history of the [Avignonian] papacy, then to French history, and reflects thereby the loss of a world-historical horizon in French historiography.[18] There is no such loss in German historiography. Here there are regional histories with a world-historical classification along with regional histories that contain no such classification. The German imperial history of the late Middle Ages represents one problem. Is it comparable to French national history or is it linked to the Latin and German-speaking imperial history of the High Middle Ages with its claim to world history?

The Saxon world chronicle has an uncertain fate in the late Middle Ages. The so-called First Bavarian Supplement is attached to the Upper German translation, which itself, however, stems not from Bavaria but, rather, from the upper Rhine region. To this Supplement is attached another, which has disparate versions in the various traditions. One such version is the Fourth Bavarian Supplement, which

---

Scriptores 11 (Milan, 1727), cols. 743–1242; Heinrich Truchseß von Diessenhofen, *Chronik, 1316–1361*, ed. J. F. Böhmer and A. Huber, *Fontes rerum Germanicarum* 4 (Stuttgart, 1868), 16–126; Martin of Fulda, *Chronicon*, ed. J. G. Eccard, *Corpus historicum medii aevi* 1 (Leipzig, 1723), cols. 1642–1732.

[16] Chesnut (1977); Grant (1980).

[17] Molitor (1921); Folz (1953); Bader (1954); Angermeier (1958); Dempf (1962); Peuckert (1948/1966); Kampers (1896/1969).

[18] Champion (1907).

will be described later. While a world-historical character can be attested in both the Saxon world chronicle and the Fourth Bavarian Supplement, such a character is lacking in the First Bavarian Supplement. The latter contains more of a listing of *emperor-gesta*, "briefly sketched portraits of rulers" from 1273–1314.[19] "The emphasis on the *emperor* profiles prevents the writing of an imperial history that maintains continuity by neglecting individual history".[20] When Rudolf von Habsburg's decision against relocation to Italy is praised, one could even interpret this as a statement against the traditional world-historical role of the German empire. Other *emperor-gesta* of the period can be similarly interpreted, such as those in Ellenhard's chronicle, which remind one of a history of the Habsburg dynasty. Similarly, the *Gesta* of Henry VII and Adolf, published by K. U. Jäschke,[21] also should be categorized as serving various dynastic, not world-historical, interests.

Thus the *emperor-gesta* introduced here are not to be taken, on the whole, as world histories but, rather, are to be compared to dynastic histories or *gesta* of public officials, as modeled primarily in church history. Despite dynastic approaches, no dynastic history can arise from these due to the character of the German kingdom. Nor do they allow the formation of a national history, as cultivated in Western Europe. We will bracket them in the following investigation.

On that note, we turn to that which can be termed world history in Germany of the late Middle Ages. The number of works is still relatively large, and since we are concerned with typical motifs and conceptions, we will be selective and limit ourselves to prominent examples.

The motifs and conceptions already mentioned can either influence the content or, over and above that, can shape the formal arrangement of the chronicle. It was advisable for the one resuming the chronicle to use the arrangement of the original. Andreas of Regensburg writes in the foreword to his world chronicle that he is writing "ad modum figure scolastice hystorie".[22] It is all the more conspicuous when this does not occur. The chronological interest allows for the

---

[19] Herkommer (1991), col. 491.
[20] Sprandel (1994), 146.
[21] Jäschke (1988).
[22] Andreas von Regensberg, *Chronica*, ed. Leidinger, 4.

use of a structuring according to the reigns of popes and emperors. The connection of world history and *Landesgeschichte* demands a structured treatment. Observations regarding structures, tendencies as regards content, and the authors' explanations regarding conceptions will be the methodological tools for transmitting the motifs and conceptions of world chronicles.

High Middle Ages	Martin of Troppau	*Flores Temporum*	Latin world chronicles in Germany	Vernacular world chronicles in Germany, Saxon world chronicle and Upper German translation
Around 1350	Johann of Viktring, Mathias of Neuenburg	Munich world chronicle, Heinrich Taube		
1350–1400	Cologne world chronicle, Heinrich of Herford, Closener, Konrad of Halberstadt, Twinger of Königshofen			
Beginning of the 15th century	Andreas of Regensburg, Gobelinus Person, Johannes Rothe, Dietrich Engelhus			
Middle of the 15th century	Thomas Ebendorfer, Platterberger/ Truchseß, Monk Albert		Fourth Bavarian Supplement of the Saxon world chronicle	
End of the 15th century	Hartmann Schedel, Nauclerus, Konrad Stolle, Rolevink, Johannes Meier			

Chronological Order of the Chronicles

The chronicles in question can be divided into several temporal categories. First one should mention those whose own period of recording is connected directly to that of Martin of Troppau, in particular Johann of Viktring and Mathias of Neuenburg.

We find the closest approximation of a German national history in the imperial history of Johann of Viktring. Indeed, he apparently worked himself slowly toward this conception, after having wanted at first to embed a younger Austrian *Landesgeschichte* in an imperial history, using refined Latin and the model of classical historians.[23]

---

[23] Moraw (1987); Fichtenau (1975).

This goal also is achieved. However, he creates a history of the Franckish and German empires by reverting to—in a second manuscript—the time following the rise of the Carolingians. The national view is apparent in the solidarity of the chronicler with the emperor, for instance in the concluding remarks on Ludwig of Bavaria 1343: "He sails by high seas, and yet remains hopeful that he will throw his anchor in a peaceful harbor and trusts in that with an unshakeable soul".[24] The world-historical task of the German empire comes often to the fore, as for instance with the election of Rudolf von Habsburg:

> This is a man, whom God chose with his heart, in divine providence from the beginning of the world forward, he is destined. The kings of England, Spain, and Bohemia were present at his election. His coronation was carried out according to the old statute of Charlemagne and in the manner in which the anointing of Solomon takes place, according to the Old Testament.[25]

Johann of Viktring is among the few chroniclers of the late Middle Ages who do not see themselves actually in the role of someone writing a continuation, even if he does have most of his material (as regards content) from previous sources, especially Martin of Troppau. He conceives of his task as literary. He wants to create a literary work of history. As if of their own accord, the materials flow for him into subdivisions according to *certae historiae*, under which he understands there to be an exchange of the actions of German emperors and Austrian dukes with the bias of a certain imperial nationalism, in which an Austrian *Landesgeschichte* is embedded.[26]

The next chronicle has another profile. Mathias of Neuenburg continued Martin of Troppau, but altered the organization of Troppau's work in his own continuation. Neuenburg does not place pope and emperor opposite each other but, rather, organizes the chronicle's overall structure according to the German emperors and builds in separate chapters for each pope appropriate to the emperor. The pope chapters are nearly inconspicuous in relation to the diverse bits of contemporary news from Spain and Scotland to Lithuania. He positively characterizes the Habsburg kings and the functioning of

---

[24] Johannes von Viktring, *Liber certarum historiarum*, ed. Schneider, II.235.
[25] Johannes von Viktring, *Liber certarum historiarum*, ed. Schneider, I.215–16.
[26] Schnell (1989).

the Habsburgers as dukes in the Alsatian region. Events from Basel and Strasbourg are also weighed heavily. A *Heilsgeschichte* is missing.

While the enhanced status of the country in the overall frame of world history certainly did play a role for Mathias, this enhanced status does not become an organizational principle for him, in contrast to others. Neither is his work characterized by imperial idealism. One must satisfy oneself with viewing Mathias in the role of a writer continuing previous work. This role gives him the opportunity to spread a sober, Christian, humanistic worldview, shaped by topoi such as the backwardness of the world and key concepts such as the *potentia* that brings everything into being.[27]

Chronicles that link up with the *Flores Temporum* should be included in this first category of world chronicles.[28] The *Flores Temporum* are a departure from Martin of Troppau, but they do include a detailed depiction of the first five epochs. The conception of *Heilsgeschichte* is thereby strengthened vis-à-vis Martin of Troppau.

In their original version, the *Flores Temporum* ordered the pope and emperor sections parallel to each other on opposite pages, as in Martin of Troppau's version. The *Flores* contained in numerous manuscripts also contain copies in which chapters on pope and emperor alternate. In contrast to Mathias of Neuenburg, the pope chapters have not been slipped into longer emperor chapters. Rather, pope chapters follow completed emperor chapters. In a third group of manuscripts, papal history and imperial history are handled subsequently in one sequence or another and are completely self-contained. We know from the studies of Anna Dorothée von den Brincken that the numerous copies of Martin of Troppau also contain both of these models that depart from the order of the original version.[29]

Current research differentiates several stages within the continuations of the *Flores Temporum*. A first stage extends to 1313. Some researchers observe in this stage a stronger consideration of imperial history than previously attested. "The death of Henry VII, unlike almost any other death of the previous 500 years, represents a great loss for the entire world".[30] In this stage of the continuation, the

---

[27] Bossard (1944); Moraw (1987); Sprandel (1994), 43–53.
[28] *Flores temporum*, ed. O. Holder-Egger, *MGH SS* 24 (1879), 226–60.
[29] Von den Brincken (1985, 1989).
[30] Mierau (1996).

pope section has been added to the emperor section according to the orders of the three previously mentioned models. The pope section deals with problems of the Catholic Church as a whole and with friction between mendicant orders and local parish priests. The author of this stage of the text also amends older sections of the *Flores* with additions of imperial historical material and, in so doing, alters the profile of the chronicle as a whole.

The latter also applies to the second stage of continuations, which extends to 1349/1350. This second stage adds not onto the first continuation but, rather, onto the original *Flores*, and it offers a different text that parallels the first stage for the period extending to 1313. It is now known in three printed versions,[31] but its tradition is wider still. Characteristics of the content include a critique of Boniface VIII and sentiment against the papacy of Avignon that succeeds him, as well as a statement in favor of Ludwig of Bavaria regarding his conflict with the papacy.

While the *Flores* continuations up to this point have, for the most part, similar content at every stage, they split after 1349/1350 into regionally colored, individual histories that vary significantly in content. In part, they still maintain the pope-emperor arrangement and still can be considered world histories in that respect. Some, however, let this drop. The former is true for the Munich world chronicle, in which pope and emperor chapters alternate.[32] The second stage of the *Flores* continuations breaks off after depicting Charles IV's ascension to the throne with the help of many gifts. The Munich world chronicle continues this tendency, in particular with regard to the papacy of Avignon. There is a gap with Charles IV, but this king is mentioned with Urban V in a critically distant tone.

Heinrich Taube occupies a special position.[33] He also continues the *Flores*, but must not be compared with the continuations considered so far, for he offers his own original text extending to 1363. Heinrich Taube also has the pope and emperor chapters following each other. Following a chapter about Innocent VI (†1362) is a chapter about Charles IV, which, however, breaks off in the middle of

---

[31] Eckhart (1723); Eysenhard (²1750); Sprandel (1994).
[32] *Münchener Weltchronik*, ed. R. Sprandel, in *Chronisten als Zeitzeugen* (Köln, 1994), Anhang 2.
[33] Heinrich Taube von Selbach, *Chronik*, ed. Breslau.

his rule in 1363. A certain Bavarian emphasis in the material is thereby established, which is also conditioned by the fact that the chronicler is located in Eichstätt. With this emphasis, Heinrich Taube's chronicle is very similar to the Munich world chronicle. Nonetheless, the emphasis already is weakened by virtue of the fact that Heinrich Taube is writing simultaneously a history of the bishops in Eichstätt, which can take up regional aspects. With the trinity of pope, emperor, and bishop history, he creates a new sequencing model that will be realized elsewhere somewhat later and independently of him. Heinrich Taube occupies a special position among the writers of *Flores Temporum* continuations also by virtue of his position toward the emperors Ludwig of Bavaria and Charles IV, as well as toward the popes of Avignon. Heinrich Taube stood in circumstances in Eichstätt that forced him to judge Ludwig negatively in the conflict with the curia and to represent Charles IV correspondingly positive. Thus, both Heinrich Taube and the Munich world chronicle demonstrate how locally conditioned *ressentiments* among authors of the same work can lead to opposingly structured texts.

To the second category belong those chroniclers who stand in the tradition of Martin of Troppau but do not link up with him directly. Rather, these chroniclers require intermediary links to his chronicle and period. First we should mention Closener and Twinger of Königshofen.[34] As Klaus Kirchert shows, Closener and Twinger connect world history and city history with each other in many respects.[35] Their works differ insofar as one can regard Closener as a preparatory work for Twinger. Closener begins with a rudimentary pope catalogue, most likely derived from Martin of Troppau. He then continues with a detailed imperial history, which he creates first out of material from Martin of Troppau, then from Ellenhard's chronicle [*Chronicon Ellenhardi*][36] and the First Bavarian Supplement of the Saxon world chronicle. The Strasbourg section that is added has a double theme: the bishop history and the civil city history. In the former, the *Bellum Waltherianum*, the author inserts the battle between

---

[34] Fritsche Closener, *Chronik, bis 1392*, ed. K. Hegel, *Die Chroniken der Städte oberrheinischen Städte, Straßburg* 1, *Die Chroniken der deutschen Städte* 8 (Leipzig, 1870), 1–151; Twinger of Königshofen, *Chronik*, ed. Hegel.
[35] Hofinger (1974); Kirchert (1993).
[36] *Chronicon Ellenhardi*, ed. P. Jaffé, *MGH SS* 17 (1861), 122–44.

bishop and city in the thirteenth century and a kind of early war monograph. The civil city history is arranged according to over-arching themes such as fires, war marches, persecutions of Jews, et al., which in turn are ordered chronologically and contain regional sources, including again the *Chronicon Ellenhardi* among others.

Twinger, in contrast, reinforced the embeddedness in world his-tory by preparing a book about the first five [world] epochs. He relies there mainly on the Latin world historiography of the German High Middle Ages. The books about emperors and popes follow this one. Already the order of both is reversed, in comparison with Closener, which also certainly is meaningful. For the younger emper-ors, Twinger relies additionally on Mathias of Neuenburg. Both parts, but in particular the pope section, are considerably amended, using also excerpts from Martin of Troppau. A history of the bishops of Strasbourg follows, as with Closener (there the third part, in Twinger the fourth part). For each, twenty-five pages became seventy-five pages in the editing. At the beginning of this bishop-history, Twinger lets it be known once more how important it is for him that the *Landesgeschichte* be anchored in world history. He reports the supposed first episcopal appointment in Strasbourg by King Dagobert and embeds this in the chain of imperial history beginning with the Romans by considering the relationship of Romans, Franks, French, and Germans.

The civil urban history of Strasbourg that follows begins again with a history of origin. Then comes the history of Christianization and the city's expansion. Increasingly, Twinger comes closer to Closener's scheme and orders the materials according to subject. The sixth part comprises a register of key words arranged in alphabeti-cal order. This register can be classified as belonging with the remain-ing lexicographical works of Closener and Twinger. Kirchert is, unfortunately, too brief with respect to the chronicles. However, he places the lexicographical works beyond the framework of mere scholastic purposes and—probably correctly—understands them as specific, tradition-rooted "organizational structures, which the mind places upon the world being depicted".[37] By virtue of their arrange-ment and classification, along with the combination of *Landesgeschichte*

---

[37] Kirchert (1993), 136.

and the need for chronological factual certainty, which we also find elsewhere, Closener, and even more so Twinger, follow an encyclopedic conception in their world history, which places these authors in a special position.

Another important author of the second category is Heinrich of Herford.[38] He uses an epochal history and in the sixth epoch continues the work of Martin of Troppau, bridging the time since the end of Martin's chronicle with western European chronicles, the dynastic history of Levold of Northof (referred to the counts of Mark in the region of Lower Rhine), and others. Heinrich of Herford provides material to the pope-chronicler Konrad of Halberstadt, but appears in turn to have borrowed material from the latter as well.[39]

Heinrich of Herford, who organizes according to emperors, markedly accents *Heilsgeschichte*. The notions of a seventh and eighth epoch, which go back to Augustine and are further developed by Konrad of Halberstadt, are indicated in Heinrich as well.[40] At the same time, the organization according to emperors is not exactly without conceptual meaning. He has an anti-papal orientation, belongs most likely to the opponents in Minden of the bishops provided by the pope, and shows a bias toward Ludwig of Bavaria. He objects to Charles IV, who was favored by the pope, yet at the same time sees in his reign close ties to *Heilsgeschichte*, as well as signs of the coming apocalypse in his election and the events of his first years.[41]

Heinrich of Herford transforms the dynastic history of Levold of Northof page by page into an imperial history, although, incidentally, this is not apparent in the otherwise-so-useful edition of A. Potthast. Konrad of Halberstadt transforms Heinrich of Herford completely into a papal history.[42] The work of Konrad of Halberstadt must be characterized, in contrast to the papal histories mentioned above, as world history, because it has the same richness of material as Heinrich of Herford and likewise is conceived within a framework of an apocalyptic *Heilsgeschichte*.

---

[38] Heinrich von Herford, *Liber de rebus memorabilioribus sive Chronicon, bis 1355*, ed. A. Potthast (Göttingen, 1859), 1–291.

[39] Leng (1996).

[40] Haeusler (1980).

[41] Sprandel (1994), 67–82.

[42] Konrad von Halberstadt, *Chronographia Interminata 1277–1355/59*, ed. R. Leng (Wiesbaden, 1996).

The Cologne world chronicle[43] is comparable in a more modest sense with Closener and Twinger of Königshofen. This world chronicle links up with older world historiography by means of the Cologne continuation of Martin, and it is arranged similarly to a Cologne bishop chronicle, just as the two Strasbourgians introduce Strasbourg histories alongside the papal and imperial history.

The emphasis of the chronicles belonging to the third category lies in the early fifteenth century. First we have to mention the world chronicle of Andreas of Regensburg. Andreas writes a pope- and emperor-chronicle in the tradition of Martin of Troppau, whose work he enriches with materials from the Latin world chronicling of the High Middle Ages. He bridges the period following the end of Martin's chronicle with *Flores Temporum* continuations and Bavarian *Landesgeschichte*. Continuations of the Saxon world chronicle are produced as well.

Andreas of Regensburg considers a three-way scheme in two ways: First, the names of popes and emperors in the manuscript are emphasized with red double circles, the bishops of Regensburg with black double circles. In places he also writes papal, imperial, and even episcopal history in two or even three columns, thereby creating a synopsis as Martin of Troppau once did. Second, he later works the material of the world chronicle into a Bavarian dynastic chronicle.

Formally speaking, Regensburg takes on greater importance with reference to the Quaternion doctrine, according to which Regensburg is one of the capitals of the empire along with Rome, Cologne, and Trier.[44] Nevertheless, one would not wish to characterize the bolstering of *Landesgeschichte* as Andreas's main intention. He ends his world chronicle in 1422 but promises to describe future events as long as he lives[45] and, indeed, argues this intention until 1438. He views the chronicler as somehow bound by duty to *memoria*. To remain silent in times of general need would be a sign of despair (659 in a dialogue about the Bohemian heresy). The pope-emperor scheme is thus merely a tradition-bound framework for a fostering of memory, which considers in particular the regional relations.

---

[43] *Kölner Weltchronik, 1273/1288–1376*, ed. R. Sprandel, *MGH SS rer. Germ.*, N.S. 15 (CITY, 1991), 33–119.
[44] Andreas von Regensburg, *Chronica*, ed. Leidinger, 8; Schubert (1993).
[45] Andreas von Regensburg, *Chronica*, ed. Leidinger, 150.

Andreas mentions in his foreword the *alveus* of papal-imperial history, through which the *rivuli* run, the "tempora sanctorum et virorum illustrium ac cetera quedam digna memoria".[46] It appears as if he were searching for a new form of historical description. Yet in the end this disappears in the annalistic scheme with regional historical emphasis.

Comparable to that is the world chronicle of Johannes Rothe, in which, however, Thuringian history carries even more weight than Bavarian history did for Andreas. Johannes Rothe proceeded, in contrast to Andreas, from *Landesgeschichte* to world history and works his previously edited Thuringian history into a world history, with which he goes back to the history of creation. To that end, he uses Ekkehard of Aura with continuations and Martin of Troppau, among others.[47] In the rhymed preface to the world history, he announces that he wishes to write about heathens, Jews, and Christians, partly also about the ruling class of Thuringia, and about "was bebiste, keiser haben gethan von wunderlichen dyngen" [what kinds of wonderful things popes and emperors have done]. The Franks drove the Romans out of this land. Following that, the landgraves of Meißen came.[48] The chronicler's main motivation was probably to place his own country in a prized position by placing it within a world-historical frame.

The world chronicle of Gobelinus Person carries the author-given title *Cosmidromius* [The Way of the World] and demonstrates thereby the claim to worldliness. Over and above that, the conception of the work is not completely recognizable today, since the edition of Max Jansen—nearly one hundred years old—is reliable only with respect to the sections on contemporary history.[49] From the previous sections, only spot samplings have been printed, and the record of sources in the introduction raises questions as well. It seems doubtful that—as Jansen believes—authors such as Eusebius, Jerome, Flavius Josephus, Prosper, and so on were used directly and not via the medium of another large world chronicle. It seems possible that the *Cosmidromius* is indeed a continuation of Martin of Troppau. However,

---

[46] Andreas von Regensburg, *Chronica*, ed. Leidinger, 4.
[47] Patze (1968), 95–168, in particular 121 seq.
[48] Johannes Rothe, *Thüringische Weltchronik*, ed. von Liliencron, 8, 9–10.
[49] Gobelinus Person, *Cosmidromius, bis 1418*, ed. M. Jansen (Münster, 1900), 1–243.

it is a chronicle of six epochs and used, along with individual writings, other world chronicles (probably Ekkehard in particular) for the pre-Christian sections.

Following the period covered by Martin of Troppau, Gobelinus Person mixes chapters on popes alternately with chapters on emperors. This scheme falls by the wayside with the eruption of the schism. The *Cosmidromius* produces a very intensive history of the Roman papacy up to the Council of Constance and also a history of Paderborn by going back and forth to a certain extent between these two foci of the history, which the author himself personally experienced. The history of six epochs becomes a sort of contemporary book; it becomes world and regional history from an individual perspective. At the same time, as he writes in the introduction, the author is driven by the notion of apocalypse ("finibus seculorum, qui in nos devenerunt") and writes, in connection with Daniel 2:35: "Visiones capitis mei conturbaverunt me".

The world chronicle of Dietrich Engelhus builds on Gobelinus Person. He also alternates between chapters about individual emperors and individual popes but goes beyond Gobelinus Person in implementing the scheme: he shortens the history of Urban VI to be proportionate to the histories of the other popes. He builds similar chapters for the popes and emperors who follow, up through Martin V and Sigismund. When he wrote his chronicle in 1422/1423, the world supposedly had only a few years left. He himself continues the chronicle up through 1433. After that, others continue the writing. Various years are given for the end of the world: 1421, which he can easily reject. He did not live to experience 1467, another year proposed.[50]

With that, we come to the next and penultimate category. In the middle of the fifteenth century, Thomas Ebendorfer splits world history into two clearly separate works: an imperial history and a papal history. The papal history, written later, is conceived of as a counterpart to imperial history: "After having depicted the *gesta* of the emperors [. . .], I would now like to work out the catalogue of the popes in a similar fashion (*similiter*)".[51] Thus, with respect to exter-

---

[50] Dietrich Engelhus, *Weltchronik, 1101/1115–1395/1420*, ed. G. W. Leipniz, *Scriptores rerum Brunsvicensium* 2 (Hannover, 1710), 977–1143, at 1142.

[51] Thomas Ebendorfer, *Chronica pontificum Romanorum*, ed. H. Zimmermann, *MGH SS rer. Germ.*, N.S. 16 (1994), 53–553, at 53–54.

nal form, one could view Thomas Ebendorfer as continuing Martin of Troppau. As regards content, one can confirm partly that both histories of Thomas Ebendorfer belong to world history, more for the imperial history and less so for the papal history. In the papal history, Ebendorfer repeatedly laments the times and the *machina mundi*, which is being shaken.[52] At the same time, this work differs in several respects from a world history. It is written at a temporal distance to imperial history and has had a separate history of transmission. The papal history stands, by virtue of the reliance on the *Liber pontificalis*, in a tradition of church historiography. Finally, it is placed in this tradition by virtue of its content, even if in a new spirit. The curia is criticized. A church without a papacy becomes conceivable. In contrast to his imperial history, Thomas Ebendorfer's papal history in the whole cannot be considered a world history.

For imperial history after 1273, Thomas combines Johann of Viktring, Andreas of Regensburg, and Heinrich Taube with Austrian *Landesgeschichte*.[53] Thomas Ebendorfer's imperial history is world history because it reaches back to the Assyrians, is organized according to four world empires, and is occupied with the High Middle Ages only in the sixth book (the seventh book constitutes an amendment of the whole with new material). The *directiones*, which are attached with a certain pedantry to every reign of an emperor, lend the book a moralistic tone, which Thomas emphasizes expressly in prefaces as well. By dedicating the work to Frederick III, it takes on almost the character of a royal mirror, which represses the *heilsgeschichtlichen* character. It remains world history because it is intended to educate an emperor. Only a world history could offer historical education for an emperor.

In Nuremberg, Platterberger and Truchseß write a chronicle that is organized according to popes and emperors.[54] In the section organized according to emperors, Nuremberg histories are included under special headings. The chronicle goes back to the creation of the

---

[52] Thomas Ebendorfer, *Chronica pontificum Romanorum*, ed. Zimmermann, 22, 53.

[53] Thomas Ebendorfer, *Chronica regum Romanorum, 1346–1458* (= *Annales imperatorum Romanorum*), ed. A. F. Pribram, Mitteilungen des Instituts für Österreichische Geschichtsforschung Erg.bd. 3 (Wien, 1890/1894), 96–112; 150–213.

[54] Johannes Platterberger and Theoderich Truchseß, *Eine deutsche Weltchronik, bis 1409*, ed. D. Kerler, *Chroniken der fränkischen Städte, Nürnberg 3, Die Chroniken der deutschen Städte 3* (Leipzig, 1864), 268–305.

world and relies mainly on Vincent of Beauvais for the Old Tes-
tament/Greek history according to earlier world epochs.[55] Research
has been concerned up to this point mainly with the first volume of
the two-volume chronicle—that is, the Old Testament/Greek history. Until 1979, the second volume was known only in excerpts
from Hartmann Schedel, and the main areas of interest were the
events that related to Nuremberg.[56] It appears, however, that this
second volume is a continuation of Martin of Troppau and that it
uses for the remaining period nearly every world chronicle that had
been written in Germany since Martin.

The main characteristic of the work is certainly the manifest task
of developing for Nuremberg that which other regions already have:
the embedding of regional history in world history. Correspondingly,
the author announces in the foreword that he will describe "the
actions and histories of the Old and New Testament for the glory
of God and the honor of the imperial city Nuremberg".[57] In the
chapter on Charles IV, the authors select, from among the various
sources at their disposal, the positive portrayal of this king provided
by Heinrich Taube. In that regard, they reveal the interests that
influence their writing of Nuremberg history, for Charles IV did
much to secure the traditional form of the council government in
Nuremberg.

The Fourth Bavarian Supplement to the Saxon world chronicle
is an individual work that has been attributed to an anonymous
author from Ingolstadt or Neuburg-on-the-Danube. This chronicle
is comparable to the Thuringian world chronicle in that events of
Landesgeschichte nearly obfuscate the horizon of world history. However,
not only the connection of this chronicle to the Saxon world chronicle but also its unmistakable connections to world history—from the
imperial "*kleinodien*" to the Hussite and the Turkish wars—give this
chronicle a place among world chronicles.

The monk Albert, who has papal history and imperial history follow each other in two sections, belongs to the chroniclers of the
fourth category.[58] He describes himself as someone who is continuing

---

[55] Schnell (1986); Weigand (1991).
[56] Schneider (1991).
[57] Platterberger and Thuchseß, *Deutsche Weltchronik* 260.
[58] Mönch Albert, *Weltchronik, 1273/1277–1454/1456*, ed. R. Sprandel, *MGH SS rer. Germ.*, N.S. 17 (1994), 37–328.

the Cologne world chronicle, which stands in the tradition of Martin of Troppau. He uses Heinrich of Herford and Gobelinus Person as sources as well. Since neither a *landesgeschichtliche* nor a *heilgeschichtliche* perspective comes to the fore, we must see the monk Albert primarily in the role of a continuator.

The last temporal category concerns world-historical incunabula and early printing. The largest in the German realm are the chronicles of Rolevinck, Nauclerus, and Hartmann Schedel, works of differing qualitative and quantitative rank but which all, nonetheless, deliver a world history.[59] Research into the sources for these works is difficult and incomplete. Especially the latter two have a strong influx of events from Italian world histories that shapes their content. Despite this, they remain conceptually comparable to earlier world histories of Germany. Rolveninck and Hartmann Schedel offer once again, as did Martin of Troppau in his original version, synoptically comparable papal and imperial history on the same or opposing pages. A portrayal of this kind is surprising, because such an external similarity to Martin of Troppau did not exist very frequently in the time between Martin and these chroniclers. One might see in this a desire for the establishment of links and for continuation, which represents a force in opposition to the marked innovations made in the content. However, even the content has strong elements of continuity. We will not delve any further into Rolevinck, for whom the research is still especially incomplete.[60]

Hartmann Schedel adds, as do Heinrich of Herford and Konrad of Halberstadt, a seventh and eighth world epoch. Before he makes a few geographical excursions after the eighth world epoch, he provides a picture of Emperor Frederick III and Pope Pius II in conversation—a symbol of mutual world rule. For the first five world epochs, Schedel's main source is Jacobus of Bergamo, who likewise ordered his work in world epochs. In the sixth world epoch, various works of Aeneas Silvius become the main source. Silvius was not a world chronicler of any sort, but wanted to transmit humanist knowledge of lands and peoples through his texts. This message is

---

[59] Werner Rolevink, *Fasciculus temporum, bis 1474*, ed. J. Pistorius and B. G. Struve, *Rerum Germanicarum Scriptores* 2 (Regensburg, 1726), 397–576; Johannes Nauclerus, *Memorabilium omnis aetatis et omnium gentium chronici commentarii (= Chronicon universale, bis 1500)* (Köln, 1579); Hartmann Schedel, *Chronicon mundi, bis 1492* (Nürnberg, 1493).
[60] Baer (1973); Johanek (1988).

taken up by Schedel and combined with the traditional scheme.[61] The generation scheme of Nauclerus should be identified as original organizational model. The generation comprises thirty years. The Old Testament has sixty-three generations. In the sixth Age dating from the birth of Christ, there are forty-five generations by 1350, and then another five by 1500. This scheme allows Nauclerus to look away from pope and emperor and to combine everything from the various sources that is worthy of being remembered in the history of mankind—to which indeed an ordering of ages refers directly.

In the same period as the authors previously mentioned, Konrad Stolle writes the most important of the various continuations of the Thuringian Johannes Rothe's world chronicle.[62] In contrast to those previously mentioned, Stolle is no longer published in the time of the incunabula and early printing, but did live on at least in the realm of Thuringian *Landes*-historiography.[63] At the same time, however, this did not reverse the expansion of *Landesgeschichte* that Johannes Rothe undertook in his world history. Rather, he pushed the contextual emphasis on the world-historical horizon even further. He does not return to the pope-emperor scheme but, rather, orders his subjects thematically by listing histories under individual headings.

The unpublished papal chronicle of Johannes Meyer represents a special case. Meyer writes a history of the Dominican Order and uses the pope-emperor scheme in order to allow the treasure of privileges and the events in Dominican history to be assigned chronologically to the popes and emperors. Something parallel to the combination of *Landes*- and world history is obviously at work here. Here, not a country but, rather, an order is placed in the world frame.[64]

Summary

The question posed at the outset regarding the conception of world history in the late Middle Ages demonstrates the considerable multi-

---

[61] Joachimsen (1910); Rücker (1988).
[62] Konrad Stolle, *Memoriale, bis 1502*, ed. R. Thiele (Halle, 1900), 31–526.
[63] Patze (1968), 107–08; Proksch (1994).
[64] Albert (1898).

facetedness and variability of historical thought in this period. We are focusing our considerations on world history in the more narrow sense. Papal histories, which belong to the clearly different but related category of church history, are bracketed in the same way as those imperial histories which do not claim to be an actual part, much less center, of a world history but, rather, wish to give prominence to personalities in the manner of a herald. Alternatively, they are approaches to dynastic history or are comparable to official *gesta* promulgated in the sphere of the Church.

Even the world histories in a more narrow and actual sense offer a plethora of conceptions. As expected, each chronicler views himself most frequently in the role of a writer continuing previous work and, especially in the first category, as a writer continuing one or several world histories of the High Middle Ages. With the later chroniclers, there is the question of links. Thomas Ebendorfer uses Johann of Viktring, and also the other chronicles presented here as exemplary come up again and again elsewhere, for example: Mathias of Neuenburg appears in Twinger of Königshofen and once again is used directly in Nauclerus. The *Flores Temporum* and the Saxon world chronicle (Upper German translation) have their own series of continuations that follow them.

Among chroniclers of the second category, Closener should be mentioned before Twinger, for whom Closener is the most important source. Closener demonstrates the growing ability of the chroniclers to combine several sources. He bridges the period between the chronicles of the High Middle Ages and his own time with material from Strasbourg as well as with a Saxon world chronicle continuation. Closener thus belongs to those who add material from other forms of chronicling into a conception of world history. The situation is similar with Heinrich of Herford, who utilizes *Landes*-historical as well as western European chronicles, and Andreas of Regensburg, who connects the *Flores Temporum* with Bavarian material.

It continues in the same way in the next category: Platterberger and Truchseß link up several of the world chronicles mentioned here with Nuremberg material. The monk Albert describes himself expressly as a writer continuing the Cologne world chronicle, which in turn is based on a Cologne continuation of Martin of Troppau. At the same time, Albert utilizes (without expressing it) Heinrich of Herford and Gobelinus Person. Gobelinus Person himself finds in Dietrich Engelhus yet another continuator. Johannes Rothe belongs to the few who do not fit in the role of a continuator, even when he is writing out sources. However, he does not annex *Landesgeschichte* to world history as the others do. Rather, he expands *Landesgeschichte* into world history. Konrad Stolle, in turn, continues him. Thomas Ebendorfer, in contrast, is similar to the continuator type. In his imperial history, he combines Austrian material with world-historical material from Andreas of Regensburg, with the *Flores Temporum* and others.

The treasury of sources is greatest at the end of the Middle Ages and is utilized by the educated chroniclers such as Rolevinck, Hartmann Schedel, and Nauclerus. Through their work they testify to the lively circulation of handwritten chronicles. At the same time, one does not wish to place them at the side of the older authors as writers of continuations or sequels. Along with the Italian sources, they consciously bring a new element into world chronicling, some more so and others less so. Despite the continuation of the pope-emperor scheme by two of them, the organization is altered according to geographical sections (in Schedel) and biographical sections (in all three).

The most important conception of world history in the Middle Ages is certainly *Heilsgeschichte* with a view to the end of the world. This conception does not come to the fore in all the chronicles dealt with here, but it remains alive in the field investigated by us and even stays intact after passing over the threshold of humanistic changes, as we see in Hartmann Schedel especially. One must differentiate between those world histories which produce the link to *Heilsgeschichte* only by means of the formal organization of world epochal or world imperial history and those which, in the end, reveal an individual occupation with the question of apocalypse. The *Flores Temporum* and the Saxon world chronicle with its continuations, Johannes Rothe, Platterberger and Trucheß, Thomas Ebendorfer, Rolevinck, and Nauclerus belong to the former, while Heinrich of Herford, Konrad of Halberstadt, Gobelinus Person, Dietrich Engelhus, and finally Hartmann Schedel belong to the latter type of world history. For Gobelinus Person, the occupation with apocalypse is embedded in a portrayal of history from the perspective of the individual, which reflects his going back and forth between Rome and Westphalia.

It also follows from that which has been presented that numerous chronicles connect world history with *Landesgeschichte*. Related to that, we can mention only briefly another question posed in the introduction, namely to what extent chronological interests allowed the world chronicles to come into existence, simultaneously connected with the need for a stabilization and maintenance of the past. More than the others, Andreas of Regensburg expresses the task of the historian as cultivator of the past. The prizing of *Landesgeschichte* is comparable with the prizing of the Dominicans in the world chronicle of Johannes Meyer.

The chronological imperative is injured at several characteristic points, in Closener and Twinger with the thematically structured city histories, in Konrad Stolle, and in the humanistically influenced chroniclers of the last category. Comparing the latter with Closener and Twinger, a moment of transformation in the Middle Ages becomes apparent: the move from the older encyclopedic interest with its strong symbolic ties (based on Isidore of Seville) to a worldly knowledge, which includes the posthumous fame of the great spirits and the information-hungry *wanderlust*.[65]

Political currents underlie the conceptions described here that influence our chroniclers. They are evident even in Mathias of Neuenburg, even if a critically neutral restraint seems to be his attitude toward them. The currents do not remain everywhere under the surface but, rather, force their way into the formal conceptions to a certain extent. This occurs, for instance, when Johann of Viktring begins his imperial history with the Franks, or when Heinrich of Herford groups the same material according to emperors which Konrad of Halberstadt arranges according to popes. The period of Ludwig of Bavaria is especially eventful. Not only Johann of Viktring and Heinrich of Herford but also the second continuator of the *Flores Temporum* and Heinrich Taube write in this period.

A direct connection of world histories to imperial ideology and imperial reform endeavors is rarely as demonstrable as it is in Johann of Viktring. However, a connection may exist nevertheless in several cases. This connection is most clear in Thomas Ebendorfer, whose imperial chronicle would not have gained such an aspect of worldliness had he not served the empire of Frederick III for many years.

---

[65] Gmelin (1927); Billanovich (1958); Kirchert (1993), 136–37.

CHAPTER SIX

HIGH AND LATE MEDIEVAL NATIONAL HISTORIOGRAPHY

Norbert Kersken

An inspection of the European cultural circle shows that, in almost all systems of rule on a national basis until the beginning of the sixteenth century, a tradition of historiography had developed that was bound formally and substantively to national criteria. Four temporal periods can be differentiated in the chronology of the documents of this historiography. These temporal emphases, in which the writing of national historical portrayals in various regions are concentrated, are the first quarter of the twelfth century, the period around 1200 and the third quarter of the thirteenth century, the fourteenth century, and the second half of the fifteenth century.[1]

Development of the National Historical Form of Expression in the First Quarter of the Twelfth Century

In the first quarter of the twelfth century a national historical historiography developed according to a remarkably similar timetable in several European regions, marking the onset of a tradition. Two groups of regions can be typologically differentiated here. First, the regions in the west of Europe, in which national historical reflection linked up with a political and geographical terminology from late antiquity and the migration of the peoples and took as its reference the *gentes* of the migratory period and their historiography. On the Iberian peninsula, in France, and in England, the traditional regional terms *Hispania*, *Gallia*, and *Britannia* and the histories of the Goths, the Franks, and the Anglo-Saxons, as well as the historical drafts

---

[1] In the following, only the text editions, as well as a very select list of the most important and newest literature, will be given. In general, see Kersken (1995).

formulated by Isidore of Seville, Gregory of Tours, and the *Liber historiae Francorum* or Bede, became prerequisites for high medieval historiography. Second, in several territories north and east of *Romania*, first attempts at national history had been formulated since the eleventh century, in which the introduction of these 'new' regions to the medieval conception of history first had to be developed and established.

In France, historiography experienced new impulses in several places in the first years of the twelfth century. The most important were the monasteries of Fleury on the Loire and Saint-Denis in Paris. At Fleury, Hugo (1118/35) wrote the *Historia modernorum*,[2] a history of the west Frankish-French empire from 842 to 1102. At Saint-Denis, the *Gesta gentis Francorum*[3] appeared, which later was taken up into the *Grandes chroniques de France*.

At approximately the same time in England,[4] under Henry I, the third ruler of Norman descent, a revival of historiographic interest began. First the monk John at the monastery at Worcester undertook the task of combining the universal chronicle of Marianus Scotus of Mainz (1028–82/83) with the *Anglo-Saxon Chronicle*, which began with its information about English history in the year 450, the traditional date for the beginning of the Anglo-Saxon conquest of the island.[5] John continued the account to 1140. An English national history arose thereby, which was to a certain extent based and embedded in universal history yet also oriented according to the annalistic skeleton of the two foundational works. Due to this minimal advance in form and interpretation, one can still speak here of a conceptionally Anglo-Saxon historical understanding.

At the same time however, in the second and third decades of the twelfth century, there arose a new historiographic beginning, which created structures for a new, Anglo-Norman conception of history. In the monastery of Malmesbury, which stood under the

---

[2] Hugo, *Liber qui modernorum regum Francorum continet actus*, ed. G. Waitz, *MGH SS* 9 (1851), 376–95. Cf. Bautier (1994), 69–72.
[3] Cf. *Repertorium fontium historiae medii aevi, primo ab A. Potthast digestum*, vol. 4 (Rome, 1976), 728.
[4] For a standard work on medieval English historiography, see Gransden (1974) and (1982).
[5] *The Chronicle of John of Worcester*, vol. 2, *The Annals from 450 to 1066*, ed. R. R. Darlington and P. McGurk; vol. 3, *The Annals from 1067 to 1140 with the Gloucester interpolations and the continuation to 1141*, ed. P. McGurk (Oxford, 1995, 1998).

patronage of the king, the monk William (ca. 1095–1142/43), librarian of the monastery who has been dubbed "the best-read man of the twelfth century",[6] developed a rich literary output.[7] Following extended travels to libraries, he wrote, around 1124/25, a comprehensive depiction of English history, the *Gesta Regum Anglorum*,[8] to which followed a systematic portrayal of the English church history in the *Gesta Pontificum Anglorum*.[9] As a contemporary continuation of the *Gesta Regum*, he wrote the *Historia Novella* in the last years of his life.[10] William of Malmesbury was supported in his historiographic activities by prominent representatives of the Anglo-Norman royal house, first by Edith-Mathilde (†1118), the wife of Henry I; following her death he was supported by Robert of Gloucester (ca. 1090–1147), an illegitimate son of Henry I. By virtue of this, as well as with respect to the conception of his historical work, William can be counted as one of the few medieval English historians close to the king.[11] He was, after Bede, the first to reflect upon and structure the totality of English history beyond a purely annalistic portrayal. He arranged his work in four books: the first, beginning in 449, describes the history of the Anglo-Saxon kingdoms up through the attainment of political unity under Egbert of Wessex; the most comprehensive book, II, describes the time from the beginning of the ninth century through the end of the Anglo-Saxon period in 1066; and the three following books finally are concerned with the reigns of the first three Anglo-Norman rulers: William the Conqueror, William Rufus, and Henry I. William of Malmesbury's historical work may be regarded content-wise as the Anglo-Norman version of English history. Against the background of a strong kingdom of Norman ancestry, he is concerned with the formation of a new kind of unity in English historical consciousness arising from the coming together of Anglo-Saxon and Norman traditions.

---

[6] Thomson (1975), (1976), and (1979), 321.

[7] An overview of his work can be found in Thomson (1975), 395–96, and (1976), 334–35.

[8] William of Malmesbury, *Gesta Regum Anglorum. The History of the English Kings*, ed. R. A. B. Mynors et al., General Intro. and Comm. by R. M. Thomson, 2 vols. (Oxford, 1998, 1999).

[9] William of Malmesbury, *De gestis pontificum Anglorum libri quinque*, ed. N. E. S. A. Hamilton, RS 52 (London, 1870); engl. trans.: William of Malmesbury, *The Deeds of the Bishops of England* (*Gesta pontificum Anglorum*, trans. D. Preest (Woodbridge, 2002).

[10] William of Malmesbury, *The Historia Novella*, ed. K. R. Potter (London, 1955).

[11] See Gransden (1975), esp. 363–64, 375, 377.

A few years after the completion of William's *Gesta*, Henry, archdeacon of Huntingdon in central England (ca. 1080/85–1155/56), wrote
independently of William a very differently oriented English history.[12]
Encouraged by his superior, Bishop Alexander of Lincoln, he worked
on this work continually from around 1130 until 1154, to which fact
six different editions testify. The different (vis-à-vis William) historical
approach announces itself already in the title *Historia Anglorum*. Henry
writes the history of *Britannia*—this geographical term had no meaning for William—as well as the history of the peoples dominant there:
the Romans, Anglo-Saxons, Vikings, and Normans.[13] Henry of Huntingdon delivers here not a mere depiction of the historical course
but, rather, a conscious and decisive interpretation of English history. Accordingly, English history is filled with the outward threat
and conquest of foreign peoples; he interprets this as plagues sent
by *ultio divina*, which bring into view God's constant involvement in
history. The *Historia Anglorum* is therefore meaningful for English
national-historical thought because it reveals an important turning
point. Henry attempted to go beyond the usual starting point of
English history and reached back to the Trojan ancestor of the British
already mentioned in the ninth century, the eponymous *Brutus*, and
also mentioned the legendary Arthur. Herewith a theme was addressed
that simultaneously provided a new basis for English historical thought.

Around 1135, Geoffrey of Monmouth (ca. 1090/1110–1155) wrote
a *Historia Regum Britanniae*,[14] in which he depicted in detail the pre-
Roman and pre-Anglo-Saxon history of the British island, a period
which had not been thematized previously in English historiography.
Henry of Huntingdon became acquainted with this book during a
trip to Rome in 1139, in the monastery of Bec in Normandy.
However, he could not decide to rework his depiction of English
history accordingly; rather, he relayed the content to the Breton
Warin in a letter, which he included later in a supplementary eighth
book.[15] The reason for this contradictory attitude can be found in

---

[12] Henry of Huntingdon, *Historia Anglorum: The History of the English People*, ed. and
trans. Diana Greenway (Oxford, 1996).
[13] Book I: *De regno Romanorum in Britannia*; Book II: *De Adventu Anglorum*; Book III:
De Conversione Anglorum; Book IV: *De Regno Anglorum*; Book V: *De Bellis Dacorum*; Book
VI: *De Adventu Normannorum*; Book VII: *De Regno Normannorum*.
[14] *The* Historia Regum Britanniae *of Geoffrey of Monmouth*, ed. A. Griscom (London,
1929; repr. Genève, 1977). See also Gillingham (1990).
[15] Book VIII: *De summitatibus rerum. Exemplar autem secunde epistole, de serie Britonum
hoc est (558–583)*.

the new approach of the Monmouth historical conception, which was not reconcilable with the previous version going back to Bede. What remains clear is that various elements and interpretatory approaches to English history developed in the years around 1120/30, which shaped English historical thought for centuries: the depiction of English history as the history of kings, the interpretation of English history as history of the British island as shaped by various peoples, and the invention of the oldest, Trojan-British period.

These themes were picked up again in further depictions in the following period. Around 1135/40, Geffrei Gaimar, a secular cleric in the service of Ralph Fitz Gilbert and his wife Constance, wrote an *Estoire des Engleis*,[16] an outline of English history in the Anglo-Norman (old French) language in the form of a chronicle in verse. In the unpreserved opening section he depicts the beginnings of English history in the version of Geoffrey of Monmouth. This innovation was also taken up in the *Historia de gestis regum Britanniae*[17] by the canon Alfred, working around 1143 in the southern border territory of Northumbria at Beverly Minster (southeast of York). This work, however, clearly shows the difficulty inherent in bringing into harmony Geoffrey's history of the British period with the depiction of its two other authorities, Bede and Henry of Huntingdon. In contrast to these and to William of Malmesbury, he introduces a new historiographic concept. He depicts the development of the *regnum Britanniae* on the *insula Britannia*, whereby he reveals a returning interest of national-historical historiography, the proof of the great age of one's own nation and its system of rule: he emphasizes that the *regnum Britonum* is older than that giant of European historical thought considered up to now to be the greatest in relation, the Roman Empire.[18]

The first attempts at writing 'Spanish' history were undertaken during this period on the Iberian peninsula.[19] These historiographic efforts awake special interest, because there was no 'Spain' either in the sense of a nation or a political entity in the Middle Ages. The

---

[16] Geffrei Gaimar, *L'Estoire des Engleis*, ed. A. Bell, Anglo-Norman Texts 14–16 (Oxford, 1960). See also Bell (1976).

[17] *Aluredi Beverlacensis Annales, sive Historia de Gestis Regum Britanniae, Libris IX*, ed. Thomas Hearne (Oxford, 1716).

[18] "Unde liquido apparet multo esse antiquius regnum Britonum quam regnum Romanorum" (I:22).

[19] For medieval Spanish historiography, see Sánchez Alonso (1947); Linehan (1993); and esp. Cirot (1904).

point of departure for all high medieval syntheses was the Gothic history of Isidore of Seville.[20] A first compilation was undertaken by Pelayo, 1098/1101–1130 and 1142–43 bishop of Oviedo, the former capital of Asturia (†1153). Around 1118, Pelayo put together a compilation of chronicles, the so-called *Corpus Pelagianum*, which began with Isidore's history of the Goths and was supplemented with a chronicle by Pelayo himself for the eleventh century.[21] The significance of Pelayo, who stands in disrepute due to his forgeries in favor of his diocese, consists in the fact that he places the Leon-Castilian kingdom in the tradition of the Isodorian Goths for the first time and thereby postulates a 'Spanish' historical context. The so-called *Crónica Nájerense*, compiled in the middle of the twelfth century in the Clunaic abbey of Santa María de Nájera (Rioja), represents a further development.[22] The three books of the chronicle offer, following a universal-historical introduction, a portrayal of 'Spanish' history up to the beginning of the twelfth century from a Castilian perspective.

The two earliest texts presented here date already from the eleventh century. They refer to the youngest system of rule at the time, the dukedom of Normandy, which underwent a politically and constitutionally independent development since 911 in the north of the West Frankish empire.[23] Commissioned by the ruling duke Richard I, Dudo (ca. 965–before 1043), a canon from Saint-Quentin who was in diplomatic legations at the Norman court, began in the years 994 to 1015 to write a comprehensive depiction of the history of the Norman rulers, a *Gesta Normannorum*.[24] Dudo refers to Frankish historical thought, which since the seventh century had claimed descent from the Trojans and, thereby, historically equal worth with the Romans, and he claims for his part that the ancestors of the Normans, the *Daci* or *Dani*, descend from Antenor, who fled from Troy. In the depiction of the Viking-Norman heroic early period, the legendary Hasting, who, as the "archetypical Northman",[25]

---

[20] Cf. the article by Pizarro in this volume.

[21] *Crónica del obispo Don Pelayo*, ed. B. Sánchez Alonso, Textos latinos de la Edad Media española 1 (Madrid, 1924). See also Fernández Conde (1971).

[22] *Crónica Nájerense*, ed. A. Ubieto Arteta, Textos Medievales 15 (Valencia, 1966).

[23] On Norman historiography generally, see Boehm (1969).

[24] Dudo of Saint Quentin, *De moribus et actis primorum Normanniæ ducum*, ed. J. Lair, Mémoires de la Société des antiquaires de Normandie III, 3 (Caen, 1865); English trans.: Dudo of St. Quentin, *History of the Normans*, trans. E. Christiansen (Woodbridge, Suffolk, 1998).

[25] Davis (1976), 54.

personifies the epoch of mass robberies and land acquisitions, stands at the center, although he is not yet connected with the history of the dynasty of later Norman dukes. The dynastic-historical aspect is first addressed in the second book, which is dedicated to the political accomplishments of Rollo (927/32), the first Norman ruler in a historical sense. The most comprehensive part deals with the portrayal of Richard I, the Norman ruler who prompted the first historical treatment of the entire context of the formation of Norman rule. Dudo's historical work is historiographically and historically meaningful, because it attempts, on the one hand, to place itself—in literary respect with the choice of the form of *gesta ducum/regum*—in the tradition of Carolingian historiography. On the other hand, it recognizes for the first time that a 'new people', a people without tradition-forming roots in the area of Roman-Frankish European culture, conceives of itself as a political unity in the early national sense and thereby tethers itself typologically through the appropriation of the Trojan genealogy to the models of older European historical thought.

One generation later, after the middle of the eleventh century, historiographic activity transferred its location from the Norman court to the cloisters. William, a monk at Jumièges, took Dudo's portrayal of Norman history as the point of departure for *Gesta Normannorum ducum*, which he had dedicated to the Norman duke William around 1070/71, after the latter's ascension to the English throne.[26] The conception of the work, to dedicate a book to every Norman duke, remained the same, but its significance was incomparably greater, because his work was much more widely distributed in written form (47 manuscripts) and, furthermore, was continued several times following the completion of William's version. The two most important revised versions originated around 1109 at Saint-Évroul by Orderic Vitalis (1075–1142/43) and around 1139 at Bec by Robert of Torigny (around 1110–86).

In the second decade of the twelfth century in the cave-monastery of Kiev, older annalistic depictions were compiled in three versions, following shortly on each others' heels, into a comprehensive portrayal of old Russian history, the *Povest' vremennych let*, the first version

---

[26] *The* Gesta Normannorum Ducum *of William of Jumièges, Orderic Vitalis and Robert of Torigni*, 2 vols., ed. E. M. C. van Houts (Oxford, 1992/95).

of which (1110/12) goes back to the monk Nestor.[27] The depiction
of the historical context of the Rus' was indebted to its imbedded-
ness in the Byzantine world chronicle (Georgios Hamartolos), which
led in the depiction to retention of the annalistic frame of depiction.
This also led to the consideration of the central paradigm of Old
Russian historical-political thought, namely that of the Russian territory (*russkaja zemlja*), while the idea of an ethnic substratum that
ensures the unity of Russian history is hardly developed.

At approximately the same time, a first attempt at writing Polish
history[28] was undertaken. The author was an unknown clergyman
of foreign, probably north French, origin, who was located at the
Krakow ducal court and is referred to as Gallus Anonymous. Around
1113/17 he wrote *Cronicae et gesta ducum sive principum Polonorum*,[29] literarily a very carefully composed work that is divided into three
books. He devotes his attention mainly to the ruling duke Bolesław
III, whose life and deeds take up more than half of the entire work.
This directs attention to the background of the writing and to the
intended reception of the work; it was written in a time of domestic-
political crisis in the rule of Bolesław, who had his older half-brother
Zbigniew blinded in 1112 after years of fighting for sole power. For
his own rehabilitation as well as for political safeguarding, he not
only underwent acts of penance such as pilgrimages but also made
the first attempt at writing Polish history, which placed his rule and
the Piast dynasty in a larger context that reflected on the entirety
of Polish history and thereby legitimated it. It should be emphasized
that Polish history begins, accordingly, not with the beginnings of
the Polish people but with the origin of the dynasty.

Shortly thereafter, in the years 1119/25, the canon Cosmas of
Prague (ca. 1045–1125) wrote a *Chronica Boemorum*.[30] The depiction
is organized with an annalistic skeleton in three books, which are
each divided into chapters. It also contains predominantly contem-

---

[27] *Povest' vremennych let. Po Lavrent'evskoj letopisi 1377 g*, ed. V. P. Adrianova-Peretc,
D. S. Lichačev, 2 vols. (Moskva-Leningrad 1950). See also Noonan (1983); Hannick
(1995).

[28] On this topic, see Dąbrowski (1964).

[29] *Galli Anonymi Cronicae et gesta ducum sive principum Polonorum*, ed. K. Maleczyński,
Monumenta Poloniae Historica Nova Series 2 (Kraków, 1952). See especially Plezia
(1947); Deptuła (2000).

[30] *Cosmae Pragensis Chronica Boemorum*, ed. B. Bretholz, *MGH SS rer. Germ.* N.S. 2
(1955). See also Třeštík (1968).

porary material and arose in the context of lengthy inner-dynastic conflicts, based on which the author pleads for a strong ducal power. The chronicle depicts the Bohemian national and territorial history from beginnings that are not to be got around, beginning—in the wave of the dispersion of peoples following the construction of the Tower of Babel—with the seizure of land in the hitherto unsettled Bohemian basin under the leadership of the ancestor Boemus (which late medieval historiography czekifies to Czech), after whom the new territory is named *Boemia*. This aspect of the history of the people and country is complemented by a discourse on the history of ruling powers, in which is depicted the end of the 'Golden Age' of societal equality under the *lex nature* by means of the establishment of ducal power and the overnatural legitimation of the ruling dynasty of the Przemyslids. The version of Bohemian history drafted by Cosmas therefore sparks particular interest because it marks the rare case in which people, dynasty, and territory are related historiographically.

Elaboration and New Beginnings in the Thirteenth Century

In the thirteenth century, especially in the decades around 1200 and in the third quarter of the thirteenth century, one observes a renewed concentration of the writing of national historical texts, whereby four developments can be distinguished: the continuation of the national-historiographic tradition founded in the first half of the twelfth century without decisive conceptional innovations; the adoption of an older tradition that is conceptionally revised; the new beginning in Norway and Denmark of comparable historiography on a national basis, where previously there had not been records of that sort; and finally the founding of a vernacular national-historical tradition in France and Spain[31] as well as in England, each in the 1270s.

In Bohemia the national historiography of the thirteenth century experienced no new impulses. The only reference text remained the chronicle of Cosmas of Prague, which was continued several times: directly following the death of Cosmas by an anonymous canon at the Prague Vyšehrad; then in the 1170s by a monk in the cloister

---

[31] See Uitti (1985).

at Sázava; and, finally, in the 1280s by a canon of the Prague cathedral chapter.[32]

In England in the first decade of the thirteenth century, the monk Gervase from the monastery of Christ Church in Canterbury wrote a *Gesta regum Britanniae*, an outline of English history from Brutus to 1210[33] as pure royal history, since no such continuations had been undertaken since the middle of the twelfth century. As regards the content, it is worth mentioning that the Monmouth draft of early British history makes up, quite understandably, the beginning part of the depiction.

Other English histories up to the end of the thirteenth century are remarkable in that they are integrated in the framework of a universal-historical beginning portion. First the writings of Ralph de Diceto (ca. 1120/30–1202/03) should be mentioned. Distinguished by his position as dean of the London cathedral church and his special closeness to the court of Henry II Plantagenet, he began work in the 1180s on a large-scale universal-historical excerpt project, the *Abbreviationes chronicorum*,[34] in which he placed the older English history in world-historical contexts. Contemporary history (*tempora moderna*) begins for him in 1147/48 with the beginning of the political influence of Henry II, which he deals with in a work of its own, the *Ymagines historiarum*.[35] In the structure of his depiction it becomes apparent that he is not interested in English history in the traditional sense; rather, his selection is geared toward the dynastic interests of his king. He thus devotes little attention to the oldest history of *Britannia* and the Anglo-Saxon period, but considers the non-English territories of the Angevin empire, the dukedom of Normandy, and the earldom of Anjou. Such a 'Plantagenet conception' of English history, a connection of historiographic conception to dynastic coincidences, then admittedly lost its basis with the end of the personal union.

---

[32] Ed. Josef Emler in *Fontes rerum Bohemicarum, Prameny dějin českých*, vol. 2 (Praha, 1874), 201–69; *Pokračovatelé Kosmovi*, ed. M. Bláhová and Zdeněk Fiala (Praha, 1974).

[33] Gervase of Canterbury, *Gesta Regum*, in *The Historical Works of Gervase of Canterbury*, vol. 2: The Minor Works, ed. W. Stubbs, RS 73.2 (London, 1880), 3–324.

[34] Ralph de Diceto, *Abbreviationes Chronicorum*, in *The Historical Works of Master Ralph de Diceto*, Dean of London, ed. W. Stubbs, vol. 1, RS 68.1 (London, 1876), 1–263. See also Zinn (1977); Duggan and Duggan (1980).

[35] Ralph de Diceto, *Ymagines Historiarum*, in *The Historical Works of Master Ralph de Diceto, Dean of London*, ed. W. Stubbs, vol. 1, RS 68.1 (London, 1876), 265–440; vol. 2, RS 68.2 (London, 1876), 1–174.

More significant in this respect was the historiography that was developed in the monastery of St. Albans in the middle of the thirteenth century. The *Flores historiarum* begun by Roger of Wendover (†1236) was developed by his student Matthew Paris (ca. 1200–59) into the *Chronica Majora*, a voluminous embedding of English history in universal history.[36] From this rich material, Paris wrote several excerpts, which demonstrate his interest in offering a whole depiction of English history: the *Historia Anglorum*[37] and the *Abbreviato chronicorum Angliae*[38] limit themselves to the Anglo-Norman period, covering the period from 1067 to 1253 and 1000 to 1255; while the *Flores historiarum*[39] begin, like the initial text, with the creation of the world.

A historiographic new beginning and the end of the monastically influenced national historiography are marked by a chronicle whose author, Robert of Gloucester, is hardly comprehensible. The rhymed chronicle in Middle English[40] attributed to him has been passed down in two versions and ends with its depiction in 1270; the independent account of the years 1258 to 1270, detailing the serious conflicts between the king and aristocratic opposition, reveals an aristocratic bias on the part of the author. With respect to the biased content as well as the choice of the vernacular, on the basis of which one can assume a noble lay public as the audience, this historiography expresses a national consciousness that is not bound to the kingdom.

In France in the time of Philip II Augustus, the ground was laid for a historiography which built up the idea of French history above the history since the beginning of the rule of the Capetian dynasty through dynastic-historical constructions. The corresponding draft goes back to Andrew of Marchiennes, who detected the *reditus regni Francorum ad stirpem Karoli* for Philip II in the *Historia succincta de gestis et successione regum Francorum*[41] in 1191/96. At the same time, the monk Rigord in Saint-Denis, which since the time of Abbot Suger (1081–1151) had developed as the location for the upkeep of the official

---

[36] Matthew Paris, *Chronica Majora*, ed. H. R. Luard, 7 vols., RS 57.1–7 (London, 1872–83). See also Vaughan (1958); Lewis (1987).

[37] Matthew Paris, *Historia Anglorum*, ed. F. Madden, 3 vols., RS 44.1–3 (London, 1866–69).

[38] Matthew Paris, *Abbreviatio Chronicorum Angliae*, in *Historia Anglorum*, vol. 3, 151–348.

[39] *Flores historiarum*, ed. H. R. Luard, 3 vols., RS 95.1–3 (London, 1887).

[40] *The Metrical Chronicle of Robert of Gloucester*, ed. W. A. Wright, 2 vols., RS 86.1–2 (London, 1887). See also Pafford (1957); Hudson (1966).

[41] See Werner (1952); Spiegel (1971).

historiography of the French crown, canonized the Trojan prehistoric concepts into the version that was later taken up in the *Grandes chroniques*.[42] This dynastic-historical process is essential for French historical thought: with its claim of a Trojan-Merovingian-Carolingian-Capetian continuity, it emphasized the tradition and legitimacy of the central political power, less than that of the *populus* and its ethnic substratum. These approaches were carried over into the vernacular by the monk Primas in Saint-Denis in the 1270s and expanded into a unified depiction, the *Grandes chroniques de France*,[43] which may be regarded as a unique foundational text of national historical thought, continued through to the end of the Middle Ages and existing in early printed form.[44]

The writing of the foreigner Gallus Anonymous should be classified as a predecessor to, rather than a foundation for, Polish national historiography. More influential was the *Chronicon Polonorum* of Vincent Kadłubek (1160/61–1223), published nearly one century later, around 1200.[45] Following studies in Paris and possibly Bologna, Kadłubek was leader of the Krakow cathedral school, provost in Sandomierz, and bishop of Krakow; after his resignation (1217/18) he died as a Cistercian monk. The first three books of the chronicle are in the form of a dialogue, unusual for a historical work, between the bishop Matthew of Krakow (1143–66) and the archbishop John of Gniezno (1146–66). Only the contemporary account from 1173 and onward in the fourth book is offered as a historical account of the author. More important than this choice of form, however, were Kadłubek's innovations in content as regards understanding of Polish history, a shift towards the history of the people.[46] His first book depicts the pre-Piastic period, which is introduced as the heroic early period of the Poles in the face of the successful confrontation with the greatest commanders of antiquity, Alexander the Great and Caesar.

---

[42] Folz (1983/84), 195–96.

[43] See Spiegel (1978), 28–29, 36–37, 40–52; Guenée (1986).

[44] Printed in Paris, 1477 and 1493.

[45] Vincent Kadlubek, *Chronicon Polonorum*, ed. M. Plezia, Monumenta Poloniae Historica. Nova Series 11 (Kraków, 1994). As for the date of origin of the chronicle, which reaches to 1202, until now it has been accepted that it was the time before its commission by the bishop of Krakow (1208); Jan Powierski (1997) now proposes the date of composition of this chronicle in the time after Vincent's resignation (1217/18), in the years 1218–21.

[46] For a compelling new interpretation of this early historical outline, see Banaszkiewicz (1998).

Furthermore, Kadłubek explains that there were already important kings of the Poles and several dynastic breaks in this time, through which the meaning of the Piastic dynasty for the unity of Polish history is relativized. Kadłubek's chronicle, written in the environment of Krakow's Duke Casimir II, remained until the end of the fifteenth century the definitive reference work for Polish history.

The political success of Castile in the Reconquista under Ferdinand III (1217–52) stands in direct relation to the foundation and achievement of a Spanish-Castilian national historiography. At the beginning stands Lucas of Túy (d. 1249), school headmaster and after 1239 bishop of Túy in Galicia, who wrote a *Chronicum mundi*[47] around 1236/39 at the request of Berenguela, daughter of Alfonso VIII and mother of the later Ferdinand III. This chronicle, embedded in universal history through the chronicle of Isidore of Seville, constitutes a depiction of Spanish history up to the seizure of Córdoba by Ferdinand III in 1236.

The historiographic break from the León perspective of Lucas to the Castilian view of Spanish history is ascribed to Rodrigo Jiménez de Rada (ca. 1170–1247), who was already active at the court of Alfonso VIII and became archbishop of Toledo in 1208. As chancellor of Castile and advisor to Ferdinand III, he was one of the most important politicians of Spain in the first half of the thirteenth century. In the last years of his life he dedicated himself to a comprehensive project of 'Spanish' history, a compendium of the history of the people who had shaped the history of the Iberian peninsula: a *Historia Romanorum*,[48] a Roman history up to Caesar, a *Historia Hugnorum, Vandalorum et Suevorum, Alanorum et Silingorum*,[49] a *Historia Ostrogothorum*,[50] and a *Historia Arabum*.[51] The nucleus was the *Historia de rebus Hispanie* or *Historia Gothica*,[52] dedicated to Ferdinand III. The

---

[47] Lucas of Túy, *Chronicon mundi ab origine usque ad Eram MCCLXXIV*, in *Hispaniæ illustratæ seu urbium rerumque Hispanicarum . . .*, ed. A. Schotti, vol. 4 (Frankfurt, 1608), 1–116. See also Reilly (1976).

[48] In Rodrigo Jiménez de Rada, *Historiae minores. Dialogus libri vite*, ed. J. F. Valverde and J. A. Estévez Sola, *CCCM* 72C (1999), 37–57.

[49] Rodrigo Jiménez de Rada, *Historiae minores*, 58–78.

[50] Rodrigo Jiménez de Rada, *Historiae minores*, 79–86.

[51] Rodrigo Jiménez de Rada, *Historiae minores*, 87–149; also Rodrigo Jiménez de Rada, *Historia Arabvm*, ed. J. Lozano Sánchez, Publicaciones de la Universidad de Sevilla, Filosofía y letras 21 (Seville, 1993).

[52] Rodrigo Jiménez de Rada, *Historia de rebus Hispanie sive Historia Gothica*, ed. J. F. Valverde, *CCCM* 72 (1987). See also Reilly (1985).

nine books can be arranged into three representative blocks, which correspond to the three epochs of 'Spanish' history: the Gothic period; the period of the supremacy of the Asturian-León empire from the beginning of the eighth to the beginning of the eleventh century; and the time of the Castilian dominance since Ferdinand I (1035–65). The historiographic construction of a political center of 'Spanish' history from the first settlement of the peninsula to the Gothic period, to the supremacy of Asturia-León and then Castile presumed the development of a Gothic tradition and legitimacy, which led to the fact that the people not classifiable here, above all the Romans and the Arabs, who also shaped Spanish history, are, while not erased, handled as *universitas oppressorum*[53] of the Spanish-Gothic people in separate writings. Within this understanding of history, the historical self-understanding of the archdiocese of Toledo and the political legitimacy claims of the Castilian kingdom found their way to each other.

This conceptual innovation found acceptance and popularity one generation later, around 1270/74, under Alfonso X the Wise (1252–84) in the most important national historical text of the Spanish Middle Ages, the *Estoria de Espanna* or *Primera Crónica General de España.*[54] Although oriented primarily around Jiménez de Rada, Alfonsian historiography evidences several important changes: The choice of the Castilian vernacular for this text suppressed Latin as the language of historiography until the rise of the influence of Humanism in the middle of the fifteenth century. The text, divided in chapters throughout, is organized into two major large parts. The first section depicts the first settlement of Spain and the history of Spain under the individual peoples, who appeared here as shaping history: the Greeks, the *almuiuces* (Celts? Normans?), the Carthagians, Romans, the Vandals, Silings, Alans, and Sueves, as well as, finally, the Goths. This systematic inclusion of all peoples having shaped history in Spain shifts the historical understanding from the older Gothic-Spanish accent to a history of the peninsula, of *Hispania*. The second section for the period since the beginning of the Reconquista under Pelayo of Asturia is organized according to rulers and displays, according to selection

---

[53] Thus Rodrigo in the foreword to his Roman History: *Historia Romanorum* (as n. 48), Prologus, 37.
[54] *Primera Crónica General ó sea Estoria de España que mandó componer Alfonso el Sabio y se continuaba bajo Sancho IV en 1289*, ed. R. Menéndez Pidal, 2 vols. (Madrid, 1955). See also Menéndez Pidal (1946); Catalán (1963); Martin (1991).

and valuation of materials, the León-Castilian interpretation of history. The *Estoria de Espanna*, as Spanish-Castilian national chronicle, subsequently stimulated several revisions and continuations up to the end of the fifteenth century.

A comparable courtly national chronicle that goes back to the beginning of the twelfth century can be reconstructed for Hungary, although it was first handed down in its late medieval textual format.[55] A decisive modification in Hungarian historical thought occurred at the end of the thirteenth century with Simon of Kéza, who probably studied in Italy and was court chaplain to Ladislas IV (1272–90). Kéza's *Gesta Hungarorum*,[56] finished in 1282/85, is the oldest surviving depiction of Hungarian history. He based this on the existing version of the national chronicle, adding the so-called Hungarian Hun-history. This history claims that the Hungarians, who settled the Carpathian basin at the end of the ninth century, stemmed from the Huns of the fifth century and are to be equated with the latter, which results in the often-used nomenclature *Huni sive Hungari*. Their eponymous ancestors, the *patres Hungarorum*, were Hunor and Magor, who descended from Noah's son Japhet and point already to the Hungarians/Magyars. The Hunnish king Attila becomes a hero of the Hungarian early period. Historiographically, this approach is interpreted such that the first of the two books of the *Gesta* is devoted to the history of the Huns, and the second deals with Hungarian history. The acquisition of Hungary at the end of the ninth century is thus legitimized as return (*reditus*) or second acquisition (*secundus ingressus*). The significance of Simon of Kéza lies in the fact that he modified the older, dynastically influenced national chronicle according to a *Volksgeschichte*. He postulated for the *natio Hungarorum*[57] an integration into the Christian world-historical view, on the one hand, and, on the other, a centuries-long connection of people and dynasty to the Pannonian settlement region.

---

[55] Generally Macartney (1953).

[56] Simon of Keza, *Gesta Hungarorum*, ed. A. Domanovszky, in *Scriptores rerum Hungaricarum tempore ducum regumque stirpis Arpadianae gestarum*, ed. I. Szentpétery, vol. 1 (Budapest, 1937; repr. Budapest, 1999), 129–94; new edition of the text with an English translation: *Simonis de Kéza Gesta Hungarorum*, ed. and trans. by L. Veszprémy and F. Schaer (Budapest, 1999).

[57] This important idea, e.g., in Keza, *Gesta Hungarorum* 2, 141. See also Szücs (1975), esp. 260–61.

Medieval Norway produced national historical texts only in the years from ca. 1180 to 1230.[58] The integration into the Old West Nordic, as well as the Latin, cultural circle, brought with it a use of both languages for historiography as well. The circumstances of the writing as well as the authorship of the two texts in Latin remain largely hidden. The author of the oldest text, the *Historia de antiquitate regum Norwagiensium*,[59] is Theodrich, possibly a monk in Nidarholm (near Nidaros/Drontheim), who is perhaps identical with the later Thórir, bishop of Hamar (1189/90–96), or with Thórir, archbishop of Drontheim (1206–14). The text is dedicated to Archbishop Eystein (Augustin) Erlendsson of Drontheim (1157/61–88). Theodrich's *Historia* depicts in thirty-four chapters Norwegian history from the rule of Harald "Harfagri" ("Fairhair"; ca. 930) to Sigurd Magnusson "Jórsalafari" ("the Jerusalem pilgrim"; 1103–30), hence he considers neither legendary beginnings nor the contemporary period. Yet the period of Olaf the Holy (1015–30) is introduced in six chapters as a central period in Norwegian history. An important concern of the historical narrative, laced with moral and evaluative comments, is the emphasis on Norway's belonging to the *orbis christianus*. The other text, the *Historia Norvegiae*,[60] presumably arose in association with the archbishop of Drontheim, Eirik Ivarsson, who was in exile in Denmark from 1190 to 1202. It contains a description of the region and history of Norway up to the year 1015. Although it remained incomplete and was handed down as such, it awakens interest on account of the regional and imperial concept developed, which forms its basis.

Along with these works attributable to the Latin cultural circle, several texts of Old West Nordic saga literature belong in this context also. In the group of so-called *Konungasögur*, which are thematically dedicated to Norwegian kings' history, several works deal with the totality of Norwegian history. Along with two anonymous portrayals that offer Norwegian history from Halfdan the Black, the father of Harald Fairhair, to the appearance of Sverre Sigurdsson

---

[58] See generally Ker (1909); Bagge (1991); Sawyer and Sawyer (1993), 214–32.

[59] *Theodrici monachi Historia de antiquitate regum Norwagiensium*, in *Monumenta Historica Norvegiæ. Latinske kildeskrifter til Norges historie i middelalderen*, ed. G. Storm (Kristiania, 1880), 1–68. The most important new study of this is Bagge (1989).

[60] *Historia Norwegiæ*, in *Monumenta Historica Norvegiæ*, ed. Storm, 69–124. See also Sandaaker (1985).

in 1177,[61] one should mention above all the major historiographic work of the politically and literarily most significant personality of medieval Iceland, Snorri Sturluson (1178/79–1241),[62] who stood in close relation to King Hakon IV of Norway and his jarl Skúli. In the 1220s, he wrote a Norwegian history, which is known as *Heimskringla*,[63] after the introductory words of the text *Kringla heimsis* ("the circle of the world"). The depiction, which is exemplary for its obvious concern for objectivity and withholding judgment, consists of sixteen individual sagas, with the focal point being the depiction of the life of Olaf the Holy (*Óláfs saga Helga*). In contrast to the other kings' sagas, this one depicts—in the *Ynglinga saga*—the legendary early history of the Norwegian kings as well and ends accordingly at 1177.

The heyday of the Danish empire in the so-called Valdemar period under Knut VI (1182–1202) and Waldemar II (1202–41) was the period in which the blueprints of Danish national historical thought were formulated.[64] The first sketch, written around 1185, stems from an author hardly identifiable as an individual, Sven Aggesen, nephew of the former archbishop Eskil of Lund (1137–77, †1181/82). His *Brevis Historia regum Dacie*[65] depicts the history of legendary ancestors of the Danish kings Skjold (*sic*) to the year 1185. The circumstances of the writing are not completely clear; he himself complains in the foreword that he has not yet found any compilations of the individual kings.

Equally unclear is the identity of the most significant medieval Danish historian. Saxo (†after 1202/08), who later received the epithet Grammaticus, was a cleric at the court of Archbishop Absalon of Lund (1178–1201) and his successor Andrew Suneson (1202–28)

---

[61] *Ágrip af Nóregskonunga sogum*, in *Ágrip af Nóregskonunga sogum. Fagrskinn—Nóregs konunga tal*, ed. B. Einarsson, Íslenzk fornrit 29 (Reykjavík, 1985), 1–54; and *Fagrskinna–Nóregs konunga tal*, ibid., 55–373.

[62] See Ciklamini (1978); Fix, ed. (1998).

[63] Snorri Sturluson, *Heimskringla*, 3 vols., ed. B. Adalbjarnarson, Íslenzk fornrit 26 (Reykjavík, 1941–51); Snorri Sturluson, *Heimskringla. History of the Kings of Norway*, trans. L. M. Hollander (Austin, Texas, 1995). See also Bagge (1990) and (1991).

[64] For an overview of medieval Danish historiography, see Jørgensen (1931); Damshold (1992).

[65] *Svenonis Aggonis filii Brevis Historia regum Dacie*, in SS hist. Dan. 1 (1917/18), 94–141. In Danish: *Sven Aggesøns historiske skrifter. Oversatte efter den paa grundlag af Codex Arnæmagnæanus 33, 4to restituerede text* by M. Cl. Gertz (Copenhagen, 1916/17; repr. 1967). See also Sawyer (1985).

and worked, during a long period beginning in the 1180s, on a monumental historical work known today as *Gesta Danorum*,[66] dedicated to King Waldemar and Archbishop Andrew Suneson. The *Gesta Danorum* may be regarded, in a historiographic as well as literary sense, as the most sophisticated text of the Scandinavian Middle Ages. The work is divided into sixteen books, of which the first eight deal with the earliest period, and Books IX–XVI consider the period of Christianization. In addition, four books form a representative block: Books I–IV deal with the pre-Christian period and offer a unique insight into the oldest saga and cultural history of Scandinavia. Books V–VIII consider the period up to the extension of the Christian mission to Denmark; Books IX–XII deal with the period from the introduction of Christianity to Denmark up through the conclusion of the Danish church organization; and, finally, Books XIII–XVI treat Danish history since the establishment of the archbishopric of Lund.[67] This conception of the internal structure of the work belies Saxo's view of the coherence of Danish history. His periodization of Danish history, determined to some extent by church history, manages to integrate Danish history into the universal Christian worldview while not negating the cultural historical inheritance present from the pre-Christian North. Finally, this approach offers the possibility of constructing a coherent Danish folk, regional, and imperial history without writing an affirmative history of rulers.

Approximately one generation after Saxo, in the middle of the thirteenth century, two anonymously delivered texts on the subject of Danish history also arose in the circle of the Icelandic kings' sagas. The *Knýtlingasaga*, the history of the descendants of Knut the Great, is a history of the Danish kings from Harald Bluetooth to the rule of Knut VI.[68] Óláfr Thórdarson Hvitaskáld (ca. 1210–59), a nephew

---

[66] *Saxonis Gesta Danorum*, ed. J. Olrik and H. Ræde, 2 vols. (Copenhagen, 1931, 1957); English trans. by Hilda Ellis Davidson/Peter Fisher: *Saxo Grammaticus, The History of the Danes. Books I–IX*, 2 vols. (Cambridge, Mass., 1979/80); also *Saxo Grammaticus, Danorum regum heroumque historia, Books X–XVI*, ed. and trans. Eric Christiansen, 3 vols. (Oxford, 1980/81). Since no medieval manuscripts have survived, the original title of the work is unknown. Important new studies include Skovgaard-Petersen (1969), (1987), and (1988); Johannesson (1978); as well as three collections of studies of Saxo: Boserup (1975), Friis-Jensen (1981), and Santini (1992).

[67] Inge Skovgaard-Petersen has called attention to this.

[68] *Skjöldunga saga, Knýtlinga saga, Ágrip af sögu Danakonunga*, ed. B. Guðnason, Íslenzk fornrit 35 (Reykjavík, 1982).

of Snorri's who was located at the court of Valdemar II during
1240/41, is accepted as the author. The depiction, in which the
story of Knut the Great serves as focal point, is divided into 130
chapters. It may be assumed that, in the context of the late medieval
transmittal of texts, the *Sköldunga saga* came before this; the latter
offered the legendary Danish history from ancestor Sköld to Gorm
the Elder, the father of Harald Bluetooth, whereby a comprehensive depiction of Danish history (*Danakonunga sögur*) was accomplished.
Even less well documented, known only through a seventeenth-cen-
tury copy, is the *Ágrip af sögu Danakonunga*,[69] written around 1241/59.
The short text offers an overview of the Danish kings from Harald
Bluetooth to Valdemar II, and it arose possibly in connection with
Ingeborg, the daughter of the Danish king Erik IV and wife of the
Norwegian king Magnus VI, at the Norwegian court. Finally there
is an early document of a vernacular national historical depiction
originating in Denmark itself, which was written at the end of the
thirteenth century in Lund.[70] It consists of a series of kings' historical biographies from the eponymous first ruler Dan to the year 1295.

Continuation and Change in the Context of Late Medieval Historiography

In the fourteenth century, especially in the period from around 1310
to 1390, one observes nearly everywhere a stabilization and re-writing
of earlier developed national historical concepts. In this context two
phenomena can be distinguished: on the one hand, the express re-
writing of base texts that had been developed in the thirteenth century; and, on the other hand, new emphases attributable above all
to the embedding of national history in universal historical presentations, which were variably historiographically successful. A new
beginning of a national historical tradition exists in this period only
in Scotland.

The re-adoption of a Danish national historical depiction followed
in close connection to the historical work of Saxo, of which an
unknown author, possibly a Jutland Franciscan, wrote an excerpt

---

[69] *Ágrip af sogu Danakonunga*, ed. B. Guđnason, 323–36.
[70] *Gesta Danorum på danskæ*, in *Gammeldanske Krøniker*, ed. M. Lorenzen (Copenhagen,
1887–1913), 1–60.

planis verbis in the middle of the fourteenth century.[71] The writer followed the book and chapter organization of Saxo but oriented himself in his *Continuato* according to the periods of rule of the Danish kings from Knut VI to the beginning of the rule of Valdemar IV Atterdag (1340).

At the center of the development of French national historiography stands the *Grandes chroniques* drafted at Saint-Denis. There, in the period critical for the monarchy under John II (1350–64), Richard Lescot continued the chronicle up to the death of Philip VI.[72] The continuation in the subsequent stage of revision until 1377/79 signified a formal and conceptual break, when the work was continued at the court under Charles V (1364–80) as the official chronicle.[73]

The so-called Hungarian national chronicle, continually taken up with interruptions since the beginning of the twelfth century, was brought into the textual condition that we know today after the middle of the fourteenth century in two editions.[74] The main manuscript of the first edition is the so-called picture chronicle (*Chronicon pictum*), a splendidly illuminated manuscript dating probably from the period between 1358 and 1370.[75] The second edition is referred to as the Ofen Chronicle. The interest in a total portrayal of Hungarian history in the middle of the fourteenth century is worthy of consideration. After the Árpáds died out, the Angevin kings Charles I (1308–42) and Louis I the Great (1342–82) attempted to legitimate their rule through the claim to Árpád tradition. According to this need, the extinction of the Árpáds in the male line with the death of Andrew III is not noted at all, and Charles of Anjou is presented only in

[71] *Saxonis Gesta Danorum ab incerto auctore in compendio redacta et continuata*, in *Scriptores minores historiæ Danicæ medii ævi*, ed. M. C. Gertz, vol. 1 (Copenhagen, 1917/18), 195–458. See also Leegaard Knudsen (1994).

[72] *Les Grandes Chroniques de France*, 10 vols., ed. J. Viard, Société de l'histoire de France 395, 401, 404, 415, 418, 423, 429, 435, 438, 457 (Paris, 1920–53).

[73] *Les Grandes Chroniques de France. Chroniques des règnes de Jean II et de Charles V*, 4 vols., ed. R. Delachenal, Société de l'histoire de France 348, 375, 391, 392 (Paris, 1910–20). See also Hedeman (1984) and (1985).

[74] Both redactions are placed side by side in the critical edition: *Chronici Hungarici compositio saeculi XIV*, ed. A. Domanovszky, in *Scriptores* (as n. 56), vol. 1, 1937), 217–505.

[75] Facsimile edition with commentary: *The Hungarian Illuminated Chronicle. Chronica de gestis Hungarorum*, 2 vols., ed. D. Dercsény (Budapest, 1969); *Képes Krónika*, ed. Gy. Kristó, 2 vols. (Budapest, 1987).

his genealogical relation to his great-grandfather, the Hungarian king Stephen V (1270–72). Building on the existing edition of the national chronicle, Henry of Mügeln, a poet with close ties to the courts in Prague, Vienna, and Visegrád, wrote two textual adaptations. Based on the manuscript of the Ofen chronicle, he wrote a Middle High German version in prose in 1358/61, which is dedicated to Rudolf IV of Austria.[76] One begun thereafter, probably 1360/62, a Latin rhymed chronicle dedicated to Louis I of Hungary, breaks off in its accounting at 1071/72 in the only existing manuscript.[77]

In Spain, the national historical draft dating back to Alfonso X remained the point of departure for further historiography. Second (*Segunda Crónica General*)[78] and third (*Tercera Crónica General*)[79] versions were completed in 1344 and around 1390. A new development of this period can be found in the all-Spanish historical drafts from non-Castilian perspective. The most important text is an anonymous chronicle, which has been designated since the sixteenth century as a chronicle from San Juan de la Peña, although in actuality it stems from the close circle of the most significant ruler of late medieval Aragón, Pedro IV ("el Ceremoniós") (1336–87), to whom a significance comparable to that of Alfonso X for Castile is attributable based on his historiographic initiatives for Aragón. The original Latin version of the chronicle, completed around 1369/72, is not preserved; a shorter version in Catalan has been handed down as well as a longer version in a Catalan,[80] an Aragonian,[81] and a Latin[82] version, which may be regarded as a retranslation from the Catalan. The chronicle is divided into thirty-nine chapters and treats in four separate depictions first the legendary early history and the Visigothic period

---

[76] *Chronicon Henrici de Mügeln germanice conscriptum*, ed. E. Travnik, in *Scriptores* (as n. 56), vol. 2 (Budapest, 1938), 87–223. See also Hennig (1972), esp. 168–94.

[77] *Chronicon rhythmicum Henrici de Mügeln*, ed. A. Domanovszky, in *Scriptores* (as n. 56) vol. 2 (Budapest, 1938), 225–72.

[78] *Edición crítica del texto español de la Cronica de 1344 que ordenó el Conde de Barcelos Don Pedro Alfonso*, ed. D. Catalán, Fuentes cronísticas de la hist. de España 2 (Madrid, 1970).

[79] See Catalán (1962), 188–193.

[80] *Crònica general de Pere III el Ceremonios dita comunament Crònica de Sant Joan de la Penya. Primera edició del seu text catalá*, ed. A.-J. Soberanas Lleó (Barcelona, 1961).

[81] *Crónica de San Juan de la Peña (Versión aragonesa). Edición crítica*, ed. C. Orcástegui Gros (Madrid, 1986).

[82] *Crónica de San Juan de la Peña. Versión latina*, ed. A. Ubieto Arteta, Textos Medievales 4 (Valencia, 1961).

to the invasion of the Arabs, then the history of the kings of Navarre and their dependents the counts of Aragón beginning in the middle of the ninth century, while the main section of the chronicle is devoted to the history of the crown of Aragón from Ramon Berengar IV (1131–62) to Alfonso IV (1327–36), the father and predecessor of Pedro IV. The work is in the end a history of the crown of Aragón, which nonetheless attests no autochthonous formation of tradition but, rather, builds upon a common Spanish point of departure, similar to Castilian historical thought. In the last years of the fourteenth century the Augustine hermit García Eugui,[83] bishop of Bayonne and confessor to Charles II of Navarre (1349–87) and thereafter to his son Charles III (1387–1425), wrote the first 'Spanish' history from a Navarrese perspective. This *Chronica de los fechos subcedidos en Espana desde su primeros señores hasta el rey Alfonso XI*, which ends with death of Charles II, begins with a universal history, but for the Spanish history leans heavily on the *Estoria de Espanna*. After the end of the latter's accounting, the contemporary account is reduced to a short chronicle of events.

English historiography of the fourteenth century[84] reveals two significant conceptual expressions: first, the *Brut*-chronicles, portraits of English history beginning with the Trojan origins of English history and the eponym Brutus—first in Anglo-Norman, then in Middle English—and, second, the embedding of English history in universal historical contexts, mostly in Latin. At the beginning of the so-called *Brut*-chronicles stands a complex of three relatively independent texts, characterized as a short Anglo-Norman prose chronicle and named *Brutus, Li Rei de Engleterre*, and *Le Livere de Reis de Engleterre*,[85] which are documented in four different, handwritten configurations of records. The time period covered ends in 1270/72, in continuations in 1306 and 1326. In textual and temporal relation to the *Rei de Engleterre* stands the so-called anonymous English rhymed chronicle from the early fourteenth century,[86] whose depiction reaches from the immigration of Brutus to the death of Edward I and the ascen-

---

[83] The chronicle has not yet been edited; see Honoré-Duvergé (1942).
[84] See Taylor (1987).
[85] Foltys (1962). See also Tyson (1975).
[86] *An Anonymous Short English Metrical Chronicle*, ed. E. Zettl, Early English Text Society. Original Series 196 (London, 1935).

sion of Edward II (1307). After Robert of Gloucester's chronicle, it is the second historiographic text in Middle English; it makes use, like the former, of the verse form and derives possibly from a cleric in the western Midlands. The portrait of English history is determined by a developed territorial consciousness and the continuity of the kingdom, untouched by dynastic breaks. At about the same time, in the years around 1300, the Augustine canon Peter of Langtoft in Bridlington (east of York) wrote an English history from the beginnings to the death of Edward I (1307) in Anglo-Norman verse.[87] With the depiction of the death of Henry III (1272), he is independent of previous works in his depiction of contemporary history. The verse chronicle enjoyed great popularity, which is apparent in the fact that the text was translated into Middle English in 1338 by Robert Mannyng of Brunne, a Gilbertine canon.[88]

Peter of Langtoft marks a final turning point in the historical thought of medieval England. Outside the circle of educated monks, clerics, and the court, a noble lay public had developed an interest in national history. The understanding of English history for this public was based neither on a concept of *Volksgeschichte* nor on a concept of a history of kings but, rather, on a notion of the territorial unity of the island, which was conceived even in its natural spatial expanse and thus included both Wales and Scotland. The main text of these *Brut*-chronicles is an anonymously handed-down text called *Brut* or *The Chronicles of England*. It was begun as a prose chronicle in Anglo-Norman, extended in its oldest version to the year 1272, and was continued during the beginning of the fourteenth century for Edward I's period of rule, to 1333. From one of these versions, a translation into Middle English was prepared in the third quarter of the fourteenth century;[89] the Anglo-Norman version was not continued further after that time. The exclusive, pragmatic organization of the text in narrative sections guaranteed an openness of form,

---

[87] *The Chronicle of Pierre de Langtoft, in French Verse. From the Earliest Period to the Death of King Edward I*, ed. T. Wright, 2 vols., RS 47.1–2 (London, 1866, 1868); new ed. of the contemporary part: *Édition critique et comentée de Pierre de Langtoft, Le règne d'Édouard Ier*, ed. J. C. Thiolier (Créteil, 1989). See also Summerfield (1998).

[88] Robert Mannyng of Brunne, *The Chronicle*, ed. I. Sullens, Medieval and Renaissance Texts and Studies 153 (Binghampton, N. Y., 1996).

[89] *The Brut or The Chronicles of England*, ed. F. W. D. Brie, 2 vols., Early English Text Society. Original Series 131, 136 (London, 1906, 1908). See also Brie (1905); Taylor (1986).

which made a continuation of the depiction to the late fifteenth century easier and made the *Brut* the standard work of late medieval English national historiography, with over 230 preserved manuscripts. Besides this main text of the *Brut*-chronicles of southern English (London) provenance, a series of conceptually related chronicles in Anglo-Norman arose mainly in England; these, however, are documented only singularly, mostly hand-written.

The most significant attempt to depict English history in a universal historical framework was undertaken in the second quarter of the fourteenth century by Ranulf Higden, a monk at Chester since 1299 (†1363/64). His carefully constructed *Polychronicon*[90] is divided into seven books. After the first introductory book, the following six books are organized firstly according to dates of the world epochs[91] and then, in Books IV–VI, according to epochal dates of English history.[92] Here he differentiates the Anglo-Saxon, the Danish, and the Norman epochs. At the same time, in Books II–IV he places the dates of the oldest English history in relation to a universal history of salvation, while in Books V–VII the dates of general history, becoming less and less frequent, especially the papal history, are integrated into English contexts. Ranulf Higden thus wrote not a traditional universal chronicle but, rather, an English history with universal historical references. English history for him is constructed not through the kingdom but through the steady territorial frame of reference, the *insula Britannica* and the nation-building ethnicities, the Anglo-Saxons, the Danes, and the Normans.

The *Polychronicon* was as successful as the *Brut*-chronicle and also was translated into Middle English at the end of the fourteenth century by John Trevisa (1362–1402).[93] In contrast to the *Brut* however, it had a much different reception, by an educated public associated

---

[90] *Polychronicon Ranulphi Higden Monachi Cestrensis; together with the English Translation of John Trevisa and of an Unknown Writer of the Fifteenth Century*, 9 vols., ed. C. Babington and J. R. Lumby, RS 41.1–9 (London, 1865–86). See also Taylor (1966); Edwards (1978–81); Brown (1998).

[91] Book II covers the time from Creation to the destruction of the Temple; Book III the time from the Babylonian captivity of the Israelites to John the Baptist; and Book IV begins with the start of the sixth age of the world.

[92] Book V begins with the Anglo-Saxon conquest and ends with the death of Aethelred I and the beginning of the Viking attacks; Book VI goes from Alfred the Great to 1066; and Book VII from 1066 until the present (1327, in continuations to 1340 and 1352).

[93] The text in the edition of the *Polychronicon* is printed on facing, right sides. See also Fowler (1995).

with monasteries, church institutions, and universities. Of less significance was the comparable *Eulogium historiarum* from the monastery
of Malmesbury, written in the 1360s.[94] Its five books follow each
other not chronologically but, rather, thematically: Book I is dedicated to biblical history, Book II to papal history, Book III to the
world empires and the Empire, and Book IV to a description of the
earth. Finally, the fifth and most comprehensive book contains a
total description of English history from the Trojan beginnings to
the rule of Edward III.

At the beginning of the fourteenth century, still before the re-
establishment of the Polish kingdom under Władysław Łokietek in
1320, a new draft of Polish history was written in Krakow. The
author, whose name is handed down as Mierswa or Dzierzwa, is a
rather unknowable person; it is suspected that he was a Krakow
Franciscan or a member of the cathedral chapter. His *Chronica
Polonorum*[95] is based mainly on the chronicle of Kadłubek, which he
reduced significantly and made more readable by giving up the dialogue form; for the period of the thirteenth century up to the pre-
mature end of the depictions in 1288, the chronicle is organized in
the form of an annal. The text is worthy of special interest by virtue
of its beginning section, in which Dzierwa carries out a new kind
of organization of Polish history. He derives the Poles from Noah's
son Japhet, gives them a progenitor *Wandalus*, which makes reference to the designation of the Poles as Vandals found already in
Kadłubek, and places this *pater Polonorum Wandalus*, who is supposed
to have lived at the time of the Old Testament Joseph, additionally
into Roman Trojan genealogy.

By virtue of the introductory integration of Polish history, the so-
called Great Polish chronicle (*Chronica Poloniae maioris*)[96] is also worthy
of consideration. The anonymously handed-down text, which was
put together possibly by Janko of Czarnków (ca. 1320–87), the former
under-chancellor of Casimir III, in the 1370s/80s, is first strongly

---

[94] *Eulogium (historiarum sive temporis): Chronic ab orbe condito usque ad annum Domini M.CCC.LXVI., a monacho quodam Malmesburiensi exaratum*, 3 vols., ed. F. Scott Haydon, RS 59.1–3 (London, 1858–63).

[95] *Miersuae Chronicon*, ed. A. Bielowski, in *MPH* 2 (1872), 145–90, 283–438; *MPH* 3 (1878), 46–52. The most important analyses of the texts are Banaszkiewicz (1977) and (1979).

[96] *Chronica Poloniae maioris*, ed. B. Kürbis, Monumenta Poloniae Historica, Nova Series 8 (Warsaw, 1970). See also Derwich (1985).

indebted to Vincent Kadłubek and is organized annalistically in the
account that follows for 1202/05–71/73. The prologue of the chronicle
formulates the notion of a common lineage of the Slavic peoples
from the eponyms Lech, Rus, and Czech, who can be further traced
back to Japhet. Pannonia is cited as the original Slavic settlement
region, the *mater et origo omnium Slauonicarum nacionum*. These two Polish
histories of the fourteenth century reinforce the shift toward *Volksgeschichte*
introduced by Kadłubek for Polish historical thought: Polish history
constitutes itself not through the territory or through unbroken dynastic lines of rule but, rather, through the age and identity of the
Polish people, which can be traced back to Japhet, as is found also
in western European historical thought.

The end of the dynasty of the Przemyslids in Bohemia in 1306
and the establishment of the foreign dynasty of the Luxembourgers
also brought forth new versions of Bohemian history. In the period
following the coronation of John of Luxembourg as Bohemia's king
(1311), an anonymous rhymed chronicle in Old Czech appeared,
which has been attributed since the sixteenth century to one Dalimil.
This so-called Dalimil-chronicle[97] depicts, in almost 5,000 verses
divided into 106 chapters, Bohemian history from the early period
up to the coronation of John of Luxembourg in 1311. In contrast
to comparable texts of this period, this text developed the national
historical view with an engaged early Czech nationalism, which is
aimed primarily against the Germans in the region (above all against
the German city-dwelling middle class and against Germans in political [advisor-] functions) and for which the Bohemian nobility moved
into the foreground as the social stratum that carried this view. At
the same time, the verse chronicle can be understood as historical-
political education for the new foreign king John.

Further late medieval attempts at new versions of Bohemian history
return directly to the kingdom, to John's son and successor in Bohemia,
Charles IV (1347–78). Correspondingly, what dominated here was not
the Bohemian perspective but, rather, the contextual understanding
of the rule and programmatic of the Luxembourger on the Bohemian
throne. The Italian Franciscan Giovanni de Marignolli (†1358/59)
undertook from 1338–53 an ambassadorial journey by order of the

---

[97] *Staročeská kronika tak řečeného Dalimila. Vydání textu a veškerého textového materiálu*, ed.
J. Daňhelka, K. Hádek, B. Havránek, and N. Kvítková, 2 vols. (Prague, 1988). See
also the ongoing historiographical classification and analysis by Bláhová (1995).

pope to the khagan of the Mongols, and followed Charles, after his coronation as emperor in 1355, as court chaplain to Prague, where he wrote a new Bohemian history by Charles's commission. His *Cronica Boemorum*[98] can be characterized as an attempt to integrate Bohemian history into a universal chronicle informed by the account of his journey to the Far East. The first of its three books is dedicated to world history up to Noah; the second book continues this history up to Augustus and describes Bohemian history; the third book depicts church history from the Old Testament prophets up to Peter, then the history of the Prague bishops to 1234. It is apparent that Marignolli attempted to unify two different conflicting tendencies: the dualism of papal and imperial history taken from Martin of Troppau; and the unification of a universal and a Bohemo-centric conception of history. Accordingly, he orders, on the one hand, Charles IV from Noah via the Trojan Romans to the medieval emperors according to a history of rulers and, on the other hand, he introduces the Bohemians as descendants of Japhet. These conceptual problems, as well as the foreignness of Bohemian history for Marignolli, deter-mine the wide failure of the chronicle, in terms of historiography.

Neplach (1322–71), abbot of the monastery of Opatovice in East Bohemia, also understood the empire of Charles as a structurally basic condition, which also must have had influence on the way Bohemian history was depicted. His purely annalistically organized *Summula cronice tam Romane quam Boemice*,[99] which ends in 1365, attempted, mainly relying on Martin of Troppau and Cosmas of Prague, the integrated depiction of imperial history, beginning with Augustus and the beginnings of Bohemian history. The unification of both strands of data ends however with the year 1000. Neplach then abruptly introduces papal and imperial history from 1003 to 1351 and later, beginning anew with Bořivoj's baptism in 894, relates Bohemian history up through 1365. However, these two attempts at rethinking—after the imperial coronation of the Bohemian king—the historiographic base structure provided by Cosmas and at widen-ing the horizon of depiction to general imperial history did not find acceptance. This is because the difficult historiographic integration

---

[98] *Kronika Jana z Marignoly*, ed. J. Emler, in *Fontes* (as n. 32), vol. 3 (Prague, 1882), 485–604; von den Brincken (1967); Hilgers (1980); Bláhová, (1987), 580–83.
[99] *Neplacha, opata Opatovickýého, krátká kronika římska a česká*, ed. J. Emler, in (as n. 32), vol. 3 (1882), 443–84. See also Bláhová (1987), 583–85.

of various political structures, of imperial history and Bohemian history, was not rigorously realized. Therefore, innovation with respect to older conceptions of Bohemian history was no longer present.

The next attempt at Bohemian history gave up this connection with imperial history. The author, Přibík Pulkava from Radenín (†1380) was headmaster at the Egidius-Seminary in Prague and drew up his *Cronica Boemorum*,[100] written around 1374, at the instigation of and in close connection with Charles himself. The author revised the text several times, so that six versions can be distinguished. On the basis of the sixth version, Pulkava himself wrote a translation into Czech;[101] in the fifteenth century it was translated twice into Middle High German.[102] The original organization in chapters later was given up in favor of a division into two books. There, the first book ends with the death of Wenzel/Václav III (1306), the second book with the death of Charles's mother Elizabeth (1330); thus, a contemporary section is missing. After the second version however, the depiction was supplemented with the history of Brandenburg and relevant excerpts from a *Chronicon Marchie Brandenburgensis*; this happened against the background of Charles's acquisition of the Mark Brandenburg in 1373. The dynastic-historical aspect of the periodization is also supplemented by a content development of the chronicle corresponding to the territorial expansion of Luxembourgian feudal politics.

The one new establishment of a national-historical tradition in the fourteenth century concerns Scotland. In the 1360/80s, John of Fordun (†ca. 1385/87), a cleric at the cathedral church of Aberdeen, wrote the *Chronica gentis Scotorum*, divided into five books and ending with the death of David I (1124–53), and the so-called *Gesta Annalia* for the period through 1385, which one may regard as groundwork for the continuation of the depiction.[103] The periodization of Scottish history, as becomes clear in the organization of the book, also of

---

[100] *Cronica Przibiconis dicti Pulkaua*, ed. J. Emler, in *Fontes* (as n. 32), vol. 5 (Prague, 1893), 1–207. See also Bláhová (1987), 572–80.

[101] *Kronika Pulkavova*, ed. J. Emler, in *Fontes* (as n. 32), vol. 5 (Prague, 1893), 209–326.

[102] These translations have not yet been published; see Bláhová (1987), 579.

[103] *Johannis de Fordun Chronica Gentis Scotorum*, ed. W. F. Skene, The Historians of Scotland 1 (Edinburgh, 1871); *John of Fordun's Chronicle of The Scottish Nation. Translated from the latin text by Felix J. H. Skene*, ed. W. F. Skene, The Historians of Scotland 4 (Edinburgh, 1872). See also Goldstein (1993), esp. 104–32; Boardman (1997).

the planned Books VI and VII, reveals an understanding of history as *Volksgeschichte* that finds few parallels up to this time in its radicality. The depiction begins with the sweeping early history, the story of the eponymous great-grandparents Gaythelos, the son of a Greek king and Scota, the daughter of a pharaoh, who initiated a migration of their people from Egypt to Albion via Spain and Ireland. Carrier and subject as well as identificatory concept of Scottish history in this context is not the *regia stirps* or individual significant kings, nor an already always firmly circumscribed region of settlement but, instead, the *gens Scotorum*, the *genus Scoticum*. This Scottish conception of history is informed by a century-long struggle for Scottish independence vis-à-vis the claims of the English crown, and, against the background of a crisis-laden development of the kingdom under David II (1329–71) and Robert II (1371–90), is implemented as a didactic device for them. History contains examples for politically positive and negative actions on the part of the rulers, *exempla ad futurorum*, the observance of which should ensure the security of the political independence of the *natio Scotorum*.

New Developments Since the Middle of the Fifteenth Century

In the fifteenth and early sixteenth centuries, with emphasis on the period following the middle of the fifteenth century, the national-historical form of depiction achieved a level of popularity not previously attested. The more than sixty texts of this period cannot even be enumerated here. Instead, one should describe the striking characteristics of national historiography towards the end of the Middle Ages.

In western Europe—in Spain, France, and England—a textual tradition of national chronicles had developed in the 1270s, which experienced its last level of reworking in the 1460/70s. The *Crónica general*, dating back to Alfonso X, underwent a revision around 1460, characterized as a *Cuarta Crónica General*, in which a vernacular version of the *Historia Gothica* of Jiménez de Rada also left its mark; the version extended to 1454.[104] The official version of French history, the *Grandes Chroniques de France*, was continued, in the last stage of revision,

---

[104] *Primera Crónica General*, ed. Menéndez Pidal, vol. 1 (as n. 54), lxix–lxxii.

to the accession to the throne of Louis XI (1461).[105] The *Brut* in England had a comparable significance, the latest revision of which ends likewise with 1461.[106] Here, however, the difference between the historiographic traditions in Spain and France as well as in England becomes apparent: if national historiography is bound closely to the kingdom with respect to the milieu of the writing as well as the conception, then one can not speak of an official historiography for England, even if one may assume a relatively stable institutional framework for the long-lasting productivity of the *Brut*, possibly a connection to the central governing body and chancellery in London.

A second phenomenon is the writing in many countries of new, large national-historical syntheses, which newly canonized the conception of history for a long time. At the beginning of the texts relevant here stands the *Scotichronicon* of Walter Bower (ca. 1385–1449), the abbot of Inchcolme (an island in Firth of Forth).[107] He linked himself to Fordun's chronicle but developed it further and continued the depiction in sixteen books up through the murder of James I (1437). In England, shortly thereafter, new comprehensive depictions appeared against the background of the dynastic conflicts between the houses of Lancaster and York. John Hardyng (1378–ca. 1465) dedicated his English rhymed chronicle, extending at first to 1457, to Henry VI; however, he dedicated a second, revised version to the former's opponent, Richard of York, as well as his son Edward IV.[108] John Capgrave (1393–1464), provincial of the English Augustine hermits, wrote an English history conceived in universal-historical terms, the *Abbreuiacion of Cronicles*, written around 1462/63 and ending with the 6615th year after the creation of the world, that is 1417, omitting contemporary history.[109]

A new development in Danish historiography dates back to the 1470s as, presumably in the Sorø Cistercian monastery, the first significant depiction of Danish history in the vernacular, the so-called

---

[105] See Avril, et al. (1987).
[106] *Brut; continuatio of 1333–1461*, ed. F. W. D. Brie, vol. 2 (as n. 89), 291–332, 335–91, 491–533.
[107] Walter Bower, *Scotichronicon*, ed. D. E. R. Watt, 9 vols. (Aberdeen, 1987–98).
[108] See Gransden (1982), 274–87.
[109] John Capgrave, *Abbreuiacion of Cronicles*, ed. P. J. Lucas, Early English Text Society 285 (Oxford, 1983), with detailed introduction by the editor and bibliography. See also Zumkeller (1992).

Rimkrønike,[110] appeared, which was printed in Copenhagen in 1495. The text depicts in over 5,000 verses the periods of rule of 116 Danish kings from the legendary Humble to Christian I.

Among the most significant late medieval national historical syntheses in the European context is the Polish history of Jan Długosz (1415–80), who performed outstanding functions first in the chancellery of the bishop of Krakow and later at the court of the Polish king Casimir IV. He had finished the first version of his *Annales seu cronicae inclyti regni Polonorum*[111] in 1458/61 and then continued the account up to 1480. His account of medieval Polish history, divided into twelve books, was the basis for all subsequent historians until the eighteenth century.

In contrast, the *Corónica abreviada de Espana* of Diego de Valera (1411/12–88?),[112] a politician and diplomat under John II, Henry IV, and Isabella, was very much bound to the concept of the *Crónica General* but, due to multiple printings since 1482, had the character of a standard work for over a century. In a similar way, János Thuróczy, (ca. 1435–ca. 1490), jurist in the king's chancellery, held himself conceptually in his *Chronica Hungarorum*[113] to the tradition of the Hungarian national chronicle but added an independent account for the last hundred years from 1387–1487. This chronicle retreated admittedly to the background after the printing of Bonfini's *Decades*. In Muscovian Russia the so-called *Chronograf* compendia were established at the end of the fifteenth century, compilation works that integrated Russian history in a universal-historical framework in the tradition of Byzantium. The oldest preserved version dates back to 1512.[114]

---

[110] *Den danske Rimkrønike*, ed. H. Toldberg, 3 vols. (Copenhagen, 1958–61). See also Nielsen (1986), 10–14.

[111] *Ioannis Dlugossii Annales seu cronicae incliti regnis Poloniae*, Bd. 1–[7] (Warsaw, 1964–[2000]). See also Koczerska (1985); Kürbis (1987).

[112] Diego de Valera, *Crónica de España abeviada*, ed. J. de Mate Carriazo (Madrid, 1927).

[113] The work had appeared in print twice already in 1488 (Brünn, Augsburg). Johannes de Thurocz, *Chronica Hungarorum*, ed. E. Galántai, G. Kristó, and E. Mályusz, 2 vols., Bibliotheca Scriptorum medii recentisque aevorum. S.N. 7, 9 (Budapest, 1985, 1988); fourth part: János Thuróczy, *Chronicle of the Hungarians*, trans. P. Engel, Indiana University Uralic and Altaic Series 155 (Bloomington, 1991).

[114] *Russkij chronograf*, part 1, *Chronograf redakcii 1512 goda*, Polnoe sobranie russkich letopisej 22,1 (Saint Petersburg, 1911; repr. Düsseldorf, 1973). See also Lichatschow (1975); Tvorogov (1975), esp. chaps. 6 and 7 and 232–34.

At the turn of the fifteenth to the sixteenth century, national-historical accounts were prepared for the first time in a series of countries. Here, the relationship to new kinds of state-building processes and an intensification of national thought is not to be overlooked. In Sweden, where contemporary rhymed chronicles had dominated up to this time, the crisis of the Nordic union and the tendencies toward Swedish independence created the background against which Erik Olsson (Ericus Olai) (ca. 1425–86), canon in Uppsala, wrote the *Chronica regni Gothorum* in the 1460s,[115] a depiction from the first king, Erik, who ruled allegedly at the time of Christ's birth, to the seventieth king, Christian I.

In the Holy Roman Empire, in view of the Rome-centered orientation of the central political power, there were only beginning attempts at a German national historiography.[116] In the context of the reception of Tacitus since its first printing of 1470 and the demand for humanistic historical interest in the court circle surrounding Maximilian I, literary formations of German national consciousness appeared in the Alsatian humanist milieu, which found its eloquent historiographic expression in the *Epitome rerum Germanicarum* of Jakob Wimpfeling (1450–1528), begun by Sebastian Murrho (†1495). This text appeared in print in 1505[117] and was mainly motivated by pedagogical patriotic interests and uncovered a genuine Germanic, non-Roman early historical connection for German history.

The internal consolidation of the confederate state system, its international implementation, and the factual removal from the Holy Roman Empire found expression in the historiography through the fact that the particular historiographic reflection of the fourteenth and fifteenth centuries, since the beginning of the sixteenth century, was supplemented by a series of comprehensive accounts of Swiss history.[118] The first texts of this kind appeared in the city republics of Zurich and Lucerne. At the beginning of this historiographic

[115] The work appeared first in Stockholm in 1615 and is now available as *Chronica Erici Olai Decani Upsaliensis*, in *Scriptores rerum Svecicarum medii aevi*, ed. E. G. Geijer and J. H. Schröder, vol. 2 (Uppsala, 1828), 1–166. See also Nygren (1953); Kumlien (1979), 126–29.

[116] Thomas (1990) and (1991).

[117] *Epitoma Germanorum Iacobi Wympfelingii et suorum opera contextum* (Argentoratae, 1505). See also Muhlack (1991), 99–103, 162–63, 240–42, 255–56; Mertens (1993), 42–43. For context and background, see Krapf (1979), esp. 102–11; Hammerstein (1989); Münkler, et al. (1998).

[118] See Maissen (1994); Feller/Bonjour (1962).

tradition stands the *Kronica von der loblichen Eydtgenoschaft* of Petermann Etterlin,[119] printed in Basel in 1507, after which followed not much later the *Chronik von den Helvetiern* of Heinrich Brennwald (1478–1551) out of Zurich.[120]

Finally, the humanist and Augustine canon Cornelius Aurelius (actually Cornelius of Gouda, ca. 1460–1531), wrote the *Chronycke van Hollandt, Zeelandt ende Vrieslant* in 1510/16, which later became the so-called *Divisiekroniek* due to its division into thirty-two sections (*divisies*).[121] It is a regional history of Holland, placed into a universal-historical framework, which—again against the background of the reception of Tacitus and in contrast to older Dutch historical thought—made the people rather than the dynasty the object of reference, by emphasizing that the Batavians, allied with the Romans, were the predecessors of the Dutch people.

In the regions of western Europe, the influence of humanism and the increasing internationalization of cultural relations since the middle of the fifteenth century had the effect that, after the vernacular language had found historiographic usage since the last quarter of the thirteenth century, one observes a return to the use of Latin. Alfonso García de Cartagena (1385/86–1456), bishop of Burgos and leader of the Castilian delegation at the council of Basel, was the first to practice this. In his *Anacephaloeosis* of 1456,[122] a draft for a larger historical work that was not carried out, he developed a conception of Castilian-Gothic history with the goal of proving that the Castilian monarchy had a longer history than did other European nations. More successful in this respect was the work of his student and collaborator, Rodrigo Sánchez de Arévalo (1404–70), who had lived since 1460 at the papal court and there wrote the *Compendiosa Historia Hispanica*.[123] He linked up directly with Jiménez de Rada and continued the depiction in a fourth book up through Henry IV.

---

[119] Petermann Etterlin, *Kronica von der loblichen Eydtgenoschaft, jr harkommen und sust seltzam strittenn und geschichten*, ed. E. Gruber, Quellenwerk zur Entstehung der Schweizerischen Eidgenossenschaft III, 3 (Aarau, 1965).

[120] *Heinrich Brennwalds Schweizerchronik*, ed. R. Luginbühl, 2 vols., QQ zur Schweizer Gesch. I,2 (Basel, 1908, 1910).

[121] See Tilmans (1989) and (1992).

[122] The *Regum Hispanorum, Romanorum Imperatorum, summorum Pontificum, necnon Regum Francorum anacephalæosis* also is printed as *Hispaniæ illustratæ ... scriptores varii*, vol. 1 (Frankfurt, 1603), 246–91. See also Tate (1960); Catalán (1982), 39–42.

[123] Repr. in *Hisp. illustr. SS*, vol. 1, 121–246. See also Tate (1960); Catalán (1982), 42–48.

Humanistic national historiography began in France with the *Compendium de origine et gestis Francorum* (1495) of Robert Gaguin (1433–1501),[124] which took the last version of the *Grandes chroniques* as its point of departure and continued the account up through Gaguin's present time. A historiographic new beginning is more strongly indicated, however, by the literarily successful *De rebus gestis Francorum libri X* of Paolo Emilio (†1529),[125] who came from Italy and was court historiographer in Paris under Charles VIII and Louis XII. In England as well, the humanistic new conceptualization of national history came from an Italian, Polidore Vergil (ca. 1470–1555), who had lived since 1502 in England and who, already commissioned by Henry VII, published the *Anglica Historica* in 1534.[126] This work was supposed to demonstrate the legitimacy of the new Tudor dynasty to the European public and, at the same time, questioned for the first time the traditional conception of the beginnings of English history, handed down since Geoffrey of Monmouth. In this context, Antonio Bonfini (1427–1502/03) must be mentioned as well. While his historiography did not signify a new revival of Latin chronicles for Hungary, it did signify a historiographic new beginning comparable to that of the aforementioned texts. From 1486 he lived in Buda at the court of Matthew Corvinus, who commissioned him to write a Hungarian history, the *Rerum Ungaricarum decades*,[127] a synthesis that, for two hundred years, became the reference work for Hungarian history.

With this integration of Italian humanists into genuine national-historical traditions, the connection is made to another new development of the fifteenth century. National history up to this point

---

[124] It first appeared in print in 1495 and underwent several new editions until 1528. See also Schmidt-Chazan (1985); Collard (1995) and (1996). A first complete French edition, which had numerous re-editions, appeared by 1514, see Collard (1994).

[125] A first incomplete edition appeared as *De rebus gestis Francorum libri IV* in Paris in 1517; the first complete edition, going up to 1488, appeared in 1539; numerous further editions appeared through the middle of the seventeenth century; see Maissen (1994).

[126] *Polydori Vergilii Anglicæ historiæ libri XXVI* (Basel, 1534); Books XXIV–XXVII: *The Anglica Historia of Polydor Vergil A. 1485–1537*, ed. and trans. D. Hay, Camden Series III, 74 (London, 1950). See also Hay (1952).

[127] Antonius de Bonfinis, *Rerum Hungaricarum decades quatuor cum dimidia*, ed. M. and P. Kulcsár, Bibliotheca scriptorum medii recentisque aevorum. Saec. XV. [22] 1–4. Series Nova 1, vols. 1–3 (Leipzig, 1936), and vol. 4.1–2 (Budapest, 1941, 1976). See also Kulcsár (1973); Cochrane (1981), 344–49.

had always been written from one's own perspective;[128] since the
middle of the century, however, texts had begun to appear that
might be regarded as foreign national histories written for a foreign
public in a foreign milieu.[129] Along with the aforementioned Italian
humanists, Jean de Waurin (ca. 1394–after 1471) from the Flemish
Artois should be mentioned as the earliest example. In the service
of Philip the Good and Charles the Bold, de Waurin fought against
the French (until 1445) during the Burgundian support of England
in the Hundred Years War and wrote the *Recueil des chroniques et
anchiennes istories de la Grant Bretaigne* in the years from 1446 to after
1471 at the request of his nephew Waleran de Waurin.[130] The text
depicts English history from Trojan beginnings up to the year 1471.
The second national history from a foreign perspective is the *Historia
Bohemica*, which Enea Silvio de' Piccolomini (1405–64) wrote in 1457
before his election as Pope Pius II.[131] His interest for post-Hussitic
Bohemia was, in view of his involvement in the imperial council,
quite political and, at the same time, thereby fulfilled an informa-
tional need on the part of the European public.

With the introduction of a foreign perspective and the dissemination of historiographic works in the printing of books, works of
historiography became, with respect to their genesis as well as their
reception, independent from the referenced milieu, from the people
or the nation whose history they write. With that, the first, the
medieval stage of national historiography comes to an end.

---

[128] This holds also for historians who lived in a political and cultural milieu that
was foreign to them, like Dudo of Saint-Quentin, the so-called Gallus Anonymous,
Giovanni de Marignolli, or Henry of Mügeln; they assumed in the new conditions
the perspective of the place and allow us to recognize only partially the view of a
foreigner.

[129] See in the first place the fundamental article by Tellenbach (1977).

[130] Jehan de Wavrin, *Anchiennes Chroniques d'Engleterre. Choix de chapitres inédits*, ed.
E. Dupont, 3 vols., Soc. de l'hist. de France 94, 102, 115 (Paris, 1858–63); Jehan
de Waurin, *Recueil des chroniques et anchiennes istories de la Grant Bretagne, a present nomme
Engleterre*, ed. W. Hardy and L. C. P. Hardy, 5 vols., RS 39 (London, 1864–91).
See also Zingel (1995), 70–75.

[131] Enea Silvio, *Historia Bohemica—Historie česká*, ed. D. Martínková, A. Hadravová,
J. Matl, Czech and English preface by F. Šmahel, Clavis Monumentorum Litterarum
(Regnum Bohemiae) 4 (Praha, 1998).

CHAPTER SEVEN

DYNASTIC HISTORY

Leah Shopkow

To compose history using the family as the organizing principle has seemed so natural to scholars that they have hardly questioned the appearance of histories so organized. All human beings are born; many reproduce; all die, and they mostly belong to families while they do so. Thus the existence in the High Middle Ages of 'dynastic' histories—genealogies, family histories, and regnal history organized around the lives of individuals—simply has been accepted;[1] indeed, some scholars have argued that genealogical thinking was a fundamental mode of thought in the Middle Ages. The Bible, with its description of all humanity as descended from Adam, along with medieval desires to fit all the peoples of the world into this scheme, conditioned this genealogical thinking, and it expressed itself even in how people viewed language. In other words, genealogy and notions of descent and generation were in the air.[2] If more of this sort of history was written after 950 than before that date and if after that date such histories treat families below the level of royalty, this is because of the spread of the technology of writing, in which members of the elite participated as quasi-literates, using the eyes and knowledge of others.[3]

---

[1] It is clear that there are other sorts of history which might be called dynastic histories: most of the works of which the Carolingian rulers were the patrons, official or unofficial; the *Saxon History* of Widukind; the Ottonian royal biographies and histories; the histories of Godfrey of Viterbo or even Matthew Paris's history; in short, any history with a quasi-official character or secular patronage of almost any kind. This article, however, considers only histories whose organizational principle is the reign of a sequence of rulers or the generations of a family.

[2] See Bloch (1986); also Angenendt (1984), whose first heading is "Genealogy as the 'Original Form of Understanding the World'."

[3] On quasi-literacy, see Bäuml (1980). The foundational works on medieval literacy are Stock (1983) and Clanchy (1993), but see some of the modifications to the notion that writing took over for memory offered in Carruthers (1990).

Another explanation for this particular flowering of genealogical
literature is more temporally and culturally specific and derives from
the work of Georges Duby, who explained the appearance of narrative histories organized around the family in the middle of the
tenth century as growing from a cultural change in the elite themselves. Around the year 1000, he asserts, they began to identify themselves as members of a lineage, descended from a common ancestor,
as well as holders of a particular patrimony, which they kept intact
by limiting succession to male primogeniture. This consciousness led
them eventually to write down their recollections of their families,
which tended to focus on the male lineage, because that was the
source of the property, but which also accommodated those women
who brought property into the family.[4] In other words, Duby ascribes
this relatively new sort of history to a reconception of the noble family. A number of scholars have accepted this hypothesis, notably
Gabrielle Spiegel and R. Howard Bloch.[5] This hypothesis suggests
that we should expect to see such histories first and most abundantly
in northern France, where noble self-consciousness had the deepest
roots (and this is, in fact, where we do see the most highly developed dynastically organized histories).

An alternative explanation for the same phenomenon has been
offered by Patrick Geary, who suggests that this change may derive
not so much from a change in the regard in which elite families
held their ancestors as from the loss of knowledge by the elite of
their ancestors. This loss occurred as the scattered holdings which
characterized the Carolingian period were consolidated into holdings
sometimes far away from the monasteries that housed the family's
dead and the memories of the family preserved in the monasteries'
libri memoriales.[6] As a result, families were forced to secure their 'memories' in other ways, including the creation of dynastic histories.

---

[4] See 'The Structure of Kinship and Nobility: Northern France in the Eleventh
and Twelfth Centuries' and 'French Genealogical Literature', in Duby (1980), 134–48,
149–57. See also Spiegel (1983).
[5] See, for example, Spiegel (1990), 78 and n. 58; Bloch (1983). Van Caenegem
(1973), 72, remarks that "Genealogies are one of the primitive forms of historical
writing in monarchical and aristocratic societies", suggesting that the growth of this
form reflects the aristocratic organization of the period. Genicot (1975), 40–42,
addresses this issue.
[6] Geary (1994), 48 ff.

However, dynastic history of any kind is, in fact, rare in relation to other kinds of history. Léopold Genicot, one of the few scholars to address a portion of dynastic historical literature at large, in speaking about genealogies has noted that, "Genealogies are spread throughout a long period of time and a broad space and they are never numerous for a period and country".[7] There are, of course, problems of survival. Genicot notes that because genealogies are small and often exist only in one copy, they are easy to miss in the manuscripts; the same factors would lead to the disappearance of many of such texts.[8] They also can be missed because of misleading titles in catalogues or tables of contents. But this would be true of many historical texts in general, so that we may not be talking about different rates of survival at all. The lengthier dynastic histories are even more rare and more limited in the places in which they arose: Normandy, Anjou, the royal court of France, but only an unpredictable scattering in other places. So the central problem is that if dynastic histories are a crucial expression of family pride, why are there not more of them?

Dynastic History

The term dynastic history is a modern one with no medieval counterpart; the category brings together works that, in all likelihood, medieval people would have seen as related, because they were all historical in nature, but would not have been considered the same type.[9] The question of whether medieval writers recognized genre at all in the modern sense is a vexed one, which I will not solve here. However, they did think in terms of models for writing works of various types, and I have found the notion of the 'horizon of expectations' helpful in understanding how the use of such models might have created some uniformity in written materials.[10]

---

[7] Genicot (1975), 35; for dynastic history as a category, see also van Houts (1995), 33–42.

[8] Genicot (1975), 33, 26–27.

[9] German scholars have used this term particularly frequently; see, for example, Johanek (1992).

[10] See Shopkow (1997), 24, for the application of the notion of the 'horizon of expectations' (originally drawn from Jauss [1982]) to history; the conventional thinking of medieval writers on issues such as truth has been explored in Morse (1991).

Thus, when someone sat down to write the history of his monastery or of his diocese and chose to write a serial biography—a *gesta*—not only did he know what the conventions of his text were (the *Liber Pontifialis* and Paul the Deacon's *History of the Bishops of Metz* providing a model)[11] but so also would those who read the text, if they had read other *gesta*, understand precisely what it was he or she was reading, even if neither historian nor reader had any particular name for the type of history being written or read.[12] When historians set out to continue the work of the great universal historians, Eusebius and Jerome, they were of course continuing in that tradition of dividing universal history into the constituent histories of individual peoples or *regna*.

Similarly, when people wrote genealogies, one of the types of history I have subsumed under the rubric of 'dynastic history', they had models as well and a name for the form—genealogy. Not only would writers have been familiar with oral genealogies, which seem to have predated the earliest written versions, but also Christian writers would have had before them the genealogical materials in the Bible. But genealogies often were not fully independent of other texts; they commonly (although not exclusively) appear as excursuses in larger historical texts.[13] Indeed, the genealogical materials in the Bible also appear as part of a larger project. Thus, even though genealogies were relatively clear in their form, their function—whether they were a sort of supporting text or belonged on their own—was ambiguous. Furthermore, their contents were variable in the information the writer felt it pertinent to include. They might consist of a sim-

[11] *Liber pontificalis*, ed. L. Duchesne, rev. C. Vogel, 3 vols. (Paris, 1955–57); Paul the Deacon, *Gesta episcoporum Mettensium*, ed. G. H. Pertz, in *MGH Scriptores*, vol. 2 (Hannover, 1829), 260–70.

[12] On *gesta* see Sot (1981) and in this volume; *Gesta Normannorum ducum: een studie over de handschriften, de tekst, het geschiedwerk en het genre*, ed. E. M. C. van Houts (Groningen, 1982), 145–57 (to my knowledge this discussion is not available in English).

[13] For example, the famous personal family histories of Lambert of Saint-Omer in the *Lamberti S. Audomari canonici Liber Floridus*, ed. A. Derolez (Ghent, 1968); and Lambert of Watrelos's account of his own family in *Annales Cameracenses*, ed. G. H. Pertz, in *Monumenta Germaniae Historica, Scriptores*, 16 (Hannover, 1859), 510–54. The *Liber Floridus* also contains Lambert's much expanded version of the Flemish comital genealogy and a French royal genealogy composed in verse, probably by Lambert himself, as well as abbatial and episcopal lists (van Caenegem [1973], 73–74). Many noble genealogies appear in monastic histories and foundation chronicles as well. On the relationship between genealogy and lengthier histories, see Genicot (1975), 13.

ple filiation consisting of one individual in each generation, with collateral relatives and women left out, or they might be fuller than that. So even in this relatively clear case, there were ambiguities and variations of practice.

It would be logical to assume that there is a consistent relationship between genealogies and more extended histories, and this seems to have been the case with serial biographies—*gesta*—of bishops or abbots: the episcopal equivalent of the string of begats—the list—preceded the fuller work.[14] However, this was not always true for secular genealogies. In some cases, for instance in the genealogies of the counts of Flanders, one can see a relatively rudimentary account of succession turn into a fuller history as it was recopied and reworked. In Anjou, genealogies predate the fuller dynastic historical tradition that began around 1100, and the later writers relied upon them.[15] In other cases, such as Dudo of Saint-Quentin's *Deeds and Customs of the Norman Dukes*, some scholars have conjectured that there was an underlying oral genealogy, or at least a collection of family tales or Norman oral lore, but the complete and lengthy text stands alone as a written text.[16] Perhaps such genealogies existed in every case and were not written down or were lost, but there are large numbers of genealogies which have survived, yet which never were expanded or continued. Thus, it would be a mistake, as Genicot warns, to see genealogies as simply a rudimentary form of longer dynastic histories.[17] The frequency with which they continued to be copied and the unpredictability with which they were reworked as longer texts suggests that they had their own significance; they were not simply minor examples of something else, although they might well be source material for another kind of history. Indeed, when the Flemish comital genealogy became a longer history, it no longer was called a genealogy but acquired a name of its own, *Flandria generosa* (*Noble Flanders*).[18]

---

[14] See Sot (in this volume); Deliyannis (1997).
[15] L. Halphen and R. Poupardin, *Chroniques des comtes d'Anjou et des seigneurs d'Amboise* (Paris, 1913), xciii–xcv; the genealogies are published in Poupardin (1900).
[16] Dudo of Saint-Quentin, *De moribus et actis primorum Normanniae ducum*, ed. J. Lair (Caen, 1865); Dudo of Saint-Quentin, *History of the Normans*, trans. Eric Christiansen (Rochester, N.Y., 1998); Searle (1984); van Houts (1984).
[17] Genicot (1975), 22–23.
[18] *Genealogiae comitum Flandriae*, ed. L. C. Bethmann, in *MGH Scriptores*, vol. 9 (Hannover, 1851), 313–34.

The genesis of the longer dynastic histories is not fully clear. What we have in most cases is a series of individual biographies, each starting with the birth or reign of its subject. Other members of the family may be invoked to a lesser or greater degree. In the *Deeds and Customs of the Norman Dukes*, few collateral relatives are mentioned: the attention is on the succession of Norman rulers. In the *History of the Counts of Guines and Lords of Ardres*, however, the marriages of most of the children of the family are related and collateral branches of the family often are mentioned.[19] These histories resemble the episcopal and abbatial histories commonly known as *gesta*, and the first example, Dudo's history, indeed may have been modeled partially on that kind of history.[20] In addition to the Norman examples, there are Angevin dynastic histories, and the imperial chronicle of Frutolf (but not of his successors) is also organized around the imperial succession. Finally, the French national history, the *Grandes chroniques de France*, takes this form, and there are a few other examples.[21] What is striking is that there is no one generic name for this kind of history as there was for genealogies, just as there was commonly no one name for histories.[22]

One might also consider family trees as a form of dynastic history, and these begin in the twelfth century and become more common with the passage of time, although there seems to have been some experimentation with the physical form of the trees.[23] However,

---

[19] Lambert of Ardres, *Lamberti Ardensis historia comitum Ghisnensium*, ed. J. Heller in *MGH Scriptores*, vol. 24 (Hannover, 1879), 550–642; Lambert of Ardres, *The History of the Counts of Guines and Lords of Ardres*, trans. L. Shopkow (Philadelphia, 2001).

[20] Shopkow (1997), 147–48.

[21] On Dudo's title, see Huisman (1984); William of Jumièges, *The Gesta Normannorum ducum of William of Jumièges, Orderic Vitalis, and Robert of Torigni*, ed. and trans. E. M. C. van Houts, 2 vols. (Oxford, 1992–95). The Angevin examples: Halphen and Poupardin, *Chroniques des comtes d'Anjou et des seigneurs d'Amboise*. Frutolf: Schmale (1972). On the *Grandes chroniques: Les Grandes chroniques de France*, ed. J. M. É. Viard, in *Société de l'histoire de France, Publications in octavo*, vols. 395, 401, 404, 415, 418, 423, 429, 438, 457 (Paris, 1920–); Spiegel (1978). Frutolf's work is regnal, in that it does not concern itself with the time before the emperor's rule, but begins each reign with a summary of the years of the reign. His successors may have chosen not to continue this organization, because they begin *in medias res*, in that in writing about contemporaries, they did not know how long a reign would last. However, both Ekkehard's chronicle and the anonymous *Kaiserchronik* might be called dynastic, even though organized in annalistic form, in that the emperors are the main concern of the chronicle.

[22] Shopkow (1997), 19–21.

[23] Klapisch-Zuber (1991).

the claim that these are "histories" or even "texts" (beyond the post-modern view that everything is a text) is problematic; one could just as easily see these as "family portraits", a sort of written version of the sculptural family necropolis, also increasingly frequent from the thirteenth century on.[24]

Finally there are works that defy easy classification into genres and probably did in the Middle Ages as well, at least to a degree. I know of no other work like the *Lignages d'Outremer*, for example, a late thirteenth-century text that records the lineages of a number of families from the kingdom of Jerusalem. The first version of the text was composed by, or following the notes created by, Jean d'Ibelin to celebrate his family, but the Ibelin family is only one of the families noted. The information given, however, is essentially genealogical.[25] And one wonders what medieval readers made of "family romances". From a modern perspective, these texts are quite variable in their factuality. *Fulk fitz-Warine*, the first version of which probably dated from the mid-thirteenth century, was composed in verse for a member of the fitz-Warren family. The surviving version is later and in prose. It commemorates three generations of the fitz-Warren family, refers to well-known historical figures and is situated in a recognizable historical context, although it contains "errors" and "fantasy".[26] In contrast, texts like *Bevis of Hampton* or *Guy of Warwick*, whose characters are not historical figures, although probably also created for the families bearing those names, are farther removed from this kind of historicity.[27] In other words, family romances cover the gamut from history to "house literature".[28]

---

[24] See Moeglin (1995) for the discussion of several family tombs.

[25] *Lignages d'Outremer*, in *Recueil des historiens des croisades, Lois*, vol. 2 (Paris, 1843), 435–74; but see Nielen-Vandenvoorde (1995), 107, for cautions about the edition.

[26] *Fouke le Fitz Waryn*, ed. E. J. Hathaway (Oxford, 1975–76); A. Kemp-Welch, *The History of Fulk Fitz-Warine* (London, 1907) Many of the historical events, however, are muddled in the retelling, and it is clear that Fulk II's deeds (actually the grandson of Guarine de Metz) are modeled on King Arthur's in places, while in other places it relates stories similar to those told in *Eustace the Monk*, the Robin Hood corpus, and Blind Harry's romance of William Wallace.

[27] Bevis of Hampton: *The Romance of Sir Beues of Hamtoun*, ed. E. Kolbing and K. Schmirgel, 3 vols. (repr. Millwood, N.Y., 1978) (Middle English); *Der festländische Bueve de Hantone*, ed. A. Stimming, 2 vols. (Dresden, 1914–20). Guy of Warwick: *The Romance of Guy of Warwick*, ed. J. Zupitza (London, 1883–91); *Gui de Warewic, roman du XIIIᵉ siècle*, ed. A. Ewert, 2 vols. (Paris, 1932–33).

[28] Hauck (1978).

The Distribution of Dynastic Histories

Although dynastic histories of any type are uncommon in general during the Middle Ages until the very end, there are some discernable patterns to their production. Before about 950, all dynastic histories are genealogical and all, with the exception of Irish genealogies, concern royal lineages.[29] Many historians are familiar, for example, with the genealogies provided by Nennius in his *Historia Britonum* and by Asser in his *Life of Alfred the Great*.[30] There is some debate whether these genealogies arise purely from indigenous cultural patterns—Germanic or Irish oral traditions of descent—or were influenced by the genealogical materials in the Bible in their creation, but that they contain biblical material and in their written form were deeply influenced by the Bible is beyond question.[31] Royal genealogies have survived from the early medieval period for both the Merovingians and Carolingians, for the Goths (reported by both Cassiodorus and Jordanes), for the Anglo-Saxons, and for the Welsh kings; the large body of Irish genealogical materials, containing the names of some 12,000 individuals, are not exclusively royal. Genicot has noted that with the exception again of the Irish genealogies, genealogical literature comes from northern, "Germanic" Europe in this period.[32]

From the end of the tenth century, however, new genealogies began to appear of families who, while they may have claimed royal or imperial descent were themselves not always royal or imperial. The earliest of these was the genealogy of Arnulf the Great of Flanders, compiled around 965, composed by Witger, perhaps at Compiègne, but preserved at the monastery of Saint-Bertin.[33] These were followed by genealogies from all over France (although more from the north than the south), from Spain, from Germany, and from the Latin territories of the east.[34]

No history organized around the family that was not simple genealogy seems to have survived from the first millennium. After 1000, however, the number slowly begins to grow, but interestingly, and

---

[29] Ó Corrain (1985).
[30] On these and other genealogies, see Davis (1992).
[31] On Ireland, see Ó Corrain (1985), 55; on England see Davis (1992), 30–31.
[32] Genicot (1975), 17.
[33] *Genealogiae comitum Flandriae*, ed. Bethmann, 302–04.
[34] For a more comprehensive account of the surviving genealogies, see Genicot (1975).

unlike the earlier genealogies, these histories concerned noble families, not kings. The first of these works was the aforementioned eleventh-century *Deeds and Customs of the Norman Dukes*. The *Deeds* was epitomized and then continued in the eleventh century by William of Jumièges in his *Deeds of the Norman Dukes*. By this time, the official history of Normandy seems to have been firmly cast in the dynastic mode; the *Deeds of the Norman Dukes* was reworked by Orderic Vitalis and then reworked and continued by Robert of Torigni in the twelfth century.[35] A similar series of dynastic histories concerning the counts of Anjou was started at the beginning of the twelfth century, including a fragment composed by a reigning count, and, as in the Norman case, the Angevin historians, once official history was cast in dynastic form, followed the precedent.[36] The twelfth century is also the period in which the earlier genealogies of the Flemish counts develop into more detailed histories, although never anything close to as fully detailed as the Norman dynastic histories. Not surprisingly, genealogical histories also were produced in Hainaut, where the ruling family was closely related to the counts of Flanders.[37] Around this time, the *Historia Welforum*, concerning the history of the Welf family of Saxony, also appeared.[38] These histories concerning princely families were joined from the middle of the twelfth century and the beginning of the thirteenth by some works concerning lesser folk, the mid-century *Deeds of the Lords of Amboise* (in Anjou) and Lambert of Ardres's *History of the Counts of Guines and Lords of Ardres* (in the Artois, then part of Flanders).[39]

From the eleventh century, then, there was a small but steady production of these fuller dynastic histories which were, however,

---

[35] See *The Gesta Normannorum ducum of William of Jumièges*, ed. Van Houts; van Houts (1981).

[36] Halphen and Poupardin, *Chroniques des comtes d'Anjou et des seigneurs d'Amboise*.

[37] Much of this activity is focused on Gislebert of Mons, the chaplain and chancellor of Baldwin V of Hainaut (Baldwin VIII of Flanders), for whom Gislebert wrote a genealogical history showing the links between the counts of Hainaut and Flanders; this text is not available yet in a printed edition (see *Narrative Sources* [2000], 'Gislebertus-Montensis'). His account of the county of Namur, however, is in print (Gislebert of Mons, *Relatio de infeodatione comitatus Namucensis*, ed. W. Arndt, in *MGH SS*, 21 [Hannover, 1869], 610–11.)

[38] *Historia Welforum Weingartensis*, ed. L. Weiland, in *MGH, Scriptores*, vol. 21 (Hannover, 1869); see Schmidt (1983), 424–53 ("Welfisches Selbstverständnis").

[39] Halphen and Poupardin, *Chroniques des comtes d'Anjou et des seigneurs d'Amboise*, 74–132; *Lamberti Ardensis historia comitum Ghisnensium*, ed. Heller; *The History of the Counts of Guines and Lords of Ardres*, trans. L. Shopkow (Philadelphia, 2001).

not very common until the end of the Middle Ages, when they are more widely found, particularly in the German lands.[40] The vernacular *Ninety-five Comital Reigns of Austria*, composed in the fourteenth century, was one such work.[41] Andrew of Regensburg in the fifteenth century composed a *Chronicle of the Princes of Bavaria*, extant in both a German and a Latin version. This flowering of dynastic historiography was not limited to Germany; there was, from the late fifteenth century, a vernacular genealogy of the Breton rulers composed by Pierre le Baud, only one of a host of writers producing Breton history.[42] Much of this late medieval production was in the vernacular.

Most royal history did not take dynastic form, with two major exceptions. Frutolf's imperial history, in which each ruler's regnal years are set out and the ruler's actions described year by year (until Henry V, Frutolf's contemporary), was composed at the beginning of the twelfth century.[43] However, Frutolf's successors did not choose a dynastic form for their histories; instead they wrote annals, albeit annals that were clearly dynastic in their intention to celebrate the imperial lineage.[44] In contrast, French royal history already tended toward the dynastic in the twelfth century. There were earlier genealogies of the French rulers, but from the beginning of the twelfth century, each French king received a biography (Suger's biography of Louis VI and his unfinished biography of Louis VII suggest that he may have intended to create a dynastic series).[45] These biographies appeared at the same time as chronicles that are strongly focused on the royal family, if not organized around them. These various Latin chronicles and biographies provided the basis for the vernacular and unambiguously dynastic *Grandes chroniques de France* of 1274.[46]

---

[40] Johanek (1992), 208, referring to Sprandel's work, mentions that there were at least 226 historians at work in this region between the plague and 1517.

[41] *Österreichische Chronik von den 95 Herrschaften*, ed. Seemüller.

[42] On the Bavarian texts, see Moeglin (1985), 42–43, 45 ff., and (1988), 106 ff.; on Breton texts, see Kerhervé (1980) and (1992).

[43] Schmale, Schmale, and Ott (1972).

[44] This did not mean that biographic forms of history were not important; Frederick I moved within a welter of biography. Moreover, the Cologne chronicler explicitly designated his chronicle, based on Frutolf-Ekkehard, as a 'chronica regia' (Wattenbach-Schmale [1976], 107–08); one exemplar contains a diagram of the descent of the Saxon emperors (Klapisch-Zuber [1991], fig. 3).

[45] Suger, *Vie de Louis VI le Gros*, ed. and trans. H. Waquet (Paris, 1964); Suger, *Oeuvres*, ed. and trans. F. Gasparri (Paris, 1996–).

[46] *Grandes chroniques de France*, ed. Viard; Spiegel (1978).

Family trees appeared in conjunction with genealogical texts, sometimes as illustrations of them, sometimes as a visual representation
of them for the purposes of memory, although diagrams of the family go back at least to Roman times. Survivals of such materials are
rare, however, before the twelfth century, when one of the most
famous trees, the Welf family tree, appeared appended to the Welf
family history.[47] Most of these diagrams were organized with contemporaries at the bottom and progenitors at the top, reversing the
norms of the modern family tree (which appeared in early modern
times). Here too the influence of religious models was felt in the
form of 'trees of consanguinity' and biblical genealogies, like those
created by Peter of Poitiers in his study aid, the *Compendium historie
in genealogia Christi*.[48]

Toward the end of the Middle Ages, as literacy became more
widespread, new families created dynastic texts. Italian merchant families of the later fourteenth century and afterwards sometimes created family trees for their *ricordanze* books, and sometimes genealogies,
and these very occasionally turned into fuller accounts of the history
of the family. Their purpose seems to have been in part to account
for families not only blasted apart by the ravages of plague but also
cut off from their ancestors and collateral relatives by their twelfth-
and thirteenth-century migration to cities.[49]

Probably one of the most marked features of dynastic history, however, was the frequency with which it might be reworked or continued, its potentially "living" quality.[50] Writers of fifteenth-century
vernacular histories were drawing on earlier rhymed vernacular chronicles and Latin foundation or patron histories; in some cases the
materials had lain fallow for two centuries before being revived.[51]
Genicot has shown with the genealogy of the counts of Boulogne,
begun in the late eleventh century, how a genealogical tradition (this
not a bare genealogy but one with a simple text) might change over
time.[52] The Norman histories were, in Elisabeth van Houts's phrase,

---

[47] Schmidt (1983), 431.
[48] Klapisch-Zuber (1991).
[49] Klapisch-Zuber (1986). Most *ricordanze* books, however, do not contain family
trees and only a very small percentage have more than a simple tree or list.
[50] Genicot (1975), 27.
[51] Johanek (1992), 207–08.
[52] Genicot (1975b).

"a history without an ending", being continued over about a century and a half.[53] The Angevin tradition too was reworked, added
to, and revised. From a simple genealogy the Flemish dynastic histories developed into a longer and fuller history over the course of
more than a century (and the final version, *Noble Flanders*, was continued in various places after its initial composition a little after 1164).
After long lying fallow, the Scheyer tradition of the Wittelsbachs was
revived and reworked.[54] I refer to a "potentially" living quality because
many such texts were never continued and, of course, most noble
families seem never to have composed such histories at all.[55]

Noble "Self-Consciousness" and Historical Writing

If the nobility of Europe in the eleventh and twelfth centuries was
undergoing an awakening to self-consciousness, they did not, by and
large, commemorate this fact by writing or having written the histories of their families, although there is ample evidence of noble
self-awareness based on a family's relationship with the past. In addition to historical forms of commemoration, we should think also of
patterns of naming; for instance, the increasing use of certain family
names in a lineage—Arnold, Baldwin, and Manasses are very common in the family of the counts of Guines—as well as the rise of
the family name itself. This was the period in which the Welfs
identified themselves *as Welfs*.[56] Family membership also was indicated by the increasing use of armorial bearings and the creation of
family necropolises.[57] The connection to the past might take many
more ephemeral forms—the story, the picture, the gesture[58]—and
might include other forms of literature than history.[59] So I do not

---

[53] van Houts (1981).

[54] On the Scheyer genealogy, see Moeglin (1985), 3–16 and 75 ff. (for its redis-
covery); see also Althoff (1988), 72 ff.

[55] There is, of course, the problem of the survival of such written records. If a
family record found itself in a monastic collection (which is the case for most of
the dynastic histories that have survived), it had a decent chance of surviving even
in a single manuscript. Where it did not, the text might be far more vulnerable.

[56] See Schmidt (1983), 424–53, for the process by which the Welfs "discovered"
that they were "Welfs".

[57] See also Moeglin (1995), 32, for the description of the Wittelsbach gravesite
at Seligenthal and that of the Luxembourgs at Prague.

[58] Johanek (1992), 197.

[59] Hauck (1978).

mean to suggest that noble families were not aware of themselves, did not attempt to enhance their status with literary works, or, most crucially, did not know or pass on stories about their past. What I do mean to say is that writing down accounts of the past organized around the descent of the family does not seem to have been a primary means for most families of creating family identity.

One possible reason for the paucity of such histories is that substantial resources were needed to produce even the most meager historical text. Learned people had to be deployed to record the text, particularly when Latin was the standard language of history. While in theory a Latin work might be composed to facilitate the comprehension of the unlearned or might be orally translated, in practice, the consumption of such works at the court, when they were intended for the court at all, seems to have been limited to the Latin *literati* at the court.[60] All of this expense was incurred for an audience that was potentially smaller than the numbers who might be reached by a purely verbal and "traditional" recitation of family stories. If the purpose of the family history was to create cohesion and to advertise that cohesion and the family's importance to other families, there might be more effective means to do this—perhaps patronizing a monastery, creating a family necropolis, keeping a splendid court, going to tournaments, and employing those who might advertise one's patronage to a wider clerical audience—at least until the increasing use of the vernacular made it possible for a work to be read easily by or to lay people, in other words, until there was a lay, literate culture.[61] The *Grandes chroniques de France* seem to stand at the beginning of this process. In short, the costs of producing a family history might outweigh the benefits.

Even in the case that a family chose to commission a history, the resultant history would not necessarily be organized around the lives of family members. Rosamund McKitterick has argued that the Carolingians invented annals as a support to the status and ambition of their dynasty, but the form focuses the attention on the control and organization and time and its passage rather than on descent.[62] To organize a history around one's family was to emphasize family connections or, in the case of the Carolingians, lack of them. To

---

[60] Johanek (1992), 203–04.
[61] See Johanek (1992), 195–96, for his comments on Viala, *Naissance de l'écrivain.*
[62] McKitterick (1997), 115–17, 127 ff.

choose another historical form was, perhaps, to stress the effective authority of one's office. Thus the chronicles patronized by kings of Castile, deeply concerned though they were with royal power, did not take a strictly dynastic form, although the fourteenth-century Aragonese chronicle of San Juan de la Peña, an official history commissioned by Pere III, was strongly dynastic in its arrangement.[63] Similarly, Henry III made sure that information came to the ears of Matthew Paris and in at least one case gave Matthew a superior vantage point from which to see (and write about) events, but the history is also not organized dynastically.[64]

The choice not to organize one's history dynastically may in many cases have been partly a pragmatic issue. It is relatively easy to write a dynastic history retrospectively but more difficult to write contemporary history in this mode. If one writes a portion while the subject is still living, events may force one to change one's text, which is what happened to William of Jumièges as he wrote his *Gesta Normannorum ducum*. His original version ended in the mid 1050s, before the Norman Conquest. He then revised his text to accommodate that new and spectacular development, at which point he dedicated his work to Robert Curthose. Robert's fall from favor necessitated another revision.[65] The successful maintenance of the *Grandes chroniques de France* required an institutionalized process of writing, in which officially appointed "historians of France" wrote the biography of each monarch after his death.[66] Most noble families would have been much less able to maintain an on-going historical project over a long period of time than the kings of France or even great nobles like the dukes of Normandy and counts of Anjou, whose history was revisited by quasi-official and official historians over a

---

[63] On the Castilian histories, see Vones (1991). Exemplary biography was an important form but seemingly not the account of the descent of a family; see, for example, those of Fernan Gonzalez (*Poema de Fernán González*, ed. M. A. Muro [Logrono, 1994]); and Pero Niño (G. Diaz de Gamez, *El Victorial*, ed. R. Beltran Llavador [Madrid, 1994]). I thank Karen Daly for calling my attention to these texts. For the *Chronicle*, see *The Chronicle of San Juan de la Peña: A Fourteenth-century Official History of the Crown of Aragon*, ed. L. H. Nelson (Philadelphia, 1991); *Crónica de San Juan de la Peña*, ed. A. Ubieto Arteta (Valencia, 1961).

[64] See Matthew Paris, *Chronica Majora*, ed. H. R. Luard, 7 vols. (repr. Wiesbaden, 1964); Shopkow (1997), 261.

[65] *The Gesta Normannorum ducum of William of Jumièges*, ed. Van Houts, xxxii–xxxv.

[66] Guenée (1980), 339 ff.

century. Most dynastic histories, particularly the genealogies, probably were written all at one time.

Choosing a dynastic history also presented the problem of how the dynasty was defined. These histories tend not only to focus on a family but also on a specific territory. What if more than one territory were involved? Lambert of Ardres solved the problem of the unification of two territories under the rule of his family by treating the descent of each family separately and by incorporating other genealogies into separate chapters as necessary (his history contains genealogies of the lords of Aalst and the castellans of Ghent, as well as of other lesser families). The strategy of the chronicler of San Juan de la Peña was similar.[67] But Robert of Torigni, after composing a biographic addition to the *Gesta Normannorum ducum* that concerned Henry I (†1135), turned to the composition of a universal chronicle, based on the work of Eusebius-Jerome-Sigebert of Gembloux.[68] While Robert's lord, Henry II of England—the count of Anjou, Poitou, and Maine and the duke of Normandy and Aquitaine, as well as the king of England—looms very large in this chronicle, the story of the ruling family is set in an annalistic form. And while Angevin history was composed for Henry II, it was similarly not composed *about* him, perhaps because he was so much more than "just" a count of Anjou.[69] The same thing is true for lesser families and also sometimes for vernacular texts. Robert of Béthune commissioned two histories, the *Chronique des rois de France et ducs de Normandie* and the *Histoire des ducs de Normandie et des rois d'Angleterre*, both of which have a great deal to say about members of his family and clearly were intended to glorify them, but Robert's writer named and organized his work not around the Béthune family but around the great lords and kings the family served, and he presented the information in chronicle form.[70]

---

[67] *Chronicle of San Juan de la Peña*, ed. Nelson; *Crónica de San Juan de la Peña*, ed. Ubieto Arteta.

[68] *The Gesta Normannorum ducum of William of Jumièges*, ed. Van Houts; *Chronique de Robert de Torigni, abbé du Mont Saint-Michel*, ed. L. Delisle, 2 vols. (Rouen, 1872–73).

[69] Jean of Marmoutier dedicated his version of the *Gesta consulum Andegavorum* (Halphen and Poupardin, *Chroniques des comtes d'Anjou et des seigneurs d'Amboise*, 162) to Henry, but that work ends with Henry's father Geoffrey.

[70] Anonymous of Béthune, *Chronique des rois de France et ducs de Normandie*, in *Recueil des Historiens des Gaules et de la France*, 24/2: 750–75 (repr. Westmead, 1967); Anonymous of Béthune, *Histoire des ducs de Normandie et des rois d'Angleterre*, ed. F. Michel (Paris, 1840). The former is not a complete edition.

Dynastic history also may have run against the twelfth-century historians' growing consensus that history should conform to particular
conventions of presentation and style to ensure its "truth". Simplicity
of rhetoric was one desirable feature of that style, in a period when
historians sometimes compared more elaborate histories unfavorably
with more straightforward chronicles.[71] Frequently accompanying this
anti-rhetorical stance was an explicit claim to impartiality or to attack
the impartiality of other historians.[72] But dynastic histories implicitly
trespassed upon these claims to impartiality, written as they often
were by intimates of the subjects. Dudo of Saint-Quentin's Norman
history was attacked as being adulatory, partly, no doubt, because
of the close relationship between the author and the subjects; its
form also may have played a role.[73] If one wished to flatter without
appearing to do so, a form that did not explicitly focus on the lineage might be preferable to one that did.

Given that the means of establishing one's truthfulness were conventional and resided as much in form as in authorial intention, it
is not surprising to find dynastic histories replaced with other sorts
of works. Robert of Torigni's decision not to continue writing dynastic history but instead to write a universal chronicle may partially
derive from a concern of this kind, as well as the practical difficulties
I have mentioned above. However, Robert also may have intended
his chronicle to serve a different purpose from his contribution to
dynastic history. Gislebert of Mons similarly composed different sorts
of works for different purposes. He did write a short genealogical
history of the counts of Hainaut, but his longest work, which is intimately related to the counts although not organized regnally, is in
chronicle form.[74] In other words, different forms of history were
required for different circumstances. And even when a work was
dynastically organized, alternative organizations might present them-

---

[71] Guenée (1980), 203–07, on chronicle. On the truth claim, see Beer (1981).
For the conventionality of such claims, see Morse (1991).

[72] See, for example, William of Malmesbury, *Gesta regum Anglorum*, ed. and trans.
R. A. B. Mynors, R. M. Thomson, and M. Winterbottom, 2 vols. (Oxford, 1998–99),
1:424; William of Newburgh, *Historia rerum Anglicarum*, in *Chronicles of the reigns of
Stephen, Henry II, and Richard I*, ed. R. Howlett, vol. 1 (London, 1884), 12–16.

[73] In fact, William of Jumièges decided to edit Dudo's text for that reason (*The
Gesta Normannorum ducum of William of Jumièges*, ed. Van Houts, 1:6).

[74] Gislebert of Mons, *La chronique de Gislebert de Mons*, ed. L. Vanderkindere
(Brussels, 1904). See also n. 37 above and van Houts (1995), 23.

selves. The *Ninety-five Comital Reigns of Austria* lists the counts of Austria beginning with the first count, who reigned 810 years after the flood, but it begins with universal history, and the five books into which the text is divided are also each dedicated to one of the five senses.[75] In other words, alternative ways of thinking about the history of a family and alternative forms of organization, particularly those which cast the history of a dynasty in the context of larger structures, intellectual or political, continually would have presented themselves.

Nonetheless, it seems clear that once a dynastic history had been produced, other histories produced in the area or in contiguity were likely to adopt the form. In other words, existing texts served as models for other similar works. Dudo of Saint-Quentin's Norman history directed Norman history into a dynastic form for the next century and a half. It also may have influenced the Angevin tradition, for the author of the *Gesta consulum Andegavorum* seems to have known Dudo's work or that of William of Jumièges, the only likely source for his contention that Rollo had married a daughter of Charles the Simple named Gisela and been granted all of Normandy and Brittany besides.[76] The counts of Anjou were intermittent enemies of the dukes of Normandy, but this does not mean that they would not imitate the form Norman history took; in fact, it might increase the likelihood of such imitation. It is tempting to see the genealogical form of the *Grandes chroniques* as arising from the Norman example as well; from 1204 the kings of France were also dukes of Normandy, and manuscripts of the Norman histories were present in Parisian libraries from at least the twelfth century.[77] Similarly, the early genealogies of the Flemish counts seem to have given rise to a host of genealogical histories, not only *Noble Flanders* but also Lambert of Saint-Omer's and Lambert of Wattrelos's genealogies of their own families and the *History of the Counts of Guines and Lords of Ardres*.

---

[75] See *Österreichische Chronik von den 95 Herrschaften*, ed. J. Seemüller (Hannover and Leipzig, 1909), 6 ff. on the seven ages; 25 on the names of Austria; 25–26 on the first count.

[76] Halphen and Poupardin, *Chroniques des comtes d'Anjou et des seigneurs d'Amboise*, 35; Dudo, *De moribus et actis primorum Normanniae ducum*, ed. Lair, 166, 168, 169.

[77] Manuscript C2 of William of Jumièges was at Saint-Victor (*The Gesta Normannorum ducum of William of Jumièges*, ed. Van Houts, 1:xcix); Manuscript E2 was composed at Saint-Denis (*Gesta Normannorum*, ed. Van Houts, civ).

The Author-Subject Relationship in Dynastic Histories

The choice of how to structure a history, of course, may not have been made by the subjects of the history; even the decision to write a history may have been made by someone else; finally, the family that was the ostensible subject of the history may not have been the intended recipients thereof. There is considerable evidence that many of the surviving genealogical and dynastic histories were composed at monasteries associated with the dynasty and that the choice of what to write and how to write it, and even whether to write it at all, lay with the clerical authors of such histories rather than with the patrons; these histories reflect the needs of the institution rather than those of the patrons. For example, the dynastic materials in the history of Frenswegen were intended to serve the foundation, not the family of the counts of Bentheim,[78] while, to use a monumental rather than historical example, the Bamberg family memorial at Holy Cross was created after the lineage died out; it was intended to remind the new patrons of the monastery, the Hapsburgs, of their responsibility to the monastery.[79]

That the writer sometimes had other patrons or potential patrons to please than the subjects of the history becomes clearer in light of dynastic histories which are not dedicated to their subjects. Dudo of Saint-Quentin included numerous dedicatory poems to members of the comital family—Ralph d'Ivry, Richard I's half-brother; Robert of Rouen, Richard I's son, and Richard I himself—but the extant copies with a dedicatory letter contain a dedication to Adalberon of Laon.[80] Jean of Marmoutier dedicated his *Historia Gaufredi ducis Normannorum et comitis Andegavorum* not to Geoffrey's son, Henry II of England, but to William the bishop of Le Mans.[81]

Even when a work indubitably was given to its subject, that does not mean that the subject commissioned it. The Scheyer genealogy of the Wittelsbachs was a monastic history created to shore up the legitimacy of the Wittelsbachs, after 1180 the dukes of Bavaria, as

---

[78] Johanek (1992), 202.
[79] Moeglin (1995), 527–28.
[80] I have argued in Shopkow (forthcoming) that Dudo intended his work to do double duty, to serve his Norman masters but also to procure his advancement at home in Vermandois and that this accounts for several oddities of the text.
[81] Halphen and Poupardin, *Chroniques des comtes d'Anjou et des seigneurs d'Amboise*, 172.

well as to reinforce good relations between the family and the monastery, but it was written upon monastic initiative.[82] In other words, a cleric or other *literatus* sometimes decided that a history of a particular family was needed. Lambert of Ardres reports that he wrote his history of the counts of Guines to placate Baldwin II of Guines whom he had accidentally offended. While this explanation, which Lambert himself says is not the most important reason he wrote, may be pretextual in that it imitates Ovid's reasons for composing the *Metamorphoses* and is thus topical, it does suggest that Lambert took on the project spontaneously, in a manner of speaking.[83]

At the other extreme, Dudo of Saint-Quentin very clearly states that he was commissioned by both Richard I and Richard II of Normandy to write his history,[84] and Pierre le Baud begins his *Genealogie des roys, ducs et princes de Bretaigne* (1486) with a direct address to Margaret, duchess of Brittany, in which he reports that he is acting upon her suggestion.[85] Therefore, in a few cases at least, the patron appears to have taken the initiative in the genesis of the work.[86]

The middle ground is more ambiguous and the issues are more complicated. William of Jumièges dedicated his *Gesta Normannorum ducum* to William the Conqueror but also mentions others with an interest in its production.[87] Yet it is very clear that his work has at least a quasi-official character, as do its later redactions drawn up by Orderic Vitalis and Robert of Torigni. Similarly, the *Gesta consulum Andegavorum* begins with no reference to the subjects of the text as patrons at all, and yet the first redaction was created during the reign of Fulk le Réchin (†1109), who not only demonstrably could read Latin but also wrote some sort of genealogical account of his family himself, now extant only in fragmentary form. And the *Gesta consulum* was continued by Thomas of Loches, probably the chaplain of Fulk V. Jean of Marmoutier, the last continuator, directly

---

[82] Moeglin (1988), 35–37.

[83] On this point, see *History of the Counts of Guines and Lords of Ardres*, trans. Shopkow, 2–3, 6; Lambert's comments come in chapter 149.

[84] Dudo, *De moribus et actis primorum Normanniae ducum*, ed. Lair, 119.

[85] Kerhervé (1992), 529–30. For Margaret, as the mother of two daughters, the important issue was whether women could succeed to Brittany.

[86] But such a statement is itself conventional. The historian may have asked the patron to commission the work. See Shopkow (1997), 183.

[87] *The Gesta Normannorum ducum of William of Jumièges*, ed. Van Houts, 182–83.

addresses Henry II, count of Anjou and king of England, who could read Latin.[88]

Whether the subject commissioned the work or not, however, the relationship between the subject and the author and/or his institution seems to have been a crucial one. Saint-Denis was famously a producer of French royal history from Suger's reign on, but earlier there seems to be a strong connection with Fleury, where Aimoinus of Fleury was active in the tenth century, Helgaud wrote the biography of Robert I in the eleventh, and Hugh of Fleury produced his *Deeds of the kings of France* at the turn of the twelfth.[89] Norman monasteries seem to have shared that role, as ducal patronage passed to them in sequence: first Jumiéges and Caen, then Saint-Evroul, and finally Bec.[90] Scheyer, the site of the first Wittelsbach genealogy, was the family burial site until the mid-thirteenth century, when the genealogical tradition created at Scheyer was forgotten.[91] Marmoutier seems to have functioned as comital historical center to some degree as well.[92] Nor was Thomas of Loches, writing at Marmoutier, the only chaplain/chancellor/notary to compose history for his lord: Dudo of St. Quentin is said in one charter to have been Richard II's chancellor and chaplain, while Lambert of Ardres, author of the *History of the Counts of Guines and Lords of Ardres*, was the chaplain of Ardres and spiritual parent of many of his lord's children, and Gislebert of Mons the chancellor of the count of Hainaut. Pierre le Baud was at the court of Brittany as secretary and confessor.[93] This trend is also apparent in simple secular biography: biographies often

---

[88] Halphen and Poupardin, *Chroniques des comtes d'Anjou et des seigneurs d'Amboise*, 25; for Fulk's fragmentary genealogical history, see 232 ff.; xxviii; xl, 171.

[89] Aimoinus of Fleury, *Historia Francorum*, in *PL*, ed. J.-P. Migne, vol. 139 (Paris, 1880), 617–791; Helgaud of Fleury, *Epitoma vitae Roberti Regis*, in *PL*, vol. 141 (Paris, 1880), 903–36; Hugh of Fleury, *Actus regum Francorum*, in *PL*, vol. 163 (Paris, 1893), 873–912. These histories were not, however, dynastically organized. Aimoinus's older contemporary, Abbo of Fleury was also an active historian; both men wrote biographies as well as histories. On French royal biography, see Carpentier (1991).

[90] Shopkow (1997), 58–60.

[91] Moeglin (1985), 5, 13.

[92] The first and last redactions of the *Gesta consulum Andegavorum* were composed there, as were some historical materials produced by William of Compiègne and used by Jean of Marmoutier in his version (Halphen and Poupardin, *Chroniques des comtes d'Anjou*, 164), and Jean of Marmoutier naturally wrote his history of Geoffrey Plantagenet there; the author of the *Liber de compositione Castri Ambazie* used materials from Marmoutier (Halphen and Poupardin, *Chroniques des comtes d'Anjou*, liii).

[93] Cassard (1985), 70.

were written at institutions that had close links to the subject and/or
by individuals who had close links to the subject.[94]

Two sorts of authors seem to emerge for dynastic histories, then:
the first an individual closely associated in a personal way with the
family commemorated; the second, the writer at an institution closely
associated with the family regime.[95] Both sorts of authorship raise
questions about who determined the content of the histories and
whether these histories represent the memories of their subjects, a
"memory" "retrieved" from documents or simply made up, or some
combination of the two.

Because dynastic histories often present themselves as memories,
it is easy to take that presentation at face value. I do not wish to
argue here that the elite (or indeed the peasants) of medieval society had no memories of their own pasts. Other scholars have argued
convincingly that they did and even that the function of preserving
these kinds of memories was entrusted to some layperson, sometimes
learned, sometimes a family member.[96] What I want to argue here
is something different, that many of the surviving dynastic histories
we have are not simple transfers of "memory" from the minds of
the collectivity to the page but are, instead, mediated, often by members of the clergy but certainly by a learned person, and not always
for the ends or at the behest of the family in question. Certainly
parts of these traditions might well slip into historical writing
unchanged—the most prominent examples being Lambert of Wattrelos
and Lambert of Saint-Omer's reports on their own families.[97] In
other cases, we may talk about mediation, as in the case of the
Anglo-Saxon royal genealogies. These may preserve an account of
descent from a Germanic god, presumably the oral portion of the
genealogy, and insert the god's ancestors. The result is to emphasize that "the god" was human and not, in fact, a god; indeed he
might be descended from Noah.[98] This treatment of pagan gods is

---

[94] For example, Otto I's biographer, Hrosvita of Gandersheim, wrote at an institution whose abbess was an imperial relative.

[95] Althoff (1988), esp. 74–75; Johanek (1992), 201–02.

[96] See, for example, Moisl (1981); van Houts (1999), Geary (1994), Johanek (1992),
201.

[97] Although it is worth noting that both men, as historians themselves, had encountered dynastic-genealogical integrated into history already—it did not appear in their
work as some kind of spontaneous invention.

[98] Genicot (1975), 39.

consistent with medieval learned treatments of the Roman gods of antiquity.[99] We may also talk about the incorporation of materials that may not have been memory but which were widespread, such as the use of epic, for example, the way epic deeds are set into the *Gesta consulum Andegavorum*'s account of Geoffrey Grisegonelle.[100] At the other extreme, in some cases the contents of these histories may not have resided in the brain of any person before they took shape in the mind of the writer, either under the influence of a researched historical record or through invention.[101]

It can, of course, be very difficult to tell precisely from where the contents of these histories come. To give one example, scholars have been arguing for some time about whether Dudo of Saint-Quentin's material was composed of family memories passed to the historian by his patrons or whether it contains mostly constructions by the historian.[102] Clearly, however, some genealogies and dynastic histories drew upon the author's research. This seems to have been the case with the Welf genealogies and was certainly the case with the *Grandes chroniques de France*. Gislebert of Mons, although an eyewitness, also drew upon the charter record. Lambert of Ardres certainly had at least read some historical texts—*Noble Flanders* at the very least—and perhaps charters as well. Research in this sense must include orally circulating material as well. When the author of the *Gesta consulum Andegavorum* included quasi-epic materials on the reign of Geoffrey Grisegonelle, he might have gotten that material from members of the family, but he might equally well have encountered them in some other oral form.

Even if we suppose that the core of the dynastic history contained nothing but the memories of the family, someone either within the family or within its circle of power would have to have decided to write this material down. We have to assume that for most members

---

[99] Veyne (1988).

[100] Halphen and Poupardin, *Chroniques des comtes d'Anjou et des seigneurs d'Amboise*, 37 ff. and 38 n. 1. Still, this "epic" story is recounted in a text liberally strewn with classical reminiscences (41 n. 1).

[101] See Althoff (1988), for a conjectural reconstruction of the genesis of several noble genealogies through the labors of learned compilers.

[102] This argument is tied into the larger question of whether the Normans were still "Scandinavian" in their institutions. For the argument that they were and that Dudo's work contains extensive Nordic memories, see Searle (1984); van Houts (1984); for the argument that Dudo based his work on Latin examples, particularly Vergil's *Aeneid*, see Shopkow (1997), 150; Bates (1982), 15 ff.; Albu (1994), 111–18.

of the elite, simply telling their family stories was enough, otherwise we would have many more of them than we do. What was important enough to cross that threshold? And if the contents of a dynastic history were not memories but were the result of careful clerical research, again what impulse gave rise to the history and gave it this shape? In fact, as Jean-Marie Moeglin has warned, genealogies could always have been different than they are;[103] indeed, in cases where dynasties produced more than one genealogy or dynastic history, that point often is demonstrated very clearly. This suggests that the criteria for inclusion or exclusion is likely to be not simply who was remembered but the context for the "remembering". In other words, we need talk about the "social logic" or different sorts of social logic for dynastic history.[104]

Functions of Dynastic History

The concerns of a family well may have lain behind certain kinds of dynastic documents, particularly family trees and rudimentary genealogies. The family tree delineated those who might have a claim on property, but other questions also might arise from relationship. For instance, a tree might be used or even drawn up in disputes over marriage.[105] In other words, the functions of these histories are various and particular. Therefore, I have selected a few texts to illustrate the possibilities, rather than to attempt any comprehensive, and necessarily faulty, generalization.[106]

The Flemish genealogical tradition offers an interesting case to use as we consider the question of social logic in dynastic histories, as it is one of the earliest and undergoes considerable development with time. The first history in the series, the genealogy of Arnulf of Flanders by Witger,[107] traces the descent of Arnulf of Flanders from Charlemagne, something that later will become typical of noble genealogies.[108] In the first of the two parts, the text provides a genealogy of the Frankish kings and emperors, specially notes Judith, the

---

[103] Moeglin (1995), 524–25.
[104] On social logic, see Spiegel (1990).
[105] See Maleczek (1988).
[106] See also Genicot (1975), 35–44, on this subject.
[107] *Genealogiae comitum Flandriae*, ed. Bethmann, 302–04.
[108] See Folz (1950), 375–80, for some examples from Germany.

daughter of Charles the Bald and the grandmother of Arnulf, and also makes special reference to the monastery of Compiègne. This part of the genealogy is simply a list, which includes women (both as wives and unnamed as concubines) as well as men, although a few personal characteristics are included (Louis d'Outremer is said to be "elegant of form"). The second part, a genealogy of the Flemish counts, is a considerably fuller as well as more sparsely peopled account, and it begins with Baldwin I's marriage to Judith. The text quickly moves to the next generation, in which Baldwin II marries an unnamed princess from "overseas" (the English princess Elftrude) and is buried at Saint-Bertin. The remaining part of the genealogy concerns the deeds of Arnulf the Great. Most of the specifics of his deeds are generally omitted in favor of an outpouring of typical late Carolingian panegyric. The specific deeds Witger mentions are his donations to the monastery of St. Mary at Compiègne: his donation to the tombs of Sts. Cornelius and Cyprian; his endowment of the clergy there; and his donation of a bell—all appropriate because Charles the Bald, his relation, founded this church. At the end comes Arnulf's marriage, the birth and marriage of his son Baldwin, and prayers for the well-being of Baldwin and Arnulf, both of whom seem still to be alive at the time of writing.

What is striking in this genealogy is how much of what might have been said has been omitted. The conquests of the Baldwins and Arnulf himself are of no interest to Witger; there is no indication of identification of these men with a particular patrimony or domain. Nor does Witger long to catalogue the deeds of any of the members of the family, apart from their religious deeds. In fact, Arnulf appears most forcefully here as the benefactor of the church at Compiègne. The genealogy, particularly if one includes the Carolingian lineage that accompanies it, does, however, show signs of considerable research on Witger's part.

If we inquire after the social logic of the genealogy, we may, rather than seeing this as an expression of "noble self-consciousness", see it as a document that safeguards the interests of at least one of the two institutions named. Arnulf was known by his contemporaries as "the Rich", but also as "the Old".[109] He became count in 918 upon

[109] Nicholas (1992), 41.

the death of his father and lived until 965; he may have been born as early as 885. By the time this genealogy was composed, between 951 and 959,[110] Arnulf was already an old man; his son Baldwin ruled the south of Flanders during this period.[111] Thus a succession was in the offing, a time of shift and change.

Compiègne was not in Flanders; indeed, it was a favored Carolingian residence under Charles the Bald,[112] and Charles the Simple was still making donations.[113] Arnulf pursued a complicated policy in relation to Charles's son and long-term successor, Louis IV, supporting him initially up until 939 and then rebelling against him. Toward the end of his life, possibly after this genealogy was written, he was again conciliatory.[114] For the monks at Compiègne, whose founders were intermittently at odds with this other desirable patron, none of whose kin lay buried at Compiègne, it might well have been a priority to stress Arnulf's earlier benefactions and offer the prayers of the monks for him and his son in the hopes that such benefactions might continue. All in all, then, family relationships as laid out by Witger serve the needs of Compiègne. But the single autograph manuscript of Witger's genealogy is preserved at Saint-Bertin.[115] Saint-Bertin also had a stake in the counts; its presence may relate to that monastery's careful collection of historical materials and also to the burial there of members of the comital family.[116]

In the next series of Flemish genealogies, political concerns swirl much closer to the surface than purely monastic concerns, and, not surprisingly, the second and third generations of comital genealogies were more widely disseminated, perhaps in some kind of quasi-official way. The genealogy composed during the lifetime of Robert II (†1111) at Saint-Bertin was preserved in five manuscripts (one now lost) and

---

[110] *Genealogiae comitum Flandriae*, ed. Bethmann, 302 n. 1; but see van Caenegem (1973), 92 n. 8 who notes that Grierson has suggested 959–60, a date accepted also by Genicot (1975), 19, while Werner (1967), 7:46 says 962.

[111] Nicholas (1992), 42.

[112] McKitterick (1983), 751–987, 193, 214; for the school, see 214.

[113] McKitterick (1983), 333.

[114] McKitterick (1983), 251.

[115] *Genealogiae comitum Flandriae* (1851), 302.

[116] Baldwin II was buried at St. Peter's in Ghent; Elftrude refused to have him buried at Saint-Bertin, because the monks would not let her be buried there as well (Nicholas [1992], 20). Baldwin III was buried at Saint-Bertin, and Witger (*Genealogiae comitum Flandriae* [1851], 303) notes that Arnulf's brother Adalulf was as well.

two versions, with several continuations.[117] The important political issue at the end of the earliest versions was the succession of Robert I "the Frisian" to Flanders; while the majority version is neutral, at least one version takes a dim view of Robert's character and rights. While this genealogy may seem to affirm the continuity of the family (Robert I was usurping Flanders from his nephew), it does document a political change important to the southern lords (including the people of Saint-Omer), who, according to *Flandria generosa*, had not supported Robert. That this tradition should be alive at Saint-Bertin, where Robert's defeated rival was buried, is hardly surprising.[118] The continuations of this genealogy similarly appear at times of crisis: one hand chronicles the succession crisis of 1127–28; another picks up until the succession of Baldwin V of Hainaut (Baldwin VIII of Flanders) upon the death of Philip of Alsace; a third carries on through the sad aftermath of Bouvines; while another later hand carries on to the succession of Guy after the long reigns of Baldwin XI's daughters. In other words, the hands change at political junctures in the history of Flanders. These genealogies and their continuations and reworkings do not always seem to represent the political interests of the family. Lambert of Saint-Omer stresses Robert II's "tyranny" toward the clergy. The story ends happily, more or less, with the count penitent (although compelled by the fear of an interdict) and then quickly dead.

This history, then, does not seem to arise from the comital family's sense of itself. Although the lineage of the counts of Flanders was a true blood lineage (albeit sometimes through the female line)—not always the case in other places—the genealogies take into their stride the abrupt changes of family branch that punctuated Flemish history. What concerned them, when they gave more than the bare succession, was political events and connections. The counts of Flanders were extremely effective rulers; their administration was more complex and professional than the French administration of the period, for example. To a great degree, the history of their family *was* the history of Flanders. In short, in this case, the genealogies are a kind of institutional history.

---

[117] *Genealogiae comitum Flandriae*, ed. Bethmann, 305–06, with continuations 306–08.
[118] Nicholas (1992), 52; *Genealogiae comitum Flandriae*, ed. Bethmann, 322.

Why the history of Flanders took this biographic form is a more difficult question. In the case of Witger's genealogy, the genealogy provides the kinship link that might encourage the continued patronage of a foundation outside the territory the counts of Flanders might hope to control. However, Witger's genealogy was not that influential, for the genealogy that supplanted it in the eleventh century traced the family's descent from the legendary Lideric of Harlebec, not Judith,[119] and represents a claim not to Carolingian descent but to a jurisdiction in Flanders that predated Judith. These new and deeper roots were set down even as political upheaval seemed to create a break, if not a complete one. In other words, history was produced at a node of crisis.[120] The familial form the history took may even be reinforced, in this case, by the familial nature of the crisis, a battle between uncle and nephew.

Once Flemish history had taken a dynastic form, however, it is relatively easy to explain its continued tendency to do so. An existing history created a template for later histories that it might be more difficult to break with than to utilize. In the Norman case, Dudo of Saint-Quentin's example was so powerful that it took Norman historians more than a century to break away from it. And, as I have suggested above, the mode in which Flemish history was cast also influenced local writers, such Lambert of Saint-Omer, Lambert of Wattrelos, and Lambert of Ardres, to write history in this fashion.

The last of these histories is particularly interesting to think about in terms of dynastic history, because it was through interpreting it that Duby arrived at many of his theories on noble marriage and noble attitudes toward family. The emphasis on family and lineage is indeed much clearer in the *History of the Counts of Guines* than it is in the comital histories, although lineage is much more broadly interpreted. Not only are the legitimate children of a particular count of Guines or lord of Ardres enumerated but also their spouses are named, and often their descendants for three or four generations. When scholars think about dynastic history, this history is one that they immediately think of.

However, it would be a mistake to see even this history as simply arising from the pride of the family in its lineage and its concern

[119] *Genealogiae comitum Flandriae*, ed. Bethmann, 305 and n. 6; also van Caenegem (1973), 73, 81–82.
[120] On this genesis of history, see Althoff-Coué (1992).

for its patrimony alone (although concern there is aplenty); the political circumstances under which it was produced are simply too sug-
gestive. Lambert implies that he began writing around 1194.[121] If so,
one obvious reason to do so was the unification of two territories,
Guines and Bourbourg, which had been in the making for a long
time. But as Lambert wrote another and more disturbing sequence
of events was unfolding, and these also might have contributed to
the creation of the history. The region of which Guines was a part
was extremely unstable in the late twelfth and early thirteenth centuries. It was part of the land contested between the count of Flanders
and the king of France and had, in fact, changed hands twice before
the end of the twelfth century. After 1202 the count of Flanders was
absent on crusade, and after 1205, the heiress to Flanders was a
minor child in the hands of Philip Augustus. Finally, Guines had a
dangerous enemy on its very borders in Renaud, count of Boulogne,
who from 1203 on attacked Guines either in person or by proxy.
In 1205, Baldwin II of Guines was captured by Renaud, and the
old man died shortly after his release, early in 1206. These events,
so threatening to the family's position, also may have inspired their
chaplain to write his history as a way of affirming the family's rights
and reassuring them in a period of trial.

Still, the reassurance must itself have been painful, for Lambert
told a remarkable number of unappetizing stories about the family.
A number of the ancestors of the family are described as being hated
by their people; one was murdered. The patron's great-grandmother
was a horrible woman who enserfed free people; Lambert says she
was "famous for the vice of cupidity and for notorious avarice".[122]
Lambert even attributes the imprisonment of his patron, Arnold II,
to Arnold's dissipation of the funds he had gathered to go on the
third crusade and his ultimate failure to go.[123] In other words, the
text takes a moral and admonitory stance toward the family. This
exemplary function, which provided both examples to avoid and
those to imitate, was often characteristic of dynastic history.[124]

---

[121] Lambert of Ardres, *The History of the Counts of Guines and Lords of Ardres*, trans.
L. Shopkow (Philadelphia, 2001), 2–3.
[122] *History of the Counts of Guines and Lords of Ardres*, trans. Shopkow, 162 (chapter
129).
[123] *History of the Counts of Guines and Lords of Ardres*, trans. Shopkow, 128 (chapter
95).
[124] Johanek (1992), 198.

So, although the French genealogies show a consciousness of family, they seem to arise not from that family self-consciousness but, rather, from political situations, and the existence of some genealogies seems to have prompted the creation of other histories taking a dynastic or genealogical form. The precociousness of these forms of history in northern France and Flanders, well before they appear in Germany,[125] may reflect not so much the greater degree of noble self-awareness in that region as the more rapid coalescence of territorial principalities and the identification of both monastic communities and princely administration with these principalities and their rulers.

The work that has been done on German genealogical material points in the same direction. For each genealogical work, a specific set of political and religious circumstances can often be educed which conditioned the creation of the work and the form the work took, that is, the individuals who were actually conceived of as being part of the family or dynasty. What is striking about the German materials, however, is that the 'dynasty' is often not a biological dynasty, that is, there are breaks and interruptions, in which new families appear. In consequence, these dynastic genealogies appear much more focused on the control of a particular piece of property than on a biological lineage. In the case of the fourteenth-century Welf genealogical table, the genealogy begins with Hermann Billung, not a Welf forebear at all, although founder of Saxony.[126] While the genealogy did serve Welf political goals, it was not "genealogical" at all in the most fundamental sense, that a family was commemorated. What the German genealogies make clear is that many genealogies and genealogical histories were the work of a "professional" who established the genealogy through "research", and that frequently these works were compiled not at the prompting of the family but at the instance of an institution.[127]

Varying historical purposes could lie below the genealogical form, so that, in a sense, to concentrate on the "natural" form of biological succession obscures as much as it reveals. The *Lignages d'Outremer* (begun in 1268) are an interesting case. They are part of a larger

---

[125] van Caenegem (1973), 73 and n. 16.
[126] Moeglin (1995), 524–25.
[127] Althoff (1988).

work, the *Assises de Jérusalem*, which was a collection of lost laws redrawn in the thirteenth century from memory at the court of Cyprus, composed by several authors, which survive in thirty-some-odd manuscripts and which was translated from the original French into other languages.[128] The *Lignages* never are found alone, and, in fact, the text explicitly situates itself with reference to the *Assises*. Even in the earliest versions, it is clear that it was a companion text. From the prologue, the relationship between these rather disparate texts appears to be that both are ways to describe a geographical, social, and political region, a land, its laws and its people.[129] The work is divided into chapters, each of which deals with a noble family and its descendants, but in the first edition, the family in whose circle the text was composed, that of Jean d'Ibelin, who was the redactor of one of the legal components of the *Assises*, is given pride of place. Noble pride in family is assuredly expressed here, but it is a pride connected to a particular polity—the kingdom of Jerusalem—and a particular service—the family's participation in the governance of the kingdom—and also at a particular time—the time when that kingdom had essentially slipped out of existence and the location of Outremer had shifted. It commemorated only the original families still in existence at the time of redaction and also added some families who were newcomers (such as the de Montforts). Once again, the existence of the tradition permitted a later writer to direct the text to new ends. This redactor, less interested in the Ibelin family and more in the structure of the kingdom, reorganized the text around 1309 to put the most important families first (the Lusignans, the kings, had been at the end in the first redaction). The text was reworked again around 1369, when its interest was purely historical.[130]

---

[128] See Nielen-Vandevoorde (1995).

[129] "Since you have heard and listened to the laws and customs of the realm of Jerusalem, and of those who first established them, it is proper that we enumerate for you the heirs who have descended and come from that good folk and by whom the land was inhabited". Venice, Biblioteca Marciana, Fr. app. 20265 (annex, no. 2) quoted in Nielen-Vandevoorde (1995), 108 (translation mine). Thus laws, country, and people all come together as one entity, suggesting again a community, rather than isolated noble families.

[130] Nielen-Vandevoorde (1995).

A Few Conclusions

I would argue, based upon what I have said above, that dynastic histories grow out of institutional history, in some cases an institution with which the members of the family are closely associated and in other cases a political territory. In other words, dynastic pride does not merely center on the *possession* of a piece of land but, rather, centers on its *rule*, and the rulers then are identified with the people they rule as well. Jules Lair, in his edition of Dudo of St. Quentin's history, named it *On the Customs and Deeds of the Norman Dukes*, not a medieval title, but Gerda Huisman has argued that the proper name, the name by which it appears in library catalogues, was the *Gesta Normannorum*, and Eric Christiansen, in his recent translation, has followed suit.[131] Since the history of the rulers was that of the people they ruled in a given territory, the crucial events then, are political; these texts are less concerned with the emergence of noble self-consciousness than with the development of territorial principalities and the association of particular families with these lands and/or the monastic communities within them. Most dynastic histories are created at predictable junctures in the relationship between a family and a domain: when the family first successfully lays claim to rule a territory (the first Norman dynastic history; the Scheyer genealogy); when a succession crisis threatens the family's control over the territory (the Saint-Bertin genealogy; the genealogy of the rulers of Brittany); in periods of threatened decline (the *History of the Counts of Guines*; the *Lignages d'Outremer*); or in periods when the history of a family is so intertwined with that of a territory that the family's history can effectively come to be that of the territory (France [with the *Grandes chroniques*] and fifteenth-century Bavaria). Under these last circumstances, dynastic histories take on a strongly national character.[132] The understanding of how such histories might be used to enhance the reputation of a court, the prestige of its prince, and the legitimacy of the ruler was fully in place by the twelfth century. One need think only of the dynastic histories of the Welfs (three separate genealogies dating from the twelfth century), the process by which

---

[131] Dudo, *De moribus et actis primorum Normanniae ducum*, ed. Lair; Huisman (1984); Dudo, *History of the Normans*, trans. Christiansen.
[132] Moeglin (1985); Kerhervé (1980).

the family chose to identify themselves as Welfs, and the literary flowering at Welf court at Braunschweig, a new court in search of an anchor.[133] But this kind of history became most fully useful when the prestige of literacy soared, the audience for learned texts expanded, and literature of all kinds became more readily exploitable by the court. Thus the author of the late fourteenth-century Austrian vernacular chronicle of the dukes flaunts his considerable erudition and mastery of Latin sources; the text opens with a reference to Seneca's work on the cardinal virtues.[134] When that change occurred in the late fourteenth century in the German lands, an explosion of dynastic history followed and, as I have argued elsewhere, a similar explosion of all kinds of history took place across western Europe.[135]

But there is no reason that the history of such a territory had to take dynastic form; there were always alternatives to such a means of forming identity, which might focus instead on common institutions like laws and customs, or on a particular monastery or bishopric. In the fourteenth century it is clear that civic chronicles receive some of these local historical energies. Consequently, the histories of regions are not often organized around their rulers, even if those rulers play a very important role in the histories. In France, dynastic history endured, and it makes a kind of sense. There was in France no common law, as there was in England to inspire a Bracton, but a scattering of common laws and Roman law. What held the French territories together, to the degree that they were held together, was the person of the king. In other words, the king was the main shared royal institution and perhaps the only possible repository for national history. The reasons why history also took on a dynastic organization in Aragon, I shall leave to a scholar of that region.

---

[133] See Schmidt (1983); Nass (1995); Hucker (1995); Moeglin (1995), 525.

[134] *Österreichische Chronik von den 95 Herrschaften*, ed. Seemüller, cclii–ccliii on the sources; cclxxvii on the author's education; 1 and n. 1 for the reference to Seneca.

[135] Johanek (1992), 205–06; Shopkow (1997), 263–71.

CHAPTER EIGHT

CONTEMPORARY AND 'EYEWITNESS' HISTORY[1]

Peter Ainsworth

The present essay attempts to chart the emergence from ca. 1170 onwards of several kinds of vernacular historical writing that are distinctive, amongst other things, for being allegedly contemporaneous with the events that they set out to recount. The authors of these works are more often than not 'eyewitnesses' of sorts, but as we shall discover, use of this term raises a number of awkward questions. The focus here will be on historiographical discourse in Anglo-Norman and Old French, initially in verse but eventually also (by the end of the twelfth century) in prose.

By 1170, Latin historiography still was largely dependent upon the Augustinian model of the Two Cities, which emphasized the immutability of the eternal and the good. The past therefore was viewed primarily in terms of the degree to which it approximated to, or offered a correlative for, the eternal present of Christian revelation. After a period of several hundred years, during which history writing in Latin had been largely universal and cumulative in emphasis, with very few writers ever managing to bring their histories as far as their own generation, we encounter the re-emergence during the final quarter of the twelfth century (and especially in the Anglo-Norman *regnum*), of 'eyewitness' historiography also composed in Latin. A short discussion of several instances of the new trend is prefaced by some reflexions on medieval attitudes to eyewitness testimony. This in turn leads into a more detailed exploration of one of the first extended eyewitness accounts to be written in a dialect of Old French, the Anglo-Norman *Chronicle* of Jordan Fantosme. Set against a cultural and literary backdrop still manifestly influenced by the *chanson de geste* and its epic vision of the past,[2] Fantosme's poem

---

[1] I am grateful to Dr. Wendy Michallat for her invaluable assistance with the preparation of both of my essays for this volume.
[2] This backdrop is explored in greater detail in my essay on "Legendary History", see p. 000 below.

is one of the first vernacular 'histories' of the Middle Ages to authenticate its content by reference to the author's physical presence at
key moments of the narrative. The essay then moves on to consider
the impact of the crusades on historiography written in both Latin
and Old French, and concludes with an examination of one of the
greatest exemplars of eyewitness history from the Middle French
period: Jean Froissart and his *Chroniques*.

For reasons discussed immediately below and elsewhere in this
volume,[3] the period running from the early twelfth century to ca.
1250 marked a watershed in the development of western European
awareness of historicity and, therefore, of the past. Several interrelated factors were involved, many of which have been explored by
Dominique Boutet in a groundbreaking study entitled *Formes littéraires
et conscience historique aux origines de la littérature française (1100–1250)*.[4]
Perhaps the most fundamental issue at stake in this context was the
growing tension between what was then understood by historical and
other kinds of truth, or as Boutet expresses it:

> la question, lancinante pour le Moyen Age, des rapports entre fiction
> et vérité historique au plan de l'écriture et, plus encore, de la récep-
> tion des œuvres, mais aussi celle des relations réciproques qu'entreti-
> ennent à cette époque l'Histoire et l'imaginaire.[5]

The term 'Histoire' (capitalized) is used here by Boutet to refer to
works whose referent is essentially historical, to distinguish them from
works referring primarily or exclusively to the literary or imaginary
(here termed 'histoire'); but as Boutet readily acknowledges, the distinction is difficult to maintain in absolute terms when one looks at
the spread of narrative works composed in the vernacular between
1100 and 1250, almost all of whose authors would claim to be *telling
the truth* in one way or another:

> In the period under consideration (from the beginning of the twelfth
> to the middle of the thirteenth century), all of these texts claim to "tell
> the truth" (a term which can cover a moral concept, a teaching, or
> an objective historical reality that the text claims to imitate); this claim
> can at times appear all the stronger for occurring in narratives that
> are ostensibly implausible in character. Fabliaux, lays, and Arthurian

---

[3] Ainsworth, "Legendary History", see p. 387 below.
[4] Boutet (1999).
[5] Boutet (1999), 3.

romances often make such claims, as do the epic poems about which Jean Bodel wrote that their subject matter, the matter of France, is manifestly true: "Cil [= les contes] de France sont voir chascun jor apparent".[6]

Boutet's prime interest lies in determining to what extent the emergent vernacular narrative literature in Old French and its varieties of formal expression may be shown to be related to a growing historical awareness. Jacques le Goff has argued that what we understand in the twenty-first century by self-consciousness and self-awareness with regard to our origins and subsequent history is largely an 'invention' of the thirteenth century, whilst Boutet himself reminds us that it is only in the late twelfth and early thirteenth centuries that medieval man begins to emancipate himself from the social, religious and philosophical collectivities of the time to emerge as more of an individual, indeed as more of a *person*:

> Medieval man is above all a 'homo historicus', a person intimately connected to the collectivity that owns him and carried along with it on the flood tide of history. But the theological notion of the 'person', which takes on a whole new meaning with the advent of auricular confession, implies that at this period a contradictory trend is beginning to make itself felt: witness the revival of autobiography along the lines of Augustine's *Confessions*, evidenced by works by authors such as Othlon de Saint-Emmeran (end of the ninth century) and Guibert de Nogent (beginning of the twelfth century). This is a trend, it may be argued, that eventually will issue in the extraordinary flowering of medieval vernacular literature.[7]

It is for reasons such as these that the study of medieval vernacular historiography cannot easily be divorced from that of other contemporary forms of narrative or 'writing about the past' and about the destiny of the individual within his or her collectivity. An inevitable part of the background to this essay must, therefore, be the perplexing but fascinating tension that obtained at this time between the historical and the imaginary (or what we would call today, broadly speaking, the fictional/literary). Neither form of expression existed in a pure state in the twelfth century; nor can either be studied in isolation from the other.

---

[6] Boutet (1999), 3; my translation.
[7] Boutet (1999), 5; my translation. For Boutet's reference to J. Le Goff, p. 21.

Early Eyewitness Histories

It is in the last quarter of the twelfth century that we begin to come across Latin and vernacular historians who claim to have witnessed at first hand the events that they recount and for whom such claims are a gauge of factual authenticity. The paragraphs that follow are, to a large extent, informed by the work of Peter Damian-Grint, a specialist in Anglo-Norman and Angevin literary history who has investigated the characteristics of this strain of historiographical writing. One of the achievements of his research has been to rectify several misunderstandings about the attitude of most Latin historians of the twelfth century towards their written sources. Recalling for us Isidore of Seville's classic definition ('historia est eorum temporum quae *uidimus*'), Damian-Grint holds with the view that for men such as William of Malmesbury, the ideal source of information was the first- or second-hand eyewitness account. The witnesses had to be trustworthy and honest individuals of sound reputation, the complete antithesis of irresponsible peddlers of mere hearsay.[8] Reliable eyewitnesses were always to be preferred to written sources. With specific reference to the latter, moreover, a few Latin historians differentiated between the activity of the *compilator* (as William of Malmesbury described himself, making it clear that the reliability of some of his sources was a matter for the reader to decide), that of the *assertor* (someone who himself vouched for the authenticity of the material he presented to the reader), and, lastly, that of the *auctor* (who for a long time had been viewed as a reliable source fully meriting the trust of readers,[9] despite the view of St Thomas Aquinas that argument from *auctoritas* was to be deemed *infirmissimus*).

From the last quarter of the twelfth century, contemporary or almost contemporary eyewitness accounts in Latin of significant events or personalities become more numerous, in some cases ostensibly because of the need to provide a "trustworthy" record of a controversial battle or military campaign, or of some other kind of cataclysmic event. The heroic culmination to William the Conqueror's

---

[8] "Indulgenti famae credere, et facilitatem auditorum fallere", William of Malmesbury, *Gesta Regum Anglorum*, ed. and trans. R. A. B. Mynors, compl. by R. M. Thomson and M. Winterbottom (Oxford, 1998, 1999), iv, 382; in Damian-Grint (1999), 70.
[9] Cf. Minnis (1984), 100.

successful campaign of 1066 is evoked for us in the Latin verse of
Gui d'Amiens,[10] the poet clearly seeking to portray William as the
very epitome of courage, military leadership and heroism.[11] Guillaume
de Poitiers wrote his equally encomiastic *Gesta Guillelmi* in Latin prose,
whilst Raoul de Caen celebrated the deeds of Tancred in the same
language (early twelfth century). North of the Channel, Richard of
Hexham's *De bello standardii* and Ælred of Rievaulx's *Relatio de stan-
dardo* (both ca. 1138) also laid claim to eyewitness authority and may
be seen as exemplars of a small but significant number of 'campaign'
histories written in Latin.

The *Vita Sancti Thomae* of William Fitz Stephen, in contrast, is a
prime example of a hagiographical text written very soon after the
martyrdom of a saint. At the beginning of the work the author
affirms his status as privileged eyewitness (at first- but sometimes second-hand) of Thomas Becket's martyrdom: "Passionem eius Cantuariae
inspexi . . . caetera plurima, quae hic scribuntur, oculis uidi, auribus
audiui; quaedam a consciis didici relatoribus".[12] Guernes de Pont-
Sainte-Maxence, author of a six-thousand-line vernacular *Vie de Saint
Thomas Becket*,[13] appears to have used a number of written sources,
including royal edicts and letters written by Henry II and Becket,
in compiling his work. His editor Walberg tells us that he also para-
phrased in verse a number of sections from the Latin biographies
of Edward Grim (1172)[14] and William of Canterbury (1172–74); and
at lines 147–50 and 6168,[15] Guernes claims to have consulted Thomas's
servants and friends at Canterbury itself, presumably the closest he
could manage to eyewitnesses of the outrage, but on the whole this
is a self-consciously literary and highly partial (if precise) account of
the martyrdom of Archbishop Thomas. The poet uses all of the
rhetorical resources of dialogue and set-piece dramatic episodes to

---

[10] *Carmen de Hastingae proelio*, ed. C. Morton and H. Muntz, Oxford Medieval
Texts (Oxford, 1972); cf. Davis (1978); Sayers (1966–67).
[11] For a lively translation into modern French of ll. 438–64 of the poem, based
on F. Michel's edition, *Chroniques anglo-normandes* (Rouen, 1840), vol. III, 1–38, see
Gally and Marchello-Nizia (1985), 179.
[12] William Fitz Stephen, ed. James Robertson, *Vita Sancti Thomae*, Rolls Series,
vol. 67/3 (London, 1877), 1–2, quoted in Damian-Grint (1999), 71.
[13] Guernes de Pont-Sainte-Maxence, *La Vie de Saint Thomas Becket*, ed. E. Walberg
(Paris, 1964).
[14] See Damian-Grint (1999), 71 n. 19.
[15] See *La Vie de Saint Thomas Becket*, ed. Walberg, x–xi.

enliven his narrative and convince his reader of Thomas's saintliness, and may even (as he tells us) have performed his poem at the
archbishop's tomb, perhaps before an audience of pilgrims. Not the
least interesting characteristics of the poem are its successful blending of Christ's Passion into the narrative of the martyrdom and its
frequent moral and spiritual reflexions. Walberg argues that Guernes's
narrative straddles two 'literary genres', those of religious poetry and
verse historiography. It is certainly hagiographical and encomiastic,
and its alexandrine metre lends it a faintly epic color, though the
poet's regular use of five-line rhyming sections rather than assonanced
laisses makes for a rather disjointed and halting style. The other principal strand of narrative writing (both Latin and vernacular) inspired
by issues of spiritual moment arose, of course, from the crusades.
We shall consider the significance of 'crusade history' later on in this
essay.

The military campaigns of the final quarter of the twelfth century
produced at least one work of vernacular history by a poet who
claimed to have participated actively in at least some of the events
that he describes. Around 1174–75, Jordan Fantosme finished his
Anglo-Norman *Chronicle*.[16] We know next to nothing about this writer,
but he may have been the pupil of Gilbert de la Porrée, bishop of
Poitiers from 1142, who certainly had a clerk by the name of Jordanus
Fantasma.[17] A few lexical forms found in the *Chronicle* relate to
Provençal, and certain aspects of the poem's metrical subtleties might
suggest that the author had had some contact with Occitan civilization. Whatever the case, we also find a clerk by the name of
Fantosme attached to the bishop of Winchester's entourage between
1150 and 1180. The *Chronicle*, unsigned but mentioning the name
Jordan Fantosme no fewer than five times, recounts the revolt of
Henry the Young King against his father Henry II Plantagenet, supported in his struggle by William the Lion, king of Scotland, and
by Louis VII of France and his vassal Philip, count of Flanders. The
poem's most recent editor, R. C. Johnston, highlights the innovative
and experimental aspects of this work, in which there is in fact no
mention of the word 'chronique'. For reasons of practicality, Johnston
stays with his provisional English title 'Jordan Fantosme's Chronicle',

---

[16] *Jordan Fantosme's Chronicle*, ed. and trans. R. C. Johnston (Oxford, 1981).
[17] Cf. MacDonald (1961).

whilst at the same time suggesting an alternative Anglo-Norman one: *Estoire del viel rei Henri*.[18] This, he argues, better reflects the subject matter as well as the poetic tone of the work. Finished shortly after the events narrated, the *Chronicle* remains an important source for the Scottish invasions of England in 1173–74. Those aspects of the narrative that deal with the campaigns of the Count of Leicester are less reliable, whilst those recounting the war in Brittany and Normandy are extremely thin on content. The opening of the poem is revelatory of the moralizing nature of the poetry and of the poet's undoubted affection and respect for Henry II Plantagenet:

> Oëz veraie estoirë: que Deu vus beneïe!
>   Del mieldre curuné   qui unkes fust en vie
> Talent m'est pris de faire vers, dreiz est que jos vus die.
>   Celui tieng a sage qui par autre se chastie.   (Johnston edn., ll. 1–4)

Nevertheless, there was not to be unqualified praise for Henry II, whose decision to have his son crowned in his own lifetime but without according him the material status of his new rank is viewed here as a signal error of judgment, beginning a conflict that would carry serious consequences for the kingdom's barons:

> Puis entre vus e vostre fiz   mortel nasquid envie,
>   Dunt maint gentil chevalier   ad puis perdu la vie,
>   Maint hume deschevalchié,   mainte sele voidie,
>   Maint bon escu estroé,   mainte bruine faillie.   (ll. 13–16)

Whilst sharing with us the pain felt by a father confronted by the disobedience of an ungrateful son,

> Li sires d'Engleterre   ad en sun cuer pesance,
>   Quant sun fiz le guerreie   qu'il nurri ad d'enfance . . .   (ll. 77–78)

the poet also implicitly censures the father for embittering the Young King (cf. Eph. 6:1–4), and this Pauline, Christian theme surely underpins the entire narrative. As far as Jordan's evocation of the preparations for battle is concerned, anyone with even a modest familiarity with the *chanson de geste* and its conventions would recognize, through the poet's deployment of demonstratives, motifs and formulae the strong influence of the epic:

---

[18] *Jordan Fantosme's Chronicle*, ed. and trans. Johnston.

Atant es vus ces chevaliers   descenduz del paleis,
   E vunt saisir ces armes   igneus e demaneis,
   Vestir haubercs e bruines,   lacier ces healmes freis,
   Prendre par les enarmes   ces escuz vianeis.
Dunc oïssiez Deu aramir   li vielz Henri li reis:
'Mar m'avrunt entreacuntré   li traitre es chaumeis!'

(ll. 153–58; cf. ll. 647–49)

Amongst the other epic and feudal motifs and themes encountered in the poem, we should mention, if only briefly, that of *mauvais conseil* which, in William the Lion's case, involves his readiness to give greater credence to untried strangers than to his own domestic advisors:

Bien sout li reis d'Escoce   adunkes guerreier,
Ses enemis en guerre   grever e damagier;
Mes trop fud acustumé de cunseilz noveler.
   La gent estrange chierisseit,   amot, e teneit chier.
   La sue gent demeine   ne volt unkes amer,
   Ki lui e sun reaume   deveient cunseillier.
   Bien i parut en haste   —ja m'en orrez parler—
   Cum avint de sa guerre   par malveis cunseillier.

(ll. 637–44; cf. ll. 673–78)

We are dealing here, manifestly, with a well-composed *estoire* and literary work. However, in the last part of his poem Jordan Fantosme takes great pains to stress to his listeners the reliability of his witness accounts ("Dehé ait Fantosmë, si ja m'orrez mentir!", l. 1146), especially when relating episodes where he himself was an active participant in the fighting. His description of William the Lion at the siege of Alnwick was not, he assures us, obtained by mere hearsay ("cum cil qui ad oï") but, rather, from his own testimony as a direct, first-hand eyewitness:

Li reis d'Escoce fud pruz,   merveillus e hardi.
   Par devant Audnewic   s'arestut desguarni.
   Jo ne cunt mie fable   cum cil qui ad oï,
   Mes cum celui qu'i fud,   e jo meismes le vi.   (ll. 1766–69)

Having rapidly donned helm and hauberk, the king mounts his warhorse and hurls himself into the press, killing the first man who gets in his way. After a fierce and bitter struggle, William falls prey to two contrary forces evoked in the poem by means of parallel *laisses*. The first is material: the lance of an English *serjant* or man at arms, which pierces the flank of the royal mount. As Fantosme and his editor both note, all would have been well had it not been for the intervention of the *serjant*'s weapon—and that of the second, moral force to which I have alluded, namely the sin of the Scots, here symbolized by the wounded horse lying on top of the body of the king, between his thighs:

190

Li reis se fait armer	tost e ignelement,
E muntad el cheval	qui n'esteit mie lent,
E vait en cel estur	par mult grant hardement.
Le premier qu'il feri	a terre l'agravent.
Li esturs fud mult fort	del rei e de sa gent.
Tut s'en fust bien alez,	par le mien escient,
Si ne fust un serjant	qui vers lui se destent;
De la lance qu'il tint	sun cheval li purfent.
Ne fait a demander	se li reis fud dolent!
Le pechié des Escoz	li fait encumbrement.
Li reis chiét a la terre	e le cheval ferant.

191

Li reis e sun cheval	a terre sunt andui,
Il ne pot relever,	le cheval jut sur lui.
Ore ad asez travail	e peines e ennui,
Quant garçon e escuier	passent ultre lui.
Il orrad novelës,	men escient, encui;
Ne purrad pru aidier	sei meismes ne autrui. (ll. 1776–92)

193

Li reis jut a la terre	abatu, ço vus di;
Entre ses quisses	giseit le cheval sur li;
Jamés n'en levera	pur parent ne ami,
Se li chevaus n'en est traiz,	dunt il est malbailli—
Il en iert a tuz jorz	avilé e huni.
Il esteit sempres pris	—*a mes dous oilz le vi*—
A Randulf de Glanvile	u il puis se rendi;
E ses chevaliers sunt	pris tut li plus hardi. (ll. 1799–1806)[19]

---

[19] My emphasis; cf. *Jordan Fantosme's Chronicle*, ed. and trans. Johnston, xvii, for a detailed commentary. I hope to publish an extended essay on Jordan Fantosme's poem in the near future.

Crusader Histories

As Damian-Grint and others[20] have argued, the First and Second Crusades had a major impact upon the development, in Latin first of all, of eyewitness historiography.[21] As Jean-Charles Payen has suggested, medieval Palestine was not solely a land of potential conquest for knights without fiefs; it was, above all, the theatre for a new Exodus to the original Promised Land.[22] 'Eyewitness' historiography of the First Crusade is represented by Baudri de Bourgueil's *Historia Hierosolymitana*, the Anonymous's *Gesta Francorum et aliorum Hierosolymitanorum* (1098–1100),[23] and Guibert de Nogent's *Gesta Dei per Francos* (composed between 1104 and 1108).[24]

A monk who eventually became abbot of Nogent in 1104, Guibert emphasised the need for an unsullied alliance between Creator and elect if the crusaders were to prove victorious in their struggle to reconquer the holy places. Comprising eight books and composed largely in prose but incorporating a number of passages in verse, the *Gesta Dei per Francos* is primarily spiritual in emphasis. Guibert was also the author of an introspective spiritual autobiography (the *De vita sua sive monodiarum libri tres*),[25] and it is, therefore, perhaps not surprising that one of the central issues in his *Gesta Dei per Francos* should be the difficulty of establishing just what it is that motivates human conduct. That said, the *Gesta Dei* extols the achievements of the Franks with gusto and provides a well-constructed and well-documented account of the First Crusade that aims to establish the causes behind events. The Second Crusade produced Odo de Deuil's *De profectione Ludovici VII in Orientem* (ca. 1140) and Raoul the Priest's *De expugnatione Lyxbonensi* (1147), the latter of which provides a mainly English perspective on the events recounted.[26]

---

[20] Damian-Grint (1999), 72; Reynolds (1990), 47–57.

[21] We should not of course forget the influence of the First Crusade, in particular, on the development of the vernacular Old French epic, exemplified by the *Chanson de Roland*.

[22] Payen (1997), 51–52.

[23] Discussed by Smalley (1974), 131–34.

[24] Guibert de Nogent, *Gesta Dei per Francos*, ed. L. d'Achery (Paris, 1651; repr. in J.-P. Migne, *Patrologia Latina*, vol. 156; see also *Rec. hist. crois., Historiens occidentaux*, vol. 4, [1879], 117–263).

[25] Guibert de Nogent, *Autobiographie*, ed. and trans. E. R. Labande (Paris, 1981); English trans. by C. C. Swinton, *The Autobiography of Abbot G. de Nogent* (London, 1924).

[26] Cf. Livermore (1990).

The impact of the Third Crusade was felt particularly keenly in the West, another factor reinforcing the need to "speak the truth" about what the crusaders had witnessed.[27] The *Estoire de la guerre sainte* was composed by the Norman minstrel Ambroise, in all likelihood between 1190 and 1196.[28] Present at the siege of Acre ("si com il vit a sa veüe"),[29] Ambroise pays enthusiastic tribute to Richard Cœur de Lion, offering his listeners a wealth of 'exotic' detail (a battalion of African warriors wearing red turbans are vividly described by the simile: "sembloient cerisiers meurs", l. 3357),[30] and occasionally waxing eloquent on the sufferings undergone by the pilgrims, which included swarms of gnats (ll. 9526–41), whilst King Richard himself was stuck with so many Saracen arrows that he "resembloit un herriçon" (l. 11630). As Damian-Grint points out, Ambroise takes care to tell us the identity of his sources for virtually all of the episodes to which he had *not* been a direct witness. It is true that his style is reminiscent of the epic, but, minstrel or clerk though he may have been, Ambroise prides himself on telling us the truth. That may be why, in the passage that follows, he takes umbrage with the *jugleor* and peddlers of mere hearsay:

> . . . vieilles chançons de geste
> dont jugleor font si grant feste
> ne vos sai mentir ne veir dire
> ne afermir ne contredire
> ne jo ne trois que le m'esponge
> si ço est veir o tot mençonge; . . .   (*Estoire*, ll. 4189–94)

When employed by another historian from this period, Richard de Templo,[31] the claim to eyewitness authority must, in contrast, be treated with caution. Richard's *Itinerarium* is remarkably close to

---

[27] As we shall see in a moment, this need would make itself felt even more insistently after the Fourth Crusade—which culminated in an attack on fellow (orthodox) Christians and the sack of the civilized city of Constantinople.

[28] For a lively discussion of Ambroise's style and handling of episodes dealing with warfare, see Hanley (2001) and (2001a), and esp. in the latter, p. 114: an intriguing episode involving a Christian battering ram so well-made that the Turks have to employ a whole series of means to destroy it (everything but the kitchen sink, in fact). Coverage also is provided in this thesis of the crusading account of the Minstrel of Rheims.

[29] Ambroise, *Estoire de la guerre sainte*, ed. G. Paris, Collection des documents inédits sur l'histoire de France, vol. 11 (Paris, 1897), l. 4568.

[30] Cf. Damian-Grint's commentary (1999), 78–79; Bancourt (1982).

[31] See Richard de Templo, *Itinerarium Regis Ricardi*, ed. W. Stubbs, Rolls Series, vol. 38/1 (London, 1864).

Ambroise's *Estoire de la guerre sainte* and was almost certainly modeled on it; whole sections appear to have been translated from it.[32]

Time and space preclude more extensive coverage of the literature inspired by or produced in the wake of the Third Crusade, not least because our principal quarry is vernacular 'eyewitness' or near-contemporary history. However, we cannot finish this section without a brief mention of one of the most important Latin works of the later twelfth century, William of Tyre's *Historia rerum in partibus transmarinis gestarum*, translated into English as *A History of deeds done beyond the sea*.[33] Born in Jerusalem in 1130, William studied in Europe before returning to the Holy Land, where he became archdeacon of Tyre in 1167, then archbishop in 1175, by which time he was also chancellor of the kingdom. This work provides an account of the history of the Latin kingdom of Jerusalem up to 1184 (William died in 1186). A major source for the history of the Latin kingdoms overseas, it was translated into French as early as 1220–23 and continued in several recensions and under various titles until as late as 1277.[34] Known for the liveliness of its narrative and its limpid style, the *Historia* grew out of conversations between William and Amalric, king of Jerusalem. Its scope was ambitious, beginning as it did with the Muslim conquest of Syria in 634–40[35] before providing a history of the First Crusade. A chronological account of each reign was provided, together with a portrait (after the manner of Suetonius) of each successive king. His subject, in the broadest of terms, is the country that he loved and saw as continuously under threat; William is arguably the first 'western' writer to use the term *patria* in this context:

> His *History* portrays a land as well as its Frankish conquerors. He worked hard to collect and sift information on what had happened when he was not present as an eyewitness. If his informants' reports varied, he set down each version, as the best he could do. He tried to write objectively, at the risk of annoying contemporaries. Mistakes in tactics or politics and irresponsible behavior get their share of blame. Nor does he spare his own feelings. . . . William does full justice to the

---

[32] Damian-Grint (1999), 71.
[33] William of Tyre, *Historia rerum in partibus transmarinis gestarum*, ed. R. B. C. Huygens, 2 vols. (Turnhout, 1986); trans. A. Babcock and A. C. Krey as *A History of deeds done beyond the sea*, in Records of Civilization (New York, 1943).
[34] See Tyl-Labory (1992).
[35] Smalley (1974), 136 ff.

excitement and pathos of his story of Overseas. A flash of eastern magic lights up his descriptions of a caliph's palace as it was described to him. He gives a first-hand and pathetic account of how he discovered that his pupil, the young heir to the kingdom, had contracted leprosy.[36]

William disapproved of campaigning bishops and was relatively poor on military history. He also resented the growing independence from diocesan control of the military orders, especially the Knights Templar,[37] but as Beryl Smalley has emphasized, his greatest achievement has to do with his percipience regarding causes and causality. Rejecting the classic explanation for the decline of the Kingdom *post* 1174, namely sinfulness and *accidia*, William looked beyond the moral to the political sphere:

> The first crusaders were expert soldiers, attacking a country whose natives had grown accustomed to peace and had forgotten how to defend themselves. Their enemies were disunited politically. The Muslim princes fought one another instead of obeying a superior. Almost every city had its own lord. Hence these isolated strongholds fell easily to the crusaders. Now, on the contrary, the Muslims were united under one ruler. The sultan had plenty of money, thanks to his conquests, and could pay his troops. Recruits were at hand in quantity, given the means to hire them. The present generation of Franks Overseas faced much greater odds than their forbears.

William realized that political unity and a full treasury will decide a conflict between two states. Modern historians of the Latin kingdom still subscribe to William's analysis of the causes of its fall.[38]

Villehardouin and the Fourth Crusade

When, shortly after 1207, Geoffroi de Villehardouin, Marshal of Champagne, began writing his *Conquête de Constantinople*, it may well have been because he felt the need to act as apologist for an army

---

[36] Smalley (1974), 140.

[37] It is worth mentioning at this juncture the recent publication of a later work that deals with the fortunes of the Knights Templar and with the reasons for the decline and fall of the Latin kingdom: the *Cronaca del Templare di Tiro (1243–1314)*, ed. L. Minervini (Naples, 2000). We should also note, in the context of this essay, the editor's own sub-title for the work: 'La caduta degli Stati Crociati nel racconto di un testimone oculare'.

[38] Smalley (1974), 141.

of which he had been one of the leaders, if not *the* leader; and which
had lost its way. With the Fourth Crusade deflected from its primary goal—a new conquest of Jerusalem undertaken from Cairo—
an explanation was needed as to how Western Christians, urged on
by the Venetians whose commercial sphere of influence had been
restricted by the hostile policies of the Byzantines, had been able to
seize Zara for their Italian allies before plundering Constantinople,
the very cradle of Byzantine and orthodox civilisation. Throughout
the narrative Villehardouin's sympathies seem to lie with Boniface,
marquis of Montferrat; we know that the chronicler became the
Marquis's liegeman in 1207 through the donation of Messinopolis.
Moreover Villehardouin had suggested that Boniface lead the expedition, and the *Conquête* ends with his death. It is thus Boniface and
his ambitions that seem to lend to the narrative its particular strategic perspective. A professional soldier and clever conciliator, always
present at councils held to determine strategy, Villehardouin was also
a skilful negotiator to whom were assigned the most delicate missions, including the embassy to the Venetians. In his work he claims
to be the faithful witness of the events that he recounts:

> Et bien temoigne Joffrois li mareschaus de Champaigne, qui ceste oevre
> dita, que ainc n'i menti de mot à son escient, si com cil qui à toz les
> conseils fu.[39]

Peter Noble is one of several critics who have pointed out how convenient is the pithy phrase *à son escient* ('as far as he is aware'); certainly, Villehardouin's narrative is far from being an impartial account.[40]
But Villehardouin no doubt believed in the strategy adopted by those
leaders who supported Boniface, and most of the commentators who
have read him carefully stop short of accusing him of bad faith, even
if they do point out several conspicuous omissions. He clearly wanted
to get at the truth as he saw it and to demonstrate to himself and
others the chain of circumstances that had brought the expedition
to its conclusion. We also should note that Villehardouin was eager
to attribute at least some significant happenings to the hand of God,
in contexts where modern interpreters probably would argue that

---

[39] Geoffroy de Villehardouin, *La Conquête de Constantinople*, ed. E. Faral, in Les
Classiques de l'histoire de France au Moyen Age, 2nd ed., vols. 18–19 (Paris, 1961),
CCV, 120.
[40] Noble (1999), 203; cf. Archambault (1974).

the more likely cause was the cynical opportunism of the expedition's leaders.

In terms of style, Villehardouin offers us a sober but nearly always coherent and consistently chronological narrative. Unlike his more modest contemporary, the minor Picard knight Robert de Clari (whose own *Conquête de Constantinople* is not so naive as many have made it out to be),[41] Villehardouin in general avoids picturesque background detail, limiting his frame of reference to the essentials of how he saw the expedition unfold. The great theme of Villehardouin's *Conquête* is the absolute requirement for cohesion within the army and the consequent rejection of anything likely to disrupt it (defections, betrayals, desertions, discord between the leaders). It is this which occasionally gives his work a moralizing tone. He must have been aware of the stinging criticism of the leaders that was doing the rounds within the army, and may have turned to writing in order to counter it with arguments that certainly are often persuasive:

> It was necessary, in his opinion, to accept the Venetian proposals and capture Zara because the crusaders, too few of whom had come to Venice, had not garnered enough finance to honour the commitments made in their name. They were victims of bad fortune which had deprived them of zealous leaders, plagued with multiple defections and undermined by a powerful element within, which sought unceasingly to destabilise the army. That the undertaking was not unjust was testified to by God's unfailing protection and the blessing of the Pope. The crusaders were manifestly justified in going on to conquer Constantinople at the request of Alexis IV. Here was a just act which, moreover, ended the reign of the monstrous Alexis III, a useful act which procured the means to liberate the Holy Land, and a necessary act which neutralised the effects of the most recent defections; in short, an act performed in the interests of justice, the papacy, the crusade and the crusaders themselves.[42]

Whilst prose steadily gained ground from around 1220, verse still was being used—and continued to be used for a long time to come— for the writing of rhyming chronicles of a biographical nature such

---

[41] Robert de Clari, *La Conquête de Constantinople*, ed. Ph. Lauer, "Classiques Français du Moyen Age", vol. 40 (Paris, 1924); cf. Dembowski (1963). For a balanced and thorough introduction to Villehardouin, De Clari, Henri de Valenciennes, the Greek chroniclers and the general background, see Noble (2001). Noble is currently preparing a new edition and translation of Robert de Clari's chronicle.

[42] Geoffroy de Villehardouin. *La Conquête de Constantinople*, ed. J. Dufournet (Paris, 1969), 9; my translation.

as the romance-like *Histoire de Guillaume le Maréchal* (ca. 1220–26)[43] or Chandos Herald's *Life of the Black Prince* (ca. 1385),[44] a mix of chivalric biography and muted polemic featuring Edward of Woodstock, prince of Wales and Aquitaine, and also John of Gaunt, duke of Lancaster, as well as the military allies of these two princes. Also of interest is the fact that the *Chronique* of 24,346 alexandrines, written between 1380 and 1385 by a clerk named Cuvelier,[45] celebrating the life of the French constable Bertrand Du Guesclin, looked for inspiration to the poetic diction of the *chanson de geste*.

Froissart

Born in 1337 or thereabouts in Valenciennes, Jean Froissart[46] spent his youth there before leaving for England in 1361 to take up a position at the court of his compatriot Queen Philippa of Hainault, wife of Edward III. It is not unlikely that the young writer had been encouraged in his literary vocation by Jean le Bel, canon at Liège and himself author of a *Chronique*[47] recounting the first campaigns of the Hundred Years War. The canon's chronicle, however, was written in prose and contained criticism of certain verse chronicles, which allegedly had sacrificed factual veracity to poetic licence. For eight years Froissart enjoyed the protection of Queen Philippa. He presented her with his first historical work, almost certainly cast in verse but sadly now lost, which (he informs us) celebrated the great military successes achieved by the English up until the battle of Poitiers in 1356.

Froissart immersed himself in the life of the English court at London, Westminster and Berkhamsted. During this period he wrote songs and ballads, virelays and rondeaux, but spent part of his time

---

[43] *Histoire de Guillaume le Maréchal*, ed. and trans. P. Meyer, 3 vols. (Paris, Société de l'Histoire de France, 1891–1901); cf. Duby (1984).

[44] Ed. Tyson (1975).

[45] Ed. Faucon (1990–91).

[46] See Zink (1998). With the kind permission of Hachette/Le Livre de Poche and Michel Zink, general editor of the *Lettres Gothiques* series, some of the material in this final section is translated from the *Introduction générale* to *Chroniques, Livres I et II*, ed. P. F. Ainsworth and G. T. Diller, in "Lettres Gothiques", ed. M. Zink (Paris, 2001).

[47] Jean le Bel, *Chronique*, ed. J. Viard and E. Déprez, 2 vols. (Paris, 1904–05).

gathering information for the historical inquiries that he intended to pursue. In particular he interviewed the French hostages held under house arrest in London to meet with the requirements of the Treaty of Brétigny (1360), four years after the battle of Poitiers and the capture of John the Good of France. It was in this way that Froissart obtained the supplementary information on the Anglo-French conflict that he would later incorporate into the first recension of his *Chroniques*, complemented by additional accounts collected during research trips undertaken with the permission and, presumably, encouragement of Queen Philippa. These journeys were ambitious. The chronicler's travels took him to King David Bruce in Scotland in 1365, to Edward Despenser's castle at Berkeley in Gloucestershire in 1366, to the Brussels court of the Duchess Jeanne and Duke Wenceslas of Brabant, again in 1366, and in 1366–67 to the court of the Black Prince in Aquitaine at Bordeaux. On his return from a journey he had made to Italy in 1368, where he had attended the marriage of Lionel of Clarence to Violante Visconti in Milan, Froissart learned of the death of his benefactress Queen Philippa, who had passed away on 15 August 1369. He once again set out for his native Hainault, where he was shortly to begin the first *prose* version of Book I of the *Chroniques* for Robert de Namur, brother-in-law to Jeanne and Wenceslas of Brabant and to Edward III of England. This version, Siméon Luce's "first redaction proper", was finished around 1373.[48]

If Froissart abandoned verse, at least for history writing, it was almost certainly because he had been influenced by the ideas of Jean Le Bel, whose *Chronique*, finished in 1361, had, as we have seen, denounced certain historical works written in verse containing "an over-abundance of often redundant words, chosen and contrived so as to embellish the rhyme". In order to lend more authority to his own account of events between 1325 and 1350, Froissart went to the lengths of transcribing practically word for word whole tracts of Jean le Bel's original text, a form of 'plagiarism' that, for the time, was seen as far from reprehensible since *citation*, generally practised without reference to sources, was a commonplace procedure heightening the prestige of a work whilst at the same time guaranteeing its authenticity. From 1373, Froissart took up residence in the presbytery

---

[48] Jean Froissart, *Chroniques*, ed. S. Luce, G. Raynaud, L. and A. Mirot, 15 vols. (Paris, 1869–), vol. 1 et seq.

at Les Estinnes-au-Mont given to him by Guy de Châtillon, count
of Blois. This enabled him to make progress with his narrative until
1378. In the opinion of Siméon Luce, the resultant text should be
seen as the "first redaction revised", but in 1376 the count of Blois
had already commissioned another version of Book I, also concluded
ca. 1377–78 (the Amiens MS version, called by Luce the "second
redaction") and containing some material of which there is no trace
in the 'previous' version or redaction. It is practically certain, however, that much of this new version is actually older than its so-
called predecessor, the "first redaction revised". Whatever the case,
these two prose editions of Book I offer us a lively account of the
origins of the great dynastic conflict between the kings of England
and France. They contain Froissart's account (obtained from eyewitnesses) of *chevauchées*, sieges, skirmishes, and pillaging, punctuated
by several pitched battles in which, during this period at least, the
knights of Edward III—led by excellent commanders and backed
up by archers from Wales or Cheshire—were generally victorious
(battles of Sluys, 1340; Crécy, 1346; and Poitiers, 1356).

Between the first and second Books of the *Chroniques* there is no
obvious break in continuity. A large part of Book II, written between
1378 and 1385, provides an account of the conflict between the
count of Flanders and his subjects of Ghent, as well as of the disagreements between this town and its rival, Bruges. There is also,
however, an account of riots and popular insurrection in France and
in England (the Maillotins in France and the Great Revolt of 1381
in England). Froissart was himself a witness to certain of these events.
We know that he accompanied Guy de Blois during Charles VI of
France's campaign against the Flemish in 1382. Although he was a
native of Hainault and not a Fleming, the troubles of the count and
county of Flanders must have affected Froissart deeply. Certain
episodes of Book II betray, if not a sympathy for the rebels (in his
eyes guilty of having tried to overturn a social order instituted by
God), at least a measure of understanding, in a narrative context
where the excesses of the masters, as well as their failure to arrest
the disturbances, are also vividly evoked.

A new journey undertaken in 1388 with the encouragement and
support of Guy de Blois allowed Froissart to visit the court of Gaston
Phébus, count of Foix-Béarn at Orthez, where he gathered information about the conflict that had just finished in Spain and which
features as the primary subject-matter of his third Book (1389). In

a subsequent redaction of the latter, he corrects this 'Castilian' version of events against fresh oral testimony secured from a Portuguese knight, don Fernand Pachéco, whom he met in 1390 at Middelburg in Zeeland. Book III heralds a major transformation in the chronicler's handling of both time and narration: "From now onwards the *Chroniques* combine poetic time with historical time, narrative time and the time of memory".[49] This is the phase during which the *Chroniques* become the recital of the chronicler's own experience as traveller and interviewer, interwoven with his account of the Spanish wars and of the political discord brewing in England between Richard II and the Commons. From Book III onwards "we move from chronicle to memoir [. . .], the chronicler's present existence and personal recollections of what he has experienced taking precedence over the objective memory of events, or at least shaping his communication of it".[50]

Froissart wrote hardly any poetry after 1389. Poetry, it seemed, would henceforward find its expression in the writer's prose. By a strange paradox, the more the chronicler's prose evinces literary or rhetorical qualities, the more penetrating and astute are his criticisms of contemporary society. In 1389 he is once again to be found in Paris, where in August of the same year he witnesses the entrance into the city of Charles VI's new queen, Isabeau of Bavaria. Between 1391 and 1392 Froissart once again changes patron. Guy de Blois, who, writes Michel Zink, was by this time "ruined, poorly advised, dissipated and obese",[51] had sold his county to the younger brother of the French king, Louis de Touraine, soon to be created duke of Orléans. Froissart thus lost a means of support upon which, in any case, he was no longer able really to rely. The humiliating ruin of Guy de Blois affected Froissart deeply. At the end of his life his patrons were Albrecht of Bavaria, count of Hainault, and his son William, count of Ostrevant.

In 1392 Froissart was present at the French court when the famous attempt was made on the life of Olivier de Clisson. Several months later he attended the peace negotiations at Leulinghem. In 1395, the chronicler returned one last time to England, but, in spite of the welcome he received, albeit from a slightly aloof Richard II, the trip

---

[49] Zink (1998), 18; my translation.
[50] Zink (1998), 78; my translation.
[51] Zink (1998), 12; my translation.

must have disappointed him because everything had changed and his old English friends had virtually all disappeared. Froissart ended his days in Hainault around 1404, probably in his *forge* at Chimay, where for some years he had held a canonry. It was at Chimay that he penned his fourth Book, which covers the reign and mental illness of Charles VI and the last years of the reign of Richard II.[52] Froissart's very last composition, however, was a rewrite of the opening section of Book I (covering the period 1325–50), a version generally known as the Rome MS redaction.[53] Here the writer appears to voice his fears about the future of *Prouesse* in a country that had been witness to the deposition and murder of its king.[54]

The modern historian treats the *Chroniques* with caution. However, anyone seeking an understanding of the social, political and cultural forces that drove aristocratic and military policy in the fourteenth century will benefit by consulting them. Without being a comprehensive and faithful reflection of a society, the *Chroniques* offer us a quite remarkable perspective on a world in which prowess, honor, and courtliness (the ideology of the knight) are pre-eminent; but the chronicler is not entirely insensitive to the miseries suffered by a populace subjected to the plundering of roving bands of mercenaries, discharged soldiery or royal raiding parties; nor is he blind to the exactions and injustices imposed on them by their sovereign or feudal suzerain, even if (most of the time) the nascent radicalism of his representation of events is tempered by conventional excuses invoking the laws of war or the unpredictable whims of Dame Fortune.

His conception of objectivity would not, of course, stand up to the scrutiny of modern historical science. He tried above all to highlight the *hautes emprises* or deeds of extraordinary valor accomplished over the course of the Hundred Years War, without favoring personalities from any particular 'nationality'. He was a teacher, seeking to educate the young and to stall the passage of time by prolonging the echo of the reverberations from these exemplary combats. However, he was also a consummate storyteller, one could even say a film director *avant la lettre*, excelling in the depiction of movement and

---

[52] See tome 16 of Jean Froissart, ed. Kervyn de Lettenhove. *Œuvres* (Brussels, 1867–77); accessible via the Internet at http://gallica.bnf.fr).

[53] Jean Froissart, *Chroniques. Dernière rédaction du Premier Livre. Edition du manuscrit de Rome Reg. Lat. 869*, ed. G. T. Diller, in Textes littéraires français (Geneva, 1972).

[54] Cf. Ainsworth (1990), Part III, 219–302.

the upheaval of the battlefield, sketching in the play of light on helms and lances, and brushing in the color of heraldic pennants fluttering in the wind. He knew also how best to convey the emotions of his characters, often by means of a simple gesture or silent gaze in the midst of a *tableau vivant* rendered dramatic by recourse to passages of direct speech.

Alongside the substantial accounts of gallantry often featured in manuals of literary history or anthologies of set pieces (Crécy and Poitiers, the Six Burgesses of Calais,[55] Charles VI's fit of madness in the forest of Le Mans, etc.), one comes across more uncertain passages that are less susceptible to easy contextualization. A number of narrative developments in Book III spring to mind where Froissart merges his historical presentation with other forms of narrative account: travel journal incorporating lively dialogue, report, anecdote, gossip, *exemplum* or mythological tale. A prime instance of this richer, more troubling, textuality is the chronicler's repeated attempts to shed light on the circumstances of the murder of the young heir of Foix-Béarn by his father Gaston Phébus. The chronicler here includes himself as a participant in the gradual weaving of his narrative during the long ride across the countryside of Béarn. Froissart continually interrogates his travelling companion Espan de Lion, who constantly puts off getting to the heart of the matter until Froissart is forced to find out the 'true' details of the crime from an alternative source. It is an old squire who, after much hesitation, finally agrees to recount his version of the facts to the chronicler. This account is thus a narrative at second hand, such that the 'facts' in question undergo a remodelling that serves both to mask and mythologize them. The same procedure is used in Froissart's account of the bewitching of Pierre de Béarn, which is in turn marked by the recirculation of the myth of Acteon, of which Froissart was so fond and which reappears in his romance *Meliador* as well as in one of his longer narrative *dits*.[56]

It is also worth underscoring the interest inherent in the three major redactions of Book I of the *Chroniques*, from the historical but

---

[55] This episode has lost none of its appeal to French audiences. See Jean-Marie Voeglin's *Les Bourgeois de Calais. Essai sur un mythe historique*, Albin Michel, coll. "Evolution de l'humanité" (Paris, 2001), reviewed in *Le Monde des Livres* du 24 mai 2002, p. VII.

[56] Zink (1980).

also—and more particularly—*literary* point of view. Recounting ca. 1400 preparations for a renewal of the War in 1333, Froissart picks up and rewrites a hitherto summary allusion to the role played in these events by the French fugitive Robert of Artois, "qui ne cessoit nuit ne jour de lui [à Edouard III] remonstrer quel droit il avoit à la couronne de France" (first redaction text), working it up into an extremely well-constructed speech to the king in full council. The chronicler is especially prone to dramatic scenes of this kind, often enlivened by imagined speeches, especially when the authority, rights, or reputation of a king are at stake.

The well-crafted work of the canon of Chimay—poetry and *Chroniques*—amounts to an attempt to comprehend (that is, to understand but also to circumscribe) the myth and the factual reality of chivalry by imposing some kind of shape upon them through recourse to the written word. Froissart in this way 'consecrates' them for all time, at precisely the moment when their continued existence seemed threatened by a new political and social order apprehended only obscurely by the chronicler. This accounts, perhaps, for an increasingly frequent recourse in the later redactions and books to mythological or didactic digressions, and for the writer's linking of a recent, ephemeral past to a more stable and somehow more *authentic* past, as an insurance against a future already auguring badly—with the great plague of 1348–49 and beyond, the popular uprisings of 1358–84, several periods of royal tyranny between 1380 and 1400, and, finally, a dramatic increase in political assassinations and depositions (1399–1400). The trait common to many aspects of this work which, on the face of it appears to be so heterogeneous, is writing itself, as foundation, creation, conservation, and communication of the truth: "car vous savez que toute la cognoissance de ce monde retourne par l'escripture, ne sus aultre chose de verité ne sommes fondez fors que par les escriptures approuvées".

We have seen how, having begun with a chronicle in verse, Froissart almost certainly was converted to prose for the composition of his *istoire* by the example of Jean le Bel and his *Chronique*. This recourse to an *auctoritas*, calculated in principle to safeguard factual accuracy, demonstrates Froissart's determination to preserve for posterity what he calls the 'recors des preux', and thereby to offer future generations a source of edifying examples. Only writing can guarantee this *translatio* or handing down to the descendants of meritorious knights both a precious fount of knowledge and a *savoir-vivre*.[57] In this respect Froissart may be compared to the secretaries of the monarchical orders of chivalry whose task it was, at the close of each year, to enroll the distinguished feats of arms performed by their members. They were also obliged to report in writing any misdeeds or derogations that may have been committed, incurring *reproche d'armes*. This aspect of chivalric ideology is set forth in the *Prologue* to Book I, where the author of the *Chroniques* warns us that:

> esploit d'armes sont si clairement comparet et achetet, che scèvent chil qui y traveillent, que on n'en doit nullement mentir pour complaire à autrui et tollir le glore et renommée des bienfaisans, et donner à chiaus qui n'en sont mies digne.

Later, when writing his third book, Froissart will defend himself in no uncertain terms against those who accuse him of bias:

> [Qu'on ne dise pas que je aye eu la noble histoire] corrompue par la faveur que je aye eu au conte Gui de Blois qui le me fis faire et qui bien m'en a payé tant que je m'en contempte, pour ce qu'il fut nepveu et si prouchains que filz au conte Loys de Blois, frère germain à saint Charles de Blois, qui, tant qu'il vesqui, fut duc de Bretagne. Nennil vrayement! Car je n'en vueil parler fors que de la verité et aler parmy le trenchant, sans coulourer l'un ne l'autre. Et aussi le gentil sire et conte, qui l'istoire me fist mettre sus et ediffier, ne le voulsist point que je la feisse autrement que vraye.[58]

Strange as it may seem, this passage shows the importance to the chronicler of Valenciennes of *oral* testimony, given in good faith and obtained from people who had actually taken part in the combats, sieges, or raids of which Froissart is so anxious to preserve a vivid memory. He lived at a time when oral testimony given in good faith still was deemed entirely dependable. Rather than criticize him for his gullibility, we should commend him for having so scrupulously interviewed the many people whom he met in royal courts or engaged in conversation in wayside inns. The picture Jean Froissart gives us of fourteenth-century society is dominated by an ideological climate that is at one and the same time royal, aristocratic, and chivalric.

---

[57] Ainsworth (1998).
[58] Froissart, *Chroniques*, ed. Luce, Raynaud, Mirot, and Mirot, 13: 223–24.

Given that the king was the leader of the body politic, the well-being of his subjects depended upon his own health and moral qualities. Numerous episodes in the *Chroniques* delineate aspects of the apprenticeship of kings or depict the progressive hardening of their moral character.[59] Conversely, the chronicler is ever ready to condemn royal tyrants guilty of excessive dependency on favorites, be they princes of the royal blood or impertinent upstarts.[60] In the same way, Froissart emphasizes the essential importance of the role played at court by the king's counselors, even as he depicts for us the dread consequences of *mauvais conseil* given by men unworthy of such trust.[61] Froissart thus evinces a strongly conservative conception of the society of his time. Yet his thinking barely differs, in this respect, from the most discontented 'reformers' of the end of the fourteenth century.[62]

That said, the society depicted in the pages of the *Chroniques* is not an entirely static one. Froissart accords a special status to those opportunistic (in the positive sense of the term) knights and squires, the careers of whom represent for him the *nec plus ultra* of chivalry: "pluiseur chevalier et escuier se sont fait et avanciet", he tells us, "plus par leur proèce que par leur linage". In short, in this world that was still feudal and strictly structured, it nevertheless still was possible to advance socially. Even so, Froissart shares the anguish, if not the pessimism, of a great number of his contemporaries, witnesses of the Great Plague and of the endemic conflicts between neighboring realms which punctuated the fourteenth century. His desire to fix forever the ideal image of *Prowess* and her leading exponents—Edward III, the Black Prince, Sir John Chandos, or Sir Walter de Manny—before they disappear forever, can be explained partly by his conviction that human existence is precarious, with only writing being capable of preserving some trace of it, however modest:

> Car bien sçay que ou temps advenir, quant je seray mort et pourry, cest haulte et noble hystoire sera en grant cours, et y prendront tous nobles et vaillans hommes plaisance et augmentation de bien.
>
> Car vous savez que toutte la cognoissance de ce monde retournent par l'escripture, ne sus aultre chose de verité nous ne sommes fondez fors que par les escriptures approuvées.[63]

---

[59] Ainsworth (1990), 272–302.
[60] Ainsworth (1990), 98–100, 241–56.
[61] Ainsworth (1990), 192–205.
[62] Cf. Lewis (1977), 42–43.
[63] Prologue to Book III; see Froissart, *Chroniques*, ed. Luce, Raynaud, Mirot, and Mirot, 12: 2, 14: 9.

The Prologue to the 'first redaction revised' recension of Book I (Luce's 'B' manuscripts version), invokes the age-old topos of the Three Orders, but in so doing replaces the *oratores* (those whose duty it was to pray for the welfare of those who bore arms: at first the bishops, later the clergy in general) with those whose function it is to record in chronicles or histories ('cronisier') the exploits of the knightly caste:

> Li vaillant homme traveillent leurs membres en armes, pour avancier leurs corps et acroistre leur honneur. Li peuples parolle, recorde et devise de leurs estas, et de leur fortunes. Li aucun clerch escrisent et registrent leurs avenues et baceleries.[64]

The Prologue to the final redaction of Book I (the Rome MS version composed ca. 1399–1404) places still greater emphasis upon the eminently honorable role fulfilled by the chronicler as recorder and memorialist:

> Or se debrise et disfere li mondes en pluisseurs manieres. Premierement, li vaillant honme travellent lors corps en armes pour conquerir la glore et renonmee de che monde; li peuples parole[,] recorde, et devise de lors estas; auquns clers escripsent et registrent lors oevres et baceleries, par quoi elles soient mises et couchies en memores perpetueles. Car par les escriptures puet on avoir la congnissance de toutes coses, et sont registré li bien et li mal, les prosperités et les fortunes des anciiens.[65]

From this perspective, Froissart's *Chroniques* can be likened to the English chantry chapels of the fourteenth and fifteenth centuries, endowed by bishops, princes, and knights to preserve the memory of their passage here on earth and to guarantee that masses for their souls are said in perpetuity. The best examples of these can still be seen today at Winchester, Tewkesbury, Hereford, Ely, and Warwick.

In the final analysis, Froissart's major preoccupation remains that of representing and, so to speak, *consecrating* the spectacle of the *apertises d'armes* of the knights whom he admired with so much passion. He even casts himself as their *clerical* disciple in so far as he could declare himself to be their secretary and celebrant. Seen from this point of view, the *Chroniques* are in themselves a great heroic *emprise*, for it is in this work that the clerk finally comes to associate his destiny with that of the knight (princes, barons, knights, and squires)

---

[64] Prologue to Book I, 'B' MSS; see Froissart, *Chroniques*, ed. Luce, Raynaud, Mirot, and Mirot, 1: 5.
[65] *Chroniques*, ed. Diller, 37; cf. Marchello-Nizia (1984).

whose likeness he preserves in the *Chroniques*. Some of his portraits
are literary *tombeaux*, reminding us of the alabaster effigies of those
who lie to this day in many English churches dating from the fourteenth century (see for example that of Sir Hugh Calveley at the
parish church of St. Boniface at Bunbury near Tarporley, Cheshire).
Here, to quote just one example, is how Froissart depicts the virtues
of his patrons Wenceslas de Brabant and Guy de Blois:

> Ce duc Winchelant fut largues, doulx, courtois et amiables, et grant
> chose eust esté de luy, s'il euist longuement vescu, mais il morut en
> la fleur de sa joennesse, car il s'arma très voulentiers, dont je, qui ay
> escript et cronisiet ceste hystoire, le plains trop grandement que il
> n'eubt longue vie tant que à IIII^{xx}. ans, ou plus, car il eust fait moult
> de biens en son temps, et luy desplaisoit grandement le scisme de
> l'Eglise, et bien le me dist, car je fuy moult privé et accointié de luy,
> pourtant que j'ai veu en mon temps que j'ay travailliet le monde CC
> haulx princes; mais je n'en vey oncques plus humble, plus debonnaire,
> ne plus traittable, et aussy avecques luy mon seigneur et mon bon
> maistre, monseigneur Guy, le conte de Blois, qui ces hystoires me
> recommanda à faire. Ce furent les deux princes, en mon temps, de
> humilité et de larguesce et de bonté, sans nul mauvaix malice, qui
> sont le plus à recommander, car ilz vivoient largement et honneste-
> ment du leur, sans grever ne travaillier leur peuple, ne de mettre nulles
> mauvaises ordonnances ne coustumes en leurs terres.[66]

The chronicler's admiration is neither unbounded nor uncritical, but
it is only towards the end of his career that Froissart betrays serious doubts as to the viability of the chivalric dream. The earlier
redactions of Book I book evince an almost uniform infatuation for
the gallantry of chivalry. Books III and IV, in contrast, betray a progressive disillusionment. Analyzing the account of the tragedy of
Richard II ('Froissart's version, not Shakespeare's') given in Book IV,
Michel Zink has highlighted the percipience of the chronicler ca.
1399–1400:

> Tout montre, ici et jusqu'à la fin du livre et de l'œuvre, le soin et
> l'efficacité avec lesquels Froissart rend, sur un ton presque neutre, la
> haine, la peur, la trahison, la dissimulation, la servilité, la violence,
> l'humiliation, les retournements de situation, les ricanements du des-
> tin, la glu du piège où se prend celui-là même qui l'a tendu. Vraiment,

---

[66] Book III; see Froissart, *Chroniques*, ed. Luce, Raynaud, Mirot, and Mirot,
14:159–60.

Froissart n'est plus le jeune homme euphorique, ébloui par la cour de la reine Philippa et par le panache chevaleresque. L'écrivain, l'historien, le moraliste ont beaucoup appris sur l'homme, sur l'homme de cour, sur la faiblesse des puissants.[67]

Conclusion

An essay of this scope will of necessity be selective. My prime aim has been to encourage readers to evaluate the historicity of the narratives discussed against their original intellectual, social, and cultural background. A second aim has been to encourage the same audience to go back to these texts in order to reach conclusions based on their own reading. Inevitably there are omissions that will cause some eyebrows to be raised. There is, for example, no reference (save this one) to Joinville's wonderful *Vie de saint Louis*,[68] or, less worryingly perhaps, to would-be imitators of Froissart such as Enguerrand de Monstrelet. No coverage has been provided of the Burgundian chroniclers and memorialists (Georges Chastellain, Jean Molinet, and Olivier de la Marche, to name only the better known of these), nor have we been able to include the fascinating *Journal d'un bourgeois de Paris*.[69] In sum, difficult choices have had to be made; I feel, nonetheless, that authors and texts such as these will not suffer unduly for having been omitted, for they still can be read in peace and with unalloyed pleasure, free of the burden of my analysis.

As we saw at the outset of this study, the use of the term 'eyewitness historian' is fraught with difficulty when applied to the Latin and vernacular 'historians' of the period that I have attempted to discuss. Even genuine eyewitnesses were strongly influenced in the composition of their works by stylistic, rhetorical and generic constraints or presuppositions. This is why I have elected, rather, to write about 'Contemporary and "Eyewitness" History': perhaps the greatest merit of this designation is that it provides a more objectively

---

[67] Zink (1998), 96.

[68] But see Jean de Joinville, *Vie de Saint Louis*, ed. J. Monfrin, Classiques Garnier (Paris: Dunod, 1995).

[69] But we can refer our readers to Colette Beaune's 1990 edition of *Journal d'un bourgeois de Paris* for the Lettres Gothiques series, based on Tuetey's original edition.

honest 'generic' or, rather, summative title for the texts considered here, whilst offering far fewer hostages to fortune. In the last analysis it has allowed us at least to bring together and shed some fresh light upon a particularly interesting body of writers, chroniclers, and historians, each of whom deserves to be studied in his own right.

CHAPTER NINE

LATER MEDIEVAL INSTITUTIONAL HISTORY

Bert Roest

Like other essays in this volume, this chapter concentrates on texts that share a comparable subject matter rather than a generic label. To be specific, this chapter deals with later medieval institutional history, defined as the official or unofficial historical writings by and for medieval religious institutions (e.g., individual cloisters, monastic and mendicant orders, the papacy, and the diocese), regardless of the generic categories to which these texts themselves can be assigned.[1]

The chosen approach enables me to evade some traditional problems of generic division and generic exclusion that traditionally form a stumbling block in surveys of medieval historiography. That is not to say that I have solved all problems with regard to the demarcation of my text corpus. Many chronicles were not conceived to present the history of a particular institution. Yet they contain so much material concerning a particular religious house or order that they can hardly be ignored. An interesting example is the famous chronicle of Salimbene of Parma. Its surviving parts suggest a universal historical conception. However, the work abounds in information regarding Franciscan houses, the early development of the Franciscan order, and the life and career of many individual friars. Moreover, this kind of information is a central part of Salimbene's narrative. Another case in point is the work of Orderic Vitalis († ca. 1142), which began in a very localised institutional format (the history of Saint-Évroul in Normandy), but expanded into ecclesiastical and universal history.[2] There are many such borderline cases. They make clear that overly refined distinctions between so-called institutional history and other forms of medieval historical writing will necessitate me to leave out many interesting works, or to separate writings that in the eyes of the medieval compiler belonged together.

[1] With thanks to The Netherlands Royal Academy for Arts and Sciences, which provided me with the means to complete my research.
[2] See the remarks in Houts (1995), 15; Chibnall (1984).

This chapter deals with developments in the later Middle Ages (ca. 1000–1500 A.D.), a period in which many religious institutions became the subject of historical reflection. To some extent, this historical reflection followed patterns established in earlier periods. This was most certainly the case with later medieval monastic and episcopal history. Hence my sketch of these forms of institutional history during the later medieval period will be relatively succinct. The bulk of this chapter is devoted to the large historiographical production in the male branches of the Dominican and Franciscan orders. That is not to say that members of other new religious movements did not engage in historical writing. My choice to focus on the Dominicans and the Franciscans is predominantly motivated by the fact that these two mendicant orders in particular nurtured a host of productive historians, several of whom for a variety of reasons have not until recently received the esteem that they deserve.

I. *Monastic History*

Between the eight and the thirteenth century, historical writing was predominantly a monastic affair. Even after mendicant and lay urban chroniclers outwinged monastic historiographers, monastic historical writing did not subside. Speaking about monastic historiography, we can distinguish between the large monastic tradition of chronographical and historiographical writing in salvation-historical perspective (with close relations to exegesis and eschatology, following the lead of Eusebius, Jerome, Orosius and Bede), and the more truly institutional forms of monastic historiography. As the first tradition is dealt with in another chapter, the latter concerns me here. Its basic formats during the medieval period were the annals and the *gesta abbatum*. Both these forms of monastic historiography, which could take on manifold different features and titles (and therefore should not be interpreted as separate genres in the strict sense), normally dealt with the foundation and history of the monastery, more often than not with particular attention for its founders, benefactors, patron saints, abbots, privileges, and possessions. In short, the monastic chronicle is the memory of the monastery's religious, judicial, and economic reality and continuity.[3]

---

[3] Houts (1995). On early and high monastic history, see also Kastner (1974); Patze (1977), 89–121.

The monastic chronicle recorded the authentic monastic life, relating the miracles performed by patron saints, and the religious habits and deeds of past generations of monks and abbots, who needed to be commemorated through meditation and prayer. This aspect explains why monastic chronicles frequently incorporate necrologies (*libri mortuum*) and *consuetudines*, and sometimes grew out of them. Throughout the medieval period, many monastic chronicles (as well as those concerning churches) have remained anonymous: a sign that not the individual but the community was important.[4]

During periods of religious reform, in the tenth-early eleventh century (Cluny) and again in the twelfth century (Citeaux and Prémontré), monastics consciously used the writing of history to depict their own reformed monastic community over against older ones, and as a means to strengthen the reform ideal among their own members. No wonder that monastic chronicles abound in ages of monastic reform. Among these are famous ones, such as the *Gesta abbatum* of Cluny, the *Gesta abbatum Gemblacensium* of Sigebert of Gembloux, and the series of monastic chronicles of Monte Cassino, which eventually found their more or less definite reworking by Petrus Diaconus after 1138.[5]

The *Gesta abbatum* were institutional histories shaped as serial biographies of the community's first abbots: the dominant authority figures, who bore responsibility for the community as a whole and often determined its success. These biographies were modelled on saints' lives, and could serve comparable liturgical, edifying and commemorative purposes. This complicates the distinction between monastic historiography and monastic hagiography. The earliest event in a monastic chronicle usually is a miracle of the founder-saint or a comparable miracle worker. Saints' lives and legendaries written in a monastic setting as well as monastic annals and chronicles frequently tell a comparable history of the places where saints lived, founded monasteries, performed their miracles, and where their relics were kept.[6]

---

[4] Houts (1995), 30–31 (also for more information concerning the authorship of monastic chronicles in male and female settings). On the relationship between monastic history and practices of commemoration, see in particular Oexle (1995), 9–78.

[5] Richter (1972); Goetz (1988), 455–88; Goetz (1989), 135–53; Waha (1977), 989–1036; Hofmann (1973), 59–162; Schmale (1985), 137–38.

[6] Houts (1995), 15 and 29, mentions for instance the *Inventio et miracula sancti Vulfranni*, produced in Saint-Wandrille in Normandy (ca. 1053–54), which "is as much a chronicle of the refoundation and growth of the monastery as it is an account of the discovery of the body of St. Vulfran". See also Houts (1989), 233–51.

Monastic chronicles also codified obtained privileges and landed possessions; the economic life-blood of the traditional religious houses. This provided incentives for incorporating documents and charters, and for including detailed reports of duly witnessed donations by generous benefactors. Hence there exists considerable overlap between monastic chronicles (or comparable forms of local institutional history) and document collections pertaining to particular institutions. Cases in point are the so-called monastic chartulary chronicles and the later medieval urban town books.[7]

Traditional monastic houses and foundations of regular canons as a rule were established with aristocratic support and kept close relations with noble benefactors. Many monastic chronicles therefore incorporate a (partial) history of the founding aristocratic dynasty, making it hard to draw the line between monastic chronicles and dynastic history.[8] If dynasties gained a supra-regional or even pan-European importance, monastic chronicles incorporating their deeds could evolve into forms of territorial history and beyond.

In the German lands, where several monasteries were imperial foundations, monastic chronicles could include a partial history of the German Empire, providing the monastic house and its imperial benefactors with a proper world-historical lineage. This was particularly fashionable during the Ottonian and early Staufen period.[9] In post-conquest England and Normandy monastic historiography and Anglo-Norman dynastic historiography were also closely linked, witness the monastic chronicles of St. Augustine's Abbey in Canterbury.[10] An almost automatic overflow from local monastic history and hagiography to a *Historia Anglorum* and world-historical compilations, is also visible in the works of Matthew Paris (ca. 1200–59), a monk from St. Albans. In the Iberian Peninsula, we can signal several literary endeavours under Alfonso X of Castile in the thirteenth century, and the fourteenth-century historiographical initiatives under Pedro IV of Aragon. In both cases, the combination of strong monastic

---

[7] Cf. Houts (1995), 16, 29 ff.; Genet (1977), 95–138; Patze (1977). Hofmann (1987), 427–28, mentions also the chartulary chronicle of John of Vincentio (1144), the so-called *Chronicon S. Vincentii Vulturensis*.
[8] Cf. Patze (1964), 8–81, and (1965), 67–128; Patze (1987), 331–70; Houts (1995), 3 ff., 32.
[9] Schmale (1985), 96.
[10] Emms (1995), 159–68.

historiographical traditions and a royal court trying to legitimate its power and to boost its literary culture brought about a significant historiographical production.[11]

In French royal monasteries comparable developments took place. Famous are the formidable historiographical activities in the abbeys of Fleury, Saint-Germain-des-Prés, Saint-Magloire, and Saint-Denis. From the early eleventh century onwards, these centres produced *Gestae* & *Vitae Abbatum*, saints' lives and royal biographies, alongside of histories of the Franks and the French realm. Good examples are the works of Aimon of Fleury and its continuations, the works of Raoul le Tourtier and Hugh of Fleury, the history of Louis VI by Suger of St. Denis, the *Roman des Rois* of the Saint-Denis monk Primat (fl. 1274), the subsequent works of Guillaume de Nangis and Richard Lescot, and the ultimate literary offspring of combined monastic and royal patronage: the thirteenth-and fourteenth-century *Grandes Chroniques de France*.[12]

For monastic historians, dynastic aspects were not the sole impetus to extend the historiographical scope. The ongoing interest in chronographical matters and the strong salvation-historical, exegetical and eschatological concerns of medieval monastic authors enticed many of them to follow the lead of Eusebius and Jerome. Hence they engaged in the production or continuation of universal chronicles and forms of ecclesiastical history. Frequently, such works were conceived as universal chronicles from the outset, for which I would like to refer the reader to other chapters. Sometimes, however, such works grew out of an ever-expanding monastic history. This was for instance the case with the aforementioned *Historia ecclesiastica* of Orderic Vitalis. Before 1120, Orderic was asked by his abbot Roger of St. Évroul to write a history of the cloister. In the writing process (which lasted until 1141), the scope of his work gradually expanded into a full-blown history of the world. Notwithstanding this evolution, Orderic composed the work as a whole primarily for his fellow brethren and for the liturgical praxis of his monastery.[13]

The work of Orderic Vitalis was not exceptional. Many monastic chroniclers placed the history of their monastic institution in a

---

[11] Cf. Dyer (1990), 141–58, 248–51; Houts (1995), 20.
[12] Spiegel (1978); Guenée (1986), 189–214; Bautier (1994), 59–72.
[13] *The Ecclesiastical History of Orderic Vitalis*, ed. M. Chibnall, 6 vols. (Oxford, 1969–80); Hofmann (1987), 415–16.

wider salvation-historical perspective. Thus forms of order history
with hagiographic overtones appeared,[14] as well as forms of ecclesiastical history in which the history of the monastery or the order
was carefully embedded in the history of the Church (as happened
in the *Historia Ecclesiastica* of Hugh of Fleury).[15] In the late Middle
Ages, comparable perspectives were developed by mendicant chroniclers, who had reasons of their own to link the emergence and the
significance of their religious orders to a (hierocratic) history of the
Church at large. To this kind of mendicant historiography, which
itself was inspired by the longstanding *Liber pontificalis* tradition, I will
return later on.[16]

In the period after ca. 1200, monastic historiography did not subside, even when it lost some of its prominence to the mendicants
and various non-religious protagonists. In fact, the late Middle Ages
abound in monastic chronicles of every kind: short annals limited to
one particular foundation (from the high Middle Ages onwards, annals
continued to be a 'basic vehicle' for local institutional history), fully-
fledged monastic chronicles with overtones of dynastic history, as
well as specimens of monastic reform historiography, in which the
perspective could be much broader than the community for which
the chronicle was intended.

No use then, to lament the decline of monastic historiography
during the late medieval period. There certainly was a breach: the
Plague epidemics of 1347/9 caused the abrupt termination of many
local monastic and non-monastic historiographical traditions. The
later fourteenth century was, in a sense, a time without history.[17]
This should not be interpreted as a full decline of monastic historical writing, as has been done in the past. Monastic historical writing was taken up again in the course of the fifteenth century, frequently
in connection with observant reforms.

The early observants, whether monks or friars, almost everywhere
turned their back on 'superfluous' learning, towards a 'more pure'
religious life. They were more concerned with the production of

---

[14] Such as the *Exordium magnum Cisterciense sive narratio de initio Cisterciensis ordinis*,
ed. Br. Griesser (Rome, 1961), by Conrad of Eberbach (fl. ca. 1200).
[15] Cf. Hofmann (1987), 413 ff.
[16] Zimmerman (1960); Hofmann (1987), 413.
[17] Sprandel (1987), passim.

meditative and pastoral texts than with historiography.[18] Only the second or third generation of observants once again saw the need for institutional history, as a means to establish a strong profile over against non-observant rivals, as a vehicle for commemorative meditation, and as a repository of predicable materials (the same motivations that had bolstered the historiographic production in the mendicant orders all along). To these purposes, the leaders of the Benedictine reform movements of Kastl, Melk and Bursfeld inaugurated a conscious reflection on Benedictine history and propagated the writing and reading of Benedictine (order and cloister) chronicles.

Well-known is the plea of abbot Gunther of Nordhausen from the Erfurt St. Peter monastery. He urged that every reformed settlement should produce a history of its own foundation, as part of an educational program in which the reading of *piae historiae* in private and in communal reading encounters was deemed to be beneficial. If a suitable historian could not be found within their communities, abbots had to seek a historian from elsewhere.[19] According to Gunther, every community had sufficient historical material to write a chronicle, and each monastery should have a *doctus historiarum magister* to teach history to novices and monks. Within boundaries, this stimulated the reading of history (with recourse to already existing compilations that were floating around),[20] the copying of venerable examples of monastic history,[21] and the production of new observant monastic chronicles, both in Latin and in the vernacular.[22] These latter chronicles, which

---

[18] In the traditional orders, this lack of historical interest partly related to lacking standards of education; see Schreiner (1988), 38.

[19] See Gunther's own *Traktat über den Wert historischer Aufzeichnungen* (1481) cf. Frank (1973).

[20] Interesting in this context is the Latin 'Sammelhandschrift' now in Paris BN Lat. 10334 containing the *Flores temporum*, the *Notitia saeculi* of Alexander of Roes and other excerpts, all of which were predominantly chosen for their moral and predicable qualities. These were compiled in 1466 by a monk of Blaubeuren on request of the Blaubeurer Abbot Ulrich Kundig; see Schreiner (1988), 60–66. Later, Christian Tubinger wrote a chronicle of Blaubeuren, the *Burrensis coenobii annales. Die Chronik des Klosters Blaubeuren*, ed. G. Brösamle, trans. B. Maier (Stuttgart, 1966).

[21] In Blaubeuren, the monk Andrew Isengrein copied in 1477 the famous chronicle of Monte Cassino (with information on early Benedictine history), which then travelled to various other observant Benedictine centres, sometimes to function as source for new *vitae* and chronicles on early Benedictine history. See Schreiner (1988), 58.

[22] In the context of the late fifteenth-century Bursfeld reform, we can point to the *Chronicon ecclesiasticum* by Nicholas Bottenbach of Siegen, the annals of Hirsau by John Trithemius, and the chronicles in Clus near Gandersheim. In the 1490s,

Constance Proksch even wants to consider as 'eine eigenständige, historiographische Gattung unter der Bezeichnung Reformchronistik',[23] share as central theme the *sacer ordo Benedictini* as the motor of religious reform that would enable wayward religious communities to return *ad sinceritatem regulae*.[24]

II. *Episcopal History*

The diocese (or rather the cathedral chapter and the *familia* of the bishop) also provided an institutional setting for the production of historiographical texts: forms of episcopal history that focussed on the succession of bishops and on the origin and development of the diocese itself. Scholars often present episcopal history as an emulation of the famous *Liber pontificalis/Gesta Pontificum Romanorum*. Hence, episcopal history would seem to follow the normative prototype of the history of the bishops of Rome. As a matter of fact, the *Liber pontificalis* is a beautiful example of medieval institutional history. Its first redactions go back to the sixth century (*Catalogus Felicianus*), and maybe even to the third or fourth century (the *Catalogus Liberianus*). After a substantial lapse between the eight and eleventh century, the work was pursued seriously in the era of Gregory VII, to be continued with adjustments and additions until 1431. The work was amplified and fuelled by additional papal biographies and chronicles, such as that of John of Salisbury and the *Vitae paparum Avenionensium* of Werner of Hasselbecke.[25] In the later Middle Ages, the pope catalogue of the *Liber pontificalis* constituted a basic source for the ubiquitous pope-emperor chronicles of mendicant stock, to which I will return. Through this reception in mendicant historical compendia, the pope catalogue had a fundamental influence on all kinds of historiographical writing between the thirteenth and the sixteenth century.

Historians signal the presence of the *Liber pontificalis* (in one form or another) in many episcopal libraries throughout the medieval

the abbot of Hirsau, Blasius Scheltrub (1484–1503), who also re-established a commemorative cult around St. Aurelius, took the initiative to gather historical knowledge about the monastery, resulting in the Hirsauer Codex. See Schreiner (1988), 69.

[23] Proksch (1994), 11, 28 ff.; Schreiner (1988), passim.

[24] Schreiner (1988), 51 ff.; Proksch (1994), 29–30. Proksch gives many additional examples.

[25] Cf. Zimmermann (1981); Prerovsky (1974).

period. As historians tend to see the papacy as the primordial episcopal institution, other episcopal histories usually are presented as
the diocesan pendant of the *Liber pontificalis*. Among these episcopal
histories the *Gesta episcoporum* in particular are singled out as generically 'quintessential'. Such *Gesta*, which frequently were written by
members of the bishop's *familia* (often his secretary) or by members
of the cathedral clergy, predominantly trace the history of the episcopal see as a succession of bishops and their religious and worldly
endeavours from the foundation of the diocese onwards.[26] As a literary genre, the *Gesta episcoporum* would have reached its apex between
the ninth and the twelfth century, notably in Northern France,
Lorraine, and Saxony: centres of Carolingian, Ottonian and Salian
imperial culture with close-knit ties between imperial and episcopal
power.[27]

Like the *Gesta abbatum* mentioned before, these *Gesta episcoporum* can
be interpreted as an intermediary between a mere catalogue and
veritable *historia*: dealing with the succession of bishops within the
diocese, but also digressing on the history of larger territories and
the vicissitudes of the Empire as a whole. Sot mentions in this regard
the *Gesta pontificum Hammaburgensis ecclesiae*, compiled by Adam of
Bremen (ca. 1070),[28] and the episcopal chronicle of Thietmar of
Merseburg (†1018). Many original *Gesta* received one or more continuations, whereas others received reprisals, or became a muster for
episcopal histories elsewhere. Again the episcopal chronicle of Thietmar
of Merseburg is a case in point. Thietmar's work formed the basis
for later *Gesta archiepiscoporum Magdeburgensium*, *Gesta episcoporum
Merseburgensium*, and *Gestae episcoporum Halberstadensium*, which were continued into the fourteenth and fifteenth centuries.[29]

As was the case with monastic chronicles, the *Gesta episcoporum*
combined a range of different objectives. They firmly grounded the
foundation of the diocese with its territory and its churches in a
saintly past, and they confirmed the legitimacy of episcopal power
in Church and Empire with recourse to historical precedent and
established rights and privileges. The former element accounts for
the fluent transition between episcopal histories and episcopal saints'

---

[26] On the *Gesta episcoporum* as a genre, see Kaiser (1994), 459–80.
[27] Cf. Handschuh (1982); Engels (1989), 135–75.
[28] Cf. Buchner (1963), 15–59; Sot (1981), 7–15, 32 ff.
[29] Cf. Lippelt (1973).

catalogues. Normally, the founding bishops are depicted as saints, who before and after their death are at work within the diocesan territory (in the proximity of their graves). Not by chance the burial or translation of a former bishop-saint frequently prompted composition of episcopal histories. The redaction normally took place on request of the living bishop or members of his circle, who saw the occasion as an opportunity to stress the sanctity of the episcopal office and to legitimise and sanctify episcopal authority in matters of administration, liturgy and politics. In other words, many episcopal chronicles constitute a *commemoratio* and an authoritative *memoria* of religious, sacramental and political efficacy, meant to establish a direct link between the present (the time of the author and his envisaged audience) and the saintly past of the diocese.[30] The concern for legitimacy and established rights and privileges, on the other hand, explain the many digressions on the history of the Empire and the insertion of many archival documents and official episcopal letters. In turn, such well-documented diocesan chronicles could function as a cartulary for episcopal usage and as a stable testimony of the possessions and privileges of the cathedral church and the diocese as a whole.[31]

Insofar as the history of the diocese coincided with the history of the town in which the cathedral church was situated, episcopal histories could evolve into urban chronicles, or at least provide a basis for the production of urban chronicles after the emancipation of lay urban authority from regional aristocratic and ecclesiastical jurisdiction. Within the Empire, this double process was accelerated after the collapse of the imperial episcopal system, which weakened the relative weight of bishops as political players.[32]

Traditionally, scholars therefore envisage a decline of the *Gesta episcoporum* as a genre; a decline accentuated by a loss of wider perspectives and a movement towards more local and modest bishop catalogues, which in the second half of the fourteenth century also saw vernacular continuations. Lately, Markus Müller has challenged this view by looking at surviving late medieval episcopal chronicles

---

[30] Sot (1981), 18–19.
[31] Cf. Sot (1981), 25–27, 48 ff.
[32] The early twelfth-century *Gesta Treverorum* were an outflow of the original *Gesta archiepiscoporum Trevirensium*. Hofmann (1987), 422. See Houts (1995), 25 ff., for a first assessment of urban history in Italy and Germany.

and by questioning scholarly assumptions about the 'proper' generic properties of the *gesta episcoporum*. As long as these *gesta* are seen to constitute a specific genre of writing in a set religious-political context, namely the Ottonian church system, it follows naturally that the genre lost significance in the aftermath of the Investiture contest. Later medieval episcopal histories, whether bearing the title *gesta episcoporum* or not, did not have the same content, nor the same imperial outlook. Nevertheless, from a quantitative perspective the writing of episcopal history flourished as never before during the closing centuries of the Middle Ages. Müller lists seventeen dioceses in the Empire where episcopal history only started between 1250 and 1450, whereas in fifteen other dioceses the writing of episcopal history was only embarked on after 1450. To this he adds substantial continuations of high medieval historiographical traditions.[33]

Müller signals definite changes in the representation of the bishop in the late Middle Ages, such as the downplay of his pastoral role and holy stature. This also shows in decline of episcopal *vitae*,[34] an increasing emphasis on the diocese as a territorial entity, and the rise of the catalogue as the standardised format for new episcopal histories under the influence of mendicant historical *compendia*. Müller also signals differences in historiographical orientation between the traditional authors of the bishops chronicle (members of the cathedral clergy), and those produced by 'new' compilers of episcopal history: mendicants and clerics of various observant movements (i.e., members of the Bursfeld and Melk Benedictine reform, and the Windesheim congregation of the Augustinian canons), as well as legal professionals and humanist scholars in service of the episcopal administration and the episcopal court. These different authors had different motives for writing and hence a variety of ways to represent the succession of bishops and the history of the diocese.[35] To check Müller's conclusions in wider European perspective, further study of late medieval episcopal chronicles is necessary.

---

[33] Müller (1998). It is impossible to summarise this rich and deep-probing study, which hopefully is the starting point for a new interest in late medieval episcopal history and related forms of institutional historical writing.

[34] Except for the holy bishops from mendicant stock. Yet the production of saints' lives for the latter group frequently was an initiative of the order rather than of the diocesan clergy.

[35] Müller (1998), passim. Nice specimens of such 'late' episcopal chronices are found in the dioceses of Frauenburg, Lübeck, and Münster; see Sprandel (1987), 301.

III. *Mendicant Historiography*

Until ca. 1970, mendicant historiography shared in the generally negative verdict that three generations of mediaevalists (between Lorenz/Wattenbach and Herbert Grundmann) had passed on late medieval historiography. These scholars duly acknowledged the increase in historiographical output during the closing centuries of the Middle Ages. Yet aside from the 'lebendige, spontane Geschichtsschreibung auf kleinere Zeiten und Räume . . .'.[36] this output was deemed to be fossilised and schematic, not able to emulate the standards and eschatological perspectives of eleventh and twelfth century historical writing. This verdict disqualified an enormous text corpus that at the same time was eagerly used as source material for the study of late medieval political, institutional and socio-economic history. For this reason, late medieval chronicles often have received partial editions that contain only the 'useful' or 'original' parts; therewith distorting the compilatory set-up of the manuscript copies.

Since ca. 1970 we are experiencing a major re-evaluation of later medieval historiographical praxis. This re-evaluation is no doubt connected with a general redemption of the late medieval period altogether. Gradually, the inherently historicist idea of a medieval autumn is left behind. We begin to appreciate the correspondence between the use value of texts and the phenomenology of literary production. The late medieval period overflowed with historiographical (sub) genres, and related forms of literature. Apparently, such literature was in tune with readers' expectations and the discursive needs of the time. No use complaining that texts from that period do not match their high medieval forerunners, or do not seem to cohere with modern notions about the proper format of medieval historiography.

New generations of (predominantly German and some French) historians have done much to emancipate late medieval historiography from the limbo to which previous generations had condemned it. Important signposts in this regard are the 1980 and 1985 studies of Bernard Guenée, the 1985 study of Rolf Sprandel, the 1985 handbook of Franz-Josef Schmale, and the 1987 volume *Geschichtsschreibung und Geschichtsbewusstsein im späten Mittelalter* edited by Hans Patze.[37] In

---

[36] Grundmann (1965), 23.
[37] Guenée (1980) and (1985) Sprandel B. Guenée, 'L'histoire et la compilation au XIIIᵉ siècle', *Journal des Savants* 78 (1985) 119–135; Schmale (1985); Patze (1987).

these volumes we find both an evaluation of the important work done after 1970 and major prolegomena for subsequent research.

The study of mendicant historiography properly speaking owes much to Anna-Dorothea von den Brincken's and Gert Melville's interest in the compilatory format and historical conceptions of successful mendicant chronicles, the re-evaluation of the architecture of Vincent de Beauvais' *Speculum Historiale* by Hans Voorbij and the scholarly circle around Monique Paulmier-Foucart, the renewed interest in later medieval historiography as a form of encyclopaedic writing, and the attention for dissemination of late medieval mendicant chronicle manuscripts by Peter Johanek and his collaborators in Münster.[38] Thanks to such endeavours, the traditional lamentations about the compilatory and 'uncritical' nature of mendicant historiography have been exchanged for a genuine fascination with the compository strategies of mendicant compilers and the incredible distribution of mendicant chronicles.

This redemption of mendicant historiography touches in particular the so-called 'kompilatorische Weltchronistik', which can hardly be depicted as institutional historiography in the strict sense of the word. However, as a typical product of 'mendicant' historiographical practice, it deserves some of our attention. The order histories and order-related hagiographic texts always have been and predominantly still remain the domain of specialists in medieval hagiography and of (mendicant) scholars interested in the literary and religious culture of the mendicant orders as such. These various forms of institutional historiography in the strict sense of the word are neglected by historians in search of general patterns in medieval historiographical writing, maybe because many such order histories on average do not seem to waver much from the traditional catalogue format. Yet they form the core of mendicant institutional history properly speaking. They constitute a considerable part of the mendicant historiographical output, and in addition have some interesting qualities of their own, reasons for which they will be central in the following sections.

---

[38] For instance Brincken (1981), 694–735, (1985), 461–500, and (1989), 551–91; Melville (1987), 57–111, and (1988), 133–53; Voorbij (1991); Meier (1992), 157–75; Mierau, Sander-Berke and Studt (1996).

III.1   *Franciscan and Dominican hagiography as institutional history*

The emergence and astonishing success of the Franciscan order in
the early thirteenth century went hand in hand with a large historiographical and hagiographic production. After the death of their
charismatic founder, the Friars Minor were keen to produce authoritative *vitae* to single out the extraordinary saintly qualities of Francis
and the unique character of his chosen life of evangelical perfection
over against older attempts of religious reform, therewith legitimising the Franciscan order and its ecclesiological mission, and empha-
sising Francis' salvation-historical significance (which to some extent
even turned Francis into a Christ-like figure). Among these authoritative hagiographic texts, we can signal the various *vitae* composed
by Thomas of Celano and Julian of Speyer, as well as the *Legenda
Major* and the *Legenda Minor* of Bonaventure that after 1263 became
the official *vitae* of Francis within the order for centuries to come.[39]

The Franciscan hagiographic production was not limited to its
founder. Other prominent members of the order received ample
hagiographic attention as well, more often than not in the context
of their official beatification. Cases in point are the *vitae* devoted to
Anthony of Padua, Clare of Assisi and Louis of Anjou, and those
vitae devoted to the foremen of the observant movement (such as
Bernardine of Siena and John Capistran). Subsequent saints' lives of
less-universal figures frequently emerged as instruments of commemoration and edification by individual Franciscan communities.

Alongside individual *vitae*, Franciscan friars embarked on the production of larger, order-related saints' catalogues. These can hardly
be distinguished from order historiography properly speaking, as the
latter also abounds in abbreviated legends of Franciscan saints. The
oldest surviving catalogue is the *Dialogus de gestis sanctorum fratrum minorum* (ca. 1245)[40] ascribed to the Franciscan missionary, historian and

---

[39] For an introduction, see Desbonnets (1967), 273–316; Clasen (1967); Campagnola
(1974), 17 ff.; Paciocco (1990); Uribe (1996), with information concerning the works
of Thomas of Celano, Bonaventure, Bernard of Bessa, Julian of Speyer, Henry of
Avrange, and the various texts of the 'spiritual' tradition. There exist several
corporate editions of such texts. See for instance *Fontes Franciscani*, ed. E. Menestò,
S. Brufani et al., Testi 2 (Assisi, 1995).

[40] *Dialogus de gestis sanctorum fratrum minorum auctore Thomas de Papia*, ed. F. Delorme,
Bibliotheca Franciscana Ascetica Medii Aevi, V (Quaracchi, 1923). The Franciscans and
the Dominicans were not alone in the production of institutional catalogues of order-

theologian Thomas of Pavia. This work, commissioned by general minister Crescent of Jesu in 1244, can be described as a collection of biographies of nineteen holy friars, the 'deeds' of whom the author intended to preserve for posterity. These deeds would reveal the power of God. They would provide examples of virtue to strengthen the vulnerable faith of fellow friars, and they would correct heresy by showing the truth of the Catholic Church signified in the lives of holy men.[41] In fact, the *Dialogus* combines the deeds of Franciscan saints with historical anecdotes concerning the Franciscan order.

Aside from the *Dialogus* there exist various other thirteenth- and early fourteenth-century Franciscan Saints' catalogues of a comparable miscellaneous character.[42] A special category in this regard is formed by the cloud of anecdotal hagiographic writings that we associate with the spiritual wing of the Friars Minor. The sometimes dissident hagiographic texts of the budding spiritual movement, such as the *Legenda trium sociorum*, the *Actus beati Francisci et sociorum eius*, and the *Speculum perfectionis* not only represent Francis in his life of utmost poverty and simplicity, but also devote much attention to several of Francis' first companions, who by later generations were often seen as the living exemplars of the founders original intentions.[43] The intricate textual history of these various compilations, their historical trustworthiness, their interdependence as well as their chronology, have been matters of contention among Franciscan scholars ever since the late nineteenth century, when Sabatier used such texts to recreate the 'original' way of life of Francis and his companions.[44] Several friars who figure in these collective biographies

---

saints. Among the Servites of Mary, we can point to the *Legenda de origine ordinis*, ed. E. M. Toniolo (Rome, 1982). Among the Augustinian Hermits, we can refer to the *Liber vitas fratrum* of Jordan of Saxony († ca. 1375).

[41] *Dialogus*, ed. Delorme, 2.

[42] Such as the *Liber miraculorum et visionum* (ca. 1300) from the Franciscan province of Saxony. For a partial edition and manuscript information see Lemmens (1909). Several friars mentioned in this collection also appear in the *Catalogus sanctorum fratrum minorum*, ed. Lemmens (Rome, 1903).

[43] Cf. *Actus beati Francisci et sociorum eius*, Collection d'Études et de Documents sur l'Histoire Religieuse et Littéraire du Moyen âge IV (Paris, 1904); *Actus beati Francisci et sociorum eius*, ed. J. Cambell (Assisi, 1988) (new ed. in preparation); *Legenda trium sociorum*, ed. Th. Desbonnets, *AFH*, 67 (1974), 38–144; *Speculum perfectionis status fratris minoris*, ed. P. Sabatier (Manchester, 1928²).

[44] On this so-called 'quaestio franciscana' see Menestò (1993), 245–67; Zanot (1997), 261–74.

and anecdote collections of 'spiritual' origin also received *vitae* of their own.[45]

The various catalogues of Franciscan saints written in the later Middle Ages make mention of several hundreds of Franciscan *sancti* or *beati*. The fourteenth-century Umbrian *Catalogus sanctorum fratrum minorum* (ca. 1335), which also stands on the borderline between order history and hagiography, makes mention of at least 200 brethren.[46] If we forego for the moment the large order histories that also incorporate many saints' lives, such as the *Chronica XXIV generalium*, the most notorious saints' catalogue and programmatic work of Franciscan order hagiography is the vast and influential *De conformitate beati Francisci ad vitam Domini Iesu* of Bartholomew of Pisa (1390).[47] It is first of all a lengthy biography of Francis, fleshing out the by then classic theme of conformity between the lives of Francis and Christ. In addition, it describes at length the sanctity of the order and its notable members. Hence, it is also a lengthy order chronicle and a catalogue of (more than three hundred) holy friars, Poor Clares, tertiaries, Franciscan philosophers, theologians, order superiors, and order provinces.[48] Comparable numbers of Franciscan saints are mentioned in the early fifteenth century catalogue of Frederick of Amberg (†1432)[49] and in the *Compendium chronicarum* (1521) written by the observant Franciscan Mariano of Florence (†1523), to which we will return.[50]

Unlike Francis, the figure of Dominic initially did not become the focus of conflicting religious ideals from within the order of Friars Preachers, at least not in such a marked way. Dominic had been more careful in establishing an institutional setting than Francis. By the time of Francis's death, there were fierce discussions about the

---

[45] See for an initial overview Roest (1996), 81–82.
[46] *Catalogus sanctorum fratrum minorum* (ca. 1335), ed. L. Lemmens, Fragmenta Minora (Rome, 1903). From roughly the same period dates the *Memorabilia de Sanctis Fratribus Minoribus*, ed. M. Faloci Pulignani, in *Miscellanea Franciscana* 15 (1914), 65–69. See also Paciocco (1990), 92–103.
[47] Edited in *Analecta Franciscana* 4 and 5 (Quaracchi, 1906–12).
[48] The compiler made an eclectic use of a wide range of spiritual and non-spiritual hagiographical and historiographical sources. The book had a wide circulation inside the order during the fifteenth and early sixteenth centuries. It became subject to harsh criticism and ridicule by sixteenth-century protestants; see Goyau (1926), 90–147; Campagnola (1974), 59 ff.; Erickson (1972), 253–74.
[49] Delorme (1911), 544 ff.
[50] Wyngaert (1921), 3–35. For more information on these various catalogues see Paciocco (1989).

role that his enactment and vision of evangelical life should play in the future development of the Franciscan order. Franciscan hagiography is a testimony to it. Dominic's own initiatives were subsumed in detailed order institutions. When he died, the Dominican order did not face the same problems. There was less need to focus on Dominic himself, and more on the order as a newly established movement of professional preachers, in which Dominic figured alongside several others.[51] It was in the context of Dominic's canonisation in 1234, a dozen years after his death, that the hagiographic memory about Dominic as founding father was revived. Between 1234 and 1260, this evolved into a definitive fixation on Dominic as the saintly inventor of the Dominican way of life. This development can be charted in the subsequent official saints' lives of Dominic written for commemorative and liturgical purposes by Petrus Ferrandi († ca. 1259), Constant of Orvieto (†1256), the Dominican master general Humbert of Romans (†1277), and Thierry of Apolda († ca. 1298).[52]

The Dominicans were keen to push the canonisation and the hagiographic commemoration of friars that in their life and deeds epitomised the Dominican ideals, and therewith confirmed the Dominican institutional self image. Insofar as the Dominican order was an organised movement of preachers and teachers, it is not surprising that beatified Dominican doctors of theology function prominently. Good examples are the *vitae* devoted to Hugh of St. Cher, Raymond of Peñyaforte, Thomas Aquinas and Albertus Magnus. Many more examples can be obtained by skimming through Kaeppeli's catalogue of Dominican authors. In addition, just as was the case in the Franciscan order, Dominicans began to stimulate the veneration and canonisation of Dominican nuns, tertiaries and influential lay fellow travellers. Cases in point are the hagiographic works devoted to Elisabeth of Thüringen,[53] and the veritable Dominican hagiographic industry around Catherine of Siena.[54] The compilers of such

---

[51] Cf. Elm (1972), 127–47; Canetti (1996).

[52] Most of these texts have been edited in the various volumes of the Monumenta Ordinis Praedicatorum Historia (MOPH). See also Kaeppeli (1970–93), 1:292–93, 2:290, and 4:128–29, 297–301; Koudelka (1972), 47–67; Barth (1984), 83–112.

[53] Cf. Rener (1993); Kaeppeli (1970–93), 4:297–301.

[54] For brevity's sake, I only refer to the *vitae* produced by Thomas Anthonius Nacci, Thomas Nesis of Siena (†1390), Raymond de Vineis of Capua (†1399), John of Ivrea (fl. 1430), and Anthony Rocca (fl. first half fifteenth century); see Kaeppeli (1970–93), 1:118, 4:155–56, 329, 342, 378–79.

texts were concerned with pushing a certain form of holiness, but also to connect this holiness with the evangelical lifestyle of the Dominican order itself.

From the outset the Dominican order as a whole was represented as an authentic subject of historiographical writing. This shows in the Dominican production of order saints' catalogues and order histories, in which individual friars are presented as witnesses of an institutionalised Dominican sainthood, with learning and pastoral care as constitutive elements.[55] The exemplary institutional Dominican saints' catalogue is Gerard of Fracheto's *Vitae fratrum ordinis praedicatorum* (ca. 1260). Gerard produced the work on request of Humbert of Romans, who had asked on the general chapter of 1255 to collect materials on the virtuous and saintly deeds of friars preachers.[56] Gerard of Fracheto deliberately modelled his *Vitae fratrum* on the famous *Vitae patrum*, a strong token of the Dominican group-image in church-historical perspective, and tried to establish the order's identity as a body of friars preachers with a specific evangelical form of life over against the traditional orders and the regular canons.[57] Throughout the late Middle Ages, Gerardo's *Vitae fratrum*, which in that regard was more successful than the comparable Franciscan *Dialogus de gestis fratrum minorum* mentioned before, remained the dominant model of Dominican collective institutional hagiography. See for instance the works of Peter Gui († ca. 1347), Peter Gallo (†1348), John Meyer from Zurich (†1485), and Jean Martin of Valenciennes (†1495).[58]

The mendicant orders also engaged into the production of hagiographic texts on non-mendicant saints. As said before, the friars had a vested interest in promoting the cult of saintly fellow travellers; whether they were exemplary lay tertiaries or saintly royals. Mendicant historians composed many individual saints' lives for the purpose of canonisation, and for the edification of novices, female religious and aligned penitential groups.[59] Moreover, they embarked on the pro-

---

[55] Canetti (1996b), 24.

[56] *Vitae fratrum ordinis praedicatorum*, ed. B. M. Reichert, MOPH 1 (Paris, 1896).

[57] Kaeppeli (1970–93), 2:35–38, 4:94. Cf. Canetti (1996b), 26. On the *Vitae patrum* as model for Dominican order hagiography see Boureau (1987), 79–100.

[58] Kaeppeli (1970–93), 2:474–75, 3:220–21, 229.

[59] It is not possible to mention all the individual texts. For more information the reader is directed to the catalogue of Kaeppeli (for the Dominicans) and to the surveys of Roest (1996) and Pacciocco (1990) (for the Franciscans).

duction of saints' catalogues for liturgical and pastoral purposes, either integrated in their chronicles[60] or separately, in independent works. In this context we can refer to (predominantly Dominican) standardised abbreviated legendaries,[61] such as the *Epilogus in gesta sanctorum* (1245) of Bartholomew of Trent and the most famous of them all: the *Legenda aurea* of Jacob of Voragine (†1298). With these and several other large-scale mendicant legendaries, trimmed to function in liturgical settings and as instruments for preaching and devotional reading, mendicant hagiographers moved far beyond the folds of institutional hagiography.[62]

III.2 *Franciscan order chronicles*

Aside from these various hagiographic texts, the mendicant orders soon engaged in the production of various types of order history, be it catalogues of leaders (Dominican generals or Franciscan general ministers), or more encompassing chronicles devoted to the history of mendicant convents, provinces, or the respective orders as a whole.

Meant for use within the order, Franciscan order histories provided the friars with useful information concerning their predecessors who had helped to bring the order into prominence. These texts abound in miracle stories and eulogies of the order founder and his

---

[60] Cf. the extensive saints' catalogue in the *Satyrica Historia* of Paulinus of Venice OFM, made accessible by a separate thematic-alphabetical index and sophisticated cross-reference systems.

[61] The tradition to compose large saints' catalogues went as far back as the sixth century. From the eleventh century onwards such catalogues developed into gigantic legendaries. Witness the thirteenth-century legendary of St. Maximin, the *Sanctilogium sive speculum legendarum* of the abbey of St. Denis, the *Catalogus sanctorum et gestorum eorum* (ca. 1370) of Petrus Natalis, the *Collectarium sanctorum monachorum* of the later abbot William of S. Paolo *fuori le mure* in Rome (written between 1372 and 1382), the lost legendary of Gilles van Damme (†1463) from the Cistercian monastery of Dunes, and the giant *Sanctilogium* of Jan Gielemans (†1487), which is heavily dependent upon the former. See Philippart (1977); Vauchez (1981), 666–67; Dubois and Lemaitre (1993), 27–54.

[62] See for example Dondaine (1946), 53–102; Abate (1949), 269–92; Kunze (1983), 448–66 (with a lot of information on the various vernacular adaptations); Boureau (1984) (which present the Dominicans as the inventors of the "légendier hagiographique universel de grande diffusion"); Fleith (1991); Dunn-Lardeau (1986); Kaeppeli (1970–93), 1:172 ff., 2:349–69, 473–74, and 4:46–47, 139–41; Guerrieri (1933), 198–241; as well as the new edition of the *Legenda Aurea*: Iacopo da Varazze, *Legenda Aurea*, ed. Giovanni Paolo Maggioni, 2 vols. (Florence, 1998).

most renowned followers. The relationship with the aforementioned hagiographic texts therefore is close. Most of these histories also celebrate what their authors saw as the essence of the Franciscan experience and emphasise the role of the order in the Church. As in some of the *vitae* (such as Thomas of Celano's second life of Francis), several order histories also take a stand on disputed aspects of Franciscan life (like the *usus pauper* controversy), the relationship with the secular masters at the university, and the sometimes uneasy relationship with the secular clergy.

It is possible to distinguish between histories that focus on the order as a whole, and those devoted to individual provinces. The Friars Minor were surprisingly quick in producing 'provincial' chronicles. The oldest of these is the *Tractatus de adventu fratrum minorum in Angliam* (ca. 1258), written by the friar Thomas Eccleston († ca. 1260).[63] For twenty-six years Thomas, who had joined the order shortly after 1229, collected materials about the early history of the English Friars Minor. He edited these materials in an accurate and edifying text, with as dominant themes evangelical poverty, study, and missionary zeal.[64]

The *Chronica Fratris Jordani*[65] (ca. 1262) contains the memoirs of the Italian friar Jordan of Giano, who took part in the second expedition of Franciscan missionaries to the German regions (1221), and thereafter made a substantial career in the new German Franciscan provinces as *custos* and provincial vicar. With this chronicle, Jordan gave in to the pressure of his fellow Franciscans, who wanted him to preserve his memories of the ascent of the Friars Minor in Germany. In the early fourteenth century, German Franciscans showed additional historiographical initiatives.[66]

The boundaries between Franciscan order histories and other Franciscan chronicles are rather vague, somewhat in contrast with

---

[63] *Fratris Thomae vulgo dicti de Eccleston tractatus de adventu fratrum minorum in Angliam*, ed. A. G. Little (Manchester, 1951). Campagnola (1974), 28–29, suggests that Thomas was inspired by the example of Gerard of Fracheto's *Vitae fratrum ordinis praedicatorum*.

[64] Roest (1996), 197–201.

[65] Gatto (1997), 425–43 enumerates the existing editions and announces a new one. On the representation of the order in such order chronicles, see Campagnola (1966), 243 ff., and (1974), 27 ff.; Berg (1985), 82–101.

[66] Cf. the *Annales minorum Prussicorum* (ca. 1330) and the *Chronicon provinciae Argentinensis*. For partial editions see Lemmens (1911), 671–87, and (1913), 702–04.

the more systematic approach to history among the Dominicans. This is revealed in some of the surviving chronicles from the Irish Franciscan province that we will encounter later on in more detail, such as the 'Kilkenny chronicle' and the Annals of friar John Clynn. Although not order chronicles in the strict sense of the word, they provide information on the establishment of Franciscan convents, the succession of provincial ministers and other dignitaries. The same holds true for the famous chronicle of Salimbene, which is one of the most important thirteenth-century sources of information for Franciscan settlements, individual friars and institutional developments in the Italian and French provinces, and yet is not an order chronicle in the strict sense of the word.

Compared with the quick emergence of provincial chronicles, the production of general order histories came relatively late. The first Franciscan general order chronicle might have been the *Historia ordinis minorum* (ca. 1290) of the Italian friar Philip of Perugia, provincial minister of Tuscany and bishop of Fiesole. Wadding and Sbaralea make mention of this work in their catalogues of Franciscan authors, but thus far this chronicle has not been rediscovered.[67] From the end of the thirteenth and the beginning of the fourteenth century, other short order histories survive, or rather concise catalogues of general ministers. Cases in point are the so-called *Catalogus generalium ministrorum* (ca. 1304–18, with later continuations), which used to be ascribed to Bernard of Bessa († ca. 1304), formerly the secretary of Bonaventure,[68] as well as to Peter of Todi. This catalogue not only lists fourteen successive general ministers and their deeds, but also gives an outline of Franciscan history from the death and the beatification of Francis to the early fourteenth century, complete with information about papal privileges, regulations and statutes concerning study, preaching activities, the celebration of the Divine Office, Franciscan missionary activities and the relationship with the secular clergy. From roughly the same period are some surviving fragments

---

[67] Wadding (1906), 196; Sbaralea (1908–36), 2:383.

[68] *Catalogus generalium ministrorum ordinis fratrum minorum*, ed. O. Holder-Egger, *MGH Scriptores* 32 (Hannover, 1908), 652–74; *Chronicon Generalium; Catalogus Ministrorum Generalium (OFM)*, in *Zeitschrift für Katholische Theologie* 7 (1883), 322–52; *Analecta Franciscana* 3, (1898), 693–707; and *Archivum Franciscanum Historicum* 2 (1909), 431–40; 6 (1913), 785; 15 (1922), 333–48. Oswald Holder-Egger showed that the work was written after Bernard's death. Maybe the author of this extant catalogue used a now-lost comparable work of Bernard.

of smaller Franciscan lists of general ministers, provincial ministers and other friars, most of which are anonymous.[69] One of these, the *Chronicon abbreviatum de successione generalium ministrorum* (ca. 1304),[70] was written by the Italian friar Peregrine of Bologna, provincial minister of Greece and Genoa. The chronicle, actually a letter to his minister general, is foremost a short list of eighteen general ministers, and major developments within the order under their rule.[71] A more substantial work is the anonymous *Chronica XIV vel XV generalium*,[72] which covers more or less the same period, and seems not so different from the *Catalogus generalium ministrorum* mentioned before. According to fourteenth-century chronicles and other sources, a comparable catalogue would have been written by the Franciscan friar Philip Brusseri of Savone (ca. 1260–1340). But neither this nor most of the other chronicles ascribed to him seem to have survived.[73] The *Chronica brevis ordinis minorum* (ca. 1350) by the Franciscan hagiographer Dominic Bonaventure de Festo shared the same fate.[74]

These order histories and catalogues of general ministers culminated in the huge *Chronica XXIV generalium* (ca. 1369), which reached back to the work of Peregrine of Bologna and is ascribed to Friar Arnold of Serrano from Aquitaine, although this attribution is uncertain.[75] This large chronicle tells the story of the Franciscan order under its various general ministers up to Leonard Giffoni "ad eruditionem praesentium et futurorum cautelam". As it contains much

---

[69] For their editions, see for instance *Analecta Franciscana* 1 (1887), 261–63, 273 ff.; *Series generalium ministrorum ordinis fratrum minorum Florentina*, ed. O. Holder-Egger, *MGH Scriptores* 32 (Hannover, 1908), 675–85.

[70] Edited in *Tractatus Fratris Thomae vulgo dicti de Eccleston, de adventu fratrum minorum in Angliam*, ed. A. G. Little (Paris, 1909), 141–45; and as *Chronicon abbreviatum de successione ministrorum ordinis minorum* (Manchester, 1951).

[71] Moorman (1968), 292.

[72] *Analecta Franciscana* 3 (1898), 693–707.

[73] Aside from the *Acta generalium ministrorum*, he allegedly wrote other topographical and historical works, such as a *Speculum terrae sanctae*, a *Compendium historiarum ordinis minorum*, and a *Chronicon Franciscanae provinciae Genuensis*. With the exception of the description of the Holy Land, none of these works seem to have survived. See Sbaralea (1908–36), 2:376.

[74] Sbaralea (1908–36), 1:235. For Dominic's *Vita S. Francisci Fabrianensis*, see *AASS* 3 (April), 89–95.

[75] Edited in *Analecta Franciscana* 3 (1898), 1–575. See Frey (1887), 229–43; Moorman (1968), 292; Campagnola (1974), 58: "Egli mostra infatti di conoscere tutta la storiografia francescana antecedente, compresa quella spirituale". Even the theme of tribulations and decadence is present.

institutional and biographical information, it is a source of the greatest importance for modern historians. In this context it is also worthwhile to refer back to Bartholomew of Pisa's *De conformitate*, which
also can be seen as an order history, notwithstanding its hagiographic
overtones.

These catalogues and order chronicles have mainly been edited
and studied to obtain information about their textual history, to identify specific 'Franciscan themes', and to extract information about
the history of the order. These works still need additional study to
understand their compository strategies and their usage in minorite
communities. For this, renewed manuscript work is unavoidable.

The disagreements concerning the interpretation of the Rule of
Francis showed in various Rule-commentaries and papal statements,
and even lead to persecution and imprisonment of critics from within.
They also stimulated 'dissident' historiography.[76] A well-known spec-
imen is the early fourteenth-century *Historia septem tribulationum*,[77]
written by the Italian spiritual leader Angelo Clareno (Pietro da
Fossombrone). It is a polemical history of seven subsequent tribulations that the Franciscan order had undergone from the days of
Francis onwards. The overall tone and choice of vocabulary show a
Joachimist inspiration, very much in line with conceptions elaborated
by other spiritual spokesmen, such as Peter John Olivi and Ubertino
of Casale. Throughout Angelo's *Historia*, the need for reform is the
central theme and battle cry, without the expectation that reform
will change the order for the better permanently.[78]

Notwithstanding its spiritual pedigree, Angelo Clareno's programmatic theme of reform influenced later order histories and related
forms of writing between the fourteenth and sixteenth centuries.[79]
All major Franciscan observant historians, who normally listed Angelo

---

[76] In the context of 'dissident' historiography, we also should note the *Chronica
Nicolai minorita* (ca. 1330): a document compilation concerning the disputes on the
poverty of Christ and the beatific vision between Pope John XXII and the Franciscan
order. See Nicholas Minorita, *Chronica, Documentation on Pope John XXII, Michael of
Cesena and the Poverty of Christ with Summaries in English*, ed. G. Gál and D. Flood,
Franciscan Institute Publications (New York, 1996); Gál (1997), 337–44.

[77] Angelo Clareno, *Historia Septem Tribulationum*, ed. A. Ghinato, Sussidi e Testi
per la Gioventù Francescana, 10 (Rome, 1959); see Campagnola (1974), 45–52.

[78] Campagnola (1974), 49. For the early history of Joachimist and non-Joachimist
Franciscan reform ideas, see Phelps (1972), and Burr (1993).

[79] Cf. Campagnola (1974), 54.

Clareno and his spiritual party among their forerunners, took over the theme of reform as leading narrative strategy in their own writings. This was true for the *Chronica fratrum minorum observantiae* (ca. 1480) of Bernardine of Fossa (Bernardino Aquilano),[80] the hagiographic *Franceschina* or *Specchio dell'ordine dei minori* (ca. 1480), of Jacob Oddi of Perugia,[81] the *Chronica ordinis minorum observantium* (ca. 1506–08) of the Bohemian friar Nicholas Glassberger,[82] the anonymous Franciscan Observant chronicle of Prague (ca. 1510), as well as for the *Fasciculus chronicarum* (early sixteenth century) of Mariano of Florence.[83] The production of these and other Observant chronicles went hand in hand with an ongoing transmission and translation of the *Actus/Fioretii*, Bonaventure's *Legenda Major*, and Francis' own writings. In 1503, the observant friar Antonio Bruni compiled in Italian a vast corpus of such exemplary hagiographic sources, which in return received continuations and followers.[84] Of interest is also Peder Olson's *Historia*

---

[80] *Chronica fratrum minorum observantiae*, ed. L. Lemmens (Rome, 1902); see Pratesi (1960), 778–80; Campagnola (1974), 89–90. Bernardine also composed saints' lives, sermons, and a convent chronicle; see below.

[81] *La Franceschina. Testo volgare umbro del secolo XV scritto dal p.Giacomo Oddi di Perugia*, ed. N. Cavanna, 2 vols. (Florence, 1931). The work is a partisan representation in thirteen chapters of the spiritual outlook. It reduces Francis' first followers to personified Franciscan virtues. Campagnola (1974), 90–91, therefore proposes to see this book as a work of affective piety in the line of *De conformitate* and the *Fioretti*; see Pasqualin Traversa (1995).

[82] Nikolaus's *Chronica ordinis minorum Observantium*, ed. in *Analecta Franciscana* 2 (Quaracchi, 1897), is only one of his historical writings. He edited the *Trilogium animae* of Louis of Prussia, in which he inserted a small diatribe against the *Supplementum chronicarum* of Jacob Philip of Bergamo. He also published a *Stammbaum der deutschen Kaiser und Könige*, on request of Conrad Celtis, and a *Maior chronica Bohemorum moderna*. See also Seton (1923) and (1926), 411–17. The *Chronica ordinis minorum observantium* was written between 1506 and 1508 on request of the Neurenberg guardian Bartholomaeus Wyer. An unknown continuator extended the chronicle until 1517, while a second continuator added a list of provincial and general chapters up till 1580. Many elements of Glassberger's chronicle were taken over by Wadding, with additional information from Mariano of Florence.

[83] The autograph of Mariano's *Fasciculus* apparently was used by Lucas Wadding for his own *Annales*, and maybe destroyed after the latter were completed. Campagnola (1974), 94–95. Mariano's chronicle only survived in an abbreviated form, known as the *Compendium chronicarum fratrum minorum*, ed. T. Domenichelli (Quaracchi, 1911). See also the first four yearly issues of the *Archivum Franciscanum Historicum*. Mariano wrote several other works with a historiographical bend. Cannarozzi (1930), 31–71; Abate (1934), 46–52; Cresi (1964), 191–99; Bertagna (1982), 473–79.

[84] Campagnola (1974), 91–92. Franciscan history writing in the fifteenth- and early sixteenth century was very much an observant affair, with the writings of Matthias Doering as notable exception. Doering continued the *Nova chronica* of Dietrich Engelhus (†1434) for the years 1420–64; see MS Leipzig, Universitätsbibl. 1310 (an. 1464), fols. 109r–124r.

de inchoatione et propagatione ordinis fratrum minorum in Dania et regionibus septentrionalibus (ca. 1520) produced in the observant friary of Roskilde.[85] It sketches the history of the Franciscan order in Scandinavia from the 1230s onwards, but emphasises the spread of the observance in the later fifteenth and early sixteenth centuries, as well as the beginning troubles with the Lutherans. The latter problem was taken up again by the Franciscan *Chronica de expulsione*, describing the process by which the Franciscan friars were expelled from the Scandinavian countries between 1528 and 1532.[86]

The sixteenth century saw the appearance of large documentary histories in the Franciscan family with a larger 'all-Franciscan' perspective, such as the *Monumenta ordinum fratrum minorum*, the *Firmamentum trium ordinum beatissimi patris nostri Francisci*, and the *Speculum minorum*, replete with editions of constitutions and other official texts; a tendency that was to culminate in the *Annales* of Lucas Wadding a century later. The *Monumenta*, the *Firmamentum* and the *Speculum minorum*, which still await their first critical study, were very much the results of teamwork.[87]

III.3 Dominican order chronicles

Whereas the Franciscans were quick in the production of provincial chronicles, the Dominicans took the lead with the production of general order histories, starting with Jordan of Saxony's *Libellus de initio ordinis fratrum praedicatorum* (ca. 1233).[88] The work, written on request of younger friars, holds a middle ground between a hagiographic encounter with the order's early saints and a full-blown history of the early Dominican order. It provides relatively little information

---

[85] Petrus Olai, *De ordine fratrum minorum*, ed. M. Cl. Gertz, in *Scriptores Minores Historiae Danicae Medii Aevi* 2 (Copenhagen, 1922), 279–324; see Rasmussen (1976).

[86] *Cronica de Expulsione fratrum minorum*, ed. M. Cl. Gertz, in *Scriptores Minores Historiae Danicae Medii Aevi* 2 (Copenhagen, 1922), 325–67. This work was written on request of the provincial superior, with in mind possible future proceedings to retrieve lost properties. Rasmussen (1998), 17.

[87] The works of these compilers (respectively Anthony of Medina, Anthony of Rincon, Francis Ledesman, Boniface of Cerva, and Gerard Zoethelme) only exist in old editions: *Monumenta ordinum fratrum minorum* (Salamanca, 1506–11); *Firmamentum trium ordinum beatissimi patris nostri Francisci* (Paris, 1512); *Speculum minorum* (Rouen, 1509); see Wadding (1906), 28; Sbaralea (1908–36), 1:88.

[88] *Libellus de initio ord. praedicatorum*, ed. H. C. Scheeben, MOPH 16/2 (Rome, 1935), 25–88 Cf. Kaeppeli (1970–93), 4:178.

about the spread of the order, the development of its institutions
and the like, matters that nevertheless must have been of great concern to Jordan of Saxony. The book reflects rather more needs of
the order in the years 1232–33, when the book was conceived (just
before Dominic's canonisation). Jordan wanted to establish the image
of Dominic as preacher and order founder, and to prevent Dominic
from becoming an overpowering fixed model of saintliness (maybe
with hindsight to the struggles in the Franciscan order) that could
harm the development of the Dominican movement in light of its
growing pastoral, educational and ecclesiastical responsibilities.[89]

After Jordan's initial undertaking, the production of order-chronicles
in the Dominican order did not abate. In the thirteenth century,
alongside of several anonymous order chronicles of uncertain provenance, the Spanish friar Peter Ferrandi († before 1259–60), and the
'official' order hagiographer and historian Gerard of Fracheto (†1271)
both produced a significant *Chronica ordinis praedicatorum*.[90] In the same
period, Stephen of Salagnac compiled his curious *De quattuor in quibus
Deus ordinem praedicatorum insignivit*, a work that only was completed
half a century later by the chronicler Bernard Gui.[91] These order
chronicles stemmed from a genuine urge to commemorate the deeds
of past generations of friars and to gain a satisfactory institutional
self-representation, both on the level of the order as a whole, and
on a provincial level. Good examples of the latter are the *Historia
ordinis praedicatorum sue Dominicanorum in Dania 1216–1246* (ca. 1261),[92]
and the early fourteenth-century *Chronica provinciae Romanae ordinis
praedicatorum* of Hugh Borgognonibus of Lucca (†1322), lector and
prior of the Roman province.[93]

Rather influential were the order histories of the prolific Dominican
historian and inquisitor Bernard Gui (†1331). As an order historian,
he compiled a *Catalogus priorum provincialium* (for the Provence, Toulouse,

---

[89] Jordan of Saxony, *On the Beginnings of the Order of Preachers*, ed. and trans. Simon
Tugwell, Dominican Sources: new Editions in English (Parable-Dublin, 1982), Intro.,
ix–xi. See also Brooke (1974), 214–32.

[90] On Petrus Ferrandi, see van Otroy (1911), 52 ff.; Kaeppeli (1970–93), 3:226,
4:230. The chronicle of Petrus Ferrandi, which according to Nadeau (1999), 138,
should be ascribed to Humbert of Romans, originally ended in 1254. Later continuations end in 1271 and 1321 respectively. On Fracheto's order chronicle, see
Kaeppeli (1970–93), 2:35–38, 4:94.

[91] Stephen of Salagnac, *De Quattuor in Quibus Deus Ordinem praedicatorum Insignivit*,
ed. Th. Kaeppeli, MOPH 22 (Rome, 1949). Stephen worked on this until 1278.

[92] Tugwell (1996), 161–64 (Appendix II: *Historia ordinis praedicatorum in Dania*).

[93] Cf. Kaeppeli (1970–93), 2:253.

Francia and Dacia), the *Catalogus magistrorum ordinis praedicatorum*, and *De fundatione et prioribus conventuum provinciae Tolosanae et Provinciae*, which was envisaged as a general history of the order but never moved beyond a series of chronological accounts of the Dominican settlements in the Toulouse and Provence areas.[94] Around 1317–18, some of Bernard Gui's materials were used by the anonymous compiler of the *Brevis historia ordinis fratrum praedicatorum*, which itself received continuations until 1367/8, and until 1483. The *Brevis historia* is foremost a catalogue of Dominican authors. As such, it stands in an intricate tradition of Dominican author catalogues (many of which subsequently became important sources for the larger Dominican order histories of Henry of Herford and Jacob of Soest). Among these author catalogues, we can signal the so-called catalogue of Stams (that incorporates some pristine author lists from the later thirteenth and the early fourteenth century), the catalogues of Uppsala and Prague, the catalogue of the Burgundian humanist Laurent Pignon (ca. 1412), and the author list of Louis of Valladolid (ca. 1413–14).[95]

---

[94] *Bernardus Guidonis de fundatione et prioribus conventuum provinciarum Tolosanae et provinciae ordinis praedicatorum*, ed. A. Amargier, MOPH 24 (Rome, 1961). On copies, continuations, and reworkings see Kaeppeli (1970–93), 1:220 ff., 4:50–51. For a first evaluation of this 'Wirkungsgeschichte', see Montagnes (1981), 183–203; Simonin (1939), 192–213. We also should mention Gui's more wide-ranging *Numerus et nomina conventuum fratrum ac monasteriorum sororum in singulis provinciis totius ordinis*, and his works devoted to the history of other orders, bishops, and counts in southern France; see Kaeppeli (1970–93), 1:223–24, 4:50–51. These works betray Gui's ecclesiastical outlook, which also shines through in his hagiography. Another interesting chronicle on another order is William of Hyporegia's *Tractatus de origine et veritate ordinis Cartusiensis* (1314), written after the author's transfer to the Carthusians. Kaeppeli (1970–93), 2:103.

[95] *Laurentii Pignon Catalogi et Chronica, accedunt Catalogi Stamsensis et Upsalensis Scriptorum O.P.*, ed. G. Meersseman, MOPH 18 (Rome, 1936). Laurent Pignon (†1449), confessor of Duke Philip the Good, not only produced the *Catalogus fratrum spectabilium ordinis fratrum praedicatorum* (1394–1412; six individual catalogues of male and female Dominican saints, church dignitaries, generals, provincials of Francia, and authors), written "Ut presentibus et futuris fratribus Ordinis Praedicatorum innotescat quales et quantos viros predictus ordo genuerit", but also a *Chronica compendiosa de capitulis generalibus et provincialibus Franciae OFP* (1412), which comes close to a statute collection; see Kaeppeli (1970–93), 3:67. For the mutual (inter)dependence of the various author lists mentioned here, the probable existence of an older communal source, and the way in which various catalogues acted as sources for the chronicles of Henry of Herford and Jacob of Soest, see Auer (1933); Scheeben (1937), 202–22; Simonin (1938), 193–214. In the traditional monastic orders, such catalogues did exist as well, as is testified by *De claris scriptoribus monasterii sui* of Jean de Liège from the St. Lawrence monastery; see Michiels (1998), 226.

Another prolific Dominican historian, Galvanus Fiamma (†1344) from Milan, compiled two order histories, normally referred to as the *Chronica parva ordinis praedicatorum*,[96] and the much larger *Chronica maior ordinis praedicatorum* (known through excerpts used by post-medieval Dominican historians, such as Borselli and Ambrogio Taego).[97] Fiamma's *Chronica maior* was not just a concise succession of Dominican saints, generals, chapter meetings and order privileges. Aside from many anecdotes concerning the early history of the order, the work also contained a detailed description of the origin and development of the Milanese St. Eusebius friary. In the later fourteenth century, the Dominican tradition of order histories was upheld by friars from Aragon and the Provence, namely Nicholas Rossell (†1362), his friend Jacob Dominici († before 1384),[98] and the lector Peter of Arenys (†1419/20), whose *Chronicon ordinis praedicatorum* initially covered the period 1349–1415, with continuations until 1453.[99]

Among the more prominent early fifteenth-century order chroniclers were the above-mentioned Laurent Pignon and the theologian and inquisitor Jacob of Soest (†1438/40). In between Jacob's rich historical 'Nachlass' (the so-called *Chronicae diversae*; a conglomerate of chronicles, historical notes and catalogues of privileges and constitutions) stands out the now lost *Chronica brevis ordinis praedicatorum* (until 1427).[100] For his works, Jacob made ample use of some of the

---

[96] MSS Rome Bibl. Casanatensia 1315, fols. 1r–36v, and Ravenna Bibl. Classense 347. B.M. Reichert used the Rome manuscript for his edition *Fratris Galvagni de la Flamma Cronica ordinis praedicatorum ab anno 1170 usque ad annum 1333*, MOHP 2 (Rome-Stuttgart, 1897). This short chronicle lists order generals, general chapter meetings, provincial chapters of the Lombardy province, and the priors of the St. Eusebius friary of Milan.

[97] Taego used a manuscript from the Dominican convent of St. Luke in Mantua. For a partial edition of the *Chronica major* on the basis of Taego's excerpts, see Odetto (1940), 297–373. See also Tomea (1997), 331–36.

[98] Nicholas Rossell from Majorca issued the collection of the *Collectanea de historia ordinis praedicatorum praesertim de provincia Aragoniae* and compiled the *Collectanea ex registris et libris camerae apostolicae et ex aliis libris et cronicis diversis*. Jacob Dominici charted the history of the Dominican Aragonese province in his *Chronica capitulorum provincialium et priorum provincialium provinciae Provinciae* and his *Chronica priorum et series capitulorum Prov. Aragoniae ordinis praedicatorum*, ed. Kaeppeli, *AFP* 14 (1944), 33–40. For the relationship between the works of Nicholas and Jacob, and their use of other Dominican sources, see Alós (1912), 15–60; Kaeppeli (1944), 19–42, and (1970–93), 2:319–20, 3:184–85, and 4:133.

[99] Kaeppeli, (1970–93), 3:217, 4:226.

[100] See Beckmann (1925); Scheeben (1930), 233–36; Guimarães (1937), 290–304; Simonin (1938), 193–214; Eckert (1986), 125–38; Kaeppeli (1970–93), 2:343, 4:138.

Dominican author catalogues mentioned above. His own writings, and in particular the *Chronica brevis*, in turn formed a major source for the early sixteenth-century order chronicles of Albert Castello.[101]

During the later fifteenth century, catalogues of Dominican generals were produced by Jerome Albertucci de Bursellis of Bologna (†1497), and by several anonymous compilers.[102] At roughly the same period, Dominican observant order historiography made its appearance with the various German chronicles of John Meyer of Zurich (1422–85), who became a staunch supporter of the observant cause in the reformed friary of Basel and in neighbouring monasteries.[103] These works of John Meyer in particular deserve further attention, also to obtain a better picture of the Dominican observant self-representation over against that of other observant movements.

III.4   *Dominican and Franciscan convent histories*

In analogy with their high monastic forerunners, mendicant houses routinely maintained necrologies and *kalendaria* in which deceased brothers, sisters and lay benefactors were enumerated for liturgical commemorative purposes. Frequently, such collections were kept with collections of order constitutions and lists of officials.[104] Based on, and alongside of these texts, more elaborate convent chronicles made their appearance. Kaeppeli's catalogue of Dominican authors mentions a substantial number of such convent chronicles. Rather impressive is, for instance, the historiographical tradition in the Florentine Dominican friary S. Maria Novella from the later thirteenth century

---

[101] Namely his *Brevis et compendiosa cronica de magistris generalibus et viris illustribus ordinis predicatorum*. Creytens (1960), 227–313.

[102] See Jerome's *Cronica magistrorum generalium ordinis praedicatorum* (working its way up to 1493/4, with continuations for the year 1495/6), his *Tabulae de magistris generalibus ordinis praedicatorum*, and *De viris illustribus ordinis praedicatorum*. Kaeppeli (1970–93), 2:245–46. Among the anonymous catalogues, we can signal the *Cronica brevis ordinis praedicatorum* (ca. 1470–75), in MS München Nationalmuseum 939.

[103] Cf. his *Buch der Reformation des Predigerordens* (1468), the *Chronica brevis ordinis praedicatorum* (ca. 1470–75), the *Deutsche Ordenschronik* (two versions, 1481 and 1484), and the *Chronicon ordinis praedicatorum*. For these works, Meyer used the order chronicles of Jacob of Soest. See Albert (1898), 255–63 and (1906), 504–10; Kaeppeli (1970–93), 2:477–80, 4:161–62; Fechter (1987), 474–89.

[104] Such as the *Liber obituum et anniversariorum* of the Dominican friary of Osnabrück. See Siemer (1937), 15–95.

onwards.[105] Of comparable significance were the historiographical traditions in the Dominican convents of Orvieto[106] and Pisa.[107]

Aside from the convent necrologies, several of which have been edited in the *Archivum Franciscanum Historicum* and sister journals, minorite convent chronicles are harder to track down.[108] Surviving Franciscan library and archive collections provide information about the existence of community books and convent chronicles, whether or not in the context of the observant reforms.[109] To my knowledge they have not been brought together, nor scrutinised in any systematic way. Here and there smaller convent chronicles (which extend well beyond the Middle Ages) have been edited.[110] Some interesting specimens survive from the Franciscan province of Dacia (Scandinavia),

---

[105] See the *Necrologium S. Mariae Novellae de Florentia*, the *Cronica fratrum S. Mariae Novellae* (1280–1307) of Scolarius of Florence (†1320), and its continuations by Paul of St. Croce (†1348) and Jacob Thomas of Florence (†1408). See also the *Libellus memorialis de rebus conventus Florentini* of John Tucci (†1348). See Kaeppeli (1970–93), 3:236, 4:138–39, 172–73, 220, 231–32, 276–77.

[106] Compilations by John Matthew Caccia (†1348) and Bartholomew of Orvieto. Cf. *Chronique du couvent des Prêcheurs d'Orvieto*, ed. A. M. Viel and P. M. Girardin (Rome, 1907); Kaeppeli (1970–93), 2:47, 4:45–46; and *Archivum Fratrum praedicatorum* 62 (1992), 140–41, 152–62, 172–74.

[107] For instance, the *Chronica antiqua* of the lector Bartholomew of San Concordio († ca. 1347) and its continuations by Dominic Peccioli (†1408) and Simon of Cassano († after 1418). See *Chronica antiqua Conv. S. Catharina of Pisa*, ed. F. Bonaini, *Archivio della Storia Italiana* Ser. I, 7/2 (1848), 399–582; Barsotti (1928); Kaeppeli (1970–93), 1:157, 168, 333–34, 3:344. For Dominican convent chronicles in Perugia (between 1327 and 1331, and later continuations, e.g., by Julian Angelo of Perugia, († ca. 1478–80), Pistoia (by Peter Anthony Cecchi, fl. ca. 1420, Jerome Anthony of Perugia, fl. 1425, et al.), Auxerre (by William of Maillaco, †1462, and Étienne Cordonnier, †1494), Florence (S. Marco), Siena, and Basel (by the observant friar John of Mainz, †1457), see Kaeppeli (1970–93), 1:18, 2:121, 473, 480–81, 3:56–57, 165, 216, and 4:120, 162, 179–80, 224; Koudelka (1959), 111–47; Morçay (1913); Panella (1995b), 235–303. A special case is the *Chronicon Mediani monasterii*, composed in 1326 by Jean of Bayonne, who left the Dominican order to end his years in the monastery of Moyenmoutier; see Kaeppeli (1970–93), 2:384. Also of interest is the chronicle of John Krawinkel (†1508), from Dortmundt; see Rensing (1936), 74, 169. Not mentioned here are chronicles produced in female mendicant monasteries, such as the Dominican monastery St. Agnes in Bologna (in or after 1254); see Tugwell (1996), 137–44.

[108] The available catalogues of medieval Franciscan authors are old and unreliable, and my own electronic catalogue is far from complete. This catalogue can be accessed at http://users.bart.nl/~roestb/franciscan/

[109] See Bernardine of Fossa's *De conventu S. Angeli de Ocra*, MS Venice, Marc. Z.L. CXLIII Bess. fols. 233–36 (on the way in which the S. Angelo convent became observant in 1481). See also the *Cronica sacriste Pysini ordinis minorum*, in MS Vienna, Österr. Landesbibl. 3284 (an. 1380).

[110] Klein (1995).

particularly the memorial books or convent diaries from the Franciscan friaries of Visby and Stockholm. A friar from Visby (Gotland) wrote some chronicles on Danish and Swedish history in the frame of the friary's *diarium*, and included a list of Franciscan provincial chapters in Dacia.[111] Of comparable significance is the *diarium* from the Franciscan friary of Stockholm in which, around 1450, the friars inserted a series of annalist notes on the history of Sweden.[112] Together with additional annals and rhyme chronicles, these notes constituted the basis for the so-called *Franciscan Prose Chronicle* and related historical writings in the Swedish vernacular about the Swedish royal dynasty, and therewith stood at the cradle of vernacular Swedish national history.[113]

A separate category is formed by the more personal notebooks, which can be rich sources for the study of convent life and the personal interaction and religious career of individuals. Surviving mendicant library catalogues mention several of these (both Dominican and Franciscan), yet most of them have not been studied in depth.[114] In both orders, the convent chronicle proved to be a suitable vehicle for other forms of historiography, be it forms of 'regionalised' universal chronicles, or forms of urban and local history, as we will see later on. It testifies to the generally outward-looking mentality of the mendicant friars, whose ideals of evangelical perfection were bound up with the political, intellectual and literary interests of their surroundings.

---

[111] Rasmussen (1998), 16; *Diarium Minoritarum Wisbyensium* (MS Holm. B99), ed. Göte Paulssom, Annales Suecici Medii Aevi (Lund, 1974), 120–48, 315–34.

[112] Rasmussen (1998), 16; *Diarium fratrum minorum Stockholmensium*, ed. Ericus Michael Fant, Scriptores Rerum Suecicarum Medii Aevi 1 (Stockholm, 1818), 67–83.

[113] Cf. Rasmussen (1998), 16; Rosén (1940), 101–30; Kumlien (1979).

[114] Attention has been paid to the 'Memorial' of Niccolò Galgani (†1424), of San Domenico in Camporegio: Koudelka (1959), 111–47. See also the *Notae autobiographicae et notae de fratribus et rebus ordinis praedicatorum sui temporis* of Stefan Irmy of Basel (†1488) and the *Notae de viris illustribus conventus S. Maria in Gradi* (Viterbo) of Giovanni dei Maiensi (ca. 1380); see Kaeppeli (1970–93), 3:356; Panella (1995), 185–233. In Franciscan circles we can, for instance, point to the so-called chronicle of Francis Venimbeni of Fabriano (†1322), and the 'autobiography' of Jacob Ptolomy of Siena (1232–1390); see Pagani (1959), 153–77; Filippini (1890), 180; Tassi (1893). The text of Jacob Ptolomy (MS Rome BAV Arch. S. Pietro F 32 fol. 351v), contains interesting details about Jacob's life in the order and the history of the Tuscan order province until 1371; see Péano (1975), 273–97.

III.5   *Other forms of mendicant historiography*

When mediaevalists speak about mendicant historiography, they often allude to the concise historical compendia or 'Martin's chronicles', and the encyclopaedic universal chronicles that stand in the *imago mundi* tradition. Both are forms of universal history rather than mendicant institutional history. Yet their paradigmatic late medieval exemplars originated in a mendicant context and are definitely the product of the mendicant educational outlook. Moreover, these mendicant compendia and encyclopaedic universal chronicles formed a major model and source for other forms of (regionally oriented) universal history.[115]

The mendicant production of universal chronicles was large, and will not be dealt with as a whole within this chapter. As a matter of fact, a comprehensive study of the overall mendicant historical production is a debitum, all the more so now that many detailed introductory studies on individual authors and texts are available, so that a comparative approach becomes feasible. Here I only will touch upon some Dominican and Franciscan specimens that are bound up with the mendicant institutional outlook or with important mendicant activities. Without making any statement about generic stature, these specimens can be put in seven overlapping categories.

A first successful category, consisting of small historical compendia or 'Martin's chronicles', has received its most intelligent analysis by Anna Dorothea von den Brincken and Gert Melville.[116] These compendia, which stand in the *series temporum* tradition, derive their name from the *Chronicon summorum pontificum et imperatorum* of Martin of Troppau (OP), which itself was inspired by prior non-mendicant pope-emperor chronicles. Martin wrote his *Chronicon* as an *adiumentum* for students and teachers of theology and canon law. For the former, the *Chronicon* provided a nice extension of Peter Comestor's *Historia scholastica*. For the latter, it provided a timetable to Gratian's *Decretum*. Thanks to its hierocratic, pope-oriented vision of history (legitimising papal supremacy as well as the activities of the papally oriented mendicant orders), Martin's *Chronicon* was more or less officially adopted by the papal curia. The papacy even sent a copy

---

[115] Schumann (1996), 245.
[116] See for instance Melville (1980), 51–104; Brincken (1981), 694–735.

to the court of the Ill-Khans, where the Persian court historian Rashid al-Din included it in his chronicle collections as the 'History of the Franks'. Its handy format and coherent hierocratic vision made the *Chronicon* extremely popular among the regular clergy, hence its wide dissemination into many mendicant libraries and its enormous impact on late medieval historiography.

The papal orientation of Martin's *Chronicon* was even more outspoken in the *Historia nova ecclesiastica*, written between 1313–17 in Avignon by the Dominican Ptolomy of Lucca. Like Martin, Ptolomy wrote this work for theologians and canonists. He presents the papacy alone as the binding chain of history since Christ. The work can therefore be interpreted as an extended pope-catalogue, with close affinities to the *Liber pontificalis*.[117] A comparable hierocratic vision was deployed in Bernard Gui's *Flores chronicorum seu catalogus pontificum Romanorum* and its abbreviation (the *Pontifices Romani*). Gui complemented these concise pope catalogues with separate short chronicles on the emperors and the kings of France.[118] Aside from these Dominican pope-emperor or pope chronicles,[119] there were also notable Franciscan specimens.[120] The most successful ones were the papally oriented *Chronica minor auctore minorita Erphordiensi* (ca. 1264–72, also known as the *Cronica Romana*),[121] and the Schwabian *Flores temporum* (ca. 1292), in which world history forms a background or 'spine' (*spina*) for the miracles of saints and the passion of martyrs (history's flowers), therewith constituting a historicized *Legenda Aurea*.[122]

---

[117] The work is partly edited in L. Muratori, *Rerum Italicarum Scriptores*, vol. 11 (Milan, 1727), 743–1242. On its impact and use by mendicant and non-mendicant chroniclers, see Schmugge (1976), 495–545.

[118] For Bernard's sources and his methods of compilation, see Lamarrigue (1981), 205–19.

[119] To which can be added others. Cf. comparable works of Bartholomew of Trente, Galvano Fiamma, Antoninus of Florence (1389–1459), Jerome Albertucci de Bursellis (†1497), and John Meyer (†1485). See Kaeppeli (1970–93), 1:79–84, 172 ff., 3:271–73, and 4:46–47, 90–91; Walker (1933).

[120] For a survey of smaller and intermediate Franciscan pope-emperor chronicles, such as the *Gesta imperatorum et pontificum* of Thomas of Pavia, see Roest (1996), 42 ff.

[121] For a partial edition, see *Cronica Minor Auctore Minorita Erphordiensi*, ed. O. Holder-Egger, *MGH Scriptores Rer. Germ.* 24 (Hannover, 1899), 486–671. On its hierocratic vision, see Roest (1996), 209–14.

[122] Not the popes but the emperors are the binding spine of worldly history, to which the deeds of holy men can be attached; see Roest (1996), 49–50. For its dissemination in southern Germany, see Mierau, Sander-Berke and Studt (1996).

These compendia share a rigorous organisation of historical materials, which appear as singular unit-histories along the grid of successive popes and/or emperors (linking the manifold historical facts
with a straightforward framework of salvation history). History therewith becomes an instrument for biblical theology, canon law, homilet-
ics, and the propagation of a hierocratic world-view. Far from naïve
compilations, these works exhibit an ideological institutional stance
that too often is ignored by modern mediaevalists.[123]

A second category consists of the larger *Imagines mundi, Specula,* and
historical *summae,* which make use of comparable organizational principles as the small pope-emperor chronicles (including an intelligent
use of graphics), but embed history in a wider geographic-historical
perspective of the world and frequently connect it to other fields of
knowledge in an encyclopaedic vision.[124] This category too had important twelfth-century representants, and therefore should not be seen
as a form of mendicant historiography *tout court.* Nevertheless, it found
its most famous expression in the *Speculum historiale* of the Dominican
friar Vincent of Beauvais.[125] In scale and success, the *Speculum historiale*
(and the *Speculum majus* of which it was only a part) was unsurpassed.
Other mendicant chronicles that traditionally are placed in this category because they exhibit comparable geographic-historical and even
encyclopaedic perspectives normally were smaller and less influential.[126]
Some of them, notably the *Satyrica historia* of the Franciscan Paulinus
of Venice, are wonders of organization and compilatory refinement,
and desperately need modern editions that do justice to their structure, their cross-reference systems and their illustrative programs.[127]

---

[123] Cf. Guenée (1980), 55 ff.
[124] On the relationship between late medieval universal history and encyclopaedism,
see Meier (1992), and Binkley (1997).
[125] See for instance Lusignan and Paulmier-Foucart (1997).
[126] Such as the *Chronica universalis Metensis* of John of Mailly OP († ca. 1254/60),
the *Chronicon* of Francis Pipino OP († after 1328), the *Cronica imaginis mundi* of Jacob
of Acqui OP († ca. 1334), the *Chronografia interminata* of Conrad of Halberstadt OP
(† after 1355), the *Liber de rebus memorabilioribus* of Henry of Herford OP (†1370),
the *Annales Stadenses* of Albert von Stade OFM (ca. 1256), the *Cronica* of friar Elemosina
OFM (†1339), the *Chronica Bohemorum* of John Marignolla OFM (ca. 1350), and the
chronicle of John of Udine OFM. See Brincken (1968), 118–86; Heullant-Donat
(1994).
[127] On Paulinus see the work of Heullant-Donat (1994), as well as Roest (1996),
245–80. Paulinus' richly illustrated *Chronologia magna,* with its twenty-six parallel
chronological series of worldly and religious rulers can also be seen as a refined
universal chronicle in the *series temporum* tradition.

An ambiguous and rather miscellaneous third category consists of the less-organised regionalised world chronicles that borrow from other historiographical types (and subscribe to the *imago mundi* ideal) but are more the idiosyncratic and often original outcome of individual interests. Especially among the Franciscans such chronicles abound.[128] The most famous example is the aforementioned chronicle of Salimbene of Parma, which is the most vivid historical work of the thirteenth century.[129] Other good Franciscan examples are the chronicle of the so-called *Anonymous Umber* ('Paulus of Gualdo'),[130] the chronicle of John of Winterthur,[131] the so-called Lanercost Chronicle,[132] and the various Anglo-Irish chronicles that combine a rudimentary universal history with a strong regional and even local Franciscan perspective. In this context we can point to the archaic Annals of Multyfarnam (*Annales de Monte Fernandi*) compiled by Stephen of Exonia (1246–after 1274), the closely connected Annals of Ossory, the Kilkenny Chronicle, the Annals of Ross and the Annals of John Clynn (himself also from the Kilkenny friary), the Annals of Nenagh, written after the mid-fourteenth century by Galfridus O'Hogan, and the Annals of Inisfallen (ca. 1360).[133] We would be equally justified to count these latter chronicles among regional or convent histories, were it not for the fact that they are not fully focused on the lives of the local friars, contrary to the annals growing out of the necrologies and diaries mentioned earlier.

A fourth category, which is closely connected with mendicant biblical exegesis and teaching of biblical theology, contains the various *Summae de aetatibus* and *Compilationes librorum historialum totius Bibliae* that are mid-way between veritable chronology and the *Historia scholastica* of Peter Comestor. Interesting mendicant specimens are the *Tractatus*

---

[128] Among the Dominican chronicles, we maybe can place in this category the *Cronica novella* of Herman Corner (ca. 1365–1438), the *Collectarium historiarum* of Jean Dupuy (fl. 1430), and some historical works of Jacob of Soest (†1438/40); see Kaeppeli (1970–93), 2:528–29, 4:168.

[129] See for instance d'Alatri (1988); d'Alatri and Paul (1992); Gujotjeannin (1995) and Roest (1996), 22–26. Guyotjeannin shows that the chronicle of Salimbene is not without organisation, but that its structuring elements are very associative.

[130] Fossier (1977), 411–83; Vauchez (1990), 274–305.

[131] Arnold (1983), 816–18; Berg (1983), 114–55, (1985), 82–101.

[132] Little (1943), 25–41; Gransden (1974), 494–96; Offler (1984), 45–89. The *Lanercost Chronicle* transmits parts of a now-lost North-English Franciscan chronicle.

[133] See for the overall relations between these various (and other now-lost) Anglo-Irish chronicles, their manuscripts and partial editions Williams (1991).

de mundi aetatibus of the Minorite friar Pontius Carbonel (ca. 1260–1350) from Barcelona,[134] the *Summa de aetatibus* of the Franciscan John of Udine († ca. 1366),[135] and the *Summa de temporibus* of the Dominican Étienne de Lessines (fl. ca. 1270).[136]

A fifth category consists of the mendicant missionary and ambassadorial histories with links to the *imago mundi* tradition. Sometimes, these works were even fully incorporated into larger historiographical works. This happened for instance with the *Historia Tartarorum* of the Dominican friar Simon of St. Quintin (fl. ca. 1247), which has survived through its insertion in Vincent of Beauvais' *Speculum historiale*.[137] Likewise, the Franciscan John Marignolla included his description and history of the Middle and Far East in his *Cronica Bohemorum*, whereas Elemosina of Gualdo and John of Winterthur also inserted such materials in their own universal chronicles. Yet such missionary and ambassadorial histories survived separately as well, witness the *Historia Tartarorum* of John of Pian Carpine, the story of William of Rubruck and the famous *Itinerarium* of Odoric of Pordenone. These works testify to the missionary exploits, ambassadorial missions and ethnographical interests of the Franciscans.[138]

A sixth category is formed by mendicant national and dynastic histories, connected with the mendicant presence at the royal courts of Europe. Good Dominican examples are the *Annales sex regum Angliae* of Nicholas Trevet († after 1334),[139] and the various historical compendia for the Aragonese court by Pedro Marsili (fl. 1315),[140] Jacob Dominici († ca. 1384), Antonio Ginebreda (†1395), and John Garcia of Calatayud (†1459).[141] Among the Franciscans, we can single out

---

[134] MS Barcelona, Biblioteca de Catalunya 545 (Dalmases 30). Wyngaert (1949).

[135] Cf. Frohne (1992).

[136] Kaeppeli (1970–93), 1:13.

[137] Cf. Guzman (1974), 87–306.

[138] For a survey of such texts see Roest (1996), 101–23; Guéret-Laferté (1994); and the introduction of Jackson (1990). On generic overflow with other kinds of travel literature, see Richard (1981).

[139] Trevet wrote several chronicles on the request of the English royal family, namely the *Annales sex regum Angliae* (ca. 1320–23, which chart the rule of the English kings from Stephen to Edward I), a wide-ranging *Historia ab origine mundi ad Christum natum* (ca. 1327–28), and the Anglo-Norman *Chronicles*, a universal chronicle with a strong English focus. Both in his *Chronicles* and in his *Annales*, Trevet treats the Angevin house and the Dominican order in detail, sometimes to the detriment of other contemporary events. Dean (1976), 328–52; Kaeppeli (1970–93), 3:187–96.

[140] On his *Chronica gestorum Iacobi I Aragoniae* see Robles (1972).

[141] See the work of Robles mentioned above, as well as Kaeppeli (1970–93), 1:113, 2:439–40. This listing is by no means exhaustive.

manifold historical works of Juan Gil de Zamora, such as his fascinating *De preconiis Hispanie*,[142] as well as the abbreviations and continuations of Saxo Grammaticus' *Gesta Danorum* by fourteenth- and fifteenth-century Danish friars.[143] The relationship between these mendicant forms of national/dynastic history and mendicant educational and political ideals (as they appear in mendicant political treatises, mirrors of princes, and other educational works) still awaits its first book-length study.

A final category is formed by mendicant urban chronicles. Both indirectly and directly, the mendicants contributed in a significant manner to the proliferation of urban history in the later Middle Ages. Indirectly through the use of mendicant 'Martin's chronicles' by urban historians, to provide their account of local affairs with a more universal-historical (and salvation-historical) embedding; directly through the actual production of urban chronicles by mendicant authors, whether or not in direct relation to the history of their own convent or the history of the diocese in which they were active as priests, teachers, confessors, counsellors or bishops.[144]

This twofold contribution has tempted historians to trace the origin of urban history to mendicant historiographical activities. They even have depicted the mendicants as the 'Lehrmeister der städtischen Geschichtsschreibung'.[145] However, the mendicants were seldom the inaugurators of local historiographical traditions. In Italy, urban communal history often goes back to earlier centuries.[146] In the German lands, the mendicant role might have had a greater pioneer character. Yet even there, urban historiographical traditions reach back to older forms of episcopal historiography, to which I have alluded to in a previous section.

Nevertheless, the mendicant production of urban and strongly 'regionalised' universal chronicles was significant. Many of these works, which sometimes only survive in a fragmentary fashion,[147]

---

[142] Cirot (1913); Roest (1996), 234–43.

[143] *Compendium Saxonis et Chronica Jutensis*, ed. M.Cl. Gertz, *Scriptores Minores Historiae Danicae Medii Aevi*, 1 (Copenhagen, 1918); Petrus Olai, *Danorum gesta post chronica Saxonis facta*, Uppsala University Library, manuscript de la Gardie 37 fol.; Rasmussen (1998), 17.

[144] To give an example: Jacob of Voragine, our famous Dominican hagiographer, became archbishop of Genoa and wrote a history of that town, as well as related works; see Kaeppeli (1970–93), 2:349–69, 4:139–41.

[145] Schmidt (1958), 14–15.

[146] Fossier (1977b), 641–55.

[147] Dr. Anton Rinzema provided me with fragments of the Franciscan chronicles

remain unedited or are only to be found in partial editions.[148] Some of them have received a preliminary analysis,[149] whereas others have been studied in relation to late medieval urban self-expression[150] and the rationalization of historical perspectives (the rise of the so-called 'städtische Weltchronistik').[151] In order to evaluate their 'mendicant' character and their interaction with other forms of late medieval urban and regional historiography, much additional work is needed. Moreover, a scrutiny of such texts probably will shed additional light on the history of the mendicant orders themselves.

IV. *Conclusion*

Throughout this chapter, it has been difficult to uphold the boundaries between history and hagiography, between order histories and regional, urban, and universal chronicles. To a large extent, these boundaries say more about modern needs to classify than about medieval generic sensibilities. It is clear that medieval genre consciousness did exist, but it was more refined and more flexible than a simple classification can deal with.[152]

---

from Groningen in MS Leeuwarden Provincial Library 9056 D (Codex Gesta Frisiorum), 261–68 (*Ex cronico conventus nostri*, 1413–1501) and 269–75 (*Ex cronico coenobii Franciscanum*, 1413–1501). Contrary to the titles, these works are not so much chronicles pertaining to convent matters as important histories of the town and province of Groningen (and Friesland) in the fifteenth century.

[148] Partial editions of predominantly Dominican urban chronicles can be found in Muratori's *Rerum Italicarum Scriptores* (and in the revised twentieth-century re-issue), whereas other Franciscan and Dominican urban chronicles found partial editions in the German series *Die Chroniken der deutschen Städte*. An exception to the rule is formed by the short *Annales Gandenses*, written by a Flemish Friar Minor from Ghent (between 1296 and 1310). This work, with its Flemish patriotic sentiments, has received no less than two full editions with additional corrections. See on this van Werveke (1959), 109–15.

[149] Such as the chronicles of the Colmar Dominicans. Köster (1952), 1–100; Kleinschmidt (1972), 371–496; Borst (1978), 264–81, 554–55. These chronicles are seen as very important sources for the history of the city and the neighbouring area, not solely because of their political information, but also because of matters pertaining to cultural and social history. See for instance Rubin (1994), 101–02.

[150] Hofinger (1974); Möhring-Müller (1993), 27–21; Hecker (1981); Busch (1997).

[151] Hofmann (1987), 465–67, and Johanek (1987), 287–330 mention for example Henry of Herford's *Liber de rebus et temporibus memorabilioribus*, the *Cronica Tremoniensium* of Johann Nederhoff, the chronicles of Detmar of Lübeck, and those of Closener.

[152] Roest (1999), 47–61.

Many medieval authors mentioned here wrote more than one work, or dealt with different genres.[153] Others dealt in one work with various forms of institutional and non-institutional history, combining universal history with catalogues of order saints, functionaries and provinces. They ensured that all this information could be retrieved from the universal format with the help of powerful indices, or through the layout of the text.[154] All such developments were connected with 1) changing conceptions of worthwhile history (from history to multiple histories along a clear axis); 2) innovative notions of brevity and *compilatio* techniques that reflect epistemological concerns and educational objectives and practices; 3) a diversified envisaged readers' public. In general, we see the rise of pragmatism and the emergence of history as handbook and reference literature.

Insofar as it can be distinguished from other forms of historical writing, later medieval institutional history contains more than meets the eye. The catalogues of abbots, bishops, and order generals, as well as the chronicles of institutional beginnings share a strong ideological subtext that frequently is kept from view in the existing (partial) editions. A further exploration of these texts will help to uncover these subtexts, and will enable us to understand medieval views of institutions and the representation of institutional self-conceptions.

---

[153] Sprandel (1987), 300.

[154] Sprandel (1987), 305, refers to a manuscript of the late fourteenth century *Gesta Trevirorum* that is divided in four columns, dealing respectively with the diocese, the popes, *nota digna* from the region and the world as a whole, and the emperors; see Melville (1987).

CHAPTER TEN

MEDIEVAL URBAN HISTORIOGRAPHY IN WESTERN EUROPE (1100–1500)

Augusto Vasina

Among the extensive and varied scientific analyses of medieval historiography in western Europe, the part dedicated expressly to annalistic and chronicle production of an urban character after the year 1000 has not been, at least in relatively recent times, very significantly developed, nor, one could say, developed with a sufficient balance between the particular historical and geographic areas concerned.

Starting in the seventeenth century, the scholarship of the Maurists promoted and published at the national level, especially for France, Germany, and England, abundant collections of medieval narrative texts, in the process also providing investigations and analytical studies of individual urban chronicles.[1] We also can consider the work of L. A. Muratori, in the collection and publication of medieval Italian chronicles from 500–1500 in his *Rerum Italicarum Scriptores* (*RIS*) to be a branch of this tradition.[2] Works in this series are of great importance, since a large number of the narrative texts that were published concern Italian cities after the year 1000, thus strongly characterizing the historiography of this peninsula in the intervening centuries.

But only in the nineteenth century, with the publication of the *Monumenta Germaniae Historica*'s section *Scriptores* (*MGH SS*), edited by G. H. Pertz and his successors, has it finally been possible to see medieval historiographical production representing sufficiently diverse European historical areas in an inclusively balanced and accurate view. Thus, only recently have scholars been able to begin to select

---

[1] Delogu (1994), 21.

[2] *Rerum Italicarum Scriptores* (*RIS*) (1723–1751). It must be remembered that, even before other Italian chronicles had been published by other scholars in volumes later than the collection, Muratori had published, parallel to the *RIS*, various narrative texts, especially about south-central Italy, in volumes 3–6 of his *Antiquitates Italicae Medii Aevi* (*AIMAE*).

and to distinguish from the very variegated compass of medieval narrative sources the various typological components of urban historiography, and to better single out the actual texts.[3]

The definition of true urban chronicle-writing has been from the
start a rather difficult task, not only because of the very heterogeneous and composite character of the texts under consideration, some
of which are given titles referring to urban centers that are not
always adequate and faithful to their individual narrative contents,
but also because of a still imprecise idea that we have of actual
urban reality, which was defined in the Middle Ages—one must
never disregard this!—as the presence of a bishop and an episcopal
see.[4] And yet, during the course of the nineteenth century, there was
undoubtedly progress toward a more appropriate recognition of historical details, of the complexity and individuality of urban phenomena. Historians of that time, inspired by the spread throughout
Europe of a lay and middle-class culture that was increasingly self-
conscious of its civic origins and of its values of liberty and autonomy, focused more attention on the medieval urban world, especially
on the decisive phase of revival that arose all over Europe from the
torment of the centuries around the year 1000 and lasted throughout the period. Sometimes more, sometimes less, historians tended
to minimize consideration of the ecclesiastical components (above all
episcopal, canonical, and monastic), which in the early medieval
urban world had expressed a determined presence by giving historiographical culture a universalistic tendency. Instead, historians
focused their attention on the great undertakings of the lay urban
forces in, for example, the more or less bold construction of communal autonomy, in the dialectic among the various social classes,
and in the economic dynamics of the merchant and artisan businessmen. History and historians thus sometimes almost confused *in itinere*
the just-recovered sense of identity in urban life with the symbolic
and effective figure of the bishop, by losing their way in a multiplicity of perspectives on realities particular to the urban world, which
were difficult to reduce to synthesis.

---

[3] *Monumenta Germaniae Historica* (*MGH SS*) (1826–1998). A large number of the
urban chronicles written after 1000 have been published, organized by national sections, in vols. 16–19 and 24.
[4] This is a connotation of particular significance above all in the course of the
early Middle Ages; on this, see Dupré (1956), passim; Dupré (1958), passim.

Between the nineteenth and the twentieth centuries, especially under the influence of positivist thought, oriented to perceive the historical process in its factuality and concreteness and in an objective form, an adequate search for the cultural aspects of the medieval urban experience was missing. Neglecting narrative sources because of their subjectivity, historians thus lost many occasions to research and define the collective identity of the urban world, the individuality of the civic spirit from community to community, the consciousness of common belonging to a unique urban reality, not just in the demographic, political, and social senses. In the process, they neglected, for the most part, the intellectual and professional profiles of the men of culture and of the ruling groups of the urban world; they did not catch their reflections in the more or less elevated level of sensibility and consciousness of the chronicle authors. Because this is the point of departure for a functional definition of urban typology within medieval European historiography, this is in a certain sense the discriminator that we can agree to use to make a convincing selection of numerous, frequently anonymous, and variegated narrative texts produced during the medieval centuries in western Europe.

In the course of the twentieth century, especially in recent decades, scholars have tried to remedy this lack of methodological and critical character, dedicating increasing attention to the personality of the already-identified chroniclers or trying to free from anonymity the still very numerous anonymous annals and chronicles. They also have investigated in a more thorough way the scholastic and cultural *cursus* and the social and professional origins of the identified chroniclers.[5] It also should be noted that the study of medieval historiography has in the meantime been in part freed from its traditional compartmentalization and from the prevalent activity of exclusively philological/literary analysis of individual texts, to assume a historico-critical dimension and a systematic consideration, through comparison of narrative and other types of sources, in an ever larger and more wide-reaching radius.[6] There have thus arisen, on both

---

[5] The contributions of Girolamo Arnaldi cover this area in many pioneering ways, in particular Arnaldi (1963). More recently in this field of interest, for its value both retrospective and prospective, we should mention *Il senso della storia nella cultura medievale italiana (1100–1350): quattordicesimo convegno di studi; Pistoia, 14–17 maggio 1993* (Pistoia, 1995), passim.

[6] An essential bibliography on this, even if not brought up to date, can be consulted in Delogu (1994), 174–75.

the international as well as the national and regional levels, numerous reviews of medieval European historiography, more and more diligent at distinguishing and modulating according to their interior logic an urban narrative typology.[7] The enlargement of the horizons of this historiographical production in ever more detailed comparisons, and at various levels of narrative sources of different historical areas, undoubtedly has been facilitated by the publication, since the nineteenth century on the initiative of several national historical institutes, of *Repertori*, as for example of the general one by A. Potthast, whose updated edition has been for some decades in process under the care of the Istituto storico italiano per il Medio Evo.[8]

Among the various publication initiatives of specific interest (particularly intense in the orbit of Anglo-American, German, and French historiography), it recently has become possible to produce a fully developed analysis of medieval sources, distinguished typologically and articulated for the various historical and cultural areas of Europe. Of specific interest here, as well as for its undoubted didactic worth, is the volume which, written by Elisabeth M. C. van Houts, has appeared recently with the title *Local and Regional Chronicles*,[9] in which "Town Chronicles" are taken into consideration specifically in section C, organized geographically, with a reconstruction of the past and the present of each chronicle, of the authors, and of the possible audiences and number of sources put to use in each narrative text in question. Van Houts includes numerous works composed variously from 500–1500, but always identified as pertinent to this specific typological field, for the most part by identifiable authors.

The distinction that she has used between civic chronicles and episcopal or monastic chronicles (section A) and dynastic chronicles or *Gesta principum* (section B) as a point of departure guarantees the rigor with which she has made the selection of narrative materials and their organized distribution in time and in historical space. But in this important book, it no doubt would have been possible to

---

[7] For a recent article on medieval historiography at the international level, see Delogu (1994), 111–74 and esp. 161 ff.; a historiographical review of a national character, regarding Italy, has been published by Capitani (1964); a census of regional chronicle-writing, almost exclusively urban, in the region of Emilia Romagna was edited some years ago by the author: cf. Andreolli et al., eds. (1991).

[8] See the two volumes of Potthast (1896), and their ample revision and enhancement conducted in more recent years in Potthast (1962–98).

[9] Van Houts (1995), 42–49.

characterize the varied and intense urban historiographical production of the medieval centuries after 1000 by factors other than differences in ethno-national and cultural areas. An acceptance and application of selective criteria suggested below could aid in defining the historiographical typology in question in yet more rigorous terms. To begin with, we should reconsider the cultural values of the emerging phenomenon of communal autonomy, which is encountered, and eventually in every city is resolved, either in some form of administrative management of the *res publica*, or in attainment of a stage of maturation in the political sense, that involves the greater part of the urban classes and in particular the intellectual classes (notaries, judges, masters, etc.). We also should consider whether this autonomy has been able always to energize the collective imagination of the *cives*, placing itself at the center of the whole experience—not just political—of each urban community; and, in a positive case, to what degree this or that chronicler has succeeded in discovering a principle of communal identity in this tendentially absorbing and unifying experience, and in transmitting a strong consciousness of it from generation to generation.[10]

It seems evident that, in order to be able to begin this examination with some hope of a positive outcome, some elementary conditions must be fulfilled. First, we must succeed in defining some essential biographical data about the chroniclers—at least those identified by name—above all about their familial, social, professional, and cultural profiles, in order to be able to establish their status and a sense of their connection with the urban world—above all, with its institutions. That is, we must determine whether we are dealing with a report of an official functionary, permanent or temporary, or with an independent and unofficial report.[11] But even at this level of inquiry we encounter notable difficulty in answering

---

[10] After the publication of the Atti dell' XI Convegno storico internazionale dell'Accademia Tudertina (11–14 ottobre 1970) on the theme "La coscienza cittadina nei comuni italiani del Duecento" (Todi, 1972), interesting considerations and observations on civic sentiment in Italian urban centers in the later Middle Ages and on their reflections in contemporary civic historiography appeared in various articles published in *Il senso della storia* (1995), passim.

[11] Arnaldi (1966) was among the first scholars to confront the issue of delineating the figure of the notary-chronicler in the medieval Italian city. Such biographical queries recur systematically in the entries of chroniclers from Emilia Romagna; cf. Andreolli et al., eds. (1991), passim.

these proposed biographical questions. Relatively difficult even for
the urban historiography of north-central Italy after 1000, the questions become decidedly less answerable for the urban chronicle production of most countries of transalpine Europe, which, in general,
is less copious, is less studied, has (for the most part) a less numerous and more fragmentary presence of witnesses, and is almost always
anonymous.[12]

Other inescapable conditions arise from the necessity of singling
out and characterizing for each city the diverse peculiarities of its
political, institutional, economic, social, and cultural development, in
order to be able to adequately situate the various historiographical
productions and the activities of each chronicler. In this case, the
task of expanding our historical knowledge of later medieval Italian
and European cities has been abundantly undertaken, above all in
the second half of the twentieth century, by specialists of medieval
urban history, through a continuous series of learned monographs,
more or less ample in both analytical and synthetic breadth.[13] As a
whole, this rich and articulate production of studies of urban history makes it less difficult, and more equivalent among the various
regions of medieval Europe, to investigate the facts of the particular surrounding conditions and of the individual processes of their
development in diverse, important urban centers, especially in the
cultural sense, and of the specific evolution of collective mentality
and civic consciousness. Even so, for certain regions and centers,
obstacles persist that are not negligible for expanding our knowledge
in these particular sectors. In fact, one must admit that in not a few
cases the indispensable operation of crossing and comparing data
acquired by the biographical investigations of chroniclers with these
results of the research of the ambient and structural character of the
city does not allow us to respond in an adequate measure to the
numerous questions which are at the base of this article.

---

[12] This is one of the aims of Potthast (1962–98), vols. 2 and 3, respectively, under
the terms *Annales* and *Chronica* or *Cronica* or even *Chronicon*. For a suitable comparison of narrative texts of medieval transalpine historiography distinguished by national
areas, one can still see the *MGH, SS* (n. 3 above). See also van Houts (1995),
"Bibliography", 9–12. The difficulty of working in this larger field of research of
the rest of Europe appears also from reading the works by Guenée (1980), passim,
which are only marginally interesting to medieval urban historiography.
[13] This is seen already in Dupré (1956) and Dupré (1958); still useful in this
regard is Ottokar (1948), 3–65 and 179–82 (above all for the Italian and French
cities); cf., in particular for Germany, Ennen (1972).

Urban Development in the Later Middle Ages

When examining the objective conditions of development of the urban world after 1000, today we are able, with greater clarity and determination than some years or decades ago, to point out a significant distinction between the cities of north-central Italy (i.e., those making part of the 'regnum Italie') and urban centers of southern Italy (Norman, Angevin, and Aragonese), which had characteristics of development analogous in many aspects to urban centers in transalpine Europe (Iberian peninsula, France, England, Low Countries, Germany, Scandinavian and Slavic worlds).[14] While we know about these analogous aspects that we see in urban centers—related, of course, to very individual historical developments—we also must consider significant differences of conditions and situations of development from the early to the later Middle Ages. Notwithstanding the common, characteristic, but ever less unifying presence of the bishop, who had more or less numerous and varied attributes in the temporal sphere, in each urban center the political, institutional, economic, social, and cultural evolutions assume pathways that are very different in the areas compared and distinguished above, above all because of the effect of very different connections between the urban world and external powers, both central and regional and local.

Numerous factors would be required to evaluate completely the varied details of the historical pathways and destinies of European cities after 1000, even if in the later Middle Ages these generally involved a common process of renewal: factors of remote or recent influence, connected, for example, to the Roman or to the more recent origins of the urban reality; factors external or internal to the civic structure, related sometimes predominantly to the initiatives and actions of men, sometimes to circumstances of natural and ambient phenomena connected to the particularities of the urban site, to its dislocation from its surrounding territories and to the varied qualities and opportunities offered by the local countryside.

It is in this context that we should direct attention to salient characteristics that connect the varied forms of urban development after

---

[14] The present article is really articulated on this essential distinction, which has not yet been adequately studied and developed in its varied phenomenology, in its motivations and in its changeable cultural, and indeed historiographical, twists and turns.

1000 to the early medieval centuries. Along with the persistence of traditional local powers—ecclesiastical and civil—there appears along the path of transformation in medieval Europe, albeit with different manifestations, a slow and not entirely linear decline of universal powers and their cultural influence expressed variously in time and space. The first of these institutions is the empire, the second is the papacy. In north-central Italy we see development of the city-state, while in other places under consideration we see the consolidation of the central powers of national monarchies. Clearly, we are dealing with political-institutional processes along completely different paths, which had an impact on the diverse class divisions in local, regional, and national society, as well as in various ethnic substrates.

In southern Italy, because of immigration from transalpine countries, and north of the Alps, for a whole series of profound reasons (not least the usual application of the law of primogeniture), the great nobility, both feudal and non-feudal, tended to prevail and to maintain power longer. They did this through widespread control of important ecclesiastical and civil posts, but from positions often external (although not foreign) to the urban world, where they were superior to, but almost never dominated, the productive artisan and mercantile classes. The great nobility (princes, marquis, dukes, and counts) frequently competed intensely against the sovereign powers of the monarchs, who often had recourse to the support of cities by means of a politics of concessions of privileges and immunities.

In north-central Italy, in contrast, due to the capillary diffusion resulting from a different system of succession, as well as because of a more complex ethnic makeup, the middle and lower nobility, feudal and otherwise, were prevalent. They displayed incisive initiatives and strong operative capacities that functioned by means of a connective web between city and country. Further, the leaders of the middle classes—artisanal, commercial, and intellectual—contributed to give a new juridical order and political autonomy to the city, which thus had to face an involved and prolonged conflict with the central powers (royal-imperial, then papal).[15] In these urban centers

---

[15] It does not seem to me that the comparison between these diverse historical realities, Italian and European, has been conducted under any rubric that applies in an effective way and with very convincing results. For the diverse lines of development after 1000 of the communal cities one must, however, take separate count of the analytical, and still valid, studies for north-central Italy of Volpe (1922); for the area of France and Flanders of Ottokar (1948), passim.

quite a mobile and composite society appeared, ever more active and dynamic in modifying the traditional orders and connections in the direction of a lay culture that was materially productive. Meanwhile, in the transalpine urban centers a more classic rigidity of connections between the various *ordines* and powers of medieval society curbed rather more strongly those instances of renewal, safeguarding the traditional equilibria that were based on an alliance at the old level between nobility and clergy. In the cities of the Italian 'regnum', the productive middle classes, frequently allying themselves with the lower and middle urban and rural nobility in the formation of the patriciate and of the local aristocracy, gave a decisively political significance and a character of permanence to the experimentation of the municipal commune, frequently becoming, among the phenomenon of the urban *signorie* and vicariates, states and even regional principalities.

In the other historical areas of medieval Europe, with the partial exclusion, perhaps, of the centers of ancient Lotharingia and in particular those of Flanders, the urban bourgeoisie, remaining for the most part socially, economically, and professionally distinct from the great rural nobility, did not succeed in going beyond the experience of community administration and of corporate management of economic and professional activities. These cities seem more influenced than others by the presence of strong ecclesiastical powers, episcopal and metropolitan, locally constituted and still firmly rooted.

Urban Historiographical Texts

The different articulation and development of municipal society in northern Italy and elsewhere could not but be reflected in the variety of forms of elaboration of urban culture found in these centers, and definitely in very different historiographical expressions. Municipal chronicle-writing, as will be seen in some measure from the basic survey of authors and texts that follows under illustrative headings, succeeded in collecting and representing, sometimes in an incisive and significant form, more frequently in an obscure and imprecise manner, the variety of images offered by individual urban societies, whether mobile or viscous and apparently static. From all this evidence we can see the presence of forms of consciousness of a civic identity manifested especially in politically advanced states and urban societies.

But before analyzing the position of some chroniclers and their works of particular representative significance, it seems to me opportune to define further the methods of separating out various historical and historiographical areas of medieval Europe. A glance at a historical map of Europe permits us, in fact, to single out some territorial regions of particular urban density, made up of centers of travel, markets, and ports, especially on the seacoasts and river courses of considerable importance; cities, nodes of intensive movement of men and goods and thus also of inter-city communications and information—just the type of exchange of information of interest to the chronicler.[16]

In the transalpine world, the manifestations of urban historiography after 1000 appear primarily in the area of France and Germany, in particular on the course of the Rhine but also, to a lesser degree, on the coasts of the North and Baltic Seas. In contrast, in north-central Italy, other than the marine cities of Genoa, Pisa, and Venice, chronicle production appears to be concentrated in the regions of Lombardy, the Veneto, Emilia-Romagna, and Tuscany, with a particular density in the plain of the Po, an area in which an exceptional network of land and riverine paths of communication developed along trade routes.[17] Other parts of Europe are placed in a marginal position, not only because production of chronicles was less common but also because they seem for many reasons to be less or not entirely qualified in a truly urban sense for the period considered here.

We must emphasize again that the region of the Po is responsible for a greater density, structure, and continuity of urban chronicle production than anywhere else, with examples ever more frequent from the communal era to the seigniorial, observable on both the

---

[16] I propose the geo-historical information that precedes and follows to be functional for drawing a map of lines of development of urban historiography in Europe in the period under consideration, on the model of the cartographic apparatus offered for the diffusion of other historiographical typologies, above all monastic, by Guenée (1980).

[17] We are dealing also—and indeed we should not forget it—with areas of particular urban density characterized by centers known generally for a strong presence of productive and intellectual classes, politically important and increasing in size. A quantitative calculation, although not exhaustive, of civic chronicles distributed by region shows in the first position Tuscany with sixteen texts, the region of Emilia-Romagna with fifteen, Lombardy with thirteen, and the Veneto with nine.

north (Lombardy and part of the Veneto) and the south (Emilia and Romagna) sides of the Po. In the course of the later Middle Ages, these regions figured prominently as centers of intense circulation of historiographical activity, characterized also by the mingling of internal and external impulses of a political as well as a cultural nature that came from beyond the Apennines, especially from Florence and from the lands of the Papal States.[18]

North-Central Italy

Coming now to a detailed list of individual chroniclers and their works, it seems opportune to start with Genoa, because of the antiquity and continuity over a long period of an urban historiographical production that presents specific characteristics, significant especially for its official status, internal to its communal institutions, and for its strong focus on the maritime and mercantile destiny of its *cives*. We are dealing, to be precise, with the *Annales Januenses*,[19] which were begun by Caffaro di Rustico di Caschifellone (ca. 1080–1166) after 1099 and were continued and brought up to date with many additions up to 1293 by other authors of the commune, according to a chronological framework of the civic consuls and on the order of the local magistrates, who ordered its transcription and conservation in the communal cartulary. The uninterrupted work of the continuators—Oberto (1169–73), Ottobono (1174–96), Ogerio Pane (1197–1219), Marchisio (1220–24), Bartolomeo (1225–38); then as coauthors together the chancellors of the commune up to 1263, the *quattuorviri* (lawyers and laymen, from 1265–79), and, finally, Giacomo Doria (1280–93)—bears witness to the character of the great interest and authority of their testimony, to the sources of information and particular amplitude of their narrative perspective that, from the Ligurian capital, follows the economic and social fortunes of the Genovese merchants and seamen along their Mediterranean routes

---

[18] These aspects of interregional circulation, within the ancient lands of the 'regnum Italie', of chronicle production in greater quantity of exchange of experiences and cultural, political, institutional, and economic-social models, have been taken under consideration for the region of Emilia-Romagna in Andreolli et al. (1991).

[19] *Annali genovesi di Caffaro e de'suoi continuatori*, ed. L. T. Belgrano (Rome, 1890).

all the way to the Holy Land and the eastern Empire.[20] The *Annales*, intended to hand down the historical memory of the urban community in an official version, were composed in Latin and subsequently enjoyed a varied fortune, above all from the nineteenth century onward. It was precisely from the nineteenth century that the peculiarities of the *Annales* began to be studied and identified, as a product of the almost two-century-long collaboration of its various authors, from upper-middle class families and communal professionals in the notariate and the chancellery. These were conditions that already by themselves could secure public dignity and credibility to the chroniclers, as faithful interpreters of the lay ideology of the new communal society, in the continuity of its transmarine and marine undertakings, in both peace and war.[21]

From Caffaro to Jacopo Doria, during the prolonged municipal experience of Genoa, are blended together the succession of *compagne* and consulates, the initial *municipalismo* and the early moralistic-pedagogical burdens, in a perspective more open to the increasing complexity and dispersion of late thirteenth-century life.

The *Annales Placentini*, by a notary of Piacenza, Giovanni Codagnello (ca. 1175–after 1235) invite us to enter into the life of the communal experience of a city of dry land, of Lombard culture, of great relevance for transport in the heart of the plain of the Po and, because of this, a city of remarkable mercantile vocations.[22] Probably a descendant of the lower nobility, local vassals of the urban church, Codagnello worked as a notary in Piacenza's commune, but there is no evidence that his chronicle production was officially commissioned by urban magistrates. Thus, his *Annales* could be considered a personal expression of his desire to pass down to contemporaries and to posterity the memory of the records of Piacenza. The *Annales* (ca. 1090–1235) seem derived only in their first part from written memory of a familial (his father also was a notary) and communal (archival documentation, especially from the urban commune) character; then they become ever more an expression of the direct experience undergone by the notary-chronicler, a participant in conflicts both internal and

---

[20] Petti Balbi (1995) has given us one of the most recent and critically up to date studies of Caffaro, the continuators and their works.

[21] Potthast (1962–98), 2:291–92.

[22] J. Codagnelli, *Annales Placentini*, ed. O. Holder-Egger, *MGH Script. rerum German. in usum scholarum*, vol. 23 (Hannover, 1901).

external to his city, between nobility and people, between guelph and ghibelline, and between clergy and laymen. An attentive re-teller of the local annalistic tradition that is now lost, Codagnello's works (also attributed to him are the *Gesta Federici imperatoris*, *De rebus gestis in Lombardia*, and *Gesta obsidionis Damiate*) seem to be the earliest survivors of an authentically local narrative thread, but also display awareness of the context of Lombard historiographical production of Guelph-Ambrosian inspiration, in strong competition with that of the Ghibelline party in the large-scale chronological arc of conflict between the communes and the Empire from Frederick I to Frederick II Hohenstaufen. Thus, in some measure his *Annales* reflect ideological themes and schemes of this central and renewed dispute in the world of the Po seem to be moderately representative in many aspects.[23]

Codagnello, from the commune of Piacenza, using a chronological outline of consulates and podestàs (although in a fitful way), in a rather monotonous notarial style, and in Latin sometimes more inclined to streaks of local dialect than to the discipline of classical rhetoric, records especially the military phases of penetration and conquest of the *contado*. His municipalist outlook, moderately pro-Guelph/nobility, usually does not widen beyond the limits of the political and territorial rivalry of his commune with the surrounding ones of Parma, Cremona, and Pavia; traces of a broader intercity Guelph solidarity, the sort of thing promoted by the Lombard League, are rather fleeting.[24] The works of Codagnello produced significant echoes in the context of historiographical production at Piacenza from the late Middle Ages to the modern era; less in the succeeding historiographical tradition of Lombardy and the Po region.[25]

The urban historiography of Lombardy, Veneto, and more broadly the Po basin, in the successive generations of authors working under the secular arc of imperial Hohenstaufen dominion in Italy, resulted in a production so intense and varied as to render it impossible to make a sufficiently articulated and detailed summary.[26] In its total

[23] Gatti (1991), 267–71.
[24] Arnaldi (1982), 562–68; Castignoli (1986), 273–302.
[25] Potthast (1962–98), 3:495–97. Studies of this chronicler and his writings took on valid scientific dimensions starting only in the late nineteenth century.
[26] On Lombard historiography in this crucial phase, see Martini (1970); on Venetian historiography in the same period see Arnaldi and Capo (1976).

panorama, without doubt the prevalent ideology and expressed in terms more or less rigid or murky, was the defense of the regime of communal autonomy and of the connected system of 'libertates', the almost exclusive affirmation of the civic *patria*, more frequently in an anti-imperial function but sometimes also with the protection and security of royal privileges. As a rule, the presence and the institutional, social, and cultural prestige of the clergy in the urban world, still somewhat significant, do not characterize urban historiography as prevalently as in the past (for example even in the period of the Investiture Controversy); we see more and more the emergence of authors of lay origin, decisively turned to pragmatism and to contemporaneity and, thus, to their personal, direct, experimentation.

Urban historiography of the communal era nevertheless is characteristically defined as 'canonical', that is, of an ecclesiastical origin, a product of the chapters of canons of the urban cathedrals; in recent years this rightly has been assumed to be a peculiarity of chronicle writing of Romagna,[27] which is worth mentioning here. Its oldest surviving witness is found in the *Chronicon Faventinum* (Faenza) (first century A.D.–1236), written by the canon of the cathedral of St. Peter in Faenza, master Tolosano (mid 12th century–1226) and continued for a decade by at least two other chroniclers.[28] A man of noteworthy biblical, classical, and juridical culture, Tolosano succeeded in writing in a decorous Latin that resounds stylistically with Vergilian epic and biblical phrases. Animated by a decidedly self-sufficient spirit of municipal *patria*, he presents the remote, early medieval, and classical past in an often-legendary form, even bringing up the myth of the Roman origins of his city.[29] It is interesting to note here that, unlike most urban historiography of an ecclesiastical tradition, his narration, ever more diverse and circumstantial when turning to the communal era, follows not the chronological framework of the sequence of local bishops but, rather, although in a non-systematic form, that of the communal magistrature. His exposition, divided into 153 rubricated chapters, generally is not schematic but discursive, and it seems focused not on the clergy of Faenza but on the entire urban community, which is rendered, even in a phase

---

[27] Ortalli (1976), 615–36 and esp. 624–25.
[28] Magistri Tolosani, *Chronicon Faventinum*, ed. G. Rossini, *RIS* 2nd ser., vol. 28.1 (Bologna, 1936–39); about the question of continuators, cf. esp. Mascanzoni (1996).
[29] Cf. on this topic Vasina (1991), 117–21.

afflicted with external and internal conflicts, clearly conscious of civic solidarity between clergy and laymen, bishop and commune, under the protection of unfailing divine providence. The communal militia of Faenza in Tolosano's *Chronicon* figures almost as a sort of *militia Christi*, animated by a crusading spirit against the rival armies of Imola, Forlì, and, especially, Ravenna; a *militia* that must ultimately achieve success. In his narration, which is not especially linear, we cannot be surprised at his departures from strictly municipal events to regional ones or at his digressions on themes of great general importance (crusades, war between the Lombard communes and the emperor, etc.), since these correspond almost always to his strategy of bringing the attention of the reader to the prestigious position of his *patria*, in the present as in the past.[30]

Without doubt the circumstances of imperial Hohenstaufen domination in the lands of the 'regnum Italie' from the middle of the twelfth century until the 1250s contributed to the fermentation of civic consciousness in a strongly ideological/political sense and started to threaten the most rigidly municipalist positions, also because of their ever more pressing involvement with the recurrent competition between the universal powers of the papacy and empire. But even in light of the renewed federalist experience of the 'Societas Lombardie, Marchie Trivixane et Romandiole', conditions were never such as to promote a super-civic historiography of true regional breadth.[31] It seems that there were other, and diverse, influences that, on this path of inter-city organization, promoted individual urban communities and, in a phase of increasing maturation of relations between urban centers, followed from the spread of the figure of the foreign podestà, from the extension of the phenomenon of political exile, and from other conditions connected with this. Changes in chronicle writing did take place, albeit partially and late, above all in the region of the Veneto, which was influenced, perhaps in a determinant measure, by the formation and expansion of despotic powers—

---

[30] On these aspects of Tolosano's works, see Vasina (1995), 87–104, esp. 89–91, 96–99. The fate of his *Chronicon* has been noteworthy, as a whole, and almost uninterrupted in the course of the modern era, and not only in Faventine culture: the works of Tolosano came to light in the late eighteenth century in the context of ecclesiastical scholarship, and detailed analytical studies have subsequently been made from the late nineteenth century up to today. See Vasina (1991), 119–21.

[31] A significant part of this annalistic production is published in *MGH, SS*, vols. 18 and 19; one should still mention, in this context, the work by Martini (1970).

certainly an inaccurate prefiguration of the so-called urban lordship in the first half of the thirteenth century.[32] Those forms of solidarity which were created temporarily between several urban centers were understood by chroniclers for what they effectively were, that is, occasional military-defensive measures performing an anti-tyrannical function, according to an orientation in many aspects similar, therefore, to the contemporary federative tradition in the Po region.[33] A center of coagulation of this more open and dynamic historiographical direction was, however, not Venice—fiercely focused on its records of the doges, on its restricted patriciate, and on its exceptional fortune on the sea[34]—but Padua—a city of dry land, re-started in a new way of life in the twelfth century, and decisively oriented after that to assume a lively presence in the Venetian region, from Verona to Vicenza up to Treviso.[35]

An interpreter of this new political and cultural climate was Rolandino of Padua (1200–76), in his *Cronica in factis et circa facta Marchie Trivixane* (ca. 1200–62).[36] His rhetorical formation (developed at Bologna), the influence of his father (which was in line with his professional aspirations and was very strong), and his considerable capacity for vigorous and independent reflection on political matters made Rolandino a notary-chronicler of indubitable importance in the context of urban historiography of the thirteenth century. These factors also made his work a unique cultural expression in every respect (beginning with the recognition of its authentic and official nature, accorded to him around 1262 by a committee of colleagues, doctors *in artibus* at the school of Padua).[37] The work, divided into a *praefatio*, twelve books (for a total of 198 chapters), and a final *recomendatio ad legentes*, was considered a *recollectio cronicorum*, a recasting of paternal records, written documents, and oral and visual testi-

---

[32] Still important for many illuminating aspects is the article, published in 1962 and reprinted more recently, by Sestan (1966), 193–223.

[33] Considerations on the evolution of federalism in the cities of the Po between the twelfth and the thirteenth century have been developed in Vasina (1996), 183–201.

[34] See on this topic Pertusi (1970), passim.

[35] On the historiography of Padua in the context of that of Venice, cf. Bortolami (1995), 53–86.

[36] For the most recent edition, cf. Rolandini Patavini, *Cronica in factis et circa facta Marchie Trivixane*, ed. A. Bonardi, in *Rerum Italicarum Scriptores* 2nd ser., 8.1 (Città di Castello, 1905).

[37] See Arnaldi (1963); more recently, Bortolami (1995), 62–74.

monies, recorded by Rolandino during his almost uninterrupted presence as notary of the seal of the commune, which began in 1231 and continued through alternating hostile regimes. The *Cronica*, which from its title would seem to have a regional dimension as its aim, was written in an elegant Latin prose, following a chronology of the consuls and podestàs of Padua; but this municipal annalistic scheme was overborne by the chronicler, by means of a rather mobile perspective that ranged from the illustration of Venetian dynasties and persons (above all the Da Romano, and among these Ezzelino III and Alberico) to general items about the empire of Frederick II Hohenstaufen and the popes of his time. These are themes that would seem, in part, to foreshadow contents privileged by later urban historiography, addressed in a courtly sense to lords and princes. But it is only a question of apparently related contents, because Rolandino's siding with the Guelph and anti-Ezzelino faction, even expressed with prudence *post facta*, namely from 1260 to 1262—after the fall of the da Romano—when in effect the work was composed, remains perfectly coherent with communal morale and with its civic values of liberty, justice, and peace; values definitely brought back and recognized *in primis* in his *patria* of Padua and also shared by other centers of communal civilization. In fact, from Rolandino's re-evocation, more anguished than lucid, of the Ezzelinian tyranny—an experience grievously endured by the people for nearly thirty years in Padua and on the border—emerges a great sense of the fragility of communal institutions under the blows inflicted by the demonic power of tyrants, and a grave warning for future generations of *cives* of any communal center.[38]

If the presence of divine providence floats mysteriously amid the documents of Rolandino's *Cronica*, not as much can be said of the works of another notary-chronicler of two generations later, who lived in several centers in the Po basin but, above all, in his own *patria*: Riccobaldo da Ferrara (1246–1318 *post*). He was largely a witness and writer of current events, endowed with a remarkable political sensibility that, far from being transformed into abstract or

---

[38] *Cronica*, ed. Bonardi, vii–xvii; see also n. 37. Since the seventeenth century, the work of Rolandino has enjoyed a notable editorial fortune and, having passed through the sieve of erudition of Muratori and his continuators, has given rise to decisive developments, above all in the historic-critical mode, only in the last decades of the twentieth century.

moralistic affirmations, rather precociously ends up examining things in the dimension of economic and social reality: a vision, in sum, certainly of lay contemporaneity, even if a vein of religiosity is not entirely absent, expressed for the most part in a rather conventional way. He also was endowed with an education in rhetoric and in a vast and varied classical culture, which stimulated his intense and multi-faceted historiographical production and has reasonably motivated scholars to count him among the pre-humanists, perhaps of the school of Padua.[39]

In this article we cannot consider indiscriminately the numerous works of Riccobaldo, most of which are strongly universalistic in tone, nor even his writings, however interesting, of antique and early medieval historical geography. Here we only can recall briefly the salient outlines of one of his works of particular narrative efficacy that enters more properly into the scope of urban historiography. I refer to his *Chronica parva Ferrariensis*, in which he evokes the events of his city from its origins to 1270—events reconstructed from remote oral traditions, from his family context, from written documentation, and, for the last years, from his youthful personal observations, subsequently rearranged and written presumably between 1313 and 1317.[40] The *Chronica* as we have it is incomplete, not revised by the author and indeed inhomogeneous. Divided essentially into a descriptive part and a second narrative part, it reflects not a few of the cultural interests of Riccobaldo: his antiquarian passion for inserting the medieval origins of Ferrara into the origins of the world and remote relations between empire and papacy; his topographical knowledge in contextualizing the settlement and demographic development of his city in the region of the lower Po; his own capacity of intuition and of characterization in discovering and pursuing the commercial life of Ferrara as a natural part of its economic-social and political problems; finally his civic passion, his loyalty to the communal institutions in opposing the invading seigniorial power of the house of Este, the early establishment of its lordship in Ferrara, and the rooting of its landowning and feudal interests in the lower Po region.[41] The most incisive and significant pages of the *Chronica* are

---

[39] Zanella (1991), 163 ff.; Zanella (1980); Vasina (1995), 93–103.
[40] Riccobaldo da Ferrara, *Chronica parva Ferrariensis*, ed. G. Zanella (Ferrara, 1983).
[41] Zanella (1991), 175–79; Vasina (1995), 93–103.

dedicated, in fact, to analyzing without reticence and with irony the process of the ascension to the urban signoria of Obizzo II d'Este (ca. 1264) and in deprecating the negative consequences not only for the communal liberty of his *patria* but also and above all for the economic and social fortunes of the *populus* of Ferrara, at the last sacrificed to the rising commercial penetration of Venice.[42]

The historiographical scope of Riccobaldo is entirely concentrated on his city of Ferrara and, although both he and Rolandino wrote in similar chronological and spatial contexts, unlike Rolandino, Riccobaldo does not consider the logic of the political marshalling of factions (Guelphs and Ghibellines, philo-papal or philo-imperial), concentrating instead on the values of autonomy, liberty, and utility of communal urban society—those virtues, in fact, which would have had to work together in an affirmation of the 'bonum commune'. The *iter* of composition of the *Chronica*, written in a lively and discursive Latin, outside of the traditional municipal annalistic schemes, can represent in a certain sense the phases of the historiographical maturation of Riccobaldo: from expressions of antiquarian erudition to forms of lucid political reflection on the recent historical experience of the Ferrarese world; in a secular vision; and pragmatic both of the past and the present. This makes him a remarkable and precocious interpreter of urban historiography between the thirteenth and the fourteenth centuries.[43]

The political and institutional evolution of regimes of communal autonomy from the thirteenth to the fourteenth century, with the diminution of forms of pluralism both within the city and in its external connections, began not rarely to favor the marginalization of chroniclers—from positions univocally or largely representative of the urban consciousness, to minority and dissonant attitudes, if not

---

[42] *Chronica parva Ferrariensis*, ed. Zanella, 184–93.

[43] His rich and varied production remained hidden for a long time, not identified and in part undervalued, and only came slowly to light during the eighteenth century, above all through the efforts of L. A. Muratori. In the nineteenth and twentieth centuries it remained almost exclusively the field of study of local scholars, and only in the last decades, amidst a sustained series of research, articles and critical editions, has his peculiar and unique character been adequately re-evaluated in the context of late medieval urban historiography, contemporary with the transition between commune and urban signoria. See Zanella (1991), 176–79. We cannot ignore here those quite valid contributions, especially on Riccobaldo's writings of a universalistic character, offered in the last decade in Ricobaldi Ferrariensis, *Compendium Romanae Historiae*, ed. A. T. Hankey, 2 vols. (Rome, 1984).

absolutely of open opposition to the new oligarchical and monocratic centers of power. At the same time, this evolution favored the separation of historiographical activity from public functions by giving life to freer and more spontaneous voices, more and more often in the arena of the private citizen.[44] In addition, there was also a re-evaluation in the political sphere of the economic dimension of the initiatives of individual businessmen, especially artisans and merchants, and of their associations of trades. An area particularly favorable to these developments opened up in the Tuscan world, above all at Florence but also at Pisa and in other centers of high economic enterprise of the region.[45] In this large area, culturally very lively, the figure of the merchant-chronicler began to affirm itself in urban historiography.

A principal interpreter of this new and emerging chronicle typology was the Florentine Giovanni Villani (ca. 1280–1348), descendant of a family of mercantile and also cultural traditions, as is evident, among other things, by the historiographical activity of his relatives Matteo and Filippo. In the development of Florentine narrative production his *Nuova cronica* (origins of his city up to 1348),[46] written in an excellent vernacular in thirteen books (for a total of 1117 chapters), from the beginning of the fourteenth century until his death from the plague, represents the culminating phase of maturation of a medieval urban historiography that had made an uncertain beginning at least from the twelfth century.[47] His is quite a diffuse text, which, beyond its annalistic schemes, ends up intermingling manifold themes—of general historical interest as well as of a regional and urban character. There is a distinct progression from the legendary origins of the world and of Florence, according to the historiographical conventions of the biblical and classical universal history

[44] Not by chance, especially from the fourteenth century on in Italian cities, historiographical activity, understood as a public and/or community obligation, gave way either to forms of courtly chronicle-writing, or towards individual diarizing or memorializing and intimate books.

[45] Without forgetting what has already been said in note 17 about historiographical production in Tuscany, we must underline the notable contribution in the area of annal-writing, of chronicle-writing and of 'historie' dating from the late Middle Ages to the Renaissance, along the entire experience of humanism, from the cities of Lucca, Pistoia, Arezzo, and Siena.

[46] G. Villani, *Nuova Cronica*, ed. G. Porta (Parma 1990), esp. vii–xxiii.

[47] Del Monte (1950).

traditions in which the literary sensibility of Giovanni is indulged, to the contemporary decades of intense political and economic-social life of his city, reconstructed with increasing concentration on the basis of the best information and experience and, thus, also authority in the complex concatenation of occurrences and changes of regime.[48] It is interesting here to show that in the relationship between the truly Florentine narrative contents and those of a general context (regional, Italian, and European), at first the latter distinctly prevails, but the text more and more tends to reverse itself, making the *patria* emerge in an almost dominant position, on an almost universal horizon, due to the enterprise and the intense industry of its *cives*.

The experience that Villani had had in the artisanal and mercantile field (affiliation with the companies of the Peruzzi and Bonaccolsi) and his *curriculum* of public office in the Florentine commune (occupying various positions from 1316 to 1329),[49] if they did not contribute to give to his work real official character, at least succeeded in rendering it authoritative in the eyes of a large public of readers, both fellow-citizens and foreigners, because of his awareness of the web that closely bound politics and economics from his Florence to contemporary Europe. Such a wide reception was probably helped also by a providential vision of history, by the favor accorded to the ecclesiastical world, and by his moderate Guelphism, which, prevalent or scarce in Florence and in the Tuscan world, succeeded in giving a charge of optimism to his narration, although this was diminished in the last years by natural calamities, bank failures, and deadly epidemic phenomena. At the same time, his roving and far-seeing merchant's perspective prevented an attitude of rigid municipal moralism and, instead, provided an accurate exposition of the economic-social facts of his city in a European projection, sometimes underscored in quantitative historical terms.[50] Based primarily on written sources, for the most part selected and sometimes reported in the text but also and in a rather important way on personal testimony, his work ends by being representative of many aspects of the Florentine world in which it matured, subsequently extending its manuscript history.[51]

---

[48] Porta (1995), 125–38.
[49] G. Villani, *Nuova Cronica*, ed. Porta, xix–xx.
[50] Porta (1995), 134–35.
[51] Many times studied and published in the last centuries, the *Nuova cronica* only recently has been made object of systematic philological investigations and of critical

Proceeding along the peninsula, it becomes ever more difficult, even in the late Middle Ages, to list authentic expressions of urban historiography—incisive voices animated by the spirit of civic and communal consciousness—as lively and numerous as those already singled out or capable of being singled out in the regions of the Po and Tuscany. The lands of the Anconetan March, of the Duchy of Spoleto, and of the Duchy of Rome, subject to the pontifical monarchy, saw their civic autonomy weakened and the related manifestations of local chronicle writing withered.[52] The city of Rome, however, provides one exception. Strong municipal demonstrations and social and economic tensions developed, due to the deep vacuum which had been created in the city that had once been capital of the empire, then—in the course of the Middle Ages—of the papacy, and now—during the fourteenth century—was entirely deprived of its effectiveness and symbolic function as guide of Christianity, due to the transfer of the popes to Avignon. The humiliation of the Romans at having lost the exceptional inheritance of the capital city, and having lost also the vital resources derived from the pilgrimage industry, re-animated political aspirations for recuperating their lost status. This they attempted by means of the reaffirmation of the republican tradition of Rome in the context of a utopian design enlarged to the papacy and to the empire, which was led by the remarkable figure of an educated Roman notary, Cola di Rienzo. He was the protagonist in his city of a popular and anti-baronial movement that involved the revival of the Senate,[53] which has left a large echo in a really unusual narrative text in the Roman historiographical tradition. That tradition had been defined almost exclusively by the production of, and additions to, the *Libri pontificales* of the church of Rome; by a production, that is, that was appropriate to universalistic norms, as in fact was done, even if in more reduced measure, also in other great ecclesiastical centers of the peninsula, such as Milan and Ravenna, by means of the continuation of urban history on the schematic base

---

studies in the context of Florentine historiography and sometimes in specific relation to the figure and works of Dante Alighieri. See Porta (1995), 129, 133–34, and passim.

[52] Following the provisory count made for urban chronicle-writing of north-central Italy, as in note 17, we can list works of urban historiography in the lands of the Papal States only in five cases in the Duchy of Rome and in only one case in the Duchy of Spoleto.

[53] On conditions in Rome in the fourteenth century, connected closely to the figure of Cola di Rienzo, cf. Dupré (1952), passim.

of a series of bishops.[54] Now, at Rome, abandoned by its bishops, some unraveling had opened in this church tradition, unexpectedly giving life and strength to a secular and popular historiographical thread, nourished by cultural suggestions and by the nostalgia or aversions of intellectuals.

Unlike the works of Villani, which were many times re-elaborated and perfected both stylistically and in terms of informative contents and expositive criteria, the Roman *Cronica*,[55] long thought anonymous and only recently attributed to Bartolomeo di Jacopo da Valmontone (beg. 14th century–after 1360),[56] has been handed down to us in a text that is incomplete, much less revised, and structurally imbalanced, as well as fragmentary. The work, written between 1357 and 1358, with an addition in 1360, was composed first in a Latin draft, then vernacularized into Romance for purposes of publicity, since it was addressed with clearly ideological finality to a large public of the chronicler's fellow-citizens. He, recognizable from his autobiographical testimony as being from the aristocratic class and a student of medicine at Bologna (ca. 1338–39), reveals an unusual classical culture and a particular predilection for Titus Livy as his model of exemplary history.[57] In his pathetic re-evocation of the Roman tradition of the City, the author of the *Cronica* aims to describe the sufferings of contemporaries in the grave crises that Roman institutions and society had undergone, with a strong polemical and anti-aristocratic spirit, particularly against the cardinal family of the Colonna. Rome and the lands of the Patrimony are frequently at the center of his attention, although sometimes in the context of relations that combine the Italian and European worlds and finds its most incisive biographical expression in the figure of Cola di Rienzo and his failed utopian adventure.[58] Events internal and external to Rome, narrated in a rambling fashion from 1327 to 1354, in twenty-eight chapters, and based on personal memories, written documents, and oral testimony of contemporaries, would console his *concives*, re-evoking the great past of Rome and recalling the imagination of the readers to the expectation of ever-imminent and important

---

[54] For this ecclesiastical production of universalistic pattern in the main sees of the Italian peninsula, see Capitani (1988), 772–76 and bibliography.

[55] Anonimo Romano, *Cronica*, ed. Porta.

[56] Miglio (1995), 187; cf. note in asterisk.

[57] Anonimo Romano, *Cronica*, ed. Porta, vii–xi.

[58] Anonimo Romano, *Cronica*, ed. Porta, passim.

novitates. But in reality his vision of history, unlike that affirmed by Villani, is pessimistic and, faced with the ineluctability of the crises of the former capital city, is resigned to the impossibility of recovering its lay, civic, and popular values. The modernity and originality of his prose are found in the author's capacity to dialogue with himself and his readers, to soothe his personal discomfort with his memories and his experience of the present by communicating it, in the conviction that his writing will be useful to his readers. His style—nervous, swift, vividly imaginative and colored, primitive and learned at the same time—succeeds also in assuming dramatic movement, almost like a romance, in the final chapters (chs. xviii–xxiii and xxvi–xxvii) dedicated to Cola, who becomes the improvident protagonist of his *Cronica*.[59] This is a work, however, that is very different from contemporary historiography, revealing among other things early humanistic predilections and suggestions, together with the ability to transmit them to those outside the restricted circle of educated readers.[60]

As I have already mentioned, in the development of urban historiography between the thirteenth and the fourteenth centuries, the investigation and biographical definition of strong men and protagonists of local and regional political life, who were capable of settling the paralyzing controversies of the urban and comital oligarchies, as well as the progressive leveling of civic and communal values to positions of conformity and opportunism regarding the strong powers that were constituted from time to time, prefigure and sometimes signal the transition of chronicle-writing from the communal age to that of the seigniorial and then princely ages. This transition, found especially in politically important centers such as Milan, Verona, Ferrara, and Rimini, sees the attention of the chroniclers transferred away from institutions and communal society to concentrate on the life of the court, sometimes conforming itself to the authority of the

---

[59] Miglio (1995), 175–87.

[60] The *Cronica* cannot be said to have remained for centuries in hiding: already known from the first half of the seventeenth century, and even partially published as the *Vita di Cola di Rienzo* and also by Muratori as *Historiae Romanae fragmenta*, it had long enjoyed subsequently a fortune more of a philological than a historical character. Only in the course of the twentieth century, amongst a flourishing series of studies and of partial editions, has it finally received a complete critical edition of the text and a full historical re-evaluation. See Potthast (1962–98), 2:356; Anonimo Romano, *Cronica*, ed. Porta, xi–xvi.

urban lord, the representative of the empire, of the pope, or of the territorial prince. In the process, in certain aspects the motives and content of late medieval historiography of the area of the 'regnum Italie' seem to approach those of transalpine annals and chronicles, and those of southern and insular Italy.[61]

The Rest of Europe

As has already been mentioned, the constituent characteristics and developments of urban historiography in Europe of the monarchical-national states are quite different. This is really as much an expression of different types of experiences—not just political and institutional but also and above all social and cultural. An examination of such a vast and complex field of research is difficult, even at a comparative level, because, among other things, it is conditioned by a series of unfavorable circumstances.[62] This corpus is, as a whole, less easily studied than that of the Italian world, partly because it is less typologically definable in its precise urban definitions, given a multiplicity and variety of historical narrations that were oriented primarily in a universal or national or ethnic direction or focused on rulers, princes, or feudal dynasties; on episcopates, monasteries, canons, convents; or on other realities for the most part external to the urban world.

Another non-negligible limitation in the recognition of such chronicles is their frequently anonymous nature, sometimes aggravated by the fact that these historiographical texts have been handed down

---

[61] On the monarchical, dynastic, signorial, and even monastic characters of the historiographical traditions of southern and insular Italy after 1000 (indeed, urban chronicle-writing had a very limited fortune, since the cities belonged to the royal demesne), cf. Capitani (1988), 783–85 and 792.

[62] The research and analysis of texts have been conducted primarily in the *MGH, SS* (see n. 3 above). Other than the text and bibliography produced by Van Houts (1995) (9–12, 42–49), the following are helpful as keys for reading transalpine chronicles: for German areas, *Die Chroniken der Deutschen Staedte von 14. bis in 16. Jahrhundert*, ed. Historische Kommission bei der Bayerischen Akademie der Wissenschaften (Leipzig, 1862–); Boulay (1981); Schmidt (1958); Patze (1987); for English areas: *English Historical Documents* (1969–81), vols. 2–4; Graves (1975); Gransden (1990–91); for France, Guenée (1980); for Spanish areas, Sanchez Alonso (1947). For a comprehensive, up-to-date, and rich survey of medieval historiography, see by varied authors the term 'Chronik', in *Lexikon des Mittelalters*, vol. 2 (Munich, 1983), cols. 1954–2028.

with titles attached presumably not by their authors but by manuscript and printing traditions and which, thus, do not really signify their orientation and contents but only the fact that they had had physical presence in this or that city. Besides, such works, by not revealing any sign of the personality of their authors, seem to have a character that is prevalently compilatory, fragmentary, heterogeneous, and with frequent usually anonymous additions, which weakens the continuity of the narrative web and the sense of a coherent expository scope, if ever it existed.

Often the continuators of base-texts adapt themselves to traditional historiographical criteria and, although working in general after 1000, do not seem to have removed themselves from early medieval schemes, thus collectively giving life to monotonous, if not uniform, narrations, inadequate to give a sense of development and change in urban life.[63] It is not an accident, in this context, that such texts arose primarily from ecclesiastical surroundings and were the work of clerics—canons, monks, or friars—who were more interested in the *continuum* of the property of their institutions than in the changes of urban life as understood in the full harmony of its component parts. It was, in other words, a strongly corporate spirit, of which no corresponding expression is found among the urban laity, among the mercantile and artisan classes, or above all among the so-called bourgeoisie of officials (judges, notaries, etc.), which was less advanced politically and culturally than in the cities of the 'regnum Italie' and, further, not successful at finding the spaces of liberty and autonomy that appeared much earlier in the communal cities of the Italian world. In fact, the middle classes in the transalpine cities were not numerous or articulate: the experts of law and the intellectuals usually were bound to the ecclesiastical *curiae*; merchants and artisans were indeed united in *hanse* and *gilde*, sometimes organized in a dense network of intercity relations, but often these were conditioned by the circumstantial city-territorial connections of the external powers of bishops, lords, and feudatories of the countryside, who through their internal and external conflicts heavily burdened the urban *compages*, long controlling and delaying movements toward autonomy. Almost never, however, do the chroniclers of the transalpine cities in the later

---

[63] We are clearly dealing with remarks of a general character that will be subject below to particular evidence in the consideration of individual narrative texts.

Middle Ages end up expressing a civic consciousness in a unitary sense: they must, in fact, record the status of the *cives* in subordination to the traditional hierarchical order, based on the high clergy and the great aristocracy, and the conditions of passivity, of danger, and of injury suffered by the *civitates* because of the increasing domestic conflicts of local potentates and the hostility of these to the actions of centralization by sovereign powers into national states.

A count made of the narrative sources in question from international and national catalogues and from principal collections of editions of medieval annals and chronicles,[64] using rigorous criteria, suggests that we are dealing with a drastic selection of texts, reduced here to a small list out of a number that initially appears quite high. Some of these could not be given an accurate and analytic description, for reasons already indicated above, and for other motives, which will be stated from time to time. Above all, the texts chosen are quite far from being adequately representative of the urban centers of the extensive and varied historical, ethnic, and national areas of transalpine Europe during the later Middle Ages. In fact, in contrast to the Franco-Germanic network along the Rhine, where there was a notable density of urban centers with relatively appropriate historiographical traditions,[65] there are other areas less or not at all covered by authentic expressions of urban chronicle-writing—for example, the British Isles (making exception, but not in an entirely satisfactory and convincing way, for London), the Scandinavian peninsula, in part the Polish and Slavic worlds, and also the Iberian peninsula, where other forms of historiographical activity prevail, or where urban annals has been exhausted or had not yet reached a point of maturation.[66]

One work, among thirty or so selected texts, that presents many characteristics which can number it among true urban chronicles is the *Annales Cameracenses* (Cambrai, 1099–1170), composed between 1152 and 1170 by Lambertus Waterlos (1108–ca. 1170), regular

---

[64] See on this notes 3, 8, 9, and 63 above.

[65] We are dealing in particular with the large and extensive river network of the Rhine, which includes ten cities or almost-cities of sufficiently pertinent, and sometimes even significant, historiographical production.

[66] Chronicle-production in question is scarce in middle-eastern Germany and in the Slavic area, while four centers in the league looking out on the North and Baltic seas have left testimonies of some importance in the scope of historiographical activity in question.

canon of St. Autbertus of this same city of Flanders.[67] In contrast
to most transalpine chroniclers, the author does not go back to the
remote past, nor does he follow the schemes of universalistic historiography; instead, he provides, to a public of presumably ecclesiastical readers, information about the lived present, covering an array
of local and regional interests, attempting to understand above all
ecclesiastical circumstances and events. In particular, Lambertus tries
to give narrative continuity to specific urban and territorial themes,
linking them to the current traditions of the local episcopate and to
the most representative of its bishops, as, for example, Nicholas. We
can see that next to the bishop of Cambrai, starting in 1137–38, is
registered the presence, ever more lively, of the *cives*, among whom
the chronicler singles out the influential classes of the *magnates* and
proceres: an urban laity that already in the twelfth century is rather
resourceful and that alternates sides—now in collaboration, now in
conflict with the local bishop. The narrative horizon of the chronicler tends to widen from strictly local conflicts (for example that
against the castle of St. Autbertus) to struggles between the urban
bishop and the counts of Flanders, to relations with the Empire, with
the crusades, and to the delicate question of the subjection of the
diocese of Cambrai first by the ecclesiastical metropolitan of Cologne,
then of Reims.[68]

A more advanced phase of the history of German cities is seen
in the *Annales Lubicenses* (Lubeck, 1264–1324), which illustrate diverse
events of a port city on the shores of the Baltic Sea.[69] Its genesis is
complex: considered a continuation of the *Annales* of Albert Stadense,
it has been attributed, for the part after the year 1267, to Conrad,
a dean of the city, a chronicler contemporary with the deeds narrated, who is quite attentive to the urban connections between clergy
and laity and, in particular, to the local episcopal tradition. He does
not neglect to illustrate also, however, in modest Latin and presumably to a large public of readers in his *patria*, the controversial

---

[67] Lambertus Waterlos, *Annales Cameracenses*, ed. G. H. Pertz, *MGH SS* 16 (Hannover, 1859), 509 ff.

[68] Lambertus Waterlos, *Annales Cameracenses*, ed. Pertz, passim. This work, already known and published in the course of the nineteenth century, has been made the object of more detailed studies in the course of the twentieth century. See Potthast (1962–98), 7:116.

[69] *Annales Lubicenses*, ed. J. M. Lappenberg, *MGH SS* 16 (Hannover, 1859) 411–29.

relations of Lubeck, recorded as *civitas Teotoniae*, with the neighboring potentates, especially with the king of Denmark. The narrative scope of the author tends to concentrate increasingly on the active presence of the *cives*—of an urban laity, that is—defined by the productive classes and led by them to carve out spaces of autonomy that were to the disadvantage of the local clergy. For example, in their conflict in 1299 with the local canons, the urban laity affirmed an urban consulate that seems to signal a strong stress on internal and external competitive connections, most evident in the first decades of the fourteenth century, which provoked an interdict of long duration from the ecclesiastical authorities. The narration of the last part of the *Annales* seems to develop to a dramatic crescendo in which unfavorable human events resound negatively in an uninterrupted sequence of natural calamities.[70]

In general terms, at least from the Ottonian age onward, transalpine urban chronicle-writing that developed in the later Middle Ages seems to proceed from an institutional framework and, from the insertion into that framework of local events in the surrounding territories, to a factual exposition of the local events that is ever more precise and uninterrupted from year to year. From such narrations, however, no signs of an authentic urban consciousness, which would give a unitary sense to the text, emerge or are developed; this is a historiographical evolution, therefore, different from that of the Italian area. It is indeed comprehensible if one considers that the territorial ecclesiastical powers (episcopal or monastic) and lay aristocratic-feudal ones, as well as the centralizing powers of sovereigns, long took away from the productive urban classes sufficient space to acquire true political autonomy and an adequate level of relative community consciousness in most of the cities, which were active on the cultural and more properly historiographical plane. This is true not only for the few chronicles described above but also for those which will be briefly illustrated below, even taking due recognition of inevitable typological variations from center to center.

The rich narrative production of the center of Colmar (France) presents characteristics that correspond in certain aspects to those indicated above and differ in others. It is made up of a series of

---

[70] *Annales Lubicenses*, ed. Lappenberg, 411–29. This work, conserved in a fourteenth century manuscript, has had in the last two centuries a fortune circumscribed to two editions and to a few critical studies; see Potthast (1962–98), 2:299.

chronicles interrelated in a complex stratification of compositional additions of up-to-date information by many authors who span the last centuries of the Middle Ages. Here should be noted, because of its large chronological spectrum, the work by the title *Annales Colmarienses maiores* (1277–1472), written by an unidentified preaching friar and continued from at least the end of the thirteenth century by another author who remains anonymous.[71] Even in the variety of perspectives that reflect its urban events, there is a constant interest in the local ecclesiastical world: no longer, however, the traditional one involving the secular hierarchy, due to the absence of an episcopal see, but rather the recent religious settlements of the regular mendicant orders, who brought into the urban world new spiritual and cultural tensions. We find a constant interest in the daily and concrete problems of the life of the urban population in its middle and lower components, including problems of food and sustenance; here there emerges a particular attention to the precarious conditions connected with the merchant economy, a denunciation which seems to spring from a pervasive anti-Semitic spirit, as well as from the motives of the religious order.[72]

Constructed from the interweaving of oral and written testimony, and intended presumably for a large public of residents, including those outside the confines of the conventual world, the *Annales*, besides expanding episodically to events far out of its general range, manifest an ever more regular consideration for the entire community of Colmar, represented in the heart of local conflicts, in its moments of difficulty and of revival. Of particular significance in this sense is the decision taken in 1291 by the *consules* of Colmar (other contemporary chronicles mention the corresponding local magistracy of the *scultetus*), which gave inhabitants of the city enough timber to build 600 houses, a true architectural renewal of the city.[73]

In the German world, the annal-writing of Cologne assumes a special position, as the city was one of the most important ecclesiastical and political centers and at the same time the seat of a lively

[71] *Annales Colmarienses maiores*, ed. P. Jaffé, *MGH SS* 17 (Hanover, 1861), 202–32.
[72] *Annales Colmarienses maiores*, ed. Jaffé, passim.
[73] *Annales Colmarienses maiores*, ed. Jaffé, passim. The fortune of this work has not been entirely negligible, at least after the nineteenth century and up to recent years of the twentieth: it has been in fact copious, published in at least three editions and made the object of a significant series of specific studies of investigation on both philological and historiographical terms. See Potthast (1962–98), 2:264.

and significant chronicle production. Among the texts ascribable to this urban narrative tradition should be mentioned the *Annales Colonienses maximi*, composed in the thirteenth century by an identified monk named Gotfried, on the basis of some narrative threads of different natures and provenances that cover the period from the origins of the world up to 1237.[74] In the first part of the text, which narrates almost the whole first Christian millennium, Gotfried alternates a list of emperors and popes, according to the norms of universal historiography. After 1000, he proceeds to an exposition that is always more focused on the events of the city, above all in institutional and social terms, ecclesiastical and aristocratic; he makes continual references to the city's archbishops, whose succession is reconstructed, and he takes note of the clashing relations they often had with the emperors and with the local churches, beginning with the canons of the cathedral of St. Peter. But Cologne's bishops only rarely seem really representative of the spirit of urban solidarity; rather, their actions often appear disunifying and destructive, because of the multiplicity of their extra-urban obligations on an international level— such as acting as papal or imperial legates; participating, together with expeditions of *cives*, in the crusades to the Holy Land between the twelfth and thirteenth centuries; or being involved in the undertakings of the Hohenstaufens in the Italian peninsula.[75] An expression of the urban ecclesiastical world and destined presumably for the use of the clergy, the *Annales* seem reconstructed essentially from written sources: from the chronicle of Ekkehard to the use of official letters, whose texts were sometimes inserted in the narrative fabric, as in the case of the crusading expedition to Damietta. Only in the last part of the work does the attention of the author appear more concentrated on Cologne and its territory, giving us some dramatic sequences of temporal crises regarding the powers of the archbishops of Cologne, because of the assault on and destruction of their castles in a scenario full of human tensions and natural calamities.[76]

Characteristics analogous in terms of historical ecclesiastical culture, but with a perspective always more concentrated on urban

---

[74] *Annales Colonienses maximi*, ed. G. H. Pertz, *MGH SS* 17 (Hanover, 1861) 723–847.

[75] *Annales Colonienses maximi*, ed. Pertz, passim.

[76] *Annales Colonienses maximi*, ed. Pertz. The *Annales Colonienses maximi*, already known, studied and published in the course of the nineteenth century, has seen a certain renewal of its fortune during a series of detailed investigations undertaken during the twentieth century. See Potthast (1962–98), 2:265.

events, appear in the *Annales Magdeburgenses* (Magdeburg) by an anonymous author, perhaps a local ecclesiastic, living in the late twelfth century.[77] His narration, which seems to refer to diverse urban historical sources of quite distinct nature and value, covers the long period stretching from the Christian origins up to 1188, interrupted in that year. From generic and fragmentary information, he moves on to provide more detailed and observed information in an urban sense after the tenth century, when, because of the presence of the Saxon emperors, Magdeburg, like other German cities, experienced a strong development, among other things coming out from under the ecclesiastical authority of Halberstadt to become an archiepiscopal see in 969. The attention of the chronicler, focused above all on reconstructing the series of local bishops and underlining the close connections of dependency on imperial authority, pauses to give useful information—on the one hand about the urban ecclesiastical reality, like the monastery of St. John the Baptist or the canons of St. Maurice; on the other hand, and particularly in reference to the twelfth century, about the presence, long dominant in the urban world, of the local counts and marquises. Again in this center and in its territory, there emerge in the late twelfth century situations of conflict that involve the temporal authority of the local bishops and seem temporarily to delay the autonomous development of the urban laity and of the productive classes of the city.[78]

Although not having all the qualifications of a medieval city, Ghent in Flanders acquired over time modality and rhythms of development of urban life. The absence, up to the second half of the sixteenth century, of a local episcopal authority undoubtedly favored the autochthonous laity and the free expansion of its economic and political activity, indeed organized in the active 'communitas Gandensis', ruled by *scabini* and *maiores*. We are told of such initiative by the productive classes in our center and its territory by the *Annales*

---

[77] *Annales Magdeburgenses*, ed. G. H. Pertz, *MGH SS* 16 (Hanover, 1859), 105–95.

[78] *Annales Magdeburgenses*, ed. Pertz, passim. Naturally the medieval historiographical production of Madgeburg, that is of a city of particular importance as a strategic base of the 'ostpolitik' of the German emperors, and of missionary actions in the Slavic world, has received the attention of scholars at least in the course of the nineteenth century: specific investigations and editions from then have been followed by important research and later acquisitions both in philological and historiographical terms in the twentieth century. See Potthast (1962–98), 2:301.

Gandenses (1296–1310), written by an author who remains anonymous but was a friar of a local minorite convent, where he composed the work from 1308 to ca. 1337.[79] Written in mediocre Latin and divided into chapters, the *Annales* offer us a dense and concentrated exposition of this important manufacturing and commercial center, following the Flemish military undertakings more than the peaceful ones, for example, against the English, then against the king of France. However, particular emphasis is placed on the alternate connections with the count of Flanders, the main regional authority, and also relations, sometimes amicable and sometimes hostile, with the nearby centers of Bruges and Arras, Naumur, Ypres, and Courtrai. In a rather mature phase of civic institutions and with the decline of the traditional institutional church (the local monasteries of St. Peter and St. Bavo), the voice of our Franciscan chronicler of Ghent is one which better succeeds in understanding from contemporary experience the signs of pride and coherence of an incipient, even if not unified, urban consciousness among the laity of Ghent.[80]

Although not the seat of a bishopric during the Middle Ages, Berne (Switzerland) also succeeded in developing over time, from its foundation (ca. 1191), a community life of an urban level, perhaps more due to the initiative of its military aristocracy than through the activity of its productive classes, although the latter was already intense in the late Middle Ages. Thus tell us the so-called *Annales Bernenses* (1191–1405), by unknown authors (one of these is thought to be identified with a certain Pfund or Phunt, otherwise unknown).[81] The narrative text is divided into two quite distinct parts: a *Cronica de Berno* (1191–1344) with around thirty quite brief notations, written in Latin by a chronicler of the fourteenth century, perhaps on the basis of personal experience, of oral traditions, and of local annalistic traditions; and a series of *Notae Bernenses* (1286–1405), a sort of bringing up to date juxtaposed on the preceding text by a presumably more thoughtful author, on the basis of analogous information. Again in this case we are dealing with generally brief and fitful information,

[79] *Annales Gandenses*, ed. J. M. Lappenberg, *MGH SS* 16 (Hanover, 1859), 554–97.
[80] *Annales Gandenses*, ed. Lappenberg, passim. The work, handed down to us in one manuscript, now lost, nevertheless has enjoyed after the nineteenth century five editions and up to the 1960s of around fifteen specific philological and historiographical studies. See Potthast (1962–98), 2:284.
[81] *Annales Bernenses*, ed. G. H. Pertz, *MGH SS* 17 (Hanover, 1861), 271–74.

written sometimes in Latin, sometimes in the Germanic language, but constantly referring to the city and to its pertinent territorial surroundings.[82] A military and mercantile center of notable importance, Berne is represented above all in its conflicts with the counts of Savoy, with the Hapsburgs, and with the emperor. With an increase of warlike undertakings, the chroniclers give succinct and precise information on the construction and destruction of military buildings in the city, in its suburbs, and in the surrounding territory, about sieges and conquests of castles, which intensified in the course of the fourteenth century after a war victoriously conducted against Berne's rival, Freiburg. But the chroniclers also mention the internal situation of the city, where, notwithstanding the appearance of disturbances in the whole fourteenth century, the aristocratic government continued to rule.[83] One cannot help but perceive how—in contrast to a good part of the medieval historiographical production in German areas, but like the *Annales* of Ghent although with different indications of social order—in this text the ecclesiastical world in its institutional reality and in its existential manifestations is almost absent.[84]

A few other transalpine chronicles can be presented and included, but only partially, in the proper pattern of medieval urban historiography. In the Slavic world, and more precisely in Poland, a representative of this is the *Annales Cracovienses compilati* or *Annales Capituli Cracoviensis* (Cracow, 966–1291), by an anonymous author of the thirteenth to fourteenth century, who provides quite varied information, mostly from written sources of heterogeneous nature, like the local Franciscan annals, now lost, and those of the Polish kingdom.[85] The principal importance of this narrative text is perhaps the strong presence of local ecclesiastical traditions—episcopal, conventual, and canonical—interlaced with those of the ducal family and of the nobility of Cracow, with close attention to dynastic bonds and values.[86]

---

[82] *Annales Bernenses*, ed. Pertz, passim.

[83] *Annales Bernenses*, ed. Pertz, passim.

[84] The fortune of these *Annales*, committed to one sole manuscript at Berne, has resulted, in the course of the nineteenth century, after a series of preparatory studies, in four editions from 1817 to 1871, followed from 1868 to 1960 by a good number of investigations and specific scientific contributions both of philological and historical nature. See Potthast (1962–98), 2:254–55.

[85] *Annales Cracovienses*, ed. R. Roepell and W. Arndt, *MGH SS* 19 (Hanover, 1866), 582–607.

[86] *Annales Cracovienses*, ed. Roepell and Arndt, passim.

A few elements, in truth, shed light on urban life and that of the surrounding territory, more diffuse in the variety of its components. It is certainly true that the urban community saw itself united in the cult of St. Stanislav, above all in moments of great danger (invasions and devastations by the Tartars, ca. 1261; defeats of local *milites*, destruction and burning of the city, etc.), but the chronicler reveals no significant traces of a precise perception of a Cracovian urban consciousness.[87]

It remains now to deal with two areas neglected in the preceding pages—the Anglo-Saxon and Iberian regions—but we find ourselves in these cases faced with a historiographical production that, however intense and varied, does not usually present the specific qualifications of properly urban chronicle production. There is, in fact, for the British Isles the case of the chronicles and annals of London, usually dominated by the presence and deeds of kings, not only English ones, while sometimes the commercial connections of the island with the continent and particularly with Flanders appear episodically.[88]

Analogous considerations, at least in certain aspects, can be made for Iberian historiography and, in particular, for Spanish: primarily religious-ecclesiastical-cultic motives, or monarchical-princely-dynastic, interweave themselves also in the annals dedicated expressly to the cities, leaving usually very little space and breadth for the voices and the authentically expressive forces of the urban world, in its tensions toward political autonomy and the modernity of economic-social life of the productive classes and of the lay components in general. In addition, the anonymity of these texts, the irregularity of times of narration, and the dispersion and generally diffuse heterogeneity of this production render problematic an appropriate treatment of the chronicle traditions of important cities like Compostella, Toledo, Barcelona, Burgos, Tortosa, Maiorca, and Oviedo.[89]

---

[87] *Annales Cracovienses*, ed. Roepell and Arndt, passim. The work, conserved for us in one manuscript, has been studied and published three times and also thoroughly re-examined through subsequent specific investigations in the nineteenth and twentieth centuries. See Potthast (1962–98), 2:267.

[88] See in this regard n. 63 above. On the chronicle writing of London, see also *Ex Arnaldi [Thedmari] cronica Londoniensi*, ed. F. Liebermann and R. Pauli, *MGH SS* 28 (Hanover, 1888), 527–47, 552–54; Potthast (1962–98), 2:298; Van Houts (1995), 43, 46–47.

[89] See in this regard notes 12 and 63 above.

The present list of chroniclers and chronicles of the city in the later Middle Ages is certainly inadequate, even when only compared with the amplitude and variety of the entire historiographical panorama in question. However, in its temporary state, it is proposed as an attempt to give new form to a rather complex body of material of research and study, according to a comparative methodology. In addition, it is intended to indicate some essential lines of development within a process of transition, through the humanistic experience, from late medieval urban annal-writing to the urban historical scholarship of the modern age.

CHAPTER ELEVEN

BIOGRAPHY 1000–1350

Michael Goodich

The chief biographical sources for the period ca. 1000–1350 may be divided into three broad categories, all of which remained closely tied to the traditions of late antique rhetoric and biographical *laudatio*: 1) saints' lives, which conform to traditional models of Christian hagiography such as the *Vitae patrum* and Sulpicius Severus's life of Martin of Tours; 2) secular biographies, largely of contemporary rulers such as Frederick Barbarossa and Edward II; and, 3) autobiographies, which are often confessional or apologetic in character. Nevertheless, biography cannot always be separated from other historiographical genres. As Gervase of Canterbury noted, even chronicles and histories focus on the exemplary behavior of historical figures.[1] Furthermore, many royal biographies merely use the subject's regnal dates as a convenient backdrop for the history of the period and, thus, may not be properly termed biographies, lacking as they do personal information. Sometimes borrowing liberally from predecessors such as Suetonius, Sallust, Jordanes, Josephus, Einhard and Apollinaris Sidonius, these portraits of contemporary rulers often display a wooden and stereotypical quality.[2] While Peter the Venerable argued in favor of the accurate recording of contemporary history in order to serve future generations, edification and the portrayal of one's subject as the personification of time-honored virtues remained the declared aims of the medieval biographer.

Among the biographers may be numbered historians, theologians, natural scientists, and others for whom biography or hagiography was only one literary genre. For example, although far better known for his great *Chronica majora*, a history of England in the thirteenth

---

[1] Coleman (1992), 299.
[2] Otto of Freising, *The Deeds of Frederick Barbarossa*, trans. C. C. Mierow (New York, 1966), 9.

century, Matthew Paris (ca. 1200–59) was the author of versified and prose saints' lives in both Latin and Anglo-Norman dedicated to SS. Alban, Amphibalus, Thomas Becket, Edmund of Abingdon, Edward the Confessor, and Stephen Langton, along with histories of the abbots and founders of his abbey at St. Albans. Lawrence notes the considerable rhetorical baggage that weighs down his life of Edmund, including oxymorons, puns, biblical quotations, and other figures of speech. Matthew was likewise an artist whose chronicles and biographies include tinted drawings and half-page illustrations.[3] Konrad of Megenberg (1309–74), the author of polemical, political, and scientific tracts, also composed lives of SS. Erhard, Dominic, and Matthew. Thomas of Cantimpré (ca. 1200/01–1270/72), author of the scientific encyclopedia *De natura rerum* (ca. 1240) and an allegorical study of bees, *Bonum universale de apibus*, also composed lives of Mary of Oignies, Christina (Mirabilis) of St. Trond, Lutgard of Aywières, and John of Cantimpré. The Dominican Giovanni of San Gemignano (ca. 1260–ca. 1323), author of sermons and of the widely consulted moral encyclopedia *Summa de exemplis et rerum similitudinibus*, composed lives of such local saints as Seraphina of San Gemignano and Peter of Foligno. In addition to his *De viris illustribus*, Sigebert of Gembloux (ca. 1028/29–1112) authored scriptural commentaries, lives of Bishop Theodoric I of Metz, Guibert, Maclovius, Theodard, Deoderic, King Sigebert, Wicbert, and Lambert, along with computational, historical, liturgical, and polemical works. William of Malmesbury (ca. 1095–ca. 1142) wrote a life of St. Wulfstan of Worcester and other saints in addition to histories of the kings (ca. 1118, at the order of Queen Matilda) and bishops of England, a monograph on the church of Glastonbury, a collection of miracles of the Virgin, and a *Liber pontificalis* (1119–25). Although William claims in his preface that Wulfstan's biography is a translation of an earlier English work by the saint's chaplain Coleman, there is nevertheless evidence of some editorial work.[4]

---

[3] Matthew Paris, *The Life of St. Edmund*, trans. and ed. C. H. Lawrence (Oxford, 1996), 114–15.
[4] Mason (1990), 290–93.

The Biographical Tradition

The medieval biographer worked within a continuing tradition that stressed the citation of historical and literary precedents, the identification of sources, the use of stereotypical *topoi*, and the exemplary role of his or her subject. Many biographies begin with a prologue in which the author provides a clear summary of the didactic role of biography and the author's methods, echoing the remarks found in other literary genres and based on such classical rhetorical models as Sallust's *Bellum Catalinae*.[5] The fullest prologue may include the following elements: 1) a dedication to the patron who had requested or urged the author to undertake its publication; 2) reference to the author's personal acquaintance with the subject or with reliable and trustworthy eyewitnesses who could vouch for the accuracy of the account; 3) the citation of biblical, classical, or hagiographical precedents on whom the life has been modeled; 4) if the subject is a saint, a summary of the many pious roles the saint may play in the scheme of salvation; 5) rhetorical protestations by the author of his own lack of skill (also found in other forms of historical writing); and 6) a summary of the structure of the life. The chapter divisions, although sometimes noted by the original author, were often rearranged by subsequent copyists and editors, who might prefer either a chronological and topical division. For example, one biography of Bishop Louis of Toulouse (1274–97), scion of the Angevin dynasty, contains several options. Although the author himself announces in the prologue that the work contains nine chapters, the first redaction nevertheless contains ten chapters, and the second redaction thirteen. The first version is organized around the following subjects: his noble ancestry (descended from the tree of Jesse!); the hidden and prophetic meaning of his name; and his childhood, exile, education, virtues, pastoral life as a bishop, death, miracles and canonization.[6] Others are didactically structured around the saint's virtues, providing anecdotal accounts of those acts, visions, miracles, and so forth which illustrate these virtues. For example, the *Vita maior* of Duchess Hedwig of Silesia (†1243) by Simon of Trebnitz, master in theology and

---

[5] Grandsden (1992), 125–51.
[6] "De vita S. Ludovici episcopi Tolosani", ed. A. Heysse, *Archivum franciscanum historicum* 40 (1947), 121.

Dominican provincial of Poland, is organized around the following: her formative years, marriage, and love of continence; followed by accounts of her humility, patience, austerity, prayer, and devotion to God; works of mercy, miracles during her life, her spirit of prophecy, death, posthumous miracles, canonization, and translation. This structure may reflect the rubrics of topics dealt with at the 1267 canonization trial, which Simon cites as his source.[7]

Protestations of modesty are exemplified by the anonymous author of the life (ca. 1220) of Hugh of Lincoln addressed to prior Robert of Witham:

> My ignorance would tell in my favour; for in attempting a theme far beyond my capacity, I should win forgiveness and even merit for my humble obedience. . . . May it please you to overlook my defects as a writer, since whatever God may inspire me to set down has only been undertaken by me at your request. . . . Everyone would agree that I am unequal to and incapable of such a task. . . . The sender and the package may have their failings and defects, but the contents, I trust, will amply atone for them.[8]

Rodulphus Glaber (ca. 985–1046), in his life of the Cluniac William of Saint Benigné, wrote:

> Indeed, the many things which we have seen and the many more garnered from the truthful narrators will shape the course of this narrative. Therefore we appeal to the common and virtue-born love of the faithful that the simple style should not be held in contempt, and that a mouthful of fine flour should not be spat out because of a poor basket, for if its material were worked by a prudent hand it would be able to drive out all lack and provide unceasing sustenance.[9]

The learned Dominican Giovanni of San Gemignano claims to employ such a literary style "that neither the rusticity of language will diminish the nobility of history, nor the ornate flow cause suspicions of untruth".[10]

---

[7] Simon of Trebnitz, *Vita maior S. Hedwigis*, in August Bielowski, ed., *Monumenta poloniae historica*, 6 vols. (Warsaw, 1864–93), 4:510–11.

[8] *The Life of St Hugh of Lincoln*, ed. D. Douie and H. Farmer, 2 vols. (London, 1961), 1:1–4.

[9] Rodulphus Glaber, *Vita domni Willelmi abbatis*, in *Opera omnia*, ed. N. Bulst and trans. J. France and P. Reynolds (Oxford, 1989), 255.

[10] John of San Gemignano, *Vita Finae*, in *Acta sanctorum quotquot tote urbe colluntur* (hereafter *AA.SS*), ed. Socii Bollandiani, new ed., 66 vols.to date (Paris, 1863–1940), 12 March 2:235.

An example of the biographer's use of the prologue as a forum to voice some of the above themes is the Cistercian Caesarius of Heisterbach's extended epistolary dedication (1226) to Archbishop Henry of Cologne in his account of the life, deeds, passion, and miracles of the martyred Archbishop Engelbert.[11] Although the author of a widely consulted *Dialogue on miracles* (1219–23), which contains about eight hundred *exempla*, Caesarius modestly notes his insufficient knowledge and writing skill. He suggests that should the diocese possess more learned men, they will in the future write a more satisfactory life, since as a monk, and not a philosopher, his rhetorical skill is limited. Citing Horace (II *Epistolae* 3.15,16), he remarks, perhaps sarcastically, that they may write more to show their skills than to edify the reader. He prefers to write in a simple, unadorned style, favoring the testimonies of Scripture over those of philosophy. An apparent tension is here voiced between monastic hagiographers and those trained in episcopal schools and, later, the universities. The early thirteenth century witnessed considerable conflict over the introduction of Aristotelianism into the schools, which at first was regarded as a threat to the faith. The same opposition to philosophy is voiced by the Cistercian Hugh of Floreffe in his life of Ivetta of Huy (†1228), who claims only to report the facts based on eyewitnesses or personal confessions, free of philosophical controversies, since falsehood is an offense to God, even if the intention may be pious.[12]

In the introduction to Engelbert's miracles (which are intended to vindicate the saint against his enemies and report the cures he performed), Caesarius argues that Engelbert's sanctity had been proven sufficiently and that posthumous miracles were not necessary, as in the cases of two martyred bishops of Cologne, SS. Evergislus and Agillolfus.[13] Nevertheless, God wanted to throw terror into the hearts of the saint's murderers and so performed miracles, particularly those that occurred in the village of Gevelsberg, where Engelbert had been killed. Caesarius nevertheless claimed only to record those cases which were reported to him by Goswin, canon of St. Peter of Cologne, who was informed by "reliable persons" and who apparently was

---

[11] Caesarius of Heisterbach, *Vita, Passio et Miracula S. Engelberti*, in *AA.SS*, 7 November 3:623.
[12] Hugh of Floreffe, *Vita Ivettae*, in *AA.SS*, 13 January 2:145.
[13] Caesarius of Heisterbach, *Vita, Passio et Miracula S. Engelberti*.

entrusted with recording these events. These miracles are sealed by a vision of the saint's passion experienced by another saint, Hermann of Steinfeld, who had been cured by Engelbert of an eye ailment.

The exemplary role of biography is a continuing *topos* in both medieval hagiography and secular biography and reflects an educational philosophy that dates back to ancient models. All of the biographical sources profess the classical view that the aim of biography is to provide models worthy of emulation. As Otto of Freising (†1158) stated in his oft-cited introduction to the life of his cousin Frederick Barbarossa:

> This, I think, has been the purpose of all who have written history before us: to extol the famous deeds of valiant men in order to excite the hearts of mankind to virtue, but to veil in silence the dark doings of the base or, if they are drawn into the light, by the telling to place them on record to terrify the minds of those same mortals.[14]

The anonymous author (1261/64) of the life of Juliana of Cornillon (†1258) wrote:

> Among the visible factors by which human nature is easily swayed toward good or evil, example seems to be the chief. For just as wax receives an impression from a seal, so morality is formed by example.[15]

He notes that the lives of more contemporary saints are the most effective spurs to piety. His work is based partly on the Walloon life by Eva of St. Martin and the recollections of John of Lausanne, a canon of Liège, and was intended to both praise the saint and promote the cult of the Corpus Christi, which was confirmed in 1264. Another spokesman for the didactic task of hagiography is the anonymous author of the life of the Praemonstratensian Hermann of Steinfeld, who wrote that his aim was:

> ... to diligently consider and to wisely distinguish what should be admired and imitated: so that the worthy action of grace should be reported to those who admire God, who is "wondrous in his saints"; [and] so that the life of the readers should be improved by the examples of virtue through imitation.[16]

---

[14] Otto of Freising, *The Deeds of Frederick Barbarossa*, trans. Mierow, 24.
[15] *The Life of Juliana of Cornillon*, trans. B. Newman (Toronto, n.d.), 25.
[16] *AA.SS*, April 1:689 cited in Rener (1994), 224.

Hagiography was a particularly important weapon in the Church's arsenal against its ideological and political opponents. In the face of the rejection of the institution of saints' cults by the heretics, and the fear that the faithful would become attached to false miracle-workers, the Church was concerned to insure that only reputable persons were venerated. In 1266/67 Abbot Philip of Clairvaux undertook an investigation into the stigmata displayed by Elizabeth of Spaalbek, a beguine hermitess living near Liège.[17] At first skeptical about third-person reports, he visited her hermitage and was aided by Abbot William of St. Trond, who served as an interpreter. In the introduction to her life, he sought to justify the composition of a biography devoted to a contemporary saint in the following way:

> Since, as is written in Ecclesiasticus 42 [.16], "The glory of the Lord is his full work", and in Tobit [12.11 and 12.7] "The works of God should be publicly honored, for the sake of his glory and honor, who is glorified in his saints"; for the sake of the edification of those who read and those who hear. Among the other deeds of the Lord which according to the prophet are universal goods, our Lord, renewing the signs and changing the miracles in these days has performed a miraculous deed in the person of a certain poor and innocent virgin. We have neither read nor heard of such a deed having been performed either in our own time or in former times. But we are unable to avoid speaking about the glory of the Lord which we have seen and heard.

Philip further argues that her exemplary acts and miracles are intended to "strengthen the faith of those who are in doubt, bring sinners to penance and the ungrateful to thanksgiving, inflame the hard-hearted and obstinate to piety and devotion".

The role of the saint's life as a didactic tool led to the mining of hagiography by preachers in need of raw material for their sermons. The Dominican John Gobi's popular *Scala Coeli* (1322/30) represents such a collection of exemplary tales and miracle stories organized under subject headings that could be easily consulted by preachers. In the prologue, he writes:

---

[17] Philip of Clairvaux, *Vita Elizabeth sanctimonialis in Erkenrode*, in *Catalogus codicum hagiographicorum bibliothecae regiae Bruxellensis*, ed. Socii Bollandiani, 2 vols. (Brussels, 1886–89), 1:362–63.

Because our souls may appear to reach up to heaven through the pleasure of the narratives and examples of the saints, I have therefore
composed this *Ladder to Heaven* for the glory and honor of the Omnipotent
God and his blessed Virgin Mother, my father the blessed Dominic
and the blessed Mary Magdalene.[18]

Piero Domenico of Baone (ca. 1340), in his life of Henry of Treviso,
noted the value of reading saints' lives and sacred history: "the
Catholic faith is strengthened; the mind is edified; the soul is raised
on high and is consoled".[19]

The exemplary role of the saint demanded a search for confirmatory
precedents in both Scripture and the lives of earlier saints and martyrs for the merits and miracles displayed by the saint. Parallel comparisons to ancient heroes likewise are found in secular biographies.
Raymund of Capua (ca. 1330–99), in his prefatory remarks to the
life of Catherine of Siena, provided a vast catalog of all those saints
found in the ancient *Vitae patrum*, the lives of the desert hermits, and
those biblical figures who represent the prototypes of Christian sainthood.[20] But, although hagiography continued to employ ancient stereotypical *topoi*, the special training of the author nevertheless may often
be detected in such works. For example, the scholastic fondness
for etymology led to the frequent discussion of the peculiar features
of the saint's name as a presage of his or her future. Caesarius of
Heisterbach derives Engelbert of Cologne's German name from the
Latin 'angelic liberty'. He argues that this signifies that the murdered "Engelbert, through his necessary death, having put aside the
burden of sin, will achieve angelic freedom".[21] The *Legenda aurea* (ca.
1260) by Jacob of Voragine is filled with such speculation. For example, the chapter on Francis of Assisi notes that, although baptized
John, his name soon was changed to Francis for a number of reasons: 1) as a child he miraculously acquired knowledge of the French
language, and when he was filled with the Holy Spirit he spoke
French; 2) the use of French hastened the spread of his message
throughout the world; 3) he and his followers could make penitents

[18] J. Gobi, *Scala coeli*, ed. Marie-Anne Polo de Beaulieu (Paris, 1991), 165.
[19] Pietro Domenico of Baone, et al., *Vita et Miracula Henrici*, in *AA.SS*, 10 June
2:362.
[20] Raymund of Capua, *Vita Catharinae*, in *AA.SS*, 30 April 3:877–88.
[21] Caesarius of Heisterbach, *Vita, Passio et Miracula S. Engelberti*. On the passion
for etymology, see Guenée (1980), 184–91.

free (*franci*) of sin and the devil; 4) Francis displayed the kind of magnanimity characteristic of the French; 5) this language assisted his spoken eloquence; 6) it filled persons with the terror and the need to drive away the devil; and 7) he displayed composure, perfect deeds, and honest talk. All of these virtues James ascribed to the French. He failed, however, to note that Francis's mother was French, which surely would explain his early eloquence in that language.[22]

One of the most important first-hand accounts of a medieval saint are the recollections of the maidservants or ladies-in-waiting of Landgravina Elizabeth of Thuringia (†1231), who had known her since childhood and who testified at her canonization trial. Their evidence was gathered together by an anonymous contemporary author and served as the foundation of her abundant biographies, providing one of the most detailed accounts of the upbringing of a medieval saint.[23] The author provides the following justification for his work:

> In order to glorify the dignity and honor of His clemency by making known to the faithful of the present generation the praiseworthy life of the blessed Elizabeth and to pass it on to posterity, we have decided to commit this material to writing and afterward to conceal it away in our hearts. [We have done this] lest her worthy memory and her behavior, so worthy of imitation, be incorrectly obliterated from history and disappear through the ravages of time; lest the road that she followed be blotted out, the example to be embraced perish and fall into oblivion through negligence, and lest future generations cease to praise her because the evil disease of heresy has again suppressed and strangled what the devotion of the church has nourished like a mother. Indeed, our Elizabeth has been a destroyer of vice, a planter [of the seeds] of virtue, a school of good morals, an example of penance and a mirror of innocence, which we will briefly explain one by one.[24]

The hagiographer's immediate role as a warrior in the polemical battle against heresy, which is noted in this prologue, was especially evident in the later Middle Ages, when many of the saints actively preached against disbelief. Elizabeth's confessor and confidant, who strongly supported her case, was the Inquisitor Conrad of Marburg, who was killed by heretics in 1233; although there is no real direct

---

[22] Jacobus de Voragine, *Legenda aurea*, ed. Th. Graesse (Leipzig, 1850), 662–63.
[23] Goodich (1996), 91.
[24] "Prologus et epilogus in Dicta ancillarum S. Elisabeth Thuringiae lantgraviae", ed. D. Henniges, in *Archivum franciscanum historicum* 3 (1910), 480.

evidence of Elizabeth's own engagement against heresy. In the same
way, Louis of Toulouse's biographer, citing 1 Timothy 2:4, John
8:12 and 14:6, claims to direct his account of the saint's life at
heretics, Jews, and pagans (although the likelihood of such wayward
souls reading these works, it should be imagined, was remote).[25]

The hagiographical biography is intimately related to two stereotypical medieval literary genres, the *exemplum* and the *miraculum*, each
possessing a fixed structure, which often robs the author of an opportunity to provide reliable, first-hand data concerning the saint.[26]
Students of hagiography continue to attempt the difficult task of dis-
entangling the data concerning the saint's life from the traditional
topoi and literary forms in which it is embedded, which reflect certain continuing themes of Christian ideology. For example, the *topoi*
of the child saved from drowning or the man saved from death by
hanging conform to an outline which demanded that the 'who, what,
when, where, and why' of the miracle reflect certain fixed standards.
Often, the saint's life may tell us more about collective *mentalités* than
provide specific data about the saint herself. Among the conventional
topoi which appear in hagiography may be noted: 1) the pious mother
who encourages her offspring's religious yearnings and the martial
father who opposes them; 2) the prophetic dream and other portents preceding the saint's birth; 3) the *puer-senex*, or child saint who
possesses the virtues of maturity despite his tender age; 4) the adolescent crisis of sexual temptation that is resolved through religious
conversion; and 5) visions of the otherworld and visitations by heavenly guests who guide the saint throughout his career. Parallel stereotypical themes may be found in political royal biographies that attempt
to sanctify the dynasty.[27] The effort to separate literary devices, folk
elements, and historical events may often prove daunting, particularly in those biographies which are not supported by other documentation.[28] Hagiography, for example, has been exploited recently
as a reflection of the conflict, cross-breeding, and mutual dependence
of learned and popular culture.[29]

---

[25] "De vita S. Ludovici episcopi Tolosani", ed. Heysse, 130.
[26] Berlioz (1992).
[27] Carpentier (1991).
[28] Fuhrmann (1963).
[29] Manselli (1975).

In order to illustrate the continuing role of the *topos* in biography, an example may be cited from the life of Douceline de Digne (1214–74), a merchant's daughter who became a penitent beguine and whose brother Hugh was an important member of the Franciscan order. Her Provençal biography (ca. 1297) has been attributed to Philippine de Porcellet, daughter of a counselor to King Charles of Anjou, Douceline's successor as head of the beguinage of Roubaud and leader of the beguine women of Hyères and Marseilles.[30] This panegyrical account of Douceline's early life contains many rhetorical elements redolent with biblical allusions:

> An important and rich merchant of Digne named Berengar was wed to a true Christian of Barjols named Huguette. These two good and upright people, in accordance with the law of our Lord God, lead proper and blessed lives, faithfully carrying out God's commandments. They received the poor with great mercy, aided the sick and those in need of comfort in their home, giving of their wealth. Through their pious deeds they spent whatever the good Lord had given them. Just as a good root produces a good tree whose fruits are good, so, as a mark of Christ who is the guarantor of truth, and as a gift of God's goodness, these true parents had good, upright and holy children. Living piously, due to their holiness they gave to our Lord two great lights that shine night and day. Brother Hugh [of Digne] of blessed memory, a Friar Minor, was, as a member of the Franciscan order, an ardent preacher of God's truth. His preaching, radiant and warming as the sun, may in a wondrous way turn people to serve God and leave this world. (Oh! These two by the brilliance of their lives and their perfection were reflected in the eyes of sinners and the eyes of the just; they were a beacon of saintliness and their Christian example enlightened the state of holy penitence.) The second light, no less brilliant and holy, was the sainted lady Douceline of Digne, who was very sweet [i.e., *douce*] and worthy [*digne*], because God "bestowed the sweetest blessings upon her".

The following *topoi* appear here: the saints' pious upbringing and the formative role of their parents; concern for the poor and acts of charity; the penitential effect of preaching; the saint as an example to others; and the prophetic nature of the saint's name.

---

[30] *La vie de Saint Douceline, texte provençal du xive siècle*, ed. R. Gout (Paris, 1927), 41–42.

Canonization and Hagiography

The institutional involvement of the papacy in the confirmation of new cults produced a radical change in the traditional *Vita et Miracula*. In preparation for canonization, biographies might be required to reflect the needs of the investigating commission. For example, it has been argued that Bernard of Clairvaux's life was reworked in order to insure a more favorable hearing.[31] The growing involvement of professional notaries and canon lawyers in the confirmation of cults and of hagiographers trained in the schools and universities in the publication of saints' lives now may be detected in such documents. Direct papal intervention in the canonization of saints has been traced back to the establishment by Pope John XV in 973 of a cult honoring Ulrich of Augsburg. After that date, although local bishops continued to hold inquiries and confirm cults, the growth of the papal doctrine of *plenitudo potestatis* led to continuing papal intervention in the confirmation of cults.[32] In many of the early extant canonization bulls, some reference already is made to the receipt of the testimony of reliable witnesses as the foundation for the papal decision to inscribe a candidate among of saints. But it was Alexander III's 1171 claim of supreme authority in the confirmation of cults and relics that is regarded as the initiation of a formal papal procedure in canonization cases; this decretal was inserted into the *Decretals* of Gregory IX issued in 1234, the standard collection of canon law. Hostiensis's classic commentary (ca. 1250) on *De reliquiis et veneratione sanctorum* clarified the consequences of the papal order: 1) relics may not be venerated without papal approval; 2) the sale of relics is prohibited; 3) the transfer of relics from place to place requires papal permission; and 4) no saint should be publicly venerated without papal approval.[33] In order to inscribe a name in the catalog of recognized saints, Hostiensis stated that an inquiry must be conducted into the life, behavior, and miracles of the candidate, and the results were to be submitted to the pope. Regarding the miracles, he noted that the issues raised in the course of such an inquiry included: 1) whether the alleged miracle was a consequence

---

[31] Coleman (1992), 303–04.
[32] Kemp (1948); Vauchez (1997); Petersohn (1994).
[33] Hostiensis [Henricus de Segusio], *Summa aurea*, ed. Nicholas Soranza (Lyons, 1537), fol. 187ᵛ.

of divine action or devilish trickery; 2) whether the miracle occurred as a result of human merit and not merely the repetition of some magical formula; 3) whether the event clearly contravenes natural law; and 4) whether the true Faith has been strengthened and corroborated as a consequence of the miracle. Less stringent standards of verification were applied to the confirmation of miracles attributed to the martyrs.

Although no complete canonization inquiries survive before the mid-thirteenth century, the establishment of judicial procedures in the investigation of the putative saint's life and miracles parallels the formation of canon law from about 1180 to 1215. The canons *De inquisitionibus* and *De testibus et attestionibus*, probably introduced during the pontificate of Innocent III (1198–1216), laid down the preferred procedure in the deposition of witnesses, the recording of evidence, and the drawing up a list of questions, whether inquiring into the errors of a heretic or the life and miracles of a saint. Although such formal procedures date from the thirteenth century, many earlier saintly biographies nevertheless suggest a similar (although otherwise undocumented) hearing, probably under episcopal auspices, as the foundation of the narrative account. And many later works continued to be based on such episcopal inquiries conducted by qualified legal professionals.[34]

Very few full canonization processes contain all the relevant documents, but a large variety of different sources survive from various stages of the inquiry. Beginning in the twelfth century such canonization inquiries and the parallel episcopal hearings were to become the foundation of many of the saints' lives. Such popular saints as Francis of Assisi, Dominic, Elizabeth of Thuringia, and Louis IX, for example, were all subject to extensive inquiries, which lay at the basis of the Latin and vernacular lives circulated by their supporters. The full dossier of a saint may include the following documents: 1) letters of postulation from parties interested in advancing the putative saint's cause; 2) the raw testimony of the witnesses or notarized statements by those who knew the saint or experienced his or her miracles; 3) papal letters connected to the inquiry, including the bull of canonization; and 4) consultative remarks by the cardinals or others concerning the reliability of the evidence. In the cases of Bernward

---

[34] Andreas Jacobi da Fabriano, *Vita Johannes a Baculo*, in *Agiografia silvestrina medievale*, ed. Réginald Grégoire (Fabriano, 1983), 216.

of Hildesheim, William of Bourges, and Gilbert of Sempringham, the extant biographies were based on the papal inquiry and included a full life and miracles, a narrative account of the events leading up to the canonization, the canonization ceremony itself, and the public's reaction. In another example, the oldest life of Margaret of Hungary, the *Legenda vetus*, has been attributed to her confessor Marcellus, the Dominican provincial prior of Hungary, who testified at her canonization trial held in 1276.[35] A fourteenth-century life by Garin de Guy l'Evêque (ca. 1340), based on the trial, simply adds the christological and mystical concerns peculiar to the later period. In the absence of an extant canonization trial, it even may be possible to reconstruct the trial on the basis of a subsequent life. For example, Bishop Richard of Chichester's (†1262) narrative life and miracles by his Dominican confessor Ralph Bocking, written at the request of the Robert Kilwardby and Isabella de Fortibus, countess of Arundel (whose son had been cured due to Richard's intervention), was based on such an inquiry. It appears to follow closely the judicial testimony of the 1267 trial, which is no longer extant.[36] Matthew Paris' French version of the life of Edmund of Canterbury likewise was dedicated to the countess, who was patroness of Wymondham priory, which was connected to Matthew's monastery at St. Albans.[37] It too was the product of a formal canonization inquiry held under papal auspices.

It is possible to detect the influence of letters of postulation in some saint's lives. Such letters were often part of an organized campaign aimed at convincing the pope to appoint a commission of inquiry, since it was extremely rare for a pope to undertake canonization without proof that an important constituency stood behind the candidate.[38] The letters include many of the arguments regarding the putative saint's merits and miracles that were to become the basis of the themes taken up at the canonization trial and were to appear in subsequent biographies. For example, a textual comparison of the letters sent to the pope by the prelates of England and the university of Oxford supporting the case of Archbishop Edmund

---

[35] Klaniczay and Madas (1994), 124–27.
[36] Jones (1993), 83–246.
[37] Lawrence (1960), 107.
[38] Schimmelpfennig (1994), 78. The only clear case of papal initiative is Gerhard of Toul (1050) Bernhard Schimmelpfennig, "Heilige Päpste-päpstliche Kanonisationspolitik," in Jürgen Petersohn, ed., *Politik und Heiligenverehrung im Hochmittelalter* (Sigmaringen, 1994), 78.

of Canterbury (†1240) indicates cooperation among the petitioners; similar echoes are found in the lives by Eustace of Faversham and Matthew Paris.[39] This source material not only was used by biographers but also was exploited for other hagiographical genres. The Dominican Inquisitor and general procurator Bernard Gui was himself a witness at the canonization trial (1318) of Thomas Aquinas. He composed a biography and chapter in his *Legenda de sanctis* dealing with Thomas, both based on this inquiry.[40] Caesarius of Heisterbach's 1237 sermon on the occasion of the translation of the relics of Elizabeth of Thuringia at Marburg suggests the use of biographical material culled from a canonization inquiry as the basis of his panegyric in praise of the saint's virtues and miracles. Elizabeth is presented as a living illustration of the biblical verse, "A town that stands on a hill cannot be hidden" (Matthew 5:14), by interweaving scriptural citations and references from the lives of the saints, Jerome, Isidore of Seville, and others into the major stages of Elizabeth's earthly and posthumous life.[41] This sermon may have provided the program for the windows illustrating her life which were installed shortly afterward in Marburg cathedral under the patronage of her cousin Emperor Frederick II.[42]

The need for more reliable evidence is clear not only in the reports of miracles found in biographies derived from canonization records but also in locally produced biographies based on episcopal inquiries or notarized statements, often collected at the site of the saint's tomb or sacred relics. Examples of medical intervention prior to the performance of a miracle and the use of direct quotations are especially prevalent in the urbanized regions of southern France and Italy, where physicians were more readily available and the notarial art was highly developed. The involvement of the notary, trained in civil and canon law, and schooled in both classical and biblical texts, enhanced the accuracy of the testimony elicited at the tomb or at a hearing. The use of physicians and of direct quotation may be illustrated in the life of the Tuscan hermit Giovanna da Signa (†1307),

---

[39] Lawrence (1960), 16, 35, 42.
[40] Pommerol (1992).
[41] Caesarius of Heisterbach, *Sermo*, in *Die Schriften des Caesarius von Heisterbach über die heilige Elisabeth von Thüringen*, ed. Albert Huyskens, in *Gesellschaft für rheinische Geschichtskunde*, 43, pt. 3 (1937) 381–90.
[42] *Sankt Elisabeth* (1994).

dated between 1383 and 1386. Around the year 1356, a *paterfamilias* named Bartolo Taviani had returned from the fields to find his wife in tears.[43] Inquiring about the reason for her grief, she replied, "Because our son has become blind". Asked by his father to come to him, the six-year-old Blasio raised his arms up in front of him in order to guide himself. Trying to reach his father, he stumbled, and it was clear that the child was blind. The boy therefore was taken to Florence to visit two physicians (*medici*), who, after consultation, agreed that the child was indeed blind and that there was no natural cure to restore his sight. Saddened by the news, Bartolo made a vow to the blessed Giovanna that if his son should be cured he would bring a waxen head as an *ex-voto* offering to her tomb. Having so vowed, he returned home only to hear his son cry out, "I can already see!" The father asked, "Who restored your sight to you?" Blasio replied, "That man whom you sent to me". The father knew that the boy believed a physician had cured him, but he himself attributed the cure to the merits of the Blessed Giovanna. He fulfilled his vow and heaped thanks on God and the saint for their benevolence. Such miracles, which also provide valuable biographical material concerning common folk, reached a wider non-learned public by means of frescoes and altarpieces. The frescoes executed at Giovanna's chapel in Signa near Florence in 1441 (perhaps attributable to Neri di Bicci) include an illustration of the restoration of sight to Anselmo Fei, although a commentary on the fresco confuses this with the episode in which Blasio was cured.[44]

The Franciscans were especially active in the commission of altarpieces and frescoes in which the life cycle of the saint was based upon published biographies. The earliest such cycles, like Bonaventure Berlinghieri's scenes from the life of St. Francis (1235) at the Franciscan church of Pescia, can be dated to the 1230s and were based upon Thomas of Celano's life. Altarpieces commissioned shortly thereafter, however, reflect the changes introduced into the saint's life by the order's Minister-General Bonaventure. It is thus possible to illustrate how a (non-extant) canonization hearing, summarized in an authorized biography, received wider currency through the visual arts.

---

[43] "Vita e miracoli della B. Giovanna da Signa", ed. S. Mencherini, *Archivum franciscanum historicum* 10 (1917), 380.

[44] Russo (1986).

One of the most widely known medieval portraits of a pope is the late thirteenth-century fresco by Giotto in the nave of the upper basilica at Assisi. Pope Innocent III is portrayed dreaming that St. Francis was propping up the decrepit Lateran basilica just prior to the decisive Fourth Lateran Council (1215), when the Franciscan order allegedly was confirmed. In fact, the episode on which this event supposedly is based does not appear in Francis's earliest biography by Thomas of Celano; only in versions of the saint's life written after 1246. Around the same time St. Dominic likewise was reported as having appeared to the same pope propping up the same church, although his earliest biographer, Jordan of Saxony, likewise fails to mention such a dream. Such rewriting of history served the need to tie the new orders to a prestigious pope at a time when they faced the opposition of the secular clergy and veteran religious orders. The newly stirred memories of the saints' early disciples may well have shaken out a few long-forgotten 'facts' necessary in order to defend these interlopers against their foes.[45] The life of the second Franciscan saint, Anthony of Padua (†1231), also was rewritten several times. Shortly after his canonization in 1232, a *Vita prima*, *Officio ritmica*, and *Vita secunda* were written. Under the Franciscan Minister-General Crescenzio of Iesi, a collection of reports concerning the early Franciscans, the *Dialogus de gestis sanctorum fratrum Minorum* (1244/46), was produced, followed in the 1270s by a life by John Pecham.[46]

New Religious Orders and Hagiography

Those persons who became the subjects of contemporary sacred biography were involved actively in the political, social, and economic changes that characterize the period 1000–1350.[47] Many were founders of the new bishoprics, religious orders, hermitages, nunneries, canonries, friaries, monasteries, hospitals, and priories established during this period in order to serve particular populations. As a form of didactic literature, the saint's life presenting the ideal virtues demanded of a bishop, monk, friar, beguine, or canon provided a graphic illustration of the religious rule as it should be lived. Each order stressed

---

[45] Manselli (1985), 224–25.
[46] Moorman (1968), 290.
[47] For a survey see Vauchez (1993).

a different set of values, which might include devotion to the ideal
of poverty and the common life, the apostolic life, pilgrimage, hos-
pitality, chastity, imitation of Christ, penance, preaching, and acts
of charity. The Church faced a series of intellectual and military
rivals, including Jews, Muslims, schismatics, heretics, religious skeptics, and pagans. The hagiographer thus often included an obligatory chapter dealing with his subject's successful defeat of the enemy,
usually through eloquent persuasion, personal example, deeds, or
miracles (*verbum et exemplum*). In the eleventh century, the struggle
against lay investiture engendered a moral crusade against simony,
clerical marriage, and concubinage in which the saints' involvement
was stressed. In the thirteenth century, this moral crusade was directed
against such lay vices as gambling, usury, prostitution, and the prohibited degrees of marriage. In order to enhance the pious potential of marriage, the saintly spouse (usually female) was characterized
by devotion to the ideal of chaste matrimony, i.e., procreation without lust. Among the saints, devotion to the papacy included mobi-
lization in support of the crusades, the Inquisition, and the advancement
of learning in monastic or cathedral schools and universities. Many
of the revelations they experienced reflected divine confirmation of
the new eucharistic theology, the penitential code, or the concept of
Purgatory.

The eleventh to thirteenth centuries witnessed the unprecedented
creation of new religious orders, each with its own particular constituency, rule, and goals. The struggle for legitimacy in the face of
competing orders, the demand for proper authorization by the clerical hierarchy, the desire to establish new cults devoted to the leading figures of the order, and the need to recall the early days of the
order's history engendered considerable diplomatic and literary material. The establishment of such orders as the Cistercians, Franciscans,
Dominicans, and Augustinian hermits called forth the composition
of an official hagiography recounting the lives and accomplishments
of the order's founders. In his account of the origins of the Cistercian
order, Conrad of Eberbach († after 1226) stressed two aims: 1) to
inform future generations, especially members of the order dwelling
in remote regions, about the order's history, in particular about the
exemplary life of Bernard of Clairvaux; and, 2) to counter a calumny
spread by the black monks in the presence of uninformed secular
persons to the effect that the earliest Cistercians had withdrawn from
the monastery of Molesmes disobediently and scandalously without

due authorization.[48] The conflict within the Franciscan order between Conventuals and Spirituals concerning the interpretation of the Rule led to the publication of several versions of Francis of Assisi's life and the collection of the memoirs of his followers in order to put an end to arguments concerning the Seraphic Father's intentions. Thomas of Celano's (ca. 1190–ca. 1260) official *Vita prima* had been composed in 1228/29 at the request of Pope Gregory IX after Francis's canonization, and reflected the points highlighted in the bull of canonization. It was followed by several other accounts, by Julian of Speyer and Henry of Avranches (a version of Celano's work in Latin hexameters), among others. Celano's work was based on the recollections of those who knew the saint personally and contains many lengthy quotations. In all likelihood, he also was authorized by Pope Alexander IV to write a life of Clare of Assisi following her canonization (1255).

At the Franciscan General Chapter at Genoa in 1244, the Minister-General Crescenzio of Iesi issued an order for the collection of materials for a new biography. This led to the largely anecdotal memoir, the *Legenda trium sociorum*, composed at the hermitage of Greccio by Francis's three companions, Leo, Rufino, and Angelo.[49] Thomas of Celano produced a *Vita secunda* (1246/47) and a *Tractatus de miraculis* (1250/53), voicing the stricter position of the Spirituals within the order. Finally, the Minister-General Bonaventure's *Legenda maior* (1260) was intended to be the authoritative life of the saint, although based largely on Celano's earlier work; a shorter *Vita minor* followed. His aim was clearly to downplay conflicts within the order for the sake of unity. The 1266 Chapter-General even went so far as to demand the destruction of all earlier manuscripts of the saint's life. But the rewriting of Francis's life continued, largely in order to remove any taint of heresy from the order. Franciscan hagiography was to have a powerful influence among the wider circle of saints associated with popular piety. The theme of *imitatio Christi* found its most spectacular expression in the miracle of the stigmata, which had appeared on the body of Francis, and which began a tradition of saints who were closely identified with the suffering Christ. Such biographies

---

[48] Conrad of Eberbach, *Exordium magnum Cisterciense sive narratio de initio Cisterciensis ordinis*, in *PL*, ed. J.-P. Migne, 185: 1198.
[49] Moorman (1968), 278–94.

often contained extensive accounts of revelations and visions of the next world, the infant child, and the battle with demons.[50]

In the same way, Jordan of Saxony's *Libellus de principiis ordinis praedicatorum*, written in 1231/33 and reworked in 1234/35, probably was intended to support Dominic's (†1221) canonization. The Dominicans had expressed discontent over the speed with which Francis's case had been handled, while their founder had failed to achieve recognition. The canonization itself led to the publication of lives by Peter Ferrand (1237/42), Constantine of Orvieto (1246/47), and the Dominican Minister-General Humbert of Romans (1254). At the Paris Chapter-General in 1256, Humbert called upon members to collect edifying material concerning the formative history of the Friars Preachers. His request seems to have produced a collection of anecdotes by Stephan of Bourbon, the *Vitae fratrum* by Gerard of Fracheto, and the *Bonum universale de apibus* by Thomas of Cantimpré. A similar request regarding the Augustinian hermits led to the publication of the *Liber vitas fratrum* (1357?) by Jordan of Quedlinburg. Because of their early composition, such collections still allowed the recording of first- or second-hand accounts of the early years of the order. As the Dominican Jordan of Saxony wrote in his prologue:

> I have conversed with and seen the blessed Dominic not only inside, but also outside the order, and knew him intimately. I even confessed to him, and at his suggestion I became a deacon and four years after its establishment, undertook the habit of the order. I have decided to write down from my own memory those things that were shown to me, which I myself saw and heard, and which I partly know through the reports of others, concerning the beginnings of the order, and about the life and miracles of that holy man, concerning our holy father Dominic and other brethren.[51]

This insistent claim of reliance on either first- or second-hand knowledge rather than hearsay is a continuing theme in contemporary hagiography.

Beginning in the thirteenth century, the establishment of female religious houses and of the new penitential orders, along with the encouragement of lay piety, led to the production of female saint's lives, often in the vernacular. Such literature may have been written

---

[50] Dinzelbacher (1991).

[51] Jordan of Saxony, *Libellus de initiis sancti Ordinis Praedicatorum*, ed. C. Scheeben, in *Monumenta ordinis praedicatorum historica*, 16 (Rome, 1935), 36 ff.

for devotional and instructional purposes, aimed at providing role
models for female piety. Evidence of a flourishing cult has not always
been found, since many of these women do not appear in calendars
of the saints.[52] Some of the authors were women, such as Margaret
of Oingt, Beatrice of Nazareth, Eva of St. Martin, and Philippine of
Porcellet, who belonged to circles of pious women, sometimes accused
of heresy, whose literary output reflects the literacy and mysticism
increasingly found in female cloisters. The rise of a lay public hungry for such devotional literature spawned vernacular biographies,
largely of the earlier saints and martyrs.[53] The translation of James
of Voragine's *Legenda aurea* into several vernacular languages beginning in the late thirteenth century, which appears to have served as
a handbook for much artistic production, attests to the growing
demand for easily accessible material outside clerical circles. While
the passions of the martyrs continued to predominate, such shortened biographies were provided in the increasing number of legendaries (some in the vernacular) that contained summarized saints'
lives to be used by preachers in the composition of their sermons,
or perhaps to be read by the laity. Bartholomew of Trent, Peter
Calo, Jean de Mailly, Gui de Chartres, Pietro de' Natal, and Bernard
Gui are among those who produced such collections.[54]

Biography and the Legitimization of Power

Much contemporary biography clearly was intended to sanctify property and political power by enshrining the claims of a monastery,
religious order, or dynasty within the life of an honored figure. For
example, the widespread foundation of monasteries following the
Norman conquest of southern Italy or the restoration of older houses
that accompanied the pacification of northern and western France,
the Low Countries, and Saxony in the eleventh century were accompanied by the composition of lives which sought to legitimize monastic

---

[52] Williams-Krapp (2001).
[53] Brunel-Lobrichon (1994), 327–58. Lives of more contemporary saints such as
Louis IX, Francis, Dominic, Elizabeth of Thuringia, Celestine V, Anthony of Padua,
Yves of Tréguier, Peter of Luxemburg, Stephan of Grandmont, Peter Thomas, and
Robert of Arbrissel were written between the eleventh and fifteenth centuries in
French.
[54] Philippart (1977), 45–47.

privileges and supply a history of the patron saint.[55] Local chroniclers often deviated from their narrative by inserting a life of the
abbot or bishop who had contributed most to the foundation of the
bishopric or monastery. Saints' lives, miracles, visions, cures, and
accounts of the ceremonial burial (*translatio*) or discovery (*inventio*) of
relics were regarded as effective propaganda for the propagation of
a cult and the enhancement of the reputation of the town, order,
or monastery and the attraction of new clients to the saint's network
of patronage. Older patron saints were also given greater currency
through the production of more up-to-date biographies. In the case
of St Martial of Limoges, for example, this effectively revived his
cult, despite justifiable doubts about his claims to a position as an
apostle.[56] Royal saints might be enlisted also, in the attempt to
enhance the reputation of a monastery or episcopate. For example,
Emperor Henry II's largess to such sees as Hildesheim, Magdeburg,
Merseburg, and Strasburg—along with his chastity, defense against
the Slavs, and assistance to the poor—are stressed in James of
Voragine's account.[57] His wife Cunegunda's patronage of the cathedral of Bamberg is recorded in considerable detail, along with the
establishment of the Benedictine monastery of St. Michael and the
canonry of St. Stephen.[58]

As a result of the sharpening struggle between Church and State
following the investiture controversy and the Gregorian reform movement of the eleventh century, many saintly biographies stress clerical willingness to undergo exile and even martyrdom in the name
of Church rights. In England, beginning with the Norman Conquest,
a tradition of anti-royal sainthood arose. Many of the saints—such
as Thomas Becket, Edmund of Canterbury, and Hugh of Lincoln—
opposed clerical taxation, the trial of clerical criminals in lay courts,
and restrictions on Church property.[59] Although he did not achieve
official recognition, Simon of Montfort, who had established a council with clerical approval to rule England during the later years of
Henry III's reign (1258–65), became the center of a flourishing cult,

---

[55] Head (1994); Coleman (1992), 297; Sigal (1985).
[56] Lemaitre (1992), 68–70.
[57] Jacobus de Voragine, *Legenda aurea*, ed. Graesse, 897.
[58] Jacobus de Voragine, *Legenda aurea*, ed. Graesse, 905–06.
[59] Russell (1929).

despite the severe disapproval of King Edward I.[60] Likewise in Italy, the continuing conflict between the Ghibelline allies of Emperors Frederick Barbarossa and Frederick II and the Guelf supporters of the pope was played out in every Italian commune. This rivalry spawned a large number of saintly partisans of the Church, in which the bishop figured as the *defensor civitatis*.[61]

The rise of the city as a center of political and economic power invariably led to the proliferation of biographies in which urban themes were predominant. Lay merchants such as Giovanni of Meda (†1159), Raymund Palmerio of Piacenza (†1200), Godric of Finchale (†1170), and Gualfard of Verona (†1127) joined the ranks of founding bishops as patrons of the city.[62] Typically, such saints gave up a life of wealth for the sake of asceticism, pilgrimage, and acts of charity. The canonization of the married merchant Homobonus of Cremona (†1197) by Innocent III in 1200 signaled a clear effort by Rome to win back disillusioned lay urban dwellers from the snares of heresy. Homobonus's biography reports that after twenty years of marriage and the death of his father, he began to contemplate the brevity of human life and the vanity of the world.[63] He then devoted himself to prayer and fasting and began a life of charity, providing for the poor and hungry. This parallels the life of the founder of the heretical Waldensians, Peter Waldo, who was inspired by the legend of St. Alexis to give up his wealth, preach the Gospel, and minister to the poor. Waldo's conversion illustrates how a legend, whose first redaction was in ancient Syriac and was rewritten in Greek, Latin, and in the local vernacular languages, could become the inspiration for a new sect.

A patriotic note was voiced by the humanist Sicco Polenton (1376–1447), chancellor and archivist of Padua and author of the lives of the lay saints Helen Enselimini and Anthony the Pilgrim.[64] He stated in the dedication of Helen's biography to his son Lazarus

[60] *Miracula Simonis Montforti*, ed. J. O. Halliwell, in *The Chronicle of William Rishanger of the Baron's War*, in *Camden Society Publications* 15 (London, 1840), 67–110.
[61] Golinelli (1994), 134.
[62] Golinelli (1994), 125.
[63] *Vita Sancti Homoboni*, ed. F. S. Gatta, in "Un antico codice reggiano su Omobono 'il santo popolare' di Cremona", *Bolletino storico cremonese* 7 (1942), 112.
[64] "Vita beati Antonii Peregrini", ed. S. Polenton, *Analecta Bollandiana*, 13 (1894), 417–25.

that he had been asked to write the life by a member of the Franciscan order and that he was proud that his own wife was a scion of the Enselmini family.[65] Such appropriation of saints by noble families was a common feature of late medieval Italian piety. Sicco struck a patriotic note by remarking that some historians may praise his native city for its antiquity (since it was built four hundred years before Rome), its great defensive walls, its commodious waters, moderate wealth, the fertility of its fields, its architecture, both public and private, and other features. He prefers to list the many relics that are housed in the city and its *contado* and to praise its saints. Sicco reports that in order to keep Julian the Apostate from destroying the relics of SS. Luke and Matthew, they were spirited out of the city by boat. A similar patriotic theme is voiced by the author of the life of John Gueruli of Verucchio: "O fortunate land of Rimini, in which such a fragrance appears and the body of such a saint answers prayers daily and performs such miracles among our people".[66]

Sicco also raises the distinction between official and popular sainthood:

> Even if neither one has been approved by a judgement of the high pontiff, nevertheless, each one performed miracles and both may in the opinion of the people be placed among the blessed.[67]

This same view is found in Canon John of Cremona's life (ca. 1272) of the lay penitent Facio of Cremona:

> The fact that he can be called a saint you ought to know, because the church is dual, i.e., militant, which we are, and triumphant, which is of the blessed. If not canonized in the church militant, one is canonized above in the church triumphant.[68]

The considerable archival material available concerning the Italian communes permits us to trace municipal regulations, council decisions, and confraternities related to local saints. In addition to the widespread veneration of such figures as the Virgin Mary and Archangel Michael, there was a growing preference for the locally bred saint.

---

[65] *Vita et visiones B. Helenae*, ed. S. Polenton, in *AA.SS*, 4 November 2:412.
[66] Turchini (1970).
[67] *Vita et visiones B. Helenae*, ed. Polenton, 412.
[68] John of Cremona, *Vita Facii*, in A. Vauchez, ed., "Sainteté laique au xiii⁰ siècle: la vie de bienheureux Façio de Crémone", *Melanges d'Ecole française de Rome. Moyen âge* 84 (1972) 13–53.

This might demand the reconstruction of his legend and even the fabrication of historical facts in order to strengthen his legendary status as an urban patron. This development is illustrated in the case of the Bolognese patron St. Petronius. Petronius was held responsible for privileges allegedly granted the city's *studium* (the foundation of the university) by Emperor Theodosius II (†450). He supposedly had assisted in the rebuilding of the city after its destruction and had demanded that it remain free of tyrannical control.[69]

Secular Biography

The vast majority of biographical sources surviving from the Middle Ages were hagiographical. The surviving secular biographies also are panegyrical in tone and were influenced strongly by such Roman historians as Suetonius (see, e.g., Einhard's life of Charlemagne). Many appear under the rubric of *res gestae*, i.e., 'deeds performed' by illustrious persons such as abbots, bishops, or kings and which focused on the institution they headed.[70] Works such as Wipo's *Gesta Conradi*, Suger's *Vita Ludovici VI regis Francorum*, or the *Vita Henrici IV* are largely political, serving clear dynastic needs, and lack many biographical elements.[71] It has been argued, for example, that the lives of the Salian emperors attempted to present a theory of imperial pontificalism in the face of growing papal claims for the subordination of kings and emperors to Rome.[72] Many of these historians were employed in royal or imperial service and thus had direct access to archival sources. Charters or other diplomatic sources may appear in their works quoted fully or in part. For example, Geoffroi de Beaulieu's (†1275) life of Louis IX of France, written at the request of Pope Gregory X, contains a short version of the *Enseignements* of St. Louis, a summary of the king's moral views. The account of the murder of Charles the Good (†1127), count of Flanders, by the notary Galbert of Bruges contains letters and charters related to the struggle for communal liberty in the Low Countries.[73]

---

[69] Webb (1996), 174–80.
[70] Breisach (1994), 100.
[71] Gruber, et al. (1977), 201.
[72] Mommsen and Morrison (1962), 14.
[73] *The Murder of Charles the Good Count of Flanders*, ed. and trans. James B. Ross (New York, 1967).

In the late twelfth century, vernacular (sometimes versified) biography (often devoted to the upper nobility) began to appear, including the lyric poet Adam de la Halle's life (1283/85) of Charles of Anjou, king of Sicily, the life of King Alfonso VII by Gil Zamora, and the life (1226) of William the Marshal, duke of Pembroke. These works belong to a courtly tradition that attempted to portray their subjects as the personification of knightly ideals. In addition, non-aristocratic biographies—such as the twelfth-century collective *vidas* of such troubadours as Marcabru and Cercamon and the later life of Dante by Boccaccio—extended the list of the subjects of biography beyond saints and sovereigns. In contrast, Walter of Burley's *Liber de vita et moribus philosophorum* (1275/1337), dealing with ancient philosophers, is entirely derivative.

Abbot Suger of St. Denis' life (1137/44) of Louis VI inaugurated a long tradition of French royal historiography in which biography served as a framework for a history of the reign rather than a personal portrait of the sovereign. In Suger's work, strict chronological order is not always followed. Each of the thirty-two chapters follows a set pattern: a summary description of a particular historical event, royal intervention, and the solution of the problem. Another loyal servant of the Capetian dynasty, Jean de Joinville, sénéschal of Champagne (1225–1317), who accompanied Louis IX to the Holy Land, was one of the witnesses at the king's canonization trial and took part in the elevation of his relics. His life of Louis, dedicated in 1309 to Philip the Fair, was based on this deposition. It was dictated to his clergy and focused on the Christian virtues and military courage displayed by the saint, including reports of the saint's edifying remarks to his entourage, which the author apparently intended to inspire Louis's successor and to satisfy the piety of Philip's wife, Jeanne of Navarre. Another life (1302/03) of Louis was written by Guillaume of St. Pathus, who had served as confessor to both Louis's widow Marguerite and his daughter Blanche, to whom the work was dedicated; it is also based on the canonization record. Many of these royal biographies do not survive in a large number of copies. Nevertheless, their impact on historiographical tradition may be enduring, since, as semi-official accounts, they were cited by later court historians.[74]

---

[74] Guenée (1980), 273.

Autobiography

Wilhelm Dilthey has remarked that "autobiographies are the most direct expression of reflection about life".[75] His son-in-law and disciple Georg Misch therefore produced a monumental history of autobiography, often based on epistles, epigraphy, and other fragmentary personal data.[76] Nevertheless, the genre of autobiography did not reach its fullest form in the Middle Ages and, following the model of Augustine's *Confessions*, usually focused on a crisis of faith that was resolved through a religious conversion or rebirth. Like hagiography, autobiography contained stereotypical motifs, and the details of the subject's life were subordinated to the Christian views of sin and salvation. For example, Margery Kempe saw her life as a reflection of God's will attempting to reach salvation in the face of a hostile environment, although some saw her as a heretical Lollard. The need for justification also motivated Angelo of Clareno's *Apologia pro sua vita* (1330). Angelo sought to explain his association with the heretical Spiritual Franciscans in the face of persecution by Rome. The autobiographical materials written by Rather of Verona (ca. 887–974) and Othoh of St. Emmeram (1010–after 1067), both of whom also wrote saints' lives, focus on religious elements and require complementary sources in order to flesh out the author's life. The large number of travel accounts, for example—such as those by Marco Polo or by missionaries to the East such as the Franciscan Odoric of Pordenone or the Dominican Jordan Cathala—are more concerned with recounting the peculiarities and strange customs of their hosts than in revealing the personality of the author. In all likelihood the widely read account by John de Mandeville was written without even leaving the comfort of Europe. Likewise, the many epistles left by such figures as Bernard of Clairvaux and Pope Innocent III may assist in the reconstruction of their lives but may not be properly classified as 'autobiographical'. Indeed, the continuing appearance of traditional *topoi* and the presence of confessors who served as intermediaries in the transcription of many 'autobiographies' raise limitations about their value as personal documents. The 'autobiography' of Beatrice of Nazareth (†1268), has been attributed to a

[75] Dilthey (1976), 212.
[76] Misch (1949), vols. 2–4, which deal with the Middle Ages.

variety of authors, although her confessor Fulger may be the most
likely candidate.[77] In any case, more attention is devoted to praising the virtues of her father Bartholomew, who endowed three
Cistercian monasteries, which he joined along with his children.

Following a long hiatus, the twelfth century witnessed a revival of
autobiographical literature. This may be related to the 'rise of the
individual' and the revival of theological and philosophical controversies and included works by Petrus Alfonsi (a convert from Judaism),
Guibert of Nogent, and Abelard. In the thirteenth century, the emphasis on contrition and penance voiced by the Fourth Lateran Council
in 1215 produced a further flourishing of confessional literature,
often associated with Franciscan circles and the women's movement.
Nevertheless, the more detailed lives of Hermann of Cologne and
Ramon Llull remain apologetical and polemical in tone, and include
extensive dialogues with religious adversaries. Hermann of Cologne
(†1160), scion of a commercial Jewish family, converted to Christianity
under the influence of the theologian Rupert of Deutz, and his work
provides an intellectual justification for his abandonment of family
and community in favor of an alien faith. It shares much in common with contemporary 'dialogues' between Jew and Christian in
which the differences between the two faiths were resolved through
the allegedly superior arguments provided by Christian theology.[78]
Nevertheless, many of the details of Jewish communal life are described.
Despite its somewhat stereotypical character, Hermann's prophetic
dreams, his occupation as a moneylender, conflicts with the community over his conversion, and anxieties over marriage, contain a
ring of authenticity. In the same way, the Majorcan nobleman Ramon
Llull (†1315) wrote of the crisis that led to his conversion from the
life of a courtier. He recounts his zealous attempt to convert non-
believers through the composition of philosophical tracts, direct confrontation with the Muslims, and the establishment of schools of
foreign language in the course of meetings with public figures. A
detailed account of Ramon's journeys throughout the Mediterranean
is laced with references to his considerable literary output. The volume

---

[77] *Vita Beatricis. De Autobiografie vaan de Z. Beatrijs van Tienen O. Cist. 1200–1268*,
ed. L. Reypens (Antwerp, 1964), 33.
[78] Kleinberg (1992a).

is characterized by a self-righteous attack on those who failed to understand the mission of a man whose intellectual capacity clearly far outdistanced his adversaries.[79]

The 'autobiography' attributed to Pope Celestine V (†1294) only deals with the first thirty years of his life. It chronicles his childhood in a small village of the Abruzzi, admission to the Benedictine order, and establishment of a new religious order that combined features of the Franciscan and Benedictine rules. In all likelihood, this work was not written by Celestine himself but was, rather, based on the recollections of his disciples, who sought to strengthen the case for his canonization. While probably containing authentic details about his large family and the difficulties of rural life, the many miracles and visions conform to standard precedents, placing the work closer to the hagiographical tradition. This work falls into a tradition of confessional literature particularly prevalent in Franciscan and penitential circles in the late thirteenth century, including the lives of Angela of Foligno and Margaret of Cortona, which were written by their confessors and contain visions and revelations. The thousands of such visions and revelations interspersed in medieval literature may be noted as a widespread autobiographical form, although the stereotypical descriptions of the otherworld, conflict with the devil, or encounters with heavenly persons often lack individuality. Nevertheless, such visions play an increasingly important part in later medieval hagiography as illustrations of the saint's inner life, produced by both lay and religious persons, and they helped to propagate the Christian geography of the otherworld. In the lives of Hildegard of Bingen, Catherine of Siena, John of Roquetaillade, and Bridget of Sweden the visions represent a medium for voicing political views.[80] While Elizabeth of Schönau's *Liber visionum*, written by her confessor Ekbert, represents a kind of spiritual biography, her *Revelationes de sacro exercitu virginum coloniensium* (1156/57) served to authenticate the relics of St. Ursula and the eleven thousand virgins buried at Cologne. Saints were not the only persons whose visions have survived, however, and the *exempla* literature in particular contains reports drawn from all sectors of the population, although those selected clearly aimed to provide a moral message or to validate Christian theology. For

---

[79] Goodich (1998), 89–103.
[80] Dinzelbacher (1991), 35.

example, the 1196 vision of the afterlife provided by the novice monk Edmund of Eynsham, who had remained unconscious for two days, refers to persons known to the visionary along with a detailed Christian account of the geography and the genres of sinners likely to suffer in the next world.[81] At the same time, both natural scientists and theologians dealt with the etiology and meaning of dreams, and this literature may assist us to understand how medieval persons interpreted the figures and symbols that appear in dreams and revelations.[82]

Investigations of heresy undertaken by the Inquisition have provided some of the most fruitful sources for personal recollections, albeit produced under coercive conditions. The widely researched investigation undertaken in 1320/23 by Jacques Fournier, bishop of Pamiers (later elected Pope Benedict XII), although focusing on heresy and its dissemination has provided rather detailed accounts of the lives of such colorful figures as Bernard Delicieux, Beatrice de Planissoles, Baruch of Languedoc, and Arnaud of Verniolle, among others.[83] If traditional literary autobiography was religious and apologetic, such trial records indirectly provide evidence concerning the eating habits, sex life, and superstitions of a wider circle of the population. In the same way, canonization trials, in which a broad range of witnesses—men and women, clergy and laity, urban and rural— testified under oath in support of a candidate for sainthood, provide the social historian with indirect information about the lives of common folk. Although the testimony dealt with the saint's life or miracles, such narratives have been employed by social historians interested in the daily life, medical problems and practical concerns of the laity.[84] In the same way, the remissions issued by the royal court of the Châtelet contain colorful reports of the Parisian demi-monde in the late fourteenth century and may provide a portrait of outcasts of medieval society. These detailed accounts may well assist us in the composition of the kind of micro-history which has long eluded historians, who have been more concerned with the use of such trials for institutional history or the history of religious ideas. The testimony of several witnesses to the same miracle in a canonization trial

---

[81] 'Visio monachi de Eynsham', ed. H. Thurston, *Analecta Bollandiana* 22 (1903), 225–319.
[82] Goodich (1991).
[83] For translations of some of these sources, see Goodich (1998), 39–52, 117–43, 201–15.
[84] Finucane (1997).

allows us to flesh out the life of a microcosmic Christian community drawn together by the presence of the divine. Putting aside the ideological and stereotypical nature of much of the testimony, such witnesses also speak about their labor, fears, leisure-time pursuits, family life etc. Due to the judicial nature of these sources, the basic information about each witness includes: age, residence, origin, connection to the saint, gender, full name, profession, date of the testimony, the names of corroborating witnesses and the officials of the court, along with other specific data normally required in a court of law. Such data bring us far closer to the non-clerical and non-noble classes than the portrait found in more traditional diplomatic sources.

The Scholarly Study of Hagiography

The scholarly study of medieval biography has focused on hagiography and began in the sixteenth century with the Société des Bollandistes.[85] These scholars attempted to apply the highest standards of Renaissance scholarship to the publication of reliable editions of the lives of the saints. The project eventually received papal patronage, despite opposition from such figures as Cardinal Bellarmine. This important Counter-Reformation figure feared the scandal of publishing some of the more outlandish miracle stories found in hagiography, which would surely drive some believers into the waiting arms of the Protestants. A second opponent was the Carmelite order, because the Bollandists had raised doubts about some of the order's historical claims. Following the order of the Catholic liturgical calendar in the publication of primary hagiographical sources, in the course of over three hundred years the *Acta sanctorum* (including a period of dissolution and dispersion between 1773 and 1836) has reached the month of November. But given the demands of modern scholarship, this project has been abandoned, although editions continue to appear in the order's periodical, *Analecta Bollandiana*. Hagiographical research continues to rely heavily on the production of critical editions of the saint's life and miracles, based on the comparative, critical codicological study of relevant manuscripts and the identification of sources.

---

[85] Delehaye (1959).

Many of the issues later taken up by social and institutional historians are first raised in the scholarly apparatus of paleographers, who are concerned with the provenance of the source, the identity of its author and his program, and the specific events and persons referred to in the text. The expanding study of hagiography in recent years has engendered the creation of a number of scholarly organizations, such as The Hagiography Society, the Associazione italiana per lo studio della Santità dei Culti e dell'Agiografia, the Arbeitskreis für hagiographische Fragen, and the Hagiographische Gezelschap Nederland, in addition to the foundation of new journals such as *Hagiographica* and the creation of many internet sites taking sainthood as their focus. Many relevant primary and secondary sources continue to appear in the journals published under the auspices of religious orders.

In recent years, hagiographical research has focused on the saint's life and miracle as a backdrop for social history. The rise of the laity and the medieval commune, the women's movement, the battle against heresy, popular religion, and the treatment of children are some of the themes that have been treated through the rich prism of hagiography, which has been seen as a more accurate reflection of societal norms than traditional diplomatic sources.[86] Despite the considerable amount of recent research, however, much remains to be done. For example, the extent to which a wider public beyond the clergy was exposed to hagiography and its relation to liturgy has thus far received insufficient attention. The term *legenda* suggests that saints' lives began as commemorative texts to be read in the course of a service. As John Beleth (1150/60) noted, "passions are to be read during the feasts of the martyrs, legends during the feasts of the confessors". One manuscript of the life of Bishop Hugh of Lincoln, for example, contains the marginal notes "legere" or "noli legere", indicating which sections were to be read aloud, and which bypassed.[87] The audience exposed to the saint's life therefore would depend upon the number of persons present at the monastic refectory, village chapel, cathedral, or other venue during the reading of the legend

---

[86] See, e.g., Vauchez (1997); Finucane (1997); Golinelli (1991); Goodich (1982); Herlihy (1985); Weinstein and Bell (1982); Dinzelbacher (1995); Bynum (1987); Krötzl (1994).
[87] *The Life of St Hugh of Lincoln*, ed. Douie and Farmer, I, l.

or its abbreviated version. The considerable number of extant hagiographical manuscripts and the wide dispersion of some cults provide
ample evidence of acquaintance with saints' lives, not simply among
the educated classes.[88] Many saint's offices clearly were based on a
summarized life and miracles and, alongside the visual arts, were the
major medium through which a wider illiterate public became
acquainted with the saint's ministry. The biography was therefore
not merely a literary document but, further, served to authenticate
and substantiate the hagiographical image that the Church sought
to propagate. The absence of reliable written data therefore could
lead to the rejection of long-venerated relics or the removal of a
doubtful saint from the calendar. Gervase of Canterbury reported
that Archbishop Lanfranc attempted to cleanse the calendar of undocumented saints and, "because reliable documents could not be found
about Bregwine, Adelard, Alfric and other archbishops, their cele-
brations ceased".[89]

The intimate tie between hagiography and liturgy is illustrated in
the frequent references to sacred music in hagiography. This includes:
1) the heavenly music which miraculously accompanied the saint's
demise, 2) the detailed reports of instruments and chants employed
during the liturgy; 3) music serving as the occasion for a religious
vision or the performance of a miracle; and 4) the composition of
sacred music by the saints themselves or instructions given (sometimes by the saint) concerning the *responsoria* or *lectiones* to be recited
during the saint's feast. Pope Innocent III himself undertook to compose the offices of several of the saints he had canonized, making
use of contemporary hagiography, and Pope Gregory IX wrote hymns
in honor of St. Francis. Commemorative volumes undertaken by a
local church that houses the saint's relics have often become the
most suitable occasion to bring together all of these literary, icono-
graphical, musical, and other sources, which may become the raw
material in order to more fully appreciate the image of the saint
over the centuries. The medieval biographer's work thus can be
placed in the context of a whole range of media that served to
enhance the *legenda*.

[88] Philippart (1977).
[89] Cited in Rubenstein (1999), 281.

CHAPTER TWELVE

LEGENDARY HISTORY: *HISTORIA* AND *FABULA*

Peter Ainsworth

There were historians in the Middle Ages, and there was a medieval historiography.
What we lack are historians of medieval historiography.[1]

The present essay is intended as a complement to 'Contemporary
and "Eyewitness" History', which appears elsewhere in this volume,
and attempts to deal with issues not covered there. In particular it
sets out to explore the reasons for the appearance in Old French,
from ca. 1100 onwards, of different kinds of writing about the past
in all of which legend and the 'recycling' of elements of the past
play a major role. It begins with a discussion of the tension between
historia and *fabula*, continues with an account of the edifying function of medieval history as understood by the scholars of the time,
and then explores in turn the appearance of the new vernacular
texts of the period 1100–1220, starting with the *chanson de geste*, continuing with the *roman arthurien* and *roman d'antiquité*, and concluding
with developments towards the end of the period studied, which led
to the separation of verse and prose and to a new emphasis in the
latter form on truth-telling. If the bill of fare proposed here seems
a strange one, in the context of a handbook of historiography, it is
because the vernacular writers of the twelfth-century Renaissance
wrote about the past in ways that are surprisingly varied and delight-
fully perplexing to a modern audience, and which tell us a good
deal about how they viewed their present.

The High Middle Ages were not ignorant of the fundamental distinction, so familiar to us, between historical and fictional account.
In the seventh century, Isidore of Seville explained to his readers
how the task of *historia* was to inform and instruct by recounting
actual facts.[2] *Fabula*, in contrast, was expected to offer a fictional

---

[1] Guenée (1977), 275; my translation.
[2] Isidore de Séville, *Isidori Hispalensis Episcopi Etymologiarum Sive Originum Libri XX*,

account. The learned still recalled Cicero's *De Oratore*, which required
every historian worthy of the title to observe a scrupulous respect
for truth, showing neither fear nor favor.[3] Throughout the Middle
Ages, the function of the historian would remain that of "establishing and relating the factual events of the past". In the opinion of
B. Lacroix, the medieval historian saw himself simply as an 'expos-
itor', his role (*opus narrationis*) being to transform facts into stories to
be listened to and read. Only worthy of featuring in historical accounts
(*historia*) were events reputed to be true and which were judged memorable because they were also edifying. Above all, these were the
acts and deeds of the great:

> Historiae sunt res verae quae factae sunt.[4]
> Non tamen omnia memorabilia notare cupio, sed memoranda tantum,
> ea scilicet quae digna memoriae esse videntur.[5]
> Historia est narratio rei gestae ad instructionem posteritatis.[6]

This conception of narrative history, conferring immortality upon
the great of this world, was commonplace in the Middle Ages. It
originated with Herodotus, who had wanted to prevent the record
of the great and marvelous exploits accomplished by the Greeks and
Barbarians from being erased from human memory. Yet, as Guenée
reminds us, medieval historiography in Latin had no place of its own
in the *trivium* of the twelfth and thirteenth centuries. An ancillary
discipline, it was associated with the study of grammar and rhetoric
and drew on the teachings of theology, law, and ethics for its edifying illustrations (*littera docet*):

---

ed. W. M. Lindsay, 2 vols., Scriptorum Classicorum Bibliotheca Oxoniensis (Oxford,
1911 and 1957), 1:40–45.
    [3] Cicéron, *De Oratore*, trans. R. Southern and H. Rackham, Loeb Classical Library
(London and Cambridge, Mass., 1967), 234–35; quoted in Hay (1977), 4.
    [4] *Isidori Hispalensis Episcopi Etymologiarum Sive Originum Libri XX*, ed. Lindsay, 1:44,
45; quoted in Lacroix (1971), 17; cf. *Isidori Hispalensis Episcopi Etymologiarum*, 1:41:
"Historia est narratio rei gestae per quam ea quae in praeterito facta sunt, dinos-
cuntur".
    [5] Gervase of Canterbury, *Opera Historica*, ed. W. Stubbs, 2 vols., Rolls Series
(London, 1879, 1880); in Lacroix (1971), 20.
    [6] John of Salisbury (Ioannis Saresberiensis), *Memoirs of the Papal Court*, trans. from
Latin with Introduction and Notes by Marjorie Chibnall [= *Historia Pontificalis*, 1st
ed.] (London and Edinburgh, 1956, 1962, 1965); in Lacroix (1971), 172.

As one of the goals of the *trivium* was to establish rules of conduct, examples to avoid or imitate, it was completely natural to look back to the past, that is, to history books, for real examples.[7]

This edifying function of historical narratives was also known to the Romans. Their rhetoric advocated regular recourse to moral anecdotes taken from model lives and brought to life by the use of—often invented—direct speech.[8] Medieval rhetoric itself distinguished between *historia* (narration of facts proven to have taken place), *argumentum* (an account more probable than true), and *fabula* (neither true nor probable); but most historians in the Middle Ages seem only to have retained the first- and last-mentioned of these categories.[9] This did not stop them, however, from blending into their accounts both attested facts and fantastic or legendary phenomena. But as Jean Blacker illustrates so well, both the Latin and vernacular historians of the twelfth century certainly believed in the existence of a series of facts (*res gestae*) beyond their *own* accounts (*historiae rerum gestarum*), even if these occasionally contained magic spells, fantasies and ghostly apparitions.[10]

Romance, Historiography, and Epic: The New Vernacular Discourse of the Twelfth Century

If, for Bernard Guenée, the first major current of medieval historiography—made up of texts written in Latin and relating the history of a monastery, crusade, or province—can be seen as a by-product of moral teaching or theology, a second current—represented this time by poems composed sometimes in Latin, sometimes in *roman* by willing humanists who, to please their patrons, adapted and translated the two or three books which they were lent by them—must, for this modern historian, be viewed as a mere 'by-product' of literature. This judgment appears severe, if only because of the relative uncertainty still surrounding those composite texts from the twelfth century that we know as the *chroniques*, *estoires*, and *romans*[11]—which

---

[7] Guenée (1977), 264; my translation.
[8] See Hay (1977), 8–10.
[9] Blacker (1994), xi and 201.
[10] Blacker (1994), xii.
[11] Damian-Grint (1999), 231, reminds us that in the twelfth century the prime meaning of *romanz* is linguistic, i.e., "non-Latin".

surely have so much to teach us about how the world was viewed by contemporaries.

In an essay published in 1975, Paul Zumthor tried to isolate and define the qualities that should enable the modern reader to make viable distinctions between vernacular epic, historiography, and romance.[12] To the purely formal criteria to which he had had recourse in an earlier study (which had, however, proven inadequate for identifying the significant differences characterizing categories of text, which, almost without exception, used the octosyllabic couplet) he now added the criterion of their respective teleologies or *finalités*.[13] For Zumthor, *roman* and *histoire* (provisionally: 'vernacular narrative texts in octosyllabic couplets with a predominantly legendary or imaginative emphasis' and 'vernacular narrative texts in octosyllabic couplets with a predominantly historiographical emphasis')—were "twins born of a certain crisis of self-awareness that affected the ruling class of western society in a relatively specific place and time".[14] He distinguished them, on the one hand, from the Latin historiographic tradition with its moralizing or annalistic tendency (as defined above) and, on the other hand, from the *chansons de geste* or epics that preceded them (but which were, of course, to remain popular throughout the Middle Ages).

Before we can attempt a more detailed examination of the new forms of discourse in *roman*, both of which used the octosyllabic couplet, we need to establish just how they may be distinguished with regard to that other form of 'retrospective' expression, viz., the *chanson de geste*. The greatest particularity of the latter, again according to Zumthor, was its memorializing function:

> The epic phenomenon . . . arises in a society as yet relatively undifferentiated in social terms and in which the collective social consciousness seeks, emotively, to identify what it is that both attaches it to the known world and distinguishes it from the same; seeks, that is, to affirm its wholeness and unity, the very conditions for and consequence of its ability to dominate it. . . . Not so much a reflection of a past reality, the *chanson de geste* may thus be seen as a means of compensation,

---

[12] Zumthor (1975), 237–48: 'Roman et histoire: aux sources d'un univers narratif'.

[13] This part of our discussion owes much to Zumthor's ideas, but reference will also be made, as appropriate, to other critics who appear to offer useful clarifications.

[14] Zumthor (1975), 238; my translation.

for the group, for the fissure which has seemingly opened up between life as experienced and the world of the imagination. It converts memory and recollection into prophecy. It takes on the diffuse ideology of a collectivity, upon which it confers the reassuring dignity of that which contrives to escape the decadence of this world. By the selfsame words that it uses to declare history to be true, it transmutes it into a timeless fiction. Thus history remains, but only by abolishing itself as historicity.[15]

This "triumphant timelessness", Zumthor argues, is guaranteed by the dramatic and, as it were, liturgical aspects of the epic *chant*, "in the here and now, in the *present*, warm, virtual dialogue between the performer-singer and those who listen to him." Composition of the poem in assonanced *laisses* only reinforces this impression:

A progression establishes itself by dint of the deep narrative structures employed; but it does not predominate: repetitions, parallelisms, breaks, contradictions, each moment of the narrative discourse is fundamentally a present, forever the same.[16]

The performers of these often very lengthy songs (comprising several thousands of lines) recounted to their listeners the *gesta principum* or acts of prowess wrought by the great men of a relatively distant past. The *chansons de geste* were ostensibly inspired by the deeds of heroes from the great noble families who had lived in the Carolingian era. The narrative of their history/story was conceived as a series of events now legendary in nature, now based upon more or less authenticated fact. The *chansons de geste* soon developed into cycles relating to particular families (the *geste* of the king or of Charlemagne; the *geste* of Garin de Montglane; the William of Orange cycle). If these tales of distant conflicts (most frequently between Christians and Muslims) found such an enthusiastic audience around 1100 and well beyond, in the royal and feudal France of the first crusades, this was doubtless because they re-awakened in contemporary minds the memory of an earlier struggle that once again was becoming highly relevant, thus helping them to make sense of the challenges faced by their own generation. They presented their aristocratic audience with a profusion of heroic acts, which were sometimes tragic but invariably glorious, acts carried out for the most part in the

---

[15] Zumthor (1975), 238–39; my translation.
[16] Zumthor (1975); my translation.

name of the Lord and in the service of the Christian faith. It is
hardly surprising that the Church did not discourage them. The *chansons de geste* are thus, at least in part, a reflection or expression of
the religious fervor of the crusades. Through their protagonists—
Roland, Olivier or William of Orange—all the aspirations and dilemmas of a warrior caste could make themselves heard.

The *chansons des geste* took the form of assonanced or rhyming *laisses*
of variable length. The meter was usually decasyllabic, but alexandrines or even octosyllabic lines are also found. The degree of poetic
invention encountered in texts such as the Oxford *Roland* is, to say
the least, impressive. Daniel Poirion has alerted us to the risks of
modern interpretations that distort the meaning of these poems by
making too little of the role played by the minstrel.[17] One cannot
but admire the sheer virtuosity implied by the almost instinctive generation, in the heat and immediacy of public performance, of each
fresh series of hemistichs, lines, and *laisses*—fed by the vast resources
of *motifs* and *formulae* that any talented minstrel had at his disposal.[18]
That said, we would agree with Poirion that the process of writing,
too, must have had its role to play from the moment it was decided
that the best of these poems (or particular versions of them) should
be preserved from oblivion and copied onto parchment. It unques-
tionably played a further role in their subsequent material development and transmission.

The aesthetic of the *chanson de geste* is largely alien to modern
notions of harmony and unity. Poirion points out that these poems
accommodate long prologues "as majestic as façades", as well as "the
juxtaposition of episodes written in different styles and set alongside
each other as though within the lead-bound panes of stained glass
windows, . . . with pauses and digressions, secondary repetitions and
contradictions—like so many side chapels".[19] Michel Zink has drawn
our attention to the hieratic to-and-fro movement so characteristic
of the epic aesthetic:

> In the *chanson de geste* there is no pure narrativity as such, no linear-
> ity of narrative development, as if what mattered most were not in
> the first instance knowing what is going to happen next. On the con-
> trary the epic seems to play on a perpetual ebb and flow that revels

---

[17] Poirion (1992), 240.
[18] Cf. Boutet (1993); Hindley and Levy (1983); Kay (1978); Martin (1987).
[19] Poirion (1992), 241; my translation.

in repetitions and echoes: we have a succession of repetitive *laisses* which differ only in terms of assonance or minute variations with respect to point of view or content, in accordance with the recourse to 'parallel laisses'; plus the incessant recurrence of formulaic phrases occupying a hemistich or sometimes an entire line.

The *chanson de geste* thus appeals to what might be called the physical effects of language: the fascination and near-hypnosis generated by repetition; the vertiginousness of the same assonance ringing out line after line throughout the *laisse* and born of a very simple melody, a repeated psalmody which never alters from line to line, with at the very most a variation in the cadence at the last hemistich of the *laisse* or in its final, shorter line.[20]

The melodies in question have not been passed down to us, but Zink highlights the rhythmic stylistic effects particular to the *chansons de geste*, singling out their:

> short, neatly turned and often end-stopped phrases, allied to the insistent, regular yet varying pounding of the decasyllabic line marrying that of the asymmetrical hemistichs: a taste for parataxis and a repugnance for subordinate clauses.[21]

He also alludes to the impression of 'enigmatic terseness' with which some of these poems leave us, a characteristic that "lacks neither seductive power nor grandeur",[22] and points out how, in two *romans* from the beginning of the thirteenth century, we encounter characters enjoying the experience of someone singing to them a *laisse* or two from a *chanson de geste*—which may perhaps give us some insight into the appeal that these structural units must have had for the audiences of that time. As for the general meaning of these poems, it is the human condition and the destiny of the hero that predominate. We shall refer just once more on this matter to D. Poirion, speaking here of the relationship between the *chanson de geste* and the objective 'reality' of its source materials—and consequently of the historical consciousness which must have inspired these poet minstrels and their audiences:

> Without doubt the *chanteur de geste* sees himself as dealing with the truth, eagerly contrasting his art with the fanciful approach of the Breton story tellers. He refers back to the *geste* as the authentic source of his song. But he magnifies the actions of his characters, the better to give

---

[20] Zink (1992), 73, 75; my translation.
[21] Zink (1992), 75; my translation.
[22] Zink (1992), 75; my translation.

the war a certain quality and meaning, traits which it does not have much of in real life.[23]

Certain *chansons de geste* seem to cast light on (or reflect) those feudal conflicts which would have been familiar to the contemporaries of a Louis VII or Philip Augustus. For example, in the *geste* of Guillaume there is emphasis on the kind of behavior that a faithful and honorable vassal should demonstrate when dealing with a hesitant lord threatened by enemies without and within; whilst *Raoul de Cambrai* represents, amongst other things, the tragic dilemma of the vassal dispossessed by his sovereign.[24]

Romans bretons and *romans d'antiquité*

In the early-to-mid-twelfth-century Anglo-Norman *regnum*, whose kings clearly were eager to impose their authority and acquire a distinctive identity for their widened domains, we find the *gesta* of contemporary princes recorded in various kinds of 'history', some of which (and pre-eminently Geoffrey of Monmouth's *Historia Regum Britanniae*, with its preoccupation with the legendary antecedents of the early British kings of the pre- and post-Roman era, including Arthur himself) had no pretensions to being 'historical'.[25] Often the aim was to justify innovation by means of written accounts of what ostensibly had happened in the past; or, again, to promote change by setting it within the context of an existing custom which, in reality, it was about to undermine.[26]

From Gaimar's *Estoire des Angleis* to Wace's *Roman de Brut* and *Roman de Rou*, and not forgetting the *romans d'antiquité*, the authors teach, creating their own truth by means of a discourse that blended together legend and 'history', fact and fiction, to serve the political needs of their masters,[27] at a time when a new public was starting

---

[23] Poirion (1992), 241; my translation.

[24] See in particular the articles by Sarah Kay in the bibliography to Francis Bar's entry on Raoul de Cambrai, in *Dictionnaire des lettres françaises (le Moyen Âge)*, rev. ed., ed. G. Hasenohr and M. Zink (Paris, 1992), 1231–35. On different approaches to the representation of the past in the *chanson de geste* and *chronique*, see Kay (1987).

[25] Geoffrey's sources include Gildas, Bede, a host of Breton and Welsh legends, various Latin sources, and an anonymous *Historia Regum Britannie*; his own *Historia* was to be used, in turn, by both Gaimar and Wace.

[26] See Zumthor (1975), 240.

[27] Marichal (1968), 463.

to *read* and no longer just to *listen*. Using an idea of H. R. Jauss, Zumthor refuses to consider the historicity of these texts in terms of veracity as it is understood today; with these authors historical events are those which have to be believed: "The opposition real/fictitious does not apply".[28] In these works, the formal constraints particular to the octosyllabic couplet imply "a certain folding back of the text upon itself, a concentration on the formalist intentions of the writer":[29]

> From this particular standpoint, the almost contemporaneous *Histoire des Anglais* by Gaimar and the *Roman de Thèbes*, Guillaume de Saint-Pair's *Roman du Mont Saint-Michel* and Chrétien de Troyes' *Erec* belong to the same 'genre'.[30]

So, how are we to distinguish pertinently between historiography and romance? Contemporary generic designations are of no help to us in this regard. Renaut de Beaujeu, for example, calls his *Bel Inconnu* both a 'roummant' and an 'istoire', and it is clear that both these terms were, in general, interchangeable.[31] Gaimar describes himself as a translator, but when referring to his own poem sometimes uses the word 'geste', sometimes 'vie', and sometimes 'estoire'—whilst at the same time referring to the *Anglo-Saxon Chronicle* as a 'chroniche'. Both Wace and Benoît de Sainte-Maure label their works 'estoires' or 'gestes'.[32] It could be ventured that certain vernacular accounts of the twelfth century have a relatively stronger narrative and aesthetic structure, a difference which becomes more discernible the closer one gets to the thirteenth century. This structure is typically built around a central theme or themes composed of courtly and/or fantastic or *merveilleux* elements. Accounts which are more markedly historiographical also comprise at least some of these elements, but as Douglas Kelly has pointed out, poems which develop a fictitious intrigue on the basis of such elements contrive to liberate the text from its conventions of pure linearity, closing the story back upon itself and upon its structuring of the marvelous.[33] Paul Zumthor summarizes this evolution as follows:

---

[28] Zumthor (1975), 245; my translation.
[29] Zumthor (1975), 244; my translation.
[30] Zumthor (1975), 244; my translation.
[31] Kelly (1974).
[32] Blacker (1994), 2–3; Marichal (1968), 450.
[33] Kelly (1974), 149.

> Historiography represents the real [elements of legend or facts vouched
> for] fragment by fragment, episode by episode, each unit, in its signi-
> fying uniqueness, in principle equaling the others in dignity. The novel
> aspires to create its global meaning [which 'superimposes itself' upon
> the *sensus litteralis*], by means of a signifying syntax.[34]

Our intention remains that of pinning down, as far as is possible,
the specificity of those *romans* whose dominant characteristic is their
preoccupation with history. But we cannot accomplish that without
first comparing them to their more overtly literary, legendary, and
imaginary counterparts. That is why, for a few paragraphs, we propose to discuss those octosyllabic verse narratives which, between
1160 and 1190 or thereabouts, developed their plots by use of the
fictitious, the legendary, and the fantastic, and which, increasingly,
concerned themselves with the destiny of a (chivalrous) hero and,
therefore, with an individual. Our approach is selective. It aims to
determine in what way these narratives might be differentiated from
predominantly 'historical' *romans*—which we will discuss in their turn
within the same analytical framework.

Let us first of all observe that the true meaning of these works of
imagination, whether they be the *Lais* of Marie de France or the
romances of Chrétien de Troyes, is not readily discernible at the
surface, so to speak, of the text. No longer laying claim to a truth
that is fundamentally or primarily referential (argues Michel Zink),
the novels of Chrétien suggest another order of truth altogether,
another type of meaning. "Distinct from the literal meaning of the
text, it nevertheless inheres within it and can only remain thus".[35]
Furthermore, as Emmanuèle Baumgartner observes, with reference
to Chrétien's mysterious literary settings, one is struck, precisely, by
the immanence of this closed world, "which rears up before us against
a backdrop of absence" and is "born, so it seems, solely at the behest
and pleasure of the writer":[36]

> Everything changes with Chrétien de Troyes, even if the revolution
> does not come about through the invention of a new form. . . . A much
> more significant break with the past, on the other hand, is his rejec-
> tion of subject matter derived from classical antiquity, even in leg-
> endary guise, in favour of the matter of Britain, and his characteristic

---

[34] Zumthor (1975), 248; my translation.
[35] Zink (1992), 145; my translation.
[36] Baumgartner (1994), 3; my translation.

textual treatment of it from the seminal *Erec et Enide* onwards. The beginning of the narration in *Erec et Enide* brutally wrenches Arthurian space and time away from the chronological and historical time in which Geoffroy of Monmouth and later Wace had inscribed their narratives, doing away with any temporal or even spatial point of anchorage: the kingdom of Logres is neither precisely England nor is it yet Great Britain. The first lines postulate without any apology and as so many 'attested facts': Arthur, his kingdom, his knights and their occupation, the latter shown as essential as it is seemingly ludicrous (pursuit of the white hart, the quest for fantastic adventure in the forest perilous.).[37]

If it is true that the romances of Chrétien de Troyes feature certain social and moral dilemmas which would not have been unfamiliar to these *bacheliers* or young knights as yet unendowed with fiefs, of whom Jean Flori has painted such an evocative portrait,[38] it is important to note with M. Zink that Chrétien's chivalric hero remains a *solitary* knight—even if he is sometimes accompanied by one or more companions. At the heart of this romance world is thus to be found an isolated figure with a mysterious destiny, the 'knight errant':

> The solitary figure of the wandering knight, invented by Chrétien practically in its entirety, reveals what is at stake in his romances: the discovery of one's selfhood, of love, and of the other.

Intended to be read (collectively, aloud, and in society; perhaps in private as well) the Arthurian romances of Chrétien were composed at the court of the daughter of Eleanor of Aquitaine, Marie, countess of Champagne (who lived between 1145 and 1198), then at that of Philip, count of Flanders (between 1181 and 1185). *Erec et Enide* (ca. 1170), *Cligés* (ca. 1176), the *Chevalier de la Charrette* and *Yvain* (ca. 1177–81), and *Perceval* or the *Conte du Graal* (ca. 1181–85) show us an imaginary world where, from one poem to another, one occasionally finds the same characters evolving around a hero whose destiny becomes clearer from episode to episode and from adventure to adventure. J.-Ch. Payen has emphasised the fact that with Chrétien, the author of *romans* "lays claim to the paternity of his work with the pride of an artisan jealously possessive of his art".[39] This essential

---

[37] Ead. See also Boutet (1999), 39: "Dans ses romans arthuriens, le règne d'Arthur devient autoréférentiel, il se constitue en un temps autonome, coupé de toute antériorité (sauf, idéologiquement, pour le respect des coutumes . . .)".
[38] Flori (1975).
[39] Payen (1997), 131; my translation.

link connecting clerk-romancer and lyric poet has been explored by
F. Bogdanow, who has demonstrated how Chrétien's first romances
can be seen as the narrativization and transmutation into plot of the
sensibility and *fin'amor* of the *trouvères* and their songs.[40] Payen points
out that Chrétien's romances, less exotic (with the exception of *Cligés*)
than the *romans d'antiquité* discussed below, were "better suited to
engagement with courtly and chivalrous values"[41] such as prowess,
honour, chivalry and loyalty to the Lady. *Perceval* or the *Conte du
graal* can be seen as the 'novel' of the discovery of self and others,
while *Erec* is a celebration but also an examination of love in marriage, as well as of love's dilemmas, challenges, and risks. *Cligés* is
famous for its portrait of political and dynastic rivalries and for the
alliance it effects between the Arthurian and Byzantine worlds. One
also finds in it a subtle analysis of how men and women fall in love
(Soredamor and Alexandre, Fénice and Cligés), undertaken via a
series of monologues and dialogues in which is made apparent all
the skill of that past master of the art of rhetoric that Chrétien had
become. The *Chevalier de la Charrette*, in contrast, features and analyzes the adulterous love of Lancelot for Queen Guinevere, without
passing judgment, exploring the behavior that the perfect lover and
knight should adopt before a cold and demanding queen. Arthurian
literature can in this way be seen to represent "the victory of culture over nature", of order over disorder:

> Arthur's court is the place where rebels submit, the place to which
> the champions of order return to recount their exploits and renew
> their vigor. The waste lands and forests that they encounter are a
> metaphor for their own, unruly impulses. What is sought through the
> trials that they undergo is first of all their own identity and a pleni-
> tude of being: herein is to be found the meaning of the romances of
> Chrétien de Troyes; therein lies also the message of the *Quest*, the real
> issue being that of deciding whether the knightly vocation involves the
> discovery of God, or of oneself.[42]

Celtic, Arthurian, or Byzantine settings; a liking for adventure, full
advantage taken of the possibilities afforded by the quest; descriptions of luxurious, fabulous, and often symbolic objects; a taste for

---

[40] Bogdanow (1981). Chrétien, of course, composed lyrics himself.
[41] Payen (1997), 131.
[42] Payen (1997), 39–40; my translation.

tournaments and the hunt, often involving fabulous animals; the subsequent passage into the Other World, realm of the fantastic; the
abolition of evil customs; finely developed portraits of chivalrous
lovers and their ladies—these are just a few of the more characteristic aspects of the romances of Chrétien de Troyes, with their enigmatic *sen* and *si belle conjointure*.[43] The backdrop for Chrétien's heroes
(and the audience's assumed familiarity with the Arthurian world
and its inhabitants) has been summarized in the following terms by
Michel Zink:

> Not only does Chrétien, unlike Geoffroy of Monmouth and Wace, not
> set out to provide a narrative of the reign of King Arthur; he assumes
> such familiarity on the part of his public with the Arthurian universe
> that explanations and information alike are rendered superfluous. Each
> individual narrative work is presented as a fragment, an uncovered
> part of a vast story whose underlying continuity, it is assumed, may
> be readily mastered by any reader. None of the romances explicitly
> depicts King Arthur, Queen Guinevere, the Round Table, its customs
> and knights. The poet is content to list these, assuming familiarity, as
> and when their presence is required to dignify a ceremony, tourna-
> ment or feast. To this is added that blend of disorientation and famil-
> iarity which accompanies the progress of the hero and his adventures.
> Hardly out of Arthur's castle and under cover of the nearest forest
> margin, he enters an unknown world, strange and threatening, but in
> which news circulates at an astonishing speed and where he constantly
> meets characters who know him (sometimes better than he knows him-
> self) and who reveal to him, in imperious and fragmentary fashion,
> his destiny. Like him, the reader evolves in a world of signs which
> perpetually refer him back, implicitly and enigmatically, to a meaning
> presented as self-evident and, for this very reason, hidden. The world
> of these romances is a world laden with meaning yet mysterious in its
> very obviousness.[44]

This is less true of the *romans d'antiquité* and their authors who, in
the words of Emmanuèle Baumgartner, "do not seem to have travelled to the very end of the adventure of fiction".[45] The earliest of
these, the *Roman de Thèbes* (composed ca. 1150–55), obviously predated Chrétien's earliest romance by a few years. Like the *Roman
d'Enéas* (ca. 1160) and the *Roman de Troie* (composed between 1160

---

[43] See in particular Chrétien's *Œuvres complètes*, ed. D. Poirion, in Bibliothèque de
la Pléiade (Paris, 1993).
[44] Zink (1992), 144; my translation.
[45] Baumgartner (1994), 2; my translation.

and 1170), the *Roman de Thèbes* aimed to impart to its aristocratic
public a not inconsiderable part of the classical narrative heritage:
"Their authors are clerks who declare their intent to make accessible to laymen ignorant of Latin a knowledge to which they would
otherwise have no means of access".[46] Their intentions are, thus,
both didactic and scholarly. If the *Enéas* author occasionally goes to
the extent of translating his source word for word, his relationship
with it is often much more casual than this. Yet the *Enéas* is not
devoid of structure: A. Petit sees in it a balanced whole involving
three major sections in a ratio of 1:2:1 (escape and voyage, the theme
of the wanderer and his quest; the war undertaken by the hero to
obtain both fief and wife; the fulfilment of his destiny).[47] Within these
larger divisions one can detect the presence—at a distance from one
another or at much shorter intervals—of parallel or symmetrical narrative units, "conferring upon the narrative a binary rhythm which
multiplies the effects of echo and antithesis". In this light one may
usefully compare the love of Lavinia and Enéas with the tragic passion of Dido:

> Thus the loves of Dido, guilty and sensual widow, are set against those
> of Lavinia, the young inexperienced girl. These two sentimental episodes,
> marking two stages in the destiny of Enéas, are set in opposition to
> one another and echo one another from either end of the romance.[48]

Inasmuch as it draws together love and prowess within the context
of narrative fiction, this occasionally scrupulous adaptation of Vergil's
Aeneid perhaps deserves to be known as 'the first French novel'. But
the (ever more elaborate) portrayal of love also finds expression in the
Thèbes and the *Troie*. Michel Zink summarizes the essential elements:

> All of these authors, abundantly and indulgently, depict the first stir-
> rings of love, the disarray of a virginal heart as yet slow to recognize
> its presence, the secrets confided to a mother or wet nurse which per-
> mit its identification, the self questioning, the timidity of the lovers,
> the recourse to ruses, and all the concealments, audacious initiatives,
> betrayals and confessions.[49]

---

[46] *Le Roman d'Enéas*, ed. Aimé Petit, in Lettres Gothiques, gen. ed. M. Zink (Paris,
1997), 7; my translation.
[47] *Le Roman d'Enéas*, ed. Petit, 12.
[48] *Le Roman d'Enéas*, ed. Petit, 13–14; my translation.
[49] Zink (1992), 135–36; my translation.

Moreover, in the *romans d'antiquité* (according to Baumgartner), poetry is most clearly visible in the guise of rhetorical embellishment—confirmation of the scholarly competence of the clerks responsible for it:

> The same is true of the 'images of the world' presented via the description of the tent of the King of Adraste and of Amphiaraüs's chariot in the *Thèbes*, of the 'descriptio mundi' or digressions provided by Benoît on the customs of the Amazons; then there is the inventory of medical knowledge carved upon Amphiaraüs's chariot in the *Thèbes*; the same goes for the importance of political speeches and thought in the *Enéas* and *Troie*. Even the lovers' soliloquies, which could be thought of as signaling the advent of the novel, reveal in the excess and minutiae of their meditations the intention to produce fragments, indeed a totality of possible discourse about love, rather than to pursue the conflagrations and uncertainties of an individual passion.[50]

In light of the interest they evince in embassies, councils, and combats, these works still have something of the *chanson de geste* about them. But their authors shared the common goal of translating their respective sources as faithfully as possible, and their work can thus be seen as an important aspect of twelfth-century humanism. The declared ambition of Benoît de Sainte-Maure in his *Roman de Troie* was to translate—in other words, to render into *roman*—a part of the only classical heritage to which he had access, namely, two works composed in Latin in the sixth century (but which he believed to be much older): the *Historia de excidio Trojae* of Dares the Phrygian; and the *Emphemeris belli Trojani* of Dictys the Cretan. Convinced that these narratives incorporated eyewitness accounts of the Trojan wars, Benoît wanted to give to his own contemporaries a reliable and unbroken chronological account of an important episode in human history.[51]

In his *Roman de Brut*, finished in 1155, Master Wace had already recounted the arrival in Britain of Brut (Brutus), the Trojan descendant of Aeneas who would soon become the eponymous king of the

---

[50] Baumgartner (1994), 2–3; my translation.

[51] Cf. Boutet (1999), 32: "Est-ce un hasard si les premières œuvres de quelque importance en langue vulgaire, chansons de geste et romans d'Antiquité, entretiennent un rapport avec l'Histoire, voire avec l'historiographie en langue latine? La référence historique, sous les différentes formes qu'elle revêt dans les textes, devrait alors être rattachée à ce désir d'authenticité, de justification du discours littéraire par une autorité extérieure à la fiction romanesque".

island of 'Bretagne'. The prologue to the *Brut* having evoked the fall
of Troy and the principal reason for it (the abduction of Helen),
Benoît's project was thus to provide a history of the founding of the
town and to relate what became of it. The most recent editors of
the *Troie* have highlighted another area of particular interest to Benoît,
to which we have already made reference, namely, the opportunity
to make a great show of his erudition:

> Benoît the clerk likes to demonstrate from time to time an encyclo-
> pedic erudition, or one which at least (ironically perhaps?) gives the
> appearance of the same: recollections of scholarly glosses, commen-
> taries, quotations of biblical origin, fragments of lapidaries, bestiaries,
> and description of marvels—wrought by man or to be found in the
> natural world.[52]

It would be unfair to tax Benoît with mere personal or professional
vanity, however. The writer has, after all, the duty to transmit his
knowledge to future generations, so that they can benefit from it.[53]
Writing in this way serves the purpose of preserving for posterity
the stories and wonders of the past:

> By evoking in language the objects, the splendors, the towns which no
> longer exist, his descriptions confer upon them an immortality that
> destiny—*Fortune* or *Aventure*, as Benoît has it—refused them.[54]

That said, Benoît's narrative still aims to please and entertain. The
descriptions of combat reveal his enthusiasm for the epic, and even
if his conception of love differs in certain respects from that of the
troubadours and *trouvères*, it would never have found its voice without
their example. A manuscript now conserved at Nottingham binds
together with the *Roman de Troie*, fabliaux, *chansons de geste*, and *romans*,
a clue perhaps to the status which at least a proportion of his public accorded the work of Benoît. An even more eloquent indicator
in respect of the literariness of this text is the way in which Benoît
elected to interpret the temporality and chronology of his principal
sources. Penny Eley has demonstrated how, in this poem of some
thirty thousand lines and in spite of the strict example furnished by

---

[52] Benoît de Sainte-Maure, *Le Roman de Troie*, ed. E. Baumgartner and F. Vielliard,
in Lettres Gothiques, gen. ed. M. Zink (Paris, 1998), 9; my translation.

[53] Cf. the Prologue to Marie de France's *Lais*, ed. L. Harf-Lancner, coll. "Lettres
Gothiques" (Paris, 1990).

[54] Benoît, *Troie*, ed. Baumgartner and Vielliard, 12.

Dares, the chronology hardly functions at all as a structuring principle.[55] The area of greatest interest is, in fact, the episode. This remains an autonomous temporal unit within narrative sequences, which—in nearly all cases—owe their respective coherence to thematic rather than chronological elements, even though within each particular episode micro-chronologies undergird the coherence proper to that unit of narration. The function of these micro-chronologies is not to relate what happens in such or such an episode to the overall narrative fabric of the poem but, rather, to heighten the importance of the episode itself and, thus, maintain the reader's interest. Further proof of this tendency is to be found in the absence, from one episode to the next, of any overtly chronological linking reference. The result is a fragmented and disorienting narrative whose constitutive episodes nonetheless make for an absorbing read. The approach recalls, to some extent, the technique of similar or parallel *laisses* employed in the *chanson de geste*, and in many respects the *Roman de Troie* is a poem of truly epic grandeur.

Although we are about to leave behind the world of the *roman breton* and *roman d'antiquité*, we shall stay within the domain of rhetoric. In texts which are primarily historical and chronological in nature, we shall occasionally find elements of a style that reminds us of the epic, lay, or romance. But in the chronicles and *estoires* which we are about to discuss, the particular blend and admixture of these elements is very different—not least because these are narratives in which recognizably esthetic patterning and 'structuration' are much less apparent.

Vernacular Historiography in Verse in the Twelfth Century

It was around 1155 that Master Wace, a clerk from Jersey working in Caen and already the author of *A Life of St Margaret*, a *Creation of Our Lady* (ca. 1130–40), and a *Life of St Nicholas* (ca. 1150) completed his *roman* of *Brut* or *Brutus*, great grandson of Aeneas—and, as such, his spiritual heir and the presumed founder of the kingdom of the Island Bretons. Possessed of considerable talent as an artist, Wace was to contribute to the subsequent development of the *roman d'aventures*.

---

[55] Eley (1994).

His descriptions of combat and storms at sea are unforgettable,[56] and his ability to make short, invented dialogues seem as though they have sprung from real-life encounters is unsurpassed. Almost half of Wace's *Brut* centers on the (hi)story of a legendary king already celebrated by Geoffrey of Monmouth in his *Historia Regum Britanniae* (finished ca. 1136–38). Neil Wright's recently published research inclines us to think that Wace could only have consulted a shortened version or 'variant' of Geoffrey's work.[57] In Geoffrey's opinion Arthur, having defeated the Saxon invaders at the beginning of the sixth century and triumphed over the Romans, was a 'national' hero. The Arthurian section of the *Brut* adapted by Wace from his written source is available to us in a bilingual edition by Emmanuèle Baumgartner and Ian Short.[58] Before we look at Wace's work, let us—with the assistance of Short and Baumgartner—briefly address his role model and source, Geoffrey of Monmouth, whose contribution we must not underestimate:

> Founding a new Troy on the banks of the Thames, according the Breton language the status of a classical tongue by describing it as a 'convoluted form of Greek', providing for the first time a history worthy of the indigenous Britons, presenting a virtually forgotten Celtic military leader as an internationally renowned conqueror capable of a triumph over Rome recalling that of his illustrious predecessors Belin and Brennus who, well before Caesar, had imposed their authority— this indeed was an ambitious historiographical project.[59]

Beyond Geoffrey and Wace, the literary fortunes of King Arthur and his knights of the Round Table (which featured for the first time in the *Brut* at ll. 9747–60) would be taken up by Chrétien de Troyes and his successors.[60] However, even if he refuses to embrace all the Breton 'marvels' inherited from Geoffrey of Monmouth, Wace still evinces confidence in the fundamental historical value of his source. With respect to certain details of the post-Roman period he refers to the *De Excidio Britannie* written by the Welsh clerk Gildas,[61]

---

[56] Grisward (1970).

[57] Geoffrey of Monmouth, *The Historia Regum Britanniae II: The First Variant Version*, ed. Neil Wright (Cambridge, 1988), xi–cxiv.

[58] Wace, *La Geste du Roi Arthur*, ed. E. Baumgartner and I. Short, in Bibliothèque médiévale 10/18 (Paris, 1993).

[59] Wace, *La Geste du Roi Arthur*, ed. Baumgartner and Short, 9; my translation.

[60] Cf. Pelan (1974).

[61] *Wace's Roman de Brut. A History of the British. Text and Translation*. Ed. J. Weiss,

one of the sources previously consulted also by Bede for his *Historia Ecclesiastica* (731), and to the *Historia Brittonum* written by another Welsh clerk, Nennius.[62] This is how, in a passage familiar to any medievalist, Master Wace begins his story of the Round Table:[63]

En cele grant pais ke jo di,
Ne sai si vus l'avez oï,
Furent les merveilles pruvees
E les aventures truvees
Ki d'Artur sunt tant recuntees
Ke a fable sunt aturnees.
Ne tut mençunge, ne tut veir,
Tut folie ne tut saveir.
Tant unt li cunteür cunté
E li fableür tant flablé
Pur lur cuntes enbeleter,
Que tut unt fait fable sembler.   (Arnold edn., vol. 2, ll. 9787–98)

Wace presents King Arthur as a model of twelfth-century feudal chivalry. Here he is arranging his troops on the battlefield and setting them an example of coolness and courage:

A cels dist li reis: « Ci estez!
Pur nule rien ne vus movez.
Si mestiers est, ça turnerai
E les altres par vus tendrai,
E si Romein, par aventure,
Turneient a descunfiture,
Puigniez aprés sis ateigniez,
Ociez les, nes esparniez! »
E cil distrent: « Bien le ferum. »
Dunc prist une altre legiun
Des nobles humes, des vassals,
Healmes laciez, sur lurs chevals,
Cels mist en un lieu plus veable,
N'i ot fors lui nul cunestable.
La fud sa meisnie privee
Qu'il ot nurrie et alevee.
En mi fist tenir sun dragun
Que il portot pur gumfanun;

"Exeter Medieval English Texts and Studies" (Exeter: Exeter University Press, 1999), xv.
[62] Ibid.
[63] Quotations taken from Wace, *Roman de Brut*, ed. Ivor Arnold, 2 vols. (Paris, 1938, 1940).

> Des altres tuz fist uit cumpaignes,
> En chascune ot dous chevetaines;
> A cheval fud l'une meitié
> E li altre furent a pié.   (Arnold edn., vol. 2, ll. 12321–42)

By a strange twist of irony, however, and in the very same breath as he affirmed his doubts concerning the authenticity of at least a part of these fantastic tales from Brittany and Brocéliande, this historian so avid for veracity launched a new *translatio* entailing serious consequences for the history of European literature:

> Leaving Antiquity and the world of the Mediterranean for Brittany and the time of King Arthur, the romance forsakes historical, referential truth and must therefore search for another kind of truth. A truth which is that of meaning; a meaning which, essentially, is fed by meditations on love and chivalry.[64]

It is thus in part thanks to the conscientious 'translation' undertaken by Wace of his Latin sources and, in particular, of Geoffrey of Monmouth, that the matter of Bretagne and its marvels were to cross over so successfully to France in the twelfth century.

At the same time as launching virtually single-handedly the enduring story of the knights of the Round Table, Wace's *Brut* is also a portrait (which its author claims to be scrupulously authentic)[65] of Celtic Britain, from its Trojan origins to the Norman Conquest. A huge fresco comprising the prophecies of Merlin as well as an account of Julius Caesar's invasions and later those of Hengist and Horsa, the work relies for its structure upon the old schema of royal and generational succession ("from king to king and from heir to heir, who were the first to govern England; whence they came and in what order the kings succeeded one another"). Its point of departure is the conquest of Troy by the Greeks:

> Ki vult oïr e vult saveir
> De rei en rei e d'eir en eir
> Ki cil furent e dunt il vindrent
> Ki Engleterre primes tindrent,

---

[64] Zink (1992), 138; my translation.
[65] "La perspective générale de l'écriture de cet auteur est bien celle de l'historiographie, et son attitude celle d'un chroniqueur qui cherche à relater une *succession* de faits véridiques, une *series narrationis* selon l'expression coutumière d'Hugues de Saint-Victor, héritée de la vieille définition d'Isidore de Séville"; see Boutet (1999), 39.

Quels reis i ad en ordre eü,
Ki anceis e ki puis i fu,
Maistre Wace l'ad translaté
Ki en conte la verité.
Si cum li livres le devise,
Quant Greu ourent Troie conquise
E eissillié tut le païs
Pur la venjance de Paris
Ki de Grece out ravi Eleine,
Dux Eneas a quelque peinne
De la grant ocise eschapa.   (Arnold edn., vol. 1, ll. 1–15)

This imperative to pen the history of a prestigious lineage[66] is a key element of Wace's other *roman*, of *Rou* or Rollo, which he dedicates around 1160 to Henry II Plantagenet of England and to Henry's wife Eleanor of Aquitaine. In the epilogue to this work (which was never completed), Wace charges the task of bringing it to fruition to the same Benoît de Sainte-Maure whose *Roman de Troie* was discussed above. Recounting the history of the dukes of Normandy, from the founding of the duchy in the tenth century by the Norman chieftain Rollo to the conquest of England by William the Conqueror from 1066 onwards, the *Rou* finishes at the reign of the last of William's sons, Henry I Beauclerc. This poem contains a narrative of the 'fact-finding visit' made by the chronicler to the enchanted fountain at Barenton, hidden in the darkest depths of the forest of Brocéliande ("donc Breton vont sovent fablant/une forest mult longue e lee"), but where he encountered neither fairies nor marvels of any kind.[67]

In his study of the vernacular historians of the twelfth and thirteenth centuries, Peter Damian-Grint evokes the way in which, in the *Rou*, Wace dismisses the witness accounts (uniquely oral) of *jongleurs* and other peddlers of rumors or fabulous tales of wonder. Nothing that is not backed up by a written source, he informs us, can be trusted or retained for his own narrative:[68]

---

[66] According to Boutet (1999, 59), the motivation behind the *Brut*, the *Rou* and the *Chronique des ducs de Normandie* was not so much 'genealogical celebration' as the desire to reconstitute the *History* of the British or Brithonic peoples, as inhabitants of the westernmost isles of Europe.

[67] Wace, *Roman de Rou*, ed. A. J. Holden, 3 vols., Société des Anciens Textes Français (Paris, 1970–73), vol. 2, ll. 6377–398.

[68] Cf. Damian-Grint (1999), 108–09.

A jugleours oï en m'effance chanter
Que Guillaume fist jadiz Osmont essorber,
Et au conte Riouf lez deus oilz crever,
Et Anquetil le prouz fist par enging tuer,
Et Baute d'Espaingne o un escu garder;
Ne sai noient de ceu, n'en puiz noient trover,
Quant je n'en ai garant n'en voil noient conter.
De la mort Anquetil ai ge oï parler,
Ochiz fu, ce soit on, n'en quier homme escouter,
Mez je ne sai comment, ne qui face a blasmer;
N'en voil por verité la menchonge affermer
Ne le voir, se jel sai, ne voil ge pas celer.
(Holden edn., vol. 1, ll. 1361–72)

The composition and writing of the *Rou* must have presented Wace
with forbidding challenges. We possess an initial version, quickly
abandoned for another written in a different meter (see the passage
quoted above) and known today as the *Chronique ascendante des ducs
de Normandie*. A second part also, written in the same style, was, in
turn, quickly abandoned, with the Anglo-Norman clerk only returning to his pen to finish it around 1170. These hesitations may explain
why Henry II was soon to charge Benoît with the task of writing a
new account of the *gestes* of his Norman ancestors.[69] The edition of
the *Rou* used today by specialists is that prepared by Tony Holden
for the Sociéte des Anciens Textes Français.[70] Anglophone readers
now have the opportunity to consult the annotated translation into
English prepared by Glyn Burgess for the Société Jersiaise,[71] whilst
francophone non-medievalists can consult extracts from the Holden
edition, accompanied by notes, plates, and a translation by René
Lepelley,[72] a brief quotation from which tells us more or less everything that is known about the life and career of Master Wace:

Si lon demande qui ço dist,
qui ceste estoire en romanz fist,
jo di e dirai que jo sui
Wace de l'isle de Gersui,

---

[69] See Van Houts (1984); Gouttebroze (1991), and *Brut* ed. & tr. Weiss, xii.

[70] Wace, *Roman de Rou*, ed. A. J. Holden.

[71] *The Roman de Rou of Wace*, ed. and trans. G. S. Burgess, Société Jersiaise (St.
Helier, 2002).

[72] Wace, *Guillaume le duc, Guillaume le roi. Extraits du Roman de Rou de Wace, poète
normand du XIIe siècle*, présentés et traduits par René Lepelley (Caen, 1987).

qui est en mer vers occident,
al fieu de Normendic apent.
En l'isle de Gersui fui nez;
a Chaem fui petiz portez,
illoques fui a letres mis,
pois fui longues en France apris.
Quant jo de France repairai,
a Chaem longues conversai;
de romanz faire m'entremis,
mult en ecris e mult en fis.
Par Deu aïe e par le rei
altre fors Deu servir ne dei—
m'en fu donnee, Deus li rende,
a Baieues une provende.
Del rei Henri segont vos di . . .
      (Holden edn., vol. 2, ll. 5299–317; repr. in Lepelley [1987], 5)

It is almost at the end of the *Roman de Rou* that we read a poignant *envoi* in which Wace tells us how Benoît de Sainte-Maure came to be entrusted with the job of finishing the history of the Norman dukes:

Die en avant qui dire en deit;
j'ai dit por Maistre Beneeit,
qui cest'ovre a dire a emprise
com li reis l'a desor lui mise;
quant li reis li a rové faire
laissier la dei, si m'en dei taire.
Li reis jadis maint bien me fist,
mult me dona, plus me pramist,
e se il tot doné m'eüst
ço qu'il me pramist, mielz me fust;
nel poi aveir, ne plout al rei,
mais n'est mie remés en mei.   (Holden edn., vol. 2, ll. 11419–30)

Benoît's own *Chronique des ducs de Normandie*, commenced around 1170, was finished around 1174 but without his going much further than the battle of Tinchebray and the death of Henry I of England. Borrowing his general structure from the Latin chronicle of William of Jumièges's *Gesta Normannorum ducum* in the redaction by Robert of Torigni,[73] it also relies on three other key sources. For the first part, ending with the death of Richard the fourth duke, it looks to Dudo

---

[73] *The Gesta Normannorum ducum of William of Jumièges, Orderic Vitalis, and Robert of Torigni*, 2 vols., ed. and trans. E. M. C. van Houts (Oxford, 1992–95).

of Saint-Quentin's *De Moribus et actis primorum Normanniae ducum*.[74] For
the reigns of the Conqueror and his sons, it is largely inspired by
the *Gesta Guillelmi* of William of Poitiers and Orderic Vitalis's *Historia
Ecclesiastica*.[75] Beginning with a distinctive cosmographical prologue,
a component previously unseen in a vernacular chronicle,[76] Benoît's
Chronique, like that of Wace, places great emphasis on the challenge
which a large-scale historical work presents to the translator of important sources: "granz est l'estuide e li labors . . . de si faite ovre trans-
later" (ll. 2,123 and 2,125). Elsewhere he writes of the *aspre labor*
(*e esmaiable e demoranz*) involved, and—by means of a metaphor evok-
ing fresco painting (the *industria* topos)—apologizes for the length of
time taken to finish the first part of the poem:[77]

> Ce peise mei que tant delaie,
> qu'ausi cum l'on plastrist e taint
> la maisiere sor quei l'on paint,
> por faire ses traiz plus formez,
> plus soutis e plus colorez,
> rai je lonc tens plastri por paindre
> sanz desveer e sanz mei faindre.
> Por c'i sui tant assiduios,
> Volenterif e dessiros
> que de ça fust l'ovre acomplie.   (Fahlin edn., ll. 42,062–71)

Unlike the *Roman de Troie*, the *Chronique des ducs de Normandie* features
neither matters of the heart nor the intrigues of romance. There are
plenty of digressions (the text comprises no fewer than 44,544 lines)
but the writer's overall approach is here completely different, as is
confirmed by several references in the *Chronique* to the authenticity
of the sources consulted. That said, the repetition (with variations)

---

[74] Dudo of Saint-Quentin, *De moribus et actis primorum Normanniae ducum*, ed. J. Lair
(Caen, 1865).
[75] Respectively: William of Poitiers (Guillaume de Poitiers), *Gesta Guillelmi*, ed. and
tr. M. Chibnall (1998); and Orderic Vitalis (Orderic Vital), *Historia Ecclesiastica*, ed.
M. Chibnall, 6 vols. (Oxford, 1969–1980), mainly Books IV and VII.
[76] P. Damian-Grint, 'Learning and Authority in Benoît de Sainte-Maure's
Cosmography.' *Reading Medieval Studies* 24 (1998), 25–52; and id., '"En nul leu nel
truis escrit": Research and Invention in Benoît de Sainte-Maure's "Chronique".'
Anglo-Norman Studies 21 (1999a), 11–30.
[77] Cf. Damian-Grint (1999), 104, for a commentary. Quotation is taken from
Benoît de Sainte-Maure, *Chronique des ducs de Normendie*, ed. Carin Fahlin, with Notes
by Sven Sandqvist and Glossary by O. Södergård, Bibliotheca Ekmaniania (ed. &
glossary); Acta Universitatis Lundensis S.1, 29 (notes), vols. 56 and 60 (edition); vol.
64 (glossary). Uppsala, 1951–54; 1967; 1979.

of the formulaic expression "Si com en l'istoire trovum" cannot disguise the chronicler's reticence to divulge their identities. For Benoît, the function of the historian is, above all, to offer to his readers and listeners a resolutely chronological narrative comprising *maint buen esample*. From this perspective, the study of history with its *buen enseignemenz* serves to improve still further the already upstanding and honest comportment of the courtly man,[78] thus distinguishing him even more clearly from the *vilain*. It is no surprise, therefore, to find in the poem an *excursus* on the Three Orders (I, 13,239–13,400) as well as some encyclopedia-like digressions categorized by Benoît as *doctrine e cognicion* (I, 2,132). He cites Isidore of Seville, Pliny, and St. Augustine as authorities. These traits seem to betray a desire on Benoît's part to write a universal history, but the overall purpose of his work still remains unclear. As Jean Blacker has pointed out, it is even difficult to determine what the notion of *estoire* meant to Benoît. Was it to do with 'writing history' in the literal sense? Or, rather, perhaps about 'telling a story' to amuse or educate his listeners, and to support the Plantagenet dynasty? Whatever the case, Benoît's poem remains a hybrid mix of historical intention and fictional subject matter.[79] However, is it not the case that most entries for 'history' in modern French dictionaries still propagate confusion in this sphere by offering their users definitions such as 'an account of real or imaginary acts and events'?[80]

The Advent of Prose

Although the *chanson de geste* had offered its readers a rudimentary form of historical discourse and was to remain—throughout the Middle Ages and well beyond—a hugely popular form of literary entertainment, the soaring popularity of the historical *roman* may be a symptom of increasing impatience with the epic form on the part of a noble audience impatient for more and more history. The *chanson de geste* was no longer valid as a historical form.[81] We have also

---

[78] Blacker (1994), 47 et passim.
[79] Blacker (1994), 52.
[80] Blacker (1994), 207–08 and n. 88.
[81] Cf. Spiegel (1987).

seen that it gave expression to the aspirations of a caste, representing its members by way of what *we* might see as an anachronistic
rather than an historically accurate ordering of events (using as its
reference the prestige of Charlemagne and his household knights),
while the historical *roman* would soon foreground the origins and destinies of lineages contemporary with its author. Meanwhile, the other
major historical form in evidence at the beginning of the twelfth
century, the hagiographical narrative, focused primarily on the relationship between God and his saints. The chronological and causal
aspects determining the destiny of an individual were, thus, a secondary consideration. The verse histories composed between 1140 and
1190, in contrast, offered aristocratic audiences unfamiliar with clerical
and Latin culture a first point of contact with their own history.[82]

However, towards the end of the twelfth century there was a critical reaction. On the one hand, certain moralizing clerks, clearly
lacking imagination, became more volubly hostile to the octosyllabic
Arthurian fiction of Chrétien de Troyes and his continuators. For
these upright critics, *historia* had become *fabula*—and even *vanitas*
('Laissiez *Cliges* et *Perceval*/Qui les cuers perce et trait à val/Et les
romanz de vanité . . .').[83]

On the other hand, in written works self-consciously presenting
themselves as 'truthful' there were protests which took the form 'nus
contes rimés n'est verais'; witness the different adaptations of the
Chronique du pseudo-Turpin written towards the beginning of the thirteenth century. The first of these, the *Chronique dite Saintongeaise* of
Nicolas de Senlis, seems to confuse recourse to verse and recourse
to the affabulating activity of minstrels in their oral performances:

> N'est si mançonge non ço qu'il en dient e en chantent cil jogleor ne
> cil conteor; nus contes rimés no est verais, car tot est mançongie ço
> qu'il en dient, car il n'en sievent rienz fors quant per oïr dire.[84]

Here, one could reasonably argue, is sufficient proof of the impend-
ing waning of the *auctoritas* of verse in the face of prose, which from

---

[82] Damian-Grint (1999), 189.
[83] See G. Spiegel, *Romancing the Past. The Rise of Vernacular Prose Historiography
in Thirteenth-Century France*, California U. P. (Berkeley-Los-Angeles-London, 1993),
12. Also Molly Lynde-Recchia, *Prose, Verse, and Truth-Telling in the Thirteenth Century*,
French Forum (Nicholasville, 2000), 18–21.
[84] Bertrand de Bar-sur-Aube, *Chronique dite Saintongeaise*, ed. André de Mandach in
Beihefte zur Zeitschrift für Romanische Philologie, vol. 120 (Tübingen, 1970), 256.

then on (it was presumably supposed), would guarantee the authenticity of any serious work. However, Damian-Grint cautions us against reaching over-hasty conclusions, reminding us that assertions of this kind were occasionally made in *verse* compositions at around the same time, an observation which he supports with a quotation taken from a short *chanson de geste*, the *Mort Aymerie de Narbonne* by Bertrand de Bar-sur-Aube (ca. 1180):

> Nus hom ne puet chançon de geste dire
> Que il ne mente la ou li vers define,
> As mos drecier et a tailler la rime.
> Ce est bien voirs, gramaire le devise,
> Uns hom la fist de l'anciene vie,
> Hues ot non, si la mist un livre
> Et seela el mostier Saint Denise.
> La ou les jestes de France sont escrites.   (ll. 3055–62, ed. Couraye
>   du Parc, Paris: Firmin Didot, 1884; Johnson Reprint, 1966)

Damian-Grint also refers us to Benoît's *Chronique des ducs de Normandie* and to its author's desire to avoid all *fauseté* and *mençonge*:

> Translatee ai l'estoire e dite
> D'eissi cum l'ai trovee escrite;
> N'ai mis fauseté ne mençonge.   (*Chronique*, vv. 42035–37)

What predominates in these assertions is the desire, always present, to speak the truth. The same is true of the prose version of the *Chronique du pseudo-Turpin* attributed to 'Jehan', in which the writer links for the first time a spurning of rhyme to the consequential integrity of his *estoire*:

> Et por ce que rime se velt afeiter de moz conqueilliz hors de l'estoire, voust li cuens que cist livres fust sanz rime selonc le latin de l'estoire que Torpins l'arcevesque de Reins traita et escrist si com il le vit t oï.[85]

What counts, after all, is not to distort the narrative—believed to be the spoken words of Archbishop Turpin himself, companion of Charlemagne and of Roland. The text of the Nicolas version even offers the reader a letter of confirmation supposedly written by the legendary archbishop himself, in which he claims that what he has written down was witnessed by his very own eyes.[86]

---

[85] See Jehan, *The Old French Johannes Translation of the Pseudo-Turpin Chronicle*, ed. Ronald N. Walpole (Berkeley and Los Angeles, 1976), 10–14.

[86] Bertrand de Bar-sur-Aube, *Chronique dite Saintongeaise*, ed. de Mandach, 257.

A second approach to this extremely controversial question has been made by Gabrielle Spiegel, who points out that all six versions of the *Chronique du pseudo-Turpin* were composed within the sphere of influence of several lords from northeast France, including the counts of Boulogne and Saint-Pol.[87] Here were patrons anxious to find renewed justification for their sense of their own aristocratic and chivalric value within the kingdom of France; to win back and safeguard their autonomy by the creation of new myths; and, by so doing, to promote an anti-Capetian, comital ideology that was needed more than ever before, at a time when a powerful king was striving to limit their means and powers of intervention.[88] The thesis is an attractive one, but may it not have been the case also that these writers, by adopting a medium that was just beginning to be viewed as unimpeachable with regard to veracity, had found the ideal way to confer respectability upon material which, in fact, bordered on the fanciful? Whatever the truth of the matter, other factors must have come into play—as Michael Zink has also suggested:

> Until the end of the twelfth century, French literature is written entirely in verse, and prose literature did not exist. The only vernacular prose texts, few in number, have a utilitarian function that is either judicial or pedagogical. These could be charters, vernacular translations of the scriptures or sermons. This situation is characteristic of all young literature. Everywhere verse appears before prose.[89]

Underlying the new distribution of literary forms at the end of the Middle Ages, Zink goes on to argue, is the idea that prose discourse, as compared to verse, is seen to be "richer and susceptible of infinite expansion or development",[90] whilst Boutet observes that prose offered more scope for reflective analysis.[91] In any case, from the thirteenth century onwards, prose is increasingly employed as the vehicle for narrative works, "whilst poetry tends to be squeezed into the corset of fixed forms".[92]

Given that prose had won credibility with several 'non-professional' historians and apologists at the beginning of the thirteenth century,

---

[87] Spiegel (1993), 13–14.
[88] Spiegel (1993), 1; cf. esp. 79–82.
[89] Zink (1992), 175; my translation.
[90] Zink (1992), 177.
[91] Boutet (1999), 5.
[92] Zink (1992); my translation.

including two very different witnesses of the Fourth Crusade, Robert de Clari and Geoffroi de Villehardouin,[93] it is hardly surprising to note a gradual extension of its use to new versions of texts originally composed in verse, such as the 'rewrite' of the romance *Fouke le Fitz Waryn*, in which one can still see the 'joins' of the verses, newly sewn together in a continuous prose form.[94] We also should remember the rather obvious fact that by the thirteenth century, Latin prose had provided for a very long time the formal vehicle for Holy Scripture.[95] This may account, in part, for the increasingly confident role that it was to play from ca. 1215 to 1220 in the great vernacular Arthurian prose cycles of Tristan, Lancelot, and, especially, the Grail. Based as they were on the interweaving of often complex and lengthy intrigues, the prose romances of the first half of the thirteenth century needed a medium that was at once versatile, malleable, and tinged with at least some of the prestige of Scripture. By the end of the Middle Ages, prose had become the normal mode of narration, without, as yet, totally excluding verse as a vehicle for historiography.[96]

Conclusion

The works examined in this essay have in common the desire to transmit a heritage, preserve a record, edify their readers, and articulate aspects of their own world to their contemporaries, by recourse to narratives ostensibly dealing with a partly or wholly legendary past. In all of them, and throughout the period considered, there is an intriguing tension between what Dominique Boutet calls *Histoire* and *histoire*, between *historia* and *fabula*.[97] What we would recognize today as written history only begins to emerge, gradually and tentatively, from the *chroniques* of the later Middle Ages, influenced to

---

[93] Discussed in my essay 'Contemporary and "Eyewitness" History' in this volume.

[94] Damian-Grint (1999), 177; *Fouke Le Fitz Waryn*, ed. J. Hathaway, P. Ricketts, C. Robson and A. Wiltshire, Anglo-Norman Texts Society, vols. 26–28 (Oxford, 1975).

[95] Zink (1992), 187.

[96] Again, see 'Contemporary and "Eyewitness" History' for a discussion of verse and prose historiography in the fourteenth century.

[97] Boutet (1999), 3, n. 2, and esp. p. 24 for a discussion of the issues involved (remote, referential *History* serving in both the *roman d'antiquité* and *chanson de geste* as a platform [*support*] for fiction allowing contemporary society to explore and reflect upon its own immediate present).

a large degree, perhaps, by the already impressive example furnished by writers such as Villehardouin in the early thirteenth century. The *mémoire* also will have an important role to play, from the recollections of Jean de Joinville to the *Mémoires* of Philippe de Commynes. What makes the twelfth century so fascinating to study, however, is the sheer variety it evinces in terms of the textual transmission of different, but in many respects complementary, visions of the past: epic, commemorative (of a golden age), apologetic, or, as we have seen, legendary. Rather than disparage these early writers about the past for their naïveté, we should perhaps read them as a means of making us more aware of the subtle processes and motivations at work in all writing that purports to tell us the truth[98] about the past (or indeed anything else of importance), in whatever age it was conceived and recorded.

---

[98] On the importance of truth-telling, truth claims and 'authenticity' in the chronicles of the late twelfth and early thirteenth centuries, see Boutet (1999), 31; also Guenée (1981).

BIBLIOGRAPHY

Note: full references to primary sources are found in the footnotes.

Secondary Sources

Abate, G. (1934). "Le fonti storiche della cronaca di fra Mariano da Firenze". *Miscellanea Francescana* 34 (1934): 46–52.

———. (1949). "Il 'Liber Epilogorum' di Frà Bartolomeo da Trento O.P." Pp. 269–92 in Miscellenea Pio Paschini I. Rome.

Ainsworth, P. F. (1990). *Jean Froissart and the Fabric of History. Truth, Myth and Fiction in the "Chroniques"*. Oxford.

———. (1993). 'Asneton, Chandos et "X": Jean Froissart et l'éclosion des mythes.' *"Et c'est la fin pour quoi sommes ensemble": Hommage à Jean Dufournet. Littérature, Histoire et Langue du Moyen Age*. Vol. I. Paris.

———. (1994). 'Collationnement, montage et "Jeu Parti": le début de la campagne espagnole du Prince Noir (1366–67) dans les "Chroniques" de Jean Froissart', *Le Moyen Age* 100, 3–4 (1994), 369–411.

———. (1998). 'Configurations of Transience in Jean Froissart's "Chroniques": Intimations of "(Old) Mortality".' *Froissart Across the Genres*, ed. D. Maddox and S. Sturm-Maddox. Gainesville.

———. (1999). 'Heralds, Heraldry and the Colour Blue in the "Chronicles" of Jean Froissart'. *The Medieval Chronicle*, ed. E. Kooper, "Costerus New Series" vol. 120. Amsterdam-Atlanta.

———. (2000). 'Froissart and His Second Book.' *War, Government and Power in Later Medieval France*, ed. Christopher Allmand. Liverpool.

Albert, P. (1898). "Johann Meyer, ein oberdeutscher Chronist des 15. Jahrhunderts". *Zeitschrift für die Geschichte des Oberrheins* N.F. 13 (1898): 255–63.

———. (1906). 'Johannes Meyer, ein oberdeutscher Chronist des 15. Jahrhunderts'. *Zeitschrift für die Geschichte des Oberrheins* 52 N.F. 21 (1906): 504–10.

Albu, E. (1994). 'Dudo of Saint-Quentin: The Heroic Past Imagined'. *The Haskins Society Journal* 6 (1994): 111–18.

Allen, M. I. (1994). "History in the Carolingian Renewal: Frechulf of Lisieux (fl. 830), His Work and Influence". Ph.D. Diss., University of Toronto.

———. (1998). "The Chronicle of Claudius of Turin". Pp. 288–319 in *After Rome's Fall: Narrators and Ssources of Early Medieval History*, ed. A. C. Murray. Toronto.

Alós R., de (1912). "El Cardenal de Aragón, fray Nicolás Rossell". Pp. 15–60 in *Escuela española de Argueologia e Historia en Roma*, Cuadernos de Trabajos 1. Madrid.

Altaner, B., and A. Stuiber (1966). *Patrologie: Leben, Schriften und Lehre der Kirchenväter*. 6th ed. Freiburg-im-Breisgau.

Althoff, G. (1988). "Genealogische Fiktionen und die historiographische Gattung de Genealogie im hohen Mittelalter". Pp. 67–79 in *Staaten Wappen Dynastie: XVIII. Internationaler Kongreß für Genealogie und Heraldik*. Innsbruck.

Althoff, G. and S. Coué (1992). "Pragmatische Geschichtsschreibung und Krisen". Pp. 95–129 in *Pragmatische Schriftlichkeit im Mittelalter: Erscheinungsformen und Entiwicklungsstufen*, ed. H. Keller, K. Grubmüller, and N. Staubach. Munich.

Amory, P. (1997). *People and Identity in Ostrogothic Italy, 489–554*. Cambridge.

Anatolios, K. (1998). *Athansius: The Coherence of His Thought*. London.

Andreolli, B., et al., eds. (1991). *Repertorio della cronachistica emiliano-romagnola: secc. IX–XV*, ed. B. Andreolli, D. Gatti, R. Greci, G. Ortalli, L. Paolini, G. Pasquali,

A. I. Pini, P. Rossi, A. Vasina, and G. Zanella, with an introduction by A. Vasina. Rome.

Angenendt, A. (1994). "Der eine Adam und die vielen Stammväter. Idee und Wirklichkeit der Origo gentis im Mittelalter". Pp. 27–52 in *Herkunft und Ursprung. Historiche und mythische Formen der Legitimation*, ed. Peter Wunderli. Sigmaringen.

Angermeier, H. (1958). 'Begriff und Inhalt der Reichsreform'. *Zeitschrift für Rechtsgeschichte, German*. Abteilung 75 (1958): 181–205.

Angus, S. (1906). *The Sources of the First Ten Books of Augustine's* De civitate Dei. Princeton.

Archambault, P. (1974). *Seven French Chroniclers, Witnesses to History*. Syracuse, NY.

Arnaldi, G. (1963). *Studi sui cronisti della Marca Trevigiana nell'età di Ezzelino da Romano*. Rome.

——— (1966). "Il notaio cronista e le cronache cittadine in Italia". Pp. 293–309 in *La storia del diritto nel quadro delle scienze storiche. Atti del Primo Congresso internazionale della Società italiana di storia del diritto*. Florence.

———. (1982). "Codagnello Giovanni". Pp. 562–68 in *Dizionario biografico degli Italiani* 26 (1982).

Arnaldi, G., and L. Capo (1976). "Cronisti di Venezia e della Marca Trevigiana dalle origini alla fine del secolo XIII". Pp. 387–423 in *Storia della cultura veneta*, vol. 1, *Dalle origini al Trecento*. Vicenza.

Arnold, K. (1983). "Johannes von Winterthur". Pp. 816–18 in *Die deutsche Literatur des Mittelalters, Verfasserlexikon IV*. Berlin and New York.

Auer, A. (1933). *Ein neuaufgefundener Katalog der Dominikaner Schriftsteller*. Institutum Historicum Fratrum Praedicatorum Dissertations Historicae 2. Paris.

Auerbach, E. (1946). *Mimesis. Dargestellte Wirklichkeit in der abendländischen Literatur*. Bern. In English: *Mimesis: The Representation of Reality in Western Literature*. Trans. Willard R. Trask. Princeton.

———. (1958). *Literatursprache und Publikum in der lateinischen Spätantike und im Mittelalter*. Bern. In English: *Literary Language and the Public in Late Latin Antiquity and in the Middle Ages*. Trans. Ralph Manheim. Princeton.

Avril, F., M.-T. Gousset, and B. Guenée (1987). *Jean Fouquet. Die Bilder der Grandes Chroniques de France*. Graz.

Bader, K. S. (1954). 'Kaiserliche und ständische Reformgedanken in der Reichsreform des endenden 15. Jahrhunderts'. *Historisches Jahrbuch* 73 (1954): 74–94.

Baer, L. (1973). *Die illustrierten Historienbücher des 15. Jahrhunderts*. Straßburg [originally published in 1903].

Bagge, S. (1989). 'Theodoricus Monachus—Clerical Historiography in Twelfth-century Norway'. *Scandinavian Journal of History* 14 (1989): 113–33.

———. (1990). 'Snorri Sturluson und die europäische Geschichtsschreibung'. *Skandinavistik* 20 (1990): 1–19.

———. (1991). "Propaganda, Ideology and Political Power in Old Norse and European Historiography: A Comparative View". Pp. 199–208 in *L'historiographie médiévale en Europe. Actes du colloque... du 29 mars au 1er avril 1989*, ed. J.-P. Genet. Paris.

———. (1991b). *Society and Politics in Snorri Sturluson's* Heimskringla. Berkeley, Calif.

Balzani, U. (1883–84). *Early Chroniclers of Europe: Italy*. London.

Banaszkiewicz, J. (1977). 'Kronika Dzierzwy—problem wykładu dziejów ojczystych w XIV wieku'. *Studia >ródłóznawcze* 22 (1977): 89–95.

———. (1979). *Kronika Dzierzwy XIV—wieczne kompendium historii ojczystej*. Wrocław.

———. (1998). *Polskie dzieje bajeczne Wincentego Kadłubka*. Wrocław.

Bancourt, P. (1982). 'De l'imagerie au réel: l'exotisme oriental d'Ambroise.' *Images et signes de l'Orient dans l'occident médiéval*. Senefiance, vol. 11, 1982, 27–39.

Banniard, M. (1978). 'L'aménagement de l'Histoire chez Grégoire de Tours: à propos de l'invasion de 451 (HL II 5–7)'. *Romanobarbarica* 3 (1978): 5–38.

Barnard, L. W. (1976). "Bede and Eusebius as Church Historians". Pp. 106–24 in *Famulus Christi: Essays in Commemoration of the Thirteenth Centenary of the Birth of the Venerable Bede*, ed. G. Bonner. London.

Barnes, T. D. (1981). *Constantine and Eusebius*. Cambridge, Mass.

——. (1982). 'Aspects of the Backgroud of the City of God'. *Revue de l'Université d'Ottawa/University of Ottawa Quarterly* 52 (1982): 64–80.

——. (1993). *Athansius and Constantinus*. Cambridge, Mass.

Barnish, S. J. B. (1984). 'The Genesis and Completion of Cassiodorus' Gothic History'. *Latomus* 43 (1984), 336–61.

Barsotti, R. (1928). 'I manoscritti della 'Cronica' e degli 'Annales' del Convento Dominicano di S. Caterina di Pisa'. *Memorie Domenicane* 45 (1928): 125–39.

Barth, H. (1984). 'Die Dominikuslegende im ersten Lektionar Humberts von Romans (1246)'. *Archivum Fratrum Praedicatorum* 54 (1984): 83–112.

Bates, D. (1982). *Normandy before 1066*. London.

Baumgartner, E. (1994). 'Vers, prose et fiction narrative (1150–1240).' *Shifts and Transpositions in Medieval Narrative. A Festschrift for Dr Elspeth Kennedy*, ed. Karen Pratt. Cambridge.

Bäuml, F. (1980). 'Varieties and Consequences of Medieval Literacy and Illiteracy'. *Speculum* 55 (1980): 237–65.

Bautier, R.-H. (1975). "La place de l'abbaye de Fleury-sur-Loire dans l'historiographie française du IXe au XIIe siècle". Pp. 25–33 in *Études ligériennes d'histoire et d'archéologie médiévale*, ed. René Louis. Auxerre.

——. (1994). "L'École historique de l'abbaye de Fleury d'Aimon à Hugues de Fleury". Pp. 59–72 in *Histoires de France, historiens de la France*, ed. Y.-M. Bercé and P. Contamine. Actes du colloque international Reims, 14 et 15 mai 1993. Paris.

Becker, Ph.-A. (1944). 'Jordan Fantosme, la guerre d'Ecosse: 1173–1174.' *Zeitschrift für romanische Philologie* 64 (1944), 449–556.

Beckmann, J. H. (1925). *Studien zum Leben und literarischen Nachlass Jacobs von Soest O.P.* Leipzig.

Beer, J. M. A. (1981). *Narrative Conventions of Truth in the Middle Ages*. Geneva.

——. *Early Prose in France*. Kalamazoo, MI: Medieval Institute Publications, 1992.

Bell, A. (1936). 'Maistre Geffrei Gaimar.' *Medium Aevum* 7 (1936), 184–98.

——. (1976). 'Gaimar as Pioneer'. *Romania* 97 (1976), 462–80.

Bennett, M. (1988). 'Wace and Warfare.' *Anglo-Norman Studies* 11 (1988), 37–57.

Bennett, P. (1997). 'La Chronique de Jordan Fantosme: épique et public lettré au XIIe siècle.' *Cahiers de Civilisation Médiévale* 40 (1997), 37–56.

Benton, J., *Self and Society in Medieval France: the Memoirs of Abbot G. of Nogent*, Toronto: Med. Acad. Reprints for Teaching, 15, 1984.

Berg, D. (1983). 'Studien zur Geschichte und Historiographie der Franziskaner im flämischen und norddeutschen Raum im 13. und beginnenden 14. Jahrhundert'. *Franziskanische Studien* 65 (1983): 114–55.

——. (1985). 'Historische Reflexion und Tradition. Die "Fioretti" und die franziskanische Geschichtsschreibung bis zur Mitte des 14. Jahrhunderts'. *Wissenschaft und Weisheit* 48 (1985): 82–101.

Berlioz, J. et al. (1992). *Les exempla medievaux*. Carcassonne.

Bertagna, M. (1982). "Per un nuovo incontro con fra Mariano da Firenze", *Studi Francescani* 79 (1982), 473–9.

Beumann, H. (1950). *Widukind von Korvei. Untersuchungen zur Geschichtsschreibung und Ideengeschichte des 10. Jahrhunderts*. Weimar.

——. (1964). "Gregor von Tours und der Sermo Rusticus". Pp. 69–98 in *Spiegel der Geschichte. Festgabe für Max Braubach zum 10. April 1964*, ed. K. Repgen and S. Skalweit. Münster.

——. (1970). "Historiographische Konzeption und politische Ziele Widukinds von

Corvey". Pp. 875–94 in *La storiografia altomedievale, Settimane di studio del Centro italiano di studi sull'alto medioevo* 17. Spoleto. [Repr. in Beumann, *Wissenschaft vom Mittelalter. Ausgewählte Aufsätze.* Pp. 71–108. Cologne, 1970].

Bieler, L. (1962). 'The Celtic Hagiographer'. *Studia Patristica* 5 (1962): 243–65.

———. (1963). "Pioneers of Irish Christianity Abroad: Columba and Columbanus". Pp. 65–94 in *Ireland: Harbinger of the Middle Ages*, ed. L. Bieler. London.

Billanovich, G. (1958). "Gli umanisti e le cronache medioevali". Pp. 103–37 in *Italia medioevale e umanistica*, ed. G. Billanovich. Padua.

Binkley, P., ed. (1997). *Pre-Modern Encyclopaedic Texts, Proceedings of the second COMERS Congress, Groningen, 1–4 July 1996.* Leiden, New York and Cologne.

Binns, J. (1994). *Ascetics and Ambassadors of Christ.* Oxford.

Blacker, J. (1994). *The Faces of Time: Portrayal of the Past in Old French and Latin Historical Narrative of the Anglo-Norman Regnum.* Austin.

Blacker-Knight, J. (1984). 'Wace's Craft and His Audience. Historical Truth, Bias, and Patronage in the Roman de Rou.' *Kentucky Romance Quarterly* 31 (1984), 355–62.

Bláhová, M., ed. (1987). *Kroniky doby Karla IV.* Prague.

———. (1995). *Staročeská kronika tak řečeného Dalimila v kontextu středověké historiografie latinského kulturního okruhu a její pramenná hodnota.* Staročeská kronika tak řečeného Dalimila 3. Prague.

Bloch, R. H. (1983). *Etymologies and Genealogies: A Literary Anthropology of the French Middle Ages.* Chicago.

———. (1986). "Genealogy as a Medieval Mental Structure and Textual Form". Pp. 135–56 in *La Litterature historiographique des origines á 1500*, vol. 1, ed. H. U. Gumbrecht, U. Link-Heer, and P.-M. Spangenberg. Heidelberg.

Boardman, S. (1997). 'Chronicle Propaganda in Fourteenth-Century Scotland: Robert the Steward, John of Fordun and the "Anonymous Chronicle"'. *Scottish Historical Review* 76 (1997): 23–43.

Boehm, L. (1957). "Der wissenschaftstheoretische Ort der historia im frühen Mittelalter. Die Geschichte auf dem Wege zur 'Geschichtswissenschaft'". Pp. 663–93 in *Speculum historiale. Geschichte im Spiegel von Geschichtsschreibung und Geschichtsdeutung*, ed. C. Bauer, L. Boehm, and M. Müller. Munich.

———. (1969). "Nomen gentis Normannorum. Der Aufstieg der Normannen im Spiegel der normannischen Historiographie". Pp. 623–704 in *I Normanni e la loro espansione in Europa nell'alto medioevo.* Settimane di studio sull'alto medioevo 16. Spoleto.

Bogdanow, F. (1981). 'The Tradition of the Troubadour Lyrics and the Treatment of the Love Theme in Chrétien de Troyes' "Erec Et Enide".' *Court and Poet: Selected Proceedings of the Third Congress of the International Courtly Literature Society, Liverpool 1980*, ed. G. S. Burgess, A. D. Deyermond, W. H. Jackson, A. D. Mills, and P. T. Ricketts, ARCA: "Classical and Medieval Texts, Papers and Monographs", 5. Liverpool.

Borst, A. (1978). *Mönche am Bodensee.* Sigmaringen.

———. (1998). *Die karolingische Kalenderreform.* MGH, Schriften 46. Hannover.

Bortolami, S. (1995). "Da Rolandino al Mussato: tensioni ideali e senso della storia nella storiografia padovana di tradizione 'repubblicana'". Pp. 53–86 in *Il senso della storia nella cultura medievale italiana (1100–1350): quattordicesimo convegno di studi, Pistoia, 14–17 maggio 1993.* Pistoia.

Boserup, I., ed. (1975). *Saxostudier. Saxo-kollokvierne ved Københavns universitet.* Opuscula Græcolatina 2. Copenhagen.

Bosl, K. (1962). "Die germanische Kontinuität im deutschen Mittelalter (Adel-König-Kirche)". Pp. 1–25 in *Miscellanea Mediaevalia. Veröffentlichungen des Thomas-Instituts an der Universität Köln I, Antike und Orient im Mittelalter*, ed. P. Wilpert. Berlin. [Repr. in Bosl, *Frühformen der Gesellschaft im mittelalterlichen Europa. Ausgewählte Beiträge zu einer Strukturanalyse der mittelalterlichen Welt.* Pp. 80–105. Vienna, 1964.]

Bossard, R. (1944). *Über die Entwicklung der Persönlichkeitsdarstellung in der mittelalterlichen Geschichtsschreibung.* Zürich.

Boulay, F. R. H. du (1981). "The German town chronicles". Pp. 445–69 in *The writing of history in the Middle Ages. Essays presented to Richard William Southern*, ed. R. H. C. Davis and J. M. Wallace-Hadrill. Oxford.

Boureau, A. (1984). *La légende dorée. Le système narratif de Jacques de Voragine (d. 1298)*. Paris.

——. (1987). 'Vitae Fratrum, Vitae Patrum. L'ordre dominicain et le modèle des pères du désert au XIIIᵉ siècle'. *Mélanges de l'école française de Rome, Moyen Âge-Temps Modernes* 99 (1987): 79–100.

Boutet, D. (1993). *La Chanson de geste: forme et signification d'une écriture épique du Moyen Age*. Paris.

——. (1999). *Formes littéraires et conscience historique aux origines de la littérature française (1100–1250)*. Paris.

Bowersock, G. W. (1995). *Martyrdom and Rome*. Cambridge.

Brandt, W. J. (1966). *The Shape of Medieval History. Studies in Modes of Perception*. New Haven.

Breisach, E. (1983). *Historiography: Ancient, Medieval and Modern*. Chicago.

——. (1994). *Historiography. Ancient, Medieval and Modern*. 2nd ed. Chicago.

Brie, F. W. D. (1905). *Geschichte und Quellen der mittelenglischen Prosachronik The Brute of England oder The Chronicles of England*. Marburg.

Brooke, C. (1974). *Medieval Church and Society*. London.

Brown, P. (1995). *Authority and the Sacred: Aspects of the Christianization of the Roman World*. Cambridge.

——. (1998). "Higden's Britain". Pp. 103–16 in *Medieval Europeans. Studies in Ethnic Identity and National Perspectives in Medieval Europe*, ed. A. P. Smyth. Houndsmill.

Brown, R. E. "Hermeneutics in the Jerome Bib. Comm.

——. (1994). *The Death of the Messiah: From Gethsemane to the Grave. A Commentary on the Passion Narratives in the Four Gospels*. 2 vols. New York.

——. (1968). "Hermeneutics". Pp. 605–23 in *The Jerome Biblical Commentary, with a foreward by Augustin Cardinal Bea*. Englewood Cliffs, NJ.

Brown, S. (1993). *The Origins of Christianity: A Historical Introduction to the New Testament*. Rev. ed. New York.

Brunel-Lobrichon, G., A.-F. Leurquin-Labie, and M. Thiry-Stassin (1994). "L'hagiographie de langue française sur le Continent ixᵉ–xvᵉ siècle". Pp. 291–371 in Philippart, et al. (1994–96), vol. 2.

Brunhölzl, F. (1991). *L'époque carolingienne*. Vol. 1/2 of Histoire de la littérature latine du moyen âge. Updated text translated by H. Rochais, with an expanded bibliography prepared by J.-P. Bouhot. Turnhout.

Brüning, G. (1917). 'Adamnans Vita Columbae und ihre Ableitungen'. *Zeitschrift für celtische Philologie* 11 (1917): 213–304.

Buchner, R. (1963). "Die politische Vorstellungswelt Adams von Bremen", *Archiv für Kulturgeschichte* 45 (1963), 15–59.

Buda, M. (1989). 'Early Historical Narrative and the Dynamics of Textual Reference.' *Romanic Review* 80 (1989), 1–17.

Büdinger, M. (1900). *Die Universalhistorie im Mittelalter. Denkschriften der Kaiserlichen akademie der Wissenschaften, philosophisch-historische Classe*, 46.I–II. Vienna.

Bullough, D. (1986). "Ethnic History and the Carolingians: An Alternative Reading of Paul the Deacon's Historia Langobardorum". Pp. 85–105 in *The Inheritance of Historiography 350–900*, ed. C. Holdsworth and T. P. Wiseman Exeter.

Buridant, C. (1973). 'Motifs et formules dans la Conquête de Constantinople de Villehardouin.' *Revue des Sciences Humaines* (1973), 355–76.

Burgess, R. (2001). "The Gallic Chronicle of 452: A New Critical Edition with a Brief Introduction". Pp. 85–100 in *Society and Culture in Late Antique Gaul: Revisiting the Sources*, ed. R. W. Mathisen and D. Shanzer. Aldershot.

Burgess, R. W. (1999). *Studies in Eusebian and Post-Eusebian Chronology. Historia Einzelschriften* 135. Stuttgart.

Burke, P. (1991). 'History of Events and the Revival of Narrative.' *New Perspectives on Historical Writing*. Cambridge.

Burr, D. (1993). *Olivi's Peaceable Kingdom. A Reading of the Apocalypse Commentary*. Philadelphia.

Busby, K. (1986). 'Courtly Literature and the Fabliaux: Some Instances of Parody.' *Zeitschrift für romanische Philologie* 102 (1986), 67–87.

Busch, J. W. (1997). *Die Mailänder Geschichtsschreibung zwischen Arnulf und Galvaneus Flamma, die Beschäftigung mit der Vergangenheit im Umfeld einer oberitalienischen Kommune vom späten 11. bis zum frühen 14. Jahrhundert*, Münstersche Mittelalter-Schriften 72. Munich.

Bynum, C. (1987). *Holy Feast and Holy Fast: The Religious Significance of Food to Medieval Women*. Berkeley.

Cameron, A. (1993). *The Later Roman Empire A.D. 284–430*. Cambridge, MA.

Campagnola, S. da (1966). "Il francescanesimo nelle cronache di Giordano da Giano, Tommaso di Eccleston e Salimbene de Adam" *Studi Francescani* 2 (1966), 243 ff.

——. (1974). *Le origine francescane come problema storiografico*. Perugia.

Canetti, L. (1996). L'invenzione della memoria. Il culto e l'immagine di Domenico nella storia dei primi frati Predicatori (1221–1260). Spoleto.

——. (1996b). "Intorno all' 'idolo delle origini': la storia dei primi frati Predicatori", in *I frati Predicatori nel Duecento, Quaderni di storia religiosa*. Verona. Pp. 9–51.

Cannarozzi, C. (1930). "Ricerche sulla vita di fra Mariano da Firenze". *Studi Francescani* 27 (1930), 31–71.

Capitani, O. (1964). "Motivi e momenti di storiografia medioevale italiana: secc. V–XIV", Pp. 779–800 in *Nuove questioni di storia medioevale*. Milan.

——. (1988). "La storiografia medievale", in *La storia: i grandi problemi dal Medioevo all'eta contemporanea*, vol. 1, *Il medioevo*, ed. N. Tranfaglia and M. Firpo (Turin, 1988), 757–92.

Carpentier, E. (1991). "Les historiens et le pouvoir Capétien: d'Helgaud de Fleury à Guillaume le Breton". Pp. 129–139 in *L'historiographie médiévale en Europe*, ed. J.-P. Genet, Paris.

Carruthers, M. (1990). *The Book of Memory: A Study of Memory in Medieval Culture*. Cambridge.

Cassard, J. (1985). 'Un historien au travail: Pierre Le Baud'. *Memoires de la Sociéte d'histoire et d'archaeologie de Bretagne* (1985): 67–95.

Castignoli, P. (1986). "Giovanni Codagnello, notaio, cancelliere del comune di Piacenza e cronista". Pp. 273–302 in *Il Registrum magnum del comune di Piacenza*, ed. E. Falconi and R. Peveri. Milan.

Catalán, D. (1962). *De Alfonso X al Conde de Barcelos. Cuatro estudios sobre el nacimiento de la historiografía romance en Castilla y Portugal*. Madrid.

——. (1963). 'El taller historiográfico Alfonsí. Métodos y problemes en el trabajo compilatario'. *Romania* 84 (1963): 354–75.

——. (1982). "España en su historiografia: De objeto a sujeto de la historia". Pp. 9–67 in Ramón Menéndez Pidal, *Los españoles en la Historia*. Madrid.

Champion, P. (1907). *Cronique Martiniane*. Paris.

Chaurand, J., 'La conception de l'histoire de G. de Nogent (1053–1124), *Cahiers de Civilisation Médiévale* 8 (1965), 381–395.

Chenu, M. D. (1927). 'Auctor, Acta, Autor.' *Bulletin Du Cange* 3 (1927), 81–86.

Chesnut, G. F. (1977). *The First Christian Histories: Eusebius, Socrates, Sozomen, Theodoret, and Evagrius*. Paris.

Chibnall, M. (1984). *The World of Orderic Vitalis*. Oxford.

Ciklamini, M. (1978). *Snorri Sturluson*. Boston.

Cirot, G. (1904). *Les histoires générales d'Espagne entre Alphonse X et Philippe II (1284–1556)*. Bordeaux and Paris.

Cirot, J. (1913). *De Operibus Historicis Iohannis Aegidii Zamorensis*. Burdeos.
Clanchy, M. T. (1993). *From Memory to Written Record, England, 1066–1307*. 2nd ed. Cambridge, Mass.
Clark, C. (1971). "The narrative mode of The Anglo-Saxon Chronicle before the Conquest". Pp. 215–35 in *England Before the Conquest. Studies in Primary Sources presented to Dorothy Whitelock*, ed. P. Clemoes and K. Hughes. Cambridge.
Clasen, S. (1967). *Legenda Antiqua S. Francisci. Untersuchung über die nachbonaventuranischen Franziskusquellen, Legenda Trium Sociorum, Speculum Perfectionis, Actus b. Francisci et Sociorum eius und verwandtes Schrifttum.* Studia et Documenta Franciscana 5. Leyden.
Cochrane, E. (1981). *Historians and Historiographers in the Italian Renaissance*. London.
Coleman, J. (1992). *Ancient and Medieval Memories: Studies in the Reconstruction of the Past.* Cambridge.
Collard, F. (1994). "Histoire de France en latin et histoire de France en langue vulgaire: la traduction du Compendium et gestis Franorum de Robert Gaguin au début du XVIᵉ siècle". Pp. 91–118 in *Histoires de France, historiens de la France.* Actes du colloques international, Reims, 14 et 15 mai 1993, ed. Y.-M. Bercé and P. Contamine. Paris.
——. (1995). 'Formes du récit et langue historique dans le Compendium de origine et gestis Francorum de Robert Gaguin'. *Bibliothèque d'Humanisme et Renaissance* 57 (1995): 67–82.
——. (1996). *Un historien au travail à la fin du XVᵉ siècle: Robert Gaguin.* Travaux d'Humanisme et Renaissance 301. Geneva.
Collet, O. (1993a). *Etude philologique et littéraire sur "Le Roman de Jules César".* "Publications Romanes et Françaises", ed. Alexandre Micha, Jacques Monfrin, vol. 207. Geneva.
Collingwood (1961). *Idea of History*. 1946. London.
Collins, R. (1991). *Early Medieval Europe 300–1000.* London.
——. (1994). "Isidore, Maximus and the Historia Gothorum". Pp. 345–58 in *Historiographie im frühen Mittelalter*, ed. A. Scharer and G. Scheibelreiter. Vienna.
——. (1998). "The 'Reviser' Revisited: Another Look at the Alternative Version of the Annales Regni Francorum". Pp. 191–213 in *After Rome's Fall: Narrators and Sources of Early Medieval History. Essays presented to Walter Goffart*, ed. A. C. Murray. Toronto.
Colson, F. H. Translated by (1935). *Philo.* Vol. 6. Loeb Classical Library. Cambridge.
Commynes, P. de. (2001). *Lettres*, ed. Joël Blanchard. "Textes Littéraires Français" vol. 534. Geneva.
Cowdrey, H. E. J. (1980–81). 'Bede and the English People'. *Journal of Religious History* 11 (1980–81): 501–23.
Cox, P. (1983). *Biography in Late Antiquity: A Quest for the Holy Man.* Berkeley.
Cresi, D. (1964). 'Elenchi di illustri Frati minori in un'opera inedita di Mariano da Firenze'. *Archivum Franciscanum Historicum* 57 (1964): 191–9.
Creytens, R. (1960). 'Les écrivains dominicans dans la chronique d'Albert de Castello'. *Archivum Fratrum Praedicatorum* 30 (1960): 227–313.
Crick, J. (1986). 'Update: The Manuscripts of the Works of Geoffrey of Monmouth: A New Supplement.' *Arthurian Literature*, ed. Richard Barber. Vol. VI. Woodbridge.
——. (1987). 'Update: The Manuscripts of Geoffrey of Monmouth's "Historia Regum Britanniae".' *Arthurian Literature*, ed. Richard Barber. Vol. VII. Woodbridge.
Croke, B. (1983). "The Origins of the Christian World Chronicle". Pp. 116–31 in *History and Historians in Late Antiquity*, ed. B. Croke and A. M. Emmett. Sydney.
——. (1987). 'Cassiodorus and the Getica of Jordanes'. *Classical Philology* 82 (1987): 117–34. [Repr. in Croke, *Christian Chronicles and Byzantine History, 5th–6th Centuries.* Pp. 117–34. London, 1992.]
Croizy-Naquet, C. (1998). 'Les figures du jongleur dans L'estoire de la Guerre sainte.' *Le Moyen Age* 114 (1998), 229–56.
d'Alatri, M. (1988). *La cronaca di Salimbene. Personaggi e tematiche.* Bibliotheca Seraphico-Capuccina 35. Rome.

d'Alatri, M., and J. Paul (1992). *Salimbene da Parma.Testimone e cronista*. Bibliotheca Seraphico-Capuccina 41. Rome.

Dábrowski, J. (1964). *Dawne dziejopisarstwo polskie (do roku 1480)*. Wrocław.

Damian-Grint, P. (1996). 'Truth, Trust, and Evidence in the Anglo-Norman "Estoire".' *Anglo-Norman Studies* 18 (1996), 68–72.

———. (1997). '"Estoire" as Word and Genre.' *Medium Aevum* 66 (1997), 189–99.

———. (1998). 'Learning and Authority in Benoît de Sainte-Maure's Cosmography.' *Reading Medieval Studies* 24 (1998), 25–52.

———. (1999). *The New Historians of the Twelfth-Century Renaissance. Inventing Vernacular Authority*. Woodbridge.

———. (1999a). '"En nul leu nel truis escrit": Research and Invention in Benoît De Sainte-Maure's "Chronique".' *Anglo-Norman Studies* 21 (1999a), 11–30.

Damsholt, N. (1992). "Tiden indtil 1560". Pp. 11–51 in *Danmarks historie*. Vol. 10 of *Historiens historie*, ed. S. Mørch. Copenhagen.

Darlington, R. R. 'Anglo-Norman Historians.' London: Birkbeck College, University of London, 1947.

Davidse, J. (1982). 'The Sense of History in the Works of the Venerable Bede'. *Studi Medievali* 23 (1982): 647–95.

Davis, C. (1992). 'Cultural Assimilation in the Anglo-Saxon Royal Genealogies'. *Anglo-Saxon England* 21 (1992): 23–36.

Davis, R. H. C. (1978). 'The *Carmen de Hastingae Proelio*', *English Historical Review*, 367 vol. 93, 1978, 241–61.

———. (1981). et Wallace-Hadrill, J. M. (eds). *The Writing of History in the Middle Ages. Essays Presented to Richard William Southern*. Oxford.

———. (1976). *The Normans and their Myth*. London.

de Lubac, H. (1959–64). *Exégèse médiévale: les quatre sens de l'Écriture*. 4 vols. Paris.

Dean, R. J. (1976). "Nicholas Trevet, Historian". Pp. 328–52 in *Medieval Learning and Literature. Essays presented to R. W. Hunt*, ed. J. J. G. Alexander and M. T. Gibson. Oxford.

Del Monte, A. (1950). 'La storiografia fiorentina dei secoli XII e XIII'. *Bullettino del l'Istituto storico italiano per il Medio Evo e archivio muratoriano* 62 (1950): 175–264.

Delahaye, H. (1959). *L'oeuvre des Bollandistes à travers trois siécles*. 2nd ed. Brussels.

———. (1962). *The Legends of the Saints*. Translated by D. Attwater. New York.

Delbouille, M. (1953). 'Le Témoignage de Wace sur la légende arthurienne.' *Romania* 74 (1953), 172–99.

Delisle, L. (1885). *Anciens catalogues des évêques des Églises de France*. Pp. 386–454. Histoire Littéraire de la France 22. Paris.

Deliyannis, D. M. (1997). 'A Biblical Model for Serial Biography: the Liber Pontificalis and the Books of Kings'. *Revue Benedictine* 107 (1997): 15–23.

Delogu, P. (1994). *Introduzione allo studio della storia médiévale*. Bologna.

Delorme, F. F. (1911). 'Catalogus Friburgensis sanctorum fratrum minorum'. *Archivum Franciscanum Historicum*, 4 (1911): 544–58.

Dembowski, P. (1963). *La Chronique de Robert de Clari, étude de la langue et du style*. Toronto.

Dempf, A. (1962). *Sacrum Imperium: Geschichts- und Staatsphilosophie des Mittelalters und der politischen Renaissance*, 3rd ed. Darmstadt.

Deptuła, C. (2000). Galla Anonima mit genezy Polski. Studium Z historiozofii i hermeneutyki symboli dziejopisarstwa średhiowiecznego, Lublin.

DeRossi, J. B., and L. Duchesne (AS). *Martyrologium hieronymianum*. Part I, Acta Sanctorum, Nov. vol. 2 (Paris, 1887); Part II (Brussels, 1931).

Derwich, M. (1985). "Janko z Czarnkowa a Kronika wielkopolska". Pp. 127–62 in *Acta Universitatis Wratislaviensis 800*. Historia 50. Wrocław.

Desbonnets, T. (1967). 'Généalogie des biographies primitives de S. François'. *Archivum Franciscanum Historicum* 60 (1967): 273–316.

Diller, G. T. (1984). *Attitudes chevaleresques et réalités politiques chez Froissart.* Geneva.

Dilthey, W. (1976). *Selected Writings.* Edited and translated by H. P. Rickman. Cambridge.

Dinzelbacher, P. (1991). *Revelationes.* Typologie des sources du moyen âge occidental 57. Turnhout.

———. (1995). *Heilige oder Hexen? Schicksale auffällige Frauen in Mittelalter und Frühneuzeit.* Munich.

Dondaine, A. (1946). 'Le dominicain français Jean de mailly et la Légende dorée'. *Archives d'histoire dominicaine* 1 (1946): 53–102.

Dörrie, H. (1938). 'Die Griechischen Romane und das Christentum'. *Philologus* 93 (1938): 273–76.

Downing, J. (1963). 'Jesus and Martyrdom'. *Journal of Theological Studies* 14 (1963): 279–93.

du Plessis, M. (1968). 'Les aveux d'ignorance de Grégoire de Tours sont-ils contradictoires du caractère de sa langue?'. *Revue des langues romanes* 78 (1968): 53–69.

Dübler, C. E. (1943). *Geschichtschreibung im spanischen Mittelalter.* Barcelona.

Dubois, B. and J.-L. Lemaitre (1993). *Sources et méthodes de l'hagiographie médiévale.* Paris.

Dubois, J. (1967). 'La composition des anciennes listes épiscopales'. *Bulletin de la Société Nationale des Antiquaires de France* 110 (1967): 74–104.

———. (1976). 'Les listes épiscopales témoins de l'organisation ecclésiastique et de la transmission des traditions'. *Revue d'histoire de l'Église de France* 62 (1976): 9–23.

———. (1978). *Les martyrologes du Moyen Age latin.* Typologie des Sources du Moyen Âge occidental 26. Turnhout.

Duby, G. (1967). *Adolescence de la chrétienté occidentale 980–1140.* Geneva.

———. (1976). *Le Temps des cathédrales. L'art et la société 980–1420.* Coll. "Bibliothèque des Histoires", ed. Pierre Nora. Paris.

———. (1980). *The Chivalrous Society.* Translated by C. Postan. Berkeley and Los Angeles.

———. (1984). *Guillaume le Maréchal ou le meilleur chevalier du monde.* Paris.

Duchesne, L. (1882). 'Le Liber pontificalis en Gaule au VIᵉ siècle'. *Mélanges d'archéologie et d'histoire de l'École de Rome de l'École de Rome* 2 (1882): 277–89.

———. (1907–15). *Les fastes épiscopaux de l'ancienne Gaule.* 3 vols. Paris.

Dufournet, J. (1966). *La Destruction des mythes dans les Mémoires de Philippe de Commynes.* Paris.

———. (1973). *Les Ecrivains de la IVᵉ Croisade: Villehardouin et Clari.* 2 vols. Paris.

Duggan, C. and A. Duggan (1980). "Ralph de Diceto, Henry II and Becket with an Appendix on Decretal Letters". Pp. 59–81 in *Authority and Power. Studies on medieval law and government presented to Walter Ullmann on his seventieth birthday*, ed. B. Tierney and P. Linehan. Cambridge.

Duggan, J. J. (1987). 'The Experience of Time as a Fundamental Element of the Stock of Knowledge in Medieval Society.' *Grundriss der Romanischen Literaturen des Mittelalters*, Vol. XI, ed. U. Link-Heer, P.-M. Spangenberg and H. U. Gumbrecht: "La littérature historiographique des origines à 1500". Heidelberg.

Dumézil, G. (1959). *Les Dieux des Germains: essai sur la formation de la religion scandinave.* Paris.

Dumville, D. N. (1983). 'Update: The Manuscripts of Geoffrey of Monmouth's "Historia Regum Britanniae".' *Arthurian Literature*, ed. Richard Barber. Vol. III. Woodbridge.

———. (1985). 'An Early Text of Geoffrey of Monmouth's "Historia Regum Britanniae" and the Circulation of Some Histories in Twelfth-Century Normandy.' *Arthurian Literature*, ed. Richard Barber. Vol. IV. Woodbridge.

———. (1985a). 'Update: The Manuscripts of Geoffrey of Monmouth's "Historia Regum Britanniae": Addenda, Corrigenda, and Alphabetical List.' *Arthurian Literature*, ed. Richard Barber. Vol. IV. Woodbridge.

——. (1985b). 'Update: The Manuscripts of Geoffrey of Monmouth's "Historia Regum Britanniae": A Second Supplement.' *Arthurian Literature*, ed. Richard Barber. Vol. V. Woodbridge.

——. (1986). 'The Historical Value of the "Historia Brittonum".' *Arthurian Literature*, ed. Richard Barber. Vol. VI. Woodbridge.

Dunn-Lardeau, B., ed. (1986). *Legenda aurea: sept siècles de diffusion. Actes du colloque international sur la Legenda aurea: texte latin et branches vernaculaires à l'Université du Québec à Montréal.* Montreal and Paris.

Dupré, E. (1952). *Roma dal comune di popolo alla signoria pontificia.* Bologna.

——. (1956). *Aspetti della città medievale italiana.* Bologna.

——. (1958). *La città medievale in Europa.* Bologna.

Dyer, N. J. (1990). "Alfonsine Historiography: The Literary Narrative". Pp. 141–58, 248–51 in *Emperor of Culture. Alfonso X the Learned of Castile and His Thirteenth-Century Renaissance*, ed. R. I. Burns. Philadelphia.

Eckert, W. P. (1986). "Jakob von Soest. Prediger und Inquisitor". Pp. 125–38 in *Von Soest-aus Westfalen. Wege und Wirkung abgewanderter Westfalen im späten Mittelalter und in der frühen Neuzeit*, ed. H.-D. Heimann. Paderborn.

Edwards, A. S. G. (1978–81). 'The Influence and Audience of the Polychronicon: Some Observations'. *Proceedings of the Leeds Philosophical and Literary Society (Literary and History Section)*, 17 (1978–1981): 113–19.

Eggert, W. (1994). "'Franken und Sachsen' bei Notker, Widukind und anderen". Pp. 514–530 in *Historiographie im frühen Mittelalter*, ed. Anton Scharer and Georg Scheibelreiter. Vienna.

Eley, P. (1994). 'How Long is a Trojan War? Aspects of Time in the "Roman de Troie" and its Sources.' *Shifts and Transpositions in Medieval Narrative. A Festschrift for Dr Elspeth Kennedy*, ed. Karen Pratt. Cambridge.

Elm, K. (1972). 'Franziskus und Dominikus. Wirkungen und Antriebskräfte zweier Ordensstifter'. *Saeculum. Jahrbuch für Universalgeschichte* 23 (1972): 127–47.

Emanuel, H. D. (1966). 'Geoffrey of Monmouth's "Historia Regum Britannie": A Second Variant Version.' *Medium Aevum* 35 (1966), 103–10.

Emms, R. (1995). "The Historical Traditions of St. Augustine's Abbey, Canterbury". Pp. 159–68 in *Canterbury and the Norman Conquest. Chuches, Saints and Scholars 1066–1109*, ed. R. Eales and R. Sharpe. London and Rio Grande.

Engels, L. J. (1979). 'Once more the *Carmen de Hastingae Proelio*', *Anglo-Norman Studies* 2 (1979), 3–14.

Engels, O. (1989). "Der Reichsbischof in ottonischer und frühsalischer Zeit". Pp. 135–75 in *Beiträge zur Geschichte und Struktur der mittelalterlichen Germania Sacra*, ed. I. Crusius. Veröffentlichungen des Max Planck-Instituts für Geschichte 93. Göttingen.

English Historical Documents (1969–81). *English Historical Documents.* Edited by D. C. Douglas, G. W. Greenaway, H. Rothwell, and A. R. Myers. Vols. 2–4. London.

Ennen, E. (1972). *Die europäische Stadt des Mittelalters.* Göttingen.

Erickson, C. (1972). 'Bartholomew of Pisa, Francis exalted: De conformitate'. *Mediaeval Studies* 34 (1972): 253–74.

Erikson, A. (1965). 'The Problem of Authorship in the Chronicle of Fredegar'. *Eranos* 63 (1965): 47–76.

Eysenhard, M. (1750). Hermanni Gygantis ordinis fratrum minorum Flores temporum seu Chronicon. Pp. 140–163 in *Flores temporum-Fortsetzung, 1355–1513*, ed. J. G. Meuschen. 2nd ed. Leiden.

Fanning, S. (1991). 'Bede, Imperium, and the Bretwaldas'. *Speculum* 66 (1991): 1–26.

Faral, E. (1936). 'Geoffroy de Villehardouin. La question de sa sincérité.' *Revue historique* 177 (1936), 530–82.

Farmer, Dom H. (1962). 'William of Malmesbury's Life and Works.' *Journal of Ecclesiastical History* 13 (1962), 39–54.

Fasoli, G. (1970). 'Rileggendo il 'Liber Pontificalis' di Agnello Ravennate'. *Settimane di studio del Centro italiano di studi sull'alto medio evo* 17 (1970): 457–95, 711–18.

Favrod, J. (1993). *La Chronique de Marius d'Avenches (455–581): Texte, traduction et commentaire.* 2nd ed. Cahiers lausannois d'histoire médiévale 4. Lausanne.

Fechter, W. (1987). "Meyer, Johannes OP". Pp. 474–89 in *Die Deutsche Litteratur des Mittelalters. Verfasserlexikon.* Vol. 6, 2nd ed. Berlin and New York.

Feichtinger, B. (1998), "Glaube versus Aberglaube: Der Untergang Roms in den Augen von Zeitgenossen". Pp. 145–66 in *Chartulae: Festschrift für Wolfgang Speyer. Jahrbuch für Antike und Christentum. Ergänzungsband* 28. Münster.

Feller, R., E. Bonjour (1962). *Geschichtsschreibung der Schweiz. Vom Spätmittelalter zur Neuzeit.* 2 vols. Basel and Stuttgart.

Fernández Conde, J. (1971). 'La obra del obispo ovetense D. Pelayo en la historiografía española'. *Boletín del Instituto de Estudios Asturianos* 25 (1971): 249–91.

Fichtenau, H. (1975). 'Herkunft und Sprache Johanns von Viktring', *Carinthia* 1 (1975): 25–39.

Filippini, E. (1890). 'Notizie storico-biografiche intorno all'archivio di San Francesco di Fabriano'. *Miscellanea Francescana* 5 (1890): 180.

Finegan, J. (1998), *Handbook of Biblical Chronology: Principles of Time Reckoning in the Ancient World and Problems of Chronology in the Bible.* 2nd ed. Peabody, Mass.

Finucane, R. C. (1997). *The Rescue of Innocents: Endangered Children in Medieval Miracles.* New York.

Fix, H., ed. (1998). *Snorri Sturluson: Beiträge zu Werk und Rezeption.* Ergänzungsbände zum Reallexikon für Germanische Altertumskunde 18. Berlin.

Fleischman, S. (1983). 'On the Representation of History and Fiction in the Middle Ages.' *History and Theory* 22, 3 (1983), 278–310.

Fleith, B., ed. (1991). *Studien zur Überlieferungsgeschichte der lateinischen Legenda Aurea.* Brussels.

Flori, Jean. 'Qu'est-ce qu'un bacheler? Etude historique du vocabulaire dans les chansons de geste du XIIᵉ siècle.' *Romania* 96 (1975), 289–314.

Flutre, L. F. (1932). *Li Fait des Romains dans les littératures française et italienne du XIIIᵉ au XVIᵉ siècle.* Paris.

Folz, R. (1950). *Le Souvenir et la légende de Charlemagne dans l'Empire germanique médiéval.* Paris.

——. (1953). *L'idée d'empire en occident du Vᵉ au XIVᵉ siècle.* Paris.

——. (1983/84). 'Sur la légende d'origine des Francs'. *Mémoires de l'Académie des sciences, arts et belles-lettres de Dijon* 126 (1983/84): 187–99.

Fossier, F. (1977). 'Les chroniques de fra Paolo da Gualdo et de fra Elemosina. Premières tentatives historiographiques en Ombrie'. *Mélanges de l'école française de Rome. Moyen âge-temps modernes* 89 (1977): 411–83.

——. (1977b). 'La ville dans l'historiographie franciscaine de la fin du xiiiᵉ et du début du xivᵉ siècle'. *Mélanges de l'école française de Rome. Moyen âge-temps modernes* 89 (1977): 641–55.

Fowler, David C. (1995). *The Life and Time of John Trevisa*, Medieval Scholar, Seattle.

Frank, B. (1973). *Das Erfurter Peterskloster im 15. Jahrhundert. Studien zur Geschichte der Klosterreform in der Bursfelder Union.* Göttingen.

Frappier, J. (1946). 'Les Discours dans la Chronique de Villehardouin.' *Etudes romanes dédiées à Mario Roques.* Paris.

——. (1946a). 'Le Style de Villehardouin dans les discours de sa chronique.' *Bulletin of the John Rylands Library of Manchester* 30 (1946a), 57–70.

Freese, J. H. ed. (1975). Aristotle. "Poetics". Cambridge.

Frend, W. H. C. (1965). *Martyrdom and Persecution in the Early Church.* Oxford.

Frey, K. (1887). 'Arnaldus de Sarano, "Chronica"'. *Vierteljahrschrift für Kultur und Literatur der Renaissance* 2 (1887): 229–43.

Friis-Jensen, K., ed. (1981). *Saxo Grammaticus. A Medieval Author Between Norse and Latin Culture.* Copenhagen.

Frohne, R. (1992). *Die Historienbibel des Johannes von Udine (Ms. 1000 Vad).* Bern.

Fuhrmann, H. (1963). 'Der Fälschungen im Mittelalter. Überlegungen zum mittel-alterlichen Wahrheitsbegriff'. *Historische Zeitschrift* 197 (1963): 529–54.

Gál, G. (1997). "The chronicle of Nicolaus Minorita". Pp. 337–44 in *Editori di Quaracchi, 100 anni dopo bilancio e prospettive. Atti del colloquio internazionale, Roma 29–30 Maggio 1995, Scuola superiore di studi medievali e francescani, Pontificio Ateneo Antonianum*, ed. A. Cacciotti and B. Faes de Mottoni, Rome.

Galbraith, V. H. (1945). 'Good Kings and Bad Kings in Medieval English History.' *History* 30, 112 (1945), 119–32.

——. (1951). *Historical Research in Medieval England*. London.

Gallais, P. (1966). 'La Variant Version de l'*Historia Regum Britanniae* et le *Brut* de Wace.' *Romania* 87 (1966), 1–32.

Gatti, D. (1991). "Codagnello, Giovanni". Pp. 267–71 in *Repertorio della cronachistica emiliano-romagnola: secc. IX–XV*, ed. B. Andreolli et al. Rome.

Gatto, L. (1997). "La cronaca di Giordano da Giano e le edizioni che la riguardono". Pp. 425–43 in *Editori di Quaracchi, 100 anni dopo*. Rome.

Geary, P. J. (1994). *Phantoms of Remembrance: Memory and Oblivion at the End of the First Millennium*. Princeton, N.J.

——. (1988). *Before France and Germany: The Creation and Transformation of the Merovingian World*. New York.

Genet, J. P. (1977). "Cartulaires, registres et histoire: l'exemple anglais". Pp. 95–138 in *Le métier d'historien au Moyen Âge. Études sur l'historiographie médiévale*, ed. B. Guenée. Paris.

Genicot, L. (1975). *Les Généalogies*. Turnhout.

——. (1975b). "Princes Territoriaux et sang carolingien. La *Genealogia comitum Buloniensium*". Pp. 217–306 in *Études sur les principautés lotharingiennes*. Louvain.

Gerberding, R. A. (1987). *The Rise of the Carolingians and the Liber Historiae Francorum*. Oxford.

Gillingham, J. (1990). 'The Context and Purposes of Geoffrey of Monmouth's History of the Kings of Britain'. *Anglo-Norman Studies* 13 (1990): 99–118.

Glasser, R. (1972). *Time in French Life and Thought*. Tr. C. G. Pearson. Manchester.

Gmelin, H. (1927). *Die Personendarstellung bei den florentinischen Geschichtsschreibern der Renaissance*. Leipzig and Berlin.

Godzich, W. and Kittay, J. (1987). *The Emergence of Prose. An Essay in Prosaics.* Minneapolis.

Goetz, H. W. (1985). "Die 'Geschichte' im Wissenschaftssystem des Mittelalters". Pp. 165–213 in F.-J. Schmale, *Funktion und Formen mittelalterlichen Geschichtsschreibung*. Darmstadt.

——. (1988). 'Zum Geschichtsbewusstsein in der alemannisch-schweizerischen Klosterchronistik des hohen Mittelalters (11.–13. Jahrhundert)'. *Deutsches Archiv* 44 (1988): 455–88.

——. (1989). "Das Bild des Abtes in den alamanischen Klosterchroniken des hohen Mittelalters". Pp. 135–53 in *Ecclesia et regnum. Beiträge zu einer Geschichte von Kirche, Recht und Staat im Mittelalter*, ed. F.-J. Schmale. Bochum.

——. (1999). *Geschichtsschreibung und Geschichtsbewusstsein im hohen Mittelalter*. Vorstellungs-welter des Mittelalters 1. Berlin.

Goez, W. (1958). *Translatio Imperii: Ein Beitrag zur Geschichte des Geschichtsdenkens und der politischen Theorien im Mittelalter und in der frühen Neuzeit*. Tübingen.

Goffart, W. (1963). 'The Fredegar Problem Reconsidered'. *Speculum* 38 (1963): 206–241. [Repr. in Goffart. *Rome's Fall and After*. Pp. 311–54. London, 1989.]

——. (1966). *The Le Mans Forgeries. A Chapter From History of Church Property in The Ninth Century*. Cambridge, Mass.

——. (1983). 'Foreigners in Gregory of Tours'. *Florilegium* 4 (1983): 80–99. [Repr. in Goffart. *Rome's Fall and After*. Pp. 275–91. London, 1989.]

——. (1986). 'Paul the Deacon's Gesta Episcoporum Mettensium and the Early Design of Charlemagne's Succession'. *Traditio* 42 (1986): 59–93.

——. (1987). "From Historiae to Historia Francorum and Back Again: Aspects of the Textual History of Gregory of Tours". Pp. 255–74 in *Religion, Culture, and Society in the Early Middle Ages. Studies in Honor of Richard E. Sullivan*, ed. T. F. X. Noble and J. Contreni. Kalamazoo, Mich. [Repr. in Goffart, *Rome's Fall and After*. Pp. 55–76. London, 1989].

——. (1988). *The Narrators of Barbarian History (A.D. 550–800): Jordanes, Gregory of Tours, Bede, Paul the Deacon*. Princeton.

——. (1995). 'Two Notes on Germanic Antiquity Today'. *Traditio* 50 (1995): 9–30.

Goldstein, R. J. (1993). *The Matter of Scotland. Historical Narrative in Medieval Scotland*. Lincoln, Neb.

Golinelli, P. (1991). *Città e culto dei santi nel medioevo Italiano*. Bologna.

——. (1994). "Italia Settentrionale (1130–1220)". Pp. 125–153 in Philippart, et al. (1994–96), vol. 1.

Goodich, M. (1982). *Vita perfecta: The Ideal of Sainthood in the Thirteenth Century*. Monographien zur Geschichte des Mittelalters 25. Stuttgart.

——. (1991). 'Oneiromantie im Mittelalter: Jüdische und christliche Perspectiven'. *Psychologie und Geschichte* 3 (1991): 1–6.

——. (1996). "Una santa bambina, una santa dei bambini: l'infanzia di Elisabetta di Turingia (1207–1231)". Pp. 91–114 in vol. 1 of *Storia dell'infanzia*, ed. E. Becchi and D. Julia. Bari.

——. (1998). *Other Middle Ages. Marginal Groups in the Medieval Period*. Philadelphia.

Gouttebroze, J.-G. (1981). 'Henry II Plantagenêt, patron des historiographes anglo-normands de langue d'oïl.' *La Littérature Angevine Médiévale, Actes du colloque du samedi 22 Mars 1980*. Maulévrier.

——. (1991). 'Pourquoi congédier un historiographe: Henri II et Wace (1155–1174).' *Romania* 112 (1991), 289–310.

Goyau, G. (1926). "Les étranges destinées du Livre des Conformités". Pp. 90–147 in *Saint Francis of Assisi: 1226–1926. Essays in Commemoration*, ed. W. W. Seton. London.

Grabar, A. (1946). 'Martyrium'. In *Recherches sur le culte des reliques et l'art chrétien antique*. Vol. 2. Paris.

Granier, Th. (1998). "Histoire, dévotion et culture à Naples (VIII^c–XI^c siècles)". Unpublished thesis. Université d'Aix-Marseille I.

Gransden A. (1974). *Historical Writing in England*. Vol. 1. C. 550 to 1307. London.

——. (1975). 'Propaganda in English Medieval Historiography'. *Journal of Medieval History* 1 (1975): 363–81.

——. (1982). *Historical Writing in England*. Vol. 2. C. 1307 to the Early Sixteenth Century. London.

——. (1990–91). 'The chronicles of medieval England and Scotland'. *Journal of Medieval History* 16 (1990): 129–50; and 17 (1991): 217–43.

——. (1990). 'Prologues in the historiography of Twelfth-Century England.' *England in the Twelfth Century*. Proceedings of the 1988 Harlaxton Symposium, ed. Daniel Williams, Woodbridge.

——. (1992). *Legends, Traditions and History in Medieval England*. London.

Grant, R. M. (1980). *Eusebius as Church Historian*. Oxford.

Graves E. B. (1975). *A Bibliography of English History to 1485*. Oxford.

Grisward, J. H. (1970). 'A Propos du thème descriptif de la tempête chez Wace et chez Thomas d'Angleterre.' *Mélanges offerts à Jean Frappier*. Vol. i. Geneva.

Gruber, J., et al. (1977). "Biographie". Pp. 199–213 in vol. 1 of *Lexikon des Mittelalters*.

Grundmann, H. (1957). *Geschichtsschreibung im Mittelalter: Gattungen, Epochen, Eigenart*. Gottingen.

Gschwantler, O. (1976). "Die Sage von Alboin und Rosimund". Pp. 214–54 in *Festschrift für Otto Höfler zum 75. Geburtstag*, ed. H. Birkhan. Vienna.

——. (1979). 'Formen langobardischer mündlicher Überlieferung'. *Jahrbuch für internationale Germanistik* 11 (1979): 58–85.

——. *Histoire et culture historique dans l'occident médiéval*. Collection "Historique". Paris: Aubier, 1980.

Guenée, B. (1973). 'Histoires, annales, chroniques. Essai sur les genres historiques au Moyen Age'. *Annales: economies, sociétés, civilisations* ns. 28 (1973): 977–1016.

——. (1977). 'Y a-t-il une historiographie médiévale?' *Revue historique* 258 (1977), 261–75.

——, éd. (1978). *Le Métier d'historien au Moyen Age*. Paris.

——. (1980). *Histoire et culture historique dans l'Occident medieval*. Paris.

——. (1982). 'L'histoire entre l'éloquence et la science. Quelques remarques sur le prologue de Guillaume de Malmesbury à ses "Gesta Regum Anglorum".' *Académie des Inscriptions et Belles-Lettres*, comptes rendus de l'année 1982 (1982), 357–70.

——. (1984). 'Histoire et Chronique. Nouvelles réflexions sur les genres historiques au Moyen Age.' *La Chronique et l'histoire au Moyen Age*, ed. D. Poirion. Paris.

——. (1985). "L'histoire et la compilation au xiii^c siècle". *Journal des Savants* 78 (1985): 119–35.

——. (1986). "Les Grandes Chroniques de France. Le Roman aux roys (1274–1518)". Pp. 189–214 in *Les lieux de memoire*, vol. 2: *La nation*, ed. P. Nora. Paris.

——. (1987). 'Histoire d'un succès.' *Les Grandes Chroniques de France. Reproduction en fac-similé des miniatures de Fouquet. Manuscrit français 6465 de la Bibliothèque Nationale de Paris*, ed. François Avril, Marie-Thérèse Gousset, Bernard Guenée. Paris.

Guéret-Laferté M. (1994). *Sur les routes de l'empire mongol. Ordre et rhétorique des relations de voyage aux xiiie et xiv^f siècles*. Nouvelle bibliothèque du moyen âge, 28. Paris.

Guerrieri, R. (1933). 'Le cronache e le agiografie francescane medioevali Gualdesi ed i loro rapporti con altre cronache et leggende agiografiche umbre'. *Miscellanea Francescana* 33 (1933): 198–241.

Guimarães, A. de (1937). 'Autour de la chronique de Jacques de Soest et de ses éditions'. *Archivum Fratrum Praedicatorum* 7 (1937): 290–304.

Guyotjeannin, H. (1995). *Salimbene de Adam, un chroniqueur franciscain*, Témoins de l'histoire. Turnhout.

Gunn, D. M., and D. N. Fewell (1993). *Narrative in the Hebrew Bible*. Oxford.

Guzman, G. G. (1974). 'The Encyclopedist Vincent of Beauvais and his Mongol Extracts from John of Plano Carpino and Simon of Saint-Quentin'. *Speculum* 49 (1974): 287–306.

Haeusler, M. (1980). *Das Ende der Geschichte in der mittelalterlichen Weltchronistik*. Beihefte zum Archiv für Kulturgeschichte 13. Cologne and Vienna.

Hammerstein, N. (1989). "Geschichte als Arsenal. Geschichtsschreibung im Umfeld deutscher Humanisten". Pp. 19–32 in *Geschichtsbewußtsein und Geschichtsschreibung in der Renaissance*, ed. A. Buck, T. Klaniczay, and S. K. Németh. Leiden.

Handschuh, G.-P. (1982). *Bistumsgeschichtsschreibung im ottonisch-salischen Reichskirchensystem. Studien zu den sächsischen Gesta episcoporum des 11. bis frühen 13. Jahrhunderts*. Diss. Phil. Tübingen.

Hankey, A. T., ed. (1984). *Ricobaldi Ferrariensis, Compendium Romanae Historiae*. Edited by A. T. Hankey. 2 vols. Rome.

Hanley, C. (2001). 'Reading the Past through the Present: Ambroise, the Minstrel of Reims and Jordan Fantosme.' *Mediaevalia* 20. Proceedings of an interdisciplinary conference held at the University of Hull, April 1999: "Framing the Text: Reading Tradition and Image in Medieval Europe", ed. and intr. by Kate L. Boardman, Catherine Emerson and Adrian P. Tudor, with a preface by Derek Pearsall (2001), 263–81.

——. (2001a). 'The Portrayal of Warfare in Old French Literature *c.* 1150–*c.* 1270', Ph.D thesis, University of Sheffield, Sheffield, 2001a.

Hannick, C. (1995). 'Povest' vremennych let'. Pp. 137–138 in *Lexikon des Mittelalters* 7.

Hanning, R. W. (1966). *The Vision of History in Early Britain: From Gildas to Geoffrey of Monmouth*. New York.

Haskins, C. H. *The Renaissance of the Twelfth Century*. Cambridge, MA.

Hauck, K. (1955). 'Lebensnormen und Kultmythen in germanischen Stammes- und Herrschergenealogien'. *Saeculum* 6 (1955): 186–223.

——. (1978). "The Literature of House and Kindred Associated with Medieval Noble families, illustrated from Eleventh- and Twelfth-century Satires on the Nobility". In *The Medieval Nobility: Studies on the Ruling classes of France and Germany from the Sixth to the Twelfth Century*, ed. and trans. T. Reuter. Amsterdam. [Translation of "Haus- und sippengebundene Literatur mittelalterlicher Adelsgeschlechter von Adelsatiren des 11. und 12. Jahrhunderts her erläutert". In *Geschichtsdenken und Geschichtsbild im Mittelalter*, ed. W. Lammers. Darmstadt, 1961.]

Haug, W. (1975). 'Andreas Heuslers Heldensagenmodell: Prämissen, Kritik und Gegenentwurf'. *Zeitschrift für deutsches Altertum* 104 (1975): 273–92.

Hay, D. (1977). *Annalists and Historians. Western Historiography from the Eighth to the Eighteenth Centuries.* London: Methuen & Co, 1977.

——. (1952). *Polydore Vergil. Renaissance Historian and Man of Letters.* Oxford.

Head, T. (1994), "The Diocese of Orléans, 950–1150". Pp. 345–57 in vol. 1 of Philippart, et al. (1994–96).

Heather, P. J. (1991). *Goths and Romans 332–489.* Oxford.

Hecker, H. (1981). *Bettelorden und Bürgertum. Konflikt und Kooperation in deutschen Städten des Spätmittelalters.* Frankfurt.

Hedeman, A. D. (1984). 'Valois Legitimacy: Editorial Changes in Charles V's Grandes Chroniques de France'. *Art Bulletin* 66 (1984): 97–117.

——. (1985). 'Restructuring the Narrative: The Function of Ceremonial in Charles V's Grandes Chroniques de France'. *Studies in the History of Art* 16 (1985): 171–81.

Heffernan, T. J. (1988). *Sacred Biography: Saints and their Biographers in the Middle Ages.* Oxford.

Heinzelmann, M. (1994). *Gregor von Tours, (538–594): "Zehn Bücher Geschichte". Historiographie und Gesellschaftskonzept im 6. Jahrhundert.* Darmstadt.

——. (1994b). "Die Franken und die fränkische Geschichte in der Perspektive der Historiographie Gregors von Tours". Pp. 326–44 in *Historiographie im frühen Mittelalter*, ed. A. Scharer and G. Scheibelreiter. Vienna.

Hellmann, S. (1935). 'Das Fredegarproblem'. *Historische Vierteljahrschrift* 29 (1935): 36–92.

Hennig, J. (1972). *Chronologie der Werke Heinrichs von Mügeln.* Hamburger Philologische Studien 27. Hamburg.

Herkommer, H. (1991). "Sächsische Weltchronik". In *Die deutsche Literatur des Mittelalters. Verfasserlexikon* 8. 2nd edition. Cols. 473–500.

Herlihy, D. (1985). *Medieval Households.* Cambridge, Mass.

Heullant-Donat, I. (1994). *Ab Origine Mundi. Fra Elemosina e Paolino da Venezia. Deux Franciscains Italiens et l'histoire universelle au xive siècle, Thèse pour le doctorat ès-lettres.* 3 Vols. Paris.

Hilgers, H. A. (1980). 'Zum Text der 'Cronica Boemorum' des Johannes de Marignolis'. *Mittellateinisches Jahrbuch* 15 (1980): 143–54.

Hillgarth, J. N. (1992), "The *Historiae* of Orosius in the Early Middle Ages". Pp. 157–70 in *Antiquité tardive et christianisme ancien (VIe–IXe siècles)*. Vol. 2: *De Tertullien aux Mozarabes. Mélanges offerts à Jacques Fontaines à l'occasion de son 70e anniversaire, par ses élèves, amis et collègues*, ed. L. Holtz, J.-C. Fredouille, and M.-H. Jullien. Études Augustiniennes, Série Moyen-âge et Temps Modernes 26. Paris.

Hindley, A. et Levy, Brian. (1983). *The Old French Epic: An Introduction.* Louvain.

Hofmann, H. (1973). 'Studien zur Chronik von Montecassino'. *Deutsches Archiv* 29 (1973): 59–162.

——. (1987). "Artikulationsformen historischen Wissens in der lateinischen Historiographie des hohen und späten Mittelalters". Pp. 367–687 in *La littérature historiographique des origines à 1500*. Vol. 1: *Grundriss der romanischen Literaturen des Mittelalters XI/1*, ed. A. Biermann, et al. Heidelberg. 2. Teilband.

Hoffmann, H. (1958). *Untersuchungen zur karolingischen Annalistik.* Bonn.

Hofinger, F. (1974). *Studien zu den deutschen Chroniken des Fritsche Closener von Strassburg und des Jacob Twinger von Königshofen*. Munich.

Höfler, O. (1938). 'Das germanische Kontinuitätsproblem'. *Historische Zeitschrift* 157 (1938): 1–26.

Hollister, C. W. (1976). 'The Strange Death of William Rufus.' *Speculum* 48 (1976), 637–53.

Holmes, U. T. (1964). 'The Anglo-Norman Rhymed Chronicle.' *Linguistic and Literary Studies in Honor of Helmut A. Hatzfeld*. Ed. A. S. Crisafulli. Washington DC: Catholic University of America, 1964, 231–6.

Honoré-Duvergé, S. (1942). 'La chronique de García d'Euguí, évêque de Bayonne'. *Bulletin hispanique* 44 (1942): 17–39.

Hucker, B. U. (1995). "Literatur im Umkreis Kaiser Ottos IV". Pp. 377–406 in *Die Welfen und ihr Braunschweiger Hof im hohen Mittelalter*, ed. Bernd Schneidmüller. Wiesbaden.

Hudson, A. (1966). 'Tradition and Innovation in Some Middle English Manuscripts'. *Review of English Studies*, n.s. 17 (1966): 359–72.

Huisman, G. (1984). 'Notes on the Manuscript Tradition of Dudo of St Quentin's Gesta Normannorum'. *Anglo-Norman Studies* 6 (1984): 122–35.

Il senso della storia nella cultura medievale italiana (1100–1350): quattordicesimo convegno di studi; Pistoia, 14–17 maggio 1993. Pistoia.

Iogna-Prat, D., C. Jeudy, G. Lobrichon (1987). *L'école carolingienne d'Auxerre de Muretach à Remi (830–908)*. Paris.

Jackson, P. (1990). *The Mission of Friar William of Rubruck. His Journey to the Court of the Great Khan Möngke*. Translated by P. Jackson. The Hakluyt Society Second Series 173. London.

James, E. (1988). *The Franks*. Oxford.

———. (1998). "Gregory of Tours and the Franks". Pp. 51–66 in *After Rome's Fall: Narrators and Sources of Early Medieval History. Essays presented to Walter Goffart*, ed. A. C. Murray. Toronto.

Janvier, Y. (1982). *La géographie d'Orose*. Collection d'études anciennes. Paris.

Jäschke, K. U. (1970). *Die älteste Halberstädter Bischofschronik*. Cologne and Vienna.

———. (1988). "Zu den Gesta Adolfi regis von 1299/1316". Pp. 221–45 in *Historiographia mediaevalis: Studien zur Geschichtsschreibung und Quellenkunde des Mittelalters: Festschrift für Franz-Josef Schmale zum 65. Geburtstag*, ed. D. Berg and H.-W. Goetz. Darmstadt.

Jauss, H. R. (1982). *Toward an Aesthetic of Reception*. Translated by T. Bahti. Minneapolis.

Joachimsen, P. (1910). *Geschichtsauffassung und Geschichtsschreibung in Deutschland unter dem Einfluß des Humanismus*. Leipzig and Berlin.

Jodogne, O. (1963). 'La Naissance de la prose française.' *Bulletin de la Classe des Lettres et des Sciences Morales et Politiques, Académie Royale de Belgique* (1963), 296–308.

Johanek, P. (1987). "Weltchronistik und regionale Geschichtsschreibung im Spätmittelalter". Pp. 287–330 in *Geschichtsschreibung und Geschichtsbewußtsein im späten Mittelalter*, ed. H. Patze. Vorträge und Forschungen, 31. Sigmaringen.

———. (1988). "Historiographie und Buchdruck im ausgehenden 15. Jahrhundert". P. 114 in *Historiographie am Oberrhein im späten Mittelalter und in der frühen Neuzeit*, ed. K. Andermann. Sigmaringen.

———. (1992). "Der Schreiber und die Vergangenheit. Zur Entfaltung einer dynastischen Geschichtsschreibung an den Fürstenhöfen des 15. Jahrhunderts". In *Pragmatische Schriftlichkeit im Mittelalter*, ed. H. Keller, K. Grubmüller, and N. Staubach. Munich.

Johannesson, K. (1978). *Saxo Grammaticus. Komposition och världsbild i Gesta Danorum*. Stockholm.

Johnston, R. C. (1976). 'The Historicity of Jordan Fantosme's Chronicle.' *Journal of Medieval History* 2 (1976), 159–68.

———. (1979). 'Jordan Fantosme's Experiments in Prosody and Design.' *Mélanges Pierre Jonin*. Senefiance Vol. 7. Aix-en-Provence.

Jones, C. W., ed. (1943). *Bedae Opera de temporibus*. Cambridge, Mass.

———. (1947). *Saints' Lives and Chronicles in Early England*. Ithaca, N.Y.

Jones, D., ed. (1993). *Saint Richard of Chichester. The Sources for his Life*. Sussex Record Society 73. Lewes.

Jørgensen, E. (1931). *Historieforskning og historieskrivning i Danmark indtil aar 1800*. Copenhagen.

Kaeppeli, T. (1970–93). *Scriptores Ordinis Praedicatorum Medii Aevi*. 4 vols. Rome.

Kaiser, R. (1994). "Die Gesta episcoporum als Genus in der Geschichtsschreibung". Pp. 459–80 in *Historiographie im frühen Mittelalter*, ed. A. Scharer and G. Scheibelreiter. Vienna.

Kampers, F. (1896/1969). *Die deutsche Kaiseridee in Prophetie und Sage*. Munich. [Repr. Aalen, 1969.]

Kastner, J. (1974). *Historiae fundationum monasterium. Frühformen monastischer Institutions-geschichtsschreibung im Mittelalter*. Münchener Beiträge zur Mediävistik und Renaissance-Forschung 18. Munich.

Kay, S. (1978). 'The Nature of Rhetoric in the Chanson de Geste.' *Zeitschrift für romanische Philologie* 94 (1978), 305–20.

———. (1987). 'Le passé défini: problèmes de la représentation du passé dans quelques chansons de geste féodales', *Au carrefour des routes d'Europe: la chanson de geste*, Senefiance 21 (1987), t. 2, 697–715.

Keller, H.-E. (1977). 'Wace et Geoffrey de Monmouth: problème de la chronologie des sources.' *Romania* 98 (1977), 1–14.

Kelly, D. (1974). "'Matiere" and "Genera Dicendi" in Medieval Romance.' *Yale French Studies* 51 (1974), 147–56.

Kelly, J. N. D. (1975). *Jerome: His Life, Writings, and Controversies*. London.

Kemp, E. W. (1948). *Canonisation and Authority in the Western Church*. Oxford.

Kendall, C. B. (1978). "Bede's Historia Ecclesiastica: The Rhetoric of Faith". Pp. 145–72 in *Medieval Eloquence: Studies in the Theory and Practice of Medieval Rhetoric*, ed. J. J. Murphy. Berkeley.

———. (1979). "Imitation and the Venerable Bede's Historia Ecclesiastica". Pp. 161–90 in *Saints, Scholars, and Heroes: Studies in Medieval Culture in Honor of Charles W. Jones*, vol. 1, ed. M. H. King and W. M. Stevens. Minnesota.

Kennedy, G. A. (1984). *New Testament Interpretation through Rhetorical Criticism*. Chapel Hill.

Ker, W. P. (1909). 'The Early Historians of Norway'. *Saga-Book of the Viking Club* 6 (1909): 238–56. [Repr. in *Collected Essays*, ed. C. Whibley. Vol. 2. Pp. 131–51 London.]

Kerhervé, J. (1980). 'Aux origines d'un sentiment national: Les chroniqueurs bretons de la fin du Moyen Age'. *Bulletin de la Société archéologique du Finistère* 108 (1980): 165–206.

———. (1992). "La 'Genealogie des roys, ducs et princes de Bretaigne' de Pierre le Baud (1486)". Pp. 519–60 in *Mélanges offerts a la mémoire de Léon Fleuriot*, ed. G. Le Menn with J.-Y. Le Moing. Rennes.

Kermode, F. (1987). "The New Testament. Introduction". In *The Literary Guide to the Bible*, ed. R. Alter and F. Kermod. Cambridge, Mass.

Kersken, N. (1995). *Geschichtsschreibung im Europa der 'nationes'. Nationalgeschichtliche Gesamtdarstellungen im Mittelalter*. Münstersche Historische Forschungen 8. Cologne.

Kirby, D. P. (1965–66). 'Bede's Native Sources for the *Historia Ecclesiastica*'. *Bulletin of the John Rylands Library* 48 (1965–66): 341–71.

Kirchert, K. (1993). *Städtische Geschichtsschreibung und Schulliteratur. Rezeptionsgeschichtliche Studien zum Werk von Fritsche Closener und Jakob Twinger von Königshofen*. Wiesbaden.

Klaniczay, G. and E. Madas (1994). "La Hongrie". Pp. 103–60 in vol. 2 of Philippart, et al. (1994–96).

Klapisch-Zuber, C. (1986). "Les Généalogies florentines du xive et du xve siècle". Pp. 101–31 in *Le Modèle familial européen: normes, déviances, contrôle du pouvoir*. Rome.

——. (1991). "The Genesis of the Family Tree". Pp. 105–29 in *I Tatti Studies: Essays in the Renaissance*. Vol. 4. Florence.

Klein, H.-W. (1995). *Die Chronik des Franziskanerklosters Calvarienberg bei Ahrweiler, 1440–1747*. Bad Neuenahr-Ahrweiler.

Kleinberg, A. (1992a). 'Hermannus Judaeus's Opusculum: In Defense of Its Authenticity'. *Revue des Études juives* 151 (1992): 337–53.

Kleinschmidt, E. (1972). 'Die Colmarer Dominikaner-Geschichtsschreibung im 13. und 14. Jahrhundert. Neue Handschriftenfunde und Forschungen zur Überlieferungsgeschichte'. *Deutsches Archiv* 28 (1972): 371–496.

Knape, J. (1984). *Historie in Mittelalter und früher Neuzeit. Begriffs- und gattungsgeschichtliche Untersuchungen im interdisziplinären Kontext*. Baden-Baden.

Koczerska, M. (1985). 'État et perspectives des recherches sur Jan Dlugosz'. *Acta Poloniae Historica* 52 (1985): 171–219.

Köster, K. (1952). "Die Geschichtsschreibung der Kolmarer Dominikaner des 13. Jahrhunderts". Pp. 1–100 in *Schicksalwege am Oberrhein*, ed. P. Wentzke. Freiburg.

Koudelka, V. J. (1959). 'Spigulature dal memoriale di Niccolò Galgani'. *Archivum Fratrum Praedicatorum* 29 (1959): 111–47.

——. (1972). 'Les dépositions des témoins au procès de canonisation de saint Dominique'. *Archivum Fratrum Praedicatorum* 42 (1972): 47–67.

Krapf, L. (1979). *Germanenmythologie und Reichsideologie. Frühhumanistische Rezeptionsweisen der taciteischen Germania*. Studien zur deutschen Literatur 59. Tübingen.

Krey, A. C. (1941). 'William of Tyre', *Speculum* 16 (1941), 149–66.

Krötzl, C. (1994). *Pilger, Mirakel und Alltag. Formen des Verhaltnis im skandinavischen Mittelalter*. Tampere.

Krüger, K. H. (1976). *Die Universalchroniken*. Typologie des sources de moyen âge occidental 16. Turnhout. [Updated 1985.]

——. (1981). 'Zur "beneventanischen" Konzeption der Langobardengeschichte des Paulus Diaconus'. *Frühmittelalterliche Studien* 15 (1981): 18–35.

Kulcsár, P. (1973). *Bonfini magyar történetének forrásai és keletkezése*. Humanizmus és reformáció 1. Budapest.

Kumlien, K. (1979). *Historieskriving och kungadöme i svensk medeltid*. Stockholm.

Kunze, K. (1983). "Jacobus a Voragine". Pp. 448–66 in *Die deutsche Literatur des Mittelalters. Verfasserlexikon*. Vol. 4. Berlin.

Kürbis, B. (1987). "Johannes Dlugosz als Geschichtsschreiber". Pp. 483–96 in *Geschichtsschreibung und Geschichtsbewußtsein im späten Mittelalter*, ed. H. Patze. Sigmaringen.

Lacroix, B. (1965). *Orose et ses idées*. Institut d'études médiévales. Publications 18. Montreal.

——. (1968). 'Guillaume de Tyr. Unité et diversité dans la tradition latine', *Etudes d'histoire littéraire et doctrinale*, 4th series, Paris.

——. (1971). *L'historien au Moyen Age*. Paris.

Lamarrigue, A.-M. (1981). 'La méthode historique de Bernard Gui d'après la chronique des rois de France'. *Cahiers de Fanjeaux* 16 (1981): 205–19.

Landes, R. (1992). 'Millenarismus absconditus: l'historiographie augustinienne et le millénarisme du haut Moyen Age jusqu'à l'an Mil (1)'. *Le Moyen Age* 98 (1992): 355–77.

Laporte, J. (1971). "Fontanelle". In *Dictionnarie d'histoire et de géographie ecclésiastique* 17. Cols. 915–52. Paris.

Lawrence, C. H. (1960). *St. Edmund of Abingdon. A Study in Hagiography and History*. Oxford.

Le Maître, P. (1980). 'L'oeuvre d'Aldric du Mans (832–857) et sa signification'. *Francia* 8 (1980): 43–64.

Leclercq, H. (DACL). "Martyrologe". In *Dictionnarie d'archéologie chrétienne et de liturgie* 10.2, 2523 ff.?

Leegaard, Knudsen A. (1994). *Saxostudier og rigshistorie på Valdemar Atterdags tid*. Skrifter udgivet af Institut for historie ved Københavns Universitet 17. Copenhagen.

Legge, M. D. (1971). *Anglo-Norman Literature and Its Background*. 2nd edn, Oxford.

Lemaitre, J.-L. (1992). *Le Limousin monastique. Autour de quelque textes*. Ussel.

Lemke, E. (1953). *Tradition und humanistische Einflüsse in der deutschen Geschichtsschreibung des Spätmittelalters*. Göttingen.

Lemmens, L. (1909). 'Ex Libro Miraculorum et Visionum in provincia Saxoniae c. 1300 conscripto", *Archivum Franciscanum Historicum* 2 (1909): 72–78.

——. (1911). 'Chronicon Provinciae Argentinensis Ordinis Fratrum Minorum circa an. 1310–1327 a quodam Fratre Minore Basileae conscriptum'. *Archivum Franciscanum Historicum* 4 (1911): 671–87.

——. (1913). 'Annales Minorum Prussicorum'. *Archivum Franciscanum Historicum* 6 (1913): 702–04.

Leng, R. (1996). *Konrad von Halberstadt, O.P. Chronographia Interminata*. Wiesbaden.

Leo, F. (1901). *Die griechisch-römische Biographie nach ihrer literarischen Form*. Leipzig.

Levine, R. (1991). 'Deadly Diatribe in the *Récits d'un ménestrel de Reims*.' *Res Publica Litterarum* 14 (1991), 115–26.

Levy, B. J. (1987). 'Pèlerins rivaux de la 3ᵉ croisade: les personnages des rois d'Angleterre et de France d'après les chroniques d'Ambroise et d'Ernoul, et le récit anglo-normand de la croisade et mort Richard Cœur de Lion.' *La croisade— réalités et fictions. Actes du Colloque d'Amiens, 1987.*

——. (2001). 'The "Updating" of the Text.' *Mediaevalia* 20. Proceedings of an inter-disciplinary conference held at the University of Hull, April 1999: "Framing the Text: Reading Tradition and Image in Medieval Europe", ed. and intr. by Kate L. Boardman, Catherine Emerson and Adrian P. Tudor, with a preface by Derek Pearsall (2001), 255–61.

Lewis, P. S. (1977). *La France à la fin du Moyen Age*. Paris.

Lewis, S. (1987). *The Art of Matthew Paris in the Chronica Majora*. Cambridge.

Leyser, K. (1993). 'Ritual, Zeremonie und Gestik: das ottonische Reich'. *Frühmittelalterliche Studien* 27 (1993): 1–26.

Lichatschow, D. S. (1975). *Der Mensch in der altrussischen Literatur*. Dresden.

Liddell, H. G., and R. Scott (1985). *A Greek-English Lexicon*. Revised by H. S. Jones and R. McKenzie. Oxford.

Lieu, S. (1998). "From History to Legend and Legend to History: The Medieval and Byzantine Transformation of Constantine's Vita". Pp. 136–76 in *Constantine: History, Historiography, and Legend*, ed. S. N. C. Lieu and D. Montserrat. London.

Lifshitz, F. (1994). 'Beyond Positivism and Genre: "Hagiographical" Texts as Historical Narrative'. *Viator* 25 (1994): 95–113.

Linehan, P. (1993). *History and the Historians of Medieval Spain*. Oxford.

Linskill, J. (1937). *Saint Léger. Etude de la langue du manuscrit de Clermont-Ferrand*. Paris.

Lippelt, H. (1973). *Thietmar von Merseburg—Reichsbischof und Chronist*. Cologne.

Little, A. G. (1943). *Franciscan Papers, Lists and Documents*. Manchester.

Lusignan, S. and M. Paulmier-Foucart, eds. (1997). *Lector et compilator. Vincent de Beauvais frère prêcheur. Un intellectuel et son milieu au XIIIᵉ siècle*. Rencontres à Royaumont 9. Grâne.

Livermore, H. (1990). 'The Conquest of Lisbon and its author', *Portuguese Studies* 6 (1990), 1–16.

Lock, R. (1985). *Aspects of Time in Medieval Literature*. "Garland Publications in Comparative Literature". New York.

Lodge, A. (1990). 'Literature and History in the "Chronicle" of Jordan Fantosme.' *French Studies* 44 (1990), 257–70.

Lucken, C. et Séguy, M. (eds), (2000). *L'invention de l'histoire*. Saint-Denis.

Lynde-Recchia, M. (2000). *Prose, Verse, and Truth-Telling in the Thirteenth Century*, Nicholasville.

Macartney, C. A. (1953). *The Medieval Hungarian Historians. A Critical and Analytical Guide*. Cambridge.

MacDonald, A. D. S. (1984). "Aspects of the Monastery and Monastic Life in Adomnán's Life of Columba". *Peritia* 3 (1984): 271–302.

———. (1997). "Adomnán's Monastery of Iona". Pp. 24–44 in *Studies in the Cult of St. Columba*, ed. C. Bourke. Dublin.

Macdonald, I. (1961). 'The Chronicle of Jordan Fantosme: Manuscripts, Author and Versification.' *Studies in Medieval Language and Literature Presented to Alfred Ewert.* Oxford, 1961, 242–58.

Macquarrie, A. (1994). "Medieval Scotland". Pp. 487–501 in Philippart, et al. (1994–96), vol. 1.

———. (1997). *The Saints of Scotland: Essays in Scottish Church History AD 450–1093.* Edinburgh.

Maenchen-Helfen, O. (1945). 'The Legend of the Origin of the Huns'. *Byzantion* 17 (1945): 244–51.

Maissen, T. (1994). "Ein 'helvetisch Alpenvolck'. Die Formulierung eines gesamteidgenössischen Selbstverständnisses des 16. Jahrhunderts". Pp. 69–86 in *Studia Polono-Helvetica II: Historiographie in Polen und in der Schweiz*, ed. K. Baczkowski and C. Simon. Zeszyty Naukowe Uniwersytetu Jagiellonskiego 1145. Kraków.

———. (1994). *Von der Legende zum Modell. Das Interesse an Frankreichs Vergangenheit während der italienischen Renaissance.* Basler Beiträge zur Geschichtswissenschaft 166. Basel.

Maleczek, W. (1988). "Echte und zweifelhafte Stammbäume bei kanonischen Eheprozessen bis in frühe 13. Jahrhundert". Pp. 123–43 in *Staaten-Wappen-Dynastien*, ed. W. Malaczek. Innsbruck.

Manselli, R. (1975). *La religion populaire au moyen âge.* Montreal.

———. (1985). "Il sogno come premonizione, consiglio e predizione nella tradizione medioevale". Pp. 219–44 in *I sogni nel moedioevo*, ed. T. Gregory. Rome.

Mantou, R. (1992). 'Philippe Mousket.' *Dictionnaire des lettres françaises*, ed. G. Hasenohr and M. Zink, Coll. "La Pochothèque", Paris.

Marchello-Nizia, Chr. (1984). 'L'historien et son prologue: forme littéraire et stratégies discursives.' *La Chronique et l'histoire au Moyen-Age*, ed. D. Poirion. "Cultures et civilisations médiévales", vol. ii. Paris.

Marcus, J. (1992). *The Way of the Lord: Christological Exegesis of the Old Testament in the Gospel of Mark.* Minneapolis.

Marichal, R. (1968). 'Naissance du roman.' *Entretiens sur la Renaissance du XIIe siècle*, ed. M. de Gandillac et E. Jeauneau. Paris and The Hague, 1968, 449–82.

Markus, R. A. (1963). 'The Roman Empire in Early Christian Historiography'. *The Downside Review* 81 (1963): 340–53.

———. (1986). "Chronicle and Theology: Prosper of Aquitaine". Pp. 31–43 in *The Inheritance of Historiography, 350–900*, ed. C. Holdsworth and T. P. Wiseman. Exeter Studies in History 12. Exeter.

———. (1988). *Saeculum: History and Society in the Theology of St. Augustine.* Rev. ed. Cambridge.

Marrou, H.-I. (1970). "Saint Augustin, Orose et l'augustinisme historique". Pp. 59–87 in *La Storiografia altomedievale. Settimane di studio del Centro italiano di studi sull'alto medioevo 17.* Spoleto.

Martin, J.-P. (1987). 'Les Motifs dans la chanson de geste. Définition et utilisation.' *Cahiers de Civilisation Médiévale* 30 (1987), 315–29.

Martin, G. (1991). "Cinq opérations fondamentales de la compilation: L'exemple de l'Histoire d'Espagne (Étude segmentaire)". Pp. 99–109 in *L'historiographie médiévale en Europe. Actes du colloque . . . du 29 mars au 1er avril 1989*, ed. J.-P. Genet. Paris.

Martini, G. (1970). 'Lo spirito cittadino e le origini della storiografia comunale lombarda'. *Nuova rivista storica* 54 (1970): 1–22.

Mascanzoni, L. (1996). *Il Tolosano e i suoi continuatori.* Rome.

Mason, E. (1990). *St. Wulfstan of Worcester c. 1008–1095.* Oxford.

Mayr-Harting, H. (1994). "Bede's patristic thinking as a historian". Pp. 367–74 in *Historiographie im frühen Mittelalter*, ed. A. Scharer and G. Scheibelreiter. Vienna.

McCormick, M. (1975). *Les annales du haut moyen âge*. Typologie des sources du moyen âge occidental 14. Turnhout.

McKitterick, R. (1983). *The Frankish Kingdoms under the Carolingians*. London and New York.

———. (1997). 'Constructing the Past in the Early Middle Ages: The Case of the Royal Frankish Annals'. *Transactions of the Royal Historical Society*, sixth ser. 7 (1997): 101–29.

McKitterick, R., and M. Innes (1994). "The Writing of History". Pp. 193–220 in *Carolingian Culture: Emulation and Innovation*, ed. R. McKitterick. Cambridge.

Meier, C. (1992). "Vom Homo Coelestis zum Homo Faber. Die Reorganisation der mittelalterlichen Enzyklopädie für neue Gebrauchsfunktionen bei Vinzenz von Beauvais und Brunetto Latini". Pp. 157–75 in *Pragmatische Schriftlichkeit im Mittelalter*, ed. H. Keller, K. Grubmüller and N. Staubach. Münstersche Mittelalter-Schriften 65. Munich.

Melville, G. (1980). 'Spätmittelalterliche Geschichtskompendien—Eine Aufgabenstellung'. *Römische Historische Mitteilungen* 22 (1980): 51–104.

———. (1987). "Geschichte in graphischer Gestalt. Beobachtungen zu einer spätmittelalterlichen Darstellungsweise". Pp. 57–111 in *Geschichtsschreibung und Geschichtsbewußtsein im späten Mittelalter*, ed. H. Patze. Vorträge und Forschungen 31. Sigmaringen.

———. (1988). "Kompilation, Fiktion und Diskurs. Aspekte zur heuristischen Methode der mittelalterlichen Geschichtsschreiber". Pp. 133–53 in *Historische Methode*, ed. J. Rüsen. Theorie der Geschichte, Beiträge zur Historik 5. Munich.

Meneghetti, M. L. (1975). 'L'"Estoire des Engleis" di Geffrei Gaimar fra cronaca genealogica e romanzo cortese.' *Medioevo Romanzo* 2 (1975), 232–46.

Menéndez Pidal, R. (1946). "La Crónica General de España que mandó componer Alfonso el Sabio". Pp. 139–202 in *Estudios literarios*, ed. Menéndez Pidal. Buenos Aires.

Menestó, E. (1993). "Per un'edizione critica delle biografie e leggende francescane". Pp. 245–67 in *Gli studi francescani dal dopoguerra ad oggi*, ed. F. Santi. Atti del convegno di studio Firenze, 5–7 novembre 1990. Spoleto.

Mertens, D. (1993). "Jakob Wimpfeling (1450–1528). Pädagogischer Humanismus". Pp. 35–57 in *Humanismus im deutschen Südwesten. Biographische Profile*, ed. P. G. Schmidt. Sigmaringen.

Meyer, P. (1985). 'Les premières compilations françaises d'histoire ancienne.' *Romania* 14 (1885), 1–81.

Meyvaert, P. (1986). "Le Libellus responsionum à Augustin de Cantorbéry: une oeuvre authentique de Grégoire le Grand". Pp. 543–49 in *Grégoire le Grand*, ed. J. Fontaine, R. Gillet, and S. Pellistrandi. Paris.

Michiels, G. (1998). "Jean de Liège". P. 226 in *Dictionnaire d'histoire et de géographie ecclésiastique*. Vol. 27. Paris.

Mierau, H. J. et al. (1996). *Studien zur Überlieferung der Flores temporum*. Hannover.

Mierau, H. J., A. Sander-Berke, and B. Studt, eds. (1996). *Studien zur Überlieferung der "Flores Temporum"*. MGH Studien und Texte 14. Hannover.

Miglio, M. (1995). "Anonimo romano". Pp. 175–87 in *Il senso della storia nella cultura medievale italiana (1100–1350): quattordicesimo convegno di studi; Pistoia, 14–17 maggio 1993*. Pistoia.

Minnis, A. J. (1984). *The Medieval Theory of Authorship*. London.

Misch, G. (1949–69). *Geschichte der Autobiographie*, 4 vols. Frankfurt.

Moeglin, J.-M. (1985). *Les Ancêtres du Prince: Propagande politique et naissance d'une histoire nationale en Bavière au moyen age (1180–1500)*. Geneva.

———. (1988). 'Die Genealogie der Wittesbacher: Politische Propaganda und Entestehung der territorialen Geschichtsschreibung in Bayern im Mittelalter'. *Mitteilungen des Instituts für Österreichische Geschichtsforschung,* 96 (1988): 33–54.

———. (1995). "Zur Entwicklung dynastischen Bewußtseins der Fürsten im Reich vom 13. zum 15. Jahrhundert". Pp. 523–40 in *Die Welfen und ihr Brauschweiger Hof im hohen Mittelalter,* ed. Bernd Schneidmüller. Wiesbaden.

Möhring-Müller, H. (1993). "Die 'Chronica Novella' des Lübecker Dominikanermönchs Herman Korner. Untersuchungen zu Gattung, Sprache, Publikum und Inhalt der lateinischen und mittelniederdeutschen Fassungen". Pp. 27–221 in *Zweisprachige Geschichtsschreibung im spätmittelalterlichen Deutschland,* ed. R. Sprandel. Wissensliteratur im Mittelalter 14. Wiesbaden.

Moisl, H. (1981). 'Anglo-Saxon royal genealogies and Germanic oral tradition'. *Journal of Medieval History* 7 (1981): 215–48.

Molinier, A. (1901–06). *Sources de l'histoire de France au Moyen Age.* 6 vols. Paris.

Molitor, E. (1921). *Die Reichsreformbestrebungen des 15. Jahrhunderts bis zum Tode Kaiser Friedrichs III.* Breslau.

Momigliano, A. (1955). 'Cassiodorus and Italian Culture of his Time'. *Proceedings of the British Academy* 41 (1955): 207–45. [Repr. in Momigliano. *Studies in Historiography.* Pp. 181–210. London, 1966.]

———. (1963). "Pagan and Christian Historiography in the Fourth Century A.D.". Pp. 79–99 in *The Conflict between Paganism and Christinaity in the Fourth Century,* ed. A. Momigliano. Oxford. [Reprinted in *Essays in Ancient and Modern Historiography.* Pp. 107–26. Oxford, 1977.]

———. (1987). "Ancient Biography and the Study of Religion in the Roman Empire". Pp. 159–77 in *On Pagans, Jews, And Christians.* Middletown.

Mommsen, T. E. (1959a). "Orosius and Augustine". Pp. 325–48 in *Medieval and Renaissance Studies,* ed. E. F. Rice. Ithaca, N.Y.

———. (1959b). "St. Augustine and the Christian Idea of Progress: The Background of the City of God". Pp. 265–98 in *Medieval and Renaissance Studies,* ed. E. F. Rice. Ithaca, N.Y.

Mommsen, T., and K. Morrison, ed. and trans. (1962). *Imperial Lives and Letters of the Eleventh Century.* New York.

Monfrin, F. (1994). "Liber pontificalis". Pp. 1042–43 in *Dictionnaire historique de la papauté,* ed. P. Levillain. Paris.

Montagnes, B. (1981). 'Bernard Gui dans l'historiographie dominicaine'. *Cahiers de Fanjeaux* 16 (1981): 183–203.

Moorhead, J. (1995). 'Gregory of Tours on the Arian Kingdoms'. *Studi Medievali* 36 (1995): 903–15.

Moorman, J. H. (1968). *A History of the Franciscan Order from its Origins to the Year 1517.* Oxford.

Moraw, P. (1987). "Politische Sprache und Verfassungsdenken bei ausgewählten Geschichtsschreibern des deutschen 14. Jahrhunderts". Pp. 695–726 in *Geschichtsschreibung und Geschichtsbewußtsein im Spätmittelalter,* ed. H. Patze. Vorträge und Forschungen 31. Sigmaringen.

Morçay, R. (1913). 'La Cronaca del convento fiorentino di San Marco. La parte più antica dettata da Giuliano Lapaccini'. *Archivio storico italiano,* 5th ser., 71 (1913): 1–29.

Morris, C. (1968). 'Villehardouin as Historian of the 4th Crusade.' *History* 53 (1968), 24–34.

Morse, R. (1991). *Truth and Convention in the Middle Ages. Rhetoric, Representation, and Reality.* Cambridge.

Mosshammer, A. A. (1979). *The Chronicle of Eusebius and Greek Chronographic Tradition.* Lewisburg/London.

Muhlack, U. (1991). *Geschichtswissenschaft im Humanismus und in der Aufklärung. Die Vorgeschichte des Historismus.* Munich.

Muhlberger, S. (1990). *The Fifth-Century Chroniclers: Prosper, Hydatius, and the Gallic Chronicler of 452*. ARCA Classical and Medieval Texts, Papers and Monographs 27. Leeds.

Müller M. (1998). *Die spätmittelalterliche Bistumsgeschichtsschreibung. Überlieferung und Entwicklung.* Cologne.

Münkler, H., H. Grünberger, and K. Mayer (1998). *Nationenbildung. Die Nationalisierung Europas im Diskurs humanistischer Intellektueller.* Italien und Deutschland, Politische Ideen 8. Berlin.

Musurillo, H., ed. and trans. (1972). *The Acts of the Christian Martyrs*. Oxford.

Nadeau A. (1999). "Devenir Frère prêcheur au XIIIe siècle d'áprès les 'Vitae Fratrum' de Géraud de Frachet". Pp. 135–52 in *Pfaffen und Laien-ein mittelalterlicher Antagonismus?* ed. E. C. Lutz and E. Tremp. Scrinium Friburgense 10. Freiburg.

Narrative Sources of the Southern Low Countries. 2000. University of Ghent. Accessed December 20, 2000. http://erlserv.rug.ac.be/cgibin/webspirs1.cgi?sp.nextform=search.htm&sp.dbid.p=D1A6.

Nass, K. (1995). "Geschichtsschreibung am Hofe Heinrichs des Löwen". Pp. 123–61 in *Die Welfen und ihr Brauschweiger Hof im hohen Mittelalter*, ed. Bernd Schneidmüller. Wiesbaden.

Nelson, J. L. (1985). 'Public Histories and Private History in the Work of Nithard'. *Speculum* 60 (1985: 251–95.

Nicholas, D. (1992). *Medieval Flanders*. London and New York.

Nielen-Vandenvoorde, M.-A. (1995). 'Un Livre méconnu des Assises de Jérusalem: les Lignages d'Outremer'. *Bibliothèque de l'École des chartes* 153 (1995): 103–30.

Nielsen, T. (1986). "The first printed book in Danish and the first library in Denmark". Pp. 9–18 in *From Script to Book. A Symposium*, ed. H. Bekker-Nielsen, M. Børch, and B. A. Sørensen. Odense.

Noble, P. (1999). 'Villehardouin, Robert de Clari and Henri de Valenciennes.' *The Medieval Chronicle*, ed. Erik Kooper. "Costerus New Series" vol. 120. Amsterdam.

Noble, T. F. X. (1985). 'A New Look at the Liber Pontificalis'. *Archivium historiae pontificiae* 23 (1985): 347–58.

Noonan, T. S. (1983). 'Russian Primary Chronicle'. *Wieczynski, Modern Encyclopedia of Russian and Soviet History* 32 (1983): 144–49.

Nygren, E. (1953). 'Ericus Olai'. in *Svenskt biografiskt lexikon* 14 (1953): 216–42.

Ó Corrain, D. (1985). "Irish Origin Legends and Genealogy: Recurrent Aetiologies". Pp. 51–96 in *History and Heroic Tale: A Symposium*. Odense.

O'Donnell, J. J. (1995). "The Holiness of Gregory". Pp. 62–81 in *Gregory the Great: A Symposium*, ed., J. C. Cavadini. Notre Dame Studies in Theology 2. Notre Dame, Ind.

O'Loughlin, T. (1997). "Living in the Ocean". Pp. 11–23 in *Studies in the Cult of St. Columba*, ed. C. Bourke. Dublin.

O'Neill, T. (1997). "Columba the Scribe". Pp. 80–106 in *Studies in the Cult of St. Columba*, ed. C. Bourke. Dublin.

O'Reilly, J. (1997). "Reading the Scriptures in the Life of Columba". Pp. 80–106 in *Studies in the Cult of St. Columba*, ed. C. Bourke. Dublin.

Odetto, G. (1940). 'La Cronaca Maggiore dell'Ordine Domenicano di Galvano Fiamma, frammenta editi'. *Archivum Fratrum Praedicatorum* 10 (1940): 297–373.

Oexle, O. G. (1995). "Memoria als Kultur". Pp. 9–78 in *Memoria als Kultur*, ed. O. G. Oexle. Veröffentlichungen des Max-Planck-Instituts für Geschichte 121. Göttingen.

Offler, H. S. (1984). 'A Note in the Northern Franciscan Chronicle'. *Nottingham Medieval Studies* 28 (1984): 45–89.

Ortalli, G. (1976). "Tra passato e presente: la storiografia medievale". Pp. 615–36 in *Storia dell'Emilia Romagna*, ed. A. Berselli. Vol. 1. Bologna.

Ott, N. H. (1980/81). 'Typen der Weltchronik-Ikonographie. Bemerkungen zur Illustration, Anspruch und Gebrauchssituation volkssprachlicher Chronistik aus überlieferungsgeschichtlicher Sicht'. *Jahrbuch der Oswald von Wolkenstein Gesellschaft* 1 (1980/81): 47–48.

Otter, M. (1996). *Inventiones: fiction and referentiality in twelfth-century English historical writing*. Chapel Hill.

Ottokar, N. (1948). *Studi comunali e fiorentini*. Florence.

Paciocco, R. (1989). "Elementi per una tipologia della santità francescana nel secolo xiv". Pp. 79–102 in *Santi e santità nel secolo XIV, Atti del XV convegno internazionale Assisi, 15–16–17 ottobre 1987*. Assisi.

——. (1990). *Da Francesco ai 'Catalogi sanctorum'. Livelli istituzionali e immagini agiografiche nell'ordine francescano (secoli xiii–xiv)*. Collectio Assisiensis 20. Assisi.

Pafford, J. H. P. (1957). "University of London Library MS. 278, Robert of Gloucester's Chronicle". Pp. 302–19 in *Studies Presented to Sir Hilary Jenkinson*, ed. J. Conwey Davies. London.

Pagani, G. (1959). 'Frammenti della Cronaca del B. Francesco Venimbeni da Fabriano'. *Archivum Franciscanum Historicum* 52 (1959): 153–77.

Page, R. I. (1978–79). 'Dumézil Revisited'. *Saga-Book of the Viking Society* 20 (1978–79): 49–69.

Panella, E. (1995). 'Cronaca antica di Santa Maria in Gradi di Viterbo: Perduta o mai esistita?' *Archivum Fratrum Praedicatorum* 65 (1995): 185–233.

——. (1995b). 'La continuazione quattro-cinquecentesca della Cronica di Perugia'. *Archivum Fratrum Praedicatorum* 65 (1995): 235–303.

Paris, G. (1875). *Les plus anciens monuments de la langue française (IXᵉ–Xᵉ siècle)*. Paris.

Partner, N. (1977). *Serious Entertainments: The Writing of History in Twelfth-Century England*. Chicago.

Pasqualin Traversa, G. (1995). *La 'minoritas' francescana nell' interpretazione della 'Franceschina'*. Assisi.

Patze, H. (1964 and 1965). 'Adel und Stifterchronik. Frühformen territorialer Geschichtsschreibung'. *Blätter für deutsche Landesgeschichte* 100 (1964): 8–81; and 101 (1965): 67–128.

——. (1968). 'Landesgeschichtsschreibung in Thüringen'. *Jahrbuch für die Geschichte Mittel- und Ostdeutschlands* 16/17 (1968): 95–168.

——. (1977). 'Klostergründung und Klosterchronik'. *Blätter für deutsche Landesgeschichte* 113 (1977): 89–121.

——. (1987). "Mäzene der Landesgeschichtsschreibung im späten Mittelalter". Pp. 347–50 in *Geschichtsschreibung und Geschichtsbewußtsein im späten Mittelalter*, ed. H. Patze. Sigmaringen.

——, ed. (1987). *Geschichtsschreibung und Geschichtsbewusstsein im späten Mittelalter*. Vorträge und Forschungen 31. Sigmarigen.

Pauphilet, A. (1950). 'Sur Robert de Clari.' *Romania* 57 (1950), 281–311.

—— and A. F. Labie-Leurquin. (1964). 'Saint Alexis (Vie de).' *Dictionnaire des Lettres Françaises*. Ed. G. Hasenohr and M. Zink, coll. "Pochothèque", Paris: Le Livre de Poche-Fayard, 1992, p. 1330.

Payen, J.-C. (1997). *Histoire de la littérature française. Le Moyen Age*. Paris.

Péano, P. (1975). 'Jacques de' Tolomei de Sienne, O.F.M. (1323–1390), Eléments de biographie'. *Archivum Franciscanum Historicum* 68 (1975): 273–97.

Pelan, M. M. (1931, repr. 1974). *L'influence du "Brut" de Wace sur les romanciers français de son temps*. Paris. Repr. Geneva.

Pertusi, A., ed. (1970). *La storiografia veneziana fino al sec. XVI. Aspetti e problemi*. Edited by A. Pertusi. Florence.

Petersen, J. M. (1996). "Ancilliae Domini in the Roman Empire". Pp. 89–279 in *Handmaids of the Lord: Contemporary Descriptions of Feminine Asceticism in the First Six Christian Centuries*, ed. J. M. Petersen. Kalamazoo, Mich.

Petersohn, J., ed. (1994). *Politik und Heiligenverehrung im Hochmittelalter*. Vorträge und Forschungen 42. Sigmaringen.

Petroff, E. A., ed. (1986). *Medieval Women's Visionary Literature*. Oxford.
Petti Balbi, G. (1995). "Il presente e il senso della storia in Caffaro e nei suoi continuatori". Pp. 31–52 in *Il senso della storia nella cultura medievale italiana (1100–1350): quattordicesimo convegno di studi; Pistoia, 14–17 maggio 1993*. Pistoia.
Peuckert, W.-E. (1948/1966). *Die große Wende*. Hamburg. [Repr. Darmstadt, 1966.]
Phelps, J. M. (1972). 'A Study of Renewal Ideas in the Writings of the Early Franciscans: 1210–1256'. Ph.D. diss. University of California.
Philippart, G. (1977). *Les légendiers latins et autres manuscrits hagiographiques*. Typologie des sources du Moyen Age occidental 24–25. Turnhout.
——, et al. (1994–96). *Hagiographies. Histoire internationale de la literature hagiographique latine et vernaculaire en Occident des origines à 1550*. 2 vols. Turnhout.
Picard, E. (1991). *Germanisches Sakralkönigtum? Quellenkritische Studien zur Germania des Tacitus und zur altnordischen Überlieferung*. Heidelberg.
Picard, J.-M. (1982). 'The Purpose of Adomnán's "Vita Columbae"'. *Peritia* 1 (1982): 160–77.
——. (1984). 'Bede, Adomnán, and the Writing of History'. *Peritia* 3 (1984): 50–70.
——. (1985). 'Structural patterns in early Hiberno-Latin hagiography'. *Peritia* 4 (1985): 67–82.
Pizarro, J. M. (1989). *A Rhetoric of the Scene. Dramatic Narrative in the Early Middle Ages*. Toronto.
——. (1995). *Writing Ravenna: a Narrative Performance in the Ninth Century*. Ann Arbor, Mich.
Plezia, M. (1947). *Kronika Galla na tle historiografii XII wieku*. Polska Akad. Umiejétnóci. Rozprawy wydziału historyczno-filozoficznego II, 46. Kraków.
Pohl, W. (1994). "Tradition, Ethnogenese und literarische Gestaltung: eine Zwischenbilanz". Pp. 9–26 in *Ethnogenese und Überlieferung. Angewandte Methoden der Frühmittelalterforschung*, ed. K. Brunner and B. Merta. Vienna.
——. (1998). "Introduction: Strategies of Distinction". Pp. 3–15 in *Strategies of Distinction: The Construction of Ethnic Communities, 300–800*, ed. W. Pohl and H. Reimitz. Leiden.
——. (1998b). "Telling the Difference: Signs of Ethnic Identity". Pp. 17–69 in *Strategies of Distinction: The Construction of Ethnic Communities, 300–800*, ed. W. Pohl and H. Reimitz. Leiden.
Poirion, D. 'Romans en vers et romans en prose.' GRMLA vol. IV, 1. 76.
——. (1992). 'Chanson de geste.' *Dictionnaire des Lettres Françaises*. 1964. ed. G. Hasenohr and M. Zink, coll. "Pochothèque", Paris.
Pommerol, M.-H. (1992). "Bernard Gui". Pp. 152–54 in *Dictionnaire des lettres françaises. Le Moyen Age*, ed. R. Bossuat, et al. New ed. Paris.
Poole, R. L. (1926). *Chronicles and Annals: a brief outline of their origin and growth*. Oxford.
Porta, G. (1995). "La costruzione della storia in Giovanni Villanni". Pp. 125–38 in *Il senso della storia nella cultura medievale italiana (1100–1350): quattordicesimo convegno di studi; Pistoia, 14–17 maggio 1993*. Pistoia.
Potthast, A. (1896). *Bibliotheca historica Medii Aevi*. 2 vols. Berlin. [Repr. Graz, 1957.]
——. (1962–98). *Repertorium fontium historiae Medii Aevi*. Vols. 1–8.2. Rome.
Poupardin, R. (1900). *Généalogies angevines du X^{ie} siècle*. Rome.
Powierski, J. (1997). "Czas napisania kroniki przez Mistrza Wincentego". Pp. 147–208 in *Krzyżówcy, kronikarze, dyplomaci*, ed. B. Śliwióśki· Gdańskie studia z dziejów średniowiecza 4. Gdańsk and Koszalin.
Pratesi, R. (1960). "Amici Giovanni (Bernardino da Fossa, Bernardino Aquilano". Pp. 778–80 in *Dizionario biografico degli Italiani* 2. Rome.
Prerovsky, U. (1974). *Il Liber Pontificalis nella recensione di Pietro Guglielmo e del cardinalo Pandolfo*. 3 vols. Rome.
Proksch, C. (1994). *Klosterreform und Geschichtsschreibung im Spätmittelalter*. Cologne.
Queller, D. E., and T. F. Madden (1997). *The Fourth Crusade. The Conquest of Constantinople*. 2nd edn, Philadelphia.

Quéruel, D., ed., (1999). *Jean de Joinville: de la Champagne aux royaumes d'outre-mer*. Paris.

Rasmussen, J. N. (1976). *Broder Peder Olson som de Deutsches Archivnske franciskaneres historieskriver*. Copenhagen.

———. (1998). "The Franciscans in the Nordic Countries". Pp. 6–21 in H. Roelvink, *Franciscans in Sweden. Medieval Remnants of Franciscan Activities*. Scripta Franciscana. Assen.

Ray, R. (1974). 'Medieval historiography through the twelfth century: problems and progress of research'. *Viator* 5 (1974): 33–59.

———. (1980). 'Bede's vera lex historiae'. *Speculum* 55 (1980): 1–21.

———. (1986). "The Triumph of Greco-Roman Rhetorical Assumptions in Pre-Carolingian Historiography". Pp. 67–84 in *The Inheritance of Historiography 350–900*, ed. C. Holdsworth and T. P. Wiseman. Exeter.

Raynaud de Lage, G. (1949). 'L'Histoire Ancienne Jusqu'à César et les Faits des Romains.' *Le Moyen Age* 55 (1949), 5–16.

———. (1957). 'Les Romans antiques dans l'Histoire Ancienne Jusqu'à César.' *Le Moyen Age* 63 (1957), 267–309.

Reilly, B. F. (1976). 'Sources of the Fourth Book of Lucas of Tuy's Chronicon Mundi'. *Classical Folia* 30 (1976): 127–37.

———. (1985). "Rodrigo Giménez de Rada's Portrait of Alfonso VI of León-Castille in the De Rebus Hispaniae. Historical methodology in the thirteenth century". Pp. 187–97 in *Estudios en homenaje a Don Claudio Sánchez Albornoz en sus 90 años*. Vol. 3: *Anexos de Cuadernos de Historia de España*. Buenos Aires.

Rener, M. (1993). *Die Vita der hl. Elisabeth des Dietrich v. Apolda*. Veröffentlichungen der Historischen Kommission für Hessen 53. Marburg.

———. (1994). "Lateinische Hagiographie im deutschsprachigen Raum von 1200–1450". Pp. 199–265 in vol. 1 of Philippart, et al. (1994–96).

Rensing, T. (1936). *Das Dortmunder Dominikanerkloster*. Münster.

Reydellet M. (1981). *La royauté dans la littérature latine de Sidoine Apollinaire à Isidore de Séville*. Bibliothèque des écoles françaises d'Athènes et de Rome 243. Rome.

Reynolds, A. (1990). 'The I of the Beholder', unpublished M.A. dissertation, Birkbeck College, University of London, London.

Reynolds, S. (1983). 'Medieval Origines Gentium and the Community of the Realm'. *History* 68 (1983): 375–90.

Richard, J. (1981). *Les récits de voyages et de pèlerinages*. Typologie des sources du moyen âge occidental 38. Turnhout.

Richter, H. (1972). *Die Persönlichkeitsdarstellung in cluniazensischen Abtsviten*. Diss. Erlangen-Nürnberg.

Riedmann, J. (1970). *Die Fortsetzung der Flores Temporum durch Johan Spies, Prior der Augustiner-Eremiten in Rattenberg*. Vienna.

Robles, L. (1972). *Escritos dominicos de la Corona de Aragón*. Salamanca.

Rodriguez Alonso, C. (1975). *Las historias de los Godos, Vándalos y Suevos de Isidoro de Sevilla: estudio, edición crítica, y traducción*. León.

Roest, B. (1996). *Reading the Book of History: Intellectual Contexts and Educational Functions of Franciscan Historiography, 1226–ca. 1350*. Groningen.

———. (1999). "Medieval Historiography: About Generic Constraints and Scholarly Constructions". Pp. 47–61 in *Aspects of Genre and Type in Pre-Modern Literary Cultures*, ed. B. Roest and H. Vanstiphout. COMERS/ICOG Communications 1. Groningen.

Ronconi, A. "Exitus illustrium virorum". Pp. 1258–68 in *Reallexikon für Antike und Christentum*, ed. T. Klausner. Vol. 6. Stuttgart.

Rosén, J. (1940). 'Studier in Stockholms Gråbrödraklosters diarium'. *Vetenskapssocietetens i Lund Årsbok* 21 (1940): 101–30.

Rothe, H. (1988). "Enea Silvio de' Piccolomini über Böhmen". Pp. 141–56 in *Studien zum Humanismus in den böhmischen Ländern*, ed. H.-B. Harder, H. Rothe, et al. Cologne.

———. (1991). "Über die kritische Ausgabe der Historia Bohemica des Enea Silvio de' Piccolomini". Pp. 29–48 in *Studien zum Humanismus in den böhmischen Ländern, Ergänzungsheft. Vorträge und Studien einer Arbeitstagung Marburg a.d. Lahn, September: 1987*, ed. H.-B. Harder, H. Rothe, et al. Cologne.

Rothwell, W. (1959). 'The Hours of the Day in Medieval French.' *French Studies* 13 (1959), 240–51.

Rouche, M. (1977). "Francs et Gallo-Romains chez Grégoire de Tours". In *Gregorio di Tours. Convegni del centro di studi sulla spiritualità medievale* 12. Todi.

Rousseau, P. (1985). *Pachomius: The Making of a Community in Fourth-Century Egypt.* Berkeley.

Rubenstein, J. (1999). 'Liturgy against History: The Competing Visions of Lanfranc and Eadmer of Canterbury'. *Speculum* 74 (1999): 279–309.

Rubin, M. (1994). "The person in the form: medieval challenges to bodily 'order'". Pp. 101 ff. in *Framing Medieval Bodies*, ed. S. Kay and M. Rubin. Manchester.

Rücker, E. (1988). *Hartmann Schedels Weltchronik. Das größte Buchunternehmen der Dürerzeit.* Munich.

Russell, J. C. (1929). "The Canonization of Opposition to the King in Angevin England". Pp. 279–90 in *Anniversary Essays in Medieval History by Students of Charles Homer Haskins*, ed. C. H. Taylor and J. L. LaMonte. Boston.

Russo, D. (1986). 'Jeanne de Signe ou l'iconographie au féminin. Études sur les fresques de l'église paroissiale de Signa (milieu du xvᶜ siècle)'. *Mélanges de l'École française de Rome. Moyen âge* 98 (1986): pt. 1, 201–18.

Sánchez Alonso, B. (1947). *Historia de la historiografía española.* Vol. 1: *Hasta la publicación de la Crónica de Ocampo (–1543).* 2nd ed. Madrid.

Sandaaker, O. (1985). 'Historia Norvegiæ og biskop Eirik av Stavanger'. *Maal og minne* (1985): 82–86.

Sankt Elisabeth (1981). *Fürstin, Dienerin, Heilige. Dokumentation, Katalog.* Sigmaringen.

Santini, C., ed. (1992). *Saxo Grammaticus. Fra storiografia e letteratura* Roma.

Sawyer, B. (1985). 'Valdemar, Absalon and Saxo: Historiography and Politics in Medieval Denmark'. *Revue belge de philologie et d'histoire* 63 (1985): 685–705.

Sawyer, B., and P. Sawyer (1993). *Medieval Scandinavia. From Conversion to Reformation, circa 800–1500.* Minneapolis.

Sayers, W. (1966–67). 'The Beginnings and Early Development of Old French Historiography', Ph.D. thesis (Berkeley, 1966–67).

Sbaralea, J. H. (1908–36). *Supplementum et castigatio ad scriptores trium ordinum S. Francisci a Waddingo aliisve descriptos.* 3 vols. Rome.

Scheeben, H. C. (1930). 'Jakob von Soest und seine Chronik des Predigerordens'. *Historisches Jahrbuch* 50 (1930): 233–36.

———. (1937). 'Untersuchungen über einige mittelalterliche Chroniken des Predigerordens'. *Archiv der Deutschen Dominikaner* 1 (1937): 202–22.

Scheibelreiter, G. (1984). "Justinian und Belisar in fränkischer Sicht. Zur Interpretation von Fredegar, Chronicon II 62". Pp. 267–80 in *ZANTIO. Festschrift für Herbert Hunger zum 70. Geburtstag*, ed. W. Hörandner, et al. Vienna.

Schelle, B. (1952). "Frechulf von Lisieux: Untersuchungen zu Leben und Werk". Ph.D. Diss., Munich.

Schimmelpfennig, B. (1994). "Heilige Päpste—päpstliche Kanonisationspolitik". Pp. 73–100 in *Politik und Heiligenverehrung im Hochmittelalter*, ed. J. Petersohn. Sigmaringen.

Schlochtermeyer, D. (1998). *Bistumschroniken des Hochmittelalters: Die politische Instrumenalisierung von Geschichtsschreibung.* Paderborn.

Schmale, F. J. (1985). *Funktion und Formen mittelalterlicher Geschichtsschreibung: eine Einführung.* Darmstadt.

Schmale, F.-J., and I. Schmale-Ott (1972). *Frutolfs und Ekkehards Chroniken und die anonyme Kaiserchronik.* Darmstadt.

Schmid, K. (1983). *Gebetsgedenken und adliges Selbstverständnis im Mittelalter: Ausgewählte Beiträge.* Sigmaringen.

Schmidt, H. (1958). *Die deutschen Städtechroniken als Spiegel des bürgerlichen Selbstverständnisses im Spätmittelalter.* Schriftenreihe der historischen Kommission beider Bayerischen Akademie der Wissenschaften 3. Göttingen.

Schmidt, R. (1956). 'Aetates mundi: Die Weltalter als Gliederungsprinzip der Geschichte'. *Zeitschrift für Kirchengeschichte* 67 (1956): 288–317.

Schmidt-Chazan, M. (1985). "Histoire et sentiment national chez Robert Gaguin". Pp. 233–300 in *Le métier d'historien au moyen âge. Études sur l'historiographie médiévale*, ed. B. Guenée. Paris.

Schmugge, L. (1976). 'Zur Überlieferung der Historia Ecclesiastica Nova des Tholomaeus von Lucca'. *Deutsches Archiv* 32 (1976): 495–545.

Schneider, J. (1991). *Heinrich Deichsler und die Nürnberger Chronistik des 15. Jahrhunderts.* Wissensliteratur in Mittelalter 5 Wiesbaden.

Schnell, R. (1986). "Zur volkssprachlichen Rezeption des Speculum Historiale in Deutschland. Die Alexander Geschichte in den Excerpta Chronicarum". Pp. 101–26 in *Vincent of Beauvais and Alexander the Great*, ed. W. J. Aerts, et al. Groningen.

———. (1989). "Deutsche Literatur und deutsches Nationsbewußtsein in Spätmittelalter und früher Neuzeit". Pp. 331 ff. in *Ansätze und Diskontinuität deutscher Nationsbildung im Mittelalter*, ed. J. Ehlers. Nationes 8 Sigmaringen.

Schöne, A, ed. (1875). *Eusebi Chronicorum liber prior.* Vol. 1 of *Eusebi Chronicorum libri duo.* Berlin. [Repr. Dublin, 1967.]

———. (1900). *Die Weltchronik des Eusebius in ihrer Bearbeitung durch Hieronymus.* Berlin.

Schreiner K. (1988). "Erneuerung durch Erinnerung. Reformstreben, Geschichtsbewußtsein und Geschichtsschreibung im benediktinischen Mönchtum Südwestdeutschlands an der Wende vom 15. zum 16. Jahrhundert". Pp. 35–89 in *Historiographie am Oberrhein im späten Mittelalter und in der frühen Neuzeit*, ed. K. Andermann. Sigmaringen.

Schröder W. (1991). 'Ist das germanische Heldenlied ein Phantom?' *Zeitschrift für deutsches Altertum* 120 (1991): 249–56.

Schubert E. (1993). 'Die Quaternionen'. *Zeitschrift für Historische Forschung* 20 (1993): 1–63.

Schulz, M. (1909). *Die Lehre von der historischen Methode bei den Geschichtsschreibern des Mittelalters (VI.–XIII. Jahrhundert).* Abhandlungen zur mittleren und neueren Geschichte 13. Berlin.

Schumann, K. P. (1996). *Heinrich von Herford. Enzyklopädische Gelehrsamkeit und universalhistorische Konzeption im Dienste dominikanischer Studienbedürfnisse.* Quellen und Forschungen zur Kirchen- und Religionsgeschichte 4. Münster.

Searle, E. (1984). 'Fact and Pattern in Heroic History: Dudo of Saint-Quentin'. *Viator* 15 (1984): 119–37.

Sestan, E. (1966). "Le origini delle signorie cittadine: un problema storico esaurito?". Pp. 192–223 in *Italia médiévale*, ed. E. Sestan. Naples.

Seton, W. (1923). *Nicholas Glasberger and his Works. With the text of his* Maior Cronica Bohemorum Moderna. Manchester.

———. (1926). 'Nicholas Glasberger et sa Chronique de Bohème'. *Revue d'Histoire Franciscaine* 2 (1926): 411–17.

Shopkow, L. (1984). "Norman Historical Writing in the Eleventh and Twelfth Centuries." University of Toronto, 1984.

———. (1997). *History and Community: Norman Historical Writing in the Eleventh and Twelfth Centuries.* Washington, D.C.

———, (forthcoming). "The Man from Vermandois: Dudo of Saint-Quentin and his Patrons". In *Religion, Text, and Society in Medieval Spain and Northern Europe: Essays in Honor of J. N. Hillgarth.* Toronto.

Short, I. (1994). 'Gaimar's Epilogue and Geoffrey of Monmouth's "Liber Vetustissimus".' *Speculum* 69 (1994), 323–43.

Siemer, L. (1937). 'Liber Obituum et Anniversariorum der Predigerbrüder in Osnabrück'. *Archiv der Deutschen Dominikaner* 1 (1937): 15–95.

Sigal, P.-A. (1985). *L'homme et le miracle dans la France médiévale (xie–xiie siècle)*. Paris.

Simon, G. (1958–60). 'Untersuchung zur Topik der Widmungsbriefe mittelalterlicher Geschichtsschreiber bis zum Ende des 12. Jahrhunderts'. *Archiv für Diplomatik* 4 (1958): 52–119; and 5/6 (1959/60): 73–153.

Simonin, H.-D. (1938). 'Notes de bibliographie dominicaine I: La Tabula de Stams et la Chronique de Jacques de Soest'. *Archivum Fratrum Praedicatorum* 8 (1938): 193–214.

——. (1939). 'Notes de bibliographie dominicaine II: Les anciens catalogues d'écrivains dominicains et la Chronique de Bernard Gui'. *Archivum Fratrum Praedicatorum* 9 (1939): 192–213.

Skovgaard-Petersen, I. (1969). 'Saxo, historian of the Patria'. *Medieval Scandinavia* 2 (1969): 54–77.

——. (1987). *Da Tidernes Herre var nær. Studier i Saxos historiesyn*. Copenhagen.

——. (1988). 'Saxo's History of the Danes: An Interpretation'. *Scandinavian Journal of History* 13 (1988): 87–93.

Smalley, B. (1974). *Historians in the Middle Ages*. London.

Sot, M. (1981). *Gesta Episcoporum, Gesta Abbatum*. Typologie des sources du Moyen Age occidental 37. Turnhout.

——. (1978). 'Historiographie épiscopale et modèle familiale en Occident au IXe siècle'. *Annales, Économies, Sociétés, Civilisations* 33 (1978): 433–49.

——. (1993). *Un historien et son église au Xe siècle: Flodoard de Reims*. Paris.

——. (2001). "La Rome antique dans l'hagiographie épiscopale de Gaule". Pp. 163–88 in *Settimane di studio del Centro italiano di studi sull'alto medio evo, La Mendola 1998*. Milan.

Southern, R. W. (1970). 'Aspects of the European Tradition of Historical Writing: 1. The Classical Tradition from Einhard to Geoffrey of Monmouth.' *Transactions of the Royal Historical Society* 20, 5th series (1970), 173–96.

——. (1971). 'The *Reditus ad Stirpem Karoli Magni*: A New Look'. *French Historical Studies* 17 (1971): 145–73.

Spiegel, G. (1975). 'Political Utility in Medieval Historiography.' *History and Theory* 14, 3 (1975), 314–25.

——. (1978). *The Chronicle Tradition of Saint-Denis: A Survey*. Brookline, Mass.

——. (1983). 'Genealogy: Form and Function in Medieval Narrative'. *History and Theory* 22 (1983): 43–53.

——. (1984). 'Forging the Past: The Language of Historical Truth in the Middle Ages.' *History Teacher* 17, 2 (1984), 267–83.

——. (1987). 'Social Change and Literary Language: The Textualisation of the Past in Thirteenth-Century French Historiography.' *Journal of Medieval and Renaissance Studies* 17, 2 (1987), 129–48.

——. (1990). 'History, Historicism, and the Social Logic of the Text in the Middle Ages'. *Speculum* 65 (1990): 59–86.

——. (1993). *Romancing the Past: The Rise of Vernacular Prose Historiography in Thirteenth-Century France*. Berkeley.

——. (1997). *The Past as Text: The Theory and Practice of Medieval Historiography*. London and Baltimore.

Sprandel, R. (1987). "Geschichtsschreiber in Deutschland 1347–1517". Pp. 289–318 in *Mentalitäten im Mittelalter*, ed. F. Graus. Sigmaringen.

——. (1994). *Chronisten als Zeitzeugen: Forschungen zur spätmittelalterlichen Geschichtsschreibung in Deutschland*. Cologne.

Stancliffe, C. (1983). *St. Martin and his Hagiographer: History and Miracle in Sulpicius Severus*. Oxford.

Staubach, N. (1995). 'Christiana tempora. Augustin und das Ende der alten Geschichte in der Weltchronik Frechulfs von Lisieux'. Frühmittelalterliche Studien 29 (1995): 167–206.

——. (2002). "Quattuor modis intellegi potest Hierusalem: Augustins Civitas Dei und der vierfache Schriftsinn". In Alvarium: Festschrift für Christian Gnilka. Jahrbuch für Antike und Christentum. Egänzungsband 33. Münster.

Stenton, F. M. (1925). "The south-western element in the Old English Chronicle". Pp. 106–15 in Essays in Medieval History presented to Thomas Frederick Tout, ed. F. M. Stenton. Manchester. [Repr. in F. M. Stenton. Preparatory to Anglo-Saxon England. Oxford, 1970.]

——. (1971). Anglo-Saxon England. 3rd ed. Oxford.

Stern, H. (1953). Le calendrier de 354: Études sur son texts et ses illustrations. Bibliothèque archéologique et historique 55. Paris.

Strickland, M. J. (1992). 'Arms and the Men: War, Loyalty and Lordship in Jordan Fantosme's Chronicle.' Medieval Knighthood, ed. C. Harper-Bill and R. Harvey. Vol. 4. Woodbridge.

Stock, B. (1983). The Implications of Literacy: Written Language and Models of Interpretation in the Eleventh and Twelfth Centuries. Princeton.

Stroheker, K. F. (1955). 'Zur Rolle der Heermeister fränkischer Abstammung im späten vierten Jahrhundert'. Historia 4 (1955): 314–30. [Repr. in K. F. Stroheker. Germanentum und Spätantike. Pp. 9–29. Zürich and Stuttgart, 1965.]

——. (1961). "Alamannen im römischen Reichsdienst". Pp. 30–53 in Eranion. Festschrift für Hildebrecht Hommel, ed. J. Kroymann and E. Zinn. Tübingen. [Repr. in K. F. Stroheker. Germanentum und Spätantike. Pp. 127–48. Zürich and Stuttgart, 1965.]

Stuart, D. R. (1967). Epochs of Greek and Roman Biography. New York.

Summerfield, T. (1998). The Matter of Kings' Lives. The Design of Past and Present in the early fourteenth-century verse chronicles by Pierre de Langtoft and Robert Mannyng. Amsterdam.

Szkilnik, M. (1986). 'Écrire en vers, écrire en prose. Le choix de Wauchier de Denain.' Romania 107 (1986), 208–30.

Szücs, J. (1975). "Theoretical Elements in Master Simon of Kéza's Gesta Hungarorum (1282–1285 A.D.)". Pp. 239–81 in Études historiques hongroises 1975, ed. Szücs. Vol. 1. Budapest. [German version: "Theoretische Elemente in Meister Simon von Kézas 'Gesta Hungarorum' (1282–1285) Beiträge zur Herausgestaltung des 'europäischen Synchronismus' der Ideenstrukturen". Pp. 263–328 in Nation und Geschichte. Studien. Cologne, 1981.]

Talbert, C. H. (1977). What is a Gospel? The Genre of the Canonical Gospels. Philadelphia.

Tanz, S. (1983). 'Orosius im Spannungsfeld zwischen Eusebius von Caesarea und Augustin'. Klio 65 (1983): 337–46.

Tassi, L. (1893). Vita del B. Francesco Venimbeni da Fabriano. Fabriano.

Tate, R. B. (1959). "The Anacephaleosis of Alfonso Gracía de Santa María". Pp. 387–401 in Hispanic Studies in Honour of I. González Llubera, ed. R. B. Tate. Oxford. [Spanish version: "La Anacephaleosis de Alfonso García de Santa María, Obispo de Burgos, 1435–1456". Pp. 55–73 in Ensayos sobre la historiografia peninsular del siglo XV. Madrid, 1970].

——. (1960) 'Rodrigo Sánchez de Arévalo (1404–1470) and his Compendiosa Historia Hispanica'. Nottingham Medieval Studies 4 (1960): 58–80. [Spanish version: "Rodrigo Sánchez de Arévalo (1404–1470) y su Compendiosa Historia Hispanica". Pp. 74–104 in Ensayos sobre la historiografia peninsular del siglo XV. Madrid, 1970].

Taylor, J. (1966). The Universal Chronicle of Ranulf Higden. Oxford.

——. (1986). "The French Prose Brut: Popular History in Fourteenth-Century England". Pp. 247–54 in England in the Fourteenth Century. Proceedings of the 1985 Harlaxton Symposium, ed. W. M. Ormrod. Woodbridge, Suffolk.

——. (1987). English Historical Literature in the Fourteenth Century. Oxford.

Teillet, S. (1984). Des Goths à la nation gothique. Les origines de l'idée de nation en Occident du Ve au VIIe siècle. Paris.

Tellenbach, G. (1977). "Eigene und fremde Geschichte. Eine Studie zur Geschichte der europäischen Historiographie, vorzüglich im 15. und 16. Jahrhundert". Pp. 295–316 in *Landesgeschichte und Geistesgeschichte. Festschrift für Otto Herding zum 65. Geburtstag*, ed. K. Elm, E. Gönner, and E. Hillenbrand. Stuttgart.

Thomas, H. (1990). "Warum hat es im deutschen Mittelalter keine nationale Geschichtsschreibung gegeben?". Pp. 165–82 in *Chroniques nationales et chroniques universelles. Actes du colloque d'Amiens 16–17 janvier 1988*, ed. D. Buschinger. Göppingen.

——. (1991). "Julius Caesar und die Deutschen. Zu Ursprung und Gestalt eines deutschen Geschichtsbewußtseins in der Zeit Gregors VII. und Heinrich IV". Pp. 245–77 in *Die Salier und das Reich*, ed. S. Weinfurter. *Gesellschaftlicher und ideengeschichtlicher Wandel im Reich der Salier*, vol. 3 Sigmaringen.

Thomson, R. M. (1975). 'The Reading of William of Malmesbury'. *Revue bénédictine* 85 (1975): 362–402

——. (1976). 'The Reading of William of Malmesbury: Addenda et Corrigenda'. *Revue bénédictine* 86 (1976): 327–35

——. (1979). 'The Reading of William of Malmesbury: Further Addition and Reflections'. *Revue bénédictine* 89 (1979): 313–24.

——. (1987). *William of Malmesbury*. Woodbridge, Suffolk.

Thürlemann, F. (1974). *Der historische Diskurs bei Gregor von Tours. Topoi und Wirklichkeit*. Geist und Werk der Zeiten 39. Bern.

Tilley, M., trans. (1996). *Donatist Martyr Stories. The Church in Conflict in Roman North Africa*. Liverpool.

Tilmans, K. (1989). 'Holländisches Nationalbewußtsein in der frühhumanistischen Historiographie: Cornelius Aurelius (ca. 1460–1531), und seine Zeitgenossen'. *Wolfenbütteler Renaissance Mitteilungen* 13 (1989): 61–68.

——. (1992). *Historiography and Humanism in Holland in the Age of Erasmus. Aurelius and the "Divisiekroniek" of 1517*. Bibliotheca Humanistica et Reformatorica 51. Nieuwkoop.

Tomea, P. (1997). "Fiamma (Flamma, de Flama). Galvano". Pp. 331–36 in *Dizionario biografico degli Italiani* 47. Rome.

Trestík, D. (1968). *Kosmova kronika. Studie k počátkum českého dějepisectví a politického myšlení*. Praha.

Trotter, D. A. (1987). *Medieval French Literature and the Crusades (1100–1300)*. Geneva: Droz, 1987.

Tugwell, S. (1996). 'Notes on the Life of St Dominic'. *Archivum Fratrum Praedicatorum* 66 (1996): 137–44, 161–64.

Turchini, A., ed. (1970). 'Leggenda, culto, iconografia del beato Giovanni Gueruli (1320?)'. *Studi romagnoli* 21 (1970): 425–53.

Tvorogov, O. V. (1975). *Drevnerusskie chronografy*. Leningrad.

Tyson, D. (1979). 'Patronage of French Vernacular History Writers in the Twelfth and Thirteenth Centuries.' *Romania* 100 (1979), 180–222.

——. (1986). 'French Vernacular History Writers and Their Patrons in the Fourteenth Century.' *Mediaevalia et Humanistica* 14. n.s. (1986), 103–24.

Tyson, D. B. (1975). 'An Early French Prose History of the Kings of England'. *Romania* 96 (1975): 1–26.

Uecker, H. (1972). *Germanische Heldensage*. Stuttgart.

Uitti, K. D. (1985). "A Note on Historiographical Vernacularization in Thirteenth-Century France and Spain". Pp. 573–92 in *Homenaje a Álvares Galmés de Fuentes*, ed. K. D. Uitti. Vol. 1. Oviedo.

Uribe F. (1996). *Introduzione alle agiografie di S. Francesco e S. Chiara d'Assisi (sec. XIII–XIV)*. Rome.

van Caenegem R. (1973). "The Sources of Flemish history in the Liber Floridus". Pp. 71–85 in *Liber Floridus Colloquium*, ed. A. Derdez. Ghent.

van Caenegem, R. C., and F. L. Ganshof (1978). *Guide to the Sources of Medieval History*. Amsterdam and New York.

Van Dam, R. (1993). *Saints and their Miracles in late Antique Gaul.* Princeton.

Van der Straeten, J. (1967). 'Hagiographie du Mons: notes critiques'. *Annalecta Bollandiana* 85 (1967): 474–501.

Van Houts, E. M. C. (1984). 'The Adaptation of the "Gesta Normannorum Ducum" by Wace and Benoît.' *Non Nova, Sed Nove. Mélanges de civilisation médiévale dédiés à Willem Noomen,* ed. Martin Gosman and Jaap van Os. Groningen.

——. (1984). 'Scandinavian Influence in Norman Literature of the Eleventh Century'. *Anglo-Norman Studies* 6 (1984): 107–21.

——. (1981). 'The Gesta Normannorum ducum: A History without an End'. *Anglo-Norman Studies* 3 (1981): 106–18.

——. (1989). 'Historiography and hagiography at Saint-Wandrille: The Inventio et Miracula sancti Vulfranni'. *Anglo-Norman Studies* 12 (1989): 233–51.

——. (1995). *Local and Regional Chronicles.* Typologies des sources du moyen âge occidental 74. Turnhout.

——. (1999). Memory and Gender in Medieval Europe, 900–1200 Toronto.

Van Mingroot, E. (1975). 'Datering van de Gesta episcoporum Cameracensium'. *Révue Belge de Philologie et d'Histoire* 53 (1975): 281–332.

van Otroy, P. (1911). 'Pierre Ferrand O.P. et les premièrs biographes de S. Dominique'. *Analecta Bollandiana* 30 (1911): 52–68.

Van Uytfanghe, M. (1987). *Stylisation biblique et condition humaine dans l'hagiographie mérovingienne (600–750).* Verhandelingen van de Koninklijke Academie voor Wetenschappen, Klasse der Letteren 120. Brussels.

van Werveke, H. (1959). "Bijdrage tot een nieuwe uitgave van de Annales Gandenses". Pp. 109–15 in *Dancwerc. Opstellen aangeboden aan Prof. dr. D.Th. Enklaar ter gelegenheid van zijn vijfenzestigste verjaardag,* ed. H. van Werveke Groningen.

Vasina, A. (1991). "Tolosano". Pp. 117–21 in *Repertorio della cronachistica emiliano-romagnola: secc. IX–XV,* ed. B. Andreolli et al. Rome.

——. (1995). "Le cronache emiliane e romagnole: dal Tolosano a Riccobaldo (secoli XII–XIV)". Pp. 87–104 in *Il senso della storia nella cultura medievale italiana (1100–1350): quattordicesimo convegno di studi; Pistoia, 14–17 maggio 1993.* Pistoia.

——. (1996). "Bologna e la IIa Lega lombarda". Pp. 183–201 in *Federico II e Bologna.* Bologna.

Vauchez, A. (1981). *La sainteté en Occident aux derniers siècles du moyen âge d'après les procès de canonization et les documents hagiographiques.* Rome.

——. (1990). "Frati minori, eremitismo e santità laica: Le 'vite' dei santi Maio m. 1270 ca.). e Marzio (m. 1301). di Gualdo Tadino". Pp. 274–305 in *Ordini mendicanti e società italiana xiii–xv secolo,* ed. A. Vauchez. Milan.

——, ed. (1993). *Apogée de la papauté et expansion de la Chrétienté (1054–1274).* Paris.

——. (1997). *Sainthood in the Later Middle Ages.* Tr. by J. Birrell. Cambridge.

Vaughan, R. (1958). *Matthew Paris.* Cambridge Studies in Medieval Life and Thought NS 6. Cambridge.

Verdon, J. (1986). *Grégoire de Tours. Le père de l'Histoire de France.* Le Coteau.

Veyne, P. (1988). *Did the Greeks Believe in their Myths?* Tr. by P. Wissing. Chicago.

Vinay, G. (1978). "Un mito per sopravvivere. L'Historia Langobardorum di Paolo Diacono". Pp. 125–49 in G. Vinay, ed. *Alto medioevo latino. Conversazioni e no.* Naples.

Vitz, E. B. (1986). 'Rethinking Old French Literature: The Orality of the Octosyllabic Couplet.' *Romanic Review* 77 (1986), 307–21.

Voeglin, J.-M. (2002). *Les Bourgeois de Calais. Essai sur un mythe historique,* coll. "Evolution de l'humanité", Paris: Albin Michel, 2001, reviewed in *Le Monde des Livres* du 24 mai 2002, p. VII.

Vollmann, B. K. (1983). "Gregor IV (Gregor von Tours)". In *Reallexikon für Antike und Christentum* 12, ed. T. Klauser et al. Cols. 895–930. Stuttgart.

Volpe, G. (1922). *Medio Evo Italiano.* Florence.

von den Brincken, A.-D. (1957). *Studien zur lateinischen Weltchronistik bis in das Zeitalter Ottos von Freising.* Düsseldorf.

——. (1967). 'Die universalhistorischen Vorstellungen des Johann von Marignola OFM. Der einzige mittelalterliche Weltchronist mit Fernostkenntnis'. *Archiv für Kulturgeschichte* 49 (1967): 297–339.

——. (1968). 'Mappa mundi und Chronographia. Studien zur imago mundi des abendländischen Mittelalters'. *Deutsches Archiv* 24 (1968): 118–86.

——. (1978). 'Die Geschichtsbetrachtung bei Vincenz von Beauvais. Die Apologia Actoris zum Speculum maius'. *Deutsches Archiv* 34 (1978): 440–41.

——. (1981). 'Zur Herkunft und Gestalt der Martins-Chroniken'. *Deutsches Archiv* 37 (1981): 694–735.

——. (1985). 'Studien zur Überlieferung der Chronik des Martin von Troppau (I)'. *Deutsches Archiv* 41 (1985): 461–500.

——. (1989). 'Studien zur Überlieferung der Chronik Martins von Troppau (II)'. *Deutsches Archiv* 45 (1989): 551–91.

Von Eckhart, J. G. (1723). *Corpus historicum medii aevi, sive Scriptores res in orbe vniverso, praecipve in Germania, a temporibvs maxime Caroli M., imperatoris vsqve ad finem secvli post C. N. XV.* Vol. 1. Cols. 1551–1640. Leipzig.

von Rad, G. (1930). *Das Geschichtsbild des chronistischen Werkes.* Beitrage zur Wissenschaft vom Alten und Neuen Testament. 4th series. Vol. 3. Stuttgart.

von See, K. (1972). *Kontinuitätstheorie und Sakraltheorie in der Germanenforschung. Antwort an Otto Höfler.* Frankfurt am Main.

——. (1981). 'Der Germane als Barbar'. *Jahrbuch für internationale Germanistik* 13 (1981): 42–72. [Repr. in von See, Barbar, Germane, Arier. *Die Suche nach der Identität der Deutschen.* Pp. 31–60 and 347–57. Heidelberg, 1994.]

——. (1988). *Mythos und Theologie im skandinavischen Mittelalter.* Heidelberg.

Vones, L. (1991). "Historiographie et politique: l'historiographie Castillane aux abords du XIV^c siècle". Pp. 177–88 in *L'historiographie médiévale en Europe,* ed. J.-P. Genet. Paris.

Voorbij, J. B. (1991). *Het 'Speculum Historiale' van Vincent van Beauvais. Een studie naar zijn ontstaansgeschiedenis.* Doct. Diss. Groningen.

Wadding, L. (1906). *Scriptores Ordinis Minorum.* Rome.

Waha, M., de (1977). 'Sigebert de Gembloux faussaire? Le chroniqueur et les 'sources anciennes' de son abbaye'. *Revue Belge de Philologie et d'histoire* 55 (1977): 989–1036.

Walker, J. B. (1933). *The 'Chronicles' of S. Antoninus.* Washington.

Wallace-Hadrill J. M. (1958). 'Fredegar and the History of France'. *Bulletin of the John Rylands Library* 40 (1958): 527–50. [Repr. in Wallace-Hadrill. *The Long-Haired Kings.* Pp. 71–94. London, 1962.]

Ward, B. (1981). "The Miracles of St. Benedict". Pp. 1–14 in *Benedictus: Studies in Honor of St. Benedict of Nursia,* ed. E. R. Elder. Kalamazoo, Mich.

Warren, J. (1998). *The Past and Its Presenters.* London.

Wattenbach W., and R. Holtzmann (1948). *Deutschlands Geschichtsquellen im Mittelalter.* Deutsche Kaiserzeit 1. Tübingen.

Wattenbach-Levison (1953). Wattenbach, W. *Deutschlands Geschichtsquellen im Mittelalter. Vorzeit und Karolinger* 2. *Die Karolinger vom Anfang des 8. Jahrhunderts bis zum Tode Karls des Grossen.* Edited by W. Levison and H. Lowe. Weimar.

Wattenbach-Schmale (1976). Wattenbach, W., and F.-J. Schmale. *Deutschlands Geschichtsquellen im Mittelalter vom Tod Kaiser Henrichs V bis zum Ende des Interregnum.* Vol. 1. Darmstadt.

Webb, D. (1996). *Patrons and Defenders: The Saints in the Italian City States.* London.

Weigand R. (1991). *Vincenz von Beauvais. Scholastische Universalchronik als Quelle volkssprachlicher Geschichtsschreibung.* Hildesheim, Zürich, and New York.

Weinstein, D., and R. M. Bell (1982). *Saints and Society. The Two Worlds of Western Christendom, 1000–1700.* Chicago.

Wenskus, R. (1986). "Über die Möglichkeit eines allgemeinen interdisziplinären Germanenbegriffs". Pp. 1–21 in *Germanenprobleme in heutiger Sicht*, ed. H. Beck. Ergänzungsbände zum Reallexikon der Germanischen Altertumskunde 1. Berlin and New York.

Werner, K. F. (1952). "Die Legitimität der Kapetinger und die Entstehung des 'Reditus regni Francorum ad stirpem Karoli'". *Die Welt als Geschichte* 12 (1952): 203–25.

———. (1967). "Die Nachkommen Karls des Großen bis um das Jahr 1000, 1.–8. Generation". In *Karl der Große*, 4, *Das Nachleben*, ed. W. Braunfels and P. E. Schramm. Düsseldorf.

———. (1987). "Gott, Herrscher und Historiograph: Der Geschichtsschreiber als Interpret des Wirken Gottes in der Welt und Ratgeber der Könige (4. bis 12. Jahrhundert)". Pp. 1–31 in *Deus qui mutat tempora. Menschen und Institutionen im Wandel des Mittelalters. Festschrift für Alfons Becker zu seinem fünfundsechzigsten Geburtstag*, ed. E. D. Hehl, et al. Sigmaringen.

———. (1990). "L'Historia et les rois". In *Religion et culture autour de l'an Mil: Royaume capétien et Lotharingie*, ed. D. Iogna-Prat and J.-Ch. Picard. Colloque Hugues Capet, 987–1987: La France de l'an mil (1987). Paris.

Westermann, C. (1985). *Genesis 1–11: A Commentary*. Tr. by J. J. Scullion. Minneapolis.

White, H. (1980). "The Value of Narrativity in the Representation of Reality". Pp. 1–23 in *On Narrative*, ed. W. J. T. Mitchell. Chicago.

Wickham, C., and J. Fentress (1992). *Social Memory*. Oxford.

Williams, B. A. (1991). "The Latin Franciscan Anglo-Irish Annales of Medieval Ireland". Doct. Diss. University of Dublin.

Williams-Krapp, W. (2001). "Literary Genre and Degrees of Saintliness. The Perception of Holiness in Writings by and about Female Mystics". In *The Invention of Saintliness*, ed. A. Mulder-Bakker. London.

Wolfram, H. (1967). *Lateinische Königs- und Fürstentitel bis zum Ende des 8. Jahrhunderts*. Vol. 1 of *Intitulatio*. Mitteilungen des Instituts für Österreichische Geschichtsforschung. Ergänzungsband 21. Graz-Vienna-Cologne.

———. (1980). *Geschichte der Goten. Von den Anfängen bis zur Mitte des sechsten Jahrhunderts. Entwurf einer historischen Ethnographie*. 2nd rev. ed. Munich.

———. (1990). *Das Reich und die Germanen. Zwischen Antike und Mittelalter*. Berlin.

———. (1994). 'Origo et religio. Ethnic traditions and literature in early medieval texts'. *Early Medieval Europe* 3 (1994): 19–38.

Wood, I. (1985). 'Gregory of Tours and Clovis'. *Revue Belge de Philologie et d'Histoire* 63 (1985): 249–72.

———. (1994). "Fredegar's Fables". Pp. 359–66 in *Historiographie im frühen Mittelalter*, ed. A. Scharer and G. Scheibelreiter. Vienna.

———. (1994b). *Gregory of Tours*. Bangor.

Wormald, P. (1978). "Bede, Beowulf, and the Conversion of the Anglo-Saxon Aristocracy". Pp. 32–95 in *Bede and Anglo-Saxon England*, ed. R. T. Farrell. Oxford.

———. (1983). "Bede, the Bretwaldas, and the Origins of the Gens Anglorum". Pp. 99–129 in *Ideal and Reality in Frankish and Anglo-Saxon Society: Studies Presented to J. M. Wallace-Hadrill*, ed. P. Wormald, with D. Bullough and R. Collins. Oxford.

Wyngaert, A. van den (1921). 'De sanctis et beatis tertii ordinis iuxta fr. Mariani Florentini'. *Archivum Franciscanum Historicum* 14 (1921): 3–35.

——— (1949). "Carbonel (Ponce)". Pp. 1000–1001 in *Dictionnaire d'Histoire et de Géographie Ecclesiastique*. Vol. 2. Paris.

Zanella, G. (1980). *Riccobaldo e dintorni. Studi di storiografia medievale ferrarese*. Ferrara.

———. (1991). "Riccobaldo da Ferrara". Pp. 163–81 in *Repertorio della cronachistica emiliano-romagnola: secc. IX–XV*, ed. B. Andreolli et al. Rome.

———, ed. (1984). *Storici e storiografia del medioevo italiano: antologia di saggi*. Bologna.

Zanot, M. (1997). "Lo stato dell'edizione degli Actus Beati Francisci". Pp. 261–74 in *Editori di Quaracchi, 100 anni dopo. Bilancio e prospettive*, ed. A. Cacciotti and B. F. de Mottoni. Rome.

Zimmermann, H. (1960). *Ecclesia als Objekt der Historiographie. Studien zur Kirchengeschichtsschreibung im Mittelalter und in der frühen Neuzeit.* Sitzungsberichte der Österreichischen Akademie der Wissenschaften, philologisch-historische Klasse 235,4. Vienna.

——. (1981). *Das Papsttum im Mittelalter im Spiegel der Historiographie, mit einem Verzeichnis der Päpste vom 4. bis zum 15. Jahrhundert.* Stuttgart.

Zink, M. (1980). 'Froissart et la nuit du chasseur.' *Poétique* 41 (1980): 60–77.

——. (1992). *Littérature française du Moyen Age.* Coll. "Premier Cycle". Paris.

——. (1998). *Froissart et le temps.* Paris.

Zingel, M. (1995). *Frankreich, das Reich und Burgund im Urteil der burgundischen Historiographie des 15. Jahrhunderts*, Vorträge und Forschungen. Sonderband 40. Sigmaringen.

Zinn, G. A. (1977). 'The Influence of Hugh of St. Victor's "Chronicon" on the "Abbreviationes chronicorum" by Ralph of Diceto'. *Speculum* 52 (1977): 38–61.

Zumkeller, A. (1992). 'Johannes Capgrave', *Biographisch-Bibliographisches Kirchenlexikon* 3 (1992): 296–99.

Zumthor, P. (1972). *Essai de poétique médiévale.* Coll. "Poétique". Paris.

——. (1975). *Langue, texte, énigme.* Coll. "Poétique". Paris.

INDEX OF AUTHORS

456 INDEX

INDEX OF ANONYMOUS TEXTS

INDEX OF TERMS

annals 4, 6, 73–75, 171, 278, 350
argumentum 3, 389
Arianism 58, 140
Aristotelianism 357
Arthurian literature 250, 397, 412, 415
asceticism 133–34, 136, 138, 140–41, 145, 149, 154
Augustinian friars 370, 372
autobiography 379–383

biography 115, 117–18, 120, 123–24, 154, 236, 353, 377–78
biography, sacred 116, 119–20, 123–24, 127, 131–33, 135–36, 140, 145, 150, 154
bishop chronicle 170
Bollandistes 383
brevitas 5, 57, 90

canonization 364–69, 375
catalogue 91, 94–5, 97, 107–09
chanson de geste 249, 264, 387, 390–94, 401–02, 410, 413
Charlemagne 11, 37, 102, 106, 158, 164, 239, 391, 412–13
chartulary chronicles 280
chivalry 271, 274, 398
Chronica pontificum 100
chronicle/*chronicon*/*chronique* 5, 59, 61–2, 64, 75, 90, 231, 295–305, 353, 389, 415
chronology 18–19, 21, 31, 53, 97, 108, 281
Cistercians 370
commemoratio 95, 112, 286
Constantine the Great 20, 22, 28, 45, 99, 131–32, 134
consuetudines 279
crusades 258–59, 261–64, 347, 391–92, 415

descriptio mundi 401
dialogue 128–29, 145, 253, 269, 404
diptych 92, 94–5
direct speech 269, 389

Dominicans 290–95, 301–14, 370
dynastic history 162, 169–70, 177, 217–48, 280, 350
dynasty 161, 188, 191, 192f, 205, 211

Easter calculation 34
Easter tables 73
encomium 150
end of the world 160, 178
epic 118, 238, 256, 389, 390, 403
episcopal list 91, 107
estoire 389, 395, 411
ethnogenesis 44–5
eyewitness 130, 151–52, 249–76

fabliaux 250, 402
fabula 3, 63, 159, 387, 389, 412, 415
family trees 222, 227, 239
Four kingdoms/empires 28, 37–8, 40–1, 158
Franciscans 290–301, 306–14, 370–71

genealogy 46, 102, 217–21, 224, 228, 234, 236, 239, 245, 247
gesta 5, 177
gesta abbatum 278–79, 281
gesta episcoporum 53, 89, 100, 106, 285–87
gesta episcoporum et abbatum 9, 220–22
gesta martyrum 99
gesta of public officials 160, 162
Gesta pontificum 100
gesta principum 391, 394
geste 395, 408
Ghibelline 329, 335, 375
Guelf/Guelph 329, 333, 335, 337, 375

hagiography 53–4, 66, 141, 145, 148–50, 154, 253, 290–95, 412
Heilsgeschichte 66, 160, 165, 169, 173, 178
histoire 250, 390, 415